GW01066351

PUBLICATIONS

OF THE

NAVY RECORDS SOCIETY

VOLS. I & II

DEFEAT OF THE SPANISH ARMADA

STATE PAPERS

RELATING TO

THE DEFEAT OF

𝔗𝔥𝔢 𝔖𝔭𝔞𝔫𝔦𝔰𝔥 𝔄𝔯𝔪𝔞𝔡𝔞

ANNO 1588

EDITED BY

JOHN KNOX LAUGHTON, M.A., R.N.

Professor of Modern History in King's College, London

VOL. I.

SECOND EDITION

TEMPLE SMITH FOR THE NAVY RECORDS SOCIETY

1987

© The Navy Records Society 1987

All rights reserved. No part of this publication may be
reproduced, stored in a retrieval system, or transmitted
in any form or by any means, electronic, mechanical,
photocopying, recording or otherwise without the
prior permission of the publisher.

First published in 1894

Reprinted in 1987 by

Temple Smith
Gower Publishing Company Limited
Gower House
Croft Road
Aldershot
Hants GUI1 3HR

Gower Publishing Company
Old Post Road
Brookfield
Vermont 05036
USA

ISBN 0 566 05540 6

Printed in Great Britain by
Richard Clay Ltd, Bungay, Suffolk

THE COUNCIL

OF THE

NAVY RECORDS SOCIETY

1893–4–5

PATRONS

HIS ROYAL HIGHNESS THE DUKE OF SAXE-COBURG AND GOTHA,
K.G., K.T., &c.

HIS ROYAL HIGHNESS THE DUKE OF YORK, K.G. &c.

PRESIDENT
EARL SPENCER, K.G.

VICE-PRESIDENTS

LORD GEORGE HAMILTON.
ADMIRAL SIR R. V. HAMILTON, K.C.B.

MARQUIS OF LOTHIAN, K.T.
PROFESSOR SIR J. R. SEELEY, K.C.M.G.

COUNCILLORS

H.S.H. PRINCE LOUIS OF BATTENBERG, G.C.B.
WALTER BESANT.
HON. T. A. BRASSEY.
REAR-ADMIRAL BRIDGE.
OSCAR BROWNING.
PROFESSOR MONTAGU BURROWS.
REV. H. MONTAGU BUTLER, D.D.
LIEUT.-GEN. SIR A. CLARKE, G.C.M.G.
VICE-ADMIRAL COLOMB.
ADMIRAL SIR EDWARD FANSHAWE, G.C.B.
C. H. FIRTH.

DR. RICHARD GARNETT.
MAJOR-GEN. GEARY, R.A., C.B.
LORD PROVOST OF GLASGOW.
DAVID HANNAY.
SIDNEY LEE.
REAR-ADMIRAL SIR LAMBTON LORAINE, BART.
SIR ALFRED C. LYALL, K.C.B.
CLEMENTS R. MARKHAM, C.B., F.R.S.
CAPT. S. P. OLIVER, late R.A.
COMM. C. N. ROBINSON, R.N.
J. R. THURSFIELD.
CAPT. WHARTON, R.N., F.R.S.
CAPT. S. EARDLEY WILMOT, R.N.

SECRETARY
PROFESSOR J. K. LAUGHTON, Catesby House, Manor Road, Barnet.

TREASURER
H. F. R. YORKE, Admiralty, S.W.

The COUNCIL of the NAVY RECORDS SOCIETY wish it to be distinctly understood that they are not answerable for any opinions or observations that may appear in the Society's publications. For these the responsibility rests entirely with the Editors of the several works.

ADVERTISEMENT.

This Second Edition is printed from the same type as the first; but the opportunity has been taken to correct a few trifling errors or misprints.

February, 1895.

INTRODUCTION.

THE defeat of the Spanish Armada in 1588 has been rightly described by Sir Edward Creasy as one of the decisive battles of the world, speaking of it as one continued battle lasting for nine days, rather than as a succession of battles. It marks alike the approaching downfall of Spain and the rise of England as a great maritime power. England had indeed always believed in her naval power, had always claimed the sovereignty of the Narrow Seas; and, more than two hundred years before Elizabeth came to the throne, Edward III. had testified to his sense of its importance by ordering a gold coinage bearing the device which is now reproduced on the title page and cover of this volume, a device showing the armed strength and sovereignty of England based on the sea. It was no mere coincidence which led to the adoption of such a device in 1344, four years after the most bloody battle and decisive victory of western war—the battle of Sluys—which, by giving England the command of the sea, determined the course of the great war which followed; determined that Crécy and Poitiers should be fought on French soil, not on English; determined that the

English—not the French—armies should consist of trained soldiers; that the French armies—not the English—should consist of raw levies of half-armed peasants.

The device thus adopted was continued by Edward's successors, and was still in use under Elizabeth, telling to those who could understand it that the might and majesty of England rested on her navy. That this was fully proved in the summer of 1588 is a familiar story, but the following pages show that few indeed of her statesmen, or warriors, or seamen, had realised the fact. They could believe that the fleet of England was capable of withstanding that of Spain; that the armada, of itself, was not a thing to be feared; but they never quite succeeded in getting rid of the notion that the Duke of Parma's army was still terrible. Wynter, indeed, with nigh fifty years' experience at sea, and memories of former expeditions to guide him, was sure that the enemy must find very great difficulty in the transport of the army, and that if the squadron in the Narrow Seas was kept up at its actual strength, 'the Prince's forces, being no other than that which he hath in Flanders at this time (20th of June), dare not come to the seas' (p. 214). Wynter's opinion is eminently practical. It was supposed that Parma might attempt a landing at Sheppey, Harwich or Yarmouth, places where 'a small charge will make a sufficient strength to withstand any sudden attempt; but in these princely actions a man cannot be too provident; and no wisdom were it to put things to an even balance, when more weight may be added' (*ib.*).

Drake's experience was, in its nature, altogether different from Wynter's. His fighting had been brisker, more adventurous, less systematic. He had seen less of fleets, little of the transport of troops. He had made attacks and found the enemy helpless to prevent him. It would almost seem that he imagined Parma might try to do for London what he himself had done for Nombre de Dios or Cartagena. And yet he fully realised the difficulties in Parma's way. He must have a spring tide to bring his ships out ; he must have fair weather, his ships being small and pestered with soldiers ; and if the Duke of Medina should return with the fleet, 'he is like, God willing, to have unquiet rest.' 'We ought,' he adds, ' much more to have regard unto the Duke of Parma and his soldiers, than to the Duke of Sidonia and his ships. . . . My opinion is that the Duke of Parma should be vigilantly looked upon for these twenty days, although the army of Spain return not this way ; for of them I have no great doubt ; although there be great cause for us all to watch carefully' (vol. ii.— Drake to Walsyngham, August 23). That in the face of a strong squadron Parma could not cross he quite well understood ; but not so well that—with Medina-Sidonia defeated and fled—he could not attempt to do so ; that the merest threat of interference was sufficient to prevent him.

But when even Drake did not see this clearly, it is not strange that the action of the fleet was for long misunderstood, and that the failure of the Spaniards should have been represented—as it often is even now—as due to a Heaven-sent storm.

Flavit Deus et dissipati sunt was accepted as at
once a true and pious explanation of the whole
thing. It was, too, a flattering and economical
belief. We were—it has been argued—a nation
peculiarly dear to the Almighty, and He showed His
favour by raising a storm to overwhelm our enemy
when the odds against us were most terrible.

From the religious point of view such a
representation is childish ; from the historical it is
false. False, because the Spanish fleet, after being
hounded up Channel, had sustained a crushing
defeat from the English, a defeat in which they lost
many ships and thousands of men before they fled
to the north ; a defeat so terrible that nothing could
induce them to turn on their pursuers ; a defeat
which forced them to a headlong flight into the unknown dangers of the northern seas, rather than
face the more certain and now known danger of the
English shot. Childish, because in affairs of State
Providence works by recognised means, and gives
the victory not by disturbing the course of nature
and nature's laws, but by giving the favoured
nation wise and prudent commanders, skilful and
able warriors ; by teaching their hands to war and
their fingers to fight.

But, in fact, much of the nonsense that has been
talked grew out of the attempt, not unsuccessfully
made, to represent the war as religious ; to describe
it as a species of crusade instigated by the Pope, in
order to bring heretical England once more into the
fold of the true Church. In reality nothing can be
more inaccurate. It is, indeed, quite certain that
religious bitterness was imported into the quarrel ;

but the war had its origin in two perfectly clear and wholly mundane causes.

The first and chief of these was the exclusive commercial policy adopted and enforced by the Spanish Government in respect of its West Indian and American settlements. That such a policy should give rise to smuggling, that the smuggling should be met by violent repression, and that, again, by bloody reprisals, was all a matter of course. Now amongst the smugglers were two men—kinsmen— who by force of character, by genius curiously well adapted to the circumstances of the age, and by un- daunted courage, were destined to achieve a fore- most place in the roll-call of English seamen. Their names were John Hawkyns and Francis Drake. In September 1568 these two men, with some few companions and a little squadron of five vessels, whilst carrying on a lucrative though illicit traffic with the Spanish settlements, were caught, in the harbour of San Juan de Lua, by a vastly superior Spanish force and were overwhelmed. Hawkyns and Drake, in two of the smallest vessels, alone escaped. Ordinary men, under the circumstances, would have digested their loss as they best might ; but these, not being ordinary men, determined by fair means or foul to exact compensation for the injury which they conceived had been done them. Hawkyns, with the cunning as well as the courage of the fox, entered into a simulated negotiation to hand over a considerable part of the navy of Eng- land to King Philip, on condition of having the men who had been taken prisoners set free, and of receiving money compensation for his loss. The intrigue forms a curious episode in the history of the Ridolfi plot in 1571. Drake, on the other hand—a man of bolder and more generous character —finding compensation not forthcoming, resolved to seek it for himself; and after some preliminary cruises, made that wonderful and adventurous voyage in which, with a mere handful of men, he took Nombre de Dios, sacked Venta Cruz, captured a convoy of mules laden with silver, and returned home with more treasure than any one ship had previously brought to England. His achievement was to be speedily surpassed, but by himself. Four years afterwards he started on a voyage for the South Sea, and, capturing Spanish ships by the score and Spanish towns by the dozen, put a girdle round about the earth, and returned to England, again bringing back an enormous quantity of treasure, to the amount, it was said, of a million and a half sterling.

The outcry of the friends of Spain was very loud. Drake, they said, was a pirate, and unless he was punished, war was inevitable. Elizabeth had probably made up her mind that, in any case, war was very likely. She positively and in the plainest language refused to admit the Spanish claim to the whole of the islands and continent of America. She herself sympathised, she knew that all England sympathised, with Drake, and held his achievements to be not only heroic but lawful. Besides, she had got the money; and to return money which she had once clutched was to her a constitutional impossibility. She kept the money and she knighted Drake. Spaniards naturally took a very different view of Drake's conduct. It is quite certain that the King of Spain, and not only the King, but every one of his subjects, considered Drake as a pirate who ought to have been hanged, and maintained that the approval and support which he received from the English crown was a distinct and valid reason for an appeal to arms.

The other and perhaps equally valid reason was the countenance and assistance which had been given by the English to the King's rebellious subjects in the Low Countries ; and though many English, whether for pay or principle, had served in the Spanish armies against the Dutch, it was not doubted that the general opinion of England and of England's Queen was in favour of the rebels. There were, of course, many other grounds of ill-will, beginning, it may be, with Elizabeth's refusal to marry Philip. The quarrel had been growing all along : Elizabeth had seized the Duke of Alva's treasure ; had allowed Dutch privateers to shelter in English harbours ; had supported the claimant to the crown of Portugal. Philip, on the other hand, had stirred up and fomented rebellion in Ireland, and had been a party to many plots in England— plots against the Queen's sovereignty, plots against the Queen's life. He had behaved with the utmost insolence to the Queen's ambassador, and had placed many offensive restrictions on the commercial intercourse of the two nations and on English residents in Spain.

It was said, too, and universally believed, that unoffending English subjects, visiting Spain on their lawful occasions, were on the most shadowy pretexts seized by the Inquisition, imprisoned, tortured, and burnt at the stake. That these stories had a very great effect on popular opinion is certain : it is as certain that they were much exaggerated and frequently grossly misrepresented. Englishmen in Spain were, of course, subject to Spanish laws ; and if they went to Spain for their own profit they were bound to submit to such laws as were there in force ; but the known instances of Englishmen residing for many years at the Spanish ports, and carrying on a lucrative business there, are too numerous to permit us to believe that the English, as such, were subject to any undue and irregular oppression ; though as aliens in blood, in customs, and in religion, they were not looked on with much favour. On the other hand, transgressors met with little consideration. On both sides sharp measure had been dealt out to pirates : the hanging of Oxenham and his fellows was a smaller analogue of the butchery at Smerwick, and both executions were quite in accordance with the custom of the age. Even prisoners in recognised war might be, and not uncommonly were, put to death, if they were judged not worth keeping for a ransom. It will be seen that, in the surrender of the Nuestra Señora del Rosario, it was especially stipulated that the lives of the prisoners were to be spared, and that when the ship was taken to Torbay the sheriff of Devon thought it a pity that the men had not 'been made water spaniels' (vol. ii.—Don Pedro to the King, August 21 ; Cary to Walsyngham, August 29). In the case of the San Mateo, no conditions were made, and whilst 'the best sort were saved, the rest were cast overboard and slain' (vol. ii.—Borlas to Walsyngham, August 3). Of course, when prisoners were a source of danger, there was no hesitation. The action of Henry V. at Agincourt was a commonplace of mediæval war, and in 1588 a similar measure was meted out to the Spaniards who were thrown, naked and destitute, on the coast of Ireland.

There would thus, according to the ideas and practice of the age, have been nothing out of the way in summarily slaying the men who, in 1568, were captured at San Juan de Lua, or were afterwards put on shore by Hawkyns. In Spanish law, as indeed in English law, smugglers forcibly resisting the king's authority were pirates, and might be put to death without more ado. It is probable that many of them were so put to death, but more seem to have been enslaved; and in after years some few returned to England with stories of Spanish tyranny and Spanish cruelty which made a great impression on their countrymen. Prisons in the sixteenth century were nowhere luxurious abodes, and Spanish prisons are not likely to have been better than those of other nations. Howard, the philanthropist, has left a description of English prisons two hundred years later, when they were presumably less barbarous than in the days of Queen Elizabeth; and from this we may understand that, without any special malice or design on the part of the Spaniards, Englishmen, and especially Englishmen of a respectable position —merchants, or masters of merchant-ships—who had the misfortune to get into a Spanish prison, did experience grievous sufferings.

Nor were the horrors of the prison-house necessarily the worst part of their lot.   The Spaniards, as also the French and Italians, had no scruples about making their prisoners useful ; and an able-bodied man was as likely as not to find himself helping to tug an oar in one of the king's galleys, without the slightest regard paid to his personal dignity or his nationality, or the cause of his imprisonment (cf. p. 181).

That many Englishmen did thus rot in Spanish dungeons, or break their hearts in Spanish galleys, is very well established, but the reason why is not so clear.   As a general rule it is attributed to the Inquisition, and is assumed to have been on a charge of heresy.   It seems, however, not impossible that there has always been a confusion of names. *Inquisicion* means equally the Inquisition and a judicial inquiry : *inquisidor* might be an inquisitor, or a magistrate, or, in the armada, the provost-marshal ; and men reported to be lingering in the dungeons of the Inquisition may have been in some other and perhaps fouler prison on a charge of smuggling or piracy, brawling or contempt of court.   And magistrates were not immaculate, even in England.   Even in England alleged criminals were sometimes allowed to lie for months without a hearing, and when heard, were sometimes wrongfully condemned.   It is not to be supposed that similar blunders—blunders of ignorance, carelessness or prejudice—did not occur in Spain.

Still there is no doubt that many fell into the hands of the Inquisition, as we understand the word, the Holy Office.   Always on the watch to detect and punish heresy, which, in Spain, was held to be as dangerous to the State as popery was in England, the Holy Office did not professedly exercise jurisdiction over foreigners who kept their religious opinions to themselves ; but the man who openly and noisily preached his false doctrine or denounced the dogmas of the Church, be he Englishman or Spaniard, was arrested with as little ceremony as ever was a popish recusant in England, and racked, imprisoned, or put to death, even as if he had been a Mayne, a Sherwood, or a Campion.   When we recollect the atrocities that were practised in England against the Papists under Elizabeth, or, a hundred years later, in Scotland, against the Covenanters under Charles II. ; that Burghley advocated the use of the rack, and that the burning of women as witches was common even in the seventeenth century, we may allow that the Spanish Inquisition, abominable institution as it was, and aggravated by political conditions and the death-struggle with the Moors, was a disease of the age, and common alike to Papist and to Protestant.

But as to the wrongs and sufferings of English prisoners in Spain, a point which does not seem to have been duly considered is that we seldom have any account of them except that given by the men themselves.   Miles Philips, for instance, and Job Hortop, two of the men who were landed by Hawkyns after the rout at San Juan de Lua, are credible witnesses when they describe how the Spaniards 'hung them up by the arms upon high posts, until the blood burst out of their finger ends,' and punished them severely for attempting to escape. breaking out of prison, or conspiring to seize the

ship. We know from such narratives as that of
Captain O'Brien, how, two hundred years later, the
French treated prisoners of war who committed
such offences; and according to Garneray,[1] who
professes to write from personal experience, the life
of a French prisoner on board a hulk at Portsmouth
was wretched beyond the power of words. But
when these two men—smugglers and pirates in the
eye of Spanish law—describe themselves and their
mates as being brought before the Inquisitors, and
as being racked, burnt, or imprisoned because they
could not say the Lord's Prayer in Latin, or give satisfactory answers to abstruse questions on the Real
Presence, their statements require corroboration.[2]

So, too, the story of Robert Tomson, who, after
residing for several years in Spain and Mexico,
was, he says, dragged before the Inquisition and
sentenced to a term of imprisonment for entering
on a religious argument at a supper party, and
denouncing images, pictures, and the invocation of
saints before a mixed company. During a long
residence in Spain, Tomson must have outwardly
conformed to the Catholic religion; as he afterwards married a Spanish woman, he must have
again conformed; so that his untimely display of
Protestant zeal was a relapse such as the Inquisition
always judged severely, and for which it would have
inflicted a heavier punishment than three years in
prison, with permission to marry a rich heiress at
the end of the time. The story is therefore sus-
picious, and—as the other—needs corroboration.[3]

---

[1] *Mes Pontons*, par Louis Garneray.
[2] Hakluyt's *Principal Navigations*, iii. 469, 487.   [3] *Ib.* iii. 447.

It is not often possible to subject such stories to a critical examination ; but the case of Thomas Cely, which has been put prominently forward, admits and is deserving of a fuller discussion. In 1575 (vol. ii. App. A.), Dorothy, the wife of one Thomas Cely, a Bristol trader, petitioned the Council, setting forth that 'her husband upon most vile, slanderous, spiteful, malicious, and most villainous words uttered against the Queen's Majesty's own person by a certain subject of the King of Spain, not being able to suffer the same, did flee upon the same slanderous person and gave him a blow ; hereupon her said husband, no other offence in respect of their religion there committed, was secretly accused to the *Inquisidores* of the Holy House and so committed to most vile prison, and there hath remained now three whole years in miserable state with cruel torments.'[1]

Dorothy Cely certainly believed that her husband was in the dungeons of the Inquisition, and petitioned the Lords of the Council and the Queen to institute reprisals specially directed against foreign Papists. Mr. Froude, too, accepting the petition as sufficient authority, has lately repeated and emphasised the narrative. He says :—

'Thomas Cely, a merchant of Bristol, hearing a Spaniard in a Spanish port utter foul and slanderous charges against the Queen's character, knocked him down. To knock a man down for telling lies about Elizabeth might be a breach of the peace, but it had not yet been declared heresy. The Holy Office,

[1] *S.P. Spain*, xvi. ; Froude's *History of England*, cab. ed. viii. 22, where the petition is assigned the impossible date of 1563.

however, seized Cely, threw him into a dungeon, and kept him starving there for three years, at the end of which he contrived to make his condition known in England.'[1] He thinks, however, that it was to no purpose, and that Cely was 'one of the many hundred English sailors who rotted away in the dungeons of the Inquisition, or were burnt to please the rabble of Valladolid.'[2]

Whether the fate of the 'many hundred English sailors' rests on a more solid foundation than that of Cely does not appear ; but Cely lived to command a ship against the Armada, to write the quaint letter (p. 262), to plunder the Spanish prisoners (vol. ii. Index), and to be granted a pension of 30*l.* a year (May 5, 1590). He was still alive and in good health in July 1591.

But Cely's letter is specially interesting from the naïve confession of the cause of his punishment, which was very different from that alleged in the petition, or the paraphrase of it : to knock a man down in a Spanish port, presumably on the wharf, for uttering foul and slanderous charges against the Queen's character can scarcely be considered the same thing as 'striking their secretary as I was before the *Inquisidores*, they sitting in judgment.' It might be well, before speaking too strongly of the cruelty to which Cely was subjected, to ask what would have been the fate of a foreign sailor in England who, in open court, struck the judge's secretary ? As to why Cely was, in the first instance, before the magistrates or *Inquisidores*, or whether the Holy Office had anything to do with the matter, there is

---

[1] *Longman's Magazine*, August 1893.   [2] *Hist.* viii. 23 *n.*

no evidence. It may have been for smuggling, or
for brawling, or possibly for contempt shown to the
Host in its passage along the street.

Much more might be said on this moot point;
but political affairs commonly depend on belief
rather than on fact, and, whatever the actual truth,
it appears fairly certain that, to the English, the
real or supposed cruelties of the Inquisition were a
principal cause of the very strong feeling against the
Spaniards and Papists; whilst, to the Spaniards, the
aggressions of the English smugglers and pirates,
and the assistance rendered by the English to Dutch
rebels, were direct causes of the war. The breach
was by no means a one-sided one, and though we
are naturally accustomed to lay most stress on our
own grievances, real and sentimental, we cannot but
admit that the Spaniards also had suffered very
substantial injuries. What brought matters to a
climax were the embargo laid on English shipping
in Spain in May 1585, and the dread of Spain, which
could now only be considered as a hostile power,
obtaining the command of the Dutch ports.[1]

The war between the two countries, which
avowedly began in 1585, anticipated, in a very
curious manner, the lines of the war of the French
Revolution two centuries later. In both cases the
immediate cause of war was the dread of a hostile
power fortifying itself in the sea-ports of the
Netherlands; to prevent this a levy of men was
ordered; the newly-raised army was sent abroad
under an incompetent general, whose sole title to
command was royal favour—it matters little whether

---

[1] *S.P. Dom. Eliz.*, clxxx. 35.

he was called Earl of Leicester or Duke of York—
and the result was ignominious failure.   But meantime the English fleet swept the West Indies, and
Drake's expedition of 1585–6 may be considered
the precursor and prototype of Jervis's campaign of
1794.   It will be seen that this correspondence was
not only in the commencement of the wars, but also
in their more advanced stages; that the flat-
bottomed boats at Dunkirk were imitated by those
at Boulogne; and that the destruction of the
enemy's ships at Cadiz in 1596 presents a very
exact analogy to the final overthrow of Bonaparte's
schemes at Trafalgar.

Drake's brilliant raid through the West Indies
determined Philip on a decided course.   For the
past fifteen years the invasion of England had been
mooted, as a thing desirable and not impossible.
It had been proposed by the Duke of Alva in 1569,
after the seizure of his treasure.   It had been
spoken of in 1579, after the exploits of Norreys in
the Low Countries had rendered the services of the
English volunteers notorious; and in 1583, after
his victory over Strozzi and his scratch fleet at
Terceira, the Marquis of Santa Cruz had urged it
as a necessary step towards the reduction of the
rebellious Netherlands.[1]   The Duke of Parma had
written to the same effect, repeating that English
soldiers were of little count in presence of the

[1] *La Armada Invencible*, por el Capitan de Navío C. Fernandez
Duro, i. 241.   In the book here referred to, Captain Duro has
done, from the Spanish point of view, what is now attempted, in
the following pages, from the English.   The two works are, in a
measure, complementary of each other, and both must be studied
for a full understanding of the events of the year.

Spanish veterans, and adding a statement, which
seems to have obtained general credence among the
Spaniards, that the English ships at Terceira had
been the first to fly; had, in fact, played a part
somewhat resembling that of the Egyptian ships at
Actium. It is quite possible that there were some
English ships at Terceira, though it is doubtful; if
there were, they rightly declined to imitate Strozzi's
ill-judged and suicidal manœuvre of closing with the
Spaniards, and—small blame to them—effected their
escape. True or not, however, it appears certain
that this reported flight of the English ships did
have very considerable weight with many of the
King's advisers; and so advised, and at the same
time impelled by wrath, Philip determined on the
attempt. The Marquis of Santa Cruz was called on
for his scheme, which extended to gigantic proportions. Everything was to be done from Spain.
The whole shipping of the empire was to be
collected. Every available soldier was to be
mustered. According to the very detailed project
submitted by Santa Cruz on the 12th of March,
1586, the numbers amounted to :—

—	Nos.	Tons	Sailors	Soldiers
Great ships of war . .	150	77,250 ⎫		
Store ships . . .	40	8,000 ⎬	16,612	55,000
Smaller vessels . .	320	25,000 ⎭		

besides—

—	Nos.	Sailors and fighting men	Rowers
Galleasses	6	720	1,800
Galleys	40	3,200	8,000

giving a total of 556 ships of all kinds, and 85,332 men,[1] to which were to be added cavalry, artillery-men, volunteers, and non-combatants, bringing up the number of men to a gross total of 94,222.

Philip could not approve of a project so vast and so costly ; he resolved on the expedition, but con-ceived the idea of doing it at a cheaper rate by utilising the army in the Low Countries. From this grew up the scheme which ultimately took form. The Duke of Parma, in Flanders, was to prepare an army of invasion, and a number of flat-bottomed boats to carry it across the sea. The Marquis of Santa Cruz was to bring up the Channel a fleet powerful enough to crush any possible oppo-sition, and carrying a body of troops which, when joined with those under Parma, would form an army at least as numerous as that which Santa Cruz had detailed as sufficient.

The necessary preparations were extensive, and it is not quite clear that, as they became more definite, Philip's ardour did not somewhat slacken. The cost was certain ; the issue was doubtful ; and even if successful, the result might perhaps not be exactly what was desired. Philip had always posed as a supporter of the Queen of Scots ; but the doubt must have suggested itself whether it was worth while, at this great cost, to conquer a kingdom for her—a kingdom which, with her French blood and French proclivities, would become virtually a French province. The death of the Queen of Scots, on the 8th of February, 1587, removed this difficulty. Even if the conquered kingdom was to be handed

[1] Duro, i. 253, 274.

over to James, James was not bound to France as his mother had been. Placed on the throne of England by Spanish arms, he might be expected or even constrained to hold it virtually as a Spanish fief. But it might not be necessary to give it to James at all. Elizabeth was, of course, outside the reckoning; once dispossessed, she was merely the illegitimate offspring of an abominable and incestuous concubinage. But Philip himself was lineally descended from John of Gaunt, and had a theoretical right to the throne of England distinctly superior to that which, in the case of Henry VII., had been held sufficient. As an abstract problem in genealogy, Philip's claim was by no means absurd. Whether it could become something more, and take a practical form, might very well depend on the fortune of war.

Preparations were therefore now hurried on in earnest. Ships were collected at the several ports, and especially at Lisbon and Cadiz. It seemed probable that the invasion would be attempted in the summer of 1587, when some months before, Drake, with a fleet of twenty-four ships, all told, appeared on the coast. The orders under which he sailed from England, on the 2nd of April, were to prevent the different Spanish squadrons from joining, and where he found their ships, to destroy them. It was a grand and masterful step, but it had scarcely been ordered before the Queen repented of it. Counter orders were sent post-haste to Plymouth, but Drake had already sailed. They followed him, but never found him; and Drake, acting on those first given, went down to Cadiz and there sank, burnt, or brought away thirty-seven of the enemy's ships. They were as yet unarmed, unmanned, and, when the forts were once passed, could offer no resistance. Other damage Drake did, insulting Santa Cruz in the very port of Lisbon, offering battle, which Santa Cruz was in no position to accept. Ships he had in numbers, but they too were neither manned nor armed; and before the guns were ready, Drake had stretched off to the Azores, where he captured the San Felipe, a very large and rich East Indiaman, whose treasures are said to have first opened the eyes of our English merchants to the capabilities of Eastern trade, and to have led to the foundation of the East India Company.

The destruction of shipping and stores at Cadiz necessarily delayed the equipment of the Spanish fleet; the year passed away, and it was not ready. In the following January the Marquis of Santa Cruz died. The loss to Spain was incalculable, for he was the only man who by birth was entitled, and by experience was competent, to command such an expedition as that which he had set on foot. His name was encircled with a halo of naval victory. He had held a high command at the battle of Lepanto, and in the action at Terceira was accredited with having put to ignominious flight these very English who were now the object of attack. The King and his court, however, do not seem to have realised their loss, and with a light heart appointed Don Alonso Perez de Guzman el Bueno, Duke of Medina-Sidonia, to the vacant command. Medina-Sidonia, now in his thirty-eighth year, was a man with no qualification for the post except his distinguished birth and a gentleness of temper which,

it was perhaps thought, would fit better with the idea
of making him subordinate to the Duke of Parma.
It had, indeed, appeared that Santa Cruz was not in
the least disposed to accept this inferior part; and
it may very well be that the King was almost relieved
by the solution of the difficulty which his death had
offered.   His successor was utterly ignorant of naval
affairs, had but little experience of military, and none
whatever of high command.   Personally brave, as
became his long line of ancestry, his total want of
experience and knowledge rendered him, as a commander, timid, undecided, and vacillating.   His
answer to the King, on being ordered to take on
himself the command, is in itself a curiosity.   The
business, he wrote, was so great, so important, that
he could not conscientiously undertake it, being, as
he was, without experience or knowledge of either
the sea or of war.[1]   His objections were, however,
overruled; and in an evil hour for his reputation,
he consented.   The equipment of the fleet was
pushed on, and by the middle of May it was ready
to sail from the Tagus.   It did actually sail on the
20th of May.

It may here be said that the name ' Invincible,'
so commonly given to this fleet, was not official.
In Philip's numerous letters there is no trace of it.
By him, by his secretary, by Medina-Sidonia and
other officers, and by all the contemporary chroniclers, the fleet is spoken of as the Grand Fleet—a
name constantly used in England during the eighteenth century for what we now call the Channel
Fleet.   In a semi-official list printed at Lisbon it

[1] Duro, i. 415.

was called *La felicísima Armada*—the fortunate
fleet. The 'Invincible' probably sprang out of the
idle talk of some of the young adventurers (cf. p.
175), braggarts as became their age, or out of the
silly gossip of the Lisbon taverns.[1]

None the less, the power of Spain was everywhere recognised as gigantic. The Spanish soldiers
were numerous, well-disciplined, inured to war ;
Spanish galleons, navigating the most distant seas,
brought to the Spanish treasury the riches of India
or Peru ; and Spanish galleys had curbed the ambition of the fierce conquerors of Constantinople.
Spanish statesmen were known to be most crafty
and sagacious ; and nineteenth century historians
had not yet discovered that the Spanish king, who
ruled one half of continental Europe and controlled
the other, was ignorant and incapable, childish if
not imbecile. In the sixteenth century he was
believed to be a far-seeing, prudent, ambitious man,
slow in council, swift in execution. His accumulated
wrath against England tempted him to listen to the
voice of his counsellors, who urged on the war, and
of his ambition, which invited him to seize the inheritance of his forefathers ; but, whilst yielding to
the temptation, he endeavoured, so far as in him
lay, to deserve that success which he hoped to win.
He had no practical familiarity with war, but he
had heard enough of English soldiers and English
sailors to be convinced that they were not the
dastards they were represented to be : he knew that
if they had fled from Terceira, they certainly had
not fled from Rymenam ; the brilliant skirmish of

[1] Duro, i. 50.

Zutphen had then a reputation not unlike that of the light cavalry charge at Balaclava forty years ago; and he was not ignorant of Drake's exploits in the West Indies, in the Pacific, or at Cadiz only the year before. He knew that the enterprise on which he was bent would not resemble a military promenade, and all the available forces of his vast empire were collected in this Grand Fleet. He hoped, too, for assistance from outside, and that, at any rate, a subsidy from the Pope would lessen the financial burden.

France, it was evident, might do much to forward his project, or to render it abortive; but already Philip exercised great influence over the party of the Guises, which his attitude as the champion of the Church and the avenger of their cousin, the Queen of Scots, confirmed. No politician has better understood the value of the maxim *Divide et impera!* and by the financial aid and moral support which he gave to the Guises, he rendered it certain that France would not take any active part against him, and not improbable that she might become a powerful auxiliary. To the last this remained a matter of doubt. It will be seen that Burghley and Walsyngham thought it not impossible, that Howard was fully convinced that a French fleet and a French army would join with the Spanish (pp. 203, 227). They knew that the French king was naturally antagonistic to the designs of Spain, but they had no trust in his steadfastness (p. 49); they could not gauge either the strength of his party or the pressure that might be brought to bear on him, and the 'day of the barricades' seemed to prostrate him before the Guises and Philip.

In England, as elsewhere, there prevailed an exalted opinion of Spanish power and of Spanish prowess. The prestige of Spanish arms stood high, and may be fairly compared with that of the Grand Monarque before Blenheim, or of Napoleon after Austerlitz or Jena. In forming a lower estimate of them the English sailors were almost alone, but their experience was exceptional. For the last twenty years they had been, in their own irregular way, fighting the Spaniards on every sea where they were to be met, and had come to the conclusion that, whatever the Spaniard might be ashore, afloat he was but a poor creature : the experiences of Drake, Hawkyns, the Fenners, and scores of others had proved that, even with great apparent odds in their favour, Spaniards were not invincible. Of all the panic-stricken accounts of the great armada which have come down to us, not one was written by a seaman or by any one who had practical knowledge of the Spaniards by sea. We are all familiar with the exaggerations of contemporary historians. The Spanish ships were so huge that ocean groaned beneath their weight ; so lofty that they resembled rather castles or fortresses ; so numerous that the sea was invisible—the spectator thought he beheld a populous town. What English sailors thought of them may be judged from a letter written by Fenner, who was with Drake when he burnt the shipping at Cadiz. ' Twelve of her Majesty's ships,' he said, ' were a match for all the galleys in the King of Spain's dominions.'

Still, not even Drake or Fenner could feel perfect confidence whilst ignorant of the magnitude

of the task before them. They had no fear of the
fleet (pp. 229, 241); of the army they were not so
sure. And then, too, the known power of Spain, the
tavern gossip and braggadocio of Lisbon, and the
reports of spies who felt in honour bound to give
full value for their hire, grossly exaggerated the
size, the might, the armament, and the equipment of
the fleet as it sailed from Lisbon. Some of these
reports (pp. 90, 122) may have been honestly
meant. They appear to be based on the first proposal of Santa Cruz, the details of which may have
been allowed to leak out. But the actual numbers
were very different, and as to the equipment, it was
so far from being perfect that by the time the fleet
reached Cape Finisterre vast quantities of provisions
were found to be bad, putrid, fit for nothing but to
be thrown overboard. The ships were short of
water, probably because the casks were leaky. The
ships themselves were leaking—strained, it was said,
by the heavy weather, but really from being over-
masted. Several of them were with difficulty kept
afloat, some were dismasted, and the distress was
so general that Medina-Sidonia determined to put
into Corunna to refit. This he did, but without
taking any precautions to let his intention be known
through the fleet.[1] The Scilly Isles had been given
out as the rendezvous in case of separation, and
some dozen or more of the ships, finding they had
lost sight of the admiral, did accordingly go to the
neighbourhood of the Scilly Isles, where they were
duly seen and reported at Plymouth (p. 221).
Their recall, the collecting the fleet at Corunna, the

[1] Duro, i. 57.

refitting, the reprovisioning, all took time. The damage was so great, the number of sick so large, the season getting so advanced, that a council of war urgently recommended postponing the expedition till the next year. The King's orders were, however, imperative, and the fleet finally sailed from Coruña on the 12th of July.

The main part of the English fleet was mean time mustered at Plymouth, under the command of Lord Howard of Effingham, the Lord Admiral of England, with whom were Drake and Hawkyns as vice- and rear-admirals ; several noblemen, includ ing Lord Thomas Howard, the admiral's cousin— his first cousin's grandson ; Lord Sheffield, his sister's son ; Sir Robert Southwell, his daughter's husband ; and most of the seamen whose names make up the maritime history of the century : Frobiser, Thomas Fenner and his cousins, Fenton and Luke Ward, Raymond, Lancaster, Richard Hawkyns, and many more. Large numbers of merchants' ships, levied by the Queen, or by their own towns, had joined the fleet, which as it lay at Plymouth consisted of about 80 sail all told. From the time of his return from the coast of Spain in the previous summer, Drake had been urgent that he should be sent out again, with a still more powerful squadron, to repeat the blow (pp. 124, 148, 166, 238). Hawkyns (p. 60), Frobiser, Fenner (p. 238)—all the seamen of experience—were of the same opinion. Howard, guided by their advice, repeatedly pressed the importance of the step (pp. 192, 200, 203), but Elizabeth steadfastly refused. It may be that she hoped for peace ; but it is difficult to believe that

she was entirely hoodwinked by the false protesta-
tions of the Duke of Parma and by the negotiations
carried on in Flanders.   She was herself too well
versed in the arts of dissimulation to be snared
by such evident pretences.   It is, perhaps, more
probable that she believed the war might still be
carried on in the same cheap and desultory fashion
as during the last three years, and was unwilling to
set Philip the example of more sustained efforts.   It
is very possible she had persuaded herself that the
preparations in Spain were merely a threat, which,
however, any aggressive action of hers might con-
vert into a reality.   And thus, notwithstanding
the prayers and entreaties of Howard and Drake,
backed up by every man of experience, no further
attempt was made on the Spanish ports.   It can
scarcely be doubted that, if Drake had been permitted, he would have kindled such a blaze in the
Tagus or in the harbour of Corunna as would have
effectually prevented even the threat of an invasion.

It has been repeatedly stated[1] that the Duke
of Medina-Sidonia was ordered by Philip to hug
the French coast, so as to avoid the English fleet
and to reach the Straits of Dover with his force
intact.   This is contrary to the fact.   The Duke's
instructions were to the very opposite effect.   They
ordered him, if he should meet Drake near the
mouth of the Channel, to fall on him and destroy
him ; it would be more easy to destroy the English
fleet piecemeal than after allowing it to collect in one.
And, so far from directing him to hug the French

---

[1] Monson's *Naval Tracts* in Churchill's *Voyages* (edit. 1732),
iii. 149.

coast, they advise the Scilly Isles or the Lizard as a
rendezvous, and suggest the propriety of seizing on
some unfortified port in the South of England.[1]
As a matter of fact, a position south of the Scilly
Isles was given out as a rendezvous in the first
instance; in the second, on sailing from Corunna,
the rendezvous was Mount's Bay.[2]

In crossing the Bay of Biscay the armada experienced some bad weather, and was a good deal
scattered; barely two-thirds of the ships were in
company when Medina-Sidonia sighted the Lizard
on the afternoon of the 19th of July. There, whilst
waiting for the fleet to collect, he hoisted the royal
standard at the fore, and at the main a sacred flag,
showing a crucifix between the figures of Our Lady
and St. Mary Magdalene. Other flags there were
by the score. The fleet was organised by provinces,
and the ships of each squadron presumably wore the
flag of its province—Andalusia, Guipuscoa, Naples,
&c.—as well as the flags of the nobles and knights
on board, and probably also the flag of the particular
saint to which they were dedicated. But the flag
which they appear to have worn in common as the
flag of the empire was, strictly speaking, the Burgundian flag, which had been adopted by Spain in
the time of the Emperor Charles V.—white, a
saltire raguled red; and it may be noted that,
amongst the great number and diversity of flags,
the one flag which was not worn, and could not be
worn, was the red and yellow ensign of the present
day, a flag which was not invented till the year
1785.

[1] Duro, ii. 8.   [2] *Ib*. ii. 27, 168.

The English flag at this time was the plain St. George's flag—white, a cross red—and this was worn by every English ship. The Ark, Lord Howard's ship, flew also the royal standard, the flag of the Queen's arms, and, probably at the fore, a flag of Howard's arms. Some of the other ships were also supplied with 'flags of the Queen's arms' and 'ensigns of silk' distinct from 'the flags of Saint George.' Many had streamers 'small and great,' and one, the Elizabeth Bonaventure, had 'a bloody flag,' the plain red flag which down to the end of the eighteenth century continued to be the signal to 'engage the enemy' (vol. ii.—September 25, Reports of Survey). That some of the ships, and especially those sent forth by the coast towns or by private individuals, wore also local or private flags, is not improbable, but the State Papers make no mention of such.

On Saturday, the 20th of July, the Spanish fleet was collected off the Lizard and moved slowly eastwards. Medina-Sidonia wrote to the King that he intended to proceed as far as the Isle of Wight, where he hoped to have word of the Duke of Parma. At present he had no intelligence, and was quite in the dark as to the enemy's movements. In passing Plymouth he hoped he might pick up some pinnace from which he could get information. In the afternoon, however, many ships were seen, though thick weather and mist prevented his counting them ; and towards midnight an English boat was brought in, with four men on board, from whom he learnt that the English fleet, commanded by the Admiral of England and by Drake, had put to sea that afternoon.[1]

Medina-Sidonia's statement is perfectly clear, connected and intelligible, and, being written on the very day, has high claims on our belief. It describes, too, conduct which is quite in keeping with the character of the man. He avowedly knew nothing of the art of war, and had now come on the enemy's coast, and was about to proceed leisurely through the enemy's sea, without taking any trouble to find out where the enemy's fleet was. His frank acknowledgment, whilst it proves him a fool, argues that he was, at least, a truthful one. On the other hand, the letter of Don Pedro de Valdes to the King (vol. ii.—August 21) speaks of a fisherman being captured on the Saturday, of a council of war being held to consider his intelligence that the English fleet was at anchor at Plymouth, and of the resolution come to, to 'make to the mouth of the haven and set upon the enemy, if it might be done with any advantage,' a design which was prevented by their discovering the English fleet at sea, some two hours later. Captain Duro accepts a still different story, according to which the council of war was held on the Friday afternoon, and they then knew that the English fleet was at Plymouth. At this meeting Recalde, Leyva and Oquendo, more particularly, urged that the destruction of the enemy's fleet was the first object, and that the opportunity ought not to be neglected ; to which Medina-Sidonia replied that the King's orders did

[1] Medina-Sidonia to the King, July 20–30 ; Medina-Sidonia's Journal, Duro, ii. 222, 229.

not permit him any latitude, and compelled him to proceed without delay to join the Duke of Parma.[1] But the reference which Captain Duro gives for this story not only does not sanction it, but confirms the statement of Medina-Sidonia ; and as Don Pedro's letter was written a month after the date, it is quite possible that his memory deceived him as to the sequence of events.

About the result, however, there is no difference of opinion. During the Friday evening the English warped out of the harbour ; on the Saturday they beat out of the Sound, 'very hardly, the wind being at South-West. About three of the clock in the afternoon they descried the Spanish fleet, and did what they could to work for the wind' (p. 288). The wind, by veering to the West-North-West,[2] and the Spaniards, by sailing large through the night, assisted their efforts. On Sunday morning, when the two fleets were first in presence of each other, the English were to windward, and by their practical skill and the weatherly qualities of their ships, had no difficulty in keeping the advantage they had gained.

And now, before the fighting begins, it will be well to examine the comparative force of the opposing fleets. We have all known from our infancy that the Spanish ships, as compared with the English, were stupendous in point of size, marvellous in their strength ; in guns and in number of men beyond all proportion. As to the numbers, the first proposal of Santa Cruz has already been given. It was never anything more than a proposal. The

---

[1] Duro, i. 67.   [2] *Ib.* ii. 230.

actual numbers when the fleet sailed from the Tagus
on the 20th of May were :—[1]

Ships	Tons	Guns	Men
130	57,868	2,431	8,050 seamen 18,973 soldiers 1,382 volunteers, &c. 2,088 rowers
		Total . .	30,493

These numbers, however, had suffered a marked
decrease before the fleet left Corunna, and a still
further decrease before the fleet came into the
Channel. Of the ships left behind there is no
exact account. Some, and some large ships
amongst them, certainly did not come on. Some,
again, appear to have parted company on the
voyage ; and of four galleys, from which much had
been expected, one was driven ashore and wrecked
near Bayonne ; the other three, making very bad
weather of it, put into different French ports, and
eventually returned to Spain.[2] Allowing for these
losses, it is doubtful whether more than 120 ships
of all sizes came into the Channel ; the number
of men did certainly not exceed 24,000 ; and in the
council of war held at Corunna it was estimated
as low as 22,500.[3] Of the ships, about half were
transports or victuallers pure and simple, and took
no part in the fighting ; many, too, were pinnaces,
or despatch boats, unfitted for fighting ; but they
all carried men, sailors or soldiers, who must be
deducted from the gross numbers. The effective

[1] Duro, ii. 66, 83.   [2] *Ib*. i. 65.   [3] *Ib*. ii. 142, 199.

total of fighting men in the Spanish fleet can thus scarcely have been more than from 10,000 to 12,000.

On the other hand, the total number of English ships, of all sizes and qualities, registered as in the Queen's service during any part of the season was 197, bearing 15,925 men; to which must be added the many recruits sent off from Plymouth on the 21st of July (p. 289), or who joined as volunteers in the passage up Channel. It is difficult to estimate the gross total at less than from 17,000 to 18,000 men. Of the 197 ships, however, by far the greater number neither had, nor were meant to have, any part in the fighting; many of them were not even present when the fighting was going on. Seymour, for instance, with all his squadron, did not join the Admiral till the 27th of July. The fifteen victuallers which went west, under Burnell, in June, were probably discharged at once, and their men pressed for the great ships. Four of the coast ships with Seymour were sent away to convoy the Stade fleet; six others were discharged during June, for want of victuals (p. 255). The eight London ships under Gorges (p. 311) and the ten under Bellingham (p. 339) did not leave the river till after the 29th of July, and joined Seymour only after his return from the north (vol. ii.—Seymour to Walsyngham, Aug. 1). The galley Bonavolia was, at the last moment, judged unseaworthy, and was sent into the river; on the 29th of July she was lying at the Nore-head (p. 338). These which are certainly known to have been absent from the battle of Gravelines account for 2,650 men, a number

not affected by the burning of eight ships at
Calais. Of the rest, whether present or not cannot
be determined, 37 had crews of not more than 30
men, and 900 in all. No one will suppose that these
pinnaces added to the effective strength of the fleet
on the day of battle, any more than the Pickle or
Entreprenante did at Trafalgar. They had their
use in the fleet, but that use was not engaging the
enemy's great ships. And many others of the
English vessels were scarcely of greater value as
men-of-war, so that the number of men who, even
in appearance, took part in the battle of Gravelines
can scarcely have been more than from eight to nine
thousand.

Our idea of the size of the Spanish ships has
been also somewhat exaggerated. According to
Barrow,[1] 'The best of the Queen's ships placed
alongside one of the first class of Spaniards would
have been like a sloop-of-war by the side of a first
rate.' In point of tonnage they were, in fact, the
same. The largest Spaniard, the Regazona, of the
Levant squadron, is given as 1,249 tons. The
largest English ship, the Triumph, is described as
of 1,000 or 1,100 tons, and many circumstances seem
to show that, whilst the reckoning of tonnage was
everywhere extremely vague, the English method
gave a smaller result than the Spanish. The San
Salvador, for instance, was classed by the Spaniards
as of 958 tons; when she fell into English hands,
she was described as, by estimation, of 600 (vol. ii.
Aug. 24). There is no doubt, however, that the
Spanish ships looked larger. Their poops and forecastles, rising tier above tier to a great height, towered

[1] *Life of Drake*, 270.

far above the lower-built English. Not that the large English ships were by any means flush-decked ; but they were not so high-charged as the Spanish. The difference offered a great advantage to the Spaniards in hand-to-hand fighting ; it told terribly against them when their enemy refused to close ; it made their ships leewardly and unmanageable in even a moderate breeze, and, added to the Spanish neglect of recent improvements in rig—notably, the introduction of the bowline—rendered them very inferior to the English in the open sea.[1]

And not only was there this inferiority of the ships ; there was at least a corresponding inferiority of the seamen. The Spaniards, and still more the Italians, were to a great extent fair-weather sailors. Some there doubtless were who had been through the Straits of Magellan or had doubled the Cape of Good Hope, but by far the greater number had little experience beyond the Mediterranean, or the equable run down the trades to the West Indies. To the English, on the other hand, accustomed from boyhood to the Irish or Iceland fisheries ; in manhood to the voyages to the north-west with Frobiser or Davys, or round the world with Drake, and semi-piratical cruises in the Bay of Biscay or in the track of the homeward-bound treasure-ships, the summer gales of the Channel were, by comparison, passing trifles—things to be warded off, but not to be feared. Even if the men had been equal in quality, the Spanish ships were terribly undermanned. The seamen habitually gave place to the soldiers ; the soldiers commanded ; the seamen did the drudgery, and not one was borne in

[1] Cf. Monson, in Churchill, iii. 312, 319.

excess of what their soldier masters thought necessary.   The absolute numbers speak for themselves,
and one comparison will be sufficient.   The San
Martin, of 1,000 tons, the flagship of the Duke of
Medina-Sidonia, had 177 seamen and 300 soldiers.
The Ark, of 800 tons, the flagship of Lord Howard,
had 300 seamen and 125 soldiers.

More important, however, than even this inferiority of the Spanish ships and sailors was the
inferiority of their guns and gunners.   It was long
believed in this country, and has been repeatedly
stated, that the Spanish guns were both numerous
and large.   They were, in fact, neither one nor the
other ; as a rule they were small—4, 6 or 9-pounders ;
they were comparatively few, and they were very
badly worked.

The guns at that time in use on board ship were,
roughly speaking, the same in the English and
Spanish navies ; and as everything was rough, as
the minimum windage prescribed was one-fourth of
the bore of the gun and as much more as pleased
the gunner, the Englishmen felt no difficulty in
assigning English names to the Spanish guns, as
shown in the following tables.   The weight of the
shot is approximate, but sufficiently accurate for
purposes of comparison (vol. ii. App. C).

I. Cannon .	.	. Perhaps a 60-pounder, but more probably 42.
II. Demi-Cannon	.	A 30-pounder.
III. Cannon-Pedro	.	A very light 24-pounder.
IV. Culverin	.	. A long 18-pounder.
V. Basilisco	.	. A 15-pounder.
VI. Demi-Culverin	.	A long 9-pounder.
VII. Saker .	.	. A 6-pounder.
VIII. Minion .	.	. A 4-pounder.

And smaller pieces under the names of fowler, falcon, falconet, &c., throwing balls of from 3 pounds to 8 ounces.

COMPARISON OF ARMAMENTS

Ships names	Tons	Men	Number of guns	Approximate weight of broadside in lbs.	Description of guns							
					I.	II.	III.	IV.	V.	VI.	VII.	Small pieces
Spanish												
S. Lorenzo . .	—	386	50	330	4	8	—	6	—	6	10	16
N.S. d. Rosario .	1,150	422	41	200	—	3	6	4	1	1	6	20
San Salvador .	958	396	25	185	4	—	4	5	—	1	—	11
Anunciada . .	703	275	26	60	—	—	—	—	—	8	—	18
Sta Maria d. Vison	666	307	24	50	—	—	—	—	—	6	—	18
English												
Triumph . .	1,100	500	44	340	4	3	—	17	—	8	6	6
Ark . . .	800	425	44	330	4	4	—	12	—	12	6	6
Nonpareil . .	500	250	40	230	2	3	—	7	—	8	12	8
Foresight . .	300	160	31	96	—	—	—	—	—	14	8	9
Tiger . . .	200	100	30	106	—	—	—	4	—	8	8	10

With the exception of the Tiger, whose armament is taken from an order[1] by Sir William Wynter in 1586, the English armaments are given from a table dated 1595-9, printed by Derrick.[2] The comparison shows that the change between 1586 and 1595 had been rather to decrease the weight of the guns. Wynter's order of 1586 also gives the armament of two ships which he distinguishes as galleon P. Pett at Deptford, and galleon Ma. Baker at Woolwich. In 1588 they were known as the Rainbow and Vanguard. Two papers[3] of 1595 give estimates for the armaments of three ships 'now in building,' the ordnance for the first two being described as 'answerable to the pieces that are in the

[1] *S.P. Dom. Eliz.*, clxxxvii. 65.
[2] *Rise and Progress of the Royal Navy*, 31.
[3] *S.P. Dom. Eliz.*, ccliii. 114 ; ccliv. 43.

Mer Honour,' whose armament is here given from
Derrick's table :—

Ships' names	Tons	No. of guns	Approximate weight of broadside in lbs.	Description of guns				
				II.	IV.	VI.	VII.	Small pieces
Galleon Pett, 1586 } Galleon Baker, 1586 } ·	500	54	300	8	10	14	2	20
Ship, September 1595 ·	?	44	300	4	16	18	4	2
Ship, October 1595, I. ·	?	44	280	—	20	20	4	—
Ship, October 1595, II. ·	?	36	220	—	16	12	8	—
Mer Honour . . ·	800	41	280	4	15	16	4	2

and comparing the armament ordered in 1586 for
the Rainbow and Vanguard, two ships which may
be classed with the Nonpareil given in the former
table, the necessary inference is that the armaments
of 1595 were not so heavy as those carried in 1588.

Another estimate, which, though inexact, is entitled to credit, is that given of the armament of the
Revenge, also a ship of 500 tons, taken by the
Spaniards in 1591, and reported by them to have
43 brass guns: 20 on the lower deck of from 4,000
to 6,000 pounds weight, and the rest from 2,000
to 3,000.[1] The greater weights correspond to the
cannons, demi-cannons, or culverins ; the smaller to
the demi-culverins and sakers.

Of the Spanish armament we cannot speak with
the same absolute knowledge ; but it seems admitted that the galleasses were the most heavily armed
ships in the fleet, and of these the San Lorenzo,
which was taken at Calais, was the largest and
heaviest.   The report of her armament given by our

---

[1] Duro, i. 76.

peuple (p. 349), who had possession of her for some time, corresponds fairly well with the official statement.[1] The Nuestra Señora del Rosario was the large ship captured by Drake and sent into Torbay. Her armament is given from the official inventory taken at Torquay (vol. ii. August 29, November 5). She is spoken of by Duro as one of the most powerful and best ships of the fleet.[2] The San Salvador was the ship partly blown up and sent to Weymouth (pp. 9, 301); her armament is also given from the official inventory (vol. ii. Aug. 24). Some of her small guns were very likely thrown overboard by the explosion. Duro tabulates her as carrying 25 in all. The inventory accounts for 19, including four old minions and one old fowler. The missing six were probably fowlers or falcons. The two remaining ships have their armament given by Duro.[3] They do not seem in any way distinguished from others of the same size; they belonged to the Levant squadron, and are classed with the San Juan de Sicilia, of 800 tons and 26 guns, which took a prominent part in the battle of the 29th of July. There is no published account of the armament of the great ships of the Portuguese squadron, and amongst them the San Martin, San Felipe, and San Mateo, of which all were in the thickest of the fight, and the two last were driven on shore in a sinking state. It was probably not very different from that of the N. S. del Rosario. There is here, of course, no suggestion that the more powerful ships were armed like the Anunciada or Santa Maria de Vison; but it

[1] Duro, i. 390.   [2] *Ib.* i. 83 *n.*
[3] Tom. i. 389.

appears a fair presumption that many of the ships which have been counted as effective were so armed.

It should also be noted that whereas the Spanish ships of below 300 tons burden carried only four or six small guns, English ships of 200 tons had a very respectable armament, and ships still smaller were not altogether despicable. Of the way in which the English merchant ships were armed we have little knowledge. The larger ones, under the command of men like Lancaster or George Fenner, may certainly be classed as efficient men-of-war. The Margaret and John, of 200 tons, is named as having rendered good service on more than one occasion; and considering that many of the others had probably been on privateering cruises, and that the Pelican or Golden Hind, in which Drake went round the world— a ship of nominally 100 tons—had 14 guns, it is allowable to question Barrow's judgment that, 'looking at their tonnage, two-thirds of them, at least, could have been of little, if any, service, and must have required uncommon vigilance to keep them out of harm's way.'[1] They were not, indeed, the ships that were to be looked for in the fore-front of the fight—no more was the Euryalus or the Naiad at Trafalgar—but there is no reason to doubt that they did, in their own way, render good and efficient service.

It was not only in the number and weight of guns that the English had a great comparative advantage; they were immensely superior in the working of them. According to Captain Duro,

[1] *Life of Drake*, 270.

whose statement is fully corroborated by original writers and by known facts, 'the cannon was held by the Spaniards to be an ignoble arm ; well enough for the beginning of the fray, and to pass away the time till the moment of engaging hand to hand, that is, of boarding. Actuated by such notions, the gunners were recommended to aim high, so as to dismantle the enemy and prevent his escape ; but, as a vertical stick is a difficult thing to hit, the result was that shot were expended harmlessly in the sea, or, at best, made some holes in the sails, or cut a few ropes of no great consequence.'[1] On the other hand, the gun was the weapon which the English sailors had early learned to trust to. Their practice might appear contemptible enough to an Excellent's gun's crew, but everything must have a beginning. With no disparts or side scales, with no aid beyond a quadrant or marked quoin to lay the gun horizontal, and with shot which—a good inch and a half less in diameter than the bore of the gun—wobbled from side to side, or from top to bottom, leaving the gun at any angle that chance dictated, the hitting the object aimed at was excessively doubtful.

Thoroughly trained gunners might perhaps have done better. In the opinion of William Thomas, master gunner of Flushing, ' Had her Majesty's ships been manned with a full supply of good gunners, it would have been the woefullest time or enterprise that ever the Spaniard took in hand, and no otherwise to be thought or doubted of but that the most noblest victory by the sea that ever was heard of would have fallen to her Majesty.

[1] Duro, i. 77.

What can be said but our sins was the cause that
so much powder and shot spent, and so long time in
fight, and in comparison thereof so little harm?'
(vol. ii.—Thomas to Lord Burghley, September 20).
But it does not appear that Mr. Thomas had any
experience on board ship; and, as a matter of fact,
there were gunners on board each of the Queen's
ships—about 8 per cent. of the ship's company—
sufficient for the captains of the guns. The guns'
crews were, of course, seamen, and, with no special
training, but firing a great many shot, they did
manage to get home with sufficient to do a good
deal of damage. The Spanish accounts, speaking
of the quickness of the English fire, estimate the
English expenditure of shot as about three times
their own.

But the Spaniards were fully warned of the
peculiar strength of the English. On this point, the
King's instructions to Medina-Sidonia before he
left Lisbon are quite clear. 'You are especially to
take notice that the enemy's object will be to engage
at a distance, on account of the advantage which
they have from their artillery and the offensive fireworks with which they will be provided; and on the
other hand, the object on our side should be to close
and grapple and engage hand to hand.'[1]   And the
determination to do so, without understanding that
the choice of closing or not closing might not lie
altogether with them, may partly explain the comparatively small quantity of shot per gun provided
for such a vast undertaking; a quantity so small
that, notwithstanding the slowness of their fire,

[1] Duro, ii. 9.

they ran short even after the skirmishes in the Channel.

In estimating the opposing forces, this great superiority of the English armament must be taken into account. Of Spanish ships of 300 tons and upwards, the number that left Lisbon was officially stated as eighty : but of these, eighteen were rated as ships of burden (*urcas de carga*) ; and though they carried troops and some guns, could not be counted as effective ships of war. Of the remaining sixty-two, many ought to be reckoned in the same category. An armament such as that of the Anunciada or Sta Maria speaks for itself. From the number of soldiers they carried, and from their lofty poops and forecastles, such ships would be dangerous enough in a hand-to-hand fight, but would be perfectly harmless as long as they were kept at a distance. But counting all these, we have the following comparison of the fleets :—

	Spanish		English	
	Nos.	Tons Average	Nos.	Tons Average
Of 300 tons and upwards	62	727	23	552
Of 200 to 300 tons .	—	—	26	210
			49	

The English ships of 200 tons being included, as unquestionably superior as fighting machines to many of the much larger Spanish ships.

We may assume that these forty-nine ships were all more or less engaged during the nine days, and especially in the battle of Gravelines. The fact that Captain Coxe, of the Delight, a pinnace of 50 tons, was slain by a round shot, is a proof that all the small ships did not keep out of harm's way; but we may fully accept the statement in Wynter's letter to Walsyngham (vol. ii.—August 1), that on the 29th of July the greater number of the merchant ships were of little use, 'otherwise than that they did make a show.' It must have been so. Ships of 150 tons and less carried no guns bigger than the saker (cf. p. 339), a 6-pounder, and their armament consisted for the most part of minions, fowlers, &c., throwing shot of four or three or two pounds, very effective against bodies of men or boats or small vessels, quite useless against the thick sides of the Spanish galleons. But when the Spaniards were driven from their anchorage at Calais, the English were left with the weather-gage. The wind was blowing fresh, and the armada streamed off before it. When their weathermost ships were attacked, those to leeward could render no assistance. It was a condition of naval warfare which had been and has been repeated over and over again, from the battle of Sandwich in 1217 to that of the Nile in 1798, and always with the same inevitable result. The weathermost of the Spanish ships were, indeed, the largest and the best, but not more than thirty-two seem to have been actually engaged (Wynter, August 1), and the brunt of the battle fell on some fifteen.[1]

It is unnecessary here to describe the fights of that eventful week. The official papers which follow tell how on Sunday morning, the 21st of

[1] Duro, ii. 390.

July, the English, having gained the wind, fell on the ships of the Spanish rear-guard, under the command of Don Juan Martinez de Recalde, in the Santa Ana, and without permitting them to close, as they vainly tried to do, pounded them with their great guns for the space of three hours, with such effect that Recalde sent to Don Pedro de Valdes for assistance, his ship having been hulled several times and her foremast badly wounded; how Don Pedro's ship, the Nuestra Señora del Rosario, in going to his assistance, fouled first one and then another of her consorts, lost her bowsprit, foremast, and main-topmast, and was left by Medina-Sidonia, who, whether from spite and malice, as Don Pedro believed, or from gross ignorance and incompetence, resolved to push on to Dunkirk, even at the sacrifice of this large and powerful ship, which was taken possession of by Drake the next morning, and sent into Torbay; how another ship, the San Salvador, of 958 tons, was partially blown up and was similarly left, to be taken possession of by order of the Admiral, and to be sent into Weymouth; how on the Tuesday there was another sharp action off Portland, and again a third on the Thursday off the Isle of Wight, when Recalde's ship, the Santa Ana, of 768 tons, received so much further damage that she left the fleet and ran herself ashore near Havre; how the English, joined as they passed along by many small vessels full of men, but finding their store of shot running short, were content for the next day with closely following up the Spaniards, who on Saturday afternoon anchored off Calais, whilst the English anchored

about a mile to westward and to windward of them.
Here Howard was joined by the squadron of the
Narrow Seas, under Lord Henry Seymour and Sir
William Wynter, bringing the number of effective
ships of war up to about forty-nine. The Spanish
numbers had been reduced by the loss of three of
their largest and best ships, and were further reduced off Calais by the loss of the San Lorenzo,
the largest and most heavily armed of the galeasses.
For on Sunday night Howard sent eight fireships
in amongst the Spanish fleet ; the Spaniards, panic-
struck, cut their cables, and by wind and tide were
swept far to leeward. In the confusion the San
Lorenzo damaged her rudder, and in the morning
was driven ashore and, after a sharp fight, captured
by the boats of the Ark and some of the smaller
ships. But the fleet was away off Gravelines ; and
there, on that Monday, the 29th of July, was fought
the great battle which, more distinctly perhaps than
any battle of modern times, has moulded the history
of Europe—the battle which curbed the gigantic
power of Spain, which shattered the Spanish prestige,
and established the basis of England's empire.

And the official relations give many of the
details of this great fight. They tell how the
Spaniards, having formed themselves into a half-
moon, convexity to the north,[1] were charged on the
wings and centre by our fleet ; on the westernmost
wing by Drake, with Hawkyns, Frobiser, Fenton,
Fenner, and others ; in the centre by Howard, with
his kinsmen and the Earl of Cumberland; and on
the eastern wing by Seymour, with Wynter and the

[1] Pine's *Tapestry Hangings of the House of Lords.*

squadron of the Narrow Seas ; how the wings were driven in on their centre ; how the ships, thus driven together, fouled each other, and lay a helpless and inert mass, while the English, with heavier guns and superior numbers, pounded them in comparative safety. 'The fight,' Wynter wrote, 'continued from nine of the clock until six of the clock at night, in which time the Spanish army bore away North-North-East or North by East as much as they could, keeping company one with another. . . . I deliver it to your Honour upon the credit of a poor gentleman, that out of my ship there was shot 500 shot of demi-cannon, culverin and demi-culverin ; and when I was furthest off in discharging any of the pieces, I was not out of the shot of their harquebus, and most times within speech one of another ; and surely every man did well. No doubt the slaughter and hurt they received was great, as time will discover it; and when every man was weary with labour, and our cartridges spent, and munitions wasted—I think in some altogether —we ceased, and followed the enemy' (vol. ii.— Wynter, August 1).

All this is told at length in the following pages. It is enough to say here, that the Spaniards were terribly beaten ; that two of their largest ships, ships of the crack Portugal squadron, the San Felipe and San Mateo, ran themselves ashore on the Netherlands' coast to escape foundering in the open sea (vol. ii.—Borlas to Walsyngham, August 3). Howard says that three were sunk, and four or five driven ashore. In one case he can scarcely have been mistaken. 'On the 30th,' he says, 'one of the enemy's great ships was espied to be in great distress by the captain [Robert Crosse] of her Majesty's ship called the Hope, who, being in speech of yielding unto the said captain, before they could agree on certain conditions, sank presently before their eyes ' (vol. ii.—Abstract of Accidents, August 7).

The actual loss of life was certainly very great—how great was never known, for the pursuit of the English and the disastrous passage round the west of Ireland prevented any satisfactory attempt at official returns. One set of depositions (vol. ii.—September 12) outlines the early losses and suggests the causes of those that followed. It is incorrect to attribute everything to the bad weather. Bad weather in August is comparative, and is seldom such as to be dangerous to well-found ships ; nor, indeed, do the accounts from Ireland or Spain tell of any wholesale losses from storm. The ships were lost partly from bad pilotage, partly from bad seamanship, but principally because they were not well found ; because they were leaking like sieves, had no anchors, their masts and rigging shattered, their water-casks smashed, no water, and were very shorthanded ; and that they were in this distressed condition was the work of the English fleet, more especially at Calais and Gravelines.

An exhaustive account of these losses among the Isles of Scotland and on the coast of Ireland has not been attempted : a few of the Irish papers will serve as indications, and amongst them, or the pages of *La Armada Invencible*, the fuller narrative must be sought. The English story ends when the Spanish fleet passed the Firth of Forth ; and for the rest, it is sufficient to say that, according to the official Spanish reports, which, in such an over-whelming disaster, are rather mixed, about half of the original 130 got home again ; some apparently by the simple process of not going farther than Corunna, some by turning back before they crossed the Bay of Biscay.

A point of more immediate naval interest regards the statements that have been made of the whole-sale death of the English seamen from starvation, or from the unwholesome nature of the victuals which the Queen's shameful parsimony compelled them to eat. Such statements have been put forward, in an authoritative manner, by our best and most popular historians, as established by sufficient evidence, which, as it appears, has been misunderstood, and, taken apart from its context, has been misinterpreted. The full evidence is now before us, and permits us to say positively that, from first to last, the Queen had nothing to do with the victualling of the fleet. No doubt she insisted on rigid economy in every-thing ; no doubt Burghley, and Walsyngham, and Howard knew that their accounts would be subjected to a strict, probably an unsympathetic, scrutiny, and that no item would pass which could be objected to ; but with this general knowledge, the management of the business was left entirely in their hands.

And almost every page of these volumes tells of the unceasing care with which it was conducted. Money is freely ordered ; bills are passed and paid ; letters are written to Darell directing him to provide for the victualling, and by Darell, explaining what is being done and how : again and again Burghley adds up the totals of men and money, or translates items and results into the Roman notation,[1] so as to have a clear idea of what was going on. To any one examining the evidence, there can be no question as to the victualling being conducted on a fairly liberal scale, as far as the money was concerned. It was in providing the victuals that the difficulty lay. What victualling yards or stores there were were still in their infancy, and of little use in a great emergency. The beef had to be salted, the biscuit to be baked, to meet the requirements of the day. When a fleet of unprecedented magnitude was collected, when a sudden and unwonted demand was made on the victualling officers, it would have been strange indeed if things had gone quite smoothly. Even in this present age, with an organised but inexperienced commissariat, the troops in the Crimea suffered grievous privations, and died by hundreds. In 1588 there was no commissariat at all, and the whole burden of the business fell on the shoulders of Darell, to whose energy, ability, zeal and goodwill Howard repeatedly bears witness (p. 197).

Howard, on his part, was very anxious that the ships should be victualled for six weeks at least, so that, by completing at frequent short intervals, they might always be ready for service. He wrote that King Henry VIII. ' never made a less supply than

---

[1] Arabic figures seem to have conveyed no definite meaning to him. In all his own memoranda the calculations are made in the Roman notation ; and on the margin of every paper he translated the numbers into that notation. It is thus not surprising that his arithmetic is frequently inaccurate. Even a practised accountant might have some difficulty in subtracting xix^m v^c iij^{xx} x from xxi^m ij^c ix (p. 298), or in finding the total charge of mm ix^c iiij^{xx} x men for xviij days at xvi^s iiij^d *per mensem*.

six weeks' (p. 137)—a statement wildly incorrect. It may be hoped that the early organisation of the navy will be elucidated in some future volume; at present little is known beyond the fact that in 1513 Sir Edward Howard complained most bitterly that some of his ships were provisioned for only a fortnight;[1] and though it is very possible that ships going on a foreign expedition, carefully arranged beforehand—such perhaps as the expedition to the Forth in 1544—were provisioned for six weeks, and were also accompanied by victuallers, we may be quite certain that for home service—as, for instance, in 1545—they were provisioned from hand to mouth, on the same system as in 1588. No other was, indeed, possible where there were no stores, and where, from the nature of the service, the necessity could not have been foreseen and prepared for in advance.

No doubt such a system was as bad as it well could be, and especially bad in the case of a great fleet which might at any moment be called on to put to sea, to meet or to follow the enemy. As early as the 3rd of March, Fenner called Walsyngham's attention to the danger. 'I fear,' he wrote, 'when we shall be hastened to go, our provision of victual needful will not be ready in a month, in which time it will be no small matter, the waste in doing nothing' (p. 92); and on the 8th of April, Howard, writing to Burghley, put it still more clearly. 'I thought good to put your Lordship in remembrance how necessary it is to have a better proportion of victual than for one month, considering

[1] Ellis's *Original Letters*, 3rd series, i. 145.

the time and the service that is likely to fall out, and what danger it might breed if our want of victual should be at the time of service. We shall be now victualled unto the 18th of May, and by the advertisements that giveth the largest time for the coming out of the Spanish forces is the 15th of May. Then have we three days' victual. If it be fit to be so, it passeth my reason ' (p. 137).

The particular danger which Howard thus pointed out did actually occur. On the 21st of July, when Howard received intelligence of the Spaniards being off the Lizard, the ships at Plymouth were employed in completing their victuals to the 10th of August ; 'only,' wrote Darell on the 22nd (p. 294), ' the haste of my Lord Admiral was such in his setting forth upon Saturday morning, as that divers of his ships had not leisure to receive the full of their last proportions.' Even so, however, things were not so bad as they seemed, for, ' by placing of more than four men to a mess and also by the mortality which hath been amongst them, the ships (having been from time to time furnished by me with their due proportions, as if that had not been) have all in them a store, which no doubt will serve them a good time after their ordinary victualling be expired.'

We must suppose that Burghley and Walsyngham were quite able to see that such a danger was no vague fancy, but to alter the system at a moment's warning was impossible. The provisions were not ready ; there were no government establishments to fall back on ; and from the 23rd of May, when the Lord Admiral went to Plymouth, Darell was scouring the country round, buying up what he could, more like a mess-steward with a market-basket than the agent-victualler of a great fleet. Every available means had to be used to eke out the supplies. A Hamburg ship laden with rice coming into the Sound, was summarily stayed and the rice bought for the use of the navy (p. 189). The 'scantyings' referred to by Howard (p. 219) was another means. The men were put at five or six in a mess instead of four. To many writers this has seemed an atrocious measure specially invented by the Queen in her rage for economy. It was—they say—stealing the men's victuals. As a matter of certain fact, the Queen had nothing to do with it. It was the established custom in the navy and continued to be so for the next 250 years. When the stowage of ships was very limited, when there were no stores in distant parts of the earth, any ship going on a long voyage or being thrown on her own resources for any length of time, placed her men at 'six upon four' as a matter of course ;[1] so much so, that it is unusual to find it mentioned in naval Memoirs. Unquestionably it was an evil. Putting the men on insufficient food lowered their vitality and made them a ready prey to scurvy and the many other diseases then supposed to be incidental to sea life ; but it was not considered by either officers or men more than a passing hardship, to be endured, not merely for the necessity, but for the convenience of the service ; though latterly convenience alone was held not to warrant it, and at the present time it could scarcely

---

[1] Cf. *Memoirs relating to the Lord Torrington,* 183 ; Thomas's *Journal of a Voyage to the South Seas,* 3.

be done except on extreme emergency. In putting the ships' companies on short allowance, Howard was adopting the most ordinary precaution, in view of a possible scarcity of provisions, and the indignation which has been expressed about it by writers ignorant of naval custom is altogether uncalled for; the more so, indeed, as the short allowance complained of was two-thirds of two pounds of beef and of a gallon of beer.

But this beer, it is said, was sour. That also was not unusual. It was nasty, it was unwholesome; but so long as beer continued to be the authorised drink on board ships of war, so long were the never-ending complaints of its being sour. Hawke's correspondence in 1759 is unusually full of such complaints, and especially of the West country beer. 'Our daily employment,' he wrote on the 4th of August, 'is condemning the beer from Plymouth'; to which the Admiralty replied that they were sorry to hear of the beer being bad, 'but the Commissioners of Victualling informed them that the uncommon hot weather this summer has occasioned the beer to spoil upon moving.' Howard's complaint, also in August, is of the beer from Sandwich. Both the man who supplied it and Darell declared that it was good when it was put on board; a survey showed that it had gone sour within a month, which Howard thought must be the brewer's fault (vol. ii.—August 26). The brewer excused it by the want of hops, a matter which Howard did not concern himself with, but wrote, 'I know not which way to deal with the mariners to make them rest contented with sour beer, for nothing doth displease them more.' Nevertheless, Howard's letter does not authorise the paraphrase of it given by Mr. Froude :—' Notwithstanding the disorder was traced definitely to the poisonous beer, it continued to be served out. Nothing better was allowed till it was consumed.'[1] What Howard says is ' The mariners have a conceit—and I think it true, and so do all the captains here—that sour drink hath been a great cause of this infection amongst us. . . . Mr. Darell makes trial to brew the sour beer again, and so to mix it with other new beer, which I hope will do well.' Between the ' mariners' conceit' of Howard and the ' definite tracing' of Mr. Froude, there appears nearly as much difference as between ' brewing the sour beer again' and ' continuing to serve it out . . . till it was consumed.'

But in such cases sailors and their officers have sometimes had very queer ' conceits,' as when, for instance, in Anson's celebrated voyage across the Pacific, the commodore and Michell and the surgeons, discussing the terrible scurvy that was raging, came to the conclusion that—' the steams arising from the ocean may have a tendency to render the air they are spread through less properly adapted to the support of the life of terrestrial animals, unless these steams are corrected by effluvia of another kind, and which perhaps the land alone can supply;'[2] whereupon Anson administered to the sick ' the pill and drop of Mr. Ward,' two abominable quack medicines[3] which seem to have been both emetic and

---

[1] *History*, xii. 432.
[2] Walter's *Voyage round the World* (1748), 294.
[3] *Gentleman's Magazine*, 1798, ii. 739.

cathartic in a high degree. The fancies of Howard
and his men may be considered as in a similar
category, for there can be no doubt that the sickness
which so terribly scourged our ships' companies was
of the nature of typhus, and had been busy in some
of the ships—especially in the Elizabeth Jonas—
before the Spaniards came into the Channel. It is
very possible that the pestilence was aggravated by
scarcity and bad provisions, but it was primarily and
chiefly due to infection from the shore and from
ignorance or neglect of what we now know as sani-
tary laws ; and it seems an interesting point, that
the ships commanded by the experienced old salts
escaped comparatively lightly. The ships named as
most heavily scourged are the Elizabeth Jonas, the
White Bear, and the Lion, commanded by Howard's
kinsmen, men splendid in the day of battle, but of
no experience in the very necessary art of keeping
a ship clean and sweet. A similar infection continued occasionally to scourge our ships' companies,
and still more frequently and more severely French
or Spanish ships' companies, till near the close of
last century. In our service, at least, it is now
happily almost forgotten.

The want of ammunition experienced by our
ships even after two days' fighting is another point
which has been brought forward as illustrating the
niggardly behaviour of the Queen. As before, it
was a detail with which the Queen had nothing to
do, and—also as before—there was no available
store in the kingdom. Anticipating the want,
Walsyngham had directed his agent to buy powder
in the Low Countries (p. 312), though little seems

to have been forthcoming from that quarter. But
the full explanation of the want seems to lie in the
rapidity of the fire which has already been mentioned. The ships had the usual quantity on board,
but the expenditure was more, very many times
more, than anyone could have conceived. Drake,
indeed (p. 125), and perhaps others of the more
experienced sailors, men who had been at Cadiz
when the King's beard was singed, or who had, for
years past, been settling their personal quarrels
with the Spaniard in their own irregular way, might
have some idea that a great deal of powder would
be burnt ; but they were probably alone in that
belief.

It has not been remembered, it needs an effort
to remember, that the off-fighting then practised by
the English was an essentially new phase of naval
war. The only thing that had at all resembled it,
and that on a very small scale, was the distant inter-
change of shots between the English and French
fleets at Spithead in 1545. But at Lepanto, the
memory of which was still fresh in men's minds, the
fighting was, for the most part, hand to hand, as it
also was in the still more recent action at Terceira,
from which the English were reported to have fled
so ingloriously ; and beyond question, not only the
Spaniards, but many of the English officers and
most—perhaps all—of the Queen's ministers expected that it would be so again. It was thus that
when Richard Drake was sent to the Lord Admiral
by the Council, he was directed to inquire how it was
that none of the Spanish ships had been boarded
(p. 355). Sir Walter Ralegh, who must have

talked with Howard and Drake and Hawkyns while
the business was fresh in their memories, has left us
what we may consider very direct testimony on this
point. He says :—

  ' Certainly, he that will happily perform a fight
at sea must believe that there is more belonging to
a good man of war upon the waters than great
daring, and must know that there is a great deal of
difference between fighting loose or at large and
grappling. To clap ships together without consideration belongs rather to a madman than to a
man of war ; for by such an ignorant bravery was
Peter Strozzi lost at the Azores, when he fought
against the Marquis of Santa Cruz. In like sort
had the Lord Charles Howard, Admiral of England,
been lost in the year 1588, if he had not been better
advised than a great many malignant fools were,
that found fault with his demeanour. The Spaniards
had an army aboard them and he had none ; they
had more ships than he had, and of higher building
and charging ; so that, had he entangled himself with
those great and powerful vessels, he had greatly
endangered this kingdom of England. For twenty
men upon the defences are equal to a hundred that
board and enter ; whereas then, contrariwise, the
Spaniards had a hundred for twenty of ours, to
defend themselves withal. But our admiral knew
his advantage and held it ; which had he not done,
he had not been worthy to have held his head.' [1]

  But this off-fighting and this rapid and continuous
fire quickly exhausted the supply of ammunition
which had seemed sufficient ; and though some was

  [1] *Historie of the World*, edit. 1736, ii. 565.

sent from the Spanish prize in Torbay, some also from the shattered prize at Weymouth, some from Portsmouth by the Earl of Sussex, some from London by Walsyngham, and more, perhaps, that has not been recorded, the magazines of the principal ships were almost depleted on the evening of the 29th of July (vol. ii.—Wynter to Walsyngham, August 1), and the pursuit of the next three days was strictly, as Howard called it, 'setting on a brag countenance' (vol. ii.—August 7).

Another stock complaint against the Queen is that the men were not paid their wages. This again was a detail with which the Queen was not concerned. The money was sanctioned by the Council and ordered by the Lord Treasurer. It was presumably paid to the Treasurer of the Navy, and if he had kept it at usance for his own advantage, he would only have been doing what was and continued to be the custom, both in the navy and the army, to the end of the eighteenth century. The prompt payment of naval officers and seamen is, indeed, a thing of the present day. But in fact, the Elizabethan seamen were very much better off in that respect than their successors under the Commonwealth, or the Restoration, or even George III. When the ship was paid off, these got a ticket which they could cash at whatever discount the Jew-agent chose to abstract. In Elizabeth's time they were paid in cash, and apparently at the end of every three months (p. 296). It may, of course, be represented as an abominable injustice that they were not paid down every Friday night, as the hands in a modern factory ; but that is not the custom of the navy, as to sea-going ships, even now, and still less was it so then; there was no clerical organization by which it could have been done, and as the men had no expectation of it, there was no hardship. After the battle, and during the fearful mortality at Dover—a mortality which even in the Ark and Triumph and Victory seems to have exceeded 35 per cent. of the ships' companies (vol. ii.—Hawkyns to Burghley, Sept. 4) —they demanded to be paid for the month ending on the 25th of August, and were greatly discontented that they had not received in full what was already due to them (vol. ii.—Howard to the Council, Aug. 22; Hawkyns to Burghley, Aug. 26). As the Treasurer of the Navy had been busy fighting and attending to the welfare of his own men, the delay does not necessarily imply any gross depravity or dishonesty on his part.

The system of pay in force throughout the century was peculiar. Many of the details are still obscure, but the broad principle was that—with the exception of the captain—every man on board, independent of his quality, should receive the same pay, the amount received by the officers being increased by allowances given under the name of ' dead-shares' or ' rewards.' Out of this had grown the custom to calculate the total amount payable to a ship's company at an average per head, which, in the earlier years of Elizabeth's reign, was 9s. 4d.[1] for the month of 28 days; but in 1586, consequent on a representation from Hawkyns (vol. ii. App. D), it was raised to 14s., and at this rate it remained in 1588. The uniform pay of every man was thus

[1] *S.P. Dom. Eliz.* xxv. 66.

raised from 6*s*. 8*d*. to 10*s*., the allowances being increased in the same proportion. As the nominal pay of the captain was thus brought up to 2*s*. 6*d*. *per diem*, it follows that previous to 1586 it was 1*s*. 8*d*. In addition to this, however, he had some allowance for his table; possibly also for lights, &c.; the whole, lumped together, formed his diet,[1] or daily pay, the amount of which varied, according to the size of the ship, and the circumstances of his command.

With this one exception, every man on board received the same uniform pay of 10*s*. a month; but an indeterminate number of non-existent men, known as 'dead-shares,' were also allotted 10*s*. a month; and these dead-shares were divided amongst the officers and petty officers, according to some scale not yet known. The master and the master-gunner seem to have each received a whole dead-share; so also probably did the boatswain; quarter-masters had half a dead-share, some of the gunners—the modern gunner's-mates —one-third. In addition to these, further payments were made under the name of 'rewards,' concerning which there seems to have been no regulation; the disbursement was probably determined partly by custom, partly by personal bargain, and partly at the discretion of the captain; though, judging by the light of later experience, there must have been some machinery for preventing his assigning an exceedingly large reward to himself.

It would appear certain that, according to the class of ship, a large 'reward' was assigned to the master, who was, in most cases, a man of high

[1] Cf. Skeat's *Etymological Dictionary*, s.v. 'Diet.'

standing and great responsibility. In the larger
ships commanded by Howard's 'noblemen,' he was
virtually the captain ; in the Ark he must have been
actually so ; so also in the E. Bonaventure, which
was commanded by Raymond before the Earl of
Cumberland joined her off Portsmouth, and after he
left her at Harwich. Towards the end of the season
Thomas Gray, the master of the Ark, commanded
a small squadron with the pay of 6s. 8d. a day,
besides probable allowances, and the style of rear-
admiral (vol.ii.—Scale of pay). It is not to be supposed that these men served for the nominal 20s. a
month, pay and dead-share, or for anything like it,
when lieutenants had their pay made up to 3l., and
chaplains to 3l. 10s. (vol. ii.—Hawkyns to Burghley,
Estimate No. 5, Sept. 12). It is suggested (p. 173 n.)
that Polwhele was promoted from being captain of a
small vessel to be master of a large one, the understanding being that the master's pay and reward in
a large ship was really higher than the captain's diet
in a small one.

The Lord Admiral's pay is returned as 3l. 6s. 8d.,
or 5 marks, a day, besides unknown allowances.
Seymour's daily pay was 2l. ; that of Drake was
30s. In early times the pay of an admiral or
general largely depended on his social rank or title.
Howard's rank was of the highest, and to it he owed
the honourable position he occupied at this critical
period. He had indeed served at sea, and had more
experience than fell to the lot of most admirals, but it
must not be supposed that it was on that account that
he was made Lord High Admiral of England. It
was rather because his father and two of his father's

brothers had previously been Lord High Admirals ; it was because both he and his wife were nearly related to the Queen ; it was because by birth or marriage he was related to or connected with almost every person of importance in the kingdom.

The Howards of the sixteenth century were remarkable by their high position, their political influence, their brilliant services, and in a scarcely less degree by their extreme fecundity. Most of them married twice ; most of them had large families, so that the number of people, men and women, who could claim near relationship with the Lord Admiral was enormous. Thomas, the second Duke of Norfolk, who commanded the English army at the battle of Flodden, had five sisters ; he was twice married, and had issue ten sons and six daughters. One of the sons, William, created Lord Howard of Effingham, was twice married, and had issue, besides six daughters, two sons, the elder of whom, Charles, born in 1536, succeeded as second Lord Howard of Effingham in 1573 ; was appointed Lord High Admiral in 1585 ; commanded the fleet against the armada of Spain in 1588, and at the taking of Cadiz in 1596, when he was created Earl of Nottingham. He retained the office of Lord High Admiral till 1619, and did not die till 1624, preserving his faculties to the last. Elizabeth Howard, one of the six sisters of the first Lord Howard of Effingham, married Sir Thomas Boleyn, and was the mother of Mary and Anne Boleyn. Anne married Henry VIII. and was the mother of Elizabeth. Mary married William Carey, and was the mother of Henry, created Lord Hunsdon, whose daughter,

Catherine, married Charles, Lord Howard of Effingham.

This relationship is more satisfactorily shown by a table, which—omitting the other members of the very numerous families—appears thus :—

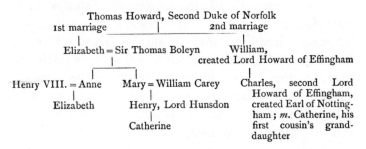

```
                    Thomas Howard, Second Duke of Norfolk
         1st marriage                          2nd marriage
             |                                      |
     Elizabeth = Sir Thomas Boleyn              William,
             |                           created Lord Howard of Effingham
         |        |                              |
Henry VIII. = Anne    Mary = William Carey    Charles,  second   Lord
         |               |                    Howard  of Effingham,
     Elizabeth      Henry, Lord Hunsdon       created Earl of Notting-
                         |                    ham ; m. Catherine, his
                     Catherine                first  cousin's  grand-
                                              daughter
```

One of Lord Howard's sisters married Edward Seymour, Earl of Hertford, eldest son of the Protector, Duke of Somerset, whose second son, Henry Seymour, commanded the squadron in the Narrow Seas through the summer of 1588, and wrote many of the letters contained in these volumes. Of the other men who served in the fleet of 1588, Lord Thomas Howard, captain of the Golden Lion, was son of the fourth Duke of Norfolk and grandson of Lord Howard's first cousin, the Earl of Surrey, executed in 1545. Lord Sheffield, captain of the White Bear, was the son of Howard's sister Douglas, who, after her first husband's death, married Sir Edward Stafford, but retained the style of Lady Sheffield. Sir Robert Southwell, who commanded the Elizabeth Jonas, had married one of Howard's daughters ; another had married Richard Leveson, then serving as a volunteer in the Ark, but afterwards Vice-Admiral of England. Sir Edward

Hoby, who was also with Howard in the Ark, had married his youngest sister-in-law, daughter of Lord Hunsdon. The appointment of all these men, without any knowledge or experience of the sea, to posts of high command, would now-a-days be called nepotism. In Howard's days it was the rule for men in office to make the public service provide for their families; and Howard would certainly have defended his right to do so on the ground that he knew his kinsmen and could depend on them. It was the custom of the age for landsmen of high rank to command afloat, and under the conditions of the navy at that time they did very well.

But men like Drake, Wynter, Hawkyns, Palmer, Frobiser, Fenner, Fenton, Luke Ward and many others, come into a different category. They had followed the sea from their boyhood, and though all men of respectable or even good family, were, by the necessities of their education and calling, of a different social rank from the others. Drake belonged to the family of Drake of Ash in Devon, and was born at Tavistock about 1540. Hawkyns, some years older, and of a family rising to wealth by trade and maritime adventure, was a native of Plymouth. The relationship between them would seem to have been on the mother's side, for Drake had family arms, Hawkyns had not. After his loss at San Juan de Lua Hawkyns retired from the sea. He had married the daughter of Gonson, the Treasurer of the Navy, and in due time succeeded him in his office, in which—according to the statements of his enemies—he enriched himself by irregular, if not by fraudulent methods.   Some of these charges, which had been persistently made, are repeated here (pp. 34–44; vol. ii. Oct. 8), but the evidence does not seem to have been sifted ; and the fact that the ships were found strong and seaworthy when they were wanted for service (pp. 79, 81) goes far to show that it was mainly the voice of spite or malice.   After the defeat of the armada Hawkyns commanded an expedition to the coast of Portugal in 1590, and later, under Drake, in the West Indies, where—off Porto Rico—he died on the 12th of November, 1595.

Drake's career was much more active and brilliant than that of his older kinsman.   Hawkyns laid the foundation of a large fortune by cheating the Spaniards, and increased it, it was suspected, by cheating his own countrymen.   Drake also founded a handsome fortune at the cost of the Spaniards, but it was by openly plundering them in what he and the generality of Englishmen considered legitimate and honourable war.   After his return from the celebrated voyage round the world in 1580, he was not at sea except in the Queen's service.   In 1585–6 he commanded a strong squadron which ravaged the West Indies, sacked Cartagena and the Spanish settlements on the mainland of Florida ; and in April 1587, with another squadron, forced his way into Cadiz, where he burnt the ships which were preparing for the intended invasion of England, and struck terror into the Spaniards and Portuguese along the coast.   William Borough, the second in command of the squadron—a man distinguished as a navigator and hydrographer, but of no experience in war—was aghast at what appeared the Admiral's recklessness, and remonstrated against his conduct in very strong terms. Drake answered by putting him under arrest on board his own ship. Borough believed, or pretended to believe, that his life was in danger, and not improbably worked on his men to run away with the ship and return to England. The quarrel was afterwards smoothed over by the influence of Burghley (pp. 74–5), and Borough commanded the galley Bonavolia through the summer of 1588, when his best service was sketching a chart of the Thames, which is here reproduced in facsimile, though smaller (p. 337). Borough's name still lives, not as that of a warrior, but of a navigator, hydrographer, and early investigator into the apparent vagaries of the compass.

In 1589 Drake, jointly with Sir John Norreys, commanded a powerful armament against Lisbon in support of the claims of Dom Antonio to the throne of Portugal. They met no enemy by sea; on shore they met the most terrible of all enemies—a wasting and deadly sickness—and, having lost many thousand men, returned helpless to England. In 1595 he was again afloat on an expedition to the West Indies. No secrecy had been preserved in fitting it out, and the Spaniards, forewarned, had everywhere prepared for it, either by removing their treasure or strengthening their defences. An attack on Porto Rico failed, and though Santa Marta, Nombre de Dios, and some other places were burnt, little harm was done and no advantage gained. The disappointment preyed on his spirits and aggravated

an attack of dysentery, which proved fatal on the
28th of January, 1596.

Frobiser, of an old Yorkshire family, seems in
early life to have been engaged in trading to the
Mediterranean. He was afterwards suspected of
piracy, though the charge was not brought home to
him ; and in 1576–7–8 he made three successive
voyages to the Arctic, where his name still lives in
'Frobiser's Strait,' now known to be only a deep
inlet or gulf. In 1585–6 he was with Drake in
the West Indies, in 1590 with Hawkyns on the
coast of Portugal. In 1594 he commanded a
squadron on the coast of Brittany, co-operating
with Norreys, and in an attack on Crozon was
mortally wounded. He died at Plymouth in the
early days of January 1595. Though he played a
foremost part in the campaign of 1588, both as a
councillor and as captain of the Triumph, the largest
ship in the fleet, and everywhere in the front of battle,
there is not one letter from him among the papers
here printed. The fact is that though a bold and
skilful seaman, a good navigator, and a man of cul-
tivated intelligence, he had neglected the more
ordinary paths of book learning, and could do little
more than write his name, which—after trying various
other forms—he decided on spelling Frobiser.

Of the volunteers who joined the fleet after the
Spaniards came into the Channel little can be said.
According to Camden, they were :—The Earls of
Oxford, Northumberland, and Cumberland; Thomas
and Robert Cecill; H. Brook, Charles Blount,
Walter Ralegh, William Hatton, Robert Carey.
Ambrose Willoughby, Thomas Gerard, Arthur

Gorges, and others.   Of these, only three are mentioned in these papers as having joined the fleet:
—the Earl of Cumberland, Charles Blount, and
Thomas Gerard.   Robert Cecill was at Dover,
writing to his father (p. 342), and, on the 30th of
July, neither was nor had been on board any of the
ships.   That Oxford, Burghley's son-in-law, or
Thomas Cecill, Burghley's son; that Northumberland, Seymour's first cousin; Robert Carey, Howard's
brother-in-law, and Sir Walter Ralegh, a man of
high repute and official rank, could be in the fleet
and not be once mentioned by Howard, by Robert
Cecill, by Seymour, or by any of the correspondents
of Burghley and Walsyngham, or by these, would
seem incredible if we had not Robert Carey's own
statement to the effect that, at the battle of Gravelines, he was on board the E. Bonaventure.[1]   It
must therefore be admitted as possible that the
others were also in the fleet, though—without
corroborative testimony—it remains extremely improbable.   That Ralegh had a command in the
fleet and 'led a squadron as rear-admiral'[2] is virtually contradicted by the evidence now before us.

   Another man who, though neither in nor belonging to the fleet, is often said to have rendered
efficient service, is David Gwynn, actually a slave
on board the Spanish galley Diana, but described as
serving on board the Bazana.   On the way from
Lisbon, in heavy weather off Cape Finisterre, the
Diana—it is said—went down with all hands.   The
other three galleys were in great danger, and the

---

[1] *Memoirs* (1759), p. 18.
[2] Edwards, *Life of Sir Walter Ralegh*, vol. i. p. xxxvii.

captain of the Bazana applied to Gwynn, whom he knew as an experienced seaman, to get them out of the mess. Gwynn consented, and as a first step desired that the soldiers should be sent below. Most of them were so sent; whereupon Gwynn, waving his cap as a signal, struck his dagger into the heart of the captain. His comrades, at the same moment and in the same manner, killed all the Spaniards who were on deck; then they killed all who were below; and having thus obtained possession of the Bazana, they attacked and won the Capitana, killing all the Spaniards on board. The fourth galley, the Princesa, made her escape, and succeeded in rejoining the fleet and getting into Corunna.

Such in brief is the story, absolutely unknown to early English and Spanish writers, which is told by the Dutch chroniclers, and has been repeated from them by later historians, notably by Motley,[1] who ought to have been warned by the many absurdities, such as the slaves being unchained and all having daggers. For, in point of fact, the story is a lie from beginning to end. Gwynn, as has been said, was serving in the Diana, not the Bazana. It was after the fleet left Corunna, not before it arrived there; it was in the Bay of Biscay, not off Cape Finisterre, that the galleys made such bad weather of it. The Diana did not go down in the open sea, but bore up for Bayonne, where in trying to run into the harbour she ran aground and became a total wreck, but without any serious loss of life. The officers and men were entertained by the

[1] *History of the United Netherlands* (cab. ed.), ii. 447.

governor of the town, and went home by land.
The other three galleys, with better success, put into
different French ports and in due time returned to
Spain.[1] Gwynn and some other English slaves, in
the confusion following the wreck, made their escape,
got to Rochelle and thence to England ; whence, as
speaking Spanish, Gwynn was sent over to Ireland
to assist in the examination of the Spanish prisoners.
His true story is told clearly enough by the Lord
Deputy (vol. ii.—Fytzwylliam to the Council, October
18). It is, perhaps, not impossible that Gwynn, after
being ignominiously sent out of Ireland as a liar, a
thief, and a lewd person, sought service in the Low
Countries, where he spun his ' galley-yarns ' to the
credulous, from whom Bor received them. It is not
often that a fable can be so completely exploded as
this now is.

Of the many other myths which have been
foisted on to the true history of the campaign, it is
unnecessary to speak. The first test of their
truth ought to be an examination of the evidence
on which they are based. It will be found that
many of them rest on no evidence at all, and others
on that of the Dutch chroniclers, more especially
Bor. It must be remembered that Dutch writers
had no special facilities for knowing what happened ;
that they were by no means crushed under a sense
of gratitude to Elizabeth, and were bitterly hostile
to the Spaniards. English and Spanish writers—
Camden, for instance, and Herrera—might be as
badly informed, but the spirit of hatred was not so

[1] Duro, i. 65 ; ii. 279.

dominant in them. They were willing to do their enemies justice.

The papers here printed are strictly what they are called on the title-page—State Papers; letters and memoranda written by or to the officers of the fleet and the high officers of State. A large proportion of the letters are written by Howard or Seymour to Lord Burghley, the Lord High Treasurer, or to Sir Francis Walsyngham, the Principal Secretary of State. Many, too, are written by Drake and by Hawkyns; others by men not so well known, but all of unquestionable authenticity. About one document alone is any doubt possible, the Relation on pp. 1–18. As stated in the note on p. 1, there are strong reasons to suppose that it emanated from Howard; but it is quite possible that it did not, and was only written from hearsay. If so, the writer was curiously well informed on points of detail which were not then public property.

Many of the letters are extremely difficult to read. Howard's writing is singularly perplexing; Seymour's is very bad; Drake's is a scrawl; Walsyngham's is atrocious. But the badness of the writing is not the worst part of them. Many of them, especially of the most interesting and important, have been very badly treated, carried about in pockets, opened and folded. read and re-read, till the edges and the folds were much frayed and torn. More than two centuries of damp afterwards tried to wash away what remained, and have too often very nearly succeeded. In 1798, John Bruce, the Keeper of State Papers, was directed by Mr. Pitt, in view of possibilities then threatening, to prepare a Report on the measures taken for the defence of the country in 1588. To his Report Bruce appended many of these documents, which he certified as examined. Since that time the papers have suffered still more from damp, sometimes also from bad mending, and no doubt many words now wanting were then still legible. The Report was thus a natural reference in cases of difficulty, but a very little experience of it showed that the transcripts were made by a very ignorant and careless man, and that, notwithstanding the official certificate, the value of them is extremely slight. With the present copies every practicable care has been taken to ensure verbal accuracy ; and though it is impossible to affirm that there are no errors, it is confidently believed that there are not many, and none of serious importance. Words which might be thought doubtful are in all cases enclosed in square brackets, and if supplied from Bruce's Report or from conjecture, the fact is duly noted.

In accordance with the resolution of the Council, the spelling has been modernised ; but wherever the original spelling seemed to have any interest, either from the social position of the writer or from its peculiar eccentricity, it is given in a note. Howard's spelling is sometimes very curious, but apparently phonetic, and is thus a guide to the Court pronunciation, as Cely's still more extraordinary spelling may be to that of middle-class society in Bristol. Obsolete or obscure words and phrases or allusions have been also noted, the Editor being instructed to act on the supposition that many members of the Society have little practice in

Elizabethan English, and have not ready access to the larger works of reference, such as the New English Dictionary (N.E.D.) or the Dictionary of National Biography (D.N.B.).

Names of men are spelt uniformly, and, wherever practicable, according to their own signatures. It is commonly supposed that the spelling of 16th and 17th century names is indeterminate : a mistake, due partly to the carelessness of other people, but still more to what seems now the curious custom of brothers, or members of the same family, differencing their names by the spelling, in much the same way that they differenced their armorial bearings by marks of cadency. Humphrey Gylberte and John Gilberte, Thomas Cecill and—after his father's death—Robert Cecyll, Marmaduke Darell and his cousin William Darrell, are some amongst many belonging to this period. The point is really one of some importance, for attention to the spelling of signatures is frequently the only way of avoiding great confusion ; as, for instance, between George Cary of Cockington, afterwards Lord Deputy of Ireland, George Carey of the Isle of Wight, afterwards Lord Hunsdon, and George Carew, Master of the Ordnance in Ireland, afterwards Earl of Totness. Each of these men, and indeed every man who could write, had an established signature, which he no more thought of varying than does anyone at the present time ; whether his peculiar spelling was dictated by reason or fancy, it marks his name, and as such, the Council has directed it to be used.

With the exception of a very few in the British Museum, with the distinguishing reference B.M., and of one at Hatfield, now abstracted from the Report of the Historical MSS. Commission, all the papers here given are in the Public Record Office, mostly in the collection of Domestic State Papers. The exact reference is in all cases given. They are arranged in nearly strict chronological order, the occasional slight deviations from it readily explaining themselves. The editorial dates at the head of the papers, in the notes and in this Introduction, are, without exception, according to the Old Style, then in use in England. The New Style, already adopted in France, Spain, and the Low Countries, which occasionally appears in the body of a document, differed by ten days from the Old. Thus the 20th of May O.S. was 30th of May N.S.; the 21st of July O.S. was 31st of July N.S.; and the 29th of July O.S. was the 8th of August N.S., which un-English date Sir Oswald Brierley has affixed to the engraving of his delightful picture of the battle of Gravelines. The legal and official year in England began on the 25th of March; but in historical writing it was frequently supposed to begin on the 1st of January, as it did on the Continent. The date 1587 affixed to the letters written between the 1st of January and the 25th of March, is historically, and according to modern usage, 1588.

Most of the papers are, of course, in English. Some, originally in other languages, have been preserved in a contemporary translation, and are referred to as 'Englished.' Others, which remain only in the original language, are referred to as 'Latin,' 'French,' &c., and have been translated by the Editor, who has endeavoured to avoid the incongruity of appearing to put new cloth to an old garment.

It only remains for the Editor to express his grateful sense of the kindness which he has received from the many friends and some strangers whom he has consulted on doubtful or obscure points. He would record his obligations to his colleague at King's College, Professor J. W. Hales; to Mr. M. Oppenheim; to the Hydrographer, Captain Wharton, R.N., F.R.S.; to Mr. C. H. Coote of the British Museum; to M. Alfred Spont; to Mr. Hubert Hall of the Record Office; to the Director of Naval Intelligence, Rear-Admiral Bridge, who has assisted him in revising the proof-sheets, and in a very special degree to Mr. Edward Salisbury of the Record Office, to whose tireless generosity and marvellous skill in piecing out words from the faintest conceivable indications the accuracy of the present transcripts is largely due.

———————

DEFEAT

OF THE

SPANISH ARMADA

ANNO 1588.

———•◇•———

A RELATION OF PROCEEDINGS.[1]

[**B.M. Cotton, Julius, F. x. ff. 111–117.**—No date, title, signature, or endorsement.   A neat, clerkly, contemporary writing.]

WHEREAS the Queen's most excellent Majesty had of late years sundry and most certain intelligences of the great warlike preparation both for sea and land which the King of Spain of late years made from all parts, not only of the mightiest and most puissant ships and vessels that he could prepare, as

[1] The MS. has nothing externally to indicate its origin; internally, there is much in favour of the opinion that it is official; and it does not seem improbable that it was drawn up under Howard's authority, as 'the more particular relation' with which he proposed 'at better leisure' to supplement 'the brief abstract of accidents' sent to Walsyngham on August 7.   It must, however, be remembered that this is only a conjecture, and that the Relation has not the authority of an authenticated document. Still, none of the statements in it are contradicted by other papers of greater value; and most of them are directly corroborated, often in the very words.

well from foreign places as in his own dominions, and by arresting of the ships of other countries that came into his dominions, but also of all kind of munition and victuals, and of captains, soldiers and mariners, and of all other provisions for a mighty army by seas, to come out of Spain and Portugal; for the more strength whereof it was notorious to the world how he had drawn into Spain and Portugal his principal and most experimented captains and old soldiers out of Naples, Sicilia, Lombardy and other parts of Italy, yea, and from sundry remote places of the Indies; the preparation whereof, with the numbers of ships, men, victuals, ordnance and all kind of munition, was made patent to the world by sundry books printed and published both in Spain, Portugal, and in many other countries of Christendom, carrying the titles of the ' Happy Armada [1] of the King of Spain,' and in some specially expressed to be against England: And in like sort, where [2] her Majesty had the like knowledge of the mighty and puissant forces of horses and footmen sufficient to make many armies prepared in the Low Countries under the conduct of the Duke of Parma, the King's Lieutenant-General, and of multitude of ships, bylanders, [3] boats and other vessels fit for the transporting and landing of the said forces, armies from the coast of Flanders, with a general publication to the world that all these so mighty forces, both by sea and land, were intended to the invasion of her Majesty's realms, and as was pretended, to have

[1] *Felicísima Armada.* It is so called in the official Relation published at Lisbon.

[2] Whereas.

[3] Bylander (Fr. *belandre*), from the Dutch *binnenlander*, was originally a small vessel adapted to Dutch inland navigation. At this time it seems to have been a one-masted craft carrying a spritsail; later on, the name was more especially applied to a kind of snow.

made therewith a full conquest : Yet for that, in
this time of their preparation, the King of Spain, by
his Lieutenant-General, the Duke of Parma, caused
certain offers to be made to her Majesty for a com-
munication of a peace betwixt their Majesties ; howsoever, by the common judgment of the world, the
same was done but to abuse her Majesty and to win
time whilst his preparations might be made complete ;
her Majesty, nevertheless, like a most godly and
christian prince, did not refuse to give ear to so
christian an [1] offer, for which purpose she sent certain
noblemen of her privy council into Flanders to treat
with certain commissioners, who continued there
without any good success by reason of the unreasonable delays of the King's commissioners ; yea, they
continued there until the navy of Spain was overcome and forced to fly.

And yet, notwithstanding this her inclination to
peace, and her princely offers of most reasonable
conditions of peace, she, like a prince of wisdom and
magnanimity, for defence of herself, her realm and
people, was not negligent of her princely office to
which God called her, and wherein He had stablished her and preserved her very many years, but
providently did prepare a princely and strong army
by sea, and put in readiness also sundry armies by
land, to prevent and withstand the foresaid attempts
so published to be made by such great armies, both
by sea and land, as never were so great made in any
part of Christendom, either by the said King or the
Emperor, his father. For which, her preparations
by seas, such diligence was used, as the same being
begun to be made but about the 1st of November,
yet the same was fully ready to take the seas
by the 20th of December, a time very short for
such an enterprise, having respect to the length

[1] MS. and.

of sundry years which the Spanish navy was in preparing.

But yet such it was as God specially favoured, and as the force thereof hath been proved to have overmatched the mightiness of the enemy's navy ; the charge whereof was committed by her Majesty to Charles Lord Howard, of the ancient house of Norfolk, High Admiral of England, who was accompanied with a great number of noblemen and others, the most sufficient and best experimented men for the seas. And after that he had continued a good time with the army upon the Narrow Seas betwixt England and Flanders, the said High Admiral, by her Majesty's commandment, sent Sir Francis Drake into the west part of this realm towards Spain, with certain of her Majesty's ships, and other ships of the subjects of the realm, to the number of fifty sail great and small, there to continue until such time as the Lord Admiral, with a great and strong force, should repair thither, if occasion should so require. And in the meantime, the Lord Admiral, with the Lord Henry Seymour, vice-admiral of that army, and many noblemen and gentlemen having charge of sundry of her Majesty's ships, continued in the Narrow Seas, having to attend upon them 20 ships of the city of London, very well and in good sort sent out, and sundry other good ships for the war which the coast towns, from the River of Thames to Newcastle northward, did send out for this service in warlike manner.

And then, upon further intelligence of the readiness of the Armada of Spain to come to the seas, the 21st of May, 1588,[1] the Lord Admiral, leaving the Lord Henry Seymour in the Narrow Seas, with a convenient force both of her Majesty's ships and of her subjects', to withstand all enterprises that the Duke

[1] Cf. *post*, May 23, Howard to Burghley.

of Parma should make by sea, did depart from the Downs towards the west with certain of her Majesty's ships and twenty other ships and barks of London, which arrived at Plymouth the 23rd of the same, where Sir Francis Drake, with the number of 60 sails, until that time under his charge, met [1] with the Lord Admiral in good order, whereupon his Lordship, commanding that fleet unto his own, made Sir Francis Drake his vice-admiral.

His Lordship, upon his arrival at Plymouth, took present order for the victualling and putting in a readiness of the whole army, being then near about the number of 90 sails of ships and barks ; which being accomplished, his Lordship put out of harbour again into the sea, and lay off and on in the Sleeve,[2] betwixt Ushant and Scilly, abiding the coming of the Spanish fleet; and afterwards his Lordship having spent long time, sometimes near the coast of France, and sometimes near the coast of England, retired with the fleet to Plymouth to refresh them.

In the meantime there were discovered betwixt Ushant and Scilly certain ships of the Spanish fleet, to the number of 14 sail, which afterward were known to be separated from their fleet by force of foul weather, and before they could be met with by any of the English army, they had a northerly wind which carried them back to the Groyne,[3] whither the rest of the fleet returned and watered. Hereupon his Lordship had intelligences sundry ways that the Spanish army was dispersed into sundry ports of Spain, distressed, spoiled, in necessity of victuals and great mortality grown amongst their people ; which

[1] Cf. *post, ib.* These details could then scarcely be known outside the official circle.

[2] The Sleeve (Fr. *La Manche*) is more properly the Channel. It will be seen, however, that Howard, like this unknown writer, always applies it to the Chops of the Channel, the sea between Ushant and Scilly.　　　　[3] Corunna.

notwithstanding did not so fall out in truth ; whereupon his Lordship, seeing our own coast clear and
the coast of France also, which he had very narrowly
searched, thought it good, with liking and advice of
his council, to take the opportunity of the next north
wind that should happen, and to bear with the coast
of Spain, there to seek out the Spanish fleet in the
Groyne or other ports of Galicia, which course was
held from the 8th of July, 1588, until the 10th of the
same, with a north wind, at which time the same
changed to southerly, 40 leagues short of the coast
of Spain, or thereabouts. His Lordship therefore,
doubting that which afterwards fell out in very deed,
and having his chief care and regard to the defence
of the realm of England, and finding that with that
wind the enemy might pass by the fleet of England
undescried, with that change of wind being prosperous for the fleet of Spain to come for the coast
of England, returned with his whole company and
arrived at Plymouth the 12th of the same, where,
with great expedition, his Lordship put divers things
in order, watered and refreshed his ships with
victuals.

The 19th of July, 1588, we had intelligence by
one of the barks that his Lordship had left in the
Sleeve for discovery, named the [Golden Hind],[1]
wherein was Captain Thomas Flemyng, that the
fleet of Spain was seen near the Lizard, the wind
being then southerly or south-west ; and although
the greater number of ships of the English army,
being then in Plymouth, with that wind were very

---

[1] Blank in MS. Flemyng is said by Sir William Monson to
have been a 'pirate,' 'at sea a-pilfering,' an idea which Kingsley
elaborated in *Westward Ho !* It is, however, distinctly contradicted by the State Papers. He was, through the Gonsons, a near
connection of Hawkyns, and is frequently named during the
following ten years as commanding a ship of war, either in the
Queen's service or with the Earl of Cumberland.

hard to be gotten out of harbour, yet the same was
done with such diligence and good will, that many of
them got abroad as though it had been with a fair
wind.   Whereupon, the 20th of July, his Lordship,
accompanied with 54 sail of his fleet, with that south-
west wind plied out of the Sound ; and being gotten
out scarce so far as Eddystone,[1] the Spanish army was
discovered, and were apparently seen of the whole
fleet to the westwards as far as Fowey.

The next morning, being Sunday, the 21st of
July, 1588, all the English ships that were then
come out of Plymouth had recovered the wind of
the Spaniards two leagues to the westward of
Eddystone,[1] and about 9 of the clock in the morning,
the Lord Admiral sent his pinnace,[2] named the
Disdain, to give the Duke of Medina defiance, and
afterward in the Ark bare up with the admiral[3] of
the Spaniards wherein the Duke was supposed to
be, and fought with her until she was rescued by
divers ships of the Spanish army.   In the meantime, Sir Francis Drake, Sir John Hawkyns,[4] and
Sir Martin Frobiser[4] fought with the galleon of
Portugal, wherein John Martinez de Recalde, vice-
admiral, was supposed to be.   The fight was so well
maintained for the time that the enemy was constrained to give way and to bear up room[5] to the
eastward, in which bearing up, a great galleon,
wherein Don Pedro de Valdes was captain, became

[1] MS. Idye Stone.
[2] This is not mentioned in any of the State Papers ; though
the Lord Admiral's pinnace Disdain is.
[3] The flag-ship.   The use of the word admiral in this sense,
common in the Elizabethan period, continued till the end of the
seventeenth century.
[4] So called by anticipation.   They were not knighted till the
26th.
[5] Room=to leeward.   It is only used adverbially, as ' to bear
room,' ' to go room,' ' roomwards,' and seems to conceal the same
idea as the still familar ' to sail large.'

foul of another ship which spoiled and bare overboard his foremast and bowsprit,[1] whereby he could
not keep company with their fleet, but being with
great dishonour left behind by the Duke, fell into
our hands.   There was also at that instant a great
Biscayan, of 800 tons or thereabouts, that, by firing
of a barrel of gunpowder, had her decks blown up,
her stern blown out, and her steerage spoiled.   This
ship was for this night carried amongst the fleet by
the galleasses.

This fight continued not above two hours ; for
the Lord Admiral, considering there were forty sail
of his fleet as yet to come from Plymouth, thought
good to stay [2] their coming before he would hazard
the rest too far,[3] and therefore set out a flag of
council, where his Lordship's considerate advice
was much liked of, and order delivered unto each
captain how to pursue the fleet of Spain ; and so,
dismissing each man to go aboard his own ship, his
Lordship appointed Sir Francis Drake to set the
watch that night.

This night the Spanish fleet bare alongst by the
Start, and the next day, in the morning, they were
as far to leeward as the Berry.   Our own fleet,
being disappointed of their light, by reason that Sir
Francis Drake left the watch to pursue certain hulks
which were descried [4] very late in the evening,
lingered behind not knowing whom to follow ; only
his Lordship, with the Bear and the Mary Rose in
his company, somewhat in his stern, pursued the
enemy all night within culverin shot ; his own fleet
being as far behind as,[5] the next morning, the

---

[1] MS. bolspreete.   [2] Await.
[3] This sentence must surely have emanated from Howard.
[4] Cf. *post*, August 10, Starke's Deposition.   Starke's word
is 'scryed.'
[5] As=that.

nearest might scarce be seen half mast high, and very many out of sight, which with a good sail recovered not his Lordship the next day before it was very late in the evening. This day, Sir Francis Drake with the Revenge, the Roebuck and a small bark or two in his company, took Don Pedro de Valdes, which was spoiled of his mast the day before; and having taken out Don Pedro and certain other gentlemen, sent away the same ship and company to Dartmouth, under the conduction of the Roebuck, and himself bare with the Lord Admiral, and recovered his Lordship that night, being Monday.

This Monday, being the 22nd of July, 1588, the Spaniards abandoned the ship that the day before was spoiled by fire, to the which his Lordship sent the Lord Thomas Howard and Sir John Hawkyns, knight, who together, in a small skiff of the Victory's, went aboard her, where they saw a very pitiful sight —the deck of the ship fallen down, the steerage broken, the stern blown out, and about 50 poor creatures burnt with powder in most miserable sort.[1] The stink in the ship was so unsavoury, and the sight within board so ugly, that the Lord Thomas Howard and Sir John Hawkyns shortly departed and came unto the Lord Admiral to inform his Lordship in what case she was found; whereupon his Lordship took present order that a small bark named the Bark Flemyng,[2] wherein was Captain Thomas Flemyng, should conduct her to some port in England which he could best recover, which was performed, and the said ship brought into Weymouth the next day.

That night fell very calm, and the four galleasses singled themselves out from their fleet, whereupon some doubt was had lest in the night they might

---

[1] These details are not found in the State Papers.
[2] Many ships are similarly named after their owner. The true name of the Bark Flemyng was Golden Hind.

have distressed some of our small ships which were short of our fleet, but their courage failed them, for they attempted nothing.

The next morning, being Tuesday, the 23rd of July, 1588, the wind sprang up at north-east, and then the Spaniards had the wind of the English army, which stood in to the north-westward, towards the shore. So did the Spaniards also. But that course was not good for the English army to recover the wind of the Spaniards, and therefore they cast about to the eastwards ; whereupon the Spaniards bare room, offering [to] board our ships. Upon which coming room there grew a great fight. The English ships stood fast and abode their coming, and the enemy, seeing us to abide them, and divers of our ships to stay for them, as the Ark, the Nonpareil, the Elizabeth Jonas, the Victory, &c., and divers other ships, they were content to fall astern of the Nonpareil, which was the sternmost ship.

In the meantime, the Triumph, with five ships, viz., the Merchant Royal, the Centurion, the Margaret and John, the Mary Rose and the Golden Lion, were so far to leeward and separated from our fleet, that the galleasses took courage and bare room with them and assaulted them sharply. But they were very well resisted by those ships for the space of an hour and a half. At length certain of her Majesty's ships bare with them, and then the galleasses forsook them. The wind then shifted to the south-eastwards and so to SSW, at what time a troop of her Majesty's ships and sundry merchants' assailed the Spanish fleet so sharply to the westward that they were all forced to give way and to bear room ; which his Lordship perceiving, together with the distress that the Triumph and the five merchant ships in her company were in, called unto certain of her Majesty's ships then near at hand and charged them straitly to follow him, and to set freshly upon the Spaniards, and to go within musket-shot of the enemy before they should discharge any one piece of ordnance, thereby to succour the Triumph; which was very well performed by the Ark, the Elizabeth Jonas, the Galleon of Leicester, the Golden Lion, the Victory, the Mary Rose, the Dreadnought and the Swallow—for so they went in order into the fight. Which the Duke of Medina perceiving, came out with 16 of his best galleons, to impeach his Lordship and to stop him from assisting of the Triumph. At which assault, after wonderful sharp conflict, the Spaniards were forced to give way and to flock together like sheep. In this conflict one William Coxe,[1] captain of a small pinnace of Sir William Wynter's, named the Delight, showed himself most valiant in the face of his enemies at the hottest of the encounter, where [2] afterwards lost his life in the service with a great shot. Towards the evening, some four or five ships of the Spanish fleet edged out of the south-west-wards, where some other of our ships met them, amongst which [the] Mayflower of London dis-

[1] Poor Coxe has had rather hard measure served out to him. Lediard, unable to distinguish an *x* from a *p* in Elizabethan writing, has changed his name into Cope; Fuller, whom Southey follows, calls him Cock; and Motley speaks of him as 'one Wilton, coxswain of the Delight.' Cf. *Don Juan*, viii. 18.

[2] 'Where' must be a clerical error for 'who.' Camden, referring probably to a copy of this Relation, says, 'Solus Cockus Anglus, in sua inter medios hostes navicula, cum laude periit;' and this has been repeated over and over again by English, French, and Spanish writers. But it will be seen (*post*, August 1, Wynter to Walsyngham) that he was alive on July 29, and that the 'navicula' was Wynter's. Motley describes his 'Wilton' as killed in boarding the great galleass. But Coxe was killed by a great shot, and Wynter's expression 'who sithen that time is slain,' clearly puts his death later. He was probably slain in the fight off Gravelines.

charged some pieces at them very valiantly, which ship and company at sundry other times behaved themselves stoutly.

This fight was very nobly continued from morning until evening, the Lord Admiral being always [in] the hottest of the encounter, and it may well be said that for the time there was never seen a more terrible value of great shot, nor more hot fight than this was ; for although the musketeers and harquebusiers of crock [1] were then infinite, yet could they not be discerned nor heard for that the great ordnance came so thick that a man would have judged it to have been a hot skirmish of small shot,[2] being all the fight long within half musket shot of the enemy.

This great fight being ended, the next day, being Wednesday, the 24th of July, 1588, there was little done, for that in the fight on Sunday and Tuesday much of our munition had been spent, and therefore the Lord Admiral sent divers barks and pinnaces unto the shore for a new supply of such provisions. This day the Lord Admiral divided his fleet into four squadrons, whereof he appointed the first to attend himself ; the second his Lordship committed to the charge of Sir Francis Drake ; the third to Sir John Hawkyns, and the fourth to Sir Martin Frobiser. This afternoon his Lordship gave order that, in the night, six merchant ships out of every squadron should set upon the Spanish fleet in sundry places, at one instant, in the night time, to keep the enemy

[1] The harquebus was a very heavy sort of musket, fired from a rest or crock. The word 'crock' is still in use, in the sense of 'a little stool.'

[2] 'The shot continued so thick together that it might rather have been judged a skirmish with small shot on land than a fight with great shot on sea.' This is Sir George Carey's account of this action, in his letter to the Earl of Sussex, of July 25.

waking ; but all that night fell out to be so calm that nothing could be done.

The next morning, being the 25th of July, 1588, there was a great galleon[1] of the Spaniards short of her company to the southwards. They of Sir John Hawkyns his squadron, being next, towed and recovered so near that the boats were beaten off with musket shot ; whereupon three of the galleasses and an armado[2] issued out of the Spanish fleet, with whom the Lord Admiral in the Ark, and the Lord Thomas Howard in the Golden Lion, fought a long time and much damaged them, that one of them was fain to be carried away upon the careen ; and another, by a shot from the Ark, lost her lantern, which came swimming by, and the third his nose. There was many good shots made by the Ark and Lion at the galleasses in the sight of both armies, which looked on and could not approach, it being calm, for the Ark and the Lion did tow to the galleasses with their long boats. At length it began to blow a little gale, and the Spanish fleet edged up to succour their galleasses, and so rescued them and the galleon, after which time the galleasses were never seen in fight any more, so bad was their entertainment in this encounter. Then the fleets drawing near one to another, there began some fight, but it continued

[1] This was the Santa Ana, Recalde's *capitana* or flag-ship. She had received much damage on the 21st, which now brought her into danger from Hawkyns' squadron, and after she had beaten off their attack was no longer able to keep the sea. She parted company unobserved during the night, and drifted over to Havre, where she became a total wreck.

[2] An English corruption of the Sp. *armada*, and in our literature is used in exactly the same sense—a fleet. Thus Shakespeare has (*King John*, iii. 4) 'A whole armado of convicted sail.' In these papers, however, it is distinctively used as meaning a galleon, a large ship out of the armada, or, in fact, 'a fleet ship,' a term suggested a few years ago for what is now called 'a battle-ship.'

not long, saving that the Nonpareil and the Mary
Rose struck their topsails and lay awhile by the
whole fleet of Spain very bravely, during which time
the Triumph, to the northward of the Spanish fleet,
was so far to leeward as, doubting that some of the
Spanish army might weather her, she towed off with
the help of sundry boats, and so recovered the wind.
The Bear and the Elizabeth Jonas, perceiving her
distress, bare with her for her rescue, and put themselves, through their hardiness, into like perils, but
made their parties good notwithstanding, until they
had recovered the wind ; and so that day's fight
ended, which was a very sharp fight for the time.

Now, forasmuch as our powder and shot was well
wasted,[1] the Lord Admiral thought it was not good
in policy to assail them any more until their coming
near unto Dover, where he should find the army
which he had left under the conduction of the Lord
Henry Seymour and Sir William Wynter, knight,
ready to join with his Lordship, whereby our fleet
should be much strengthened, and in the meantime,
better store of munition might be provided from the
shore.   On Friday, being the 26th of July, 1588, his
Lordship, as well in reward of their good services in
these former fights, as also for the encouragement of
the rest, called the Lord Thomas Howard, the Lord
Sheffield, Sir Roger Townshend, Sir Martin Frobiser
and Sir John Hawkyns,[2] and gave them all the
order of knighthood aboard the Ark.   All this day
and Saturday, being the 27th of July, the Spaniards
went always before the English army like sheep,
during which time the justices of peace near the sea-
coast, the Earl of Sussex, Sir George Carey, and the

----

[1] 'Wasted' frequently occurs in the sense of 'expended,'
'consumed.'

[2] Sir George Beeston was also knighted at this time, though
his name is here omitted.

captains of the forts and castles alongst the coast, sent us men, powder, shot, victuals and ships to aid and assist us. On Saturday, in the evening the Spanish fleet came near unto Calais on the coast of Picardy, and there suddenly came to an anchor over against betwixt Calais and Calais Cliffs,[1] and our English fleet anchored short of them within culverin shot of the enemy.

The Spaniards sent notice of their arrival presently unto the Duke of Parma, but because[2] there should be no time detracted[3] to permit their forces to join, the Lord Admiral, the 28th of July, 1588, about midnight, caused eight ships to be fired and let drive amongst the Spanish fleet; whereupon they were forced to let slip or cut cables at half and to set sail. By reason of which fire the chief galleass came foul of another ship's cable and brake her rudder, by means whereof he was forced the next day to row ashore near the haven's mouth and town of Calais; whereupon the Lord Admiral sent his long boat, under the charge of Amyas Preston,[4] gentleman, his lieutenant, and with him Mr. Thomas Gerrard[5] and Mr. . . . .[6] Harvey, together with other gentlemen, his Lordship's followers and servants, who took her and had the spoil of her. There entered into her above 100 Englishmen. And

---

[1] MS. Scales Cleeves.   [2] MS. by cause.

[3] Drawn out, spun out.

[4] Was here severely wounded. He continued serving during the war; commanded an expedition to the Spanish Main in 1595; and in 1596 was captain of the Ark under Howard, in the expedition to Cadiz, when he was knighted.

[5] Not improbably the eldest son of Sir Gilbert Gerard, Master of the Rolls; created Baron Gerard of Gerard's Bromley in Staffordshire in 1603.

[6] Blank in MS. Bor and others give his name as William. Probably, therefore, the William Harvey who was knighted at Cadiz in 1596, and commanded the Bonaventure in the Islands voyage in 1597.

for that she was aground and sewed[1] two foot, and could not be gotten off, they left her to Monsr. Gourdan, Captain of Calais, where she lieth sunk.

Now that the Lord Henry Seymour and Sir William Wynter were joined with us, our fleet was near about 140 sail—of ships, barks and pinnaces &c. During the time that this galleass was in taking by the Lord Admiral, Sir Francis Drake in the Revenge, accompanied with Mr. Thomas Fenner in the Nonpareil and the rest of his squadron, set upon the fleet of Spain and gave them a sharp fight. And within short time, Sir John Hawkyns in the Victory, accompanied with Mr. Edward Fenton[2] in the Mary Rose, Sir George Beeston in the Dreadnought, Mr. Richard Hawkyns[3] in the Swallow, and the rest of the ships appointed to his squadron, bare with the midst of the Spanish army, and there continued an hot assault all that forenoon. Sir George Beeston behaved himself valiantly. This fight continued hotly; and then came the Lord Admiral, the Lord Thomas Howard, the Lord Sheffield, near the place where the Victory had been before, where these noblemen did very valiantly. Astern of these was a great galleon assailed by the Earl of Cumberland and Mr. George Raymond[4] in the Bonaventure most worthily, and being also beaten with the Lord Henry Seymour in the Rain-

---

[1] Dried : akin to the modern sewer = a drain, and Fr. *essuyer* = to wipe dry. 'A cow when her milk is gone is said *to go sew* ; a ship is *sewed* when she comes to lie on the ground or to lie dry. To *sew* a pond is to empty or drain it' (Wedgwood). 'A ship resting upon the ground . . . is said to be sewed by as much as the difference between the surface of the water and the ship's floating mark. If not left quite dry, she sews to such a point' (Smyth).

[2] Hawkyns' brother-in-law.   [3] Hawkyns' son.

[4] MS. Ryman. He commanded the expedition which sailed for the East Indies in April 1591, and was lost, in the Penelope, off Cape Corrientes.

bow, and Sir William Wynter in the Vanguard, yet she recovered into the fleet. Notwithstanding, that night she departed from the army and was sunk. After this, Mr. Edward Fenton in the Mary Rose and a galleon encountered each other, the one standing to the eastward and the other to the westward, so close as they could conveniently one pass by another, wherein the captain and company did very well. Sir Robert Southwell that day did worthily behave himself, as he had done many times before; so did Mr. Robert Crosse [1] in the Hope, and most of the rest of the captains and gentlemen. This day did the Lord Henry Seymour and Sir William Wynter so batter two of the greatest armados that they were constrained to seek the coast of Flanders, and were afterwards, being distressed and spoiled, taken by the Zealanders and carried into Flushing. In this fight it is known that there came to their end sundry of the Spanish ships, besides many other unknown to us.

After this Monday's fight, which was the 29th of July, 1588, the Lord Admiral on the 30th of July appointed the Lord Henry Seymour, Sir William Wynter and their fleet to return back again unto the Narrow Seas, to guard the coasts there, and himself, determining to follow the Spanish army with his fleet until they should come so far northward as the Frith in Scotland if they should bend themselves that way, thought good to forbear any more to assault them till he might see what they purposed to do, verily thinking that they would put into the Frith, where his Lordship had devised stratagems to make an end of them; but the Spaniards kept a course for the Isles of Scotland,

---

[1] Was with Drake in the West Indies in 1585, and continued serving during the war. Was knighted at Cadiz in 1596.

and of purpose, to our seeming, to pass home that way, by the north of Scotland and west part of Ireland.

When we were come into 55 degrees and 13 minutes to the northward, 30 leagues east of Newcastle, the Lord Admiral determined [1] to fight with them again on the Friday, being the 2nd of August, but by some advice and counsel his Lordship stayed that determination, partly because we saw their course and meaning was only to get away that way to the northward to save themselves, and partly also for that many of our fleet were unprovided of victuals; for our supply, which her Majesty had most carefully provided and caused to be in readiness, knew not where to seek for us. It was therefore concluded that we should leave the Spanish fleet and direct our course for the Frith in Scotland, as well for the refreshing of our victuals as also for the performing of some other business which the Lord Admiral thought convenient to be done; but the wind coming contrary—viz. westerly—the next day the Lord Admiral altered his course and returned back again for England with his whole army, whereof some recovered the Downs, some Harwich and some Yarmouth, about the 7th of August, 1588.

[1] This is surely official optimism. It appears certain that he had little or no ammunition remaining.

STATE PAPERS.

Dec. 21, 1587.—*COMMISSION TO HOWARD.*

[Patent Roll, 30 Elizabethæ, part 17, m. 7 d; S.P. Dom. Eliz. ccvi. 41.—Latin.[1]]

Elizabeth, by the grace of God, &c., to all to whom &c., greeting :

Know ye that we, reposing special trust and confidence in the fidelity, prudence, zeal, experience, circumspection, industry and diligence of our beloved Councillor, Charles, Lord Howard, Baron of Effingham, knight of our illustrious order of the Garter, High Admiral of England, Ireland, Wales, and of the dominions and islands thereof, of the town of Calais and the marches of the same, of Normandy, Gascony and Aquitaine, and Captain General of the Navy and mariners of our said kingdoms of England and Ireland—do, by these presents, assign, make, constitute, ordain, and depute the said Charles to be our lieutenant-general, commander-in-chief, and governor of our whole fleet and army at sea,

[1] An extraordinary conventional jargon, setting grammar and dictionary alike at defiance. The present translation has been made after a careful comparison with other commissions of the same or nearly the same date—including one to the Duke of Buckingham in 1625—drawn up in an English only less extraordinary than the Latin.

now fitted forth against the Spaniards and their
allies, adherents or abettors, attempting or compassing any design against our kingdoms, dominions
and subjects; and also of all and singular our vice-
admirals, captains, sub-captains[1] and lieutenants, of
our barons,[2] lords and knights, of the masters of our
ships, our mariners and men at arms, employed or
to be employed,[3] of our gunners,[4] and of any others
whatsoever, retained or to be retained in our royal
fleet and army : Giving and granting to this same
Charles full power and authority to lead and command all and singular our lieges and subjects of
whatever estate, degree, or dignity they be in our
said fleet or army, and in whatsoever way they have
been or may be retained, or in whatever way they
have been engaged in this present service for resisting and destroying the Spaniards and others,
their allies, adherents, abettors or assistants, attempting or compassing any design against our kingdoms,
dominions and subjects ; as also—with our fleet and
army aforesaid, and our subjects assembled or arrayed for war[5]—according as there shall be occasion,
and wherever and whenever he shall deem it fitting,
to invade, enter, spoil and make himself master of
the kingdoms, dominions, lands, islands and all other

---

[1] Sub-capitaneorum. It is impossible to say what were meant,
in the days when post-captains were not ; but the distinction
seems to correspond to captains and commanders. It does not
occur anywhere else.

[2] Baroniorum, baronettorum, dominorum : greater and lesser
barons, and the sons of barons (lord by courtesy), or lords of
manors. What is perhaps the same phrase appears elsewhere as
' earls, viscounts, barons.'

[3] Delectorum sive destinatorum.

[4] Sagittariorum : bows and arrows are frequently mentioned
among the stores, but never 'archers' as a distinct class of men.
The ships' companies are always divided into mariners, gunners,
and soldiers.

[5] Ad bellum congregatos sive arraiatos.

places whatever belonging to the said Spaniards and others, their allies, adherents or abettors, attempting or compassing any design against our kingdoms, dominions and subjects ; and with force of arms to spoil, offend, repress, subdue and make war upon the Spaniards, their allies and adherents : And for the spoiling and utter subduing of these, whether by invasion, or in some other manner as heretofore set forth, to direct, rule, order and command our said fleet, army and subjects ; and if need be, to go and to sail with our said fleet, army and subjects, to our said kingdom of Ireland, or to any other place, according to his own will and pleasure : Giving and granting to the same Charles full power and authority to muster, direct, lead, order and command all and singular our vice-admirals, captains, sub-captains, lieutenants, barons,[1] lords, knights, masters of ships, mariners and gunners,[2] and all others soever in our aforesaid fleet and army, which are armed in our service or appointed thereto : and also to hear, examine, discuss, order and determine all suits, causes, quarrels and other matters of all and each of them, so far as they pertain, either by right or by custom, to the office of our said lieutenant-general at sea : Also to make, constitute and ordain laws and ordinances for the effective good conduct of our said fleet and army ; and furthermore, to make proclamations and enforce the due execution thereof ;[3] and to punish, repress, reform and incarcerate any belonging to our said fleet and army who shall, in any manner, offend ; and if it shall seem meet to him, to pardon, release, dismiss and deliver those

---

[1] As before—barones, baronettos, dominos.

[2] Sagittarios.

[3] Eademque debitum executionem : passing over the false concord, the ' eadem ' would seem to be the translation of the Elizabethan ' which.'

incarcerated : further, to enquire into, examine, hear and judge all capital or criminal charges relating to loss of life or limb, and cases of murder in any manner occurring in our said fleet and army, with all matters connected therewith or rising out of the same ; and also to determine, pass or publish sentences or decrees of whatsoever nature, regarding the same ; and to command and order, and cause such sentences or decrees[1] to be fully and effectively executed ; and according to his own will and pleasure, freely to do, ordain, forward, decree and execute all other things needful for the good conduct and government of our said fleet and army, as in his wise discretion they shall from time to time seem fitting, and with full power of coercion : And also with power and authority, as often as it seemeth to him fitting or necessary, to nominate, ordain, make, constitute, assign, and appoint other deputy-lieutenant or deputy-lieutenants to execute, perform, forward or carry out, in our stead and in our name, the aforesaid services or any of them ; and to recall him or them if the case should require it, and to order and appoint other or others in his or their place, for the services aforesaid, or any part of them.

Moreover, by these presents, we strictly command and enjoin all and each of the vice-admirals, captains, sub-captains, lieutenants, barons, lords, knights, masters of ships, mariners, gunners, and all others soever in our said fleet and army, in whatever manner they have been levied, retained or may be retained, that as need shall be, from time to time, they shall be attendant, counselling, helping and at the commandment of the said Charles, our High Admiral and Lieutenant General at sea, in the

---

[1] Easque sive ea executionem . . . demandandum . . .

execution of the aforesaid services, as they shall answer for it at their peril.[1]

In witness whereof &c. at Westminster, the 21st day of December.   Per ipsam Reginam.

December 22.—HOWARD TO BURGHLEY.

[ccvi. 42.—Signed. Addressed.]

My very good Lord :—I now remain aboard the Bear ; and as yet the provisions for the ships could not be taken all in by reason of the weather, which hath been so tempestuous as that no boats could lie aboard them to put in the same ; yet I hope that within two or three days all things will be in a readiness.

Here is a very sufficient and able company of sailors[2] as ever were seen ; and because their long journeys out of all places of this realm, and this bad season, makes them unprovided of apparel and such necessaries, it were good for their relief to pay them one month's wages before hand.

Many great charges extraordinary hath grown this quarter, which I could hardly have believed unless with mine own eyes and good examination I had seen.   Wherefore in respect of those causes, and for the furtherance of service, I am to entreat your good Lordship to give order that the rest of the warrant lately granted for the whole navy may be paid to Mr. Hawkyns, and 2,000*l.* more upon the old warrant of 29,000*l.* for the furnishing of those extraordinary charges, wherein your Lordship shall further a good service.

---

[1] Sub pœna gravissimi contemptus : *i.e.* under the penalty due to a most gross contempt of our authority ; *lèse-majesté.*

[2] MS. saylers.   In these papers the word is rare, 'mariners' being more commonly used.

We have entered into sea victuals this day, being the 22nd of this instant December, and not before, for the preserving of the six weeks' victuals. And Mr. Quarles [1] hath sent down divers supplies more than allowance—for the numbers were great before we entered into the six weeks' victuals.[2] Wherefore I pray your Lordship that he may be paid the rest of his allowed warrant, and that consideration for the rest which I spake to your Lordship for heretofore. And so I bid your good Lordship most heartily farewell. From aboard the Bear, the 22nd of December, 1587.

Your Lordship's most assured
loving friend to command,
C. HOWARD.

December 22.—LIST OF CAPTAINS.

[**ccvi. 43.**—Endorsed :—The names of the captains that have charge of her Majesty's ships particularly sent to the seas.]

1. The Lord Admiral.
2. The Lord H. Seymour.
3. The Lord Thomas Howard.
4. The Lord Sheffield.
5. Sir Robert Southwell.
6. Sir W. Wynter.[3]
7. Mr. John Hawkyns.
8. Mr. Borough.
9. Mr. Beeston.[4]

[1] James Quarles, Surveyor of Victuals.

[2] 'For the numbers . . . victuals,' is interlined in Howard's own hand. 'Great numbers' as distinguished from 'small.' Cf. *post*, p. 31.

[3] Had been in the service of the navy for nearly fifty years ; was knighted in 1573, and was at this time Master General of the Ordnance.

[4] Had been serving as a naval captain since the beginning of the reign.

10. Mr. Frobiser.
11. Sir Henry Palmer.[1]
12. Mr. Roger Townshend.[2]
13. Captain Crosse.
14. Mr. Henry Ashley.[3]

December 24.—HOWARD TO BURGHLEY.

[**B.M. Harl. MS. 6994, f. 102.**—Holograph. Addressed.]

My honourable good Lord :—I do understand by Mr. Cæsar[4] how much I am bound unto your Lordship for your honourable favour. I have no ways to recompense it but with my love and service, which your Lordship shall be most assured ever of.

It may be there hath been some report made to your Lordship of some chance[5] that happened here, before my coming down, by fire in one of the ships ; and because I do understand that it is reported that it should be[6] done by Ascott, I do assure your Lord-

[1] Is first named as commanding a squadron of the Queen's ships in 1576. In 1584 he was one of the commissioners for Dover Harbour, and in 1587 was knighted while commanding a squadron off Dunkirk.

[2] Though named in this list of captains, he had no experience of sea affairs, and did not command a ship either in 1588 or in any other year. He was knighted on July 26 (*ante*, p. 14), and was probably then serving on the personal staff of the Lord Admiral, but his name does not appear elsewhere in these papers. He died in 1590. His great-grandson, Horatio, was created a viscount after the Restoration.

[3] Probably the brother of Sir Anthony Ashley, Clerk of the Council, translator and editor of *The Mariners' Mirrour* (1588), knighted at Cadiz in 1596, and grandfather of the first Earl of Shaftesbury.

[4] Dr., afterwards Sir Julius Cæsar, Judge of the Admiralty Court.

[5] Mischance.

[6] This use of the conditional in oblique relation was very general.

ship it was after this manner.   There were two poor
knaves that came from Westchester [1] that strived for
a place to hang up their netting for to lie in, and the
one of them had a piece of a candle in his hand, and
in striving, the candle fell down where there lay
some oakum.   It might have bred some mischief,
but it was quickly put out.   It was in the Elizabeth
Bonaventure ; but I hope to make them a warning
to others to beware.

I am bold to send you by this bearer, my man,
the copy of a proclamation which I have drawn and
proclaimed in my own ship, and shall be this day and
to-morrow proclaimed in the rest.   I am but a bad
drawer of a proclamation, but it shall serve, I hope,
for to prevent some ill that might happen.

My good Lord, this bearer, my man, shall always
attend at the court, and shall attend on your Lordship always to know your pleasure, if you will command him anything unto me.   And so, resting
always most beholden unto your Lordship and most
ready to do your Lordship any service, I humbly
take my leave.   Aboard her Majesty's good ship the
White Bear, the 24th of December, 1587.

Your Lordship's most assured to command,

C. Howard.

[1] Chester.

January 5.—*DISPOSITION OF SHIPS.*

[**ccviii. 6.**   Rough list ; captains' names scribbled in
in Burghley's hand.]

5th of January, 1587.

Ships to remain at Queenborough with their
numbers diminished, in the charge of the Admiral :

[Men]		[Men]	
500	The Bear . .	275	Lord Admiral
500	Triumph . .	275	Lord Henry
500	Elizabeth Jonas	275	Sir Robt South-well
400	Victory . .	225	Lord Sheffield
400	Ark Ralegh .	225	Lord Thomas
250	Mary Rose .	125	Edward Fenton
250	Lion . .	125	Borough
250	Bonaventure .	125	John Hawkyns
250	Vanguard .	125	Sir Wm Wynter
200	Dreadnought .	100	Beeston
250	Rainbow . .	125	with Sir H. Palmer
160	Foresight .	80	Cap. Frobiser
30	Merlin .	15	
24	Sun . .	12	
36	Brigandine .	20	
20	George .	12	

4,020   A 2,139   rest in charge

1,881 abated

£3,208. 10s.

Ships for the Narrow Seas and Flushing, to serve under Sir Henry Palmer :

			[Men]
The Antelope	. Ch. Baker	.	160
Swallow	. Benjamin	.	160
Bull .	. Turner	.	100
Tiger.	. Bostocke[1]	.	100
Tramontana	Luke Ward[2]		70
Scout.	. Henry Ashley		70
Achates	. Capt. Riggs		60
Charles	.	. .	40
Moon	.	. .	40

B 800 rest in charge

At Portsmouth for Sir Francis Drake :

[Men]				[Men]
250	The Hope	. . .	.	140
250	Nonpareil.	. .	.	140
35	Advice	. . .	.	20
535				300

At Queenborough for Sir Francis Drake :

			[Men]
The Revenge	. Rob. Crosse	.	140
Swiftsure	. Fenner	.	100
Aid	. Fenner	.	80

[Men]
550 { whereof to be dis-charged 230 } . 320

total 1,085 for Sir Fr. Drake   C 620 in charge

465 abated

[1] John Bostocke. A Thomas Bostocke was Sir George Bond's agent at St. Jean de Luz.

[2] Had been employed against the pirates in the Channel in 1578, and commanded the Edward Bonaventure with Fenton in the voyage of 1582.

In wafting of the Artillery   [Men]

The Spy 35

Upon the Coast of Spain

The Makeshift .   .   .   . $\frac{35}{}$

D 70 rest in charge

A 2,139 �️ 3,629 men. Note when the 3 ships[1] sent
B   800 ⎟ westward shall have their numbers full,
C   620 ⎟ which are 1,085,[1] then the total monthly
D   70 ⎠ charge will be 4,657*l*.

$$
\begin{array}{r}
\text{\textsterling} \\
3{,}208 \\
1{,}200 \\
930 \\
\underline{105} \\
\text{\textsterling}5{,}443\,^{2} \\
\text{add} \quad \underline{637} \\
\text{\textsterling}6{,}080 \\
\end{array}
$$

January 6.—THE CHARGE OF THE SHIPS.

[ccviii. 7.]

To continue in charge with the Lord Admiral:
16 ships, the number of 2,139.

To continue upon the Narrow Seas under the
charge of Sir Henry Palmer: the Antelope and 8
other ships, with the number of 800.

Total, 2,939 in men, 4,408*l*. 10*s*. in money.

[1] So written in Burghley's hand. He includes, however, not
only the three ships at Portsmouth with Drake, but also the three
ships at Queenborough, under orders to join him. And where
the 4,657*l*. comes from does not appear. The charge really
amounts to 6,141*l*.

[2] This is the monthly charge for the men under A, B, C and
D, at 30*s*. a month. The charge for the additional men (465) in
the western squadron, which should be 697*l*., is added in as 637*l*.,
giving, of course, a false total.

To be sent to Sir Francis Drake : the Revenge, the Swiftsure and the Aid, with the numbers only of 320.

To be sent also from Portsmouth to Sir Francis Drake : the Hope, the Nonpareil and the Advice, with the number of 300.

Total, 620 in men, 930*l.* in money.

To continue in charge : the Spy with 35, and the Makeshift, on the coast of Spain, with 35.

Total, 70 in men, 105*l.* in money.

Total in charge presently   .   3,629

Her Majesty is to continue the charge hereof, being monthly   .   .   . .£5,443 10*s.*
To be added the charge of Sir Francis Drake's ships to the number of   . .   ¹

The charges of wages and victualling after the rate of 30*s.* a man is per month   ¹

January 8.—*ESTIMATE OF CHARGES.*

[ccviii. 8.]

An estimate of the charge of the ships that serve under the charge of Sir Francis Drake westward, viz. :

Her Majesty's ships.

Men		Men
250	The Revenge	140
250	Hope	140
250	Nonpareil. . . .	140
180	Swiftsure	100
120	Aid	80
35	Advice	20
35	Makeshift. . . .	20
1,120		640

¹ Left blank.

Men	At London.		Men
120	The Edward Bonaventure	.	60
120	Roebuck		60
100	Hopewell		50
80	Galleon Fenner . .		40
100	Golden Noble . . .		50
520			260

Men	At Plymouth.		Men
180	The Merchant Royal . .		40
100	Griffin		20
80	Minion		20
80	Thomas		20
80	Bark Talbot . . .		20
80	Spark		20
70	Hope		16
70	Bark Bond [1] . . .		16
70	Bark Bonner [2] . . .		16
60	Elizabeth Founes [3] . .		12
40	Unity		12
30	Elizabeth Drake . .		8
70	Bark Hawkyns . .		15
250	{Five hulks or other ships to make up 30 sail, which have in charge in harbour}		80
1,260			315

The great Numbers	The small Numbers
1,120	640
520	260
1,260	315
2,900	Soldiers 100
	1,315

[1] Belonging, probably, to Sir George Bond, the Lord Mayor.

[2] The Bonners were a family of shipowners at Leigh in Essex. Robert Bonner, the head of the family at this time, married Elizabeth, sister of Launcelot Andrewes, afterwards Bishop of Winchester, and one of the translators of the Bible.

[3] Humphrey Founes was Mayor of Plymouth the next year, 1588-9.

	£	s.	d.
First, the great numbers are 2,900 men, which for charge of wages, after the rate of 14s. the man, diets,[1] dead shares and reward accounted, is monthly, after 28 days to the month, amounteth to	2,030	0	0
For the tonnage of 23 merchant ships accounted in 4,000 ton may amount unto, by the month of like days	400	0	0
	2,430	0	0
For the sea victual of the said 2,900 men at 16s. 4d. every man, by the month of 28 days, amounteth to	2,368	6	8
For transportation monthly	50	0	0
	2,418	6	8

Wages 2,430 0 0
Victuals 2,418 6 8
4,848 6 8 {The monthly charge of the great numbers

For the small numbers, which are 1,315 men, the month's wages, after the rate of 14s. the man, diets, dead shares and rewards accounted, is	920	10	0
For the tonnage of the merchant ships, being 23 ships accounted in 4,000 ton, amounteth to by the month	400	0	0
	1,320	10	0

[1] Roughly speaking, diets were equivalent to the modern table-money ; dead-shares seem to have been the pay of fictitious men, similar to the 'widows' men' of the eighteenth century, with the essential difference that they were borne, not for any charitable purpose, but to increase the pay of warrant and petty officers, who

For the victual of the said 1,315 men   £   *s.*   *d.*
    monthly, as aforesaid, at 16*s.* 4*d.*
    the man, after 28 days per month,
    is   1,073   18   4
For transportation monthly   .   .   20   0   0
                                         1,093   18   4

        1,320   10   0
        1,093   18   4

        2,414   8   4 { The monthly charge of the small numbers

January 18.—*HAWKYNS TO BURGHLEY* (?)

[ccviii. 14.—Holograph. No address nor endorsement.]

My bounden duty humbly remembered unto your good Lordship :—This day with God's favour I shall make an end of the pay to all such as be discharged through the navy, and have reduced them to the numbers your Lordship did appoint. The Revenge, the Swiftsure and the Aid's company were reduced to 320 men, as was appointed, and they departed and were well over the Land's End [1] the 16th day of this month, God be thanked.

Yesterday my Lord Admiral accompanied with the Lords went over the Land's End towards Dover, with the Vanguard, the Rainbow, and sundry of our small pinnaces ; and mindeth to see Dover, Harwich and other places, before his Lordship return. His abode, I think, will not be long ; for his Lordship

also received special allowances under the name of rewards. The subject is more fully discussed in the Introduction.
[1] Writing from Queenborough, he probably meant the Land's End in Sheppey, which is Shell-Ness ; but he may have meant the Land's End by Margate, which would seem to be Fore-Ness, or possibly the North Foreland.

told me he would return within four days, if weather served.

The treasure went over the 16th day of this present, accompanied with the Bull, the Tiger and the Charles ; so as there remaineth there at Queenborough 11 great ships, as followeth :—

	Men		Men
The Bear . .	275	The Mary Rose .	125
Triumph .	275	Bonaventure .	125
Eliz. Jonas .	275	Lion . .	125
Victory . .	225	Dreadnought .	100
Ark Ralegh .	225	Antelope .	160
	1,275	which is to go into the Narrow Seas.	
	715		
	1,990	Swallow . .	80
			715

As there shall be any occasion grow here worthy the writing I will inform your Lordship, and so humbly take my leave. From Queenborough aboard the Bonaventure, the 18th of January, 1587.

Your Lordship's humbly to command,

JOHN HAWKYNS.

THE AGREEMENT WITH MR. HAWKYNS.

[ccviii. 17.—Endorsed : Mr. Hawkyns, the conditions for the bargain for the Navy upon the dormant warrant for 5,714*l.* ; 1579.]

The bargain of John Hawkyns for the navy, viz. :

Conditions in the behalf of her Majesty.

1. First, all that which was ordinary in such time as it was 5,714*l.* yearly John Hawkyns shall perform :

2. As first.—To pay and continue the same number of ship-keepers that hath been since the said ordinary was reduced to the said sum of 5,714*l.* together with the same number of gunners in Upnor Castle, the clerks &c., the watchmen, and rent that now is paid in the ordinary.

3. Item.—To keep in repair all her Majesty's ships, so as, upon a grounding, they may be ready to serve at the seas, until some one of them come to be new made in a dry dock.[1]

4. Item.—To moor the navy sufficiently, so that the ships may ride without danger.

5. Item.—To repair all manner of storehouses and wharves at Chatham, Woolwich, Deptford and Portsmouth, until any of them shall fall into such decay as they must be new built.

6. Item.—To continue all her Majesty's navy in serviceable order, and every year to do such reparations as shall be needful, either in making of a new ship, repairing in dry dock, or any way otherwise that shall be needful, so that the full number be kept as they are now at this present. If any ship be decayed, another to be put new in her place, of like length and breadth, sufficiently builded.

[None at all were made new by him.][2]

7. Item.—To ground the ships upon all occasions of sea-service, leaks or other needful causes.

8. Item.—All the boats, cocks,[3] pinnaces and lighters shall be kept in serviceable order; and as the old do decay, new to be made in their places.

9. Item.—He shall find Norway masts for all the small ships under the Aid;[4] and the topmasts and topsail yards of all the ships.

10. Item.—That at All-Hallowtide every year

---

[1] MS. docque. [2] Marginal note in Burghley's hand.
[3] Cock-boats. [4] That is, of less than 250 tons.

there shall be presented unto the Lord Treasurer, the Lord Chamberlain, Mr. Secretary and Sir Walter Mildmay, the names of twenty skilful men— as captains, owners, shipwrights, and masters—of which number the foresaid commissioners shall appoint such a number as they will to make report of the estate of the navy, and to show their opinion what shall be needful to be done to the navy the year following, which shall be likewise performed.

Conditions in the behalf of John Hawkyns.

1. First.—The said John Hawkyns shall have paid him for the service to be done of the other side, the old ordinary warrant of 5,714*l*. 2*s*. 2*d*. monthly as it was, in *Anno* 1578.

2. Item.—He shall be holpen with the commission, as in *Anno* 1578.

3. Item.—It shall be lawful for him to entertain as many shipwrights as he will, and as few as he will, and at all seasons and times as the service shall require, and no more.

4. Item.—If any of the ships shall come to a mischance—as God forbid—either by fire, wreck, spoil in war, or such like ; or the boats, cocks, or pinnaces ; then the said John Hawkyns shall have allowance for the supply of such ships, boats and pinnaces, as the charge shall require, and be judged by the commissioners or officers of the navy.

5. Item.—That if the whole navy shall go to the seas, or a great part of them, whatsoever provisions of timber, board and plank, shall be taken into them for sea service, the said John Hawkyns shall not be charged with above the value of 40*s*. in such stuff for every ship ; to say boards, planks, fishes [1] for masts, spare masts for topmasts, and such like.

[1] MS. fyshers.

6. Item.—The said John Hawkyns shall have the assistance of the shipkeepers for the help of grounding of the ships, loading and unloading of provisions, and such like; the use of the hoy for carriage, launching-tackles and crane-ropes &c., as hath been in time past.

7. Item.—He shall also have the use of the wharves, storehouses, forges, and lodgings at Chatham, Deptford, Woolwich, and Portsmouth, for those ministers that shall be needful to attend this service, and for the laying of all manner of provisions readily for the said service.

8. Item.—That if the ships shall ride in any other place by her Majesty's order, then, by the discretion of the commissioners, it may be judged what shall be increased for the same mooring, calling unto them the officers and masters of the navy.

9. Item.—That when a new ship shall be made and ready to be launched, the said John Hawkyns shall make his commodity[1] of the old.

10. Item.—If any ambiguity or doubt shall happen of either part that ought to be considered in equity and conscience be omitted in this bargain, and that the same cannot be agreed[2] upon amongst the officers, that then the commissioners aforesaid shall, by their discretions, moderate the doubt and order the same.

[1] Advantage, profit.
[2] If on either part there shall happen any . . . doubt on some point omitted in this bargain, it ought to be considered &c. ; and if the same cannot be agreed &c.

January 22.—REPORT BY PETT AND BAKER.

[**ccviii. 18.**—Endorsed, in Burghley's hand : An opinion of Peter
Pett [1] and Matthew Baker [2] the shipwright upon certain articles
of Mr. J. Hawkyns. Torn and frayed away at the edges.]

The examination of the bargain of Mr. John
Hawkyns, how far it is performed and accomplished.

First, to the behalf of her Majesty ; the condition
divided into [ten several articles] in the first page.

1. First.—All that which was ordinary at such
time as it was 5,714*l.* yearly &c.

In this article is to be noted how this 5,714*l.*
yearly was employed ; as first the ordinary of the
carpentry was undertaken by the master shipwrights
for 1,000*l. per annum* ; the moorings by Mr. Hawkyns
for 1,200*l. per annum* ; the shipkeepers' wages, clerks
&c. for 1,814*l. per annum* ; so was spared and remained
to her Majesty's farther uses 1,700*l.* yearly ; which
whole warrant is continued in Mr. Hawkyns' hands
to this day.   It is said that he employed this 1,700*l.*
yearly during 6 years in provision of cordage,
canvas, anchors &c., to furnish the storehouse with a
double furniture, to be in readiness for all suddens.
How the same is performed there resteth a question.
And touching the 1,000*l.* a year undertaken by the
shipwrights, Mr. Hawkyns is to perform the conditions, for that he took from them the benefit
thereof from the first day they entered, and they are

[1] Master builder of the navy from the time of Queen Mary.
The office remained in his family for the next hundred years.

[2] Son of James Baker, master shipwright under Henry VIII.,
and himself master shipwright early in the reign of Elizabeth. He
is described by John Davys in the dedication to his *Seaman's Secrets*
as one who, 'for his skill and surpassing grounded knowledge for
the building of ships advantageable to all purpose, hath not in any
nation his equal.'

to abide his reward.   After the time of 6 years to this time, being two years and a half, Mr. Hawkyns undertook for that 1,700*l.* [a year] to discharge her Majesty of all extraordinary reparations, new building of ships, as shall come to be said more in place following.

2. Item.—To pay and continue the number of shipkeepers &c.

Touching this article, the condition may be observed so long as the number of the ships are continued and remain in harbour.   But being of late often and long time at the seas, so are the number decreased and the charge greatly eased.

3. Item.—To keep in repair all her Majesty's ships so as upon a grounding &c.

This article was much better observed before Mr. Hawkyns undertook the extraordinary than now it is; for before, the master shipwrights did direct, but now they are to be directed ; and being but hirelings were glad to please their master, feeding his humour so long as they doubted to hazard all and reap both shame and dishonesty ; for such ships as had been tried at the seas and their weak state discovered, to remedy the same the shipwrights could not be suffered ; but that which was done was drawn by force and reported to be more than needed, and besides the shipwrights restrained from grounding of divers ships, which notwithstanding was done [by] force, without order from Mr. Hawkyns.   Nevertheless, five of the greater ships are departed from Chatham very foul and not grounded, which is both dangerous, and great hindrance to their working and sailing.   How this condition is performed may easily be judged.

4. Item.—To moor the navy sufficiently, so as the ships may ride without danger &c.

Touching this article, as the ships hath not been

damaged one way by want [of] good moorings, so
hath they been in dangerous state by reason of ill
oakum,[1] [which] heretofore was had out of the old
moorings that now is made into ropes [again] to a
great gain, whereby no oakum is to be had but at
the hands of such as [make] it of rotten ropes so
that the good hemp oakum that was accustomed to
be used [is] banished.

[The best ocom is called pocket-ocom.][2]

5. Item.—To repair all manner storehouses,
wharves &c.

Concerning these reparations, they are easily
maintained, being lately new builded [at] her
Majesty's charge.

6. Item.—To continue all her Majesty's navy in
serviceable order &c.

Touching this article something is said in the
third; but concerning any one new ship builded at
Mr. Hawkyns' charges, it is unknown; though there
hath been a nomination of 3 or 4 to be new builded
ere this time; and the Elizabeth Jonas[3] as this year;
but divers were repaired in dry docks, as shall be
noted in the sequel hereof; but the greatest part
was done at her Majesty's charge, so that Mr.
Hawkyns kept himself within the compass of his
1,700 a year. And the greatest and [chargeable]
building now being at hand, good time it is to
revoke. And for the continuing of [the number of]
ships, he hath put away one old ship and put
another in her place. [Whether this be] answerable
to the condition or no, let it be judged.

7. Item.—To ground the ships upon all occasions &c.

[1] MS. ocome.
[2] Marginal note in Burghley's hand. 'Pocket' perhaps means
'picked.'
[3] To be rebuilt must be meant. She was thirty years old.

Touching this article it hath relation to the third.

8. Item.—That all the boats, cocks, pinnaces and lighters, shall be kept &c.

Concerning boats, cocks, and pinnaces, there hath been a late supply of divers and many new ones to answer such as were decayed and wanting. At whose charge the same is, may easily be known.

9. Item.—He shall find Norway masts for all the small ships, &c.

What masts hath been found at his charge is uncertain ; but well known it is that there hath been above 20 thrust in among the Queen's Majesty's masts at Chatham, of Norway trees, and an entry made of 200*l.* for the same, at her Majesty's charge.

10. Item.—At All-Hallowtide every year there shall be presented unto the Lord Treasurer &c.

Touching this article, the condition is not observed, unless it may have relation to the two master shipwrights' late survey, which is far more favourable than otherwise it would have been, being laid open to so many ; which, if it had so come to pass, many do doubt that divers of the ships now upon the way to sea should have tarried behind.

The conditions tending to the behalf of Mr. John Hawkyns, divided into 10 several articles.

First.—The said John Hawkyns shall have paid him for the services &c.

Touching this article, if Mr. Hawkyns had performed his bargain and contented himself with a reasonable gain, then the warrant of 5,714*l.* 2*s.* had been well bestowed. But having a further allowance not less than a 1,000*l.* a year, as his fellows the officers affirm, and yet thinketh all too much that is done, saying the ships are in good state and order for these 7 years, and their state known to the contrary,—who can say in truth this money well bestowed, the condition on the other side not performed ?

2. Item.—He shall be holpen with the commission as in *Anno* 1578 &c.

This commission hath been very beneficial unto him, not only in furnishing her Majesty's yard with planks, timber, boards &c. ; but also one other yard in Deptford, which he reapeth benefit as a partner ; which yard hath and doth consume more than her Majesty's yard hath done within 2 years, in serving the subject ; which breedeth ill speeches in the country, and may hinder the service to come. Besides let it be examined how he exacteth of her Majesty in the prices of such stuff as is proper to the service, either at Deptford or Chatham. Let it be at this instant viewed at Chatham, and truly reported what stuff there is which is taken account of for the charges of this quarter to come. All shells and imperfect timber is vented[1] there. The shipwrights must use it, but cannot remedy it ; so it will continue in disorder still in making an officer a purveyor.

3. Item.—It shall be lawful for him to entertain as many shipwrights as he will &c.

In this condition he spared himself and charged her Majesty. For upon the late setting forth the ships, when the Lord Admiral would have the workmen augmented, he said there were too many, and more than could be well occupied. And such other as he kept in ordinary, divers of them he promised much and performed nothing.

4. Item.—If any of the ships come to mischance, as God forbid &c.

This condition her Majesty hath accomplished

---

[1] Discharged, shot out.

to the uttermost. In the Revenge, which ship, by beating upon the ground at Portsmouth, had some decayed place in her keel, which was perfected for a matter of 40, but he had a recompense of 70; the rest was easily borne. As for boats, cocks, and pinnaces, it is to be thought a sufficient allowance is given for such as are lost.

5. Item.—If the whole navy should go to the seas, or a great part of them &c.

In this article Mr. Hawkyns is not charged at the setting forth of the ships for [all[1]] sea store above 40s. The rest is borne by her Majesty. But who hath the dividing [the sea[1]] store, the examining of the quantity, the manner of the stuff, and the rates of the [same[1]]? Most times his partner or his man. The master shipwrights may look upon them and [open[1]] their eyes, but cannot remedy it; but it will be seen and easily perceived when the d[ividing[1]] is made.

6. Item.—The said John Hawkyns shall have the assistance of shipkeepers &c.

This condition is not denied him, though it be with grief of poor men, which he at the first did gratify, and giveth nothing now.

7. Item.—He shall have the use of the wharves, storehouses &c.

Although the use of her Majesty's wharves, yards, storehouses were proper and incident to his bargain, so, that being void, they are at liberty for any service to come, and no condition broken.

8. Item.—If the ships shall ride in any other place &c.

If he shall require a recompense of a small matter in his moorings, he may consider what hath been spared by those ships that hath been abroad at the

---

[1] These words in brackets are conjectural. A piece of the margin of the MS. is quite torn away.

seas and spent nothing; besides the yearly gain gotten by the moorings, not so little as 500*l.* a year, all pensions and charges paid.

9. Item.—When a new ship shall be made and ready to launch &c.

That new ship is yet to make at Mr. Hawkyns' charge; but he hath made the commodity of an old one aforehand, as it is noted in the first page, the 6 article.[1]

10. Item.—If any ambiguity or doubt shall happen of either part &c.

If the premises be well considered according to equity and conscience, her Majesty hath great cause to call the conditions in question and be resolved of the same; which the honourable [2] at their discretions are to consider of, as God shall move them.

Ships repaired in the time of Mr. Hawkyns' bargain for 2 or 3 y[ears] at the most, except the Revenge:

The Elizabeth Jonas} The charge of these ships
The Triumph } was borne by the venturers with Sir Francis [Drake] at the setting forth of the Bonaventure, Sea Dragon and the Aid, the last of July 1585.

The Antelope}
The Hope }
The Victory } For those ships he had so large allowance by the officers, as a small charge besides was bestowed.
The Aid }
The Swallow}

The Revenge.—For the Revenge he had allowed him 700*l.*, and the whole charge was under 1,000*l.* lately done at Woolwich.

The Merlin
a small pinnace.

[1] P 40.   [2] 'Commissioners' seems to be omitted.

January 23.—*HOWARD TO BURGHLEY.*

[**B.M. Harl. MS. 6994, f. 112**.—Holograph. Addressed.]

My honourable and good Lord :—I have received your Lordship's favourable letter, and am much bound unto your Lordship for your Lordship's favours. I would to God your Lordship's health and strength were answerable to your mind ; then I am sure this company here with me should be happy to see your Lordship here.

My Lord, on Wednesday last I went to Harwich to see the town and the haven, which I had not seen this 27 years. My Lord, it is a place to be made much of, for the haven hath not his fellow in all respects not in this realm, and specially as long as we have such enemies so near us as they be in the Low Countries, and not more assured than we are of Scotland. My Lord, we can bring all the ships that her Majesty hath, aground there in 3 springs. I know not that we can do so in any place else but here at Chatham. That which is a-doing above the town will be to very good purpose for any sudden [attack [1]], and for my part I wish it were as strong as Flushing.

I received a letter from my Lord Cobham, of an enterprise that is sent down to burn all such ships of her Majesty's as shall ride before the Rammekens or thereabouts. I received this letter as I was half the way coming homewards from Harwich. I presently sent away a pinnace, with John Wynter in her, your Lordship's servant, and did send the advertisement unto Sir William Russell, [2] with a letter

[1] Word omitted.
[2] Fourth son of Francis, Earl of Bedford, the godfather of Sir Francis Drake. At this time Governor of Flushing ; Lord Deputy

of my own; and likewise I did write unto the captains of her Majesty's ships, with certain instructions, which, if the device be attempted, I believe you shall hear they shall smart for their device. There is two ships and a pinnace : their victuals cometh out about an eight days hence, so that then they will come away. In the meantime, if nothing be done already, I doubt not but they shall safely come away. My good Lord, God send you ever well to do : and so I bid your Lordship most heartily farewell. From aboard the Bear, the 23rd of January, 1587.

Your Lordship's most assured always to command,

C. HOWARD.

January 24.—HOWARD TO WALSYNGHAM.

[ccviii. 22.—Holograph.   Addressed.]

Sir :—I most humbly thank you for your letters. I cannot tell what to think of my brother Stafford's[1] advertisement ; for if it be true that the King of Spain's forces be dissolved, I would not wish the Queen's Majesty to be at this charges that she is at ; but if it be but a device, knowing that a little thing maketh us too careless, then I know not what may come of it. But this I am sure of ; if her Majesty would have spent but a 1,000 crowns to have had some intelligence, it would have saved her twenty times as much. Assure yourself he[2] knoweth what we do here ; and if the army be or do dissolve, it is the preparation that her Majesty

of Ireland in 1594 ; raised to the peerage in 1603, as Baron Russell of Thornhaugh, in Northampton ; died in 1613.

[1] Sir Edward Stafford, the English ambassador in Paris, had married Howard's sister Douglas, the widow of Lord Sheffield.

[2] The King of Spain.

hath made that is the cause; for he cannot abide this heat[1] that is provided for him. He did never think that we would thus have provided for his coming, but that the number of false alarums that he hath given her Majesty would have made her to have taken no alarum, and so to have had the vantage; and the chopping[2] up of his friends here I am sure he doth not like; and if they be up, I wish they should continue so till there be a good peace, which I pray to God to send us.

Sir, if your next advertisements do assure the dissolving of the army in Spain, then it were good we did so here; yet if the Duke of Parma continue his, and that there be any doubt of anything intended for Scotland, put but three or four more ships to them in the Narrow Seas and I dare assure you it shall beat any power he shall be able to make, and impeach him of any attempt in Scotland; and I will take upon me the service myself; for I assure you it doth grieve me to see her Majesty at more charges than is needful, and this charge will not be great. I would fain keep the Narrow Seas three or four months; I persuade myself I shall do some service.

Upon your next advertisement, as the cause upon that shall require, I will write to you, Sir, my good friend, my opinion, and then you may use it as you shall think best. And so I pray you to write me frankly; for I do assure you I will take it kindly and friendly at your hands, and think myself much beholden unto you for it; for I may sometimes, upon a good conceit in my opinion, make such a journey as I did now to Harwich; and yet it may not be so well taken there; but I know no cause

---

[1] MS. heet.

[2] MS. chappyng. The arrest of; to chop = to seize, to lay hold of. We still speak of 'a fox chopped in cover.'

why it should be but well taken. I do assure you,
on my honour, it cost not the Queen's Majesty one
halfpenny, nor shall not, when I make any such
journey. I will rather spend myself one hundred
pounds than to spend her one penny. Thus, good
Mr. Secretary I am bold with you, as my special
good friend ; and so bid you most heartily farewell,
and God send you health and strength. From the
Bear, the 24th of January.

Your assured loving friend to use,
C. HOWARD.

January 27.—HOWARD TO WALSYNGHAM.

[**ccviii. 30.**—Signed.   Addressed.]

Sir :—I most heartily thank you for your letter
and for your advertisements. If it were not for you
I should live in a dead place for hearing of anything.

Touching Sir Francis Drake, I have likewise
received a letter from him with the like advertisement. There happened a mischance in one of his
ships at Portsmouth, that a piece broke and killed a
man, with some other hurt. If you would write a
word or two unto him to spare his powder, it would
do well.[1]

Sir, I send you herewith enclosed all the copies
of the letters from my Lord Chamberlain again,
which I most heartily thank you for, and I pray to
God the Scottish King do deceive me, but I am
afeared he will not. For my own part, I have made
of the French King, the Scottish King, and the

---

[1] This scarcely seems to warrant Mr. Froude's inference of the
Queen's parsimony. ' Drake,' he says, ' had offended her by con-
suming ammunition at target practice. She would not give him
a second opportunity ' (*History of England*, xii. 369).

King of Spain, a Trinity that I mean never to trust to be saved by ; and I would others were, in that, of my opinion.

Sir, there was never, since England was England, such a stratagem and mask made to deceive England withal as this is of the treaty of peace. I pray God we have not cause to remember one thing that was made of the Scots by the Englishmen ; that we do not curse for this a long grey beard with a white head, witless, that will make all the world think us heartless. You know whom I mean.[1]

I have received a letter from Sir Henry Palmer, that there is at Dunkirk divers hoys and lighters, that be filled with ballast and great stones, surely [means [2]] for the stopping of some haven. I will have a watch on them.

I pray you, Sir, send me word when you think the Commissioners will be sent over, that I may have all things ready for them ; and I pray you let me know if any go in Sir Amyas Poulet's [3] place ; for if he be able to go himself, if I may know of it, I will have especial care of him, that he may go at ease.

[1] Motley thinks that Lord Burghley is here indicated. More probably it is Sir James Croft, comptroller of the household, and one of the commissioners for the treaty. He was suspected of holding traitorous correspondence with Parma, and on his return in August was sent to the Tower, where he remained till December 1589. He was very old, and perhaps dotard rather than traitor. He died in 1591.

[2] Torn away.

[3] Of Hinton St. George, Somerset, grandson of that Sir Amyas Poulet who is reputed to have set Wolsey in the stocks. He had himself earned the hatred of the Catholic party by the strictness of his conduct when charged with the custody of the Queen of Scots. At this time he was Chancellor of the Order of the Garter, Governor of Jersey and Guernsey, and one of the commissioners for the treaty. His failing health prevented his going to the Low Countries. He died September 26, 1588, and was buried in London, in the church of St. Martin's in-the-Fields.

Sir, if there be at any time any matter of importance wherein I may do any service there with you, I can be quickly there and here again.

I pray you, Sir, let it be thought on, as you see cause upon your advertisements, it will ask a good time[1] to furnish our fleet again with men as they were. I do not look to see it ever bettered. I pray God it be as well when there shall be cause. And so giving you most hearty thanks for your most friendly dealing with me in all causes, and your friendly remembrance, I bid you most heartily farewell. From aboard her Majesty's good ship the White Bear, the 27th of January, 1587.

Your assured loving friend,
C. HOWARD.

January 28.—*HOWARD TO WALSYNGHAM.*

[ccviii. 31.—Holograph.   Addressed.]

Sir :—I had forgotten in my last letter to answer the matter you did write in touching Captain Morgan, my man. If he had been here I would have sent him unto you ; but he is extreme sick at London, and, as I do understand, in some danger ; which I am very sorry for, for he is a tall gentle-man. He hath the charge of all my soldiers in my ship, and hath done his duty very well. I hope he will answer all honestly and well.

Sir, if the Commissioners be once[2] gone over and that there be a surcease of arms, it shall be but folly and to no purpose for me to lie here. I think both I and the noblemen, leaving sufficient lieu-tenants in our ships, and the officers, as Sir W.

---

[1] Let it be borne in mind that it will need a good time &c.
[2] MS. wonse.

Wynter, Mr. Hawkyns and Mr. Borough,[1] remain
here with the navy will be sufficient[2]; for before
these ships can have their full number of men again
it will be a month to gather them, do what we can.
And I pray to God we have them when we shall
need; for many are gone abroad, and specially the
chiefest men; God send me to see such a company
together again when need is. I protest it before
God I write not this to you because I am weary
with being here; for if it were not for her Majesty's
presence I had rather live in the company of these
noble ships than in any place. And yet would I be
glad that there were something to do. I am more
sorrier for the noblemen than any ways for myself;
for I would have them save, to spend when need
shall be. I do assure you they live here bountifully,
and it will be hard finding of such noblemen as
these be, so well affected to this service and that
will love the sea so well as they do.

Sir, if you think that my continuing here with
the navy serve to good purpose, I shall like well of
it; but methinks if there be a surcease of arms, then
my lying here will make a jest to many, and they
have reason. I think it will be a most fittest time
to ground our ships in, for now, at our coming out,
it was you know on such a sudden as we could not
ground but two or three of the middle sort, so as the
great ships were not grounded. I have, with the
advice of the officers and masters, thought good to
begin with some the next spring, and so in a three
springs dispatch them all, and have them all in most
excellent order by the midst of March, all save the

---

[1] MS. Bowros.
[2] His meaning is—I and the noblemen (see *ante* p. 24) may
come up to the court, leaving our ships in charge of the lieutenants,
the principal officers of the navy remaining in command of the
fleet, which will be sufficient.

men ; and I doubt not but the ships shall prove some [1] notable liars, and if cause fall out, do a better day of service for England than ever ships did for it yet.   But this assure yourself, if the forces of Spain do come before the midst of April, there will be as much ado to have men to furnish us, as ever was ; but men we must have, or else the ships will do no good.   God knows it is but a bare sight to see us now to that it was, and I would not wish any to take the pains to come to see us till we are newly supplied, when cause shall be.   Sir, God send you well to do and continuance of your health, and so I bid you most heartily farewell.   From aboard her Majesty's good ship the Bear, the 28th of January.

Your assured loving friend,
C. HOWARD.

Jan. 29.—*CONDITIONS OF JAMES QUARLES.*

[ccviii. **35.**]

XXIXmo die Januarii 1587.—The humble petition and demand of James Quarles, surveyor of the victuals for her Majesty's navy, if it be her Highness' pleasure that he shall serve by rate :— videlicet—

First, he desireth to be allowed from the first of July last, 7*d.* the man at the seas, and 6½*d.* in harbour, as Mr. Baeshe [2] then had by virtue of privy seal, and so to continue unto it shall please God to

---

[1] Some persons to be &c.—viz. those who have spoken ill of Hawkyns.   See *ante*, p. 38 *et seq.*

[2] Edward Baeshe, of an old Gloucestershire family, was Surveyor-General of Victuals for the navy for upwards of forty years. He was twice sheriff of Hertfordshire, and died in April 1587. The fact that he left his widow but poorly provided for seems to speak of an integrity then far from common.

send mitigation of the dearth of victuals that now
be, to such reasonable prices as are here underwritten ; where it doth appear what they were at
such time as Mr. Baeshe did first serve by rate, and
so did continue a long time, until late years, and
what now they be ; whereby then he was able to
serve for 5½d. in harbour and 6d. at the seas, and
so will I do most willing her Majesty the like
service.

Item, whereas Mr. Baeshe had two thousand
pounds to continue with him to amplify his store for
all sudden service, I do but desire to have 500l. to
furnish two thousand men for one month upon 16
days warning.

Item, forasmuch as the store of clapboard [1] is
for the most part wasted, and that it is most
necessary that her Majesty should not be unfurnished, to have in readiness to make three thousand
tons of cask, I would pray for the speedy performance of the same, to have one thousand pounds
delivered unto me, to make provision of the said
cask ; which thousand pounds I will repay again
into her Majesty's Exchequer at the end of 6 years
next following.

Item, I desire that I may have all such her
Majesty's brewhouses, bakehouses and storehouses,
with the grounds thereunto belonging, in such
manner and form as the said Mr. Baeshe had.

The charges of one man's victual at the seas for
one flesh day :

Biscuit, 1 lb. . . . 1d. ⎫
Beer, 1 gallon. . . 1¾d. ⎬ 8¼d.
Beef, 2 lb. . . . 5½d. ⎭

[1] Small oak boards used for cask staves. The word still
appears in Customs' schedules.

The charges of one man's victuals at the seas on the fish day :

Biscuit, 1 lb. .	.	.	1d.
Beer, 1 gallon .	.	.	1$\frac{3}{4}d$.
Butter, $\frac{1}{4}$ lb. .	.	.	$\frac{1}{2}d$.
Cheese, $\frac{1}{4}$ lb. .	.	.	$\frac{1}{2}d$.
Stockfish, $\frac{1}{4}$ fish	.	.	1d.

4$\frac{3}{4}d$.

Mem : in these two days victuals there is nothing demanded for biscuit bags, necessary lading charges, clerks' wages, surveyors' wages and all other incidents pertaining to sea service, which maketh a further increase of money.

A declaration of the prices of sea victuals that was at such time as Mr. Baeshe first served at a rate and so continued a long time till these late years, and what prices be at this present.

	What they were	What they are
Wheat . . .	16s. the qr. .	20s.
Beer	18s. the tun .	26s. 8d.
Beef, being good .	12s. the cwt. .	17s.
Butter . . .	{40s. & 42s. . the dearest	4l. 10s.
Stockfish . . .	11l. the last .	20l.
Casks . . .	5s. 4d. the ton .	8s.
Canvas for biscuit bags	3$\frac{1}{2}d$. the ell .	8d.

When hereafter it shall appear unto your Honours that the high prices of victuals which now be are in any remarkable sort mitigated, and especially beef, I will serve her Majesty most willingly at such rates as hath been heretofore ; otherwise I am not able to serve without extreme loss and undoing, as by due proof I am able to make it appear unto your Honours.

MEMORANDA BY LORD BURGHLEY.

[ccviii. 43.—Autograph. Not dated.]

That the whole navy be ready to go out of Thames by the 10th of March ; to be in Portsmouth by the end of March ; to pass with the 3 part of their charges.[1]

That the Swallow pass from Portsmouth westward with mariners and gunners.

That soldiers be in readiness upon the coasts to be shipped.

That two men be found out to pass to Lisbon for intelligence.

That all English ships of subjects meet for service be stayed and put in order to be in readiness against April, to serve as cause shall require.

To provide muskets out of Holland at 23s. 4d. a piece.

That Nicholas Gorges[2] and some such as Thomas Digges[3] may, by order of the Earl of Leicester, make a view through Holland and Zealand of all kind of ships, and of the number of mariners.

[1] To be paid an imprest, or advance.

[2] Great-grandson of Sir Edmund Gorges of Wraxall, in Somerset, by his wife Anne, eldest daughter of John Howard, first Duke of Norfolk. He was thus third cousin of the Queen, second cousin once removed of the Lord Admiral, and first cousin of Edward Gorges of Wraxall, the father of Sir Ferdinando Gorges, who has been styled 'the father of English colonisation in America.' In July and August he commanded the ships fitted out by the city of London.

[3] A mathematician, surveyor and military engineer of high repute ; muster-master general of the English forces in the Netherlands, 1586–94 ; died 1595. He was the author of many works on mathematical and military subjects ; among others, of *A Treatise on the Art of Navigation ; A Treatise of Architecture Nautical ; A Treatise of Great Artillery and Pyrotechny ; A Treatise of Fortification.*

That the Earl of Leicester do solicit the States to arm a power of ships to attend on the Queen's navy.

A bargain for 2 great galleons and one meaner, and 6 pinnaces.

MEMORANDUM OF SPANISH SHIPS.

[**ccviii. 44.**—In Howard's hand.   Not dated.]

These in Guipuscoa.

In Santander	. .	16 new ships between 100 and 140.
In the Passage	. .	14 of the like burden.
In Laredo	. .	8 pataches.
In San Sebastian	. .	6 ships of 300 and 4 of 200.
In Bilbao	. .	6 pataches.
In Figuera	. .	4 ships of 100.

Some built in the River of Fuenterrabia.

In the River of Seville,	8 ships of 300 and 200 apiece and 4 pataches.
In Saint Mary Port .	2 galleys made short and broad and 4 pataches.

February 1.—*HOWARD TO WALSYNGHAM*

[**ccviii. 46.**—Signed.   Addressed.]

Sir:—I have received your letter, and by the same messenger, a letter from my Lord Treasurer, and my Lord Steward,[1] whereby I perceive the great preparation in Dunkirk for Scotland.

I am advised by their Lordships to have care of it, which I will do to the uttermost of my power.   It

---

[1] The Earl of Leicester.

doth appear no less by your letter but that we may assure ourselves that Scotland is the mark which they shoot at to offend[1] us, and therefore most necessary to provide for that. I have written mine opinion at large in mine answer to that their Lordships' letter, which I know you shall be acquainted with; and therefore, if you do think it reasonable that I have written for her Majesty's service, I pray you let it have your furtherance, knowing that you are so well bent to spend her Majesty's purse, rather than to hazard her honour; and for my own part, had rather be drawn in pieces with wild horses than that they should pass through for Scotland and I lie here.

Sir, thus her Majesty shall see what will come of this abusing peace in hand.

For your advertisements of Spain which should come in April, if we cut off this matter of Scotland, I hope we shall not need to fear the forces in Spain, neither in April nor in May.

Sir, I pray you bear with me that I remember you of this. It doth appear by mine instructions, as also as a matter determined in Council, that the setting forth of this fleet which we have here was for these two purposes:—the one for an invasion from the Duke of Parma upon this part of the realm; the other for going with forces into Scotland. Now what did move her Majesty, or upon what ground, I know not, to diminish our forces here; for if any of both those should happen upon the sudden, we shall be able to do even as much good for the service as the hoys[2] which lie at Lyon Quay[3]; for there is no master in England that will undertake, with those men that are now in them, to carry back again the ships to Chatham; and I do warrant you our state is well enough known to them in Flanders, and as

[1] Injure.   [2] MS. whoyse.   [3] Just below London Bridge.

we were a terror to them at first coming out, so do they now make but little reckoning of us; for they know that we are like bears tied to stakes, and they may come as dogs to offend us, and we cannot go to hurt them.   But as I would be loth to be any deviser of her Majesty's charge, so do I thank God I was no counsellor of this that is done; and I hope that if things fall not out according to your expectation and the rest of my Lords, that I may be excused. Yet will I not fail with the uttermost of my power to be ready to impeach any mischief that may be intended.

I have a good company here with me, and so good willers to her Majesty's service, that if the Queen's Majesty will not spare her purse, they will not spare their lives and that which they have. And so I leave; looking every hour to hear from you of more mischief coming by this disputation of peace than any good that ever shall come of it, I bid you most heartily farewell.   From off aboard her Majesty's ship the White Bear, this first of February, 1587.

Your most assured and
affectionate friend,
C. Howard.

February 1.—*HAWKYNS TO WALSYNGHAM.*

[ccviii. **47**.—Signed.   Addressed.]

My duty humbly remembered unto your Honour : Having of long time seen the malicious practices of the papists combined generally throughout Christendom to alter the government of this realm and to bring it to papistry, and consequently to servitude, poverty and slavery, I have a good will from time to time to do and set forward something as I could have credit to impeach their purpose. But it hath prevailed little, for that there was never any substantial ground laid to be followed effectually, and therefore it hath taken bad effect, and bred great charge, and we still in worse case and less assurance of quietness.

I do therefore now utter my mind particularly to your Honour how I do conceive some good to be done at last. I do see we are desirous to have peace, as it becometh good christians, which is best for all men ; and I wish it might any way be brought to that pass ; but in my poor judgment the right way is not taken.

If we stand at this point in a mammering[1] and at a stay, we consume, and our Commonwealth doth utterly decay. I shall not need to speak of our estate, for that your Honour knoweth it far better than I do : neither need I to rehearse how dead and uncertain our traffics be ; most men in poverty and discontented, and especially the poorer sort ; our navigation not set on work ; but the French and Scots eat us up, and grow in wealth and freights, and not assured to us in friendship. Our treasure doth consume infinitely with these uncertain wars, and nothing assured to us but new and continual charge. We have to choose either a dishonourable and uncertain peace, or to put on virtuous and valiant minds, to make a way through with such a settled war as may bring forth and command a quiet peace.

This peace which we have in hand hath little likelihood to be good for us, but to win a better time for them. They may easily see how glad we are to embrace peace, and might dissolve their forces without fear of any danger if they meant well. But they do rather increase their forces ; and

[1] Hesitating.

although they do nothing, yet in keeping us in charge both abroad and at home, they will both shake our store and impoverish the poor commons.

Therefore, in my mind, our profit and best assurance is to seek our peace by a determined and resolute war, which no doubt would be both less charge, more assurance of safety, and would best discern our friends from our foes both abroad and at home, and satisfy the people generally throughout the whole realm.

In the continuance of this war I wish it to be ordered in this sort, that first, we have as little to do in foreign countries as may be but of mere necessity, for that breedeth great charge and no profit at all.

Next, that there be always six principal good ships of her Majesty's upon the coast of Spain, victualled for four months and accompanied with some six small vessels, which shall haunt the coast of Spain and the Islands, and be a sufficient company to distress anything that goeth through the seas. And when these must return, there would be other six good ships, likewise accompanied, to keep the place. So should that seas be never unfurnished ; but as one company at the four months end doth return, the other company should be always in the place.

The charge of these companies would not be above 1,800 men in one fleet, which may be 2,700*l.* a month for wages and victuals. And it will be a very bad and an unlucky month that will not bring in treble that charge, for they can see nothing but it is presently their own.

If this may be done with so easy a charge, and recompensed double and treble, why should we stick at it ? Some will say, the King will always make a fleet to beat us from the coast. There is no doubt but, with an infinite charge, he may make an army. But it shall be sufficient that this small company shall live daily in their sight and weary them, and gain daily upon them. For an army, as he provideth, cannot continue any long time. His fleet from the Indies and all places can have hard escaping ; which if we might once strike, our peace were made with honour, safety and profit.

For these six ships, we shall not break the strength of the navy ; for we shall leave a sufficient company always at home to front any violence that can be any way offered unto us. I do herewith send a note how the ships may be fitted, and what they are, and what will be left at home. In open and lawful wars, God will help us, for we defend the chief cause, our religion, God's own cause ; for if we would leave our profession and turn to serve Baal (as God forbid, and rather to die a thousand deaths), we might have peace, but not with God. By open wars all the subjects of this realm should know what to do. They would not only be satisfied in conscience, but they would, every man that loveth God, the Queen and his country, contribute, set forward, fight, devise, and do somewhat for the liberty and freedom of this country. By open wars, all the Jesuits and ill affected persons would be discerned and cut off from the hope of their malicious practices. Many things more might be said to the preferring of open war before a dis-sembled peace, which God doth best allow, and the well affected people of the realm do desire, even to the spending of a great portion of their substance. And therefore I conclude that with God's blessing and a lawful open war, the Lord shall bring us a most honourable and quiet peace, to the glory of his church and to the honour of her

Majesty and this realm of England ; which God for his mercy's sake grant.   And so I leave to trouble your Honour.   From aboard the Bonaventure, the first of February, 1587.

>Your Honour's humbly to command,
>JOHN HAWKYNS.

February 5.—*LIST OF SHIPS TO BE IN ORDER OF SERVICE.*

[ccviii. 52.—Endorsed.]

Ships to be in order of service with their full numbers at the seas, as followeth :
At Queenborough with my Lord Admiral.

	Men
The Ark Ralegh	400
Bonaventure	250
Mary Rose	250
Lion	250
Vanguard	250
Dreadnought	200
Swallow	160
Foresight	160
Spy	35
Merlin	35
Sun	30
Cygnet	20
Fancy	20
Two Ketches	20
The George	20
Men	2,100

With Sir Henry Palmer.

				Men
The Rainbow .	.	.	.	250
Antelope .	.	.	.	160
Bull .	.	.	.	100
Tiger	.	.	.	100
Tramontana	.	.	.	70
Scout	.	.	.	70
Achates .	.	.	.	60
Charles .	.	.	.	40
Moon	.	.	.	40

		Men
Sum .		890
		2,100

All the men at sea   2,990

The whole numbers of men serving at the seas, besides the ships with Sir Francis Drake, are 2,990 men, which makes in charge monthly, for wages and victuals [1]   .   .   .   .   4,534*l.* 16*s.* 8*d.*

Ships to remain at Chatham with 200 men as followeth :

			Men
The Elizabeth Jonas .	.	.	50
Triumph .	.	.	50
Bear .	.	.	50
Victory .	.	.	50

200 men

Which may be a charge monthly for wages and victuals .   .   .   .   .   .   303*l.* 6*s.* 8*d.*

The monthly charge of the whole is

4,785*l.* 1*s.* 8*d.*[2]

[1] At 30*s.* 4*d.* per man for the month.

[2] The Merlin, in the Queenborough list, was at first omitted and afterwards written in between the lines. In the other places affected, the totals of men and money were corrected ; but in this final result the error was allowed to remain. It should be 4,838*l.* 3*s.* 4*d.*

Feb. 5.—*ESTIMATE OF CHARGE OF SHIPS*

[ccviii. 53.]

The 5th of February, 1587.
The charge of the ships with Sir Francis Drake:

The Revenge	250	The Advice .	35
Hope .	250	Makeshift	35
Nonpareil	250	Twenty - three	
Swiftsure	180	other ships	
Aid . .	120	which have	
		in number	1,780
	1,050		1,850
			1,050

Total 2,900 men

The monthly charge of these 2,900 men is for wages and victuals . . . 4,398*l.* 8*s.* 8*d.*

By the last conclusion before my Lord Treasurer it was agreed that there should be continued in charge only 1,315 men, which is a charge for wages and victuals monthly . . . 1,994*l.* 8*s.* 4*d.*

There is already order given to Mr. Quarles for to victual all the ships under my Lord Admiral's charge and Sir Henry Palmer's to the 14th day of March next.

Now there is a new order to be given to the said Mr. Quarles to victual the ships which are to be wholly under my Lord Admiral's charge, which have in them 2,955[1] men and shall be victualled to the 20th day of April next which is 37 days, to begin the 15th of March next and to end the 20th

---

[1] The Merlin being omitted.

of April following, both days included, which victualling is a charge of   .   .   3,188*l.* 14*s.* 9*d.*[1]

The 200 men left in the four great ships may be victualled from time to time upon the ordinary.

Feb. 11.—*HOWARD TO SIR F. WALSYNGHAM.*

[**ccviii. 64.**—Holograph. Addressed.]

Sir :—I was no sooner come down but I imparted unto my Lord Sheffield that which you had told me, who went presently aboard with no small care to find out his party ; and I assure you, with much grief that any such thing should happen in his ship. Himself was to depart to London that afternoon upon very earnest business, which I gave him leave for ; but he left such a strait commandment with Mr. Ha. Sheffield, his lieutenant, for the finding out of the truth of this, as he said to him, being his kinsman, if he had care of his honour or well doing, he would take pains in it. And yet my Lord himself, as great haste as he had, made the barber, and three or four more which he suspected, to be sworn ; and so they were ; and they utterly[2] renounced the Pope's authority.[3]

Mr. Sheffield, after my Lord's departure, took great pains and did examine the barber, and found that a two or three years agone, he was something inclined to papistry, but being matched by his wife with a honest race,[4] as it seems they converted him. I have talked with the man myself. He offers to receive,[5] and to do anything that a good Protestant should do.

This was the cause I think that bred the doubt

---

[1] At 7*d.* a day, or 16*s.* 4*d.* a month of 28 days, this should be 3,188*l.* 18*s.* 9*d.* No known rate can give the 14*s.*

[2] MS. outerly.   [3] MS. atoryte.

[4] His wife's relations.   [5] The Blessed Sacrament.

in him. He had a book that was done by an English papist beyond the seas; a bad book; but he brought it to the preacher, with dislike of the book; and the preacher is counted to be a most zealous man and very honest. The barber had many good books, as the New Testament, the Book of Common Prayer, the Book of the Psalms which he daily sang with the company. The man was prest by the Company of Surgeons, for he is a barber-surgeon, and not by my Lord; and he hath sailed often in her Majesty's ships, and accounted a very honest man. I think my Lord Sheffield will send you the party, and I believe you will not mislike him.

Mr. Ha. Sheffield, who is very earnest and zealous in religion, sware unto me that it made him rejoice at the heart to see how earnest my Lord Sheffield was in it, and to hear him use those words he did, which was most vehement [1] against papists, so be-traitoring them, saying he that was in his ship that would not be sworn against the Pope, he would take him for a traitor, and so use him. And this I dare assure you: no man whosoever is readier to communicate than my Lord Sheffield is, which I thank God for.

Sir, Newton,[2] my man, who came from Dover yesterday, telleth me that one that came from Calais doth report for certainty that the Duke of Guise hath sent down to St. Omers 20 ensigns [3] of soldiers, and that they are to come to Dunkirk. If it be true, I think my Lord Cobham [4] hath certified you. I hope this next spring, which will be on Friday next, if the wind suit us, to go into the Narrow Seas; but this wind, as it is, locks us in fast enough. The Antelope and the Swallow, which should have gone to Sir Ha. Palmer this day

[1] MS. vemente.

[2] This is probably the William Newton who appears in the list as master of the admiral's pinnace Marygold.

[3] MS. ansynse.   [4] Lord Warden of the Cinque Ports.

sennight, could never since stir, if a realm had been on it. Therefore you may see, in time of service, it is better to be at sea, than locked up in harbour. This wind, a Dunkirker cannot stir out ; they are fast locked in as well as we are.

We have had much ado here in changing out of one ship into another [1] ; but now it is done, victual and all.

If it be true that I do hear there is 900 mariners come to Dunkirk, it may be, whilst the treaty is, they will attempt something to Walcheren ; or if it be true of these forces to be come down of the Guiseans,[2] they will make a short treaty for manners' sake, and presently, upon the breaking up, they will put into Scotland. I hope, with God's goodness, to have a eye to both. But this would I fain know of you, if there be a surcease of arms betwixt her Majesty and the Duke, and not with the States, if in the meantime they attempt anything to the isle of Walcheren, I hope it is not meant but that I should seek to relieve [3] it ; for I mean to do so, except I have contrary commandment. If there be no surcease of arms, if the Dunkirkers come out, I mean not [4] to follow them, and if they come out with any number, whereby I may perceive that they carry soldiers with them, although there be a surcease of arms, I mean if I can to stay them, till I know more. Sir, I pray let me have your good advice in this ; for whatsoever I shall do it will fall out as it doth continually all things as it is taken.[4]

Sir, I will trouble you no more at this time, but God have you in his keeping, and so I most heartily bid you farewell. The 11th of February.

Your most assured loving friend,

C. HOWARD.

[1] From the White Bear to the Ark.
[2] MS. Gwysans.
[3] MS. syke to relyve.
[4] So in MS.

Feb. 12.—*MR. HOLSTOK TO JAMES QUARLES.*
[ccviii. 65.—Copy.]

Mr. Quarles :—These are to pray you to deliver victuals for 3,035 men to serve the Queen's Majesty in the ships hereunder written, being now appointed to the seas under the charge of the Lord High Admiral of England, for 37 days, to begin the 15th day of March, and to end the 20th day of April then following; which ships, some are at Queenborough, and some at the Narrow Seas. Thus, fare you well. Written the 12th day of February, 1587.

Queenborough.

	Men
The Ark	425
Elizabeth Bonaventure .	250
Lion . . .	250
Vanguard. . .	250
Mary Rose . . .	250
Dreadnought . . .	200
Antelope	160
Swallow	160
Foresight. . . .	160
Charles	40
Spy	35
Merlin	35
Sun	30
Cygnet	16
Fancy	16
Two Ketches . . .	8
The George Hoy . . .	10
White Lion . . .	50
	2,345
	690
	3,035

Ships at the Seas.

					Men
The Rainbow	.	.	.	.	250
Bull	.	.	.	.	100
Tiger	.	.	.	.	100
Tramontana	.	.	.		70
Scout	.	.	.		70
Achates	.	.	.	.	60
Moon	.	.	.	.	40
					690

Total men in all . . . 3,035

For 37 days' victuals at 7*d.* the man per diem, 3,220*l.* 10*s.* 9*d.* Your loving friend,

WILLM. HOLSTOK.

Mem. 40*l.* of this sum above written is for transportations.[1]

Feb. 14.—*HOWARD TO SIR F. WALSYNGHAM.*

[**ccviii. 67.**—Holograph. Addressed.]

Sir :—I have received your letter with the advertisement from my Lord of Hunsdon,[2] which I thank you most heartily for, and I am very glad to hear that the King[3] doth run so good a course. I pray to God to continue it. And, Sir, if the Queen's Majesty should stick to relieve him[4] in this

[1] The charge of thirty-seven days' victuals for 3,035 men at 7*d.* amounts to 3,275*l.* 5*s.* 5*d.*, which, with 40*l.* added for transportation, gives a total of 3,315*l.* 5*s.* 5*d.*

[2] Henry Carey, born about 1524, created Lord Hunsdon in 1559, was, by his mother, Mary Boleyn, the Queen's first cousin. He had been since 1568 Governor of Berwick and Warden of the East Marches towards Scotland, and since 1583 Lord Chamberlain of the Household. He died in 1596. His eldest daughter, Catherine, was the wife of the Lord Admiral.

[3] Of Scotland. Lord Hunsdon's letter is missing.

[4] MS. styke to relyve.

small matters, she is no good housewife for herself ; for I do not see but this small matter, which my Lord Chamberlain writeth of, if it be supplied, but that it is like and most certain to save her 100 thousands of pounds, besides a great deal of blood of her Majesty's subjects.   For I hold it certain if the neck of that be broken in Scotland, it will break all their intent in Spain.   But it must be done in time, that it may be known in Spain before they be ready to come out.   And this being done by her Majesty, she shall be sure that the King of Spain will never be at that charge he hath been at, upon any Scottish promise.

Sir, where [1] you write to me that you wish I were at the seas, I do assure you I long for it ; but the weather hath been and is so extreme here, the wind being at East, that we were not able to have our victuals out of the hoys into the ships before yesterday ; and yet all is not in.   But as the wind is, it is so in our teeth, as [2] if a realm lay on it we could not get out.   But assure yourself I will not lose an hour.

I hear for certain that the Duke [3] hath now gotten a great number of mariners together, and his ships full rigged, and victuals and all in, so it is like the next wind that [4] is fit for them they will attempt something.   But if they do, I hope I shall meet with them.   My Lord Ha. Seymour hath had an extreme cold, but yet he will not forbear to do all services and to be stirring abroad.   I brought him and old Gray,[5] my master, who was very ill of the

---

[1] Whereas.   [2] That.   [3] Of Parma.   [4] MS. at.
[5] Thomas Gray, the master of the Ark. In 1585 he petitioned, in the name of the masters of the navy and on behalf of the seamen of Norfolk and Suffolk, for the maintenance of a watch-light on the steeple of Winterton, in the town of Great Yarmouth.   He was a man of some substance ; a shipowner in a small way.   Towards the end of this year he was in command of the Rainbow.   See *post*, Howard to Burghley, and also Hawkyns' Note of Ships, August 28.

cold, to Rochester, whilst the ships received in their victuals ; and I thank God they are much amended. I think if I had not made them come to Rochester, they would not have been able to have gone to the seas with me; but I found by my Lord Harry that how sick[1] so ever he were, he would not tarry behind me.

Sir, I do hear by report that Campvere[2] and Arnemuiden hath sworn to the Queen's Majesty. If it be so, I am glad of it ; and if Middelburg do not the like, Flushing may easily make them weary. I pray to God to bless her Majesty, and send her to agree and to do that which is best. And so, Sir, with my most hearty thanks unto you for your favours, which I will requite in anything that shall be in my power, God send you health ; and so I bid you most heartily farewell. Chatham, the 14th of February.

Your ever assured and loving friend,
C. HOWARD.

February 15.—HOWARD TO BURGHLEY.
[ccviii. 70.—Copy.]

My very good Lord :—The late bitter time[3] hath sharply handled our men, for that many of them are but ill apparelled ; and the wind is now very bad for us and not likely to change hastily. We may also be forced to seek the coast of Scotland before our return. Therefore I think it fit, with your Lord-ship's good liking (which all of them earnestly desire), that before their going forth there may be paid unto every of them, for their further relief, six weeks' wages, which is ended since the 11th of this present month of February. The money that is

---

[1] MS. syk.
[2] Or Vere. Arnemuiden or Armuijen is here generally written Armew or Armu.   [3] Time=weather. Cf. Fr. *temps.*

already received was employed for the making of a general pay through the whole navy, from the first of December to the first of January, and for the wages and conduct in discharge of 2,000 men out of the navy to the 18th of January, upon the last diminishing of our numbers.

The sum now required for 6 weeks pay is, for 3,015 men, as I have hereafter noted, at 21s. every man, the sum of 3,165l. 15s.; which I pray your Lordship may be paid to the Treasurer of the navy, or such as he shall appoint. And so I bid your Lordship right heartily farewell. From Rochester the 15th of February, 1587.

At Queenborough.	Men	The Narrow Seas.	Men
The Ark Ralegh .	425	The Rainbow .	250
Bonaventure .	250	Antelope .	160
Lion . .	250	Bull . .	100
Mary Rose .	250	Tiger . .	100
Vanguard .	250	Tramontana .	70
Dreadnought	200	Scout . .	70
Swallow .	160	Achates .	60
Foresight .	160	Charles . .	40
Spy . .	35	Moon . .	40
Merlin . .	35		
Sun . .	30		Men 890
Cygnet . .	20		
Fancy . .	20		
Two Ketches .	20		
The George . .	20		

Men 2,125

Total: 3,015 men at 21s. per man is 3,165l. 15s.

Your Lordship's assured to command,
C. HOWARD.

Feb. 17.—*WM. HAWKYNS*[1] *TO J. HAWKYNS.*

[ccviii. 72.—The bill is signed ; the rest in autograph.]

I have received of Anthony Goddard of Plymouth, merchant, the sum of twenty and five pounds of current money of England—I say 25*l.*—which is to be paid him or to the bringer hereof in London, at sight of this bill, by the hands of the right worshipful John Hawkyns Esquire, Treasurer of her Majesty's navy. Dated in Plymouth, the 17th of February, 1587.

Your loving brother,
Wm. HAWKYNS.

The Hope and Nonpareil are both graved, tallowed and this tide into the road again ; and the Revenge, now aground, I hope she shall likewise go into the road also to-morrow. We have, and do trim one side of every ship by night and the other side by day, so that we end the 3 great ships in 3 days this spring. The ships sit aground so strongly, and are so staunch as if they were made of a whole tree. The doing of it is very chargeable, for that it is done by torchlight and cressets, and in an extreme gale of wind, which consumes pitch, tallow and firs abundantly. I wrote you two days past by Clayton who is gone post. Yesterday I received your letter sent with Sir Francis Drake ; and so I take my

[1] William Hawkyns, elder brother of the more celebrated John, was at this time Mayor of Plymouth, an office he had held twice before. It was he, rather than John, who, as the owner of numerous privateers, rendered the name of Haquin, Achines, Acle, or de Canes, the terror of French and Spanish merchant ships. He died in October 1589, and was buried in the church of St. Nicholas at Deptford.

leave, this 17th of February, 1587, at 7 of the clock at night.   Your loving brother,
WM. HAWKYNS.

Our barrel pitch is all spent 3 days gone, and very scarce to be had here. If you send 4 or 5 last, it will serve well for sea-store. These hulks here have none. If they had, I would buy some.
W. H.

February 21.—*WM. BOROUGH TO BURGHLEY.*

[**ccviii. 77.**—Signed.   Addressed.]

Right honourable and my very good Lord :—
Inasmuch as I am most deeply bound unto you, well might I be reputed blameworthy if I should not, by all good means that possibly I can, acknowledge the same in dutiful wise, and endeavour to show myself thankful for so great favour and kindness extended towards me in my late distress,[1] even in such sort as you did, both in time and place, when and wheresoever great need required, which I well understand to be far greater than I expected, and even as much as I could in reason desire. Wherefore, with faithful heart and loving mind, I yield most humble and hearty thanks, confessing myself as much beholden unto your Honour as I am or may be to any man in the world; which I cannot, nor will not be unmindful of, God willing, while breath is in my body. Although I be unable (I would I were not) to make such requital as I earnestly desire, yet nevertheless, I am your Lordship's at command in whatsoever you please, and

---

[1] This refers to his quarrel with Drake in the expedition to Cadiz, an account of which is given in the Introduction.

will be most ready to do you any service I am able or shall be while I live ; yea assuredly, I shall not think my life too dear to do your Honour such good as I desire.   Unfeignedly I protest it, humbly desiring your Lordship to accept my good will. As touching the great discontent I have received through Sir Francis Drake's injurious, ungodly, and extreme dealings, which are insupportable, though I have suppressed my grief in the respect of the com- mandment and charge given me, hoping upon re- dress for the restoring my credit ; and that, inasmuch as I was openly defamed, and causelessly condemned in so vile and shameful sort, I should, likewise in public manner, upon due examination of my guilt- less cause, have had the innocency thereof made manifest, so as it might have been apparently known how unjustly and injuriously I have been slandered and abused ; but yet I find it is not, neither can I conjecture it is like to be ; and there- fore must be fain to ease my grief as I may, hoping in good time I shall ; who desire not of God any longer to live than I shall show myself a faithful and true hearted subject to my sovereign prince and native country, whose welfare and happy main- tenance I beseech the ever living Lord long to continue.

Herewith I send your Honour mine answer[1] touching an objection against me for the coming away of the Lion.

Now it may please your good [Lordship[2]] to be advertised that this day about noon, the Lord Admiral set sail from hence with his fleet, being 8 ships of her Majesty's, viz.—the Ark, the Bona- venture, the Golden Lion, the Vanguard, the Mary Rose, the Dreadnought, the Swallow, and the Foresight, besides the White Lion of my Lord's,

[1] This is missing.   [2] Omitted in MS.

and six pinnaces and a ketch. The four great ships remain here at Queenborough, and with them Mr. Hawkyns, myself, and Captain Beeston; which ships we are to bring up to Chatham as soon as we can, and then to ground them and make them ready, as we shall be appointed.

Furthermore, my very good Lord, concerning Mr. Hawkyns' bargain for the navy, Sir Wm. Wynter and I delivered a writing of late to my Lord Admiral, desiring to be resolved therein by his Lordship; who willed us to acquaint your Honour withal. Whereupon I do send you hereinclosed the copy [1] thereof, beseeching your Honour we may understand your Lordship's resolutions touching the same, so as we may be directed by some special warrant. And thus I cease from troubling you, my good Lord, any further, but shall not cease to pray unto Almighty God for your welfare, happiness and bliss; to whose most blessed tuition I commend your Honour, humbly taking my leave. Aboard the White Bear, at Queenborough, the 21st of February, 1587.

Your Lordship's most bounden,
W. Borough.

February 17.—*SIR WM. WYNTER AND WM.*
BOROUGH TO THE LORD ADMIRAL.

[ccviii. 77, I.—Copy.   Signed by Borough.   The enclosure
referred to in the foregoing.]

Whereas upon speeches had at Greenwich, before your Lordship and the rest of the Lords of her Majesty's Privy Council, touching a bargain which was offered to be taken by Mr. Hawkyns for the yearly charge of ordinary and extraordinary

---

[1] The next letter.

in harbour, for keeping and maintaining all her
Majesty's ships and vessels that she then had, there
passed an agreement by your Honours with Mr.
Hawkyns for the said bargain in form as he had set
it down, as himself did shortly after inform us ; and
thereupon he proceeded in the execution thereof,
and hath ever since continued the same ; till of late,
finding the charge far to surmount the demand
which by his said bargain he required, in such sort
as he was not able to continue it, did therefore (as
he hath informed us) signify the same to the
Queen's Majesty and your Honours, and became
humble suitor that he might leave it at Christmas
last, which he hath done, and maketh account from
that time forwards the office and charge for the navy
is to be ordered and borne as it was in former time,
before any bargain was undertaken.

The charge of the office of late hath grown
great and very intricate by means of the often
rigging, grounding &c., and the number of new
ships and vessels added to those that were there
when the bargain was spoken of ; by which means
we are somewhat troubled in dividing the charge.
True it is, that of the said bargain we never saw
any warrant in writing from her Majesty, your
Lordship, nor from any her Majesty's Privy Council ; neither have we received any such warrant for
his leaving the same at Christmas last as he accounteth he hath done. We know that it were
hard for him to continue it ; nay, that he is not able
to continue it ; yet notwithstanding, it must be
left by order ; and therefore we desire your good
Lordship, to be directed by special warrant what to
do therein, which we will observe as becometh
faithful servants to her Majesty.

17th of February, *Anno* 1587.
W. Wynter.   W. Borough.

February 21.—*HOWARD TO BURGHLEY.*

[**ccviii. 78.**—Signed.   No address nor endorsement.]

My very good Lord :—My son-in-law, Dick
Leveson,[1] hath acquainted me how his father is
about to make sale of some portion of his living, for
the discharge of 2,300*l.* ordered by us presently to
be satisfied to a Dane, in respect of his suggested
losses ; whereunto we were drawn by an opinion
we had conceived of Sir Walter Leveson's victualling and furnishing of the ship, that he had taken
the goods disorderly.   But now, finding, by certain
examinations taken in the Admiralty Court, cause
to conceive far otherwise than was then determined,
and that he is not to be charged but in respect of
the discharge of the promise made by Mr. Dr.
Cæsar and her Majesty's pleasure ; and finding himself unable to pay the same presently without such
sale so made before, I am earnestly to pray your
Lordship, both on the behalf of Sir Walter Leveson
and my son-in-law, whose successive inheritance it
doth in like sort concern, to take some such course,
as in your Lordship's wisdom shall seem best and
most convenient, that her Majesty may discharge the
present payment unto the Dane, and that he again,
in some reasonable time, may repay the same unto
her Majesty, whereby the inheritance may be
reserved unto my son-in-law, whose well doing I
must needs be careful of.   And so hoping of your

[1] Richard Leveson, of Lilleshall in Shropshire, born in 1570,
married Margaret, daughter of Howard, in December 1587. At
this time he was serving as a volunteer in the Ark. He was
knighted at Cadiz in 1596 ; served continuously through the war ;
was Admiral of the Narrow Seas in 1600, and Vice-Admiral of
England in 1604. He died without issue in 1605, and was buried
in the old church at Wolverhampton, where there is a monument
to his memory.

Lordship's favourable furtherance to effect this my request, I bid your Lordship most heartily farewell. From aboard her Majesty's good ship the Ark Ralegh, the 21st of February, 1587.

Your Honour's most assured to command,

C. HOWARD.

February 21.—*HOWARD TO BURGHLEY.*

[**ccviii. 79.**—Holograph. Addressed.]

My honourable and good Lord :—I have received your letter even as I was weighing to go out ; and for the first part, I am most heartily to give your Lordship thanks for your honourable favour. I will acknowledge it with all my love, and ready to do you any service.

For Mr. Hawkyns' bargain : he is presently to repair to the Court, where he shall be best able to answer in his own defence ; but this much I will say to your Lordship : I have been aboard of every ship that goeth out with me, and in every place where any may creep,[1] and I do thank God that they be in the estate they be in ; and there is never a one of them that knows what a leak means. I have known when an Admiral of England hath gone out, and two ships in fleet could not say so. There is none that goeth out now but I durst go to the Rio de la Plata[2] in her ; and yet the Mary Rose and the Swallow be with me, who were ships in the King's Majesty's her father's time.[3] And therefore I dare presume

---

[1] MS. krype. [2] MS. Ryall de Plato.

[3] Howard was certainly wrong in this. The Mary Rose of Henry VIII.'s time was sunk at Spithead in 1545, and this Mary Rose was not launched till after Elizabeth's accession. Cf. Derrick's *Memoirs of the Royal Navy*, pp. 16, 19, 20, 25. The Swallow seems to have been rebuilt once, if not twice, since the

greatly that those that have been made in her
Majesty's time be very good and serviceable, and
shall prove them arrant liars that have reported the
contrary.   And I thank God her Majesty, I hope,
may be well assured of their goodness ; yet everything hath his time, and must be helped as need
requireth.

My Lord, I had no meaning to carry away all
the officers.[1]   I have none with me but Sir W.
Wynter.   I leave Mr. Hawkyns and Mr. Borough
behind to wait on your Lordship, and to put the
four great ships in readiness, which we shall greatly
need if the Spanish forces come out.   And so, my
Lord, having no more leisure to write at large,
being under sail, I bid your Lordship most heartily
farewell.   The 21st of February, at 12 o'clock the
afternoon.

Your Lordship's most assured to command,

C. HOWARD.

February 28.—*SIR WILLIAM WYNTER TO
THE PRINCIPAL OFFICERS.*

[**ccviii 85.**—Signed.   Addressed :—To my loving fellows, John
Hawkyns, Wm. Holstok and Wm. Borough, Esqrs., Officers
of the Queen's Majesty's Admiralty.]

Since my last letters sent unto you there is
nothing happened worthy the writing other than

death of Henry VIII. ; once in 1558, and again about 1580. Cf.
Hatfield MSS. No. 846, *Otho* E. ix ; and *S.P. Dom. Eliz.* cciv. 20.
    [2] The principal officers of the navy, viz. : the Treasurer
(Hawkyns), Master of the Ordnance (Wynter), Comptroller
(Borough), and Comptroller of Victualling (Wm. Holstok).   In
the next century these officers, with some additions, *e.g.* the
Surveyor and the Clerk of the Acts, formed the Navy Board,
which, under the control of the Board of Admiralty, continued to
administer much of the details of the affairs of the navy, until it
was abolished by Act of Parliament in 1832.

that the Commissioners did pass away under the charge of Sir Henry Palmer upon Sunday night last past, and as we think, landed the next day following, having a most pleasant passage.

You shall do well to call upon the Lords that it would please their Honours to be mindful that provisions might be made in time to supply the wants which will grow amongst the navy if we make any long continuance abroad, for I dare assure you that which we have and was thought to be sufficient (as it was indeed) at our coming forth, will grow by reason of our too timely coming abroad not to be able without a great supply to serve us out this summer. This winter's weather, although we have been but a while abroad, hath so stretched our sails and tackle, torn many of our blocks, pullies, and sheevers, stretched our boats, and destroyed some of our pinnaces—as the Lion's for one, who is utterly lost and must be furnished of another—as[1] a man would never believe it unless he doth see it ; these be the fruits that the seas bring forth, especially in this time of the year, as it is not unknown to you. If you be not careful to call for these things to the Lords, although they are unpleasant suits for her Majesty or them to hear of, you shall not do that that becometh you, nor avoid the peril and danger that may grow thereby ; for learn this of me : Lords will be found in no fault if matters come in question.

I trust you do not forget to set forward the masts that should serve for the great ships, although I hope in God we shall not greatly need them.

Our ships doth show themselves like gallants here. I assure you it will do a man's heart good to behold them ; and would to God the Prince of

[1] That.

Parma were upon the seas with all his forces, and we in the view of them ; then I doubt not but that you should hear that we would make his enterprise very unpleasant to him.   But with sorrow I speak it, I am afraid that they will keep me from the baths of Bath by their long detraction,[1] where I meant to have been to seek health by the beginning of May next.

My Lord Admiral being accompanied with the lords [2] and other captains, and I also waiting upon his Lordship, not with much ease did land at Dover pier and viewed the same ; where I must tell you I saw nothing that pleased me but only the Pent.[3]   I had well hoped that it should have been a harbour for good shipping, but now I see it is made a place for passage boats.   I do not discommend the harbour for that there will want water ; but I do mislike it in respect that the coming into it is not laid in good soil, which time will discover.

Thanks be to God, my Lord Admiral with all his followers do keep themselves in good health, which I pray God to continue.   And thus leaving for this time, I bid you farewell.   Written aboard the Vanguard, being in the Downs, ready to cut sail,[4] the wind at East and by North, to bear over with the other coast, 28th of February, 1587.

Your loving fellow,

W. WYNTER.

[1] Delay.

[2] Lord Henry Seymour, Lord Sheffield, and others serving afloat.   See *ante*, p. 24.

[3] The eastern basin of Dover harbour, still so called.   It was first constructed in 1583 (cf. *S.P. Dom. Eliz.* clxi. 36, 39), as a sluiced basin or 'large pent to contain water enough to let out to scour the haven's mouth.'

[4] To loose and let fall.   When a sail was farthelled or furled, it was bound to the yard with rope yarns, which were cut to loose the sail.   See Manwayring's *Seaman's Dictionary*.

February 29.—*HOWARD TO BURGHLEY.*

[ccviii. **87.**—Signed.   Addressed.]

My very good Lord :—Upon Tuesday, being in the Downs, the wind came to the east, that we were fain to put over to Blackness.[1]   This day, being the last of this present, being up alongst the coast towards Calais, I met Sir Henry Palmer, who had wafted over the Commissioners, and afterwards went to Flushing.   I have sent your Lordship a packet of letters that he brought from thence.   I perceive by a letter that I have received from my Lord Governor of Flushing that the Count Maurice is come to Middelburg ; his errand is, as it is thought, to persuade them of Campvere and Arnemuiden from her Majesty, but by my Lord Governor's letter it doth appear they will stand fast for her Majesty. I also perceive by his letter that Famars[2] and Villiers have besieged Colonel Sonoy,[3] and that

---

[1] Gris-nez.   [2] MS. Famus.

[3] MS. Coronall Snoye.   When the Earl of Leicester returned to England in December 1587, though without formally resigning the authority which the States General had conferred on him, Prince Maurice of Nassau was elected Stadtholder and Captain General of the States' army.   On this, Sonoy, who commanded in North Holland, declaring himself bound by his oath of obedience to Leicester, refused to acknowledge Maurice, and shut himself up in Medemblik, where he was promptly besieged by Maurice's troops, under Marshal Villiers : it does not appear that Famars was with him.   About the middle of March 1588 Sonoy received tardy orders from Queen Elizabeth to surrender the fortress and submit himself to the Prince, which he did.   He was deprived of his command, and shortly afterwards took refuge in England, where the Queen allotted him a congenial piece of fenland in Lincolnshire.   Owing to his ignorance of English, and perhaps also to his impracticable temper, his attempt to drain it proved a failure.   He returned to his own country and settled in East Friesland, on a small pension from the States.   Afterwards he

if he have not some comfort, it will go hard with
him.   I do wonder I have not heard some answer
touching my letter which I sent by Kirkman ; but
the case being as it is, I mean the first wind that
shall serve, to send two ships thither[1] ; for I had
rather adventure to send, than the gentleman that is
so well devoted to her Majesty should therefore
perish.   I have his man aboard with me, and hath
been these four days ; and if the wind had served
anything these two days, I had sent him and two of
her Majesty's ships to his master.

The first wind that doth serve I do mean to put
with[2] Flushing, and I hope thereby to encourage her
Majesty's good friends of Campvere and Arnemuiden
and to discourage Count Maurice and his followers.
I perceive by Sir Henry Palmer that my coming
thither will do good many ways, and I think our
being here alongst the coast hath done much good.

There are two French ships that are come out
of Spain, that doth report wonders of the Spanish
army, and that upon pain of death every man must
be ready to cut sail the 25th of March, and that
their coming is for England, and that they bring
some galleys with them hauled[3] at ships' sterns.   If
this be true, it is sure for the Isle of Wight or Sluys.[4]
If I may have the four great ships come to me in
time, and 20 good hoys, but with[5] 20 men apiece,
which is but a small charge, and each of them but
with two iron pieces, I doubt not but to make her
Majesty a good account of anything that shall be

became imbecile, and died in 1597, of the effects of falling into the
fire.   The countenance which the Queen appeared to give Sonoy
and other rebels against the States, during the early months of
1588, naturally estranged Maurice from the English for the time.

[1] To Medemblik.

[2] With, following a verb of motion, means towards or to.   To
put with = put over to.

[3] Towed.   [4] MS. Scluse.   [5] With but.

done by the Spanish forces, and I will make him wish his galleys at home again.

If the Commissioners bring peace it is the happiest thing that can be; but if they come without it, look for great matters to ensue presently upon it; for the charge is so great that the King is at, both in Spain and here, in the Low Countries, that it cannot continue long, if he had five times the treasure he hath.

Rowland Yorke[1] is dead of the small-pox. I would Stanley[2] were with him.

The Dunkirkers dare not stir abroad. Sir Henry Palmer this day did rescue a man of Dort[3] from them, which they had taken, and one of the Dunkirkers ran into Dunkirk and the other two into Calais; he that went into Dunkirk had his errand[4] with him to his smart. If we keep them in thus, they will starve.

I protest before God, and as my soul shall answer for it, that I think there were never in any place in the world worthier ships than these are, for so many. And as few as we are, if the King of Spain's forces be not hundreds, we will make good sport with them. And I pray you tell her Majesty from me that her money was well given for the Ark Ralegh,[5] for I think her the odd ship in the world for

---

[1] A soldier of fortune, distinguished alike by his impetuous courage and the impudence of his treachery. His last achievement in this line had been the betrayal of the Zutphen fort, of which he was governor, to the Spaniards, in January 1587.

[2] Sir William Stanley, a man of family and influence, had been employed in Ireland; and afterwards, in the Low Countries, had been appointed by Leicester Governor of Deventer, which he betrayed to the Spaniards in January 1587. See Motley, *History of the United Netherlands*, vol. ii. chap. xiii.

[3] Or Dordrecht.   [4] MS. hat his arrant.

[5] She was bought from Sir Walter Ralegh for 5,000*l.*, which, however, was not paid in cash. The amount was struck off Ralegh's debt to the Crown in May 1592 (*S.P. Dom. Eliz.* ccxlii. 21).

all conditions ; and truly I think there can no great
ship make me change and go out of her.   We can
see no sail, great nor small, but how far soever they
be off, we fetch them and speak with them.   And so
I bid your Lordship most heartily farewell.   From
aboard her Majesty's good ship the Ark, the last
of February 1587.

Your Lordship's most assured to command,

C. HOWARD.

February 29.—RICHARD BARREY [1] *TO LORD
BURGHLEY.*

[ccviii. **88.**—Holograph.[2]   Addressed.]

My most humble duty unto your Honour remembered :—This day there arrived from Ostend one
of the barks of this town that transported the Earl of
Derby's stuff.   The master and owners of the bark is
William and Henry Tydyeman.[3]   In their coming
from Dunkirk, a man of war of Dunkirk, of the burden
of three score tons, with 60 men in her, very well appointed, boarded them and have rifled [4] and spoiled
them of all the money they had ; and that one Thomas
Baker of Folkestone and one   Thomas Hurleston
of Sandwich, who went over for pilots.[5]   That which
is taken from them in money and other furniture
and apparel is worth 30*l.* ; and they have carried
William Tydyeman unto Dunkirk, and the passport
of the Earl of Derby.   A letter from the Earl of

---

[1] Lieutenant-Governor of Dover Castle.

[2] A very difficult scrawl.

[3] It may seem a fair presumption that these were of the same
family as the Sir Thomas Teddeman of Charles II.'s time.

[4] MS. ryfeled.

[5] The meaning is doubtful.   Perhaps it is :—and that (rifling
and spoiling) they did also to one Thomas Baker &c.

Derby unto your Honour was nailed under the bytack,[1] so as they could not find it, the which was brought unto me by Baker of Folkestone, the which I send unto your Honour here enclosed. They have done divers other spoils unto these that came from Ostend, the which your Honour shall hear of. Most humbly ceasing[2] from troubling your Honour, praying for the continuance of your Honour's health with long life. Dover, the last of February.

Your Honour's most loving at commandment,
RICHARD BARREY.

March 3.—HAWKYNS TO BURGHLEY.

[**ccix. 5**.—Holograph. Addressed.]

My bounden duty humbly remembered unto your good Lordship :—I have been very ill since I was with your Lordship, but now better I thank God.

I do daily hear good report of the good estate of the ships abroad, as it may appear to your Lordship by the letters I send herewith enclosed ; so do I hear many of good judgment that have served now in them report, wondering how these lewd bruits[3] could have been cast abroad, and the ships in that sufficient and strong estate. But not to be troublesome to your Lordship, when the shipwrights saw I took a course to put the navy in such order as there should be no great cause to use any extraordinary reparations upon them, then they saw the multitude of their idle followers should lack their maintenance, and so began to bruit[4] out weakness in the state of

---

[1] So in MS. It is probably the Sp. *bitácula*, whence the Eng. bittacle, now binnacle.
[2] MS. sessyng.   [3] MS. brewtes.   [4] MS. brewt.

the ships ; but they knew not where ; and then every man tare[1] up that which was sufficient, and said this[2] we will weary Hawkyns of his bargain. And as this shall be a thing most manifest to your Lordship and the whole world, that the navy is in good and strong estate, contrary to their hypocritical practice and vile reports, so your Lordship shall find the rest of their informations much like unto this.

I would to God her Majesty were so well provided of all furniture that belongeth to the ships as her Highness is of good carcasses of ships, which indeed is the least matter I fear.   But the provisions[3] that come from foreign countries, and such as require long time to provide, do most trouble me—as great cables, anchors, cordage, canvas, great masts, and such like ; waste and spoil of boats and pinnaces by this winter weather, as Sir William Wynter doth well note.

I am now about to gather together the great issuing that hath been this year of *anno* 1587 of cordage, canvas, and other provisions out of her Majesty's store, which I think will be 12,000 or 13,000 pound, which must be cared for and supplied in time, without the which the ships cannot serve.   There hath been great service abroad these two years past, and the ships mightily supplied from time to time with many provisions, and now call daily in such sort as I am both afraid and sorry to present it to your Lordship.   Howbeit, it must be done and care had to do it in time.   The expenses extraordinary have been great, and such as before this time hath seldom come in use ; for the navy is

[1] Tore : spoke evil of, disparaged, condemned.
[2] In this way : thus.
[3] Provisions means stores ; what we now understand as provisions were, in 1588, distinguished as victual.

great, and men more unruly and more chargeable than in time past, so as it doth not only amaze me to answer everything, but I do grieve at the charge as much as it were to proceed from myself.

I have been careful to replenish the store, for I found it not worth 5,000*l.* ; and now I think with this year's issuing, it is worth 16,000 pound. So likewise the ships I found in weak estate, and now they are as your Lordship doth see ; and this is done in effect upon the sparing out of the ordinary warrant of 5,719*l.*, yet I am daily backbited and slandered. But your Lordship doth know what a place this is to hold, that I am in. Many are to receive out of this office, and among a multitude, there are some bad and unreasonable ; and although I endeavour myself to pay and satisfy all men with order and equity, yet some be displeased.

The matters in the office are great and infinite. My men are sick and dispersed. The trust I am forced to commit abroad and at home is very much ; and with great difficulty I keep things in that order as [1] I can give reason for the things that are paid ; and many losses I receive by negligence of servants, by such as I put in trust, and by prests [2] which be without number.

Therefore, my good Lord, consider in your wisdom the burden I bear. My service to her Majesty I grudge not, but all my ability and life is ready to be employed in her service. When it shall be your Lordship's pleasure, I will give mine attendance to inform your Lordship substantially what is to be done touching the provisions that are to be provided for the navy, and the debt that the office

---

[1] Such order that.
[2] A prest, or imprest, was an earnest, or advance paid on account. A prest-man was really a man who received the prest of 12*d.*, as a soldier when enlisted.

doth and will daily grow into ; and so, wishing your Lordship health and prosperity, I humbly take my leave. From London, the 3rd of March, 1587.

Your Lordship's humbly to command,

JOHN HAWKYNS.

March 3.—*FENNER TO WALSYNGHAM.*

[**ccix. 6.**—Holograph. Addressed.]

Here cometh advertisements daily from out of Spain, most of them running upon one point. Amongst others, by the way out of Brittany, as from Nantes,[1] by reason of a Portingal there dwelling, who sent his son unto Lisbon, and by one his special kinsman there, having to do for the King's provision, gave understanding, as followeth :

At Lisbon and forthwith to be there and to serve the enterprise :

	Ships
Of ships out of divers parts provided to the number of .	400
Of galleys	50

Footmen.

	Men
Out of Italy	5,000
the Indies . . .	3,000
Spain	17,000
Portugal . . .	12,000
Flanders . . .	25,000
More to be levied in Italy . .	12,000
	74,000

Horses.

Light horse	1,200
Horses garnished . . .	1,400
	2,600

[1] MS. Naunce.

Men for the service of the artillery　1,200
Mariners and sailors　.　　.　　.　8,912
_____

10,112

Biscuit.[1]

Quintals

From Andalusia.　　.　　.　　.　27,557
　Malaga　.　　.　　.　　.　.　12,000
　Cartagena and Murcia　.　　.　12,000
　Seville　.　　.　　.　　.　.　25,000
　Burgos and Tierra de Campos　56,000
　Naples　.　　.　　.　　.　.　40,000
From all the Islands　.　　.　　.　12,000
_____

184,557

Bacon and pork, from five
　several places　　.　　.　23,000 quintals.[2]
Wines, from four several
　places　.　　.　　.　　.　26,000 butts.
Cheeses, out of four several
　places　.　　.　　.　　.　43,000 quintals.
Fish, from three places　.　19,000 hogsheads.
Beef, from three places　.　11,000 quintals.
Roves[3] of oil, from two
　places　.　　.　　.　　.　23,000 roves.
Beans, from four places　.　36,000 haniks.[4]
Barley, from two places　.　35,000 haniks.
Rice, from Genoa[5] and Va-
　lencia　.　　.　　.　　.　24,000 roves.[3]
Great store of horseshoes, nails and girths.

[1] MS. bysquet. This list of stores may be compared with that given by Duro (i. 275), as suggested by Santa Cruz in March 1586.
[2] MS. kintals. The quintal is 100 (five score) Spanish pounds, or 102 lbs. av. nearly.
[3] Arrobas. The arroba is a measure of nearly four gallons, or a weight of 25 pounds.
[4] Hanegas or fanegas. The hanega is about a bushel and a half.　　[5] MS. Jenovaye ; from the Spanish Génova.

Captain Coxe[1] came from the coast of Spain within
five days before the date hereof, in a pinnace of Sir
William Wynter's. [He reporteth[2]] the like number
of ships, or little different ; as also of a great number
of flyboats that keepeth the coast of Spain, thereby
their provisions coming in fleets together to Lisbon
in safety.   Their intents are known unto your
Honour.   I would to God we had been now upon
that coast ; the impediments would have been great
unto their army gathering together, more than I
dare presume to write, in my poor opinion.   We
rest here, a great number of valiant men, and to
great charge unto my gracious mistress, and a great
grief of mind to spend her Majesty's treasure and
do nothing upon the enemy.

I fear when we shall be hastened to go, our
provision of victual needful will not be ready in a
month ; in which time it will be no small matter, the
waste in doing of nothing.   If there were three
months' provision ready for the proportion of 3,000
men, it would not amount unto above 9,000*l.* ; and if
there should need no use of it, there would not be
1,000*l.* lost by it ; and the contrary, the time of stay
before it be ready, if cause move the proceedings,

[1] Cf. *ante*, p. 11.   In 1576 William Coxe of Limehouse commanded the Bear in a voyage to the Spanish Main under Captain
Andrew Barker, who, after quarrelling with his master and other
officers, was put on shore by Coxe in the Bay of Honduras, and
there killed by the Spaniards.   The Bear was afterwards lost, with
the greater part of her men ; but Coxe and eight others escaped,
and, after much suffering, arrived in England only to be accused
of the murder of Barker, and condemned to a term of imprisonment. How long Coxe remained in prison does not appear ; but in
1583 he was master of the Golden Hind of 40 tons, Edward Hayes
captain and owner, in the tragic voyage of Sir Humphrey Gylberte
to Newfoundland (see Lediard, 163, 197).   In 1588 he proved
himself a good navigator and bold man, and was slain, probably
— as has been said — in the great fight off Gravelines.
[2] Omitted in MS.

will cost half so much money and more in victuals and wages before victual can be provided, as also the opportunity of time to encounter the enemy lost.

I had rather have occasion to be at service, that your Honour might hear of some happy success in beating down the pride of the enemy, wherein we are assuredly strengthened in God of good and happy success. God grant it to his good pleasure, and send your Honour your heart's desire ; craving pardon of your Honour for my boldness herein, not doubting your taking in good part the rude lines that cometh from a soldier. Plymouth, from aboard her Majesty's good ship the Nonpareil, this 3rd of March, 1587.

Your Honour's in all duty,
THOMAS FENNER.

OPINION OF SIR FRANCIS DRAKE.

[ccix. 128.—Signed.]

Mine opinion touching those notes delivered by Captain Coxe.

1. First these flyboats are those which were reported to have the carrying of those pilots from Dunkirk which were provided by the Prince of Parma for this fleet now prepared at Lisbon and now employed by the Cardinal[1] and Marquis of Santa Cruz, as men of war upon that coast, until the fleet be ready, that thereby their passage for all manner of victuals and other provisions may be the safer, as also that there shall be no certain advertisements from thence, and in what readiness their fleet is for what their pretence[2] is.

[1] The Cardinal Archduke Albert, Governor of Portugal ; a younger son of the late Emperor Maximilian, King Philip's first cousin, and of the Empress Maria, Philip's sister.
[2] Design.

2. It is the likelier, for that the said Captain Coxe likewise affirmeth that both French and Dutch men have vowed unto him that they are sworn, before they depart Spain, that they shall not strike sail to any English man of war ; and if they be not able to make resistance, then to throw all their letters whatsoever overboard.

3. He also thinketh that there are by the least 30 sail of those flyboats, men of war, which he hath at sundry times seen ; and that the said flyboats have in every one of them some Spaniards, for that they are all full of small shot.[1]

4. He farther reporteth that the Rochellers told him at his first coming upon that coast that there were flyboats men of war, and that they durst not abide upon that coast for fear of them. And farther he himself confesseth that, upon consultation had with his company, they were contented to come away for their better safety, which otherwise they had not done, for that they had good store of victuals left.

5. In my poor opinion it were not amiss that the Lords did think of the continual going to the seas of the smaller sort of our shipping daily upon letters of reprisal, which can do little good ; for that all men of war which come home report that there is no shipping to be seen upon the coast of Spain but such as bring victuals and other provisions in great fleets for Lisbon, and they are wafted with [2] men of war ; but [3] those Flemish flyboats, which go in fleets, by the least five, seven and nine in company, which will not leave one English man of war untaken upon that coast, and I doubt lest some are taken already.

6. At this instant there arrived a bark of this town from Bordeaux, who reported that the King of

[1] Musketeers.   [2] Convoyed by.   [3] And also.

Navarre is with his army within five leagues of the town and stoppeth the passage of the river, so as little recourse is had thither, and that the inhabitants of the city are every night in arms, and divers alarms made among them.

Fra. Drake.

March 6.—JOHN HAWKYNS TO BURGHLEY.

[**ccix. 7.**—Holograph.   Addressed.]

Right Honourable mine especial good Lord :— I have herewith brought unto your Lordship a brief note of the material things that hath issued this last year by warrant of the officers out of her Majesty's store ; and as I can overcome it, your Lordship shall see it more particularly, as we have been accustomed in all our demands yearly for the supplying of the same.

There is already taken into the storehouse and provided to the value of 5,000*l.*, which is unpaid for ; and order given for great cables to be made this winter in Muscovia, for the value of 3,000*l.*, which will be most needful.   If your Lordship do give order for the one half[1] of this demand to be paid, the credit of the office may be satisfied ; and so, with some time and leisure the rest may be paid, as your Lordship shall from the office have information, as the necessity requireth, and not before.

For[2] the great masts is a matter of importance, and requireth some speedy order to be taken in it, your Lordship may speak with Mr. Allin[3] in it,

---

[1] MS. hallf.   [2] For=since, because.
[3] Thomas Allin, officially described as ' her Majesty's merchant for Danzig.'   His name is frequently mentioned in connection with the supply of masts, cordage, &c.

which [1] doth know how they may best be had and with the most speed ; and for that purpose there would be some prest delivered as the necessity shall from time to time require. I will attend upon your Lordship to know what order your Lordship shall think meet to be taken herein, and to satisfy your Lordship of any doubt that may be had in these matters ; and so leave to trouble your good Lordship.   The 6th day of March, 1587.

Your honourable Lordship's humbly to command,
JOHN HAWKYNS.

March 9.—*HOWARD TO BURGHLEY.*

[ccix. 9.—Signed.   Addressed.]

My very good Lord :—On Friday, being the first of March, riding under Blackness [2] on the coast of France, the wind came out of west, so as we did put off to have borne over to the coast of England ; and being half seas over, the wind came to the West-South-West and a very hard gale, so as we were driven to put over either for Yarmouth or Flushing.   And because Yarmouth was so much to the northwards, we rather chose Flushing.   So on Sunday about 12 of the clock in the forenoon, we came in with much wind and passed by the town to the Rammekens.   The Elizabeth Bonaventure in coming in, by the fault of the pilot, came aground on a sand where there had been a hulk cast away but a month before, having in her one of the best pilots in the town.   I must commend my Lord H. Seymour wonderfully for his honourable mind ; for although many of the ship went out to save themselves for fear, he would by no means stir out of

---

[1] Which=who.   [2] Gris-nez.

her, but said he would abide her fortune, and so encouraged them all. I and Sir Wm. Wynter came presently aboard of her, where we found my Lord Harry sparing no labour for her help. Myself and Sir Wm. Wynter remained still in her and devised all helps that might be ; but that tide could do no good. The next tide, by the goodness of God and great labour, we brought her off, and in all this time there never came a spoonful of water into her well. My Lord, except a ship had been made of iron, it were to be thought unpossible to do as she hath done; and it may be well and truly said there never was nor is in the world a stronger ship than she is, and there is no more to be perceived or known any ways of her being aground than if she were new made. She is 27 years old; she was with Sir Francis Drake two voyages [1] ; and there hath been no voyage which hath been, but she hath been one. Your Lordship shall find it so in your books. And this is one of the ships which they would have come into a dry dock, now before she came out. My Lord, I have no doubt but some ships which have been ill reported of will deceive them as this ship doth. And for that which Sir Wm. Wynter and I have seen now, we will take upon us that the good ship the Elizabeth Bonaventure shall serve her Majesty these 12 years ; and I do not know but that the Triumph, the Elizabeth Jonas, the Bear and the Victory should be in better case than this ship ; for they are no elder, nor as yet they never had journey to wring them as this ship hath had. Well, my Lord, they will be found good ships when they come to the seas.

Upon Tuesday my Lord Governor [2] intreated me and all our company to dinner with him, which

[1] To the West Indies in 1585-6, and to Cadiz in 1587.
[2] Sir William Russell.

we did. There came to me thither all the States of Zealand and Mons. de Valke, their Councillor, who presented from all the islands and towns all service to her Majesty, and by especial speech from the town of Middelburg, that they were all her Majesty's, and that none shall come into the town but such as shall always please her Majesty, and that Campvere nor Arnemuiden shall any ways show their duties more than they will do. I gave them thanks on her Majesty's behalf; and yet I spared not to let them know how in some things they had forgotten their duties.

The Count Maurice being there, as soon as ever we came in went his way to Lillo, where some of his fleet lay, and carried with him all that he had, yet he did send a gentleman of his to me with the most humblest message that ever he sent to any, offering all his service to her Majesty, which way soever I would appoint him. I took occasion upon this offer of his, to write a letter unto him touching Mo. Sonoy, and also sent my brother Hoby[1] with it, with a message concerning it. He wrote unto me again. His letter and also the copy of mine, I have sent to Mr. Secretary, which your Lordship may see. He hath promised to do what he can in it,

[1] Sir Edward Hoby, born in 1560, was the eldest son of Sir Thomas Hoby, ambassador in France in 1566. His mother, Elizabeth, daughter of Sir Anthony Cooke, was sister to Lady Burghley and to Lady Bacon. Hoby was thus first cousin of Sir Francis Bacon (Lord Bacon), and of Sir Robert Cecill, afterwards Earl of Salisbury. After his father's death, his mother married John Lord Russell, elder brother of Sir William Russell; her younger sister was the wife of Sir Henry Kyllygrew, the English Resident at the Hague. Hoby himself had married the youngest daughter of Lord Hunsdon, and was thus Lord Howard's brother-in-law. He was serving at this time as Howard's secretary, and seems to have had a position somewhat analogous to that of the modern Captain of the Fleet. He was the author of some polemical pamphlets, and died in 1617.

and said if it were in his own power he would, but
he must deal with the States ; and so went the next
morning into Holland to deal with them. I dealt
also with the States of Zealand in it ; and privately,
with Mo. de Valke. I believe they will deal well in
it, for so they have promised him. My Lord
Governor and I thought it best to forbear four or
five days the sending of any ships thither,[1] to see
what they will do. I have the Tramontana and the
Charles ready, and shall go to Flushing and do as
my Lord Governor shall see cause. My Lord, it is
very hard to get a pilot in Flushing that will go
thither ; for I desired Mo. Sonoy's agent to see
what he could do to get two pilots, but I could not
hear of any. Upon Wednesday, all the captains
and chiefest men of Campvere and Arnemuiden came
aboard to me to dinner. I did never see men show
more love than these do to her Majesty. The captains
give her Majesty most humble thanks for her boun-
tiful goodness to them. They of Campvere invited
me to dinner with them ; and they of Arnemuiden, to
supper. I could not deny them, they were so
earnest ; but the next morning, it was so foul
weather that I was driven to send my excuse. That
same day there came to me the two burgomasters
of Middelburg and five of the principal men of the
town, and invited me to dinner to them on the
Sunday, which I could not at that time deny them ;
but with condition that if the wind should serve me
to go out, they would pardon me. My Lord, the
preparations which were made were very great ;
such as, our merchants said, the like was never in
that town at any time.

On Friday, when the wind came to serve our
turns, I sent my son Leveson[2] and three or four
gentlemen to them, to make my excuse, and also to

---

[1] To Medemblik.   [2] MS. Lewson.

visit the Princess of Orange.[1]   My Lord, all the
mariners and seamen of Campvere and Arnemuiden
came to the governors and captains and told them
that they would all serve under me, and be commanded by none but by me ; and said whensoever
I would send for them, they would come from
Count Maurice or any, to me.   They of Middelburg heard of it, and they did the like.   My Lord,
this I dare assure her Majesty, at this hour she is
no more assured of the isle of Sheppey to be at her
devotion any ways, than she is of the whole isle
of Walcheren and all the towns.   Our merchants
find, as they say, a great change ; for they were
never so kindly handled as they are now.   My
Lord, I think we have had aboard our ships, to
view and look on them, 5,000 people on a day.

My Lord, in my going to Flushing, I took a
vessel of Nieuport, and released him again with
money in his purse, and told him that I was not on
the seas to offend any of them if they would not
give occasion ; and that I hoped, ere it were long,
we should be all good friends.   I told them they
saw whether I was able to starve both them and
Dunkirk if I listed ; for I could impeach all victuals
coming to them, and not suffer any to stir to fish ;
but I had no such meaning, if they gave not first
cause.

The Charles, coming from the coast of England,
met with a Dunkirker, half seas over, chasing two
English barks.   The Charles rescued them, and
had a good fight together ; but the Charles at
length made him run on ground under the town of
Dunkirk, for he was surely sped.   We will not
meddle with them except they come out and seek it,
for I would be loth to do anything in this time of

---

[1] Louise de Colligny, widow of William the Silent, and step-
mother of Count Maurice.

treating, that might hinder it; but yet I must not suffer her Majesty's subjects to be spoiled. We had but one in the Charles which was ill hurt. He is hurt, even like Sir Philip Sidney,[1] above the knee, and the bone all broken; a very great hurt. I have him aboard mine own ship, and am in hope to recover him.

There came into Flushing on Monday a Dane that came from Lisbon, who doth affirm that the Marquis de Santa Cruz is dead[2]; but he saith the preparations go on very great.

My Lord, as I was in writing hereof entering into Margate Road, Sir Henry Palmer came aboard and told me for certainty that there are letters come into Middelburg and to Mo. Sonoy's agent that the siege of Medemblik[3] is raised; which I am persuaded upon the hearing of my coming they did. I [had] forgotten to write unto your Lordship that they of Campvere and of Arnemuiden offered to suffer me to bring into their towns what English companies I would, and what number I listed. In like sort I had forgotten Count Maurice, at his departure out of Middelburg, bade them of the town farewell, and told them that he went out of that town as his father did out of Antwerp. He left behind him neither bed-hanging nor anything else, but carried all away with him.

There is much more than I am able to write. This gentleman, Mr. Browne's relation, who will more at large impart the rest unto your Lordship. And this[4] I bid your Lordship most heartily well to

[1] The author of *Arcadia*; Leicester's nephew and Walsyngham's son-in-law; mortally wounded in the thigh at the battle of Zutphen.
[2] He died on Jan. 30–Feb. 9.
[3] MS. has Middlebecke.
[4] With this, thus.

fare.   From aboard the Ark, this 9th of March,
1587, at Margate road.

Your Lordship's assured to command,

C. HOWARD.

March 9 (?).—*HOWARD TO BURGHLEY.* (?)

[ccix. 10.—Holograph.]

My good Lord :—I thought good to advertise
your Lordship of a flyboat and a hoy.   The flyboat
is of Calais, the hoy of Dort.   The flyboat was
very lately in Spain.   They are laden with a 1,000
quarters of wheat of the best.   Their cocket is for
Rochelle or Middelburg, neither of both the places
any great friends to us.   This cocket passed from
Mr. Wauton.[1]   The Flemings report there is as
much to come away to-morrow by the like warrant.
If wheat go away in such plumps, the market will
rise quickly, and the poor in hard case, after such a
year as the last was.   I have stayed it till I hear
from your Lordship, and as you will let me know
your pleasure and it shall be done.   My good Lord,
it is much that the enemy is relieved withal after
this manner.   Their great army could not continue,
nor their ships be victualled, if it were not by these
means.   I pray your Lordship let me know your
pleasure by this bearer ; and so I bid your Lordship
most heartily farewell.   Aboard the Ark, thwart of
the Naze.[2]

Your Lordship's assured friend to command,

C. HOWARD.

[1] Probably Roger Walton, a merchant of Calais, and a Catholic,
suspected of being in correspondence with the Duke of Parma.

[2] Orfordness.   The letter is not dated, but would seem to
have been written on the passage from Flushing to Margate, and
sent with the preceding letter of March 9.

March 9.—*HOWARD TO WALSYNGHAM.*

[ccix. 12.—Holograph.   Addressed.]

Sir :—As I had made up my other letter,[1] Captain Frobiser doth advertise me that he spake with two ships that came presently from Lisbon, who declared unto him that for certainty the King of Spain's fleet doth part from Lisbon unto the Groyne the 15th of this month, by their account. Sir, there is none that comes from Spain but brings this advertisement ; and if it be true, I am afraid it will not be helped when the time serveth.   Surely this charge that her Majesty is at is either too much or too little ; and the stay that is made of Sir Francis Drake going out I am afraid will breed grave peril.[2] And if the King of Spain do send forces either into this realm, Ireland or Scotland, the Queen's Majesty shall say the Duke of Parma is treating of a peace, and therefore it is not princely done of his master to do so in the time of treaty.   But what is that to the purpose, if we have by that a *casado*[3] ?   And if her Majesty cannot show the King's hand, his servant's hand will be but a bad warrant, if they have their wills.   Sir, for myself I am determined to end my life in it, and the matter is not great.   I protest my greatest care is for her Majesty's honour and surety.

I send you a letter that now as I write I received from a man of mine which affirmeth the like ; and so, Sir, I take my leave.   From aboard the Ark Ralegh, the 9th of March, at 12 a clock at night.

Your very loving friend,

C. HOWARD.

[1] A duplicate of that to Burghley of same date.   [2] MS. parell.
[3] So in MS.   He probably thought he was writing *camisado*, a sudden, unexpected attack in the dark.

March 10.—*SEYMOUR TO WALSYNGHAM.*

[**ccix. 13.**—Holograph.   Addressed.]

Sir :—Being assaulted as well with grief as with
joy, I stand doubtful whether of them both I should
embrace; either to conceal or to open such accidents
as befell unto the Lord Admiral and the rest of his
navy ; but leaving the same unto your honourable
judgment, do proceed accordingly.

The Lord Admiral, being earnestly laboured
and solicited by letters from the Lord Governor of
Flushing to provoke him to ride there with his
navy, the wind being also contrary to all his other
harbours, thought good to take the same as it
served.

Sunday, being the third of March, his Lordship
entered into the harbour of Flushing, where, by
great misfortune, the Elizabeth Bonaventure came
on ground betwixt 12 and one of the clock in the
day time, and could not that tide get off.   But by
the goodness of God, with the presence of the Lord
Admiral, and help of the rest of the captains and
masters, the same was recovered at the next tide,
which was twelve hours after, to the great admiring
of the whole island.

The next day after, being the 5th of this month,
his Lordship dined with the Lord Governor, where
he was very honourably entertained and feasted.
There repaired unto his Lordship during his harbour
at Flushing, divers of the States and companies of
Middelburg, Arnemuiden, and Campvere, who earnestly desired his Lordship's presence in every of
their towns, making great protestation and offers of
their sincere love and affection which the whole island
bare unto her Majesty, so much the rather (as I
gather and find) for that the Lord Admiral brought

thither his navy to their great liking, and greater discouragement of the enemy, for presently Count Maurice being at Middelburg, departed suddenly with all his stuff and furniture to Lillo, and was assured by divers soldiers and mariners that if he enterprised anything against the Queen they would leave him and stick and serve her Majesty.

Whereupon the Lord Admiral, well advising himself before that he would attempt anything for the relieving of Monsieur Sonoy, wrote very honourably and wisely to the Count Maurice, desiring and wishing him to desist his action and enterprise ; which if he would conform himself thereunto her Majesty would be very thankful. Otherwise in not regarding the same, her Majesty should be enforced to relieve them whom she knew and took to be her good friends. Hereupon Count Maurice returned answer by letters with Sir Edward Hoby (who was the messenger) altogether excusing himself, and condemning Monsieur de Sonoy, who did very much forget himself towards him and the rest of the States, whereby he was enforced to proceed as he did ; yet meaning (as I think) to advise himself with the rest of the States to make good satisfaction to her Majesty.

Now the eight of this month the wind coming very aptly about at the North-North-East, my Lord Admiral omitted no time to make his return to our English coasts, and thanked be God is well arrived to Margate road.

To conclude : I wish that this honourable ship, being grounded 12 hours upon the sands, had been as long in fight and trial with the Spaniards in good sea-room, where with the help of the Lord Admiral and the rest of his fleet, every one of us (I hope) should have acquitted ourselves in duties both to God, her Majesty and country.

So meaning no further to trouble you, being glad to understand of your good health, desire that my humble commendations may be presented to the Lord Chancellor, the Lord Treasurer and the Lord Steward.

From aboard the Elizabeth Bonaventure, the fortunate ship where Sir Francis Drake received all his good haps, the 10th of March, 1587.

Your assured friend to command,

H. SEYMOUR.

March 10.—*HOWARD TO WALSYNGHAM.*

[ccix. 15. and I.—Holograph.   Addressed.]

Sir :—Mr. Frobiser is now come in to the road here in Margate, who hath passed up and down in the Narrow Seas to see who passed and whither. He met with 4 hulks that came from Rochelle, who told him for certain that the Prince of Condé is dead,[1] and that they saw the mourning for him, and great sorrow in the town for it.   Within 5 days after word was brought to the town that the King of Navarre was also in great danger.   They were both poisoned much about one time, yet they were not together.   It is but 10 days since they parted from Rochelle.   I pray God the King be not dead. It is too great a loss of the other, if it had pleased God.   I pray God that her Majesty take good care

---

[1] The Prince of Condé died at St. Jean d'Angely on Feb. 24. It was believed then that he had been poisoned, and two servants were executed.   The Princess was also suspected, and was kept in prison for seven years before she was declared innocent.   It is now considered more probable that he died of fever (see the Duc d'Aumale's *Histoire des Princes de Condé*, ii. 179–182).   The report of the poisoning of the King of Navarre seems to have been unfounded.

of herself, for these enemies are become devils,[1] and care not how to kill.

Yesternight there came one to me of purpose from Dunkirk, who doth assure me that on Wednesday last there came a Scottish gentleman out of Spain to the Duke of Parma, and brought a packet from the King and declared that the Spanish forces by sea are for certain to part[2] from Lisbon the 20th of this month with the light moon,[3] and that the number of the fleet when they all do meet, of great and small, will be 210 sails ; and the number of soldiers, besides the mariners, are 36,000.   I am sorry Sir F. Drake is not in more readiness than he is.   I know the fault is not in him.   I pray to God her Majesty do not repent this slack dealings.   It had been good he had been ready, though he had but lien[4] on our coast.   I am afraid he will not be ready in time, do what can be done.   All that cometh out of Spain must concur in one to lie, or else we shall be stirred very shortly with heave and ho.[5]   I fear me ere it be long her Majesty will be sorry that she hath believed some as much as she hath done, but it will be very late.   By all that I can gather it should be Hunter that is come out of Spain.   The party saw the Scottish gentleman, and describeth him much like Hunter.

For her Majesty's four great ships, I am out of hope to see them abroad, what need soever shall be. If things fall out as it is most likeliest, they shall be to keep Chatham Church when they should serve the turn abroad.   I protest before God, I speak not

[1] MS. dyvles.   [2] Depart.
[3] Mowne.   [4] MS. lyne.
[5] MS. hev and o.   Howard seems to have rather affected the phrase. Cf. *Hist. MSS. Com.*, XI. Appendix iii. 124 : ' If you despatch not these things forthwith, I will send for you with heave and ho.'

for myself any ways, but for her Majesty's service and surety; for whensoever they should come, I mean not to change out of her I am in for any ship that ever was made.

Sir, I pray you let me hear from you how the peace is like to go on; for if I may hear in any time that it is not like to come to pass, I will make some provision for the choking of Dunkirk haven, although it serve but for a month; for from thence do I fear most. They look daily at Dunkirk for 1,200 mariners out of France; but if I have knowledge in any time, I hope to stop their coming out, and so the better able to look some other way.

Sir, if her Majesty think that her princely preparation of Sir F. Drake's fleet, and this that I have, should be a hindrance to a peace and that the King of Spain should take it ill, why should not the King of Spain think that her Majesty hath much more cause to think ill of his mighty preparations? It will peradventure be said he hath many ways to employ them, and not to England. That is easily answered, for it is soon known by the victualling; and he never prepares so many soldiers for the Indies. Sir, I will for this time bid you farewell. From Margate road, the 10th of March.

Your assured loving friend,
C. HOWARD.

Sir :—I pray you that there may be order taken for the staying of all shipping in England for a cause that I will write more at large hereafter.

March 13.—*MEMORANDUM AS TO VICTUALLING.*

[**ccix. 16.**—Rough note in the autograph of Lord Burghley.]

The proportion of victualling to the seas:

Nota 28 days to 1 month ; whereof—

Fish days . 10⎫ Whereof 4 Fridays that have but
Flesh days . 16⎭ 4 meals ; so there wants 2 days.[1]
Fish days . 20 meals.
Flesh days . 32 meals.

The fare of fish days for every man per diem :

Biscuit . 1 lb.   Beer . . [1] gallon.
In fish . 1 qr. of stockfish, or the 8th part
of a ling.
In cheese, per diem, 1 qr. of a pound.
In butter, half qr. per diem.

The flesh day :

Beer and biscuit, ut supra.
Flesh, 2 lbs. salt beef per diem, so as every man hath 1 lb. for a meal, and 4 men have 4 lbs. for a meal.

For one day in the week :

A device for bacon for 1 day in a week.
1 lb. of bacon for a man per diem.
A pint of pease for 1 man for a meal.
1 pottle of pease for 4 men.

4,000 cask will serve for 10,000 men for beer and beef for 3 months.

[1] This was ingenious. On Fridays only half allowance was to be issued, so that the saving on four Fridays amounted to whole rations for two days ; and the victuals for twenty-six days served for twenty-eight.

So there will be 3 days in the week—viz. Sunday, Tuesday and Thursday—for beef; and 3 fish days—Wednesday, Friday and Saturday ; and Monday, for bacon and pease.

March 12.—*SUGGESTIONS FOR REDUCING EXPENDITURE.*[1]

[**ccix. 17.**—Noted, in Burghley's hand :—Saving by . . .[2] of beef.]

For the saving of her Majesty 2,666*l.* 13*s.* 4*d.* by altering the provision of beef into other victuals, the manner whereof ensueth.

Every man's victual of beef standeth her Majesty 4*d.* the day, at 2*d.* the pound, besides cask and salt. And so the mess, being 4 persons, amounteth to 16*d.* the day for their meat, besides bread and drink.

By altering that kind of victual as before, to fish, oil and pease, her Majesty's charge will be but 3*d.* for 3 fishes the day, at 10*s.* the hundred of newland-fish ; 2*d.* in oil for the mess the day, and 2*d.* in peasen at 2*s.* the bushel, with one penny upon every mess the day for cask and other charges; which amounteth to in all but unto 8*d.* the day. So do you save the other 8*d.* on every mess the day, which is half the charge that the beef did stand. Which for the 20,000 men aforesaid, according to her Majesty's allowance, did amount unto 5,333*l.* 6*s.* 8*d.* The moiety wherof saved is, as before,

2,666*l.* 13*s.* 4*d.*

---

[1] This is an early instance of the sort of suggestions that all officials are probably familiar with, as well as newspaper readers during the silly season. It is certainly unjust to attach the dis-credit of them to either Burghley or the Queen. Mr. Froude has called the writer a 'miserable scoundrel' (*History*, xii. 369) ; 'ignorant blockhead' would perhaps be more appropriate ; he could not even work his arithmetic correctly.   [2] Torn away.

March 12.—*JOHN HAWKYNS TO BURGHLEY.* (?)

[**ccix. 18.**—Holograph.]

My most honourable and very good Lord :— Although I doubt not but your Lordship is advertised of the coming over of the navy with my Lord Admiral to Margate, yet I thought good your Lordship should see what my Lord doth write, for that daily they consume and call for that which I did always fear.

The Bonaventure, which was condemned before your Lordship for a decayed ship, doth prove far contrary ; yet I desire not they should come to such trials.

I will take order to send my Lord 200 men with speed, if they be to be had in Thames.

I have already made a new shift of sails for the Rainbow, for they have not been renewed since she was made ; and were at the first single, but now double.

If I had known the purpose that is meant for the two hoys, I could have fitted them thereafter ; but it is like they are to sink in some place, or to beat in shoal water with great ordnance. This will be a matter of some charge, therefore I do acquaint your Lordship with it ; for it may be your Lordship is advertised of the purpose.

I do prepare and am doing for 20 great anchors, which is a very great work and costly. So do we take up canvas and other provisions upon credit, which is not the best way. If the service continue, we shall not be able to supply the want without your Lordship's help.

My Lord doth specially commend the Ark Ralegh, which indeed is the best ordered ship that

I have seen for all conditions and purposes, although there be many others most excellent ships.

I would be glad to follow your Lordship's opinion for the hastening of the four great ships, and so in all the rest ; for your Lordship can best discern what is of necessity ; and so praying God long to preserve your Lordship in health, I humbly take my leave.   From my house in Mincing Lane, the 12th of March, 1587.

Your honourable Lordship's humbly to command,
JOHN HAWKYNS.

March 20.—REPORT OF CHARGES.

[**ccix. 25.**—Signed.]

For John Hawkyns :

	£	s.	d.
The charge of the four great ships for one month sea wages, harbour wages, prest and conduct, sea-store, with a supplying of sea-store to the ships serving now at the seas under the charge of the Lord Admiral, and conduct in discharging, is . . .	3,092	10	0

For James Quarles :

	£	s.	d.
The charge of the victual for one month for these 4 ships for 1,900 men is	1,551	13	4
The charge of the victuals for 2,990 men serving under the charge of the Lord Admiral now in the Narrow Seas for one month, is	2,441	16	8
For transportation of these victuals	200	0	0
	4,193	10	0

For these parcels we humbly pray your Lordship to give order to Mr. Peter to make an order for
payment of money,—

	£	s.	d.
To John Hawkyns . £3,092 10 0 }	7,285	0	0
To James Quarles . 4,193 10 0 }			

So the business may proceed according to her
Majesty's pleasure and your Lordship's order.

We also humbly pray your Lordship to be a
mean that the supply of .cordage, canvas, masts,
anchors and such like, may be supplied, whereof
your Lordship hath a note; without the which we
cannot furnish the navy but for small time.

JOHN HAWKYNS.
WILLM. HOLSTOK.
JAMES QUARLES.

March 20.—*VICTUALLING ESTIMATE.*

[ccix. **26.**—Endorsed.]

Sir Francis Drake, two months' victuals:

The victual for two months for
2,900 men to serve in the ships under
the charge of Sir Francis Drake, after
32s. 8d. the man, amounteth to the sum

	£	s.	d.
of	4,736	13	4
And for transportation &c. . .	150	0	0
Sum total	4,886	13	4

Ships with my Lord Admiral, one month's victuals:

For the victualling of one month for
all her Majesty's ships now in the
Narrow Seas under the charge of the
Lord Admiral, and for the four great
ships now at Chatham, being in all

4,890 men, to begin the 21st of April   £   *s.*   *d.*
next and to end the 19th of May ; after
the rate of 16*s.* 4*d.* the man per month,
amounteth to the sum of   .   .   . 3,993 10 0
    And for transportation &c.   .   .   200 0 0

Sum total 4,193 10 0

Sum total of both the victuallings, £9,080   3   4

March 20.—*ESTIMATE OF CHARGES FOR THE
FOUR GREAT SHIPS.*

[ccix. **27.**—Holograph of John Hawkyns.]

An estimate of the charge to prepare four of her
Majesty's great ships to the seas, and the furnishing
of the navy serving under the charge of the Lord
Admiral.

	Men	
The Elizabeth Jonas .	500	
Triumph . .	500	in all 1,900 men.
Bear . . .	500	
Victory . .	400	

                                    £   *s.*   *d.*

For prest and conduct of 1,200
sailors to be had out of sundry shires,
at 8*s.* every man, with the prester's
charges 480 0 0
    For the prest and conduct of 500
gunners and soldiers at 2*s.* 6*d.* the man,
with the prester's charges .   .   .   62 10 0
    For harbour wages of 200 men for
20 days 75 0 0
    For sea-store for the said ships at
50*l.* the ship 200 0 0
    For sea-store to renew the ships'
provision serving with the Lord Admiral in the Narrow Seas .   .   . 500 0 0

	£	s.	d.
For conduct in discharge of the 1,200 men at 7s. the man . . .	420	0	0
For conduct in discharge of the 500 men at 12d. the man	25	0	0
	1,762	10	0

	£	s.	d.
For the sea wages of the 1,900 men abovesaid serving in the said ships, at 14s. the man per month . . .	1,330	0	0
Total	3,092	10	0

JOHN HAWKYNS.

	£	s.	d.
The victual for one month of these 1,900 men serving in the 4 ships abovesaid is, at 16s. 4d. a man per month .	1,551	13	4

March 22.—ESTIMATE OF CHARGES.

[**ccix. 29.**—Signed.]

22nd of March, 1587.

An estimate of the charge of the augmenting of 2 months' charge, to be increased for the ships that are now westward under the charge of Sir Francis Drake, Knight; together with other charges for the furnishing of our four great ships, and our navy abroad under the charge of the Lord Admiral.

Sea wages.

	£	s.	d.
First, for the sea wages of 2,900 men by the space of two months, at 18s.[1] the man; diets, dead shares, and rewards in the same accounted . .	4,060	0	0

[1] So in MS. It should be 14s. for one month, or 28s. for the two months, and is so calculated in the total.

Tonnage.

For the tonnage of the merchant ships taken to serve with her Majesty's ships, being 23 ships for 4 months being esteemed at 400 ton, which is 400*l.* a month 1,600 0 0

£ *s. d.*

Sea-store and Grounding.

For an increase of sea-store for all the ships there, and for the trimming aground with tallow, being all 30 ships with her Majesty, at 10*l.* every ship with one another 300 0 0

Prest and Conduct.

For the prest and conduct of 1,200 sailors which are to serve in her Majesty's four great ships at 8*s.* every man. with the prester's charges . . 480 0 0

For prest and conduct of 500 gunners and sailors at 2*s.* 6*d.* a man, with the prester's charges . . . 62 10 0

Sea-store.

For the sea-store of the said four great ships at 50*l.* every ship . . 200 0 0

For sea-store for to renew the provision in the 24 ships and pinnaces serving in the Narrow Seas under the charge of the Lord Admiral . . 500 0 0

Conduct in discharging.

For conduct in the discharging of the 1,200 men, at 7*s.* every man . . 420 0 0

For conduct in the discharging the 500 men abovesaid, at 12*d.* every man 25 0 0

7,647 10 0

Victuals.

	£	s.	d.
For the victuals of the abovesaid 2,990[1] men for two months serving in the ships westward under the charge of Sir F. Drake, at 32s. 8d. every man	4,736	13	4
For transportation of the said victual	150	0	0
	4,886	13	4
John Hawkyns	7,647	10	0
James Quarles	4,886	13	4
The whole sum	12,534	3	4

JOHN HAWKYNS.
JA. QUARLES.

March 23.—*FENNER TO WALSYNGHAM.*

[ccix. 30, 31.—Holograph. Addressed.]

Right Honourable :—I have sent you the names
noted on the other side of such captains as are here
and have had places heretofore ; as also lieutenants
and ancients.[2] And as there are of them that are
now, if the service go forward, to proceed as
captains, their experience and deserts deserving the
same, so there are a great number of serviceable
gentlemen and soldiers that are to step up into
place ; which is left undone, until perfect directions
from your Honour of the proceedings be known ;
which I pray God be not pretermitted, but to take
the opportunity of time. And thus, as one in all
duties wishing most happily unto your Honour, I

[1] The number should be 2,900 ; 2,990 agrees neither with
the statement p. 64, nor with the arithmetic here.
[2] MS. auntients.

commit your Honour unto the Almighty. From aboard her Majesty's good ship the Nonpareil, Plymouth, this 23rd of March, 1587.

Your Honour's always to command,

THOMAS FENNER.

Captains in her Majesty's ships :

Sir Francis Drake, Knight, General in the Revenge

Thomas Fenner, Vice-Admiral in the Nonpareil

Robert Crosse, Rear-Admiral in the Hope

Edward Fenner   ,,   in the Swiftsure

William Fenner   ,,   in the Aid

Captains:

Platt	Erisey [1]	Hawes [1]
Marchant [1]	Hawkyns [1]	Baker [1]
Whyte [1]	Sydenham [1]	Pepper
Poole [1]	Rivers [1]	Wilson [1]
Spindelow [1]	Yonge [1]	Seager [1]
Acton [1]	Whiddon [1]	Harris [1]
Polwhele	Roche	Flicke [1] } both being
	Manington [1]	Lancaster [1] } in London

Lieutenants:

Scudamore	Jugge	Frost
Williams	Rottenbury	Nichols
Martin	Vernothrey	

Ensigns:

Strowde	Tether	Nicholson
Snicklowe	Tomson	

[1] Commanded a ship during the summer. The others, as well as the lieutenants &c., presumably served in some capacity, but it has not been recorded. A few of the names, which there is no way of checking, seem impossible in the spelling here given.

Sergeants :

Moon	Fenner	Judson
Deckham	Jones	Gowen
Austin		

March 29.—*EARL OF SUSSEX TO SIR F. WALSYNGHAM.*

[ccix. 39.—Signed. Addressed.]

It may please your Honour :—Whereas I sent forth a boat for discovery, and that the weather grew so stormy and tempestuous that they were not able to continue and abide the seas, but to return with small advertisements, nevertheless I have thought good to send unto your Honour herein enclosed the note of the captain's declaration. I have also sent unto you herein the declaration of the master of a hoy, who came into this harbour yesterday from Newhaven.[1]

I have also thought good to advertise your Honour that this morning I have sent a bark, and therein one in whom I repose some trust, to learn news and also to discover what he may. And for that I perceive these actions will not well be brought to pass, without some action by other matters to colour the same, I have put into her fifty quarters of wheat, and have willed him to make two ports, whereof St. Malo, or some port near to the same, to be one, the other as he may, and both to be as wind and weather will serve.

[The rest of the letter refers to other matters, especially the examination of Mr. Richard Cotton of Warblington, described as 'an obstinate recusant.' The letter is signed at ' Portsmouth, the 29th of March, 1588.']

[1] Havre.

[ccix. 39, I.—Copy.   First enclosure in Lord Sussex's
letter of March 29.]

Captain Story his note of the voyage made in a small boat for discovery the 10th of March, 1588.

Imprimis, upon Sunday, being the 10th of March, the boat was brought on ground to be trimmed and made ready for the voyage.

Item, on Tuesday at night, she being made ready, we hauled her out into the channel, pretending to have gone the same night to sea ; but the wind was easterly.

On Wednesday morning we rowed out of the haven, the wind being easterly ; with sail and oars, we gat St. Helen's Road, were we rid with the wind at South-East and could not get out until it was Thursday morning.

On Thursday, we rowed to sea as far as Dunnose, where we descried a fleet of ships to the windward, the wind being easterly, and bare towards them with sail and oars till we fetched up one of them, which was a ship of London come from Rochelle, whom we asked what the other were, and he said they were hulks bound home from Brouage.

News from Rochelle he could tell none, but that the Prince of Condé was dead.   Then the wind came to the North-East, and we went over with the coast of France, so near the East as we could lie, thinking we could have fetched to Seine Head, but we could but fetch to the Bay of Hogges,[1] for that wind blew so and that sea went so high, that we could maintain no sail save our main course [2] very low set.

On Friday morning we saw the land, which was between Barfet-nes [3] and the Bay of Hogges, and sailed alongst the shore till we came to Cherbourg,[4]

[1] La Hogue.
[2] Cape Barfleur.
[3] MS. mayne crosse.
[4] MS. Sherbrooke.

where we met with two tall ships of Cherbourg bound for Spain, as we think; but we could not speak with them by reason of the foul weather. And from thence we went to Alderney, thinking to have gotten some harbour; but the weather was so extreme foul that we could not. Yet the same night we got to Herm,[1] where we rid Saturday, Sunday and Monday, with very foul weather, not able to look out. Yet I sent over to that castle to know if there were any news, and the soldiers came aboard and told us that there were many great fleet passed by, both of Frenchmen and Flemings, both to the eastward and to the west. Then the weather being fair, we came to sea and met a southerly wind, that blew so sore that we were able to maintain no sail but our main course.[2]

On Wednesday morning we met with a great fleet of ships betwixt Portland and the Isle of Wight, fifty sail or thereabouts. Five of them gave us chase, and the headmost man of them we bare with him and spake with him and asked of him whence the rest were. He said they were all Dutch ships bound for Brouage. Other news they could tell none. And from them, we came in at Needles and went to speak with the men of war at St. Helen's, and so came in.

[ccix. 39, II.—Copy.   Second enclosure.]

The declaration of Robert Keble, master of a hoy, part of Ipswich and part of Harwich, called the William, 28th of March 1588, who came from New-haven upon Tuesday last.

He saith he arrived at Newhaven upon Saturday next shall be a fortnight, being the 16th of March, laden with coals; and the next day after his arrival

---

[1] MS. Arme.   [2] It is here written 'course.'

a Frenchman told him that the French King was marching towards Normandy and the sea coast; and other told him that it was against the King of Navarre.   And that there was a flyboat of Danske,[1] which came from Cadiz in Spain, who arrived at Newhaven this day sennight, and had been at sea about 18 days, who saith that all the French shipping is stayed in Spain and Portugal, for the service of the King of Spain; and thinketh that all other ships be stayed, for he himself had been stayed, if he had not stolen away.   Also he saith that a Frenchman did swear to him by God that the King of Spain would come, and that they would be ready the 24th of this month; and the man answered 'Tush, he will not come yet.'   'Yes,' saith he.

2. He also saith that he spake with a man of Marseilles, who did also affirm the same and said that there was in that fleet 24 great galleasses; and they both affirmed that the whole fleet was between 4 and 500 sail.

3. He also saith that he heard both the Scots and French say that they looked for them of Spain daily; and that when they came, they would join with them.

There were now, at his being at Newhaven, 56 or 57 sail of Scots there, who were there before his coming, and, as they said, bound for Brouage; but whether, he could not justly learn; but they might have gone out at his coming away, if they would; and therefore, why they tarry, he knoweth not.

He saith the Scots fell out with him and caused him to pay 30 crowns to the church there and other places, by order of the Governor's officers; and that the Governor would not hear him speak for his answer and trial.

He saith that the Scots said unto him that if

[1] Danzig.

they might catch him at sea, they would heave him and his overboard, and all other Englishmen, and would pull their hearts out of their bodies ; calling them ' English dogs,' saying they would be revenged of the blood of their queen.

The Governor of Newhaven doth not trust the townsmen there, and is now building of a fort to command the town, and is a very hard man against Englishmen.

He saith that he heard him that came from Marseilles say that Andrew Doria, Prince of Mellita,[1] was come unto Lisbon with a great sort of galleys, and should be admiral of the King of Spain his fleet, and that, as he remembereth, the number of the Spanish army should be 50 thousand.

March 30.—*DRAKE TO THE COUNCIL.*

[cciх. 40.—Signed.   Addressed.]

Right honourable and my very good Lords :— Understanding by your good Lordships' letters her Majesty's good inclination for the speedy sending of these forces here unto the seas for the defence [2] of the enemy ; and that, of her Majesty's great favour and your Lordships' good opinion, you have made choice of me (although the least of many) to be as an actor in so great a cause, I am most humbly to beseech my most gracious Sovereign and your good Lordships to hear my poor opinion with favour, and so to judge of it according to your great wisdoms.

[1] Presumably Melfi ; but none of the family served in the Armada.   It will be noticed, too, that the numbers given in this report are grossly exaggerated.
[2] The fending off.

If her Majesty and your Lordships think that
the King of Spain meaneth any invasion in England,
then doubtless his force is and will be great in
Spain; and thereon he will make his groundwork
or foundation, whereby the Prince of Parma may
have the better entrance, which, in mine own
judgment, is most to be feared.   But if there may
be such a stay or stop made by any means of this
fleet in Spain, that they may not come through the
seas as conquerors—which, I assure myself, they
think to do—then shall the Prince of Parma have
such a check thereby as were meet.

To prevent this I think it good that these forces
here should be made as strong as to your Honours'
wisdoms shall be thought convenient, and that for
two special causes :—First, for that they are like to
strike the first blow; and secondly, it will put great
and good hearts into her Majesty's loving subjects
both abroad and at home; for that they will be
persuaded in conscience that the Lord of all strength
will put into her Majesty and her people courage
and boldness not to fear any invasion in her own
country, but to seek God's enemies and her
Majesty's where they may be found; for the Lord
is on our side, whereby we may assure ourselves
our numbers are greater than theirs.   I must crave
pardon of your good Lordships again and again,
for my conscience hath caused me to put my pen
to the paper; and as God in his goodness hath put
my hand to the plough, so in his mercy it will never
suffer me to turn back from the truth.

My very good Lords, next under God's mighty
protection, the advantage and gain of time and
place will be the only and chief means for our good;
wherein I most humbly beseech your good Lordships
to persevere as you have began, for that with fifty
sail of shipping we shall do more good upon their

own coast, than a great many more will do here at home ; and the sooner we are gone, the better we shall be able to impeach them.

There is come home, since the sending away of my last messenger, one bark whom I sent out as an espial, who confirmeth those intelligences whereof I have advertised your Lordships by him ; and that divers of those Biscayans are abroad upon that coast wearing English flags, whereof there are made in Lisbon three hundred with the red cross, which is a great presumption, proceeding of the haughtiness and pride of the Spaniard, and not to be tolerated by any true natural English heart.

I have herein enclosed sent this note unto your Lordships, to consider of our proportions in powder, shot and other munitions, under the hand of the surveyor's clerk of the ordnance ; the which pro- portion in powder and shot for our great ordnance in her Majesty's ships is but for one day and half's service, if it be begun and continued as the service may require ; and but five lasts[1] of powder for 24 sail of the merchant ships, which will scant be sufficient for one day's service as divers occasions may be offered. Good my Lords, I beseech you to consider deeply of this ; for it importeth but the loss of all.

I have stayed this messenger somewhat the longer for the hearing of this Dutchman who came lately out of Lisbon, and hath delivered these ad- vertisements herein enclosed, under his hand the 28th of this March, before myself and divers justices.

I have sent unto your good Lordships the note of such powder and munition as are delivered unto us for this great service ; which, in truth, I judge to be just a third part of that which is needful ; for if we should want it when we shall have most

[1] The last was twenty-four barrels of one cwt. each.

need thereof, it will be too late to send to the Tower for it. I assure your Honours it neither is or shall be spent in vain. And thus resting at your Honours' further directions, I humbly take my leave of your good Lordships. From Plymouth, the 30th of March, 1588.

Your good Lordships' very
ready to be commanded,
FRA. DRAKE.

March 26.—NOTE OF POWDER.

[ccix. 40, I.—Enclosed in Drake's letter of March 30 ; with autograph postscript.]

Powder remaining aboard her Majesty's ships appointed to the seas in her Majesty's service under the charge of Sir Francis Drake, Knight, viz.:—

Powder : Aboard

The Revenge	$1\frac{1}{2}$ lasts 2 cwt.	
Nonpareil	$1\frac{1}{2}$ lasts 5 cwt.	
Hope	$1\frac{1}{2}$ lasts 1 cwt.	
Swiftsure	1 last	
Aid	$\frac{1}{2}$ last	$6\frac{1}{2}$ lasts

Remaining in the castle of Plymouth for the furnishing of the merchant ships likewise appointed to the seas under the charge of the said Sir Francis . . . . . 5 lasts

$11\frac{1}{2}$ lasts

Jo. DAVEY.

Forget not 500 muskets and at least one thousand arrows for them ; with such other munition, as by the particulars you shall find most wanting and best to be procured.   FRA. DRAKE.

MEMORANDA

[**ccix. 41.**—Rough notes in Burghley's autograph. Not dated nor endorsed.]

One thousand mariners to be brought to the ships, 1,075*l.*

That musters be made of all the watermen upon the Thames.

That letters be written to $\begin{cases} \text{Essex} \\ \text{Kent} \\ \text{Suffolk} \\ \text{Cambridge} \end{cases}$

That all ships be stayed in every port of the realm.

Essex	.	.	.	.	1,000
Kent	.	.	.	.	1,000
Sussex	.	.	.	.	500
Hampshire	.	.	.	500

April 2.—WM. COURTENEY [1] *TO WALSYNGHAM.*

[**ccix. 59.**—Engrossed.]

To the Right Honourable Sir Francis Walsyngham, Knight, Principal Secretary to her Majesty.

May it please your Honour to take into her Majesty's service certain hoys of the burden of 120 tons and upward apiece, to the number of 15 or 20; which hoys will carry, to their burden, cannon,

---

[1] A master mariner of Dover, whose ship, the Katharine, had been taken by a privateer of St. Malo in or about 1580. His name frequently occurs in reference to proceedings, about this capture, in the Admiralty Court.

demi-cannon, culverin, demi-culverin and saker ; for that the number of mariners will be few ; for the same hoys will not ask above 20 or 25 mariners apiece, and 50 or 60 soldiers in every hoy with the small shot. And these 20 sail of hoys shall not stand her Majesty in so much charges as the setting out of 6 sail of ships ; and 500 mariners will serve the 20 sail of hoys, and 800 will not serve 5 sail of ships ; and these 20 sail of hoys shall do as good and rather better service than 40 sail of ships shall.

Imprimis, 15 or 20 sail of hoys to be set forth with their spar-deck or netting to be made musket free by the sides, from the mast afterward, and with light spardeck or netting overhead for the safeguard of the men.

Item, these 15 or 20 sail of hoys, to be set in order five and five in a rank, and to be half shot one from another, will make as good service for the enemy as 40 sail of ships ; for that if they may have any wind to turn them, they will shoot twice to a ship's once, and the more wind the better they are.

Item, they are good to be set foremost of a fight, that shall happen if the enemy come ; and for the Narrow Seas, your Honour cannot desire better ships than these hoys.

Item, I will not have above 4 or 6 guns in a hoy ; for that 5 or 6 men will serve to stand by her sails, and the rest of her mariners to help the gunners to traverse the ordnance ; and to have the soldiers stand by their small shot.

Item, your Honour cannot have a ship of 100 or 120, but they must have 10, 15 or 20 gunners, and 150 or 200 men in a ship, besides others to help to tackle her about ; which in every hoy 20 mariners will serve for all turns.

Wherefore if any service in her Majesty's affairs be required, if it shall please your Honour to accept of my poor service in these hoys, I will rest at her Majesty's or your Honour's commandment.

Your Honour's most humble at commandment,
WILLM. COURTENEY.

April 5.—THE MAYOR AND ALDERMEN OF POOLE TO THE COUNCIL.

[ccix. 70.—Signed. Addressed.]

Our obedient duties unto your Honours in most humble wise remembered :—Your Honours' letters of the first of this present month of April to us directed, we have received the third of the same ; the contents whereof is that her Majesty doth understand that there are a good number of very apt and serviceable ships and vessels appertaining to this town, and that we should make choice of one serviceable ship of the burden of 60 tons, and one pinnace, to be furnished for two months, to be in a readiness by the 25th day of this present month ; and further importing that some merchants of this town have set forth certain ships in warlike sort, by way of reprisal, whereby they have received no small profit. May it therefore please your Honours to be advertised that there is but one ship in this harbour at this present above the burden of threescore tons ; which ship is called the Primrose of Poole, and is of the burden of 120 tons or thereabouts, being ready rigged and victualled to depart for the New-found-land, having in her two sakers, four minions, one falcon, and two falconets, with shot for the same and 500 pound weight of powder, and eight calivers. And for a pinnace, there is one small bark of this town, of the burden of 30 tons or thereabouts, called the Elephant, able to serve for that purpose, if she had munition and other furniture to set her forth. Both the which we have made stay of until we shall receive further order from your Honours. And for the merchants of this town there is not one that hath set forth any ship by way of reprisal, or otherwise gotten anything that way. Our humble suit and petition unto your good Lordships now is, that it may please the same to consider of the great decay and disability of this poor town, by reason of embargoes, want of traffic, loss at sea, and by pirates, which have and do continually lie at Studland Bay, being the mouth of this harbour, robbing both our poor neighbours and others resorting to this town. And lately having been at great charge in making of necessary provision for the defence of the enemy, whereby we are utterly unable to perform your Lordships' commandment for setting forth of a ship and pinnace, most humbly beseeching your Honours to discharge us of the same, being compelled to set down the truth of our poor estate to our great grief. Wishing that we were as able as willing in all dutiful and obedient services as becometh good and faithful subjects, we most humbly pray for the preservation of your Honours in prosperous estate, long to continue. From Poole, the 5th of April, 1588.

Your Honours' most dutiful at commandment,

JOHN BERGMAN, Mayor.

WILLM. NEWMAN.	JOHN BRAMBLE.
WILLM. DICKER.	EDWARD MAN.
ROGER MUNDLEY.	WM. REDE.
	THOMAS TUPPER.

April 6.—SIR G. CAREY[1] TO WALSYNGHAM.

[ccix. 71.—Signed. Addressed.]

My duty to your Honour humbly remembered :—
Having received letters from the Lords of her
Majesty's Council the fifth of this present, by the
which it appeareth that the preparation of the
Spanish forces are continued, and thereupon their
resistance intended in their honourable wisdoms, by
arming a competent number of ships out of the
maritime cities and places of good shipping within
this realm ; and that it seemeth an advertisement
hath been exhibited to her Majesty that there are a
good number of very able and serviceable ships
appertaining to the merchants and inhabitants of
this island ; whereupon their Lordships have thought
good to require of the inhabitants of this island the
furnishing of a warlike ship and pinnace, fit and able
for service, furnished for two months with victuals,
mariners, munition and other necessary provisions,
by the 25th of this present, to be in readiness to
attend the Lord Admiral :

It may please your Honour to understand that
—albeit I shall, for mine own part, be most ready,
by any service, to testify my dutiful and zealous
affection towards her Majesty and my native
country, as also the inhabitants of this place are
most desirous, by all possible means, to maintain
her Majesty's good opinion so graciously conceived
of them ; yet for that the island is utterly unprovided
of any warlike ships or vessels fit for employment in
such services, the greatest thereunto belonging not
exceeding the burden of seventy tons, and that the

[1] The eldest son of Lord Hunsdon, whom he succeeded in
1596. At this time he was Captain of the Isle of Wight.

insufficiency and great poverty of the merchants of
Newport is such (being rather a poor market than a
merchant-like town) as may hardly extend to the
furnishing of one quarter of a ship fit in so warlike
manner to be set forth—I have thought it fit first to
advertise your Honour of the error of that information by the which I conceive the direction of
your letters grew of this place,[1] before I would
terrify the minds of this country with so great a
charge, neither usual nor accustomed, which might
breed discontentment and work no effect, seeing
they continue the burden of continual charge in
their daily preparations for defence of this place.

Wherefore I shall humbly beseech your Honour
to acquaint the Lords with the poor state of this
country, [and [2]] the difficulty of effecting their
commandment; and if they shall [will that [2]] we
proceed with this preparation, to send me your
further direction, whether by way of subsidy, or in
what sort this charge intended should be levied;
being of opinion that my authority will neither
stretch to charge them with a matter of so great
innovation, nor that it may be done without the
general taxation of the island, which I conceive is
not meant, in respect the like is not done by the
inland men of the mainland. Besides, out of this
place no shipping hath been sent by way of reprisal
at any time, saving only by myself; and having
sustained more loss than gain thereby, I hope it be
not their Honours' pleasure to charge me with what
I shall be so hardly able to bear.

And so presuming to crave from your Honour
farther direction, in a matter so strange and unapt
to be offered to this place, before I shall proceed, I

[1] Information concerning this place, which I conceive has
caused the directions given in your letters.
[2] Words omitted in MS.

shall rest most ready to perform what may be in my power to accomplish in this and in all other matters, upon your farther honourable directions ; and so humbly commit you to the tuition of the only Almighty. From Carisbrooke Castle, this 6th of April. Your Honour's most humbly
and assured to command,
GEORGE CAREY.

April 7.—HOWARD TO WALSYNGHAM.

[ccix. 74.—Holograph. Addressed.]

Sir :—By your other letter I find her Majesty cannot be brought to have for her surety, to lie near unto her, the 4,000 footmen and the 1,000 horse. I am sorry her Majesty is so careless of this most dangerous time. I fear me much, and with grief I think it, that her Majesty relieth upon a hope that will deceive her and greatly endanger her ; and then will it not be her money nor her jewels that will help ; for as they will do good in time, so will they help nothing for the redeeming of time being lost.

For the setting out of the galley,[1] I think there is no man of judgment but doth think it most meet for her to be abroad now, being summer ; and when should she sail if not at such a time as this is? Either she is fit now to sail, or fit for the fire, and I will never hereafter wish her Majesty to be at the charge of the keeping of her, for I hope never in my time to see so great cause for her to be used. I dare say her Majesty will look that men should

---

[1] The galley Bonavolia. It will be seen (*post*, Borough to Walsyngham, July 28) that she proved utterly useless, and at the critical moment of the campaign had to be sent into the river as unable to keep the sea.

fight for her, and I know they will. At this time the King of Spain doth not keep any ship at home either of his own, or any other, that he can by any means get for money. Well, I pray heartily for a peace, for I see that which should be the ground of an[1] honourable war will never appear; for sparing and war have no affinity together.

Sir, touching the releasing of the Scottish ships and the French,[2] in my opinion it were not amiss to have them stayed a while; and better to have them stay there, than for me to stay them when they are come out; for I know for certain, there is none of the Scots nor French but they carry in their ships Englishmen and colour them for Scots; but for the Scots that are to go into Scotland, they may be suffered to depart; but for the French, I pray let us stay as well as the King of Spain. He hath stayed all, but with their will; for I am sure a great number of them went of purpose. I am afraid we shall find them all false in France, from the highest.

Sir,[3] the great Swede[4] that is stayed, and hath goodly masts in her, and most fittest for her Majesty, otherwise her Majesty should have been fain this next year to have sent a ship of her own for masts into the East Countries,[5] which would have been a great charge, I mean as soon as I can, to send her up to Chatham or to Blackwall; but I do assure you the chiefest matter of all is that we keep them from serving the King of Spain's turn. There be many things else in her that will serve well the turn now; but it must be considered how they shall be contented; for I mean not in this time to let any such ship to pass into Spain. She is a very great ship, and well appointed with ordnance;

---

[1] MS. a honourable. [2] Cf. *ante*, p. 127.
[3] As to the great Swede &c. It is a common Elizabethan idiom.
[4] MS. Swethen. [5] Danzig and the neighbourhood.

she hath many things in her, and I believe for
certain, much belonging to Spaniards. I would
wish when she cometh up, that some order might
be taken for her unlading, and then to return to
me to serve; and so, for this time, I leave you to
the Almighty to bless you with health. Margate,
Easter day. Your loving friend to use,

C. HOWARD.

*April 7.—THE MAYOR AND ALDERMEN OF
KINGSTON-UPON-HULL TO THE COUNCIL.*

[ccix. 75.—Signed. Addressed.]

Most Honourable, our most humble duties
remembered :—We have received your Lordships'
letters by David Jenkyns, her Majesty's pursuivant,
dated at Greenwich the first of this instant month,
wherein your Honours do require us to make
choice of two serviceable and good ships, not to
be under the burden of three score tons, and of
one pinnace ; and to cause the same presently to be
put in a readiness and furnished for two months, with
victuals, mariners, munition, and other necessary
provision and furniture, by the 25th of this present
month of April, to join with her Majesty's navy in
the seas, or to be otherwise employed as we shall
receive further directions from your Honours or
from the Lord Admiral of England.

May it therefore please your good Lordships to
be advertised that, before the receipt of your Lordships' said letter, all the mariners now in the town
any way able to serve, to the number of ninety
and four, were and are pressed the sixth of this
present month, to serve in her Majesty's navy, by
Christopher Chapman, by virtue of a commission
under the Great Seal of England, directed to John
Hawkyns, dated at Westminster the 2nd of February

in the two and twenty year of her Majesty's reign ;
and of a deputation from the said John Hawkyns to
the said Christopher Chapman, bearing date the first
of April, *Anno Domini* 1588; which said mariners
were appointed by him to be at Chatham the 20th
day of this instant month.   And forasmuch as all
the best ships meet for service belonging to this port
be abroad in the parts beyond the seas and at
London, and the town destitute of mariners at this
present (as appeareth by a note hereinclosed[1]), we
are no way able, as most willingly we would, to
accomplish your Lordships' appointment in so short
time, until God send the ships and mariners (now
being abroad) to be comen home.   Whereof we
have thought it our duties (in most humble manner)
to certify your Honours.   Nevertheless when it
shall please God to send some better store of shipping
and men home, we shall, to the uttermost of our
powers, show all readiness and willing disposition
to the performance thereof, as becometh good and
dutiful subjects, upon further direction from your
Lordships, and warrant for taking of such ships and
men as shall be thought meet, with all other furniture
meet for that service.   And thus most humbly we
take our leaves.   Kingston upon Hull, the 7th day
April, 1588.

Your Lordships' humbly at commandment,

WILLAM BRAYE, Mayor.

WILLM. WILSON.   JOHN THORNETON.
EDWARD WAKEFIELDE.   WILLM. GEE.
LEONARD WYLLAN.   JOHN SMYTHE.
LUKE THORSCROS.   ROBT. GAYTON.
ROBART DALTON.

[1] This enclosed note (75, I.) is a statement of the names of the
ships and number of mariners belonging to the town of Kingston-
on-Hull, which are at present on distant voyages ; with the
number of mariners pressed into the navy.

April 8.—*HOWARD TO BURGHLEY.*

[ccix. 78.—Holograph. Addressed.]

My honourable and very good Lord :—I thought good to put your Lordship in remembrance how necessary it is to have a better proportion of victual than for one month, considering the time and the service that is likely to fall out ; and what danger it might breed if our want of victual should be at the time of service.[1] We shall be now victualled, beginning the 20th of this April, unto the 18th of May, at which time the last month's victual doth end ; and by the advertisements that giveth the largest time for the coming out of the Spanish forces, is the midst of May, being the 15th. Then have we three days' victual. If it be fit to be so, it passeth my reason. I think there is none that will venture to carry these ships to Portsmouth[2] under a month's victual. My Lord, this would[3] be cared for in time ; for whensoever our victual shall come, it will ask 4 or 5 days, the taking in of it ; and the weather may so fall out as in 10 days we shall scantly take it in. I think since ever there were ships in this realm it was never heard of that but a month's victual was prepared for to victual withal. King Harry, her Majesty's father, never made a lesser proportion of supply than 6 weeks[4] ; and yet there was a marvellous help upon any extremity ; for there was ever provisions at Portsmouth, and also at Dover ; and his baking and brewing there ; so as, for the service then, which

[1] This is exactly what did happen. See *post*, Darell to Burghley, July 22.
[2] MS. Porchmouth.   [3] Should.
[4] Howard's information as to the practice in King Harry's time was strangely at fault. See Introduction.

was only for France, it was ever at hand upon any necessity.

My good Lord, let me be borne withal for the writing this plainly. It is my duty; and your Honour knoweth what danger want in such a time may do, and how people are disposed upon want to be mutinous; yet have I great cause to think they would suffer much hardness before they would do so. My Lord, I think there was never a more willing company to venture their lives in her Majesty's service than be here. Therefore it were pity they should lack at the time of service. If it be thought fit for us to be victualled for a longer time, it would[1] be gone in hand withal.

The Ark is arrived this morning here at Margate, wonderfully well trimmed and mended of her leak, which was a bolt forgotten to be driven in, and the outside covered with pitch, so it could not be seen; and when the sea had washed it off, then brake in the leak; and she was not well caulked in any place, but now most perfect. So I end to trouble your Lordship any further, praying God to send you health with your little strength. Margate Road, the 8th of April.

Your Lordship's most assured at command,

C. HOWARD.

.

April 9.—THE MAYOR OF LYME REGIS TO THE COUNCIL.

[**ccix. 81.**—Signed. Addressed.]

Right honourable Lords, our duties in most humble manner remembered:—It may please your Honours to understand that your honourable letters

---

[1] Should.

of the first of this April concerning making choice, putting in a readiness, and furnishing of certain ship-ping to serve under the conduct of Sir Francis Drake, Knight, were received the third of this said April, at 8 of the clock at night; upon receipt whereof— for that there was not at the present, nor as yet, any ship here at home of the burden of 60 tons, but three small vessels far under that burden—we have made choice of one of the best and fittest of the same vessels for a pinnace, being handsome for the purpose and of the burden of 40 tons or thereabouts, called the Revenge of Lyme, whereof is owner and captain Richard Bedford. The which bark we have caused and appointed to be manned with thirty good mariners, and furnished for two months of victuals, munition, and other furniture, as with minions, falcons, fowlers, muskets, calivers, and with all other necessary provision for the wars. And so being furnished in a readiness, shall (by God's grace), with wind and weather convenient, be sent unto her Majesty's navy at Plymouth, by the time limited by the said letters accordingly.

And as concerning order for the levying of this charge—The said three towns of Lyme, Axminster and Chard, upon conference had together of the matter, have agreed that the whole charge thereof should only rise upon those persons amongst us that are set in subsidy to her Majesty, proportionably; all which persons so set in subsidy do yield here-unto, saving certain persons of Axminster aforesaid, of sufficient ability, which refuse. Whereupon our humble request unto your Honours is that your Lordships would take further direction concerning those persons of Axminster so refusing, that they might likewise be contributory with us in the premises accordingly. And furthermore, we finding amongst us, of the said three towns, none that have received any benefit by reprisals, except one stranger very lately come in amongst us ; as also, divers of our merchants having received of late great losses in foreign countries, and chiefly in France, do humbly request your Honours that if hereafter we shall be further charged in like sort as afore, that we might by your honourable direction (to be taken in that behalf) have aid therein by others sufficient, dwelling in the towns near ad-joining and trading amongst us.   Thus leaving further to trouble your Lordships, do commit the same to the protection of the most Highest.   From Lyme Regis, this 9th of April, *Anno Domini* 1588.

Your Lordships' at commandment,
with all obedience,
JOHN JONES, Mayor.

April 10.—*A NOTE OF CHARGES.*

[ccix. 82.—Copy.]

A note of the charge of one month's wages and victuals for all her Majesty's ships and other vessels that serve under the charge of the Lord Admiral.

Ships at sea with the Lord Admiral :
First, for the sea wages of 2,990 men for one month of 28 days, serving under the charge of the Lord Admiral ; to begin the 11th day of March last, and to end the 7th of April following, both days included, at 14s. the man, *per mensem* 2,093 0 0

Elizabeth Jonas, Triumph, Bear, Victory :
For the sea wages of 1,900 to serve for one month of 28 days in her

Majesty's said four great ships;
to begin the 19th of May, 1588,
and to end the 15th of June, both
days included, after the said rate
of 14*s.* the man, *per mensem,* is .

£   *s.*   *d.*

1,330   0   0

Sum 3,423*l.*, which was paid unto Mr. Hawkyns
the 8th of May, 1588.

Ships with the Lord Admiral:
For the sea victuals for one month
of 28 days, for 2,990 men; to
begin the 19th of May, and to
end the 25th of June, 1588, both
days included, at 16*s.* 4*d.* the
man, *per mensem*   .   .   .

£   *s.*   *d.*

2,441   16   8

The 4 great ships:
For the sea victual of one month
of 28 days, for 1,900 men serving
in the four great ships; to begin
the 19th of May, and to end the
15th of June, both days included,
at 16*s.* 4*d.* the man, *per mensem* .

1,551   13   4

For transportation of the said
victuals   .   .   .   .   .

200   0   0

Sum 4,193*l.* 10*s.*, which was paid to him[1] the
13th of April, 1588.

C. HOWARD.   JOHN HAWKYNS.
                           JAS. QUARLES.

April 10.—*BURGHLEY TO WALSYNGHAM.*

[**ccix. 83.**—Holograph.   Addressed.]

Sir:—I cannot express my pain newly increased
in all my left arm. My spirits are even now so

---

[1] Quarles.

extenuated, as I have no mind towards anything but to groan with my pain. Therefore pardon me for not answering to you.

I am sorry to see more respect had to accidents than to the substance. Surely, Sir, as God will be best pleased with peace, so in nothing can her Majesty content her realm better than in procuring of peace; which if it cannot be had, yet is she excused afore God and the world. I have received many letters from the Lord Cobham urging my furtherance for resolution[1] of things; but I can only answer his expectation with my prayers. I am bold to send you two letters from Robert Cecill. When you have leisure to read them, I refer the longest to your consideration; only I would not that thereby we should be made slower in our preparations.

If you have an alphabet in cipher which I sent to her Majesty by Windebank,[2] to decipher Sir Edward Stafford's letters to her, I pray you let me have the use of it but for a day or two, and I will return it again.

And so, even forced with pain, even from my arm to my heart, I end.   10th of April, 1588.

Yours most assured,
W. BURGHLEY.

[1] Settlement.

[2] Thomas Windebank was in 1560 travelling tutor and governor to Burghley's elder son Thomas, afterwards first Earl of Exeter. In 1568 he was appointed Clerk of the Signet, and so continued till the death of the Queen. On his retirement, he was knighted by James I. Sir Francis Windebank, Secretary of State under Charles I, was his son.

April 11.—*THE MAYOR AND CITIZENS OF EXETER TO THE COUNCIL.*

[ccix. 84.—Signed. Addressed.]

Our most humble and bounden duties remembered :—Having received your Honours' letters for the setting forth of three ships and a pinnace, to attend on Sir Francis Drake, we caused a present view to be taken of all our shipping, but found none left fit for that service, saving two only bound for Newfoundland, which were gotten out of the haven, and being still upon the coast are now stayed for this purpose ; which ships being of good burden, Sir Francis Drake, whom we have made it known unto, accepteth, rather than three others of lesser portage. But by reason your Honours' letters are directed only to Exeter and Topsham, all the rest of the places and creeks belonging to the Port of Exeter, whereunto the most number and best ships of the whole harbour doth belong, do allege that because they are not specially named in your Honours' letters, this service concerneth them not ; whereas in truth, there is but one serviceable ship of the said harbour in all, belonging in part to some of the inhabitants of this city, namely the Rose of Exeter, of the burden of one hundred tons or more ; which, being one of the two ships aforesaid, together with a fine pinnace, we mind, according to your Honours' direction, to cause to be thoroughly furnished and prepared by the appointed time, although the same will be to our very great charge ; most humbly beseeching your Honours to direct your honourable letters unto Topsham, Kenton, Exmouth, Lympstone, Sidmouth, Seaton, Colyton, Dawlish, Teignmouth, Tiverton and Collumpton, for the preparing of that other ship so stayed, or some other like, for the better furtherance of this her Majesty's service, which God prosper. To whose most gracious protection we most humbly recommend your Honours, with all humble dutifulness. Exon, the 11th of April, 1588.

> Your Lordships' most dutiful and
> humble at commandment,
> The Mayor and Citizens of Exeter,
> Jo. PERYAM, Mayor.
> G. PERYAM.   NICHOLAS MARTIN.
> GEOFFREY THOMAS.   RICHARD PROUZ.[1]

April 12.—*THE MAYOR AND ALDERMEN OF KING'S LYNN TO THE COUNCIL.*

[ccix. 87.—Signed.   Addressed.]

Right Honourable :—After we, the Mayor, Aldermen, and Company of the borough of King's Lynn, had received your honourable letters which were directed to this town of King's Lynn and the town of Blakeney, concerning the furnishing of two ships of war, either of them of the burden of 60 tons at the least, and one pinnace fit for that service, we had conference with some of the chiefest of the said town of Blakeney, and with some of the towns of Cley and Wiveton, which be members of the same town of Blakeney, and we find that they are unwilling to be at any charge near the furnishing of a ship. We sent also to the town of Wells, which is a member of our port, a town very well furnished with shipping, within which there be many rich men inhabiting ; but they have denied altogether to contribute to our charge ; and we made diligent enquiry if any of our port had sent forth any ship of war or

---

[1] The modern name is Prowse ; this citizen of Exeter wrote it Prouz. Cf. *Visitation of Devon*, 1620 (Harl. Soc.), p. 223.

taken any goods by way of reprisal, but we cannot find that there is any such. And we received your Honours' said letters the 7th of this month, before which time there were gone out from hence, for Iceland, six of the best ships of our town, and divers others into Holland and other places, so that we were left destitute of all ships fit for that service except one, called the Mayflower of Lynn, being of the burden of one hundred and fifty tons, of which we have made choice ; and we have chosen also one pinnace, of the burden of forty tons, and we intend, God so permitting, to furnish the said ship and pinnace with 100 men and all other things fit and necessary for her Majesty's wars. Howbeit, the truth is that our town is very unable to bear the charge thereof without assistance. Wherefore we humbly crave your Honours' letters to be directed to the towns of Cley, Wiveton, Blakeney, Wells, and other the coast towns towards Lynn, and to the dealers with corn, merchandise, and marine causes, in the towns near adjacent, commending them to join herein in the charge with us; and we shall, according to our bounden duty, pray to God for your Honours' preservation. King's Lynn, this 12th of April, 1588.

Your Honours', in all humbleness,

THOMAS SANDYLL, Mayor.

RICHARD CLARCK. ROBART HULLYOR.
THOMAS BOSTON. THOMAS OVEREND.

April 12.—THE BAILIFFS OF IPSWICH TO SIR F. WALSYNGHAM.

[ccix. 88.—Signed. Addressed.]

After our bounden duties to your Honour humbly remembered :—Where[1] we lately received letters

---

[1] Whereas.

from your Honour, and other of her Majesty's most honourable Privy Council, for the furnishing of two ships and one pinnace presently to be put in readiness and furnished by the towns of Ipswich and Harwich for two months with victuals, mariners, munition, and other necessary provision and furniture, to join with her Majesty's navy on the seas, or to be otherwise employed as we should be directed from their Honours or from the Lord High Admiral of England, mentioning therein that such merchants of those towns who had set forth ships in warlike sort by way of reprisal, supposed to have received great profit thereby, should bear the greater part of that burden :

And where [1] sythens it hath pleased the said Lord Admiral, by his letters to us and the inhabitants of the said town of Harwich directed, to require us to make choice of three sufficient and serviceable hoys instead of the said ships and pinnace, and to furnish them with six or eight of the meetest great serviceable ordnance for each of the same hoys, besides forty men in every such hoy, whereof most to be musketeers, as by the said letters this bearer hath ready to show to your Honour may appear :

We thereupon, according to our bound duties, have endeavoured ourselves to the uttermost of our power and abilities about the accomplishment of the premises, and cannot find or get sufficient great ordnance serviceable for the same. It would therefore please your Honour, for our better service of her Majesty, whereof we have a care, to be a mean for the obtaining of that kind of munition out of her Majesty's store in London or elsewhere.

And as touching the charge meant by the said letters to be imposed upon the said merchants who set forth ships by way of reprisal, we have imparted

[1] Whereas.

the contents of the said letters to the said merchants, who, for answer thereof, affirm that they have thereby rather sustained loss than gain ; so as there is no hope of obtaining any greater help of them towards that contribution than of the other inhabitants of the said town of Ipswich, rate for rate, unless we have further direction in that behalf from your Honour. And forasmuch as heretofore, in like cases of charge, we have found some very unwilling to contribute, and fear to find some such at this time, we humbly beseech your Honour's direction in that matter, what order we shall take with such as we shall find obstinate therein. And thus being willing in every behalf to the uttermost of our power to accomplish your Honour's former commandment, we humbly take our leaves of your Honour ; praying to Almighty God for your Honour, in health and goodly felicity, long to endure. Ipswich, this 12th of April, 1588.

Your Honour's most humble to command,

JOHN BARKAR
EDWARD GOODDINGE } Bailiffs of Ipswich.

April 13.—*SIR F. DRAKE TO THE QUEEN.*

[**ccix. 89.**—Signed. Addressed.]

Most gracious Sovereign :—I have received from Mr. Secretary some particular notes, and withal a commandment to answer them unto your Majesty.

The first is that your Majesty would willingly be satisfied from me how the forces now in Lisbon might best be distressed.

Truly this point is hardly to be answered as yet, for two special causes : the first for that our intelligences are as yet uncertain ; the second is, the resolution of our own people, which I shall better understand when I have them at sea. The last insample at Cadiz is not of divers yet forgotten ; for one such flying now, as Borough did then, will put the whole in peril, for that the enemy's strength is now so great gathered together and ready to invade.

But if your Majesty will give present order for our proceeding to the sea, and send to the strengthening of this fleet here four more of your Majesty's good ships, and those 16 sail of ships with their pinnaces which are preparing in London, then shall your Majesty stand assured, with God's assistance, that if the fleet come out of Lisbon, as long as we have victual to live withal upon that coast, they shall be fought with, and I hope, through the goodness of our merciful God, in such sort as shall hinder his quiet passage into England ; for I assure your Majesty, I have not in my lifetime known better men, and possessed with gallanter minds, than your Majesty's people are for the most part, which are here gathered together, voluntarily to put their hands and hearts to the finishing of this great piece of work ; wherein we are all persuaded that God, the giver of all victories, will in mercy look upon your most excellent Majesty, and us your poor subjects, who for the defence of your Majesty, our religion, and native country, have resolutely vowed the hazard of our lives.

The advantage of time and place in all martial actions is half a victory[1] ; which being lost is irrecoverable. Wherefore, if your Majesty will command me away with those ships which are here already, and the rest to follow with all possible expedition, I hold it in my poor opinion the surest

---

[1] Compare Nelson's ' Time is everything ; five minutes makes the difference between a victory and a defeat.'—Nicolas, iv. 290.

and best course; and that they bring with them
victuals sufficient for themselves and us, to the
intent the service be not utterly lost for want
thereof; whereof I most humbly beseech your most
excellent Majesty to have such consideration as the
weightiness of the cause requireth; for an Englishman, being far from his country, and seeing a present want of victuals to ensue, and perceiving no
benefit to be looked for, but only blows, will hardly
be brought to stay.

I have order but for two months' victuals,
beginning the 24th of April, whereof one whole
month may be spent before we come there; the
other month's victual will be thought with the least
to bring us back again. Here may the whole
service and honour be lost for the sparing of a few
crowns.

Touching my poor opinion how strong your
Majesty's fleet should be to encounter this great
force of the enemy, God increase your most excellent
Majesty's forces both by sea and land daily; for
this I surely think: there was never any force so
strong as there is now ready or making ready
against your Majesty and true religion; but that
the Lord of all strengths is stronger, and will
[defend] the truth of his word for his own name's
sake; unto the which God be all glory given.
Thus, in all humble duty, I continually will pray to
the Almighty to bless and give you victory over all
his and your enemies. From Plymouth, this 13th
of April, 1588.

Your Majesty's most loyal,
FRA. DRAKE.

April 13.—*HOWARD TO BURGHLEY.*

[**B.M. Harl. MS. 6994, f. 120.**—Holograph.   Addressed.]

My honourable good Lord :—I received even
now a letter from Captain Frobiser ; the effect was
that there is come from the river of Seine, in France,
six English ships, who declared unto him that there
was great forces of soldiers come down to the sea
coast, and that it is spoken there that word is
brought by one that came out of Spain that the
Spanish fleet is at the sea, and that, upon the news,
the Frenchmen made great jollity and bravery, and
came down to the English ships and cut their cables,
and used them so badly as that they were driven to
come away with all speed and leave all their business.   And also Mr. Frobiser hath written that on
Friday last, being the 5th of this present, there
passed by Calais a hundred pilots, whereof two
were Englishmen : they came in a flyboat from
Dunkirk, and are gone to meet the Spanish fleet.
Her Majesty's pleasure was that this letter should
be sent to Sir Fr. Drake, for the wind being as it
hath been ever since, it is like they should not be
past the islands of Guernsey and Jersey, and therefore that he should send two or three nimble barks
to intercept them, if it be possible, and also if
they meet with any that cometh out of Spain, to
learn what they can of the readiness of the army
there, which in my opinion is readier than we
do think they be.   I would have been very glad
to have seen your Lordship myself, but I could
not obtain leave of her Majesty ; and yet it were
fit that I should make your Lordship acquainted
with her Majesty's resolution touching the service
on the seas, which, God willing, I will do before

I depart, if no sudden alarm[1] come, which I fear hourly.

My good friend Mr. Robert Cecill[2] did write me a letter, which I thank her Majesty she did read it over to me twice, with words of him that I was not sorry to hear. I am bold to send the letter unto your Lordship, praying your Lordship that after you have read it, that you will send it me again, for after her Majesty had read it twice unto me, she called for it again and read it to my Lord Steward.[3] I pray to God to send your Lordship strength and health, and so I take my leave of your Lordship. From Hackney, the 13th of April.

Your Lordship's most assured to command,

C. HOWARD.

April 16.—*THE MAYOR AND CORPORATION OF WEYMOUTH TO THE COUNCIL.*

[ccix. 94.—Signed. Addressed. Endorsed.]

Right Honourable, our humble duties remembered:—Whereas we have received direction from you—for that it is supposed that divers merchants of this place have had great benefit by setting forth their ships in warlike sort by way of reprisal—that this port should furnish her Majesty with two ships and one pinnace, men, munition and victuals, for two months, and forthwith to join with her forces in the fleet under the conduct of Sir Francis Drake, Knight, admiral thereof: And[4] before received order from the Lord Admiral for the like furnishing of two ships and one pinnace to join with her

---

[1] MS. alaroume.
[2] Burghley's younger son, the future Earl of Salisbury.
[3] The Earl of Leicester.   [4] And whereas we had.

Highness's navy royal in the east parts. And whereas the 13th of this present, a general press of
mariners hath been in this port, by means whereof
this place, at this instant, is much destitute :

May it please your good Lordships to be advertised that the benefit of those reprisals hath not
been in this place of that great estimation, although
some quantity of such merchandise hath been here
landed ; for that the proper owners thereof, in the
greatest part, are of other places and not inhabitants
in this port, being a town of small ability and in
part decayed. And it may further please your
Lordships, of our own industry, to our very great
charge, we have builded a platform for some defence of this town and country, at this instant not
thoroughly furnished with needful ordnance, by
reason of our poverty not able thereunto. Yet notwithstanding, our very good Lords, tendering in
all duty her Majesty's service, with desire to satisfy
as near as we can your honourable commands in this
behalf, [we] have at our own charge provided one
ship of the burden of 80 tons, furnished with fifty
men and victualled for two months, to join with Sir
Francis Drake, and one pinnace of 30 tons, furnished
with thirty men and victualled for two months, to
attend the Lord Admiral, and now ready to depart
this harbour according to their direction ; besides
two other ships providing likewise for the Lord
Admiral, by order from his Lordship. In consideration whereof, we beseech your Lordships to accept
our willingness in any service we shall be commanded ; and for that the charge is very great to
us only and the benefit general to inhabitants out
of this place, it may please you in your grave consideration, partly to disburse us, by adding some
townships near adjoining to be contributory towards
the same, being so general service, and as well

their goods as others; wherein we shall as heretofore most humbly acknowledge ourselves bounden unto your Lordships for your great care in relief of us. And so most humbly do take our leaves. Weymouth and Melcombe Regis, this 16th of April, 1588.

Your Lordships' most ready to command,

RYCHARD PITT, Mayor.

WILLIAM PIT.   JOHN MOKET, Bailiff.
BARNARD MAJOR.   JOHN ALLEN.

April 17.—SIR ROBERT WYNGFELD[1] TO THE COUNCIL.

[ccix. 95.—Signed. Addressed.]

Pleaseth it your Honours to understand that where it pleased you to direct your honourable letters to the towns of Aldborough, Orford and others, for the furnishing and setting out of a ship and a pinnace to the sea, meaning thereby, as it is supposed, that only those people that use the trade to sea should be chargeable to that service, and not those that are charged to find any furniture to land service: yet notwithstanding, the inhabitants of Orford have, for their own ease and to levy a far more sum than will suffice to that service, charged one Reuben Collye, and one Gilbert, and their servants, who are otherwise charged by land, to be contributories to their charge, and have threatened to compel them to appear before your Honours to answer such complaints as they will exhibit against them. And for that I know the men of small ability and charged otherwise, as abovesaid, I have

---

[1] Justice of the Peace and Commissioner of Musters for the county of Suffolk, knighted in 1553.

thought good to signify so much unto your Lordships, most humbly entreating you that you will
receive no information against them to their prejudice, for that I know them as ready any way
to serve her Majesty as duty requireth.   And so
humbly take my leave, this 17th of April, 1588.

Your Honours' to command,

ROBERT WYNGFELD.

PETITION OF ORFORD AND DUNWICH TO THE COUNCIL.

[ccix. 96.—Not dated nor endorsed.]

To the Right Honourable the Lords and others
of her Majesty's most honourable Privy Council.

In most humble wise beseeching your Honours,
your poor and daily orators,[1] the chief officers
and commonalties of the towns of Orford and
Dunwich &c., in the county of Suffolk, that where [2]
among themselves they cannot agree in the dissever-
ing [3] of the contribution and charge towards such
shipping for her Majesty's service as on them and
the town of Aldborough, in the said county, by your
Honours' late letters was imposed ; and only through
Aldborough, as your Honours' said orators hope
shall be adjudged ; which notwithstanding, there
is such order taken that the preparation in effect is
ready which at all their hands was required : it [4]
would therefore please your Honours to address
your letters to such knights and worshipful gentlemen as are next adjoining to those coast towns, who
best know their several estates, for the imposing of
every several town's charges for this service, ac-

---

[1] Suppliants.
[2] Whereas.
[3] Apportioning.
[4] We pray that it.

cording to the validity of their several estates. And that it would please your Honours that the town of Woodbridge, their next neighbour, which was omitted, and which your Honours upon former humble petition granted, may contribute unto the charge of the said towns, and not to Ipswich, which is not so charged as your said orators be ; neither is Woodbridge—as they account themselves—a limb of that port of Ipswich, as Ipswich hath alleged. And your said orators, according to their bounden duty, shall and will daily pray for the continuance of your Honours in all health and honour.

April 17.—*THE MAYOR AND ALDERMEN OF SOUTHAMPTON TO THE COUNCIL.*

[**ccix. 97.**—Signed. Addressed.]

May it please your good Lordships :—Immediately after the receipt of your letters of the first of this present,[1] which came to our hands the 6th of the same, whereby is signified her Majesty's pleasure that this town should prepare, furnish, man and set forth, at the proper charge of us and the rest of the inhabitants here, two ships and one pinnace to be employed in her Majesty's service, and for the defence of the realm, by the space of two months, we did, according to our duties and the abundance of our zeal and desire to do her Majesty faithful service, assemble ourselves together, as we have often done sithence the receipt of your Lordships' letters, to consider as well of the charge, as how the same might be levied among so poor and insufficient a number of inhabitants any way able to contribute

[1] See *Hist. MSS. Com.*, Report XI., App. pt. iii. 123.

towards the same ; and finding the charge to amount
to five hundred pounds or thereabouts, we see it
not possible how the same (no not the fourth part
thereof) can be levied among us, in respect of the
disability and poverty of the town, which ever
sithence the embargue [1] in Spain, being about 16
years, hath grown from time to time so to decay, as
within the half of that time there hath been almost
no trade or traffic within this town ; whereby not
only those among us that were of any reasonable
estate of wealth or stock to exercise trade of merchandise are so low drawn and impoverished as [2]
they have been constrained in effect to give up and
forsake their traffic, but even the handicrafts men,
which, by the common trade to this town, were in
some competent sort maintained, are wonderfully
decayed, and so the town dispeopled of many of her
Majesty's natural subjects ; in whose places some
few strangers of foreign countries are come to
inhabit here, and they (God knoweth) but very poor,
living with the labour of their hands.

Your Lordships will best consider the insufficiency of this place to furnish to so great a
charge as five hundred pounds, when the whole
subsidy within the same doth not amount to about a
hundred and twenty pounds, and that gathered with
much difficulty [3] and murmurs of the people ; who,
besides the said subsidy, have been of late charged
by direction from your Lordships with the provision
of certain powder and other munition to the sum of
250*l.*, which remaineth dead and without profit to
the town ; and now lately charged with reparations
about the town upon the sea banks, to defend [4] the
violence of the waters, with some little fortifications
to strengthen the town against the enemy.   And

---

[1] Embargo   [2] That.   [3] Difficilitie.
[4] Fend off, guard against.

whereas your Lordships are of opinion that benefit hath grown to some of the inhabitants in this place by way of reprisals against the Spaniard, we dare assure your Lordships, upon our poor fidelity and credit, that the town hath thereby been impoverished at the least four thousand pounds.

Thus, our very good Lords, after we had often assembled ourselves, considered, and propounded the effect of your Lordships' letters to the principal and best able of the inhabitants,[1] and finding the state of this town so weak and unable to be strained to the charge of the preparation required, and that the motion[2] thereof made to the people doth cause them greatly to murmur and grieve thereat, having nevertheless travailed therein hitherto to our utmost, we have thought it necessary, under your Lordships' humble correction, as well in discharge of our duties towards her Majesty, as finding the necessity and poverty of the town so great, with all humility to entreat your good Lordships to be a means to her Majesty, that it will please her, of her princely bounty and clemency, to discharge this town wholly of that burden and charge, because if the same should be laid upon us, it must grow out of the purse of a very few of us so utterly unable to bear the same, as that it would tend greatly to our impoverishment and beggary.

And whereas your Lordships have happily been informed that there should[3] be divers gentlemen inhabiting within this town of good ability whom you would have to contribute towards this charge, it may please your Lordships to be advertised that there is not above one gentleman that is inhabiting or remaining within the town that is not of the

---

[1] MS. inhabitauncie.   [2] Proposal.
[3] This use of the conditional as denoting hearsay is very common.

bourgeoisie of the same ; and the rest are very few, who have only hired some lodgings and houses in the town for some part of this winter past, and are either now gone or shortly do depart to their houses and charge in the country ; so as if for our better ease they should be taxed towards the furnishing of the charge aforesaid, it would be but a small relief that would thereby grow unto us.

Furthermore, if the town were able to reach to so great a contentment, whereof we should be right glad, as well for that her Majesty's service might be furthered and advanced thereby, as that our town were in case of ability thereunto, yet we must let your Lordships understand that sithence the receipt of your letters before mentioned there have been prested and taken up within this town by John Thomas and John Younge, having her Majesty's commission under the Great Seal of England, above a hundred and ten mariners ; whereby, if we were able to levy the charge among us, it were not possible for us to find so many fit mariners in those parts as might serve to man the meanest of the three ships required.

These lacks and impediments therefore considered, we do most humbly pray and hope that her Majesty and your Lordships will have compassion of the poverty and inability of this poor town in remitting and discharging the same of the shipping, charge and furniture required, assuring your Lordships that it will be an act of great charity towards us, and we shall be bound to pray for her Majesty and your Lordships (as we do daily), and to be ready to expose our lives and slender substance to do her Majesty service when and where it shall please her Majesty to employ and command us, as knoweth God ; to whose holy protection we do most humbly leave your good

Lordships. From Southampton, the 17th of April, 1588.

Yo^r Honours' most bounden at commandment,
                    ANDREW STUDLEY, Mayor.

JOHN CROOKE.	JOHN BOLLACKAR.[1]
ROBT. KNAPLOCKE.	JOHN FAVOR.
JOHN JACKSON.	ALEXANDR. PENTE.
RICHARD BESUN.	WYLLM. EDMONDS.
WILLIAM BARWYKE.	

April 17.—HOWARD TO BURGHLEY.

[**ccix. 99.**—Signed. Addressed.]

My very good Lord :—It is now determined that I shall go westward with the greatest part of her Majesty's ships, whereof I have thought good to advertise your Lordship. The purpose and conclusion of her Majesty's intent, Sir William Wynter or Mr. Hawkyns will advertise your Lordship at large.

I wrote to your Lordship before this long since of sundry extraordinary charges that were then grown in furnishing of the navy, which doth daily increase many ways ; therefore I heartily pray your Lordship that there may be paid 2,000*l.* out of the warrant of 29,000, bearing date the second of February, 1586 ; whereby her Majesty's navy may be the better furnished, and thereby more able to do her and this realm service. And so I bid your good Lordship most heartily farewell. From my house at Deptford, the 17th of April, 1588.

Your Lordship's most assured to command,
                                    C. HOWARD.

---

[1] Mayor the next year. *Hist. MSS. Com.*, XI. iii. **124.**

April 19.—*THE BAILIFFS OF IPSWICH TO
SIR F. WALSYNGHAM.*

[**ccix. 100.**—Signed.   Addressed.]

After our bounden duties to your Honour humbly
remembered :—Where we lastly received your
Honour's most favourable letters on the behalf of
the town of Ipswich, for the obtaining of great
ordnance for our better furnishing of three serviceable hoys for her Majesty against her Highness's
enemies, by your Honour's means, of[1] the Right
Honourable the Lord High Admiral of England ;
for which we render to your Honour our most
humble and dutiful thanks.   And therefore we have
hereby made so bold, eftsoons[2] to commend the
same to your Honour for further remembrance
towards my said Lord Admiral in that behalf, by
your Honour's letters to his Lordship, or otherwise
as shall seem best for the accomplishment thereof,
at the time and place by his Honour appointed ;
for that otherwise, we cannot furnish the same as
we most willingly would, according to our duties.
And therefore have sent this bearer to attend your
Honour's direction therein, for that the time
appointed for that service approacheth so nigh at
hand.

And further, if it shall like your Honour, we
having considered of the great charge of the said
hoys, do perceive that the charge thereof will amount
to four whole subsidies, to be borne by the said
inhabitants ; and thereupon, having sithence proportionably rated ourselves and the other inhabitants of the said town of Ipswich able to contribute,
according to their abilities, for the setting forth of

[1] From.   [2] Forthwith, at once.

the said hoys in warlike manner, one Ralph Morrys, gent and inhabitant of the said town, and a man of sufficient ability to bear the burden and charge set upon him, hath most obstinately refused to pay his said rate cessed upon him, to the evil example of others, if he shall so pass away. Whereupon we, according to your Honour's direction, have bound him by obligation herewith sent, to her Majesty's use in the sum of one hundred marks to make his personal appearance before the Lords and others of her Majesty's most honourable Privy Council on Saint Mark's day[1] next coming, to abide their Honours' order, whereunto as duty bindeth us we submit ourselves. And thus humbly taking our leaves of your Honour, we cease; praying to Almighty God to preserve your Honour long in health and goodly felicity. Ipswich, this 19th of April, 1588.

Your Honour's most humbly to command,

JOHN BARKAR
EDWARDE GOODDINGE } Bailiffs of Ipswich.

April 20.—THE MAYOR AND BURGESSES OF KINGSTON-UPON-HULL TO SIR F. WAL-SYNGHAM.

[ccix. 101.—Signed. Addressed.]

Right Honourable, our duties humbly remembered :—Understanding to our great grief your Honour's misliking of our late certificate, made to the Lords and others of her Majesty's most honourable Privy Council, of the lack of sufficient ships and mariners here to furnish from hence two ships and one pinnace, according to their Lordships' direction, by

---

[1] April 25.

means of their absence upon their traffic, and the late press made by one Christopher Chapman :— We therefore, encouraged by your Honour's accustomed good affection to this town and the inhabitants thereof, and the good liking you have had of our readiness and willingness in her Majesty's service, and being very sorry to minister any cause whereby the same, your Honour's good affection and liking should be any way withdrawn, are emboldened to trouble your Honour with these few lines, and thereby to advertise you that in truth the lack was no less than was at that time certified, which we shall be ready evidently to prove, if it shall so please your Honour, and that we could not by any means have furnished the said ships and pinnace ; but that sithence that time, there be both ships and mariners returned from London and Newcastle ; whereupon, in part discharge of our bounden duties, and in accomplishment of the contents of their Lordships' letter in that behalf to us written, we have appointed for that service two ships and one pinnace, as most willingly we would have done at the first if by any means possible we could ; which, with as much expedition as possible may be, shall be furnished and set forth, which we trust will be the 25th of April instant ; for we, for the more speedier dispatch therein, have hired and set to work of them all the ship-carpenters in this town or in any place within twenty miles thereof. The names of the ships and pinnace and their burdens and in what sort they are furnished is set down in a particular note enclosed in our letter [1] to the Lords and others of her Majesty's most honourable Privy

---

[1] Their letter to the Council (ccix. 104), dated April 22, contains the same assurance as to the two ships and one pinnace, and the efforts making to set them forth ; but the enclosure here referred to is missing.

Council, which the bringer hereof hath to deliver to your Honour. And thus, humbly beseeching your Honour to accept this our boldness, to continue your accustomed good affection to us and this town, and to impute our slackness in this service to the lack of serviceable ships and mariners, the true and only cause thereof, we humbly take our leaves ; beseeching the Almighty to preserve your Honour in long health, with much increase of honour. Kingston-upon-Hull, the 20th of April, 1588.

Your Honour's humbly at commandment,

WILLAM BRAYE, Mayor.

JOHN THORNTON.	WILLM. WILSON.
WM. GEE.	WYLLYM SMYTH.
JOHN SMYTHE.	EDWARDE WAKEFIELD.
ROBT. GAYTON.	LEONARD WYLLAN.

April 20.—THE JUSTICES OF EAST BERGHOLT TO THE COUNCIL.

[**ccix. 102.**—Signed. Addressed.]

Right Honourable :—May it please you to vouchsafe the reading of a most humble petition which the township of East Bergholt, in Suffolk, have instantly required us to present unto your Honours in answer of your letter of the tenth of April, wherein they are required to make some reasonable contribution towards the furnishing of a ship and pinnace to be sent out of Colchester, in Essex ; and we the justices of these limits, at whose hands all due vigilancy for her Majesty's service may be required, have thought it our parts and bounden duties, under your favourable correction, to lay open some particularities that may move your honourable com-

passions towards the said township and decayed
state of this poor corner, growing chiefly (if we be
rightly informed) by restraint made by a statute
prohibiting that no Suffolk cloth should be transported, and not here dressed before they were
embarked, thereby changing the accustomed gainful
trade, and traded with such cloths making [1] as were
best saleable in Spain ; and now through long want
of vent into those parts, we find not only the stocks
and wealth of the said inhabitants greatly decayed,
but withal they, being very charitable and godly
bent, are driven, out of their own purses, to see all
the poor and needy artificers pertaining to the trade
provided for sufficiently with meat, drink and clothes,
without trouble of any other parts ; which amounts
to so great a charge, the number of the poor being
very many, as [2] we hope according to your accustomed
wisdoms you will take favourable regard of them.
Their readiness and forwardness otherwise, in all the
good services of God and her most excellent Majesty,
are and hath been always such as deserveth the
testimony of our hands, in hope thereby to purchase
your Honours' good and gracious favour towards
both them and ourselves, who in all humility will
become humble suitors to your honourable good
Lordships as far as we may without offence, that we
may not weaken our country to strengthen another,
and our coasts and coast men already so weakened
as we hold it fit for us rather with all due care and
circumspection to foresee how to strengthen the
services of her Majesty in these parts for such
shipping as is in like manner allotted hither, in the
furtherance whereof there had been ere this used
the help of the said town of Bergholt and others if
their estate would so have borne it. And so, our
most humble duties recommended, with our hearty

[1] Which was in the making of such cloths.   [2] That.

prayers to the Almighty for your long preservation, we humbly take our leave, this present 20th of April, 1588.   Your Honours' at command,

CHARLES FRAMLYNGHAM.   PHILL. PARKER.
PHILIPP TYLNEY.   EDMUND POLEY.
JOHN LANG.   JOHN MUNDEN.[1]

April 28.—*DRAKE TO THE QUEEN.*

[ccix. 112.—Signed.   Addressed.]

Most gracious Sovereign :—Sithence my last dispatch of Mr. Stallenge to the Court, I have three sundry ways received advertisements that the enemy continueth his preparations very mightily.   The first report cometh by a man of Dartmouth who very lately came from St. Malos, and saith that he heard it reported there by divers Frenchmen returned home from Spain over land, that fifteen ships of that town and as many (at least) of Rosco,[2] besides many more of divers nations, are stayed there ; affirming that their fleet is in number between four and five hundred sail, ready furnished with seventy or eighty thousand soldiers and mariners[3] ; and that for their better encouragement the wages of all the companies is advanced.

The second was delivered by one coming lately from Bayonne, who upon conference there had with another Englishman that dwelt at Bilbao doth con-

---

[1] This name is blotted, and quite uncertain.

[2] Roscoff.   It seems at this time to have had a considerable trade (cf. *post*, Seymour to Walsingham, July 18), which afterwards died out, leaving the town to dwindle to 'an insignificant hamlet,' till, in 1769, it suddenly started to life again as the depôt of smugglers.   See Shore's *Smuggling Days and Smuggling Ways*, p. 87.

[3] It is perhaps unnecessary to call attention to the gross exaggerations in this and other similar reports.   They were, however, the best intelligence that either the Queen's ministers or the officers of the fleet could get.

firm in effect the substance of the former reports ;
adding also that there went to Lisbon out of Biscay
between forty or fifty sail of tall ships to increase
their fleet.

The last report is certainly declared [1] in France,
and brought over by a merchant of Lyme, named
Hasserde, that a Frenchman lately coming out of
the Straits meant to put in at Cadiz ; and sending
in his boat in the night, to discover such doubts as
might annoy his entry there, had intelligence by one
of his countrymen that they and their shipping were
generally stayed in all ports of the coast, and their
sails and yards landed ; and that if he came also in,
he might not pass thence.   Farther he reported that
there were within that harbour twelve great argosies,
the least of a thousand tons, and so upwards to the
burden of fifteen hundred ; taking into them (for the
most part) straw, barley, and other forage for those
horses and asses which were ordained for their
necessary carriage.

Most renowned Prince, I beseech you to pardon
my boldness in the discharge of my conscience,
being burdened to signify unto your Highness the
imminent dangers that in my simple opinion do
hang over us : that if a good peace for your Majesty
be not forthwith concluded—which I as much as
any man desireth—then these great preparations of
the Spaniard may be speedily prevented as much as
in your Majesty lieth, by sending your forces to
encounter them somewhat far off, and more near
their own coasts, which will be the better cheap [2] for
your Majesty and people, and much the dearer for
the enemy.

Thus much (as duty bindeth me) I have thought
good to signify unto your Majesty, for that it im-

[1] Publicly spoken of as certain.
[2] The more advantageous.

porteth but the hazard or loss of all. The promise
of peace from the Prince of Parma and these mighty
preparations in Spain agree not well together. Un-
doubtedly I think these advertisements true, for that
I cannot hear, by any man of war or otherwise, that
any ship is permitted to depart Spain, which is a
vehement presumption that they hold their purposed
pretences.[1] And for farther testimony of these
reports, I have sent this bearer, a captain of one of
your Majesty's ships, who (if it shall please your
Highness to permit him) can deliver some things
touching the same.

Thus resting always most bounden unto your
Majesty for your gracious and favourable speeches
used of me both to Mr. Secretary and others (which
I desire God no longer to let me live than I will be
ready to do your Majesty all the dutiful service I
possibly may), I will continually pray to God to
bless your Majesty with all happy victories. From
Plymouth, this 28th of April, 1588.

Your Majesty's most loyal,
FRA. DRAKE.

April 29.—LIST OF SHIPS.

[ccix. 113, 114.—In Howard's hand.]

The ships that shall go with the Lord Admiral
towards the west country :—

1. The Triumph.	The 20 ships of London.
2. E. Bonaventure.[2]	Chichester . 1
3. Bear.	Southampton 1
4. Ark Ralegh.	Lyme . . . 1
5. Victory.	Exmouth . . 2 and
6. Mary Rose.	a pinnace.

[1] Designs. [2] In error for the E. Jonas.

7. The E. Bonaventure.
8.   Lion.
9.   Vanguard.
10.   Dreadnought.
11.   Foresight.
12.   Charles.
13.   Moon.
14.   Fancy.[1]
15.   White Lion.
16.   Disdain.
17.   Younker.[1]
18.   Duffield.[1]
19.   Monk.[1]
20.   Trumpet.[1]

The ships remaining in the Narrow Seas under the charge of Lord Henry Seymour:

1. The Rainbow.
2.   Antelope.
3.   Swallow.
4.   Bull.
5.   Tiger.
6.   Tramontana.
7.   Scout.
8.   Achates.
9.   Galley Bonavolia.
10.   Merlin.
11.   Spy.
12.   George.
13.   Sun.
14.   Cygnet.

The 5 ports .   . 5 ships and one pinnace.
Newcastle   .   . 3 ships and one pinnace.
Hull   .   .   . 2 ships and one pinnace.

[1] Are not mentioned in any list as having served.

Lynn   .   .   . 2 ships and one pinnace.
Aldborough .   . 1 ship and one pinnace.
Ipswich and Harwich 3 hoys of 60 tons apiece.

And all such as shall come out of the Low Countries.

April.—ADVERTISEMENTS FROM ROUEN.

[ccix. 127.—Endorsed.]

First, these are to certify you that yesterday there arrived here a Breton called Roderigues Haimond, who 13 days past departed from Cadiz in Spain, at which time all the ships, as well French as Flemish, were stayed until such time as the Spanish fleet should be departed, so that if a ship of Marseille had not touched at Cadiz in passing that way, neither this party nor none else could have come out of Spain by sea, until after the departure of the army. Which time, stay was made, for that no news should be carried for England. Touching the news he hath brought, what the army is and when they purpose to depart, and whither the talk went that they meant to shape their course,—First, he saith that in all there may be 200 sail of ships, whereof the more part is almost all arrayed at Lisbon, if, since he be come away, they be not departed; and that 14 of the greatest galleons are at St. Lucar. Also that to man these ships, as the talk goeth in Spain, there are 30,000 men ready to go aboard when time serveth. Secondly, for the time of their departure, he saith that the common voices was that the galleons should depart from St. Lucar, and all the rest of the fleet, about the end of this month; and he thinketh it to be the more certain, for that the news was there that the Duke of Medina, Admiral of Spain, had already received the King's packet, which

was not to be opened till he should be at sea with all
the fleet, so that no man could certainly tell to what
place they should go after the departure from Spain ;
but the place whither, according to the common bruit,
it was by most men in Spain said that they meant
to go for Scotland there to land, but of this there
is no certainty that the party now arrived could
tell.   I demanded him if corn was cheap and victuals
in Spain.   He said that it was very reasonable
for price, and plenty sufficient; and that this year
there is like to be great plenty by reason of the
moist spring.   Finally I prayed him to tell me what
news he heard of Sir Francis Drake ; and he said
that whilst he was at Cadiz the Spaniards made two
alarms, and put themselves all in arms, because they
saw certain great ships making in towards the bay,
which they thought had been Sir Francis Drake ;
and for his own opinion, being one who loveth
Englishmen, he thinketh that the Spaniards will
never be able to accomplish their determination, for
he thinketh they are too weak at sea, and I do not
doubt, God willing, they shall be overthrown.

May 10.—*RESOLUTIONS OF THE COUNCIL.*

[ccx. 11.—Endorsed.]

1. To appoint a proportion of money to be
delivered unto the Treasurer to provide victual in
case of necessity.

2. The ships furnished by the port towns, so
many as have two months' victual, to remain in
the Narrow Seas ; and the other, furnished with
three months' victual, to attend upon the Lord
Admiral.

3. The instructions to refer the employment of

the navy that is to repair to the west parts of this realm, to the Lord Admiral's consideration ; to be employed as by his Lordship shall be thought meet, upon such intelligence as he shall receive from time to time ; having care, so much as lie in him, to impeach any attempt in Ireland, in Scotland, and England.

May 12.—*FENNER AND CROSSE TO DRAKE.*[1]

[ccx. 17.—Signed.   Addressed :—For her Majesty's service.]

Sir :—There arrived this 12th May in the morning Captain Polwhele[2] and the rest of the ships in company, all saving the caravel.   He was at Cape Finisterre and encountered with certain French ships, the ladings of many of them supposed to be Spaniards' goods ; as also one flyboat ; which ships came from several places out of the kingdoms of Spain and Portugal.   So as therefore he thought meet to return with them, for the better advertisement of the estate of the King's forts and fleet, and of their readiness, as by the examinations of divers of the masters and merchants by this bearer sent unto you at large appeareth.   And in that they generally, coming out of many several places, confirm in effect all one matter, we thought it very meet to despatch away a messenger with all haste, and therefore have taken their examinations briefly for the speedier despatch.

Most of them marvelleth that the fleet is not upon this coast.   There are six French ships and one flyboat brought in by Captain Polwhele ; he hath great care to keep everything in good order,

---

[1] It does not appear where Drake was at this time ; nor yet how this letter addressed to him came among the State Papers.

[2] MS. Powlewheele.

without spoil. Presently after this messenger's despatch we mean to take special order for the safety of everything, and to take as due examination of the parties unto whom the goods doth appertain as our knowledge can bring to pass.

Here are arrived all the ships from Bristol and all the west parts with Sir Richard Greynvile [1] and Mr. St. Leger, for which two we pray your consideration in moneys they demand for victual. We take order upon this news that the fleet shall be maintained until Saturday next with petty warrants, so as the two months' store shall be kept whole.

We have observed the order of your letter sent by my cousin William Fenner, and we despatch of the worst men with as much speed as we may, notwithstanding there will be above the numbers. All the ships here are wonderfully well manned with mariners.

We will take a special care as may be to our charge in your absence ; foreseeing, as much as may lie in us, that all be kept in good order and with as much readiness as the place will yield. We ride in a hole [2] where we cannot get out if the enemy should come. Divers of the best ships shall remove out of that place with as much speed as we may under the island,[3] to be the readier for their coming, or to follow them as occasion shall move. The mariners shall be kept aboard, and the soldiers in as great readiness as may be. We will order some powder and weapons aboard such ships as have not already.

Captain Polwhele had performed this message himself, but that we thought it meet, such his great care [4] in good order for the safety of the goods as

---

[1] MS. Greenfeild. [2] Sc. Catwater.
[3] Sc. St. Nicholas, or Drake's Island.
[4] Notwithstanding this high testimony to Polwhele's merits, or perhaps in consequence of it, he had no command during the

will be to your good liking, and therefore to continue the same, that no fault may be found in him.

We do most humbly commend ourselves unto
you, wishing honour and happiness in all your
actions. All in generality do greatly desire your
return ; and in great love, many of the captains and
gentlemen commend them to your good favour.
And so we commit you to the Lord of Lords, who
preserve and keep you in his favour for ever.
Plymouth, this 12th of May, 1588, at 7 of the clock
in the evening.

Your faithful and loving friends,
to be commanded by you for ever,
THOMAS FENNER.
ROBART CROSSE.

May 16.—*SEYMOUR TO WALSYNGHAM.*

[**ccx. 19.**—Holograph. Addressed.]

Sir :—Where news be daily current, be they
good or bad, true or false, such I receive them,
such I deliver them. This evening there came a
pinnace into the Road which came from Cadiz in
Spain this day fortnight. He delivereth unto me
for certain there be in Lisbon 300 sail, half of them
victuallers and the other half men of war ; besides
which they are greatly infected with sickness and
mortality, and that they stand greatly upon their
guard, hearing but of the name of Drake to approach them ; further, that they be marvellously
beset both with Moors and Turks, insomuch as

operations of the summer. He was probably promoted to be
master of one of the large ships, but there is no further mention
of him this season. He is named by Hakluyt (*Principal Navigations*, iii. 840) as being lost with Chidley in the expedition to the
Straits of Magellan in 1589.

the Moors have within these six weeks overthrown 20,000 Spaniards, obtaining three notable towns besides in that country.[1]   He addeth further that the Great Turk doth presently make a great army ready to set the same forward to some great purpose, whereof the Spaniards stand in some fear. So as truly, Sir, in my poor opinion, if these news be true, her Majesty cannot but in manner make what peace she list; so much the rather, when her forces shall be seen ready upon the coasts everywhere, which me thinketh is too long deferred.

The author of these news is a Frenchman dwelling at Cadiz, laden with good Spanish wines and sacks,[2] and so cometh to London with some leisure as the wind will give him leave.   This leaving any further to trouble you, do recommend me always to your honourable good favour.   From aboard the Bonaventure, this 16th of May, 1588.

Your assured loving friend to command,

H. SEYMOUR.

Post.—If it please you to have any further conference with this Frenchman, you shall hear of him at one Gerald Malines, a Fleming, who is resident always at London, and doth receive these wines at his hands.   The names of the towns that are conquered by the Moors he knoweth not, but surely,[3] Sir, all things be not current with the Duke of Parma, if her Majesty had a honourable peace.

[1] This comes under the head of 'false'; it had no foundation in fact.

[2] The wine, the familiar drink of Sir John Falstaff.

[3] MS. saerely.

EXTRACTS OF LETTERS WRITTEN FROM LISBON.

[ccx. **20.**—Englished.]

Antonio de Taso Aquereis,[1] Alferez of two hundred soldiers, writing three letters out of Lisbon into Andalusia, saith as followeth :—

In the first letter:

Do you pray to God that in England he doth give me a house of some very rich merchant where I may place my ensigne, which the owner thereof do ransom of me in thirty thousand ducats. But I do fear that seeing us they will presently yield and agree unto all that the King will demand of them, for that the King's force is marvellous great as well by sea as by land.

In the second letter:

Do you incommend[2] me in your prayers to God that he give me a good voyage and fortune that I may get wherewithal to repair to my house to live at ease. I am embarked in the admiral of the hulks, a very good and new ship; only I do fear we shall not join battle, for that the great force the King hath is such; and again that the Prince of Parma hath, who stayeth for us with thirty thousand men in the field, and hath sent unto the King craving leave that he only may give the onset, and the King will not grant it him until the Duke do join with him. All things are embarked even to the mules[3] that must draw the artillery; and commanded here, upon pain of death, no man to go

---

[1] The name seems to be hopelessly corrupt; Duro has nothing even remotely resembling it.

[2] Incommend=recommend.   [3] MS. Moyles.

ashore; only we do tarry for a fair wind to go to sea. There is given every day two and twenty thousand rations of victual unto the people for sea and land, all Spaniards.

The third letter:

As touching the voyage, it is impossible to signify unto you the people that are therein, as well soldiers, gentlemen, as of noblemen; only I can say that every day is given twenty two thousand rations of meat, and this only to Spaniards, besides strangers. All things are embarked, only tarrying for a wind; and is commanded upon pain of death no man to disembark himself. I pray you to write me when our supply doth come, which now is making ready.

May. 20.—THE STRENGTH OF THE ARMADA.

[ccx. 25.]

Relation of the Spanish Armada which departed from Lisbon the 30th of May, 1588, *stilo novo*, even as it is certified from Lisbon:

First, great hulks	40
Item, galleons	60
Item, great ships	30
Item, galleasses	4
Item, galleys	8
Item, pataches	24
In all	166
Item, Castilians, soldiers	16,000
Item, Portingals, „	3,000
Item, mariners	6,128
Item, pioneers	2,000
In all of men	27,128

In the same armada their cometh
    friars   180
In all the said armada there is of
    artillery pieces   1,493

General of the armada, the Duke de Medina Sidonia. There cometh in the same as commanders, the Prince de Ascoli, the Conde de Fuentes, the Conde de Paredes,[1] and 25 knights of the second order, being sons and brothers of marquises and earls.

May 22.—SEYMOUR TO BURGHLEY.

[ccx. 27.—Holograph. Addressed.]

My very good Lord :—The Lord Admiral and I parted our companies on the Narrow Seas the 21st of this month, his Lordship taking his course to Plymouth, having a very good wind for the purpose, and myself to Blackness, where I anchored the same day. Presently Monsieur d'Aumale[2] sent a messenger unto me, desiring me to command anything what I lacked, either for victuals, munition, powder or shot. I heartily thanked him, and told the messenger that her Majesty was well stored of

---

[1] Antonio Luis de Leyva, Príncipe de Ascoli, an illegitimate son of the King : he served as a volunteer on the staff of the Duke of Medina Sidonia, on board the San Martin, but was sent from Calais to join the Duke of Parma (Duro, ii. 282, 372). Pedro Enriquez de Acevedo, Conde de Fuentes, took an active part in fitting out the fleet, but it does not appear that he sailed in it ; he was certainly still at Lisbon on June 29 (*ib.* ii. 179). The Conde de Paredes served, apparently, with Alonso de Leyva, and perished with him on the coast of Ireland (*ib.* ii. 364).

[2] The Duke of Aumale, cousin of the Duke of Guise, and at this time besieging Boulogne, which surrendered to the forces of the League a couple of months later.

all necessaries to offend her enemies ; adding further
that her Highness could not but take his message
in better part, considering the league between her
and the French King ; yet marvelling not a little
that so honourable a house as the Guise, being
advanced by French kings heretofore, could forget
themselves so far as to put themselves in arms,
thereby to rob him of one of his principal towns,
which was most like to be done without warrant
or commission from his sovereign. To this was
answered that the French King and the Duke of
Guise were both at Paris, within these four days,
and become great friends ; assuring me further that
he would not fail to bring me letters from Monsieur
d'Aumale that should witness the same; as also
farther authority from the French King to wish[1]
him to expel the Duke of Parma his lieutenant out
of Boulogne ; all which I have expected all this
morning until noon, at which time the wind changed
at North and by West, and thereby enforced [us] to
sail over to our own coasts again.

I am further advertised that they of the higher
town of Boulogne are able to hold out a twelve
months, being furnished of all necessaries to withstand the siege. Besides they made a sally forth
upon the Duke d'Aumale the same day he came
first to Boulogne in person, which was on Friday
last was sennight, and slew 16 persons outright,
hurting many, besides taking a prisoner of some
account, with his ensign.

Now, my Lord, touching our fleet, I would
gladly understand your pleasure for the revictualling
our navy, as also what order shall be taken for our
coast men ; whether her Majesty or the towns shall
continue the charge. It is time to consider hereof,
for our victuals and days wear away apace. I have

[1] To desire, order.

nothing else to trouble your Lordship, but leave you to the merciful protection of the Almighty. From aboard the Rainbow,[1] this 22nd of May, 1588. Your Lordship's assured friend to command,

H. SEYMOUR.

May 23.—HOWARD TO BURGHLEY.

[ccx. **28.**—Signed, and autograph postscript. Addressed.]

My honourable good Lord :—Although I have not much matter worthy the writing unto your Lordship at this present, yet I thought good to let your Lordship understand how that upon Tuesday last, being the 21st of this instant, the wind serving exceedingly well, I cut[2] sail at the Downs, assigning unto my Lord Henry Seymour those ships appointed to stay with him on the Narrow Seas ; and so parting companies the same morning athwart of Dover, and with a pleasant gale all the way long, came and arrived this day, being the 23rd, about 8 of the clock in the morning, at this port of Plymouth, whence Sir Francis Drake came forth with 60 sail very well appointed to meet with me ; and so casting about, he put with me into the haven again, where I mean to stay these two days to water our fleet, and afterwards, God willing, to take the opportunity of the first wind serving for the coast of Spain, with intention to lie on and off betwixt England and that coast, to watch the coming of the Spanish forces ; which I doubt not, if God send us the good hap to meet them, but that in like sort he will send us a good success to conquer and overcome them. Unto

---

[1] Between May 16 and 21 he moved from the Bonaventure to the Rainbow, in which he remained. The Bonaventure had gone to Plymouth, with Howard.

[2] Loosed (see *ante*, p. 82, *note*).

whom I commend your good Lordship, and so bid you most heartily well to fare.   From Plymouth, the 23rd of May, 1588.

Your Lordship's most assured to command,

C. HOWARD.

My good Lord, I pray you bear with me that I have not written[1] with my own hand.   I am so busied as[2] I have no leisure, for now there is no losing of time.

May 27.—WYNTER TO BURGHLEY.

[ccx. 32.—Signed.   Addressed.]

My singular good Lord :—It doth appear to me by a letter which I received of late written by your Lordship and Mr. Secretary Walsyngham as from her Majesty, how greatly I am bound to her Highness, which I know is increased by the honourable favour that doth always continue in you towards me. I do and will pray for her Majesty to Almighty God, and ever live, by his goodness, as her most bounden, humble and dutiful servant, and always honour and love you.

Since my Lord Admiral's departure, I have been a-land at Dover pier to behold the works, as one that wisheth well to it ; and I do find that the works which is done are great, and the same which doth want will be overcomed with a reasonable charge being now followed.   There is a place in the entering of the harbour, which lieth on the north side, to the eastward, that is fallen into decay, which would[3] be taken in hand forthwith and mended ; for otherwise it would put the harbour in danger in short time, and that I would be very sorry to hear.

[1] MS. wryghten.   [2] As=that.   [3] Should.

The sending of victuals from London or Chatham to such of her Majesty's ships as serveth in the Narrow Seas is a great charge to her Highness; beside the uncertain coming of it, and the danger the vessel doth run in, which transporteth the same; and besides, the hurt the victual receiveth or [1] it can be laid aboard. Which matter, in my opinion, would be easily holpen, as by taking order that the victuals, to serve the ships which should be here, be made in Dover, from which it will be very easy for the ships to fetch it, or else for the victualler to send the same to them.

And as for other matters belonging to our Admiral's charge, I know his Lordship doth acquaint your Lordship and the rest of my good Lords with that which is needful, and therefore I leave to trouble your Lordship therein; and so most humbly taking my leave, I desire God to make you ever happy. Written from aboard the Vanguard, the 27th of May, 1588.

Your honourable Lordship's most bounden,

W. WYNTER.

*May 28.—THE DECLARATION OF
GILES NAPPER.*

[ccx. 33.]

The declaration of Giles Napper, come out of Spain the sixth of May,[2] by their computation, and arrived here at Portsmouth the 28th day of May, after our computation.

He saith he was first taken by the Turks, in a ship of Sir Thomas Leighton's; and afterwards, rowing in the Turks' galleys, taken by the Spaniards and put in the Spanish galleys, and

---

[1] Ere.   [2] April 26.

remained there a year and a half; and afterwards, he procured a Fleming to write to the King in his behalf, that for so much as he had been in captivity in Barbary two years and a half, to know his pleasure whether he should be released or kept still in the galley. And the King answered that he should serve in the galleys as a mariner, and not as a captive; but he being unwilling thereunto, desired to be released out of the galleys, which the general did grant, paying his duties. And so he was put to serve in the country, and served a Venetian a month, and afterwards agreed with a Frenchman to bring him to St. Malo. And there were there 30 sail of Flemings, Frenchmen, and Scots, that were there imbarred[1] under the Castle of Puntales, which was lately made[2] for fear of Captain Drake; and they came all away together; and the Castle shot at them and smote never a man; but a piece broke in the Castle and smote many of the soldiers.

Upon the last of March,[3] after the Spanish computation, there came a Scot from Lisbon to Cadiz, and he asked him what store of shipping there was at Lisbon; who told him that there was a hundred great ships and some galleasses, so that they were 200 sail of great and small; and they looked to come away, by report of the common people, the 16th of May,[4] by their computation; and they looked for more ships out of Italy to be ready at that time.

Also he saith that he spake with one Mr. Fletcher, at that time, being an Englishman at Cadiz, in April last, who hath a factor in Lisbon who desired his master to send for him from thence. The sickness increased, so that there died in a day,

---

[1] Stayed, arrested.
[2] To command the anchorage at Cadiz.
[3] March 21.   [4] May 6.

in the fleet and in the town, four score or a hundred. And then there was such hate between the Portingals and the Spaniards that they were almost at open wars.

Also he saith that the report amongst the common people is that they think the Englishmen will be hard for them at sea; but if they set their foot on land, they hope to find some friends; and they say they look for help of the Scots. And the King of Spain himself commended Sir Francis Drake very much, to be a valiant man of war, saying that if he had him there he would use him well enough.

Also he saith that they make great account of the Dunkirk fleet, which is thought to be about 30 or 40 thousand men; and that they make as great account of that company as that which they bring from Spain.

Also they talked closely[1] that there was a fleet preparing to go to Guinea and the Indies; and he saw ten ships lading wines for that voyage; they appointed to go about midsummer. The wine they carry is called . . . .[2] a strong wine, and is bound with iron hoops.

Also he saith that Antonio Olivarez and Pedro Castillo be the principal officers for the King at Cadiz and St. Mary Port, and that they demanded of those French ships and others that came away a hundred of oldernes,[3] which was worth there 900 ducats, and then they should depart; which when they had provided and delivered, they answered they could by no means suffer them to pass.

---

[1] In secret, privately.   [2] Blank in MS.

[3] No such coin is known. It was perhaps a trade name for a money of account. In these papers a ducat is always taken as another name for a pistole; that is the golden ducat, worth about 9*s.* The intrinsic value of the olderne would thus be about 4*l.*, or 100 pesetas.

Whereupon the French and others found themselves grieved; which they perceiving, commanded presently their sails to be taken from them; nevertheless, they conveyed some of their sails into casks, with the which they came now away.

Also he saith that the 25th of this present he came from St. Malo in Brittany, where the report was that the Parisians demand of the King whether they should accept of the Duke of Guise. And the King answering nothing, nodded his head; whereupon some of them afterwards pronounced *Vive le roi Guise !* [1]

Also he saith that many of the better sort there do judge that all this is but a policy and device between the King and the Guise for some greater matter. And although the Guise be favoured of some, yet is he disliked of many.

May 28.—*SEYMOUR TO WALSYNGHAM.*

[ccx. 34.—Holograph. Addressed.]

Sir:—According to your direction, I send you here enclosed a perfect particular of our coast men, both of shipping, numbers of men, as also the proportion of victuals, as well the beginning as the ending thereof. So as all that I am to desire you is that, hereafter, we be supplied of victuals at the least for six weeks, if so be that her Majesty make any account of service to be done; for truly, Sir, without care and regard had of us, what with taking our months' victuals in, there are so many days spent in vain, that no manner of service can be attempted, by reason they consume so fast. And

---

[1] This refers to the events of May 2-12, *la journée des barricades.*

great reason is there to consider hereof; specially when any exploits are to be tendered either for the Low Countries, Scotland, or the west parts. Thus, having nothing else to trouble you, do take my leave. From aboard the Rainbow, this 28th of May, 1588.

Your assured friend to command,
H. Seymour.

Post.—Sir William Wynter doth humbly desire you to put his letter within your packet, when you have any occasion to send unto my Lord Admiral.

May 27.—*THE PERFECT PARTICULAR OF COAST MEN.*

[ccx. 34, I.—Enclosure in Seymour's letter of May 28.]

27th of May, 1588.—The names of the ships, hoys &c. set forth by the several towns underwritten, with the captains' names,[1] number of men,[1] their several tonnage,[1] and the quantity of victuals in them remaining the day of the date hereof; which ships, hoys &c. do serve under me, the Lord Henry Seymour, admiral of her Majesty's navy serving in the Narrow Seas, viz. :—

Newcastle.—Daniel (24); Galleon Hutchins (24); Bark Lamb (24); Fancy (24).

Hull.—Griffin (25); Little Hare (25); Handmaid (25).

Ipswich.—Hoys : William (30); Katharine (30); Primrose (30).

Lynn.—Mayflower (35); Susan (35).

[1] These particulars are given in the list of the fleet, and are here omitted. The figures following each ship's name denote the number of days' victuals she had.

Yarmouth.—Grace (35).
Lowestoft.—Matthew (21).
Alborough.—Marigold (21).
Colchester.—William of Brightlingsea.[1]
Dover.—Elizabeth [2] (50).
Sandwich.—Reuben (50).
Feversham.—Hazard (30).
Hythe.—Grace of God (34).
Romney.—John ([3]).
Rye.—William (31).
Hastings.—Anne Bonaventure (24).

May 28.—*HOWARD TO BURGHLEY.*

[ccx. 35.—Signed, and autograph postscript.　Addressed.]

My very good Lord :—I have received a letter
from my man Burnell,[4] whom I left to come after us
with the ten ships with victuals.　I perceive by his
letter that the ships, and also the victuals, be nothing
in that readiness that I looked they should be in,

---

[1] MS. Brickelsey.　The number of days' victuals is not given.

[2] Here, and in some other lists, this ship appears as Elinathan,
or Ellen Nathan.　Elizabeth, as in ccxv. 76 and elsewhere, is no
doubt correct.

[3] Not stated.

[4] Francis Burnell is in the list of the fleet, as captain of the
Mary Rose, the largest of the fifteen ships that transported victuals
westward.　From Seymour's letter to Howard of August 19, it
would seem that he afterwards rejoined the Ark.　The family of
Burnell belonged to Acton-Burnell in Shropshire, the manorial
rights of which were granted to the second Duke of Norfolk on
the restoration of the title after the battle of Flodden.　From
one branch of this family, which took the name of Acton, were
descended the Acton, prime minister of Naples, who was so
closely connected with Lord Nelson in 1798-9, and also the
present Lord Acton.　Another branch, keeping the name of
Burnell, is now represented in the navy by Captain John Coke
Burnell.

nor as Mr. Quarles did promise me; for he did ensure me that within seven or eight days at the farthest, they should be dispatched after my departure from the Court, which was the 14th of this month. Burnell's letter unto me beareth date of the 20th, and signifieth unto me that Mr. Quarles and Mr. Peter told him that it would not be ready to depart in 12 or 14 days after; and besides, that the ships were in no readiness that should bring it, and that there would be no mariners gotten for them. My Lord, I judged it would be so; for when there is more care had of the merchants' traffic than there is of such matter of importance as this is, it is like it will be no better.

My Lord, we have here now but 18 days' victual, and there is none to be gotten in all this country; and what that is to go withal to sea, your Lordship may judge; and to tarry, that we must not. For even this morning, Mr. Cary,[1] the sheriff of Devonshire, and Sir Richard Greynvile have brought me word of a bark that is come newly from the South Cape,[2] and was there within these seven days, and did take two or three fishermen off that place, who told them that the Spanish fleet was to come out with the first wind. And therefore very likely that, now the wind being so good for them, they are coming out. And therefore, God willing, the first wind that will serve to put us out, we will be gone towards them; for we have done watering and only are watching here for a wind, all things else being in a readiness. God send us a wind to put us out; for go we will, though we starve. The fault is not mine. We must do as God will provide for us. But, my Lord, it would have done well that they

[1] George Cary of Cockington, Lord Deputy of Ireland in 1603; died in 1617.
[2] Cape St. Vincent.

that are gone or going to Stade or Russia[1] had
staid until these ships with our victuals had come to
us.   Your Lordship doth know what want of
victuals did breed once in Ireland, when there were
but four of her Majesty's ships with George Wynter[2];
and in like sort, when Sir William Wynter was
there.   God knoweth what this may do; and our
ships that should have come with victual, if they had
come hither, we might have taken it well in; but it
will be now hard for them to find us, for God
knoweth which way the Spanish fleet will bend,
either to England, Ireland, or Scotland.   But I
mean to leave a bark here to bring them after us,
for we will lie in the Sleeve[3] as long as we may,
except there be cause to the contrary.

There is another bark come from the coast of
Spain, belonging to Sir George Carey,[4] and past by
this way towards the Isle of Wight; who doth
report that the Spanish forces, for certainty, do set
out as yesterday.   We have the like advertisements
out of France, by divers several barks that are
come thence.   God send the wind to serve to put
us out; for I believe surely, if the wind hold here

[1] The Russian trade at this time was to St. Nicholas in the
White Sea.

[2] George Wynter, brother or cousin of Sir William, commanded a squadron of *three* of the Queen's ships on the coast of
Ireland in 1577.   He was ordered to cruise between the Cape of
Cornwall and the River Shannon, looking out for a Frenchman
named La Roche, who was reported to be preparing some private
expedition against Ireland; and to stay out as long as his victuals
lasted.   The squadron went to the seas on July 20, and returned
on October 18; but there does not seem to be any record of the
trouble to which Howard refers.   *S.P. Dom. Eliz.* cxiv. 60;
cxvii. 1.

[3] See *ante,* p. 5, *note.*

[4] Afterwards second Lord Hunsdon, Howard's brother-in-law
and Governor of the Isle of Wight; not to be confused with
George Cary of Cockington.   Both names frequently recur in
these papers.

but six days, they will knock at our door.   If they
do so, the fault is not ours ; for I hope [1] we have lost
no one hour nor minute of time, nor will suffer any
hereafter to be lost.   Therefore I pray you, good
my Lord, to cause our victuals to be hastened after
us with all speed ; and to speak to Mr. Quarles that
there may some supply be made again against anything that may happen.   And so I bid your good
Lordship heartily farewell.   From Plymouth, the
28th of May, 1588.

Your Lordship's very loving friend to command,
C. HOWARD.

I pray you let this messenger be returned with
some speed ; for although the wind do come to suit
us and that we be gone, I will leave a pinnace to
bring him after me.

May 28.—*HOWARD TO BURGHLEY.*

[**ccx. 36.**—Signed, and autograph postscript.   Addressed.]

My very good Lord :—I have received your
Lordship's letter of the 22nd of this instant, wherein
you desire that a certain ship, called the Mary of
Hamburg, stayed at Plymouth, may be suffered to
pass with her lading of rice, almonds, and other
goods, to London, whither she is bound.

Your Lordship shall understand that we have
scarcely three weeks' victuals left in our fleet, being
bound in by the wind, and watching the first opportunity of the same to go forth unto the seas ; and
that therefore, for our better provision and prolonging of our victuals, I have caused the said rice
to be stayed and taken for her Majesty's use, paying

---

[1] Feel sure, dare affirm.   The word is still used in this sense
in Cumberland.

for the same as it is valued at. And for the ship, and the rest of her lading, I will give order that she may pass hence to London, according to your Lordship's request. And so I bid your Lordship most heartily well to fare. From Plymouth, the 28th of May, 1588.

Your Lordship's very loving friend to command,

C. HOWARD.

My good Lord, there is here the gallantest[1] company of captains, soldiers,[2] and mariners that I think ever was seen in England. It were pity they should lack meat,[3] when they are so desirous to spend their lives in her Majesty's service.[4]

I would to God I did know how the world went with our Commissioners; for if I know nothing I must do thereafter, and think of the worst. I pray God all things be in best readiness, if the worst do fall out. And God send us the happiness to meet with them before our men on the land discover them, for I fear me a little sight of the enemy will fear the land men much.

REASONS WHY THE SPANIARDS SHOULD ATTEMPT THE ISLE OF WIGHT.

[ccx. 47.—Endorsed. Not dated.]

Reasons why the Spaniards should rather land in the Isle of Wight than any other place of England.

If by this preparation of the ships and the galleys, an invasion be intended to any part of England—then, entering into consideration what ports are fittest for his advantage, and most dan-

---

[1] MS. gallants.   [2] MS. sogers.
[3] MS. lake meet.   [4] MS. sarvis.

gerous to work our annoyance, let us look into these ensuing circumstances, and we shall the better judge where he will make his first descent.

Three things he will principally respect.

First, where he may find least resistance, and most quiet landing.

Secondly, where he may have best harbour for his galleys, and speediest supplies out of Spain, France and Flanders.

Thirdly, where he may most offend the realm by incursions, and force her Majesty, by keeping many garrisons, to stand upon a defensive war.

To the first, It carrieth no appearance in reason that he will land in any part of the realm where he shall not be able so soon to put himself on shore, and to intrench himself in strength, but [1] that the whole body and force of that shire, with their neighbouring aids, may and will so disturb him, or prevent him with a battle, that he must either retire to his ships, or hazard his greatest forces and the overthrow of his wearied army ; we being daily to be reinforced with fresh men and greater supplies ; small strength being sufficient to keep them awaking and busied, until a strong head may be made against them.

To the second point, What place can be assigned that may stand indifferent for Spain, Flanders and France, but that they are too remote from the one and too near the other, except the Isle of Wight, Hampton or Portsmouth ? To the latter two places, the precedent reason may give cause of security, which holdeth not in the first; but by all winds may be supplied out of one of the three countries before specified.

To the third, There is no doubt to be made, but landing in the Wight—which with an army of 8,000

---

[1] Without.

men, divided into four parts, he may easily do, the
force of the Island being unable to resist them with
that force—in very short time they may so fortify
themselves and possess those parts and places that
lie convenient for passing over our supplies, and are
by nature more than three parts fortified, that he
may keep in safe harbour his galleys to make daily
invasions into the firm[1] lands, where they shall perceive the standing of the wind will impeach her
Majesty's ships to come to their rescue.   So that all
the castles and sea towns of Hampshire, Sussex
and Dorsetshire will be subject to be burnt, unless
her Majesty will keep garrisons in those places, the
number and charge whereof will be no less exceeding[2] than how long they shall be forced to continue [will be] uncertain.

June 9.[3]—WALSYNGHAM TO HOWARD.

[ccxi. 8.—Copy.   Endorsed.   Nearly obliterated by damp.]

My very good Lord :—Her Majesty, perceiving
by your Lordship's late letters to me that you were
minded to repair to the Isles of Bayona, if the
wind serve, there to abide the Spanish fleet or to
discover what course they meant to take, doubting
that in case your Lordship should put over so far
the said fleet may take some other way, whereby
they may escape your Lordship, as by bending their
course westward to the altitude[4] of 50 degrees, and
then to shoot over to this realm, hath therefore
willed me to let your Lordship understand that she
thinketh it not convenient that your Lordship should

---

[1] *Terra firma*, the mainland.   [2] Very great.
[3] The endorsement has a smudged 7 ; but Howard in his
letter of the 15th (*post*, p. 202) refers to this as of the 9th.
[4] Latitude.

go so far to the south as the said Isles of Bayona,
but to ply up and down in some indifferent place
between the coast of Spain and this realm, so as you
may be able to answer any attempt that the said
fleet shall make either against this realm, Ireland or
Scotland.   And so &c.

*June 9.—THOMAS BOSTOCKE TO SIR
GEORGE BOND.*[1]

[**ccxi. 11.**—Endorsed:—The copy of a letter written to Sir George
Bond from St. John de Luz, the 19th of June, 1588.]

Jesus in St. John de Luz, the 19th of June, 1588.
Right Honourable, my duty considered &c. : —
It may please your Honour, my last I wrote per
your son, William Bond, in the Black Dog, of
whose arrival at Falmouth, in company with the
Jane Bonaventure, we have understood by your
son ; as also in my other letters I have wrote your
Honour at large as concerning your affairs here ;
and according to my request, I doubt not but that
your Honour and my friend Mr. Howe will furnish
me with a ship and commodities, as to your said son
and to my letters I refer me[2]; provided for the
copper you send[3] let it be all in squares and rounds,
and to send me as little in bricks as possible you
can.

I doubt not but that my friend here will accomplish[4] with me for the wools according to our
concert,[5] so that all my doubt is that any good
shipping may not be suffered to come out of

[1] Sheriff of London, 1578 ; Lord Mayor and knighted,
1587–8.
[2] As to which, I refer you to your said son &c.
[3] MS. sent.   [4] Conclude the business.
[5] MS. consorte.   The meaning is clearly agreement, or bargain.

England ; for we hold it here for most certain that the Spanish army departed out of Lisbon of the 29th and 30th of the last ; and the report goeth that they be bound for our country of England, or else for some other place whereby to annoy her Majesty ; and they are 150 sails with men. I pray God of his mercy to prevent them of their purpose, and that we may have the victory of them ; which I doubt not, through the help of Almighty God, if her Majesty have intelligence of their coming.

Now if the Spanish army be arrived in her Majesty's dominions or other ways, to her Majesty's disliking, I pray your Honour to inform some of her Majesty's Council that here, in these parts, betwixt Fuenterrabia and the Groyne, there is preparing 50 or 60 sails of ships, small and great, and do lade only victuals for a new supply to refresh their foresaid army, as biscuit, cider, bacon and wines. If they could be met withal, but with six or eight good ships with their pinnaces, no doubt they would take them, although they come together [1] ; for they be most of them very small shipping. But I do think rather they will go in three or four fleets, because some of them will be assured to pass, as they report, to the north parts of Scotland, where they say their army is. And thus your Honour may partly guess in what order we remain, until it please God we hear of her Majesty's good proceeding against our enemy ; which God grant according to our heart's desire. And thus, doubting the conveyance will not be very speedy, I rest— praying God to prosper your Honour in all your proceedings with continuation of health.

Your Honour's servant,
THOMAS BOSTOCKE.

[1] Even if they sail all together.

June 13.—*HOWARD TO WALSYNGHAM.*

[ccxi. 17.—Signed. Addressed. In bad condition.]

Sir :—I have received your letter by this bearer, of the 8th of this present, with two advertisements therein ; the one, out of France, of the demands that the Duke of Guise doth make and require of the King ; the other, of Scotland from my brother Carey,[1] which I most heartily thank you for ; but for the abstract that you write of, of the news sent you from Lisbon from the man that I know, that came not with your letter.   Notwithstanding, I perceived by your letter that by all likelihood the King's fleet is come out ; that you doubt, by the number of Irishmen that [they have with] them, that they are like to come for Ireland.

Sir, if they [should do] so, or for Scotland, if all the world lay on it, we can do [no] good as this wind is ; for it holdeth here at West and South-West, and bloweth up so as that no ship here but her Majesty's great ships dare ride in this Sound, but are fain to go into the haven.   If it begin to show any likelihood to be northerly or easterly, I do go out straight and all my company ; but we are not able by any means to get the weather[2] of this harbour, but fain to come in again, or else we should be driven to the

[1] His brother-in-law, Robert Carey, born 1560, youngest son of Lord Hunsdon, was at this time ambassador to the Scottish King. He was created Earl of Monmouth in 1626, and died 1639. He is said, by Camden, to have served as a volunteer against the armada, but the statement seems very doubtful.   These papers give it no support, and it appears (B.M. Calig. D. 1, f. 156) that he started for Scotland on July 16.

[2] To get to windward of &c.   The expression was still in use a century later, as :—'The enemy had a great squadron to weather of the Prince's and Sir John Harman's divisions' (*Relation of the Engagement . . . on August* 11, 1673).

leewards, either to Portland or to the Isle of Wight. I know not what weather you have there with you, but here is such weather as never was seen at this time of the year.

Sir, I protest before God I would I had not a foot of land in England, that the wind would serve us to be abroad ; and yet it is a hard matter and a thing unpossible [for] us to lie in any place or to be anywhere to guard England, Ireland and Scotland ; and I would to God her Majesty had [thought] well for it that she had understood their plot, which w[ould] have been done easily for money.   And then it would have been [an] easy matter to have made him [1] not able to have troubled [her] Majesty again in one seven years. And if the wind had been favourable unto us, we had been long since before their doors, [that] they should not have stirred but we would have been upon their jacks.[2]   The wind hath continued so bad these 15 days, [that] we could by no means send any pinnace into the Trade.[3] [God] will alter it when it shall please him.

Sir, if they h[ave] been at the sea so long as you are advertised, and as I [think] it most true [4]—for there were three hulks that stole out of Spain, and as they came along the coast, they saw the fleet off the Rock,[5] a 12 or 15 [leagues distant].   That was on the 20th of May.   It did confirm that which

[1] The King of Spain.

[2] Jack is a coat of mail. ' To be on one's jack ' is explained by Latham as ' to be down on one,' in the colloquial sense.   ' To dust his jacket ' would seem an almost exact equivalent.

[3] The name, down to the beginning of the seventeenth century, of that part of the sea between Ushant and Brest afterwards known as the Broad Sound, and now the Passage de l'Iroise. See vol. ii. App. B.

[4] He breaks off to tell why he thinks it true : the conclusion of the sentence is nine lines lower down—' And if they mean to go for Scotland or Ireland ' &c.

[5] Lisbon

another ship did advertise before, and therefore very likely [to] be true. The fleet did bear, and ran off West and by North, which they did to get the westerly winds, and the best course that they could keep either for Ireland, Scotland, or England. And if they mean to go for Scotland [or] Ireland, they are there before this; and if I do hear of [it] I will not be long after them, if God will send us wind to do it.

But, Sir, I pray you see in what case we are. Our victuals are not yet come to us; and if this wind continue, God knoweth when it will come. The time of our victualling that we have doth come out[1] on Saturday next; but by the good means and wise and well doings of Mr. Darell,[2] we have been refreshed here with some 12 or 14 days' victual at times, or else it would have been hard to have put to the seas any time these ten days, with 15 or 16 days' victuals. But yet we were and are resolved to go whensoever the wind shall serve, and to be as near as we can where we may meet with the King's fleet, which I pray God to send us to do; for, Sir, since the world began, I think there was never a willinger company to do their prince service than these be.

[1] Come to an end

[2] Marmaduke Darell, knighted in 1603, was at this time victualling agent for the navy, or Assistant-Surveyor, apparently subordinate to Quarles. He was formerly a clerk in the Queen's avery, or stables, and in 1585 was appointed by the Council to attend upon Sir Amyas Poulet, 'and to have the defraying of all such sums of money as should concern the diet, charges and expenses of the Scottish Queen'—*Accounts relating to Mary, Queen of Scots* (Camden Soc.), p. 1. In February 1587 he was still at Fotheringay, where he witnessed the execution of the Queen of Scots, as he wrote to his cousin, William Darrell of Littlecote—a very different man in sober history from the Wild Darrell of poetry and tradition. Cf. *Rokeby*, v. 36, and Hall's *Elizabethan Society, passim*.

Sir, if you can by any means learn, or if we can, that they be in the Groyne, I doubt not but by God's grace we will make sport with them. If you hear that they be landed in Ireland or Scotland, I pray you let me have word with all possible speed. If the wind hold here you must send hither; if it change we are gone. Sir, I will never go again to such a place of service but I will carry my victuals with me, and not trust to careless men behind me. We came away scarce with a month's victuals; it had been little enough but to have gone to Flushing. We think it should be marvelled at how we keep our men from running away, for the worst men in the fleet knoweth for how long they are victualled; but I thank God as yet we are not troubled with any mutinies, nor I hope shall not; for I see men kindly handled will bear want and run through the fire and water; and I doubt not but if this month's victual come unto us from London before we depart, we will make it to serve us to continue very near three months. And if it does not come, yet assure yourself we will not lose any opportunity, nor we will not lack; there is good fishing in the seas. And if we be driven upon any occasion upon the coast of Spain, I durst meet with the King of Spain's 18,000 men on the land in any reasonable place; and therefore, fear not, we will not want. God send us wind. And if the wind had favoured us when we went out from hence, which was on the 29th of May, they should not have needed to have come thus far to have sought us.

Sir, I forbear to write unto my Lord Treasurer, because I am sure he is a very heavy man [1] for my Lady his daughter,[2] which I am most heartily sorry

[1] Heavy of heart.
[2] His eldest daughter, Anne, wife of Edward, 17th Earl of Oxford, died June 5, 1588.

for. And so I bid you most heartily farewell. From aboard her Majesty's good ship the Ark, the 13th of June, 1588.

Your loving friend,
C. HOWARD.

[**ccxiii. 88.**—Signed. A small slip of paper, without date, address, or endorsement. Probably a postscript to the preceding. It is in the same writing, on the same paper, and has suffered from the same bad usage.]

Sir :—Most of the ships do presently come out of their victuals, which Mr. Darell will presently supply, and the rest he cannot possibly victual as yet ; which, because they be better provided,[1] shall stay until he can provide for them, which will be within these 30 days at the farthest.

Sir, I pray you send to the committee of London for to send down hither some money for the relief of their soldiers and mariners, who have done their duties hitherunto very well.

Sir, You would not believe what a wonderful thing it is to victual such an army as this is in such a narrow corner of the realm, where a man would think that neither victuals were to be had, nor cask to put it in, which I believe is little thought on there.

C. HOWARD.

June 14.—*HOWARD TO WALSYNGHAM.*

[**ccxi. 18.**—Signed. Addressed. In bad condition.]

Sir :—The extremity of the weather in this place where it hath [held], hath caused me to continue here longer than I had meant. I have not marvelled

---

[1] Sc. than the others which ' do presently come out ' &c.

a little, continuing here so long, that I have not
heard how the proceedings in the Low Countries
have gone; for in my opinion it had been very
necessary, that I might have carried myself thereafter in the actions.[1] For if the weather had served
me to have gone out, or whensoever it shall serve,
I will do my best endeavour to learn where the
fleet is, and afterwards to find them out; and
according as either I shall hear from you or find
by them, thereafter to deal with them.

The opinion of Sir Francis Drake, Mr. Hawkyns,
Mr. Frobiser, and others that be men of greatest
judgment [and] experience, as also my own concurring with them in the same, is that [the] surest
way to meet with the Spanish fleet is upon their
own [coast], or in any harbour of their own, and
there to defeat them; for if [they have] been so
long at the sea as the advertisements do declare,
they must [now] be landed either in Ireland or
Scotland ere this, or else somewhere [on] the coast
of France. But I [am] verily persuaded they mean
[nothing] else but to linger it out upon their own
coast, until they understand [that] we have spent
our victuals here; and therefore we must be busy
[with] them before we suffer ourselves to be brought
to that extremity.

Sir, it is very strange that, in this time, the
Commissioners cannot perceive whether they mean
a peace without fraud, or use the same [2] to detract a
time for a further device. And if our Commissioners
do discover any detraction in them, only to serve
their own turns, methinks her Majesty should use
the like policy, and devise to beat them with their
own rod. Then could I wish with all my heart

---

[1] In my actions; have guided my conduct thereby.
[2] The negotiation; detract = to draw out, to spin out the
time. So also detraction=a spinning out of the time.

that King Anthony [1] were with us, that he might set foot in his own country, and find the King occupied [2] there, which we might easily do. Thus I do adventure to [offer] my mind privately unto you, as unto my especial good friend, pray[ing you that] I may hear from you speedily again of such proceedings as the Commissioners have, of such advertisements as you hear, and privately, of your own advice and judgment herein.

Sir, we have endured these three days, Wednesday, Thursday and Friday, an extreme continual storm. Myself, and four or five of the greatest ships, have ridden it out in the Sound, because we had no room in Catwater, for the lesser ships that were there; nor betwixt the shore and the Island, [3] because Sir Francis Drake, with four or five other ships, did ride there. Myself and my company in these ships do continually tarry and lie aboard in all the storm, where we may compare that we have danced as lustily as the gallantest dancers in the Court. And if it may please God to continue her Majesty's ships as strong to the end of the journey as they have done hitherunto, her Majesty may [be su]re (what false and villainous reports soever have been made of them) [she hath] the strongest ships that any prince [in] Christendom hath. A[nd all the] masters and skilful men here say that it had been better to have [been of] late in any of the Spanish seas, than to have ridden out these storms here, wherein we do not find that any one ship complains.

Sir, our victuals be not come yet unto us; and if this weather hold, I know not when they will come.

[1] Dom Antonio, the popular claimant to the throne of Portugal.
[2] Occupation.　　　[3] St. Nicholas or Drake's Island.

Sir, I must not omit to let you know how lovingly and kindly Sir Francis Drake beareth himself; and also how dutifully to her Majesty's service and unto me, being in the place I am in; which I pray you he may receive thanks for, by some private letter from you.

And so, praying you to present my most bounden and humble duty unto her Majesty, and that I will not trouble her with my letters before some matter of greater moment do fall out, I bid you heartily farewell. From off aboard her Majesty's good ship the Ark, in Plymouth Sound, the 14th of June, 1588.

Your assured loving friend,

C. HOWARD.

June 15.—*HOWARD TO WALSYNGHAM.*

[**ccxi. 26.**—Signed. Addressed.]

Sir :—Within three hours after I had written my letter, which herewith I send you, [I] received your letter of the 9th of this present[1] by a pursuivant. Which letter I do not a little marvel at; for thereby you signify that her Majesty, perceiving by a letter I sent you heretofore, that I was minded to go on the coast of Spain, to the Isles of Bayona, her pleasure is that I should not go so far, but only off and on, betwixt the coast of Spain and England; lest the Spanish fleet should come into the height[2] of 50, and then should bend their course directly to this realm.

Sir, for the meaning we had to go on the coast of Spain, it was deeply debated by those which I think [the] world doth judge to be men of greatest experience that this realm hath; which are these:

[1] See *ante*, p. 192.   [2] Latitude.

Sir Francis Drake, Mr. Hawkyns, Mr. Frobiser, and Mr. Thomas Fenner ; and I hope her Majesty will not think that we went so rashly to work, or without a principal and choice care and respect of the safety of this realm. We would go on the coast of Spain ; and therefore our ground was first, to look to that principal[1] ; and if we found they did but linger on their own coast, or that they were put into the Isles of Bayona or the Groyne, then we thought in all men's judgments that be of experience here, it had been most fit to have sought some good way, and the surest we could devise, by the good protection of God, to have defeated them.

[For] this, we considered that the Spanish forces, being for so long [time] victualled as they are, might in very good policy detract [time, to] drive us to consume our victuals, which, for anything we [can see], is not to be supplied again to serve the turn, by all the means that her Majesty and all you can do. And if her Majesty do think that she is able to detract time with the King of Spain, she is greatly deceived ; which may breed her great peril. For this abusing [of] the treaty of peace doth plainly show how the King of Spain will have all things perfect, [as] his plot is laid, before he will proceed to execute. I am persuaded he will see the Duke of Guise bring the French [King] to his purpose before he will [act]. If his intention be so, I pray you, when our victuals be consumed in gazing for them, what shall become of us? Whether this [may] not breed most great danger and dishonour, I leave it to her Majesty's wisdom ; but if it should fall out so, I would I had never been born ; and so I am sure many here would wish no less, [on] their own behalf.

And if [we] were to-morrow next on the coast

[1] Principally.

of Spain, I would not land in any place to offend
any ; but they should well perceive that we came
not to spoil, but to seek out the great force to fight
with them ; and so should they have known by
message ; which should have been the surest [way]
and most honourable to her Majesty. But now, as
by your directions to lie off and on betwixt England and Spain, the South-West wind, that shall
bring them to Scotland or Ireland, shall put us to
the leeward. The seas are broad ; but if we had
been [on] their coast, they durst not have put off,
to have left us [on] their backs ; and when they
shall come with the south-westerly wind, which
must serve them if they go for Ireland or Scotland,
though we be as high as Cape Clear, yet shall we
not be able to go to them as long as the wind shall
be westerly. And if we lie so high, then may the
Spanish fleet bear with the coast of France, to
come for the Isle of Wight ; which for my part,
I think, if they come to England, they will attempt.
Then are we clean out of the way of any service
against them.

But I must and will obey ; and am glad there
be such there, as are able to judge what is fitter for
us to do, than we here[1] ; but by my instructions
which I had, I did think it otherwise. But I will
put them up in a bag, and I shall most humbly
pray her Majesty to think that that which we meant
to do was not rashly determined, and that which
shall be done shall be most carefully used by us ;
and we will follow and obey her Majesty's commandment. But if we had been now betwixt Spain
and England, we had been but in hard case, the
storm being so strong and continuing so long as it
hath done ; but upon the coast of Spain, we had
had a land wind and places of succour. We meant

[1] He means, of course : what is fit for us to do, better than &c.

not to have spoiled any town or village ; only we must of necessity water ; and when we lie betwixt both coasts, we must come to this coast to water, for so we are enjoined ; and if the wind do not serve us to come on our own coast, then in what case shall [we be, now] that we must not go on the coast of Spain ? We lay seven days in the Sleeve, which was as long as we could continue there without danger, as the wind was ; and if some had been with us, they should have seen what a place of danger it is to lie on and off in.

Sir, you know it [hath] been the opinion both of her Majesty and others, that it was [the sur]est course to lie on the coast of Spain. I confess my error at that time, which[1] was otherwise ; but I did and will yield ever unto them of greater experience. Yet you know it was thought by her Majesty that we might go into Lisbon to defeat them, which was the strongest place. Therefore I thought that if we had heard that they had been at the Isles of Bayona, or the Groyne, which be ten times more easy to defeat them in, I think it would have been good service.

But, Sir, I will persuade no [more], but do as I am directed ; and God send the wind do not force us thither ; otherwise, upon my duty, we will not go thither, now we know her Majesty's pleasure. And so I bid you most heartily farewell. From aboard her Majesty's good ship the Ark, in Plymouth Sound, the 15th of June, 1588.

Your assured loving friend,
C. HOWARD.

[1] When my opinion.

June 17.—*SEYMOUR TO WALSYNGHAM.*

[ccxi. 33.—Holograph. Addressed.]

Sir :—So long as I am in this action of service, [at] such times as will give me leave to consider advisedly thereof, [I] do bethink myself thereafter, by delivering my opinion touching the effect of your letter to Sir William Wynter, wherewith you wished me to be acquainted ; and so much the rather I busy my head, because yesterday hasty news flew from Calais to Dover of the Spanish fleet[1] being at Ushant.

But touching the Duke of Parma his intent for the annoyance of England, I am fully resolved[2] his enterprises will never go forward, but where beforehand he doth assure himself of a strong party of the contrary side ; which for England, God himself (I hope) doth prevent, as otherwise assisteth your Honours all with his Spirit, by restraining the papists' governments through every several shire,[3] whereby the same is avoided by that course.

And were it so that he might have a faction in England, surely those places remembered by Sir William Wynter are very likely to be attempted ; but yet I have bethought myself of a far more convenient hold, most fit above any yet set down, the Isle of Wight by name, aptest for a rendezvous.

And where Sir William Wynter doubteth the main chance for London by the Thames mouth,

---

[1] The ships that were reported by Godolphin on the 21st as having been met with off Scilly. See *post*, p. 221.

[2] Persuaded.

[3] Referring generally to the repressive policy of the Government, but more especially, perhaps, to the resolution of the Council on the previous day, to commit a dozen of the principal recusants to the Tower.—*S.P. Dom. Eliz.* ccxi. 28.

adding his opinion for sconces and bulwarks, thereby to front the enemies, the charge growing thereof can not be but great; besides, the weakness of those places shall be thoroughly discovered, where now, for the most part, the same are concealed. For remedying whereof with a far less charge, twenty such hoys as Harwich and Ipswich do set forth, lying in the Thames mouth in several places, being nimble of sail and quick in turning to and fro, will prevent and greatly withstand any sudden attempt ; and I am sure these twenty sails will be defrayed under the rate of four such ships as the Rainbow.

But to proceed with the Duke of Parma. We suspect, and I fear we shall find his great faction with the Duke of Guise, by reason of the Holy League. And where most commonly he giveth forth his determinations, the same for the most part doth fall out contrary ; as by the last year's experience, he made show for Ostend, and yet went to Sluys. So likewise now, he would busy our heads sometimes for Scotland, at other times for Ireland, otherwise for Norfolk or Suffolk, the more to blind our eyes by bending our forces those ways, and taking his further advantages, for his inward conceits ; the same, no doubt, being resolutely determined for Holland and Zealand, or for Picardy ; in which both places he presumeth to have strong factions.

To prevent all which, in time, is[1] to call home our Commissioners, if you stand doubtful of your expectations for their proceedings. With all, her Majesty shall ease her purse, by giving general liberty to make open wars. Otherwise, in prolonging these actions with such charges, gaining a peace fit for heretics, her Majesty, whom I beseech God long preserve, will be in danger both of the foreign

[1] The way is &c.

enemies, as otherwise stand in great contempt among her subjects, who do now manifest their duties and good wills apparently.

Thus referring my opinion to better judgments, and desiring to be excused for intermeddling so far, with my most loving commendations, I betake[1] you to God.   From aboard the Rainbow, the 17th of June, 1588.

Your assured friend to command,

H. SEYMOUR.

Post.—Sir, I would be glad you would procure her Majesty or my Lords to send the letters for these hoys; but rather I wish you would send me word to take order to send them to Greenwich, where they may be seen before her Majesty remove from thence; and I am sure my opinion will be confirmed among you.   They may be better spared now.   Their victuals do expire within eight days.

June 19.—*HOWARD TO WALSYNGHAM.*

[ccxi. 37.—Holograph.   Addressed.]

Good Mr. Secretary :—You see it is very likely to come to pass, my opinion that I always had of the French King; as also of the treacherous treaty of peace, which was never to any other end but that the King of Spain might have time, and not be troubled in gathering his forces together, and her Majesty's noble and princely nature most greatly abused.   And therefore, good Mr. Secretary, let every one of you persuade her Majesty that she lose no more time in taking care enough of herself, and to make herself, every way that is possible, as strong as she can; for there is no question but the

---

[1] Commit.

King of Spain hath engaged his honour to the
uttermost in this, for the overthrow of her Majesty
and this realm, and doth employ all the forces, not
only of his own, but also all that he can get of his
friends, for this exploit; and if he be put back from
this this year, her Majesty may have a good and
honourable peace. If not, yet she shall be sure he
shall not be able to trouble her Majesty in many
years after.

You see it is made in the world greatly for his
honour that he is able to make such a power as that
he will enterprise to invade England. Thanks be
to God, the world shall also see that her Majesty
hath provided sufficient forces to beat him by sea;
so would I wish that in time[1] her Majesty should
gather some great force together for her defence on
the land. It would be a great surety, and to the
world most honourable. For if it come that her
[Majesty] should draw the forces together on the
sudden, it will breed a marvellous confusion[2]; and all
sudden causes breeds many doubts in multitudes. I
hope in God the manifest discovery of their determination, as it may well happen by the arch-traitor
Allen's book,[3] will awaken all men. If there be

[1] In good time.

[2] The sense is: But if her Majesty should neglect to do so,
and afterwards have to gather her forces together in a hurry, on a
sudden emergency, it will cause much confusion.

[3] William Allen, born at Rossall in 1532, was in Queen
Mary's time Principal of St. Mary's Hall, Oxford. He resigned
this office in 1560, and quitted England in 1561. He became a
priest in 1565, and in 1568 founded the English college at Douay,
where, in 1570, he was appointed Professor of Divinity. In 1582
he threw himself warmly into the polemical politics of the day,
and was mixed up in the schemes of the Guises and in the plots
in favour of the Queen of Scots. After her death he publicly
asserted the title of the King of Spain to the throne of England,
and—having been made a cardinal in 1587—published, in 1588,
a violent and offensive pamphlet, entitled, 'An Admonition to
the Nobility and People of England and Ireland concerning the

that will not awake with this, I would to God when they are asleep they might never awake.

Sir, because in service of so great moment as this is, it were not requisite that many should be privy of our counsels, I made choice of these whose names I here write, to be councillors of this service; made them all to be sworn to be secret:—Sir F. Drake, Lord Thomas Howard, the Lord Sheffield, Sir Roger Williams,[1] Mr. Hawkyns, Mr. Frobiser, Mr. Thomas Fenner. I chose Sir Roger Williams for his experience by land, what occasion soever might fall out to land in Ireland, or Scotland, or in England; for God willing, if it please God to send us wind to serve us, we mean to land some with them wheresoever they land in any of her Majesty's dominions. I do assure you, Sir, these two noblemen[2] be most gallant gentlemen, and not only for-

present wars, made for the execution of his Holiness' sentence by the high and mighty King Catholic of Spain.' It is to this that Howard here refers. It has been suggested that the violence of the style and the brutality of the matter are altogether alien to Allen's nature, and that he could not have been the real author. This is possible; but he acknowledged it, gave it the weight of his reputation as a man of piety, learning and rank, and must bear the odium which attaches to its publication. He died at Rome in 1594.

[1] A native of Monmouthshire; educated at Oxford. A soldier of fortune, he served for some time with the Duke of Alva. In 1585 he was with the Earl of Leicester in the Low Countries; was knighted in 1586; died in 1595. According to Camden, ' He was perhaps no way inferior to the best soldiers of that age, could he have put bounds to his courage, which ran away with his conduct and discretion.' He wrote *Actions of the Low Countries* and other military works (see Somers' *Tracts*, i. 329). He did not now remain long with the fleet, but joined Leicester in the camp at Tilbury: see *post*, Leicester to Walsyngham, July 25.

[2] Lord Thomas Howard, born in 1561, second son of the 4th Duke of Norfolk, was at this time captain of the Golden Lion, and was knighted on July 25. In 1591 he commanded the fleet at the Azores, when Sir Richard Greynvile was slain and the

wards, but very discreet in all their doings. I would
to God I could say for her Majesty's service, that
there were four such young noblemen behind to
serve her. God bless them with life, and they will
be able to do her Majesty and the realm good
service.

Sir, I am glad that the ships sent out by the
towns are victualled for a month more. I would it
were two. And for the love of God, let not her
Majesty care now for charges, so as it be well used.
And strengthen my Lord Harry in the Narrow
Seas with as much force as you can, sike[1] by force
of the sea to keep any from landing; for landing
will breed, I am afraid, great danger.

Sir, I pray send to us with all speed. But I
hope to be gone before I hear from you, for I will
not tarry one hour after our victuals do come to us,
and if the wind will serve us; for there must be no
time lost now, and we must seek to cut off their
time, which I hope in God to do.

Sir, as I have ever found you to be my most
especial good friend, and the man that, for your
honourable and faithful doings ever with me, hath
made me to think myself ever greatly beholden unto
you, I therefore now do most earnestly pray you to
stand my good friend, as to move her Majesty this
my humble suit and request: that if it please God

Revenge captured; and in 1596 took part in the expedition
against Cadiz. He was created Earl of Suffolk in 1603; was
Lord High Treasurer 1614-19; and died in 1626. Edmund
Sheffield, born in 1563, succeeded as 3rd Baron Sheffield in
1568. His mother was Howard's sister, at this time the wife of
Sir Edward Stafford. He was now in command of the White
Bear, and was also knighted by Howard on July 25. He was
created Earl of Mulgrave in 1626, and died in 1646. Portraits of
both are given in Doyle's Baronage.

[1] Such=such as, so as. The omission of the 'as' is not
uncommon in Elizabethan English. Cf. *Richard III.* III. ii. 26:
'I wonder he is so fond to trust the mockery' &c.

to call me to him in this service of her Majesty, which I am most willing to spend my life in, that her Majesty of her goodness will bestow my boy upon my poor wife.[1]   And if it please her Majesty to let my poor wife have the keeping either of Hampton Court or Oatlands,[2] I shall think myself more bound to her Majesty.   For I do assure you, Sir, I shall not leave her so well as so good a wife doth deserve.

Thus, Sir, I have been bold to trouble you, and can yield you no other requital but my love and good will as long as I live ; and so I recommend me most heartily unto you, and bid you farewell. [From] aboard the Ark, the 19th of June.

Your most assured loving friend to use,

C. Howard.

June 20.—WYNTER TO WALSYNGHAM.

[**ccxi. 38.**—Signed.   Addressed.]

I do most humbly thank your Honour for your letters I received yesterday in the evening, bearing date the 18th of this present, whereby it appeareth that my letters lately written to your Honour, in answer of yours, had favourable construction, both by her Majesty, yourself, and all my very good Lords of the Council, which doth glad me greatly, and I, as becometh me in duty, by God's favour, will ever acknowledge your honourable kindness used therein towards me, as also for many other your favours.

---

[1] As ward : to assign the boy as ward of his own mother, who would thus receive the revenue of the estate.

[2] In Surrey.   The park is now broken up and built over, and a big hotel stands on the site of the old palace.

It seemeth by your Honour's letters that the Prince of Parma his intention is towards Sheppey, Harwich, or Yarmouth; two of the which I know perfectly, as Sheppey and Harwich; the other not so well. And yet, if I do not mistake the situation of the said places, they are such as a small charge (in manner of speaking) will make a sufficient strength to withstand any sudden attempt. And whereas it is said the Prince's strength is 30,000 soldiers, then I assure your Honour it is no mean quantity of shipping that must serve for the transporting of that number and that which doth appertain to them, without the which I do not think they will put forth; 300 sail must be the least; and, one with another, to be counted 60 ton. For I well remember that in the journey made to Scotland, in the Queen's Majesty's father's time, when we burned Leith and Edinburgh,[1] and there was in that expedition 260 sail of ships; and yet we were not able to land above 11,000 men, and we then in fear of none that could impeach us by sea. It may be said the cut[2] between Flanders and the places named is shorter than out of England to the Frith in Scotland, which is true; but, Sir, men that do come for such a purpose, being so huge an army as 30,000 men, must have a mighty deal of all sorts of provisions to serve them, as your honourable wisdom can well consider.

But, Sir, I take the Prince's case to be far otherwise. For I suppose, if the countries of Holland and Zealand did arm[3] forth but only the shipping which the Lord Admiral at his departing delivered unto our admiral in writing that they would send from those parts to join with us here, and that was 36 sail of ships of war, and that it

[1] May, 1544. See Froude, iv. 32.   [2] Cut=division, distance.
[3] Arm=equip; so in French, *armer*.

were known to the Prince those did nothing but remain in readiness to go to the seas for the impeaching of his fleet whensoever they did come forth, I should live until I were young again or [1] the Prince would venture to set his ships forth.

And again, if her Majesty's ships, and such others as doth but now remain under our admiral's charge, may be continued in the state we are in, and not to be separated, the Prince's forces, being no other than that which he hath in Flanders at this time (upon whom we mean to keep as good watch for their coming forth as possible we can), dare not come to the seas. But the sorrow we have is that we think these dealings of his to be rather a scare-crow, to hasten or bring to pass such an end of the treaty as may be most for his master's advantage, than that he meaneth to set forward the thing he giveth out in show.

Your honourable opinion that 1,000 footmen and 200 horsemen might [2] be assigned to each of the three several places before rehearsed, to make head upon any attempt, and to remain until it be seen what the Prince's designs may be, is in my poor conceit very good. For in these princely actions, a man cannot be too provident ; and no wisdom were it to put things to an even [3] balance, when more weight may be added.

There was news sent over from Calais of late to Dover, by one Skofield,[4] an English merchant lying there (as it is said), that there arrived at Dunkirk lately certain Brittany ships, whose mariners should [5] give out that they came in company from Cape Finisterre with 150 ships of war of the King

---

[1] Or=ere.   [2] MS. moughte.   [3] MS. ayeven.
[4] The name is so written, and it cannot be verified. It was probably Scholefield.
[5] Should=did, as we are told.

of Spain's ; and how that they parted from them
upon the coast of Brittany near the Trade.[1] Since
which time we have had perfect intelligence that the
Queen's Majesty's ship, the Elizabeth Bonaventure,
hath been within the Trade and thereabouts. Likewise we have spoken with the masters and company
of three flyboats of Hoorn and Enkhuysen,[2] that
were in Rochelle five days past, and came along all
the coast of Brittany, and through the Trade ; and
they said there was none upon that coast. Further,
they declared to us that there was a report at
Rochelle, seven days before their departing, that part
of the Spanish army, to the number of 150 sail,
were come to the Groyne, and stayed there for the
rest which should come from Lisbon to them. But
afterwards there was certain news brought thither
by ships of Rochelle, men of war that came home
and brought very good prizes of Spaniards with
them, that the army remained still in Lisbon,
and the infection continued very great among them.
It is a bad season of the year for any ships that
are in Lisbon, and to the southwards of it upon
the coast of Spain, to come to the northwards, by
reason of the north and north-westerly wind that
bloweth commonly from the middle of May until
the latter end of August upon that coast ; after
which time it will not be wholesome for a Spanish
army to seek to the north part.

The men of the foresaid three flyboats informed
us that the King of Navarre was in Rochelle ; and
that they were in hand with a great fortification
without the town, whereupon daily, men, women,
and children did work, and the King himself. They
spake it as witness of sight.

We are informed that my Lord Admiral is at
Plymouth with his whole army, which is but a bad

[1] The Passage de l'Iroise. [2] MS. Yackewson.

place for my Lord to be in, if the King of Spain's navy should come. For that wind which would serve to bring them for England, Ireland, or Scotland, will not suffer my Lord to get out; and the country is not very good to yield them that relief of victual that they may need of. The ships that lately went with their provision of victuals from London are with them, or else very near by this.

If we cannot have a good peace by the treaty now in hand, and that shortly, which I wish for my part might be, then if her Majesty, with the Low Countries, as Holland and Zealand, did make a sharp war out of hand (entertaining Scotland as our friend), and to spare the pride of our backs and some of our gluttons' fare, I do not doubt (by God's grace) we should then make her Majesty's enemies to come to reason shortly; and if this be not done, I fear me it cannot do well; for that we shall be wearied out with charges. And that I take to be their only policy they have; into the which I know your wisdom can sound deep, and therefore I leave it to your honourable discretion, and humbly pray your Honour to bear with my boldness.

If Mr. Hawkyns hath not left your Honour, or my very good Lord, the Lord Treasurer, the book of the issuing out of the store [1] of the storehouses, to the end your Honours may know what the same is, as [2] a supply may be made, he hath not well remembered himself; for it is needful there were a care had of it in time; for the year will now slide away apace.

If it will please your Honour to cause some one of your good friends hereabouts near the seaside to bestow a buck upon me and Sir Henry Palmer, [3] your poor well-willers, we should think ourselves

[1] Issuing of the store out of &c.   [2] So that.
[3] The buck was duly bestowed. See *post*, July 27.

greatly beholden to your Honour, whom I beseech God to prosper and increase with much honour and good health. Written from aboard the Vanguard, in the Downs, the 20th of June, 1588.

Your Honour's most assured to command,

W. WYNTER.

June 22.—HOWARD TO THE COUNCIL.

[ccxi. 45.—Signed. Addressed. In bad condition.]

May it please your Lordships, I have received your Lordships' letters of the 17th this morning, being the 22nd of this instant, whereby I do perceive her Majesty's gracious goodness that she thinketh us to be so careful of her s[ervice] as that she hath referred it unto me and such other my assistants here to do that which I and they shall think fittest and most convenient to be done for the more surety and service of her Majesty and [the] state. And her Majesty shall be well assured, and your Lordships also, as it shall please God that wind and weather shall serve us, we will [take such] course that we may learn by all intelligence to find the [enemy], yet not so rashly to deal with them if we meet with the[m but that] her Majesty shall well perceive that it is done with judgment. And yet [ho]wsoever we shall do it by the wisdom and [discretion] of man, yet God is he which disposeth all, who I doubt not [will favour] her Majesty and his people, and send her a most honourable victory.

I pray your Lordships to pardon me that I may put you in remembrance [to] move her Majesty that she may have an especial care to draw [ten or] twelve thousand men about her own person, that may not be men [un]practised. For this she may well assure herself, that 10,000 men that be practised and trained together under a good governor [and] expert leaders, shall do her Majesty more service than any 40,000 which shall come from any other parts of the realm. For, my Lords, we have here 6,000 men in the fleet, which we shall be able, out of our company, to land upon any great occasion, which being as they [have] been trained here under captains and men of experience, and each man knowing his charge, and they their captains, I had rather have them to do any exploit than any 16,000 out of any part of the realm.

My Lords, our victuals are not yet come, but we hope shortly to hear of them if this wind continue 40 hours, or else we cannot tell what to think of them, or what should become of them ; and yet we have sent three or four pinnaces to seek them out.   If they come not, our extremity will be very great, for our victuals ended the 15th of this month ; and if that Mr. Darell had not very carefully provided us of 14 days' victuals, and again with four or five days' more, which now he hath provided, we had been in some great extremity.   Mr. Hawkyns hath disbursed money for all that, and for many other charges more, wherein Sir Francis Drake hath likewise disbursed some ; and therefore to avoid that danger and inconvenience that may fall out the thereby, it would do very well that her Majesty would send five or six thousand pounds hither, for it is likely we shall stand in great need of it.

[Several] men have fallen sick, and by thousands fain to be discharged, [and] other pressed in their stead, which hath been an infinite charge [with] great trouble unto us, the army being so great as it is, the ships so many in number, and the weather so ext[reme] foul as it hath been ; whereby great charges have risen and daily do.   And yet I protest

before God we have been more careful of her
Majesty's charges than of our own lives, as may
well appear by the scantyings [1] which we have made.
And thus leaving to trouble your Lordships any
further, I take my leave. From off aboard her
Majesty's good ship the Ark, the 22nd of June,
1588.

Your Lordships' loving friend to command,

C. HOWARD.

June 22.—HOWARD TO WALSYNGHAM.

[**ccxi. 46.**—Holograph. Addressed.]

Sir :—I am very sorry that her Majesty will not
thoroughly awake in this perilous and most dangerous time ; and surely it will touch her Majesty
greatly in honour if the noblemen and the rest of
the Commissioners should not safely come back
again. It is to me a strange treaty of peace, but
the end is like unto the beginning. There is not
anything that ever cometh to a good end that hath
not a good and sure foundation, which I could
never discern in this work of Mr. Comptroller's. [2]
A good will I think he had, but surely no good
workman.

For the advertisement of the Bretons that came
to Calais, [3] I think it cannot be true, for we have
had pinnaces off and on, so as we should by some
means have heard of it, but I will send presently
some small pinnaces thither.

[1] It seems to be a stronger term than 'savings,' and includes
putting the men on short allowance, or six men to a mess instead
of four—that is, in familiar language, 'six upon four.'

[2] Sir James Croft, Comptroller of the Household, and one of
the commissioners for the treaty.

[3] Cf. *ante*, p. 206. It appears to have been his first news of
the Spanish ships reported by Godolphin, as detailed in the next
paper.

I put out on Wednesday to the sea in hopes to have met with our victuallers, but on Friday we were put in again with a southerly wind. I hope now shortly we shall hear of our victuals, for the wind doth now serve them. I pray God all be well with them, for if any chance should come to [them], we should be in most miserable case. For the love of God, let the Narrow Seas be well strengthened, and the ships victualled [1] for some good time. This one month's victual is very ill, and may breed danger and no saving to her [Majesty]; for they spend lightly seven or eight days in coming to meet their victual and in taking of it in; and if the enemy do know of that time, judge you what they may attempt. Great hurt may come by it, but no good.

Sir, I pray let her Majesty be earnestly persuaded withal to have some forces of ten or twelve thousand soldiers near to her, that may know one another and their leaders. I had rather have ten thousand such, well trained and kept together, than forty thousand that shall be brought on the sudden, half amazed, as her Majesty shall be sure to find them. Her Majesty must assure herself she is not now in peace; and therefore most priceless service, and most to her honour, to provide as in war.

Sir, I pray you to present my most bound and humble duty to her Majesty; so, God willing, I will not trouble her Majesty with my rude writing till the matter be something worth. God, of his mercy, bless her Majesty with health and to have honour over her enemies. Fare you well, good Mr. Secretary, and God send you health. From aboard the Ark, the 22nd of this June.

Your assured loving friend,
C. HOWARD.

[1] MS. vyteled.

June 23.—*ADVERTISEMENT OF THE SPANISH FLEET.*

[**ccxi. 47, 48.**—In duplicate, with some verbal differences. Endorsed :—From the Lord Admiral.]

On Friday last, the 20th[1] of this instant, Sir Francis Godolphin[2] wrote unto my Lord Admiral, that the Thursday before, a bark of Mousehole[3] in Cornwall, being bound for France to lade salt, encountered with nine sail of great ships between Scilly and Ushant, bearing in North-East with the coast of England. Coming near unto them, he, doubting they were Spaniards, kept the wind of them. They perceiving it, began to give him chase. So in the end, three of them followed him so near that the Englishman doubted hardly to escape them.

At his first sight of them there were two flags spread which were suddenly taken in again, and being far off could not well discern the same. They were all great ships, and, as he might judge, the least of them from 200 tons to 5 and 800 tons. Their sails were all crossed over with a red cross. Each of the greater ships towed astern them either a great boat or pinnace without mast.

The same morning, or the evening before, the Englishman had speech with a flyboat, who demanding of the Englishman whither he was bound, told him for France to lade salt. He willed him in any wise, as he loved his life, not to proceed ; for, said he, the Spanish fleet is on the coast. He

---

[1] So in MS., but Friday was the 21st.

[2] Member of Parliament for Cornwall ; great-grandfather of the Lord High Treasurer in the reign of Queen Anne.

[3] In Mount's Bay.

further told him that he had spoken with some of his countrymen that had been two years with their ships imbarged[1] in Spain, and were there come in the fleet. The Englishman, little regarding his speeches, or at least to see the farther truth thereof, proceeded, and found some more likelihood of the same, as is before said.

On Saturday, there came another Englishman from the west part of Cornwall, who likewise had been chased with[2] a fleet of ships, being shot at by them, but recovered the shore with little hurt.

On Sunday, one Simons of Exeter gave advertisement to my Lord Admiral that on Friday last he was chased with a fleet of great ships, having some of his men hurt with shot from them; escaping their hands, landed in Cornwall, and came post to Plymouth unto my Lord Admiral.

Each of their ships have red crosses on their sails. The two latter fleets which were discovered were, in the one, six sail, and in the other, fifteen sail.

June 23.—SEYMOUR TO WALSYNGHAM.

[ccxi. **49**.—Signed. Addressed.]

Sir :—I can advertise you but little since my last writing more than I have been at Gravelines some thirty hours, during which time issued forth from Dunkirk two small vessels, bending their course to Gravelines haven. Two of our pinnaces chased them, with the discharging of some saker shot, and yet would [they] not strike, till at the last one of our shot strake down the mainmast of one of their vessels, being a French bottom belonging to Calais, and had Monsieur Gourdan's[3] hand for his pass.

---

[1] Embargoed.   [2] By.   [3] Governor of Calais.

I demanded what he meant not to strike his sails and to come to the Queen's ships, knowing us so well. He answered that he took us for the King of Navarre's fleet, making himself ignorant what to do. I replied that if the Duke of Parma, or the Duke of Guise, should do the like, I would sink them, or they should distress me; adding further that my Sovereign Lady was able to defend her country against the Holy League, besides able to master any civil discord; and so dismissed them, with some little choler.[1]

The other ran himself hard aground right over against Gravelines, and voided themselves out of their vessel, wading through the water, and cut their sails from the masts, taking them also away. My boat, which I manned with some shot,[2] came upon their skirts, but a little too late; yet came there very near a hundred men, horse and foot, but durst not approach our shot[2]; by which time our men had some little leisure to cut down their masts, and would have fired her, but that suddenly the wind arose at North and by East, enforcing us to weigh for Blackness, where we anchored, with marvellous foul weather, some thirty hours.

These actions befell yesterday, the 22nd of this month, so as now the wind is come three points more, being North-North-East,[3] and thereby enforced to take our best harbours upon our own coasts; yet in the passage, far from us, we did descry 30 sail, to our judgment Hollanders, taking their courses westwards, which I would gladly have pursued, but that I feared they would have brought us too far west, being[4] not able to recover those coasts which we are to look unto.

This, having gathered out advertisements by

---

[1] MS. collor.   [2] Musketeers.   [3] So in MS.
[4] Sc. so that we should not be able.

private examinations a-seaboard within my own cabin, which also I send you here enclosed,[1] do take my leave.　From aboard the Rainbow, this 23rd of June, 1588.

Your assured loving friend to command,

H. SEYMOUR.

Sir :—I have strained my hand with hauling of a rope, whereby as yet I cannot write so much as I would, and therefore am enforced to use the manner to *dictare*.

There are ten days expired of this last victuals, and when ten days more are spent, eight days will be little enough to come home and take in our victuals ; and the service that is to be done is most likely at the time of our revictualling, which I have often desired should be at the least for six weeks.

Sir, it is more than time our coast men were victualled, which was promised by your last letters should be forthwith supplied.

June 23.—*HOWARD TO THE QUEEN.*

[ccxi. 50.—Holograph.]

To the Queen's most excellent Majesty.

May it please your most excellent Majesty :—I have forborne this long time to write unto your Majesty, hoping that the wind would have served that on this I might have certified your Majesty of something worth the writing.　We have often put to the sea, and have been fain to run off and on the Sleeve[2] with contrary winds ; and in the end, not being able to continue out for fear of being driven to the leeward as far as the Wight, were forced in again,

---

[1] Missing.　　　　　[2] MS. Slyve : cf. *ante*, p. 5, *note*.

into Plymouth. Our victuals were spent, and the wind not serving our victuals to come to us, we expected the goodness of God to change the wind, which did happily change on Friday morning, so that on Saturday, late at night, they came to us. They were no sooner come, although it were night, but we went all to work to get in our victuals,[1] which I hope shall be done in 24 hours, for no man shall sleep[2] nor eat till it be dispatched ; so that, God willing, we will be under sail to-morrow morning, being Monday, and the 24th of this present. I humbly beseech your Majesty to think that there was never men more unwilling to lose any time than we are.

Even as I had written this much of my letter to your Majesty, I received this letter[3] from a man of mine, which I did send to lie with a pinnace betwixt the Land's End and Ushant.[4] The party himself[5] that was chased did bring the letter, who is a wise man and of good credit. There was also another ship in this man's company that was also chased with him. The ships they met withal, seven of them, were ships of eight and nine hundred.[6] The others were Biscayans of 300. It is very likely that this stormy weather hath parted the fleet.[7] I hope in God we shall meet with some of them ; we will not stay for anything. I trust we shall meet with them on the coast of France, for I have some intelligence that for certain they mean to come thither, and there to receive many Frenchmen into their ships.

For the love of Jesus Christ, Madam, awake thoroughly, and see the villainous[8] treasons round about you, against your Majesty and your realm, and

[1] MS. geet in our vyttelse. [2] MS. slype.
[3] Probably Godolphin's letter referred to *ante*, p. 221.
[4] MS. Youshant.
[5] It would seem that this was Simons of Exeter (cf. p. 222), though he is nowhere else mentioned as a man of Howard's.
[6] Sc. tons. [7] MS. flyte. [8] MS. velynous.

draw your forces round about you, like a mighty prince, to defend you. Truly, Madam, if you do so, there is no cause to fear. If you do not, there will be danger. I would to God nobody had been more deceived in this than I ; it would have been never a whit the worse for your Majesty's service.

I humbly beg your Majesty to pardon me that I do cut off my letter in this sort. I am now in haste, and long to set sail. I beseech the Almighty God to bless and defend your Majesty from all your enemies, and so I do most humbly take my leave. From aboard the Ark, ready to weigh, this Sunday night at 12 of the clock.

Your Majesty's most humble
and obedient servant,
C. Howard.

June 23.—HOWARD TO WALSYNGHAM.

[ccxi. 51.—Holograph. Addressed.]

Sir :—This Sunday, about 7 of the clock at night, I received your letter of the 22nd of this present, and the advertisements with them, which I do most heartily thank you for ; but I perceive by your letter there should another letter come from my Lords to Mr. Darell, and also a warrant that the pursuivant should bring, which should be open for me, but he neither brought the Lords' letter nor any such warrant.

Sir, I pray you pardon me that I do not send you the names of the towns divided, such as be willing, and such as be not. Sir F. Drake hath the names of them. Now at this hour [he] is full occupied, as I am also. Our victuals came to us this last night about 12 of the clock, and we will not eat nor sleep till it be aboard us. We must not lose

one hour of time. You shall see by a letter that I
have sent her Majesty what advertisement I have.
I mean to weigh presently and set sail. This foul
weather that was on Thursday, that forced us in,
surely dispersed the Spanish fleet. It shall go hard
but I will find them out. Let her Majesty trust no
more to Judas' kisses ; for let her assure herself there
is no trust to French King nor Duke of Parma.
Let her defend herself like a noble and mighty
prince, and trust to her sword and not to their word,
and then she need not fear, for her good God will
defend her.

Sir, I have a privy intelligence by a sure fellow
that this fleet of Spain doth mean to come to the
coast of France, and there to receive in the Duke of
Guise and great forces ; and it is very likely to be
true. I mean, God willing, to visit the coast of
France, and to send in small pinnaces to discover all
the coast along. If I hear of them, I hope ere it be
long after you shall hear news. Good Mr. Secretary,
let the Narrow Seas be well strengthened. What
charge is ill spent now for surety ? Let the hoys of
Harwich go with all speed again to my Lord Henry
Seymour, for they be of great service.

Sir, for these things here, I pray take order with
Mr. Darell, for I have no leisure to think of them.
I pray you, Sir, deliver my letter unto her Majesty
with my humble duty, and so in haste I bid you farewell. Aboard the Ark, this Sunday, at 12 of the
clock at night.

Your assured loving friend,
C. Howard.

Sir, God willing, I will cut [1] sail within this three
hours.

[1] Loose sail. See *ante*, p. 82 *note*.

June 23.—LORD HOWARD TO THE COUNCIL.

[ccxi. 52.—Signed.   Addressed.]

May it please your Lordships :—Even as I had made up a packet of letters unto Mr. Secretary, one Richard Swansey, a pursuivant, came unto me. Two hours after, another pursuivant, with your Lordships' letters.   I will take what order I can, as the shortness of the time will permit me, for I mean, God willing, to set sail within these two hours, having received some advertisements which make me to make all the haste I can out unto the sea.   My victual came but this last morning about two of the clock ; and since, we have laboured very hard for the taking of them in, for we were very bare left before they came.   And yet we meant, if they did not come this day, to have gone out to the sea, although we had but three days' victual.   I pray your Lordships that some money may be speedily sent down unto Mr. Darell, for the avoiding of all danger if the towns do not prove so ready to revictual their ships as your Lordships do expect.   And so most heartily praying your Lordships to bear with my hasty and short writing, being overcharged with business now at our setting forth, I take my leave, the 23rd of June, 1588.

Your Lordships' loving friend to command,

C. HOWARD.

June 24.—DRAKE TO WALSYNGHAM.

[ccxi. 53.—Signed, and autograph postscript.   Addressed.]

Right Honourable :—Although I do very well know that your Honour shall be at large advertised by my very good Lord, the Lord Admiral, that the Spanish forces are descried to be near at hand in several companies on our coast, as it is reported for certain by three barks unto whom they gave chase and made shot, yet have I thought it good also to write these few lines unto your Honour; nothing doubting but that, with God's assistance, they shall be so sought out and encountered withal in such sort as (I hope) shall qualify their malicious and long pretended[1] practices. And therefore, I beseech your Honour to pray continually for our good success in this action, to the performance whereof we have all resolutely vowed the adventure of our lives, as well for the advancement of the glory of God, as the honour and safety of her Majesty, her realms and dominions. And thus, resting always ready to perform what shall lie in my power, either in duty or service to my prince and country, I humbly take my leave. From aboard her Majesty's ship the Revenge, this 24th of June, 1588.

Your Honour's very ready to be commanded,

FRA. DRAKE.

I leave the bearer, my servant Jonas Bodenham,[2] to solicit your Honour as occasion shall be offered.

Your Honour's faithfully,

FRA. DRAKE.

[1] Intended, designed. Cf. Shakespeare, 1 *Henry VI.* iv. 1: 'Such as shall pretend malicious practices against his state.'

[2] He continued a close follower of Drake, was with him, in the Defiance, in his last voyage, and witnessed the codicil to his will, by which Drake left him the manor of Samford Spiney, near Tavistock (*Wills from Doctors' Commons*, Camden Soc.). It is very probable that he was the nephew of Mary Newton, Drake's first wife, married in 1569, at St. Budeaux, where in 1560 Margaret Newton married John Bodenham. On the father's side he would seem to have belonged to Hereford, of which county Roger Bodenham was sheriff in 1585 and again in 1593. A Roger Bodenham commanded the Anchor in a Mediterranean voyage in 1551 (Hakluyt, ii. 99), settled in Seville, married there, made a voyage to Mexico in 1564 (*ib*. iii. 447), and was still living at San Lucar in 1580 (*S P. Spain*, xvi.).

June 24.—MEMORANDUM OF DUTCH SHIPS.[1]

[**ccxi. 54.**—Endorsed.]

24th of June, 1588.

A memorial for the Lord Admiral of the names of all the ships, with their men and tonnage.

Flushing:

Cornelis Lonck,[3] Admiral . .	. 75	130
Adrianson Cornisen Conoper .	. 75	140
Legier Jacobson . . .	. 85	160
Legier Pieterson . . .	. 52	120
Lucas Dano	. 45	120
Adrian de Doe	. 45	120
Marten Francis . . .	. 45	120
St. Pieterson Skoyen . .	. 45	120
Hans Cornelis Mortman . .	. 45	65

Campvere:

Cornelis Harmonson Calis, Vice-Admiral	. 85	150
Evarte Pieterson . . .	. 45	80

Middelburg:

Walter Longuevale . . .	. 45	130
Pieter Jonson	. 45	110
	732	1,565

[1] These are the ships ordered to join Seymour for the guard of the Narrow Seas. They were prevented crossing over by the strong westerly wind, and seem to have afterwards formed part of the squadron under Count Justin.

[2] It will be noticed that the names are not of the ships, but of their commanders.

[3] Cornelis Lonck van Roozendaal. With this one exception, none of these names can be identified here, and the wild spelling of the original remains. About half of them reappear in similar lists of the ships with Justin in the Scheldt and off Dunkirk, in August (*S.P. Holland*, lvi.).

Hollanders.

Rotterdam :

Ewke Denbowte	.	.	.	.	76	120
Jacob Jonson Bacanela	.	.	.	75	130
Pieter Marten .	.	.	.	.	60	115

Enkhuysen :

Symond Jacobson	.	.	.	.	76	140
Jacob Jeretson .	.	.	.	.	45	60
Frederick Adrianson.	.	.	.	45	100

Amsterdam :

Arnold Rovere .	.	.	.	.	65	130
					442	795
Totalis	.	.	.	.	1,174	2,360

June 26.—SEYMOUR TO WALSYNGHAM.

[**ccxi. 58.**—Holograph.   Addressed.]

Sir :—To iterate my opinion, with confirmation of better judgment, I fear no attempt for England this year more than still I doubt the continuance of private practising, policies wherewith these Italians have continually been trained.

To urge pro and contra this.

The Duke of Parma hath ready 30,000 expert soldiers, to transport either for England or Scotland. His own private strength (without the assistance of Spain or France) doth not exceed 40 sails of fly-boats and 220 bylanders.   A time must be to land them and a time to back them.

Answer.

England, I least doubt, because he is cut off from faction within our own country ; besides, one of our men upon defence is worth two of an enemy for offence, being not supported through civil discord. Also our strength of shipping, being not severed, with some longer continuance of victuals, must cross and thwart the foresaid attempts, if wind and weather assist us to attend them.

All I fear is they will never offer themselves, specially on the seas, in place where service may be tried. And to that end, we have twice showed ourselves at Gravelines, desiring nothing more than to suffer them come out, rather than to stop them in by sinking vessels with stones or timber, which will be recovered again upon every ebb, and will serve them for their strength and better fortification.

Concerning Scotland, if the news be true which a Scot this day informed me from Dundee, it seemeth that the King doth take a course to keep friendship with us, by some acts lately performed four days past, videlicet, the executing the Lord Maxwell [1] his brother, and imprisoning the Lord Maxwell himself; which if the same be current and sure, I doubt not but your honourable wisdom will back the continu-

---

[1] Lord Maxwell, born in 1553, who had for many years been intriguing with Spain in the interests of the Queen of Scots, and had repeatedly suffered imprisonment or fine for offences against the King's government, had left Scotland in April 1587, on an undertaking not to return without the King's license. Notwithstanding this, he did return in April 1588, and began to assemble his followers, to be in readiness to assist the Spaniards, either in Scotland or England. He was declared a public enemy, was arrested (June 5), and kept a close prisoner till September, when he was released on giving caution to do 'nothing tending to the trouble or alteration of the state of religion presently professed and by law established.' He was killed in an affray with the Johnstones in 1593. Robert Maxwell, his bastard brother, escaped, and on June 23 a reward was offered for him alive or dead. David Maxwell, captain of Lochmaben Castle, with five of his dependents, was hanged, and a great many of the clan were bound over under heavy caution, or security (*Register of the Privy Council of Scotland*, iv. 275–292 ; Sir Wm. Fraser's *Book of Carlaverock*, i. 278–9).

ance of such good actions. Where otherwise they should join and take part with Spain, I hope their attempts shall cost more than one battle or two, before they should approach London.

Thus having answered your letter by delivering my private opinion, do wish that Zealand be circumspectly looked into ; for I understand that companies of Arnemuiden and Campvere are dismissed lately, which may give the enemy great advantages to lie in wait for the same. So expecting some seasonable weather and more favourable winds, do take my leave. Aboard the Rainbow, this 26th of June, 1588.

Your assured loving friend to command,
H. SEYMOUR.

The two brothers Musgrave, the one captain for Yarmouth the other for Lynn, as well by their own accord as the general consent, voluntarily yield another month's victuals, desiring in no sort to have her Majesty charged ; and truly, Sir, if you knew them as well [as [1]] I, they deserve special thanks.

Tomson,[2] a great agent for Archibald Douglas, is much resident in Dover ; to what end I know not.

June 26.—SEYMOUR TO WALSYNGHAM.

[ccxi. 59.—Holograph.[3] Addressed :—To the Right Honourable Sir Francis Walsyngham, Knight, Principal Secretary to her Majesty. H. Seymour.]

I do what I can to lay in wait for the vessel that should go out of Dunkirk to Spain, but it is a hundred to one she may escape me ; yet I think

[1] As : omitted in MS.
[2] Not to be confused with Richard Tomson, the lieutenant of the Margaret and John.   [3] An almost illegible scrawl.

she may sooner fall into the hands of the Lord Admiral; and as yet the wind being so contrary hath retained all the shipping in Dunkirk; likewise the Spaniards, if they have intention to set forward. Thus much I return with speed, because my servant Floyd[1] brought me letters from you to have care thereof. So having unfolded my packet which was ready to go, do leave you better satisfied herewith. Haste.

June 30.—*A DECLARATION AS TO THE VICTUALLING.*

[**ccxi. 70.**—Endorsed: 'For my Lord Treasurer'; and in Burghley's hand: 'Ulto. Junii, 1588. Mr. Quarles' book of the victualling of the Lord Admiral [and] Lord Henry.']

30ᵐᵒ die Junii 1588.

A declaration unto your Lordship how and unto what time her Majesty's ships be victualled, as well those that be with my Lord Admiral southward as also those ships that be with my Lord Henry Seymour on the Narrow Seas, videlicet :—

Ships 16 of her Majesty's which went with my [Lord] Admiral.
Men in the said 16 ships, 3,736.

First, my Lord Admiral had one month's victual which he took with him for all her Majesty's ships, which victuals began the 19th day of May and ended the 15th day of June, his Lordship being at Plymouth, where Mr. Darell did presently victual the said fleet for 6 days longer, which ended the 21st of June. The 22nd of June arrived at Plymouth

---

[1] The MS. here has Flud: in other places Seymour wrote Fludd, or Floyd; the true name was probably the more familiar Flood or Lloyd.

15 ships sent from London with one month's victual more, which doth serve the said fleet until the 20th day of July; and then, as it appeareth by Mr. Darell's letter dated the 2nd day of June, he had both order and money by my Lord Admiral and Sir Francis Drake to provide one month's victual more, which beginneth the 21st of July, and doth end the 18th of August.

Besides this, his Lordship hath sent him by the said 15 ships a proportion for 14 days for biscuit and beer; and more, as it do appear by Mr. Darell's letters dated as aforesaid, his Lordship hath, for a convenient time, biscuit, newland fish, wine, cider, rice, oil and pease, to serve the whole fleet.

Ships of her Majesty with my Lord Henry
Seymour, 15.
Men with my Lord Henry Seymour on the Narrow
Seas in the [15] ships, 1,471.

My Lord Henry Seymour had one month's victual sent him to the Narrow Seas, which began the 16th day of June and is to end the 14th day of July.

Likewise, by your Lordship's order, there was a supply of victual sent to my Lord Henry Seymour for 18 days more, which beginneth the 15th day of July and is to end the last of the said month, and so is to begin a new proportion the 1st of August.

Ships of sundry ports with my Lord Henry
Seymour, and victualled for one month, 18.
Men in the ships from the ports, 800.

More, there is victualled by your Lordship's order divers ships, which serve under my Lord Henry Seymour, for one month, which doth begin their victuals the 25th of June and is to end the 23rd of July.

Money sent into the West Country, to Mr. Darell:

	£	s.	d.
Received and sent into the West Country out of the Exchequer, by three privy seals, for service down there	11,161	13	4

ADVERTISEMENT[1] TO WALSYNGHAM

[ccxi. 95.—Endorsed.]

It is reported that all those ships that are seen for Spain, and from Spain hither, have aboard the English flag, the French flag, and the Bourgogne[2] flag ; and when they are hailed by her Majesty's navy, they say that they are French, and so speak French, by which means they go and come. It were very necessary that my Lord Seymour had word to command all his fleet that what boat soever they meet, that [they[3]] should bring him to him to be examined ; and my Lord should have aboard of himself some one discreet person, that had of late haunted these ports, thereby to discover their men and ships, and such as could speak Flemish. By these means, it is assured me you shall meet with many.

The three ships that I wrote unto you that were going out of Dunkirk, are manned with pilots to be distributed among the navy. My hope is that [they[3]] shall be met withal. They lads[4] be shipped;

---

[1] The writing and spelling are singularly bad.

[2] The Burgundian flag—white, with a red saltire raguled—was adopted as the Spanish flag, on the accession of the Emperor Charles V., and so continued till the accession of the Bourbons.

[3] Omitted in MS.

[4] Those pilots are shipped, which seems an indication that presently &c.

and truly by that it may be thought presently they will do somewhat.

It is here said that the Spanish navy shall be reinforced with a number of French ships; and that they shall have all the favour that may be in all the French havens; and I do sooner believe it, for that I hear that all the captains of these haven-towns are sworn to the League.

July 4.—MEMORANDUM BY DRAKE.

[**ccxii. 9.**—Copy. Endorsed :—Sir Francis Drake's opinion
touching our going to the coast of Spain.]

To maintain my opinion that I have thought it meeter to go for the coast of Spain, or at least more nearer than we are now, are these reasons following : written aboard her Majesty's good ship the Revenge, this fourth of July, 1588.

The first, that hearing of some part of the Spanish fleet upon our coast, and that in several fleets, the one of eleven sail, the other of six sail, and the last of eighteen, all these being seen the 20th and 21st of June ; since which time, we being upon the coast of France, could have no intelligence of their being there, or passing through our Channel ; neither hearing, upon our own coast, of their arrival in any place, and speaking with a bark which came lately out of Ireland, who can advertise nobody of their being in those parts, I am utterly of opinion that they are returned, considering what ways [1] they have had since that time ; otherwise they could have been here without our knowledge.

[1] MS. wayes : possibly a mistake of the clerk who copied it, for weather. In Elizabethan writing *th* is very apt to be mistaken for *y* ; and Drake's writing, at the best, is a very difficult scrawl.

I say further, that if they be returned, our staying here in this place shall but spend our victual, whereby our whole action is in peril, no service being done. For the lengthening of our victual by setting a straiter order for our company, I find them much discontented if we stay there; whereas, if we proceed, they all promise to live with as little portion as we shall appoint unto them.

Our being upon the coast of Spain will yield us true intelligence of all their purposes.

The taking of some of their army shall much daunt them, and put a great fear amongst them.

My opinion is altogether that we shall fight with them much better cheap [1] upon their own coast than here; for that I think this one of the unmeetest places to stay for them.

To conclude, I verily believe that if we undertake no present service, but detract time some few days, we shall hardly be able to perform any matter of importance.   FRANCIS DRAKE.

July 14.—*CONSIDERATIONS BY FENNER.*

[ccxii. 10.—Holograph.[2]   Endorsed.]

Considerations to move the proceedings of her Majesty's fleet to go for the coast of Spain, to take there opportunity of the accident fallen out by the return of the Spanish fleet, the rather thereby utterly to dissolve them.

First, I set down to your Lordship the reasons we have of their return. They were seen the 19th of June, thirty of their fleet, in their general com-

---

[1] Cheap=market: much better cheap means, on better terms, more advantageously.

[2] Fenner's language is always curiously involved and careless; in this instance, more than usually so.

panies, with crosses painted red on their foresails ; they chased some of Falmouth, and near thereabout, not many leagues South-West of Lizard, the parties chased witnessing the same in their own persons.

The 21st of June, a bark of Dublin taken by them some 15 leagues South-West of Lizard ; which bark, being by them towed in foul weather, the cable breaking, escaped with three persons, and six of their company being into the Spaniards, and so bare unto the sea South-West ; being 18 sail in number, great hulks and very full of Spaniards, not less than ten thousand by composition.[1]

From the 21st of June until the sixth of July we could not intercept any news of their arrival in England, France, Ireland, or Scotland, which argueth plainly their companies dispersed. As also one Mr. Hawes of London (if I mistake not his name) met with several companies of them dispersed at sea ; so as that they cannot be but returned, in that they have had sundry times large[2] winds to enter Sleeve again.

Which causes considered, it was thought meet the 5th of July to bear out into the sea, until Ushant bare of us East-South-East, and Scilly North-West and by North, some 15 leagues of either, with pinnaces placed between the body of the fleet and Ushant, as also Scilly, thereby none to enter the Sleeve but that we must have sight of them. Otherwise, lying in the middle of the Channel, as we did before, with the body of the fleet, and Ushant as also Scilly thereby, if the wind came southerly, they might haul[3] the coast of France, if the North-

---

[1] Estimation.   [2] Fair ; we still say 'to sail large.'
[3] MS. hale. The expression was still in use 150 years later. Burchett, writing in 1720, has 'which ship hauling the shore on board more than the rest of the fleet did, she lay becalmed' (*Transactions at Sea*, p. 484), and Lediard repeated it in 1735 (*Naval History*, p. 676). We still say 'to haul the wind.'

West, they might haul the coast of England, and not by us for the present to be impeached.

In the mean season, some of our fleet had been at Plymouth, as also at Conquet in France, and no news but that they were dispersed and returned in great misery, as by sickness and foul weather much beaten and spoiled. Also we understood of their return by a pilot of Conquet; the like in effect from the Mayor of Rochelle, in that he certified many of their fleet to be seen about Cape Finisterre some days after the sight of them upon the coast; withal [by] three English mariners now in our company, which came from Rochelle in a bark of Millbrooke. Upon their coming from thence, [they] were aboard a pinnace of Rochelle then coming from the sea,[1] and had taken two Spale[2] Spaniards of 30 tons apiece, laden with wine and oil, who did deliver the certainty of the dispersion of the fleet into many harbours of the coast of Biscay and other places.

Which several advertisements considered, and lying in the place aforesaid as between Scilly and Ushant, the wind coming up northerly, it was thought meet by my Lord Admiral and the rest of us of council to take the benefit of time, and not to lose the opportunity of so happy an accident, but to persecute[3] their waste and dissolving, by our going upon the coast of Spain to seek the place of their dispersed companies, and to seek by all possible means their waste.

It is to be considered so mighty an army of three years' preparation, and with so many estates and provisions of horsemen, being gathered together by so great a prince and so great colleagues out of so many and so far countries, wherein there are in

---

[1] From a cruise.
[2] Seville. The Latin forms are Hispalis, Spalis.
[3] Thoroughly to follow up; to complete.

number above twenty thousand that have not tasted the seas before. And now, by the providence of God, the burdens aforesaid laid upon them have so abated the pride of their minds, so as no doubt it hath stirred a deadly grief in the secrets of their hearts against all those that have been the procures of their enterprise, wherein they have wasted themselves, touching their reputation, spent the colleagues' treasury, and abated (by their return) the pride of the Prince of Parma his forces, in that the thread of both their hopes by this accident is cut asunder. Therefore more meeter to be followed with effect.

Now were utterly to be beaten down the hope of any good success to them, by visiting their coast and following their ruin ; my most gracious Majesty thereby delivered of their malicious determinations and practices against her royal person and country. We should now have to do with amazed and discontented companies, so as they cannot (in my poor opinion) proceed against[1] this summer season, in that their provisions are wasted, their companies wearied, their fleet not to be relieved in the several places where they are of their distresses. Their great companies considered, not in season to be refreshed with water for such a journey ; in that they must use at least six thousand butts of water, wherein no doubt they shall have great want of cask, considering the use at sea in such journeys to save[2] their casks, for keeping of their ships unpestered.

Withal their mariners, being of sundry nations, and by all the advertisements we can gather very

[1] Again. This use of the word is noted in the *N.E.D.* as very rare ; not improbably it is here a slip of the pen.
[2] To save their casks would seem equivalent to the modern 'to shake' them ; that is, to knock the hoops off and let them fall to pieces, for convenience of stowage.

unwilling to meet with our forces at sea, have been, since their first proceedings, by severe punishment and political orders kept together, otherwise their minds have been to run away, both Spaniards and Flemings, Portingals and French, by all which nations they are but means [1] suited with mariners.

Many of the causes aforesaid have moved the most part of us earnestly to give counsel to lose no time in the proceeding to their coast, to the effect aforesaid, so as no man to make estimate of their lives, or burdens in want of victual, respecting [2] the weightiness of the cause, and to relieve ourselves upon the enemy, the greater to our reputation. To have stayed and gone for the coast of England to have relieved the wants of victual in some, by that means the rest had been in the same predicament ; and therefore, the wind being northerly, the 7th of July at three of the clock in the afternoon [it was] concluded to go for Spain, Ushant bearing of us East-North-East, next hand [3] some 15 leagues off.

The 9th of July being shot [4] some ten leagues off South and by West of Ushant, the wind came up at South-West, blowing much wind. Thereby bear [5] up for England again, in that divers of the small shipping were but meanly victualled, so as to refresh them and the rest, and so, at the first wind, to seek them out on the coast of Spain, and as [6] her Majesty may hear no news of them again. For this their army at sea being thoroughly dissolved, he shall never be able to gather together the like again, which easily satisfy her Majesty and ease a mighty charge, which may hereafter lie upon [her] Majesty and

---

[1] In a middling way ; moderately.
[2] Having regard to ; considering.   [3] So in MS.
[4] Pushed forward, advanced. Cf. *Psalms*, xxii. 7, 'They shoot out the lip' ; and Spenser, *Faërie Queene*, V. vi. 19, 'Well shot in yeares he seemed.'
[5] It was resolved to bear up.   [6] In such sort that.

[the] realm, if they be not now thoroughly dissolved. And therefore, since God hath made manifest the means, I pray unto the Lord to continue your willingness in mind to the execution thereof, which now is to be done (the fleet being together) with a far more easier charge and adventure than at another time. THOMAS FENNER.

July 5.—DARELL TO THE COUNCIL.

[ccxii. 16.—Signed. Endorsed.]

Right Honourable :—According to your Lordships' commandment signified to me by Mr. Quarles, I have sent herewith a note of the ships now at sea under the charge of the Lord Admiral, with their numbers of men and time of victualling, so near as of myself I know or can learn. Wherein what shall remain doubtful unto your Lordships touching the determination[1] of the victuals for that fleet which came down with my Lord, it may please you to be more fully informed thereof by those that have had the charge of their former proportions, who, understanding by this note what hath been delivered here, will soon set down what ought to remain. As for the ships set forth by the port towns, forasmuch as the charge thereof did nothing concern me, I have not acquainted myself much with it; only now, understanding your Lordships' pleasures, I have set down as much thereof as of late by credible report I have learned; and also have required Richard Swanson, a messenger of the Chamber sent hither by your Lordships about those causes, in his return by the towns to bring unto your Lordships a certain note of the rest.[2]

It may please your Lordships also to understand

[1] Ending.   [2] See *post*, p. 259.

that by reason the ships which are at her Majesty's charge have been all supplied with fresh victual here, in this long time of their stay in harbour, I am grown indebted in the country near to the sum of 900*l.*, as hath appeared particularly unto my Lord Admiral, and thereof I think he hath already informed your Lordships. I humbly therefore beseech you to give your speedy order for the discharge thereof, whereby your Lordships shall much help my poor credit amongst them. And so, with remembrance of my duty, I most humbly take my leave. At Plymouth, the 5th of July, 1588.

Your Lordships' most humble,

MAR. DARELL.

July 6.—DARELL TO WALSYNGHAM.

[ccxii. 17.—Signed. Addressed.]

Right Honourable:—Having received commandment from the Council to certify what number of ships and men are now at sea under the charge of the Lord Admiral, and for what time they are severally victualled, I have performed the same as directly as I could, and do send your Honour herewithal a copy thereof, wherein if anything may [yet] seem doubtful unto their Lordships touching the victualling of the ships at her Majesty's charge, Mr. Quarles may inform their Lordships of it more particularly. Only I have omitted to set down in that note the number of men in the coast ships, the certainty whereof I could not learn ; and therefore have presumed to refer the same unto this bearer [1] (one of the messengers sent down by your Honour about those causes), who is to bring their

---

[1] Richard Swanson : see *post*, p. 259.

Lordships a true report thereof from the towns that have set them forth. And so leaving to trouble your Honour further at this time, most humbly take my leave. At Plymouth, the 5th of July, 1588.

Your Honour's most bounden,

[MAR.] DARELL.

July 6.—HOWARD TO WALSYNGHAM.

[ccxii. **18.**—Signed. Addressed. In very bad condition.]

Sir :—Being here in the midst of the Channel of the Sleeve, on Friday, being the 5th of this month, I received your letter of the 28th of June, and another of the same date which was written after you had made up your packet. The cause of the long time that these letters were in coming unto me was because the pursuivant, embarking himself upon Monday at Plymouth, was fain to beat up and down the [sea] with a contrary wind until Friday [before] he could [find me].

By your first letter I find how greatly you stand assured that neither the French King, nor the havens and port towns that stand for the King, will give any help or assistance unto the Spanish army. As for Newhaven, it is not a place to serve their turns.

By your other letter you perceive from an advertisement you have from my brother Stafford,[1] that there is money sent down to Brest and Conquet for the relief and assistance of the Spanish fleet if they arrive there. I [wish with all] my heart that they were there with the [best welcome they could] give them. [It should not be long] after but that I would give them another welcome ; for if it be they mean to touch there, then assuredly they have a

---

[1] Sir Edward Stafford, the ambassador at Paris.

meaning to join forces with the Duke of Parma.   I
have no doubt but that my Lord Henry Seymour,
being [so] strong as he is, will have a care that he
shall not start any whither to meet them.   And it
shall be very well that you have some trusty espial [1]
there to give certain intelligence when the Duke's
forces shall be ready, [that then, my Lord] Henry
Seymour may lie in the [mouth of] their haven to
interrupt their coming forth.

I am sorry to perceive by your letter that [her
Majesty hath] no more care to have forces about
her, considering the great peril that may come by
neglecting that which should be done in time.   I
have written again unto her Majesty very earnestly
about it, and I hope that God will put into her
mind to do that which may tend most to her safety.

I am sure you have seen the letter which I sent
unto her Majesty of the discovery of certain of the
Spanish fleet not far off of Scilly, which made me to
make as much haste out to sea as I could ; for upon
Sunday our victuals came to us, and having the
wind at North-East, I would not stay the taking in
of them all ; but taking in some part of them, I
appointed the rest to follow with me, and so bare to
Scilly, thinking to have cut off those Spanish ships
[seen] there from the rest of their fleet ; but the
wind continued not 16 hours there, but turned
South-South-West, that we were fain to lay it off
and on in the Sleeve, and could get no further.
Then did I send Sir Francis Drake with half a score
ships and three or four pinnaces into the Trade, to
discover it.   In his way, hard aboard Ushant, he
met with a man of mine, whom I had sent out in a
bark ten days before to lie off and on there for discovery, who had met with an Irish [bark and] stayed
her, which had been with the [18] great ships of the

[1] Spy.

Spanish fleet 16 [leagues South-South[1]]-West of Scilly. They had taken out of the said [bark] five of her most principal men, and left in her but three men and a boy. One of the greatest Spanish ships towed her at her stern by a cable, which in the night time, the wind blowing somewhat stiff, brake, and so she escaped in the storm. This did assure us greatly that the Spanish fleet was broken in the storms which had been afore ; and by all likelihood, we conjectured, if the wind had continued northerly that they [would have] returned back again [to the] Groyne ; but [as the wind] hath served [these] six or seven days, [we] must look for them every hour if they mean to come hither.

Sir, I sent a fine Spanish caravel an eight days agone to the Groyne to learn intelligence, such a one as would not have been mistrusted ; but when she was fifty leagues on her way, this southerly wind forced her back again unto us. Therefore I pray you, if you hear or understand of any news [or] advertisements by land, that I may hear of them from you with expedition.

I have divided myself here into three parts, and yet we lie within sight one of another, so as, if any of us do discover the Spanish fleet, we give notice thereof presently the one to the other, and thereupon repair and assemble together. I myself do lie in the middle of the Channel, with the greatest force. Sir Francis Drake hath 20 ships and four or five pinnaces, which lie towards Ushant ; and Mr. Hawkyns, with as many more, lieth towards Scilly. Thus are we fain to do, else with this wind they might pass by and we [never] the wiser.

Whatsoever hath been made of the S[leeve, it] is another manner of thing than it was taken for ; we find it by experience and daily observation to be

[1] So Bruce ; there is now nothing to guide conjecture.

an hundred miles over ; a large room for men to look unto. And whereas it is thought that we should have regard [unto the] forces of the [said] fleet, if [they] should bend for Scotland, they would in their [way] thither keep so far away westward off Cape Cl[ear] as they would be farther from us at any time than [it] is betwixt England and Spain ; so that the best advertisement that we must hope for must be from you by the knowledge that you shall have over land out of Scotland, if they be discovered there. And then our best and nearest course will be unto them through the Narrow Seas, where I have no doubt but we shall defeat them of their fleet, whatsoever they do with [their land] men. But for my own part I can not [persuade myself but tha]t their inte[nt is for Ireland]. Where there are so many doubts, we [must proceed] by the likelier ways, and leave unto God [to] direct for the best. And so I bid you most heartily farewell. From off aboard her Majesty's good ship the Ark, the 6th of July, 1588.

Your assured loving friend,
C. Howard.

July 8.—*THE COUNCIL TO DARELL.*

[ccxii. **23**.—Endorsed.   A rough draft with many interlinear corrections.]

After our hearty commendations :—We find by a late note you have sent us, bearing date the 4th of July, of such ships as serve in those parts under our very good Lord the Lord Admiral, that for such of the said ships as were brought into those parts by his Lordship, you cannot set down a true estimate for what time they are victualled, unless you were made acquainted with their former victualling ; but

for the rest of the ships that serve under Sir Francis
Drake, and others that are entertained in her
Majesty's pay there, as also the coast ships, it
appeareth by your said note that they are victualled
but until the 14th of July, saving that Sir Francis
Drake hath a supply of seven days' victual more for
the number of ships appointed to serve under him.
Which being true, we do not see but the most part
of the ships shall be forced to give over the service,
a matter we do very greatly mislike of; and therefore we think it very convenient that you should
provide a month's victual for all the whole navy
serving there under his Lordship, wherein there
would[1] be all diligence possible used, especially if
they be furnished for no longer time than the 14th
of this month, as is contained in your said note.

And for such money as doth appear by your
letters to be due there, amounting to the sum of
900l., as also such further sums as shall be necessarily employed in the provision of the said month's
victual, we will take order that the same shall be
sent down with all speed by our loving friend
Richard Quarles, Esq., whom we think very meet to
repair to those parts for the better advancement of the
service. In the meantime, we would have you take
up, upon your credit, such provisions and other
necessaries as the said service shall require. And
for your better assistance therein, we send you certain commissions directed unto the Lieutenants[2] and
other principal officers in the counties where the
said provisions are to be made.

And so requiring [you] to advertise us by what
time the said month's victuals will be ready, and
whether in the meantime the provisions in the said
ships will be able to hold out, whereby the service
may not be given over. . . .

[1] Should.   [2] The Deputy-Lieutenants.

July 8.—*THE COUNCIL TO THE DEPUTY-LIEUTENANTS AND OTHERS.*

[ccxii. **23, I.**—Rough draft.]

Whereas Marmaduke Darell, gentleman, a servant of her Majesty in household, is appointed to make certain provisions within the county, as well of grain as of flesh and other necessaries, for the victualling of her Majesty's navy serving in the western seas under our very good Lord the Lord Admiral, and is also to use divers necessary ministers [for] the said service :—

These are to will and require you, as also, in her Majesty's name, straitly to charge and command you, to afford the said Darell and his deputies bearing this placart under our hands, your uttermost aid and assistance—for such service requireth expedition—as well in taking up the said provisions as also for the transporting of them to Plymouth or other place upon the sea coast, where he shall appoint.

And such sums of money as shall be due to any of her Majesty's subjects, either for provisions taken of them or for their labour and pains employed in the carriage of the same or otherwise, we will take order the same shall be repaid unto them out of hand, to their contentment.

And therefore we are to require both you and them not to fail in the furtherance of this service, as you will answer to contrary at your perils.

To the Deputy-Lieutenants in the County of . . , and to all Justices of Peace, Mayors, Sheriffs, Bailiffs, Constables, or any other her Majesty's Officers, Ministers, and loving subjects, to whom it may appertain, and to every of them.

July 10.—*CHARGES OF THE LONDON SHIPS.*

[**ccxii. 30.**—Endorsed.]

There are in the sixteen ships and four pinnaces set forth by the City of London, 1,340 men.

	£	s.	d.
The wages of which men per month, after 14s. per man, one with another, amounteth to	938	0	0
The like we account for each man's victuals per month, after 14s. the man	938	0	0
The tonnage of the said ships and pinnaces amounteth to 4,150 tons, which, after 2s. the ton per month, amounteth to the sum of	415	0	0
Sum per month	2,291	0	0
Besides powder, muskets, calivers, pikes, shot, and divers other furnitures put into the same ships and pinnaces, which at the least hath cost the City	2,000	0	0
There was paid in wages to men, and for victualling of them, from the time they were prest to serve her Majesty until the first day of May last past	1,000	0	0

The Lord Mayor of London and the Common Council are contented, and do yield to victual the said ships for one month longer.

THOMAS CORDELL.

July 11.—*DARELL TO THE COUNCIL.*

[**ccxii. 32.**—Holograph.   Addressed.]

My duty unto your most honourable Lordships humbly remembered :—Understanding by your letter of the 8th of this month (which came to my hands yesternight) that it is your Lordships' pleasure to have a month's victual more provided for the whole navy now in service under my Lord Admiral with all speed, and to be advertised from me in what time the same may be ready ; as also whether in the meantime, without it, the ships will be able to continue at sea :—

It may please your Lordships there shall be all diligence possible used in the performance of it, according to your commandment.   The commissions from your Lordships I do send away this morning ; and will also despatch away such other purveyors as shall be meet, with all the expedition I can.

Yet, forasmuch as I do judge the whole number of men that do serve in this fleet to be about 9,500, which, to be furnished for a month, will require a great mass of victual, I think it cannot be well performed in less space than a month ; and very true it is that, according to the note I sent your Lordships, the time of their former victualling will end in them all long before.   But so it is, Right Honourable, that my Lord Admiral and Sir Francis Drake, to prevent this want and inconvenience, which else must of necessity now have been, did long since— as I do certainly understand—take order for the placing of six men to a mess at sea ; which no doubt hath been observed, and thereby their victual much lengthened.   By means whereof, as also because myself, expecting of late some further service, have already provided many things here beforehand, I hope to furnish them with this month's victual in due time, and without the inconvenience which your Lordships do doubt of. Only I will presume in the meantime, until I may understand your Lordships' further pleasure, to write forthwith unto my Lord Admiral that it may please him to send those ships hither for their victual first that have most need; who no doubt—the fleet lying so near unto this coast—may return unto him again in short space, almost howsoever the wind be, and carry with them some store also for the rest. His Lordship may send, as he pleaseth, eight or ten sail at once, upon whose return others may come; and to want so many for a short time, I trust will be no great weakening unto the whole fleet. Otherwise I do not know how I shall be able to send it from hence to them, the shipping that is left here is so small and unfit for such a purpose. And so leaving the rest unto your honourable considerations, I do most humbly take my leave. From Plymouth, this 11th of July in the morning, 1588.

It may please your Lordships, the Mayors of Bristol and Lyme have written unto me to furnish their ships with two months' victual more, according to your Lordships' last letters to them in that behalf.

Your Lordships' most humble,
Mar. Darell.

July 12.—*SEYMOUR TO WALSYNGHAM.*

[ccxii. 34.—Holograph. Addressed.]

Sir :—Such summer season saw I never the like; for what for storms and variable unsettled

winds, the same unsettleth and altereth our determinations for lying on the other coast, having of
late sundry times put over, with southerly winds,
so far as Calais ; and suddenly enforced, still with
westerly great gales, to return to our English coasts,
where, so long as this unstable weather holdeth,
and that [1] the same serveth well many times for the
Spaniards to come (*vix credo*), yet shall they be
as greatly dangered by the raging seas as with their
enemies.

And to heap on braveries for conquering little
England, that hath always been renowned, and now
most famous by the great discovered strength, as
well by sea as by land, the same also united with
thousands resolute civil minds, how can the same
enter into my conceit they should any ways prevail ? when heretofore, our country, being divided
with many kings, the people barbarous and un-
civil, resisted mightily long before they could be
conquered.

But to digress from my own singular opinion,
and to give place to your honourable further authorities, I received letters from Sir William Russell,
which I send here-inclosed, hoping that all your
Honours will be most careful to regard those
quarters, the same being of so great weight and importance for the enemy's advantages.

This, also returning a note of all our coast ships
discharged and that are absent, do leave any further
to trouble you.   From aboard the Rainbow, the 12th
of July, 1588, in the small Downs, where I have much
ado to send my letters ashore.

Your assured friend to command,
H. Seymour.

The Duke levelleth at many marks, yet shooteth

---

[1] And that=even though.

but at one, I mean Zealand ; which, once obtained, his attempts for England will be far easier.

Sir, I pray you return me all my original letters both of Justinus Nassau[1] and of Sir William Russell.

July 10.—*NOTE OF THE COAST SHIPS.*

[ccxii. **34, I.**—Enclosed in Lord H. Seymour's letter of July 12.]

10th July, 1588.—Ships of the coast that served in this fleet amongst others, which were discharged upon the considerations hereinunder written :—

Newcastle .	The Daniel . .	Sent away by the Lords of the Council's letters, for wafting the cloth fleet to Stade.
	Galleon Hutchin	
	Bark Lamb .	
	Fancy . .	
Hull . .	Griffin . .	These ships were discharged for want of victuals, 17th June.
	Little Hare .	
	Handmaid .	
Aldborough .	Marigold .	This ship was discharged for want of victuals, 13th June.
Lowestoft .	Matthew .	Discharged for want of victuals, 13th June.
This pinnace is not worth the charge.[2]		
Lynn . .	Susan . .	Do., 3rd July.
Nor this of Lynn.[2]		

[1] The Admiral of Zealand, illegitimate brother of Prince Maurice.

[2] Autograph notes by Seymour.

July 13.—*HOWARD TO WALSYNGHAM.*

[**ccxii. 42.**—Holograph.   Addressed.   In deplorable condition.[1]]

Sir :—I have received your letter of the 3rd of
the present [this day [2]], being the 13th of the same,
within two hours after I [had despatched [2]] Sir E.
Hoby.   The messenger had been at the sea to
[seek me ever [2]] since Friday.   I am very sorry to
perceive by your [letter that [3]] her Majesty [doth
think [3]] that we have not [sufficiently sought [3]] to
understand some certainty of the Spanish fleet.
Sir, we are here to small purpose for this great
service, if that hath not been thought of.   Both
before my coming, by Sir Francis Drake, and since
my coming, there hath been no day but there hath
been pinnaces, Spanish caravels, flyboats, and of all
sorts, sent out to discover there.   The winds hath
been so southerly, and such foul weather as that
they could not [recover [3]] the coast of Spain so near
as to take any of their fisher boats ; and to send
some of our fisher boats to discover there, they
would do as [much good [2]] as to send oysterboat of
Billingsgate ; for neither can they bear sail [at all,
nor able to [3]] brook the seas ; [and if any had [2]] been
at the seas when the pinnaces were abroad, [they
would not [3]] have seen home again ; and if the
weather had [been such that [2]] some fisherman might
have gone, yet as soon as ever they had been seen,
they would have been taken up, with their boats,
which [be the worst [3]] of the world.

---

[1] Much torn, and badly mended with opaque paper.   Some
of the missing words are supplied from Bruce ; others by conjecture.
  [2] Bruce.   [3] Conjecture.

Sir, I did send a caravel of Sir F. Drake's [fourteen days [1]] agone, which was of any other least to be mistrusted ; but [before he [2]] could come to their coast, he met with a contrary wind [that turned [1]] him back and brake [his] mast and yard, and much [to do to rec[1]]over home again. I [sent] within three days after, a flyboat which is an excellent sailer. A man of Sir Walter Ralegh's went in her, one Hawes,[3] a very proper man. He met off Ushant 16 leagues with certain of their ships, as it shall appear by his letter which I send you. My own pinnace hath been well beaten [and] hath had 18 [grea]t sh[ot, which hath torn her hull and [1]] sails ; and by all likelihood, a Frenchman that served in their fleet ; for she was double manned and came from Spain, and a good tall ship. We have at this time four pinnaces on the coast of Spain ; but, Sir, you may see what [may co[2]]me of the sending me out with so little victuals, and the [evil of the same [2]]. For had I [not then [2]] been driven in for [lack] of victuals, we had met just with some of them not far [off Ushant [4]] ; for we came in with the storm at South the 22nd, and they fell with Scilly the next day after, an 18 sail of them. But, Sir, by all likelihood they be returned with very great harms.

Sir, I am now sending out two pinnaces more, and I trust her Majesty will think that shall be done

[1] Bruce.   [2] Conjecture.
[3] Possibly Ralph Hawes, who appears in the list of ships as captain of the Unicorn of Dartmouth.
[4] Conjecture. Bruce has 'off Scilly,' which seems inadmissible. Howard here says he came in to Plymouth on the 22nd and the Spanish ships were off Scilly on the 23rd. From his letter and advertisement of the 22nd (ante, pp. 220-1), it appears that he came in on the 21st and that the Spaniards were seen near Scilly the same day. Had he not been driven back on the 20th by a storm at South, he must have met them off Ushant rather than near Scilly.

that may be possible. I send you an advertisement that came to me even now, and I look every hour for more.

Sir F. Drake and all here do think no [gain] in sending any fishermen ; for as many as shall be sent, we [can] never look for any again. I know not what weather you have had there, but there was never any such summer seen here on the sea. God of his mercy [1] keep us from sickness, for we fear that more than any hurt that the Spaniards will do [this fleet], if the advertisements be true. Well, Sir, I would her Majesty did know of the care and pains that is taken here of all men for her service. We must now man ourselves again, for we have cast many overboard, and a number in great extremity which we discharged. I [have] sent with all expedition a prest for more men. And so I bid [you most] heartily farewell.

Your assured loving friend,
C. HOWARD.

It [2] hath pleased my Lord Admiral to command me to write my knowledge touching our espials. I assure your Honour there could not have been more care taken than his Lordship hath from time to time given order for ; and it is now certainly known that they are all returned back, much distressed ; and as for fisherboats, they are neither meet and can [not [3]] endure the seas.

Your Honour's faithfully to be commanded,
FRA. DRAKE.

[1] MS. marsy. [2] In Drake's autograph.
[3] Omitted in MS.

July 14.—*ABSTRACT OF THE ANSWERS OF THE MAYORS.*

[ccxii. **43.**]

The Answer of the Mayors of the Coast Towns on the West parts to the letters of the Lords of her Majesty's most honourable Privy Council, touching the re-victualling of the shipping set forth by them. Taken by me, Richard Swanson, one of her Majesty's messengers :—

Robert Brockinge, deputy to the Mayor of Bridgwater, answereth, that upon receipt of letters from the Right Honourable the Lord High Admiral of England, the contents of your Honours' letters were accomplished before the receipt thereof; and further answers, that if need require so, they will strain themselves for two months' more re-victualling.

Sir John Barron's answer, Mayor of Bristol, was that, after conference had with the rest of his brethren, both your Honours and Mr. Darell should be certified of their determination ; and upon my return thither, he said that one was sent to take order for re-victualling.

John Jones, Mayor of Lyme, sent one forthwith to take order for re-victualling; but most humbly craveth at your Honours that the towns of Axminster and Chard, refusing to yield both to the first and this last victualling, may by your good Lordships be brought thereunto ; being towns appointed to be contributories thereunto. Answering further, that if need so require, the merchants of the town of Lyme are contented to disburse in whole two subsidies, so that the towns of Axminster and Chard may be brought to disburse but one subsidy ; which, as they judge, will be sufficient to discharge this past, and two months more to come.

John Peryam, Mayor of Exeter, answereth that order is taken, according to your Honours' letters, for the re-victualling of two months longer.

John Wyse, Mayor of Totness, answereth that order is taken, according to your Honours' letters, for the re-victualling of two months longer.

William Hawkyns, Mayor of Plymouth, answereth that order is taken, according to your Honours' letters, for the re-victualling of two months longer.

John Porter, Mayor of Saltash, answereth that order was taken with Sir Francis Drake, Knight, for the sum of 150*l.*, to discharge them of all manner of charges of victualling; which money is already paid. But this composition, I learned, was taken at the first setting forth of their ship.

The names of the Ships set forth by the Coast Towns on the West parts, with the number of men [1] belonging to every of them :—

Bristol :—The Minion ; Unicorn ; Handmaid ; Aid.

Bridgwater :—The William.

Lyme, Axminster and Chard :—The Revenge ; Jacob.

Weymouth and Melcombe :—The Galleon ; Katharine.

Exeter and Apsam [2] :—The Bartholomew; Rose ; Gift.

Dartmouth and Totness :—The Crescent ; Flying Hart.

Plymouth :—The Charity, 80 men ; Little John.

Saltash :—The John Trelawney.

Fowey and Looe :—The Frances.

---

[1] For the number of men, see the list of ships.
[2] Topsham.

July 15.—*ORDER FOR VICTUALLING.*

[ccxii. **50.**—Signed.]

An estimate of the money for the victualling 1,471 men at the Narrow Seas, her Majesty in her own ships,[1] under the charge of my Lord Henry Seymour, as also 850 men being there in sundry ships from divers ports, viz. :—

For the Narrow Seas, *mensis Augusti*:

	£	s.
First.—The victualling of 1,471 men, in 16 of her Majesty's own ships at the Narrow Seas, for one month of 28 days, beginning the first of August and ending the 28th of the same, at 14s. the man per month . . .	1,029	14
For the transportation thereof . .	150	0
For the victualling of 850 men, serving in sundry ships out of divers ports at the Narrow Seas, at the like rate; beginning the 26th of June and doth end the 24th of July . . .	595	0
For transportation thereof . . .	80	0
Sum total . . .	1,854	14

Men, 2,321.
Money, 1,854*l.* 14s.

15th July, 1588.[2]

Mr. Peter, I pray you make an order for the payment of these sums to Mr. Quarles, for the victualling of her Majesty's ships under the charge of the Lord Henry Seymour; and to return unto me this note again, or a copy thereof.

W. BURGHLEY.

[1] So in MS.   [2] Note in Burghley's autograph.

July 16.—*MEMORANDUM BY SIR E. HOBY.*

[ccxii. 51.—Endorsed.]

The occasion of my Lord Admiral his sending me up hath been only to signify unto her Majesty what hath passed in all this season, and to resolve her Highness of the present estate of her army ; as also to bring down with me her Majesty's resolution and free liberty how she would have him to lie, or attempt aught on the enemy's coast.

July 17.—*THOMAS CELY* [1] *TO BURGHLEY.*

[ccxii. 57.—Holograph. Addressed.]

Right Honourable, my duty remembered :—My very good Lord,—I would write unto your Honour more oftener than I do, but I am not in place where I may do it. My Lord Admiral and Sir Francis Drake doth employ me to sea, for to see if I can meet with any shipping[2] coming out of Spain, which I have done divers times, and the intelligence[3] that I have gotten from time to time I have done[4] my Lord to understand of them. I am bound unto my Lord and to Sir Francis, for that they have such trust in me to do those things which standeth a trusty subject to do. I pray God I may deserve unto her Majesty, and to my Lord and to Sir Francis, the credit and trust that they suppose in me.

Your Honour hath had letters of late that their

---

[1] Some account of this man is given in the Introduction. At this time he was captain of the Elizabeth Drake.

[2] MS. to see for to sye yf I can myte wt eny shyppynge.

[3] MS. entelyjenes.   [4] Done=made.

fleet is dispersed. Truth is, I have been four times in France, and have brought[1] intelligence from time to time unto my Lord, and brought the ships with me sometimes, for that my Lord should get out some more matter than I could do. Captain Fenner[2] hath done the like, and Captain Crosse. I learn by these three hulks that Fenner and Crosse hath brought in, that the news which I had before is all one, and that there is two of their four galleys left, and two of their galleasses hath rolled their masts overboard, and many of their fleet hath broken their yards and other their tackling; notwithstanding, I learn by these men that they have a new supply of victual from Lisbon,[3] and that they arm[4] themselves as fast as they can to proceed in their wicked and malicious attempt. Therefore I think it good for us to arm ourselves to sea with all speed,[5] and to meet with them at sea, if God will give us leave.

My Lord was in a good way, if God had not sent a contrary wind. Our fleet was 80 leagues South and by West off Ushant. If the wind had holden[6] two days and two nights longer, we had had them in the Groyne, and within three leagues of the Groyne, all their whole[7] fleet in three sundry harbours, saving 30 hulks which we hear not of.

My Lord doth make what speed he may do to get out again to sea with the most part of the fleet. Truth[8] is, victual did fall out very short with many of our fleet, and very many contrary winds; and so they continue; God send better. If your Honour do write unto my Lord before we go to sea, haste us away. Good my Lord, I fear me we shall have

[1] MS. browethe.   [2] MS. Venard. Cf. p. 171.
[3] MS. Lysheborne.   [4] Arm=equip.
[5] MS. spide.   [6] MS. howelden.
[7] MS. hoell.   [8] MS. Trothe ys vytell dyd faull owet.

contrary winds and foul weather until we have a full moon.

My good Lord, a sharp war and a short, although it be chargeable, and that is fit for England. The Queen's subjects doth desire it. If I might a[1] been heard, it had been done ere this day, with a great deal less charges.[2] Our action hath not gone so forward as it might a done, if things had been furnished[3] to my desire. There is none that knoweth what I mean but her Majesty and myself; but this I will say unto your Honour and to all the rest of the Privy Council: that the King of Spain will make our mistress wise within few years, if it be not prevented. It might a been done ere this day if it had pleased her Majesty; and yet it may be done if the Duke of Parma[4] and the Guise and their friends be foreseen for doing us hurt upon the coast of England, or to enter our country: I say, if they may have the repulse for the year, and my Lord Admiral to defend[5] their fleet, as I trust in my God he shall do, for this year likewise, her Majesty shall have made for them the next year that they shall have desire to keep their own country.

Do not think to have any quietness with the King of Spain as long as his moneys comes out of the Indies. It is easily to be redressed. I have been desirous to have it known, and yet have I been afraid to move it; for that I have moved unto some of the Council, or at the least way was very willing; and when I have begun to enter into any matter of any importance, one of them told me and said this unto me: Cely, it is told me that you mell[6] with Councillors' matters. A rebuke I had, and so went my way. Another told me that if I could do

---

[1] Have.　　[2] MS. gredell les charjes.
[3] MS. foorneshed.　　[4] MS. Pallma & the Guies.
[5] Defend=fend off, repel.　　[6] Meddle.

her Majesty any service, so that it did cost[1] money, or that if charges should rise[2] upon it, never speak of it, for she will never consent unto it. So I went my way with a flea in mine ear.[3]

Another told me that if I did not make this and this of my counsel, and not to go unto the Queen, I should lose all the Council's good will. Why, my good Lord, if I have or had commandment that I should not open some matter which her Majesty would not have known, should I utter it? No, truly, if I should lose my life for my labour; and peradventure it may be so. My good Lord, I am a poor man, and one that hath been brought up without learning, and one that hath but a patched carcase[4]; for I had thirty-two sundry torments in the Inquisition with the apretados[5]—you term them in English rackings; and eight[6] years in prison lacking but two months. I take it, it was for her Majesty's sake and her subjects.

I have been towards her father and her brother and herself this sixty and two years. I have been no great craver, for I cannot spend one groat by the year by her; and yet her Majesty hath promised me good things; but I have been desirous to do her good, and not always begging, as some be. And yet have I lost above two thousand pounds since I served her Majesty, besides the great and cruel imprisonments in the Inquisition, and in the King of Spain's most filthy galleys, and seven other prisons; and God I take to witness without desert, more than that they approved that I was her

[1] If it were to cost.
[2] MS. ryes : arise.
[3] MS. a flee yn my neer.
[4] MS. karkes.
[5] *Apretado*, past part. of *apretar*, is rather one who is pressed or racked. A pressing or racking is *apretura*.
[6] It is doubtful whether the MS. has viii or xiii; one seems to have been written over the other. But cf. Cely to the Queen, Dec. 12, 1579 (*post*, App. A).

sworn man. Truth is, I did strike their secretary as I was before the Inquisidores, they sitting in judgment. I had great reason to do it.

Let these things pass. I am now to crave your Honour that you will be a mean to help to abate the malicious intention of the Spaniard. If her Majesty will, she shall have him brought to pass[1] that he shall be glad to entreat her Majesty to have a peace. And if it do cost her a hundred thousand sovereigns,[2] she shall have two hundred thousand again, and all of them of the action[3] well contented. God is the only giver of victory. My trust is only in him. I will not say but God may have put the same secret[4] into another man's head as he hath done into mine; but I believe that there is no creature can do it but myself. I once[5] moved her Majesty that she might have such a thing done. Her Majesty looked very sadly upon me; so I think, in my conscience, she thought it impossible to be done. For in very truth there was a piece of paper which her Majesty did read, and she answered me and said, It cannot be done in time. I asked her if I should show it to two persons in the world living at this present. She said, No. I think in my conscience it was more for that [she] stood in doubt that I could not accomplish [it], and that her Majesty would not have me to come to any foil[6]; for that I am assured her Majesty doth love me. I take it, it was for this, more than for any other thing. He that looks a man in the face knoweth not what is in his purse.[7] I am of that opinion, that

---

[1] To such a pass.   [2] MS. soferanes.
[3] Those concerned, or who take part in the action.
[4] It nowhere appears what the secret was.   Probably, to look out for the treasure fleet, but if so, it got into other men's heads. See *post*, Seymour to Walsyngham, July 20.
[5] MS. wouenes.   [6] MS. foyell.   [7] MS. pores.

no man can do it but myself. Within one year after it is done, it will bring her Majesty to more quietness, and her countries, than all her Council in seven years.

Good my Lord, bear with my rude and bold[1] manner in writing this word so boldly. I have the very same paper that her Majesty did read; but I do not send it to your Honour. Good my Lord, tell her Majesty from me that I have not yet told the Spaniards what we be doing in England, but when God sends me to meet with them, I will tell them. But I promise your Honour when I have told them, I will bring them home with me into England.

My Lord, there is three barks taken of late by the Frenchmen, and one of the three is a son's of mine, taken in the road of Lamoster,[2] near unto Nantes.[3] Good my Lord, send my Lord Admiral word whether I may not take a Frenchman for him. Desire her Majesty to request my Lord Admiral and Sir Francis Drake to continue the goodness towards me; and your Honour's words will be a great credit unto me, favourably written. In haste, this present 17th of July, 1588, by

Yours to command,
Thomas Cely.

I doubt your Honour will have much ado to read this letter. Desire her Majesty to help your Honour; her Majesty will. My[4]—but few words.

[1] MS. roed & boweld.
[2] Les Moutiers in the Baie de Bourgneuf.
[3] MS. Nans.
[4] It would seem as if he was going to break out again—My good Lord &c.; but as he began, it struck him that he had perhaps written enough.

July 17.—*BURGHLEY TO WALSYNGHAM.*

[**ccxii. 58.**—Signed, and holograph postscript. Addressed.]

Sir :—I have at good length, as you may perceive, written to Darell, that hath the dealing for Mr. Quarles at Plymouth for the victualling of the navy. When you have read the letter, I pray you to cause it to be sealed and sent unto him by such means as you have. And so I commend me most heartily to you. From my house near the Savoy, this 17th of July, 1588.

Your assured loving friend,

W. BURGHLEY.

I am very sorry that our counsel for sending one expressly from her Majesty to the Duke of Parma doth not like her. It will be hard for our Commissioners to be informed[1] with such certainty as largely instructed both by speech and writing from hence ; but *fiat voluntas sua.*

I am at this present, by this last night's torment, weakened in spirits, as I am not able to rise out of my bed ; which is my grief the more because I cannot come thither where both my mind and duty do require.

July 17.—*BURGHLEY TO DARELL.*

[**ccxii. 58, I.**—Draft, with corrections in Burghley's hand. Endorsed :—Memorandum of my Lord's letter to Mr. Darell at Plymouth.]

I commend me unto you :—Since[2] such time as, this other day, you have been directed to make a new provision for the victualling of her Majesty's

---

[1] Sc. in any other way . . . as if they were fully instructed &c.
[2] Sc. since the other day, when you were directed &c.

fleet there under the charge of the Lord Admiral
and Sir Francis Drake, and money sent down to
you for that purpose, the merchants here, of the
city, have been dealt withal for a new victualling of
their ships for one month more, which they have
assented unto ; and are well contented to make the
same allowance, after the rate of 14*s.* the man, as
her Majesty giveth ; the numbers whereof, as the
same is delivered unto me by a note from them,
amounteth unto 1,340 men, who were victualled by
them, as they say, until the 10th of the month of
August, after the rate of four men to a mess ; which
being reduced to five to a mess, as they understand
my Lord Admiral brought them and the rest, for the
drawing out of the victuals, they have good reason
to think, together[1] considering the death of many of
their men, that the same should reach at the least to
a fortnight more.

But howsoever that falleth out, they are content
to allow for one month more after the rate aforesaid ;
wherein I pray you to use your best means and
credit for the speedy victualling of them ; and for
the money due for the same, I will undertake either
to have it to be sent down thither unto you, or paid
here, or made over by exchange to you, as you shall
appoint. And in like sort, I pray you to help, in the
best sort you can, the ships of the ports to be
victualled, who have also assented to re-victual their
own ships for one month more ; and therefore, what
furtherance you can give them, by your commissioners or otherwise, I pray you let them find it.

I do not doubt but, considering the order that
my Lord Admiral took for the putting of four first
to a mess, and afterwards increasing them to six to
a mess ; and withal the mortality of a great many,
whereof I was sorry to understand, that those

[1] As also.

numbers, both in my Lord Admiral's fleet and Sir Francis Drake's, will be victualled for some good time with this new supply for one month more; and that the money sent down to you will be more than sufficient for your purpose; but how to judge hereof, I know not; for that there was some fault in you, in that you made not your last certificate, which you sent up hither, so perfect as had been requisite; for that you neither particularly mentioned the numbers of men, nor the vessels wherein they serve; which I pray you by your next certificate to reform, so that it may be understood what numbers serve in every of the ships that were there with Sir Francis Drake, before my Lord Admiral's coming to Plymouth; as also of those numbers brought by my Lord Admiral in every of the ships with him, and of any new numbers supplied by his Lordship after his coming thither. And, as near as you can, what the number at this present are in every of the said ships chargeable to the Queen [for] victualling, with all things otherwise needful for the better understanding and explaining of your doings.

For[1] surely, by your diversity of your certificates, as Mr. Quarles showed them here to me, by your first, we made account that the ships were victualled to the 1st of August or farther, until, by your last, you certified that the ships under Sir Francis Drake, containing 2,821 men, and eight other ships, containing 299 men, being retained into her Majesty's charge by the Lord Admiral, were victualled but to the 14th of July; a matter so strange to us, as Mr. Quarles, considering your former letters, imagined that you had written July for August; but to our grief here, we find it as you did write, which I am right sorry for.

You write also that my Lord Admiral took with

[1] This paragraph is inserted in Burghley's own hand.

him 10 sail of the victuallers; but what men or victuals they have, you know not; a matter also not well ordered; for I am sure my Lord Admiral, if you had demanded of him the knowledge thereof, he would have certified you.

Though you write that the Mayors of Bristol and Lyme have written to you to furnish their ships with two months' victuals more, according to certain letters of the Council's written to them, yet it was not meant that the charge thereof in money should be upon the Queen; but the provision[1] of the victuals to be made by you for more surety, and the money to be afterwards paid by those two towns. And so have the officers of those towns, and of the rest of the ports, sent word to the Council that they do mean to be at the charges. And therefore you shall do well, if you do make the provision for them yourself, to acquaint them with the charge thereof. If otherwise, they will not[2] make their own provisions

July 17.—*HOWARD TO BURGHLEY.*

[ccxii. 59.—Signed. Endorsed.]

My very good Lord :—I have caused Sir Francis Drake and Mr. Hawkyns to consider of your charges, for that our companies grow into great need, and many occasions in such an army doth breed sundry great and extraordinary charges. I have sent herein enclosed an estimate thereof, praying your Lordship that there may be some care had that we may be furnished with money, without the which we are not able to continue our forces

---

[1] That the provision . . . should be made &c.
[2] This 'not' would appear to have slipped in, in error. The meaning is evidently the exact opposite of what is written.

together.   And when it shall please her Majesty
that this army shall be dissolved, it shall be most
beneficial to her Majesty that money be had here in
a readiness to discharge such as be of this country ;
whereby a great sum of money may be saved in
lessening of the companies, which will ease very
much the charges of victuals, wages and conduct ;
which, without money, we shall not be able to do.

If your Lordship do give order to pay the money
to Mr. Dr. Hussey, Mr. Hawkyns hath written to
him that so much as shall discharge her Majesty's
ships serving on the Narrow Seas until the 28th of
July, shall be sent to Sir William Wynter, to Dover ;
for in this estimate those ships are included until
that day.   And so I bid your good Lordship heartily
farewell.   From Plymouth, the 17th of July, 1588.

Your Lordship's assured loving

friend to command,

C. HOWARD.

July 17.—*HOWARD TO WALSYNGHAM.*

[ccxii. 60.—Signed.   Addressed.   In bad condition.]

Sir :—I must write as I have occasion by advertisements.   I had brought in to me two flyboats of
Enkhuysen, which came from Aveiro, and in their
coming they did put into the town of Bayona.   This
was within these twelve days, long since the return
of the fleet from our coast.   There were none of the
fleet there.   There was one galley that had been
there all this year [to] keep and discover on that
[coast [1]].   He reported that the whole fleet [were] in
the [Groyne, saving a few that be [2]] in some other
places.   He also [said] that they do make ready to

---

[1] Conjecture.   [2] Bruce : conjecture.

put out again; and that [the K]ing doth send to
them daily to put out. And, in my opinion, it is
very like that they are [not [1]] divided into sundry
places, as it was reported; for if they had, some
would have been at Bayona.

Sir, I make all the haste I can possible out; and
I, and all my company that came from London, will
[not [1]] stay for anything. Sir Francis Drake and
some of those ships will be ready; and the rest within
three or four days after. And seeing the advertisements be no surer, I mean to keep the three great
ships with me yet awhile, to see what will come
of it. Some four or five ships have discharged [their
men; for the [2]] sickness in s[ome] is very great, so
that we are fain to discharge some ships, to have
their men to furnish the others.

If it had not been to water, and that all the
ships set out by the coast towns wanted victuals, I
would not have seen this town, for it is hot, being
here. Extreme business, which doth belong to
such an army, enforceth me to be here more than I
would; but there shall be neither sickness nor death
which shall make you [3] yield until this service be
ended. I never saw nobler minds than be here [in
our] forces; but I cannot stir out but I have an
inf[inite number] hanging on my shoulders for
money. We do all we [can to re]lieve them. There
was a fault, which I will not write of; but how, I
will tell you when I come up; and if I had not in
time looked into it, we should have had much more
misery amongst some than we have.

Sir, I have heard that there is in London some
hard speeches against Mr. Hawkyns because the
Hope came in [to] mend a leak which she had.
Sir, I think there were never so many of the prince's

---

[1] Not: omitted in MS.   [2] Conjecture.
[3] So in MS., but the sense seems to require 'me' or 'us.'

ships so long abroad, and in such seas, with such weather as these have had, with so few leaks ; and the greatest fault of the Hope came with ill grounding before our coming hither ; and yet it is nothing to be spoken of. It was such a leak that I durst have gone with it to Venice. But may they not be greatly ashamed that sundry times have [so] disabled her Majesty's ships, which are the only ships of the world ? [Sir,] if you did know the leaks and weakness of other [ships that] be in this fleet, in respect of them it would be said the Queen's Majesty's ships were and are strong. For when the weather hath been bad and rough, the most part of all the navy have besought me that I, and the rest of her Majesty's ships, would bear less sail, for they could not endure it, when we made no reckoning of it. And so I bid you most heartily farewell. From Plymouth, the 17th of July, 1588.

Your very loving and assured friend,

C. HOWARD.

July 17.—HAWKYNS TO BURGHLEY.

[ccxii. 61.—Holograph. Addressed :—For her Majesty's service.]

My bounden duty remembered unto your good Lordship :—By the letter and estimate enclosed, your Lordship may see how charges doth grow here daily. My Lord Admiral doth endeavour by all means to shorten it, and yet to keep the navy in strength.

In this demand is the ships serving under the Lord Henry Seymour included ; and I do write to Mr. Hussey to stay so much money as may clear them.

The four great ships—the Triumph, the Elizabeth Jonas, the Bear, and the Victory—are in most royal and perfect state ; and it is not seen by them, neither do they feel that they have been at sea, more than if they had ridden at Chatham. Yet there be some in them that have no goodwill to see the coast of Spain with them, but cast many doubts how they will do in that seas. But, my good Lord, I see no more danger in them, I thank God, than in others. The Bear one day had a leak, upon which there grew much ado; and when it was determined that she should be lighted of her ordnance, her ballast taken out, and so grounded and searched, and that my Lord Admiral would not consent to send her home, the leak was presently stopped of itself; and so the ship proceedeth with her fellows, in good and royal estate, God be thanked. I was bold to trouble your Lordship with these few words touching these four ships, because I know there will be reports as men are affected; but this is the truth.

The strength of the ships generally is well tried; for they stick not to ground often to tallow, to wash, or any such small cause, which is a most sure trial of the goodness of the ships when they are able to abide the ground. My Lord Admiral doth not ground with his ship, but showeth a good example, and doth shun charges as much as his Lordship may possible. And so I leave to trouble your good Lordship. From Plymouth, the 17th of July, 1588.

Your honourable Lordship's humbly to command,

JOHN HAWKYNS.

July 17.—*ESTIMATE OF CHARGES.*

[ccxii. 61, I.—Enclosure in Hawkyns' letter to Burghley of same date. Signed.]

An estimate of the charge of the wages growing for the companies serving under the charge of the Lord High Admiral of England, viz. :—

The last pay was made to the companies serving

in the Narrow Seas under the Lord Admiral to the
11th of February last; since which time there hath
been a pay made to the Treasurer, of those ships
for those companies, to end the 5th of May last, for
2,990 men, being 3 months, amounting unto 6,279*l.*

For the four great ships, being 1,900 men, there
is paid to the Treasurer three months' pay, to end
the 13th of July, which amounted to the sum of
3,990*l.*

	£	s.	d.
To bring the pay of the first number of 2,990 men to end the 28th of July, is 84 days, which is three months' pay, and amounteth to the sum of	6,279	0	0
To bring the 1,900 men serving in the four great ships to the 28th of July, is 15 days' pay, and amounteth unto the sum of .	712	10	0
For grounding, tallowing, sea-store, carpentry, masts, repairing of boats and pinnaces; for cordage, canvas, and such like emptions [1]	2,500	0	0
For conduct in discharge of 1,000 sick men, that were discharged out of the fleet, and for the prest and conduct of others taken up to serve in their places, by estimation. . .	700	0	0
Summa . . .	10,191	10	0

This sum is to be sent to Plymouth.

The ships that were under the charge of Sir
Francis Drake :—

There is received for the 2,900 men that were

[1] Purchases, things bought.

in Sir Francis Drake's charge, by the Treasurer, two months' pay, from the 24th of April to the 19th of June, saving there is yet to pay above 800*l.* (as I think) of the last warrant for the charge; which is 4,060*l.*

	£	s.	d.
To bring the pay of this number of 2,900 men to the 28th of July, is 39 days' pay, and doth amount of the sum of	2,827	10	0
The ships will have been in pay for tonnage, to the 28th of July, 236 days; of which there is allowed by the warrants for 4 months, which is 112 days; so rest to pay for 124 days, which is 4 months 12 days, and amounteth to	1,771	8	8
For grounding and tallowing of all those ships that were under Sir Francis Drake's charge, sea-store for them, carpentry, re-forming of masts, boats and pinnaces, cordage, canvas, and such like, for her Majesty's ships in that company . .	2,500	0	0
More, for the wages of 700 men entertained by Sir Francis Drake, Knight, for the space of four months in ships of Sir Richard Greynvile's and others, to the number of eight ships taken up to serve with the fleet of her Majesty, which were appointed to continue, by the Council's letters, ending the 28th of July, 1588, amounting to the sum of .	1,960	0	0

	£	s.	d.
For the tonnage of the said ships, being by estimation 800 ton, the sum of	320	0	0
	9,378	18	8

This sum is to be sent to Plymouth.

How the 6,000*l.* that was imprested to be carried with my Lord Admiral is defrayed :—

	£	s.	d.
Imprimis, there was sent to Sir Francis Drake, Knight, to Plymouth, for the provision of victual, by Mr. Secretary his order, the sum of	2,000	0	0
Item, there is imprested to Mr. Darell, by my Lord Admiral's order, for the victualling of all the navy	2,900	0	0
Item, paid by my Lord Admiral's warrant, for one month's pay to 1,000 soldiers entertained by Sir Francis Drake, Knight, the sum of	500	0	0
Item, more, by like warrant to relieve certain captains likewise entertained by Sir Francis Drake, Knight, the sum of . . .	100	0	0
	5,500	0	0

So as there resteth in my hands of this 6,000*l.*, only the sum of .	500	0	0

An abstract of the money that is now to be paid and sent to Plymouth :—

£   s.   d.

First, for the charge growing upon the ships that served under the

	£	s.	d.
charge of the Lord Admiral in the Narrow Seas &c., as appeareth by the first estimate .	10,191	10	0
Item, for the charge growing upon the ships that served under the charge of Sir Francis Drake, Knight, westward, as by the second estimate appeareth . .	9,378	18	8
	19,570	8	8
Of which there remaineth in my hands of the 6,000*l*., as appeareth by the account above written	500	0	0
Which being taken out of the former sum, there will remain to be paid from her Majesty . . .	19,070	8	8

C. HOWARD.   JOHN HAWKYNS.

July 17.—*THOMAS FENNER TO WALSYNGHAM*

[**ccxii. 62**.—Signed. Addressed. Sealed with the arms of the Sussex Fenners—Between 4 eagles displayed, a cross charged with a cross [1] potent.]

My letter of the 12th of July with the advertisements therein enclosed, I hope are come unto your Honour's hand, by Sir Edward Hoby. I was commanded at the sea upon the sudden, to go for the coast of Brittany, moved thereby to send your Honour letters and advertisement by a pinnace to Plymouth, delivered as before, assureth my hope that your Honour have received the same. Since that time I intercepted three great flyboats which

[1] In Burke's *General Armoury* the charge on the cross is given as ' a cross formée.' The device on the seal is, however, perfectly distinct.

came from San Lucar the 7th of June. Their advertisements which I gathered, I send your Honour herein enclosed.

Understanding by them of seventeen hulks and flyboats more, coming after within some three or four days by their supposition ; as also I gathered, by very politic means and liberality, a great secret in one of those ships ; which the name of the ship being a Hollander, which had my Lord of Leicester his pass, which ship is sold unto Spaniards in San Lucar, and now bound for Dunkirk, laden with wools, and secretly in her, two tons of silver.   If the wind and spring serve him not to put in with Dunkirk, he makes no care to put for England or Flushing, in that he hath pass, and is a Hollander.

The Sweden captain which your Honour wrote unto Sir Francis Drake to let pass is one of the company of that fleet.

The ship's name that hath the silver is called the Golden Rose of Enkhuysen.   A rose painted in her stern and in her head.

I write your Honour thus largely in that, if it please, you may advertise with speed Sir William Russell to have regard to these points.   As also advertise (as your Honour think meetest) her Majesty's ships in the Narrow Seas.

There is a very great Hollander also in company, laden with Spanish goods.   By conference with divers other of the three flyboats, I understood the said ship to be one of the company ; but sifted not the secret ; yet found by them that she was sold to the Spaniards.

I am appointed as this day to put over, if wind serve, with the Galleon Leicester in company, for the coast of France, to check [1] with this fleet.   God

---

[1] To clash, fight.   In this sense it is always followed by 'with.'

send me the happiness to do some effectual service for my gracious mistress and country. There never happened the like opportunity to beat down the Spanish pride, if it be effectually followed. If not, I would to the Lord I had not been one of the company, for our reputations thereby is overthrown. I would I were one of the thirty sail to put it in execution.

This, I betake[1] your Honour to the Almighty, most humbly craving pardon for tedious writing. From aboard the Nonpareil, this 17th of July, 1588.

Your Honour's in all duty to command,

THOMAS FENNER.

Since my letters of the 12th to your Honour at my being at the sea, I spake with three English ships of Dartmouth, who came from Rochelle, bringing certain intelligence of the dispersion of the Spanish fleet into the Passage,[2] the Groyne, and divers other places thereabouts. Withal a pinnace of Rochelle, taking two of their victuallers, within two hours after met with two of the galleons with their mainmasts overboard. They reported further, that many of them were beaten with a wonderful storm in the north part of Ireland.

This present morning a little caravel of Sir Francis Drake arrived which was sent for the coast of Spain for discovery, who met with two French which came from Lisbon the 6th of this month, who confessed six of the Spanish fleet came back into Lisbon before their departure, full of sick men ; the rest of the fleet, some in Bayona, some in the Groyne and in Passage, and in great sickness and mortality. Now is the time, I beseech God move your Honour

---

[1] With this, I commit.

[2] Los Pasages, about four miles to the east of San Sebastian ; formerly a good harbour, but now almost silted up.

to further and hasten our departure.   If not all, yet some.

The King of Navarre hath good success upon the river of Bordeaux.

July 18.—*SEYMOUR TO WALSYNGHAM.*

[**ccxii. 64.**—Signed, and autograph postscript.   Addressed.]

Sir :—I find no manner of difference between winter and summer, saving that the days be now longer, and to deliver our hard water works[1] most stormy and tempestuous the same will hardly be credited to fall out such in the season.

Being informed from Calais, the 15th of this month there should come from Rosco 50 sails to join with them of Dunkirk, I laboured, as much as wind and weather would give me leave, to attend them by intercepting their shipping, which was given me to understand should repair either to Calais or Dunkirk the next day.

The 16th of this present, I observed the full tides where they might harbour themselves, but lost my labour and returned to the Downs.

The next day, the 17th of this instant, I plied up the former course and anchored between Calais Cliffs[2] and Blackness, where no usual road was, as it appeared after by the great storm that happened. In the interim came Gourdan's ships with two Rosco flyboats under sail, which I made strike and ride at anchor with me.

The storm arose presently most outrageous, and such as, during my [being[3]] aboard the seas, this winter, I never saw greater.   These sails seemed

---

[1] This may perhaps mean :—For the performance of our hard work upon the water, stormy &c. to a degree that will hardly &c.
[2] MS. Cleives.   [3] Omitted in the MS.

deep laden, and certainly came from Lisbon, but the extremity of weather was such as I could not send any boat aboard. Yet did Gourdan, with a very nimble sail of shallop, covet to send aboard his ship; but I waved him to come unto me first, which he little regarded; whereby I was enforced to discharge a fair[1] shot over him, and so [he] came room unto me.

Upon further examination of Gourdan's men, they confessed their master's ship full freighted with merchandise at Lisbon, and so gave him leave to go aboard to work the best advantage for his master in this extremity of storm. The other two smaller vessels of Rosco which came in company, I took better care to look unto them, hoping that some of them may answer the charge of the storm which hath scattered many of our fleet, if they be well searched. This, because our navy is not yet gathered together, whereby I cannot yet advertise our fortunes, with my very loving commendations, do betake you to God. From aboard the Rainbow, the 18th of July, 1588, at anchor in the Downs, in most foul weather.

Your very loving assured friend ever,

H. Seymour.

To move the Lord Treasurer.

Sir, You shall do very well to help us with a pay for our men, who are almost 16 weeks unpaid; for what with fair and foul means, I have enough to do to keep them from mutiny. Our coast men likewise would be resolved whether their pay and other necessaries shall be defrayed at her Majesty's charges, as their victuals now are.

---

[1] MS. fayre.

July 19.—*BURGHLEY TO WALSYNGHAM.*

[**ccxii. 66.**—Holograph. Addressed.]

Sir :—I find my mind as much troubled to write as now I do, as commonly my stomach is against purging [1]; but I cannot conceal from you the causes which will shortly bring forth desperate effects.

I have received letters from my Lord Admiral and Mr. Hawkyns, with a schedule declaring that they have great lack of money for wages, besides victuals ; for [2] Mr. Quarles hath 6,000*l.* this last week, and now Mr. Hawkyns' declaration that, to make a full pay to the 28th of this month, there must be paid 19,070*l.* ; and of that 6,000*l.* which he had, there remaineth with him but 500*l.* I marvel that where so many are dead on the seas the pay is not dead with them, or with many of them.

And how the reckoning for victuals will fall out I know not, but I fear that 6,000*l.* will not serve ; and yet, as I perceive, my Lord Admiral's company are victualled until mid August, and if Sir Francis Drake was victualled, his Lordship might go to the sea without delay. At this time also is demanded by the office of the admiralty, for to pay an old debt for provisions, 7,000*l.* ; and to restore their lacks 6,000*l.* ; *in toto*, 13,000*l.* ; and I have moved them to content the creditors for the 7,000*l.* with one-third now, one other third in the end of August, and the later at Michaelmas ; which is a charitable relief, and so there might [be [3]] leisure in paying the other 6,000*l.* for new provisions. There is also paid to Quarles for one month's victual for the ships in the Narrow Seas, 1,854*l.*

[1] The meaning seems to be :—The writing this letter is as sickening as the swallowing a nauseous potion would be.

[2] As though he had said :—Which seemeth to me strange, for &c.   [3] Omitted in MS.

The office of the ordnance demandeth for furniture of habiliments &c., for to serve an army by
land, about 8,000*l.* There is also, beside 2,700*l.*
lately paid to the creditors, the sum of 2,379*l.* to be
paid. I know that the towns and the army have
also great need of money.

A man would wish, if peace cannot be had, that
the enemy would not longer delay, but prove, as I
trust, his evil fortune : for as these expeditions do
consume us, so I would hope, by God's goodness,
upon their defeat we might have one half year's
time to provide for money.

I have had conference with Palavicino and with
Saltonstall[1] how 40,000 or 50,000 might be had for
10 per cent. ; but I find no probability how to get
money here in specie, which is our lack, but by
exchange, to have it out of the parts beyond sea,
which will not be done but in a long time; yet
there is some likelihood that our merchants of
Stade might practise for 20,000 or 30,000, for
which there shall be some profit very secretly. I
shall but fill my letter with more melancholy matter
if I should remember what money must be had to
pay 5,000 footmen and 1,000 horsemen for defence
of the enemy landing in Essex.

Yours most assured,
W. BURGHLEY.

July 20.—*SEYMOUR TO WALSYNGHAM.*

[ccxii. 69.—Holograph. Addressed.]

Sir :—Your last received letter of the 18th of
this month doth in manner answer your two former

---

[1] Richard Saltonstall, Governor of the Merchant Venturers ;
Sheriff of London 1588-9 ; Lord Mayor 1597 ; knighted 1617.

letters of the 17th of this instant; for the flat bottomed boats meant to be transported from Gravelines to Dunkirk or Nieuport, the same doth very well agree with many my letters heretofore written, declaring the Duke intent only to employ them for Wakerland [1]; for otherwise they be no boats to be hazarded to the seas, no more than wherries or cockboats; and assuredly the Flushingers reinforcing their strength by sea doth confirm my opinion. I am very glad likewise that Sir William Wynter doth concur with me in judgment touching the Isle of Wight, which heretofore he did not so well regard, and which in my letters last sent unto you I remembered the same a special place for a rendezvous, wishing besides hoys instead of sconces for defence of the Thames and the City of London.[2] Also I mistrust Sandwich, which is a strong situation by nature.

These two places, the Isle of Wight and Sandwich, will very hardly be recovered of the enemy, being once obtained. But I fear them not this year nor the next, if her Majesty will not still be entertained with peace, but rather to proceed to intercept the India fleet which is shortly to return. This, having due regard to your last advertisements of Mr. Thomas Fenner's, do take my leave. From aboard the Rainbow, the 20th of July, 1588, returned to the Small Downs, where we may daily [espy [3]] any sails upon the coasts of Calais.

Your assured friend to command,

H. SEYMOUR.

There is wanting of our fleet by reason of this storm, the George, a old hoy of her Majesty's; the Sun, her Majesty's pinnace; the ship of Yarmouth,

[1] Walcheren.   [2] Cf. *ante*, p. 207.
[3] Word omitted in MS.

the ship of Rye, the pinnace of Feversham, the fly-boat which I stayed, and five of my company in her, and two Bretons of Rosco, which I stayed in that distress, and in which one of them[1] are 6 or 7 English mariners of our fleet. These, without question, are either put to Flushing or Harwich, hoping[2] by the next fair weather to hear of them. The galley and the men within her, being 280[3] persons, may thank God I stayed her going out at that time, for there is no question but she had perished.

July 21.—*NOTE OF CHARGES.*

[**ccxii. 79.**—Endorsed :—The charge of certain works[4] to be done upon the Thames.]

	£
21st of July, 1588.—Richmond.	
120 masts, at 6*l.* the piece	720
Anchors to moor the same: 20, of 6 and 7 hundred weight, at 26*s.* the hundred .	180
20 smaller anchors, of 5 hundred weight .	140
Ironwork for chains to lock them together, 1,000 weight at 25*s.*	250
Cables to moor the masts, of 9 inches: 20, at 13*l.* the cable	267
Workmanship of the masts	50
6 lighters and 6 ships or hoys, to serve for wages according to the rate of tonnage: Workmanship for this proportion of shipping, at 40*l.* a ship	480
Sum of this, besides the ships . .	2,087

[1] In one of which.   [2] So that I hope.
[3] So in MS.   Her complement was 250.
[4] The construction of a boom at Tilbury. See *post*, p. 298, Leicester to Walsyngham, July 22.

July 21.—*HOWARD TO WALSYNGHAM.*

[**ccxii. 80.**—Signed, and autograph postscript.   Addressed.]

Sir :—I will not trouble you with any long letter ;
we are at this present otherwise occupied than with
writing.   Upon Friday, at Plymouth, I received
intelligence that there were a great number of ships
descried off of the Lizard ; whereupon, although the
wind was very scant, we first warped out of harbour
that night, and upon Saturday turned out very
hardly, the wind being at South-West ; and about
three of the clock in the afternoon, descried the
Spanish fleet, and did what we could to work for the
wind, which [by this] morning we had recovered,
descrying their f[leet to] consist of 120 sail, whereof
there are 4 g[alleasses] and many ships of great
burden.

At nine of the [clock] we gave them fight, which
continued until one.   [In this] fight we made some
of them to bear room to stop their leaks ; notwithstanding we durst not adventure to put in among
them, their fleet being so strong.   But there shall
be nothing either neglected or unhazarded, that may
work their overthrow.

Sir, the captains in her Majesty's ships have
behaved themselves most bravely and like men
hitherto, and I doubt not will continue, to their great
commendation.   And so, recommending our good
success to your godly prayers, I bid you heartily
farewell.   From aboard the Ark, thwart of Plymouth,
the 21st of July, 1588.

Your very loving friend,
C. HOWARD.

Sir, the southerly wind that brought us back
from the coast of Spain brought them out.   God

blessed us with turning us back. Sir, for the love of God and our country, let us have with some speed some great shot sent us of all bigness; for this service will continue long; and some powder with it.

July 21.—*THE MAYOR*[1] *OF PLYMOUTH AND MR. DARELL TO THE COUNCIL.*

[ccxii. **81**.—Copy. Endorsed.]

Our last intelligence[2] that we gave to your Lordships was that the Spanish fleet was in view of this town yesternight, and that my Lord Admiral was passed to the sea before our said view, and was out of our sight. Since which time we have certain knowledge, both by certain pinnaces come from his Lordship, as also by plain view this present morning, that my Lord being to the windwards of the enemy, are in fight, which we beheld. As for that we suppose that his Lordship will find in this action great want of men, we have thought most meet to send such forth as the town and country will yield, and in that behalf we have provided divers ships and bottoms to carry them so fast as they come. And so &c.

July 21.—*DRAKE TO SEYMOUR.*

[ccxii. **82**.—Signed, and autograph postscript. Addressed :—To the Right Honourable the Lord Henry Seymour, Admiral of her Majesty's Navy in the Narrow Seas ; or in absence, to Sir William Wynter, Knight, give these with speed. Haste, post, haste.]

Right Honourable and my very good Lord :—I am commanded by my very good Lord, the Lord

[1] William Hawkyns, John's elder brother.
[2] This letter is missing.

Admiral, to send you the caravel in haste with this letter, giving your Lordship to understand that the army of Spain arrived upon our coast the 20th of this present. The 21st we had them in chase, and so coming up unto them, there hath passed some cannon shot between some of our fleet and some of them, and as far as we perceive they are determined to sell their lives with blows. Whereupon his Lordship hath commanded me to write unto your Lordship and Sir William Wynter, that those ships serving under your charge should be put into the best and strongest manner you may, and ready to assist his Lordship for the better encountering of them in those parts where you now are. In the meantime, what his Lordship and the rest here following him may do shall be surely performed.

His Lordship hath commanded me to write his hearty commendations to your Lordship and Sir William Wynter. I do salute your Lordship, Sir William Wynter, Sir Henry Palmer, and all the rest of those honourable gentlemen serving under you with the like; beseeching God of his mercy to give her Majesty, our gracious sovereign, always victory against her enemies. Written aboard her Majesty's good ship the Revenge, off of Start, the 21st, late in the evening, 1588.

Your good Lordship's poor friend
ready to be commanded,
FRA. DRAKE.

This letter, my honourable good Lord, is sent in haste. The fleet of Spaniards is somewhat above a hundred sails, many great ships; but truly, I think not half of them men-of-war. Haste.

Your Lordship's assured,
FRA. DRAKE.

July 22.—JOHN POPHAM[1] *TO WALSYNGHAM.*

[**ccxiii. 1.**—Holograph.[2]   Addressed.]

My duty unto your Honour most humbly remembered :—It may please you to understand that
upon Friday last the Spanish fleet was discovered
towards the west parts, and upon Saturday they
were all, to the number of eight score and two sail,
over against Falmouth ; and yesterday, being more
easterly, towards Dartmouth.   I am advertised
from my Lord Chief Justice Anderson[3] that my
Lord Admiral continued in fight with them from
nine of the clock in the forenoon until three in the
afternoon, and the Spanish fleet is said to endeavour
themselves what they can towards the east.   Whereupon my Lord Chief Justice hath written unto me
to understand my opinion what were fit to be done
touching our journey towards Ireland, whither we
resolved to take our voyage upon Monday next in
the morning, and do so resolve still, unless we
receive contrary directions from your Honour.   And
for my Lord Chief Justice's better satisfaction therein, I have thought good with all expedition to
despatch this bearer, Cottrel, my servant, to your
Honour to receive your directions whether it shall
be convenient for us to hold on our journey, or
otherwise to make stay thereof until her Majesty's
pleasure be further known in that behalf; which I
pray your Honour I may be advertised of by this

[1] Second son of Alexander Popham, of an old Somerset
family. A successful and unscrupulous lawyer ; became Attorney-
General in 1581, and in 1592 Lord Chief Justice and was knighted.
See Hall, *Elizabethan Society*, pp. 142–6, 277.

[2] A very difficult scrawl.

[3] Sir Edmond Anderson, Chief Justice of the Common
Pleas.

bearer, so as it may be with me here by Sunday next.   My Lord Chief Justice doth advertise me that the course towards Ireland is very full of pirates, in respect whereof he saith it behoveth us to pursue somewhat strongly.

I have herewithal sent unto your Honour a letter[1] written out of St. Sebastian by one Redbird, of the date of the 18th of this July,[2] by their account. It came from St. John de Luz, whither it was conveyed by the same Redbird the 12th of this July, by our account.   The bark that brought it to Bridgwater arrived there the 21st of this July, and upon Wednesday last discovered the most part of the Spanish navy 25 leagues west the headland of France, holding their course towards England.

With the same letter this other note[3] enclosed was sent.   The man I take to be honest, and your Honour can best discern what good is to be collected by the knowledge of what is comprised in them.   But with your favour I may write thus much : that these forces of themselves are not fit, as I think, to enter England until they adjoin themselves to greater aids ; and whatsoever the forces were (with good assistance) they are not to be doubted, the country I find everywhere so readily and willing.

I beseech[4] God, her Majesty, in this so dangerous a time, may, with the good advice of my Lords, have a special care of herself ; which being had, we have such an united strength through her Highness, as her enemies, being never so many, they can never prevail against so gracious a Queen.   I beseech[4] you, Sir, to pardon me, in that the abundance of my loyalty and dutiful affection to her

---

[1] This letter is missing.   [2] July 8.
[3] Also missing.   [4] MS. beseke.

Majesty hath moved me to write thus much to your Honour, and so do most heartily take my leave. At Wellington, the 22nd of July, 1588.

Your Honour's humbly at commandment,

Jo. Popham.

July 22.—DARELL TO BURGHLEY.

[**ccxiii. 2.**—Holograph. Addressed. Endorsed :—Mar. Darell, from Plymouth. Rd. the 12th of August.]

My duty unto your Honour most humbly remembered :—I did receive yesterday a letter from your Lordship with direction to provide a month's victual for 1,340 men serving under my Lord Admiral in the ships of London, who are already victualled by the city but till the 10th of August; and that the city will allow for the same after the rate of 14*s.* a man, as her Majesty doth; which money, how it may best be conveyed hither, your Lordship doth refer unto me.

The month's victual shall be prepared in a readiness for them, God willing, in due time; and for the money, I wish them of London to deal with some merchant of Exeter for delivery of it there by exchange; a course most easy for them and very convenient for me, in that I do make sundry provisions in places near thereabouts. If any of the coast towns that have set forth ships in this service shall require, in like sort, to have them victualled here, it shall be also performed according to your Lordship's commandment.

Your Honour writeth[1] that the note I sent last of the number of ships and men in service under my Lord Admiral did seem very unperfect, and

[1] See *ante*, p. 270.

disagreeable from my former presentments; and
therefore your Lordship requireth to be further
certified thereof in some more plain and direct sort
than before. It may please your Lordship, I trust
it hath been and always shall be most far from me
to abuse your Honour with any untrue information.
I might well omit the setting down of some ships
and men with whom, being not set forth at her
Majesty's charge, I had not to do; but I do greatly
hope your Honour shall not find I have erred
wittingly in any material point concerning the
charge committed here unto me. And therefore,
until by proof the contrary shall appear, I do most
humbly beseech your Lordship not to condemn
me.

I do now send unto your Lordship herewith
two several notes[1]: the one importing the state of
the whole navy, both for the number of ships and
men, according to the allowance given, as also for
the time of their victualling, which is now reduced
to end all together, in all the ships at her Majesty's
charge, upon the 10th of August. Only the haste
of my Lord Admiral was such in his setting forth
upon Saturday morning, by reason he had then
received some intelligence of the Spanish fleet, as
that divers of his ships had not leisure to receive
the full of their last proportions. And the other
note containeth an estimate what money will remain
of the last warrant towards the victualling of the
7,079 men now at her Majesty's charge from the
10th of August forwards. In both which notes I
have not (I hope) set down anything but what your
Lordship shall find to be true.

Touching the sparing of the ordinary allowance
of victuals in the ships by placing of more than 4

---

[1] These notes (ccxiii. 2, I. and III.) are omitted, as merely
repeating, in imperfect detail, the statements here made.

men to a mess, and also by the mortality which hath been indeed amongst them, as your Lordship writeth,—what in all this time it hath amounted unto, the captain and officers of every ship do only know, who (that notwithstanding) have been from time to time furnished by me with their due proportions, as if that had not been. Only, by that means, they have all in them a store, which no doubt will serve them a good time after their ordinary victualling be expired. And yet this sparing hath been only at such times when there hath been fear of want; otherwise the mariners will hardly endure to be abridged of any part of their allowances.

I did become a suitor unto your Honour and the rest of the Council, for nine hundred pounds which is owing upon my former reckoning; which it pleased you, by your next letters, to promise me should be sent hither soon after. I do humbly beseech your Honour to have the same in remembrance; and in the meantime I will presume to disburse so much out of this last money granted, because I know it is not your pleasure the country shall be unpaid. And so I humbly take my leave, beseeching God to send your Lordship long life with increase of much honour. From Plymouth, this 22nd of July, 1588.

Your Honour's most humble,

MAR. DARELL.

July 22.—*MEMORANDUM OF CHARGES.*

[**ccxiii. 3.**—Rough notes in Burghley's hand. Endorsed by
  Burghley :—Memorials for money. The navy : the provision
  for the storehouse : for the office of the ordnance.]

A computation of the numbers as Mr. Hawkyns
accounteth to be paid until the 28th of July :—

For 2,990 men from the 5th of May,
  to the day they were paid, until
  the 28th of July, being 84 days : 6,279*l.*
  3 months . . . . .
For 1,900 serving in four great
  ships, which was paid to the 13th
  of July, now for 15 days, that is   712*l.*
  to the 28th of July . . .

To be paid.

The numbers total to be paid are . 4,890 men ;
              whereof

There are serving in the Narrow
  Seas under the Lord Henry
  Seymour . . . . . 1,471 men.
So are serving under the Lord
  Admiral on the Broad Seas . 3,419
But yet by Darell's book there are 3,770
So misreckoned   351

An account of the pay due to the ships serving
under Sir Fr. Drake :—

The number certified by Mr. Hawkyns are . . . . . 2,900 men.
Which number was paid until the
  19th of June, saving 800 ; so as
  there was answered with the 800 4,060*l.* pd.
Item, to bring the pay of these from
  the 19th of June until the 28th of 2,827*l.* to be
  July, which is 39 days, requireth .   paid.

Total to be paid to the 28th of July
    for wages . . . . . 9,818*l.*
Total 7,790 men.
As thereto certified by Hawkyns,
    serving in ships of Sir Richard
    Greynvile's &c., 700
Total 8,490 men, which cometh by
    the month, after 28*s.* a man, to
    11,890*l.*, besides tonnage, and
    about 705*l.* a month, grounding,
    tallowing, carpentry.
Add for wages of 700 men, newly
    increased in 8 ships with the Lord
    Admiral and Sir Fra. Drake, to
    the 28th of July . . . . 1,960*l.*
Total of wages due at the 28th of
    July for 8,490 men . . .   11,778*l.*

Other demands of Mr. Hawkyns :—

For grounding, tallowing, sea-
    store, carpenter, masts, repair
    of boats, cordage, canvas &c.,
    for the ships under my Lord   2,500*l.*
    Admiral and Lord Henry's
    charge . . . . .   5,000*l.*
For the like charges for the ships
    with Sir Fras. Drake . . . 2,500*l.*
For tonnage for the ships for 236[1]
    days, until the 28th of July, which 1,771*l.*
    is 4 months[1] . . . .   3,731*l.*
For tonnage of the 8 ships taken up
    in the west country, for 4 months, 1,960*l.*
    ending the 28th of July . .
Item, for conduct in despatching of
    1,000 men, and in presting of men   700*l.*
                                         21,209*l.*

[1] So in MS. Burghley's arithmetic is frequently inexplicable.

But Hawkyns summeth the
    same to be but .   . 19,570*l*.
      So varieth .   . 1,779*l*.[1]

The Office of the Admiralty.

There is a debt   . 7,000*l*. for provision ⎞
There is a demand   ⎬ 13,000*l*.
  for new provisions . 6,000*l*.   .   . ⎠

Office of the Ordnance.

	£	s.	d.
There is a demand for provisions for to serve for an army :			
The sum of	8,049	0	0
Whereof in emptions presently	2,700	13	4
There is a debt in the said office .	5,211	15	$1\frac{1}{2}$
Whereof is already imprested .	2,761	11	3

Notanda.

Mr. Quarles hath had from his beginning in Feb. 1587, until the last of June, 1588, 49,808*l*. 2*s*. $3\frac{1}{2}d$.

And in July now presently 6,000*l*. for the west, and for the Lord Henry Seymour, 1,854*l*.

July 22.—LEICESTER TO WALSYNGHAM.

[ccxiii. 9.—Signed.]

Abstract.

[He has conferred with Peter Pett about the lighters and chain to be sent down to stop the river at Tilbury. He finds that these will not be sufficient, 'unless they may be strengthened with a competent number of masts before them; for otherwise, if two or three ships made of purpose should come against it with a full tide and a good strong

---

[1] So in MS.

gale of wind, no doubt they would break all and pass through.' He has taken Pett to view the place, so that he knows what should be provided. He begs that the lighters and barges to be employed may be sent down with all expedition.]

July 22.—*HOWARD TO SUSSEX* (?).

[**B.M. Cott. MS. Otho E. ix, f. 185*b*.**—Copy. Fragment, damaged by fire.]

. . . . them by Sunday in the morning about . . . them and continued it until one of the clock in the . . . . did some good, and I dare say they think some harm. I pray [you send] out unto me all such ships as you have ready [for sea at] Portsmouth, with all possible speed, and though they have not ab . . . two days' victuals, let not that be cause of their stay, for they shall have victuals out of our fleet. They shall find us bearing East-North-East after the fleet. We mean so to course the enemy as that they shall have no leisure to land. I pray your Lordship to send in those ships from Portsmouth as many tall men as you can get in so short a time. And so I bid your good Lordship most heartily farewell. From aboard her Majesty's good ship the Ark, the 22nd of July, 1588.

Your Lordship's very loving friend,

C. HOWARD.

The ships you send shall find me East-North-East, following the Spanish fleet.

Since the making up of my letter there is a galleass of the enemy's taken with 450 men in her ; and yesterday I spoiled one of their greatest ships, that they were fain to forsake it.

I pray your Lordship send her Majesty word hereof with speed, as from me. The captain's name is, as I hear say, Don Pedro de Alva, general of the field.

The messenger saith that there is an hundred gentlemen in the galleass which was taken, who for the most part were noblemen's sons.

July 23.—*SEYMOUR TO THE COUNCIL.*

[ccxiii. 12.—Signed.   Addressed.]

May it please your Lordships :—I mean not to trouble you with many lines, because I do send your Lordships the original, Sir Francis Drake's letter,[1] by the which you shall understand the state of the Spanish army, how forward they be ; and to[2] our opinions here, we conjecture still their purpose may be to land in the Isle of Wight, to recover[3] the same—which God forbid.   Thus humbly praying your Lordships to send us powder and shot forthwith, whereof we have want in our fleet, and which I have divers times given knowledge thereof, I humbly take my leave.   From aboard the Rainbow, at anchor a quarter seas over against Dover, the 23rd of July, 1588, at 11 of the clock at night.

Our victuals do end the last of this month ; yet upon extremity, now we know the enemy at hand, we will prolong that little we have as long as we can.

Your Lordships' humbly to command,

H. SEYMOUR.

I do send forthwith to the fleets of Zealand and Holland, to wish[4] them to repair unto us.   Also I have made the Lieutenant of Dover acquainted therewith, to the end he may have a better care thereof.

[1] See *ante*, p. 289.   [2] As to.
[3] Gain possession of.   [4] Desire.

July 23.—*NIC. OSELEY*[1] *TO WALSYNGHAM.*

[**ccxiii. 13.**—Holograph.   Addressed.]

Right Honourable, my duty remembered, &c. :—
Presently after your Honour gave me license to
follow my Lord Admiral, with all expedition I
followed the fleet ; whereas[2] presently Sir Francis
Drake requested him I might go in the Revenge,
where Sir Francis hath now found all to be of most
truth, that I advertised your Honour at my coming
out of Spain.   And for that I do know he doth
write your Honour of that we past with the Spanish
fleet the 21st, and this day, 23rd of July, as well of
the fights, as the taking of the gallega wherein was
Don Pedro de Valdes, who is third person in this
army of the Duke, and Juan Martinez de Recalde,
vice-admiral, I do think it not needful to repeat.
Neither of the other ship which we have also of
theirs, who spoiled herself with her powder.   Both
of them, so Don Pedro saith, are of their principal
ships.   Of that we found aboard them, I refer me
to Sir Francis, assuring your Honour they are not
in such good order in their putting themself in
battle[3] ; but aboard they have as much evil[4] order,
as I did see, who by Sir Francis' commandment was

---

[1] He had apparently been settled in Spain as a merchant, but
had of late years acted as a spy for the Government, sending such
intelligence as he could pick up.   On January 5, 1588-9, Lord
Howard wrote to Burghley concerning him :—' It hath pleased
her Highness, in respect of his good service heretofore in Spain,
in sending very good intelligence thence, and now since, in our
late fight against the Spanish fleet, to grant unto him a lease of
the parsonage of St. Helens in London.   These are therefore to
pray your Lordship to stay the same parsonage, that no lease be
in the meantime granted out of the Exchequer which should
prevent the reward of one that hath so well deserved in adventuring his life so many ways in her Majesty's service.'—*Lansdowne
MS.* lix. 4 ; Ellis's *Original Letters*, 3rd S. iv. 67.
[2] Where.   [3] Sc. order of battle.   [4] MS. yevell.

the first went to them.   They have reported to me
they are now left a hundred and fifty sail, divided,
as I do see, twelve in squadron, and do keep such
excellent good order in their fight,[1] that if God do
not miraculously work, we shall have wherein to
employ ourself for some days.

The desire I have to do my duty unto your
Honour hath emboldened me to do this.   If I may
have your Honour's license, from time to time as
we do proceed in this action, I will show myself of
no inferior to any, in hope to serve your Honour ;
most humbly beseeching your Honour to have your
obedient servant in remembrance, so that I be not
the first and only man denied that hath put himself
unto your Honour's protection, but that there may
be consideration of the long time I was prisoner for
a spy, for writing the letters to London that came
to your Honour's hands ; which being proved, could
not I have [2] release but with great expenses and
bribes ; as also the three months I spent in riding
to most ports where this army was made, whereof
I have given true relation unto your Honour ; anything that your Honour shall think convenient for
me, either in England or Ireland,[3] I shall willingly
receive wherewithal, and my person to serve your
Honour wheresoever it shall please your Honour to
use [4] of me ; assuring myself God will give me
grace to do my duty towards your Honour, for
whose long life and increase of honour I daily do
and will pray for.   From the Revenge of her
Majesty's, right against Portland, the 23rd of July,
1588.   Your Honour's obedient servant,

NICHOLAS OSELEY.

[1] So in MS. It seems to contradict the previous sentence,
which must be supposed to refer only to the prizes, the evil order
of one of which is described *ante*, p. 9.

[2] Sc. I could not have.   [3] MS. Yerlande.

[4] MS. yowse.

July 24.—*REQUISITION FOR POWDER AND SHOT.*

[ccxiii. **59**, I.—Copy.]

Whereas I have received letters from the Right Honourable the Lord High Admiral of England, advertising unto me that his Lordship hath taken two great carracks or ships from the enemy, sent to the shore, wherein is great store of powder and shot in either of them; and requireth that all the said powder and shot be sent unto his Lordship with all possible expedition, for that the state of the realm dependeth upon the present supply of such wants :— These are therefore, in her Majesty's name, straitly to charge and command you, forthwith, upon receipt hereof, you make diligent enquiry to what place the said carracks or ships are gone; and if they shall arrive near you, to cause the said powder and shot to be conveyed to his Lordship with all good speed ; further charging and commanding you to take the like order by giving intelligence hereof from port to port, until his Lordship's command shall be therein performed. Whereof fail you not upon your allegiance. Weymouth and Melcombe Regis, this 24th of July, 1588.

RICHARD PITT, Mayor.

You shall find the English fleet on the seas, between this place and the Isle of Wight or eastwards.

To the Mayor of Lyme Regis, and in his absence to her Majesty's officers in that place.

Received this same day by 9 of the clock in the morning, and have sent out for the same purpose to seek out the same ships; and we see one great ship alone to lie in sight of this town of Lyme, and we think it is one of the ships.

JOHN JONES, Mayor.

Received the said 24th day at two of the clock in the afternoon. ROBERT DENYS.

Mr. Upton, repair I pray you forthwith to Dartmouth, and despatch away the powder and shot according to the contents of this direction, with all haste.

JOHN GILBERTE. GEORGE CARY.

Received the 24th of July about 9 of the clock.

July 24.—*PALAVICINO*[1] *TO WALSYNGHAM.*

[ccxiii. **19**.—Holograph. Italian. Addressed.]

Right Honourable :—If I err, I beseech your Honour to pardon me and to be a mean that her Majesty and the rest of the Lords may likewise pardon me—especially my very good Lord, the Earl of Leicester, to whom I was a suitor to serve a-land under his charge. But the greatness of my zeal, which desireth to be amongst those who do fight for her Majesty's service and for the defence of her kingdom, doth constrain me, with an honourable company, to depart as this night toward Portsmouth, there to embark and join the Lord Admiral, where I hope to be present in the battle, and thereby a partaker in the victory or to win an honourable

---

[1] Sir Horatio Palavicino, a Genoese banker settled in England, where he had made a large fortune, and was largely employed in the financial business of the Government. He was knighted in 1587.

death, thus to testify to the whole world my fidelity to her Majesty. Especially do I commend my affairs to your Honour, and pray God to give you every happiness. From the Court, the 24th of July, 1588.

Your Honour's most assured friend to command,
HORATIO PALAVICINO.

July 25.—LEICESTER TO WALSYNGHAM.

[ccxiii. 27.—Holograph. Addressed.]

Mr. Secretary :—We have here news commonly spread abroad that my Lord Admiral hath taken either admiral or vice-admiral and the great galleass, besides one great ship sunk. The Almighty God be praised therefor, and to give further victory, to his glory and the comfort of his poor church, as no doubt it must be, with the greatest renown and perpetual fame to her Majesty that ever came to any prince. And this being true,[1] I would gladly know what her Majesty will do with me. I have here now assembled in camp 4,000 footmen, as gallant and as willing men as ever was seen ; with the horse yet only of this shire. The lying in camp will do them much good, though it be but for a short time ; and in my poor opinion, not good to dismiss them over suddenly, though the fleet be defeated, till ye see a little also what Parma will do. I am here cook, cater and hunt[2] ; for as[3] I myself have not only set the men a-work here about the forts, and was present among them all the first day, but also did peruse[4] and made choice of the ground fittest for the encamping of the soldiers ; and yesterday went to Chelmsford, to take order

[1] If this be true.
[2] Caterer and huntsman.
[3] That.
[4] Did examine.

for the bringing of all the soldiers hither this day ; and this day came with the most part of them hither by 10 a-clock this morning, with very good provision for them, through the care and diligence of sundry the justices of peace here, which hath deserved great thanks, if their pains had been seen to [1] others as to [1] me. But if the news be true of this good beginning, which [2] I cannot but suspend till I hear from you, and be sorry that all men shall receive them before myself, yet I pray you be not forgetful to resolve what shall be done here, and let me know it as soon as may be, for many respects.

I assure you I am angry with Sir John Norreys [3] and Sir Roger Williams. They were both appointed by mine own [4] desire, as well as otherwise, to offices of great charge ; Mr. Norreys, as marshal of our companies, the other of the horsemen. Sir John, at his arrival yesterday morning at 3 a-clock, told me that in respect of [5] the Spanish fleet were passed hitherward and not impeached, as now we hear it is, he was willed to go to Dover to see if the Lord Admiral did pass that way, to relieve him with men and to assemble the forces there ; which I did like very well, albeit altogether without anybody to

[1] By. [2] My belief in which.

[3] Second son of Lord Norreys, and grandson of Sir Henry Norreys, executed on a charge of adultery with Anne Boleyn. He had served with great distinction in command of English volunteers in the Low Countries, afterwards in Ireland, and again in the Low Countries under Leicester, who conceived a special hatred for him, possibly because he was a competent soldier, which Leicester was not. The feud had been patched up by Walsyngham's good offices, but, if we may judge from this letter, the reconciliation was very hollow. In the following year Norreys was with Drake, in joint command of the expedition to Portugal. He was afterwards Lord-General in the Low Countries, and, later on, in Ireland, where he died in 1597.

[4] MS. my none. [5] Seeing that the Spanish fleet.

supply his place, being marshal; but for a day or two content to travail the more myself as I have done; willing him and Sir Roger Williams both in any wise to return this day early to me again, for that all our forces would be assembled at the place for our camp; which they promised faithfully, especially Sir John Norreys. But yet neither ot them both do I hear of, myself returning this morning with most of our men; nor anybody to order the camp, either for horse or foot, but only Edmund Yorke [1] and myself. Which manner of dealing, I assure you, doth much mislike me in them both; for, except my Lords of the Council did give Sir John such special order, as he saith, to go to Dover, I am ill used, having so many men to take charge of, and not one officer here, but only my cousin Leighton [2] and myself; and that the country must now needs see me so hardly accompanied as I am; for it is now 4 a-clock, but hears not of them. If they come not this night, I assure you, for my part, I will not receive any of them into office, nor bear such loose careless dealing at their hands. If you saw how weakly I am assisted, you would be sorry to think that we here should be the front against the enemy, that is so mighty, if he should land here. But I see the mighty God doth behold his little flock, and will do all things to his glory, not re garding our sins. And seeing her Majesty hath appointed me her Lieutenant-General, and numbers of men to govern, and officers accordingly, I look [3] that respect to be used toward me that is due to my place.

I am herein somewhat to entreat you to consider

[1] A brother of Rowland Yorke (see *ante*, p. 85), but seems to have remained true to his allegiance. His son, also Edmund, preferred to follow in the footsteps of his uncle.

[2] Sir Thomas Leighton, knighted in 1579; afterwards Governor of Guernsey.   [3] Look for.

of this service, and albeit her Majesty hath summoned all her Lords to attend her person, yet were it meet in so great a conference as this is, wherein her surety and the whole realm doth consist, that as much countenance as may be, be given thereto. Among other, though he be no man of war, yet I find the country doth much respect and love him, especially that he is a true faithful subject to her Majesty and known to be zealous in religion. His presence with me would do much good. It is my Lord Rich,[1] whom I pray you send back, with her Majesty's good liking to me. You have all the rest of [the][2] nobility and their forces ; and if you could procure my Lord Wentworth's[3] coming also, I would think they should well further this service.

Even as I had written thus much, being 5 a-clock, I received this letter[4] from Mr. Norreys. You will see whether there be such necessity of his special journey for that he writeth of, but I could have directed by my letters to the lieutenants there. But surely, Mr. Secretary, he makes me conceive that there is other matter in it, that having an honourable place under me and no authority elsewhere, for aught I know, more than as a supervising muster master, should deliver himself thus from me to command apart, without commission, rather than with me, in the honourable place appointed him.

[1] Robert, Lord Rich, a justice of the peace for Essex : was created Earl of Warwick in 1618 and died the same year. He married the Lady Penelope Devereux, sister of the Earl of Essex, whom he divorced for adultery ; and was, by her, the father of that Earl of Warwick who was Lord High Admiral for the Parliament during the Civil War.

[2] Omitted in MS.

[3] Thomas, 2nd Lord Wentworth, was deputy of Calais when it was taken by the French in 1558. For that loss he was tried and acquitted. He sat as one of the judges of the Duke of Norfolk in 1572 and of the Queen of Scots in 1586. He died in 1590.   [4] Missing.

And where[1] he promised faithfully to be here with me this morning early, it appears by his letter that he means to stay longer to receive my further opinion. Before God, I am much troubled with this dealing ; you knowing how well I have dealt with him since our reconcilement. But I pray you judge evenly whether this be not cause to think strangely of his doings, to leave me thus to myself, being my principal officer. If my Lords did appoint him to this, I must say they do me the more wrong, to alter and change in these cases without acquainting me with the matter. And albeit I do complain to you in this matter, yet mean I not but to use it well, and hear what he can say ; but that I must deal frankly with you, for you were a doer between us, and this is a time you know for all officers under me to show their care and love, if the matter were of less moment. I have little backing or countenance enough beside, and therefore we ought to join the better together in so needful a service. And so, with my paper, at this time to end my letter. In hot haste going to our camp again, this 25th of July.   Your assured,

R. LEYCESTER.

July 25.—SEYMOUR TO WALSYNGHAM.

[ccxiii. **30.**—Holograph. Addressed.]

Sir :—I am most glad of this most happy beginning of victory obtained of her Majesty's enemies, but most sorry I am so tied I cannot be an actor in the play. But if the Duke be as good as his threats, he will now show his courage, for hitherto he hath only played with surprises of towns

---

[1] Whereas.

more undirectly than directly. I pray God it may be my fortune to light upon himself, the same being so given out, but I fear me this matter will daunt him.

We are here very carefully cared for by Sir John Norreys, for munition, men, and powder, which is not yet come unto us. In the mean [time][1] we are assisted with the presence of worthy gentlemen that are of purpose come to serve her Majesty with the venture of their lives ; which I thought necessary to acquaint you therewith, to the end her Majesty may give them thanks. Their names be Sir Charles Blount,[2] Francis Carey,[3] Richard Lee,[4] Brute Brown.[5]

[1] Omitted in MS.

[2] Second son of the 6th Lord Mountjoy, born in 1563. On coming to the Court in 1583, his good looks attracted the Queen's notice and won for him her favour. He is described as then ' of a brown hair, a sweet face, a most neat composure, and tall in his person.' He was knighted by Leicester for service in the Low Countries in 1587, and succeeded as 8th Lord Mountjoy on the death of his elder brother in 1594. He commanded the Lion at Cadiz in 1596, and the land forces, under Essex, in the Islands' Voyage in 1597. In 1600 he was appointed Lord Deputy of Ireland, and Lord-Lieutenant in 1603, when he was created Earl of Devonshire. Died in 1606, leaving no legitimate issue, but several children by Lady Rich (see *ante*, p. 308), whom he afterwards married.

[3] The spelling of the name is uncertain, and there is no other mention of him. He may have been a son of Sir Francis Carew, then in command of the Surrey militia (ccxvii. 75). It does not appear that he was any relation of Lord Hunsdon, whose youngest son, Robert, joined the E. Bonaventure with the Earl of Cumberland (*Memoirs*, ed. 1759, p. 18).

[4] He may have been a younger cousin of Sir Henry Lee, afterwards Master of the Ordnance ; or the name may have been Leigh. It is impossible to identify him.

[5] Brute seems to have been a common Christian name in a family of Browns of Tavistock. The parish register shows the birth of John son of Brute Brown in 1616 ; also the burial of Brute son of Brute Brown in 1620. This particular Brute Brown was probably the man slain by a great shot at Porto Rico in 1595, as he was sitting at supper with Drake, who, as he started up, exclaimed, ' Ah ! dear Brute, I could grieve for thee, but now is no time for me to let down my spirits.'

Thus preparing myself for the service, do commit you to God. From aboard the Rainbow, a pretty way in the sea, in Dover Road, but shifting further forth, the 25th of July, 1588.

Your assured friend &c.

H. SEYMOUR.

Post.—Sir, upon this extremity I am bold to retain certain ships for this service, which can not be long ; hoping, if you will, a means to see the charge answered ; for by intelligence we daily look for them. I have sent Monsieur Gourdan of these news.

July 25.—MEMORANDUM BY BURGHLEY.

[**ccxiii. 34.**—Endorsed, in Burghley's hand :—Memorial at Richmond.]

Nich. Gorges:—That Holstok and Mr. Hawkyns' deputies may take care for preparing and setting forth to the seas the 8 ships hereafter following, to be sent the Lord Henry Seymour :—

George Bonaventure, Violet, Vineyard, Anne Francis, Jane Bonaventure, Samuel, Susan Parnell, Solomon.

The number of the men are 530.

That some money be delivered in prest to Hawkyns' deputy for this purpose.

For 14 days' wages,   185*l*. 10*s*.} 556*l*. 10*s*.
For 1 month's victuals, 371*l*.

Every ship to have 20 barrels of powder.

For other furniture, as calivers &c. for [1] tonnage.

Bellingham :—To choose out 12 more strong ships above 100 tons out of the Stade fleet.

For men in the same, for 14 days.

For victual for one month.

[1] According to.

July 25.—ED. BURNHAM [1] *TO WALSYNGHAM.*

[S.P. Holland, lv.—Holograph.   Addressed.]

Right Honourable:—According to your Honour's commandment by your last letters I have informed myself of the price of all sort of armours here in Middelburg, which differeth something from that it is worth in Holland, being somewhat better cheap there than here, but not much.   The musket with the band-roll and rest, 22*s.* sterling ; the caliver and furniture, 12*s.* and 13*s.* sterling.   The horseman's armour complete, with cuissants, the breast petronell proof, and the backpiece proof, 3*l.* and 3*l.* 6*s.* 8*d.* sterling.   There is one Finch [2] that hath bought 30 for Sir Thomas Heneage at 3*l.* sterling the piece ; but since they are grown dearer, for that he bespake them a good while ago.   Powder is here at 4*l.* 10*s.* sterling the quintal, which is a hundredweight.   In England is 8*l.* more than this.   There is no great quantity to be had here ; but the greatest store that is for these countries is in Amsterdam.   By some of our merchants I do understand that there is good quantity at Hamburg and Stade,[3] and better cheap than in these parts. . . .

We understand here that the great galley which the enemy hath made at Sluys, going out before the last tempest, was forced to put in to the Texel, wherein there is a hundred Italian soldiers and 200 *forçats.*[4]   Yesternight here arrived a drum from the

[1] An agent of Walsyngham's.   He was back in England in September.   Probably the Mr. Burnham named by the Queen in October 1591, when 'it was her pleasure to have some honest person sent to Brittany to view and report on the forces there.'
[2] If Sir Moyle Finch (see *post*, p. 320), it is strange that Burnham should speak of him as an unknown man.
[3] MS. Stoades.   [4] MS. forsats.

enemy about certain prisoners of theirs which be here, who saith that the galley hath been long missing and they cannot tell what is become of her, which makes us think to be true. They of Enkhuysen have of late taken a Scots pirate who had 94 men aboard of him and 25 pieces of ordnance. It is thought that they will execute most part of the men. I have, since my last to your Honour, spoken to Monsr. de St. Aldegonde,[1] who telleth me that he can do nothing with the Count Maurice, and that he is altogether led by Villiers the marshal, Monsr. de Famars,[2] and Villiers the preacher. By reason of my sickness which hath held me long, I could not as yet go into Holland, but I sent my despatches to Mr. Kyllygrew, of whom I have answer that he had received the same, and since that time I have received letters from him, by the which he writeth me that the Count Maurice would have me to come, which I will not fail to do, as soon as it shall please God to send me health. I find St. Aldegonde to be in a very bare estate, and was resolved if the Princess [3] had gone in France, to have gone with her, and to have presented his service to the King of Navarre. Her stay is the cause of his. He desired me to write to your Honour to know your Honour's advice whether he should proceed in this determination of himself, since that now the Princess doth not go, but findeth many difficulties. Among the rest, the lightness and unconstance of that nation ; want of means to provide himself for such a journey ; the small means that the King hath now in this time to do for him.

[1] Had been the confidential minister of the Prince of Orange, and on repeated missions to England.

[2] MS. Famasse.

[3] The Princess of Orange. See *ante*, p. 100 *n*. She was still at Middelburg in the end of August.

This last tempest forced all the ships of war of these countries, that lay before Dunkirk and Nieuport, to come in. The like hath not been seen by any at this time of the year. But this day it is thought they will all go forth again. The corn of this island is in danger to be spoiled by reason of the great store of rain that is fallen of late.

By others I know your Honour shall be advertised of the pacifying of the mutiny in Gertruidenberg.[1] The States, they have paid their money; assurance they have none but the honesty of the mutineers. They have railed very much against all the States, especially against Barnevelt, whom they name Barrabas, and Brasser of Delft. They advised Count Maurice, who lay before the town, to take heed of them all, and that they would betray him as they had done his father. Sir John Wingfeild[2] they have been content to accept for their governor. Herewith I send your Honour a pacquet which I received yesternight from Mr. Kyllygrew, with my most humble duty; and as I am bound, I beseech the Almighty long to bless and preserve your Honour. Flushing, the 25th of July, 1588.

Your Honour's most humble
and obedient servant,
EDW. BURNHAM.

[1] MS. Gettenbergen. With many others, the garrison of Gertruidenberg had revolted in February on much the same grounds as Colonel Sonoy (see *ante*, p. 83), declaring that they recognised no authority but that of the Queen of England, and would not treat except with Lord Wyllughby. By his mediation, an agreement was come to, by which they were to return to their duty on being paid 216,000 fl. The money was paid, but the garrison mutinied again and delivered the town to the Prince of Parma. See De Thou (Fr. edit. of 1734), x. 162-3.

[2] In 1591-2 Master of the Ordnance in the expedition to Brittany; slain at the storming of Cadiz in 1596

July 26.—SHIPS TO BE SENT TO SEYMOUR.

[ccxiii. 35.]

A note of the 8 ships appointed to be sent to the Lord Harry Seymour into the Narrow Seas the 25th July, 1588, under the command of Mr. Nicholas Gorges, Esquire.

The names of the ships and their number of men after :

	Men
The Susan Parnell of London .	80
Solomon	80
George Bonaventure . .	80
Anne Francis . . .	70
Vineyard	60
Violet	60
Samuel	50
Jane Bonaventure . .	50
Sum of the men	530

The 26th of July the ships and men entered into pay, and from that day was victualled for one whole month.

	£	s.	d.
The victualling of 530 men for one month, after 14s. the man, amounteth to	371	0	0
For prest of 530 men at 12d. per man	26	10	0
For the pressers due at 4d. per man	8	16	8
Sum	406	6	8

July 26.—WINCHESTER [1] *TO THE COUNCIL.*

[ccxiii. 36.—Signed.   Endorsed.]

Right Honourable :—Having according to the tenor of your Lordships' late letters signified your Honours' pleasures unto the deputy lieutenants of Dorset for the present dispatch and sending of one thousand men to be employed in Essex, do find by answer returned from the said deputies that the strength of that county, being of itself very small, to be thereby greatly weakened and the present state thereof to require all places of danger to remain fortified, having the enemy so near them at sea and in sight, as besides, advertisement being given them of the great preparations of the French, likewise ready to put to the sea in assistance of the Spaniard.   There is already drawn out of the said county, by warrant from the Lord Admiral, for his better supply, 400 men.   With all which I have thought it my part to acquaint your good Lordships, leaving the same to your Honours' considerations, humbly praying your further pleasures to be returned touching the said 1,000 men so required, to be either supplied out of Wilts, Somerset, or Devon, or otherwise to be stayed at home for the present guard of that county, for the causes before alleged.   And even so do leave your good Lordships to the tuition of the Almighty.   Basing, this 26th of July, 1588.

Your Lordships' at commandment,

WINCHESTER.

[1] William Powlett, Marquis of Winchester, Lord Lieutenant of Dorset and Hampshire, married Agnes, Lord Howard's half sister.

July 26.—*THE COUNCIL TO HOWARD.*

[**B.M. Addl. MS. 33740, f. 2.**—Signed. Addressed.]

After our right hearty commendations to your Lordship :—Forasmuch as the Queen's Majesty is informed that the enemy is very well provided of shot,[1] and it may be that your Lordship is not at this present furnished with such a number to answer them as is meet, her Highness, being very careful that your Lordship should be supplied with all the provisions that may be had, hath given order that in the county of Kent a good number of the best and choicest shot of the trained bands in the said county should be forthwith sent to the seaside, to the intent that upon any notice to be given from your Lordship they may be brought unto you to double man the ships that are both with your Lordship and the Lord Henry Seymour, which her Majesty hath thought good to signify unto your Lordship by this bearer, Sir Thomas Gorges, Knight, who is of purpose dispatched unto your Lordship for that cause. And so beseeching Almighty God to send your Lordship a happy and honourable end of this service, we bid you right heartily farewell. From Richmond, the 26th of July, 1588.

Your assured loving friends,

CHR. HATTON, Canc.   W. BURGHLEY.
F. KNOLLYS.   T. HENEAGE.
A. POULET.   J. WOLLEY.

[1] Musketeers.

July 26.—LEICESTER TO WALSYNGHAM.

[**ccxiii. 38.**—Holograph. Addressed.]

Mr. Secretary :—The 4,000 men of Essex are all come together and lodged here together at West Tilbury upon a very good ground for aptness for the defence of this coast. They be as forward men and all willing to meet with the enemy as ever I saw. Some want, their captains showed in themselves, that being suddenly removed to this place, brought not so much as one meal's provision of victual with them, so that at their arrival here there was not a barrel of beer nor loaf of bread for them. Enough after 20 miles' march to have been discouraged and to have mutinied, but all with one voice, finding it to be the speediness of their coming, said they would abide more hunger than this to serve her Majesty and the country.

I did send to have Robert Arderne[1] come down and to bring a hundred tuns of beer, and to be here this day ; but I hear not of him yet, and if he fail it will be the greater ill hap, seeing all this part, on this side and the other, within 4 miles of the water, cannot yield drink enough for them. And for that I hear the 1,000 men from London will be here this night also, I have sent presently to stay them till we may provide for them here, except they have provision with them.

And touching the resolution of my Lords for their captains to continue their leadership I am sorry for it ; because it must now light upon me, their displacing ; but rather than I will hazard her Majesty's safety and the whole realm's service, I

---

[1] Officially styled 'Assistant to the Clerk of the Acatery'— i.e. the office of buying provisions for (catering for) the Sovereign.

would displace my brother or any man. As for the account of the regiments, I do yet scarcely see how I shall bring it to pass without getting other manner of persons than goldsmiths and mercers are ; and yet if it may be so there is not place for half such captains as so great a service requires. And for that it hath pleased God to begin graciously with us and to give hope of comfortable victory, yet let us not be too secure when the substance of their forces remain yet whole, and being so resolutely bent as they be ; but that we continue our defensive preparations, rather more than less, against them.

And because I see and find many causes now to increase my former opinion of the dilatory wants you shall find upon all sudden hurly-burleys, for which respect I am in duty bound to move her Majesty and humbly to beseech her, that as these cases that touch her honour, life, and state, that there may be such due regard had for all provisions as in times past hath been. But in no former time was ever so great cause as at this time. And albeit her Majesty hath appointed on shore an army to resist her enemies if they land, yet how hard a matter it will be to gather the men together, I find it ; and may judge, if it will be 5 days to gather the very countrymen,[1] what will it be and must be to look in short space for those that dwell 40, 50 and 60 miles off ; and this must be warning that considerations of victuals as well as anything else be provided at the place of assemblies &c. I did two whole days before the coming of these make proclamation in all market towns for victuallers to come to the place where the soldiers [2] should encamp, and to receive ready money for it ; but there is not one victualler come in to this hour. I have sent to all

---

[1] The men of the immediate neighbourhood.
[2] MS. soldyers.

the justices about it from place to place; but I
speak it to this end, that timely consideration is to be
had of all these things, and not to defer and put off in
hope, till the worse come and the time do [1] overpass.

And that it may please her Majesty, of her
princely magnanimity, now above all other former
times, to show herself careful and provident not
only for her own person, which is the stay of us all,
but also of all her whole realm and people, whom
God hath committed to her protection. And were
she secured, and all about her did counsel her to
have presently a convenient force both of horse and
foot about her, that she will not defer the time upon
any supposed hope both to assemble them in time,
and to appoint some special nobleman about her to
govern and direct them; for her Majesty cannot be
strong enough too soon; and if her navy had not been
strong and abroad, as it is, whatsoever cost hath been
bestowed, what case had herself and her whole
realm been in by this time? Or if God do [1] not
miraculously give her victory there, what case will
she be in, if her forces be not, not only assembled,
but an army perfectly dressed, with all the officers
appertaining, to withstand that mighty enemy that
is to approach then her gates? I pray you, Mr.
Secretary, with humble pardon, deliver thus much
to her Majesty; for God doth know I speak it not
to bring you to charges. I would she had less cause
to spend than ever she had, and her coffers fuller
than they be; but I will prefer her life and safety,
and the defence of the realm, before all sparing and
charges, being in the present danger it is in.

There is a portion of money appointed I perceive to the charge of Sir Moyle Finch [2] to be

---

[1] MS. to.

[2] Eldest son of Sir Thomas Finch, of Eastwell in Kent, by
right of his wife Katharine, daughter and heiress of Sir Thomas

brought hither.   I am glad of it, and do desire the
gentleman may be our Treasurer here ; and whether
the extraordinary charges, as for platforms, fortifications and such like, shall be paid by him or no, and
Peter Petts' charge.   And so with my paper I end.
At Gravesend this 26th of July.

Your assured friend,
R. LEYCESTER.

July 26.—LEICESTER TO WALSYNGHAM.

[ccxiii. 39.—Holograph.   Addressed :—For her Majesty's affairs.]

Mr. Secretary :—After the writing of my other
letters, here is arrived Sir Roger Williams, and
perceive Mr. Norreys will be this night with me.
In the meanwhile, they have put me to more
travail than ever I was in before.   I perceive by Sir
Roger, that my Lord Henry Seymour is departed
toward Rye, to assist my Lord Admiral, but doth
want both men and powder.   Good Lord, how is
this come to pass, that both he and my Lord Admiral
is so weakened of their men ?   I hear their men be
run away, which must be severely punished, or else
all soldiers will be bold.   He saith also that the
Prince [1] is looked to issue out presently.   He hath
suffered no stranger this seven or eight days to come
to him, or to see his army and ships, but he hath
blindfolded them.

I beseech you assemble your forces, and play
not away this kingdom by delays, and hasten our

Moyle of Eastwell.   He was, at this time, officially styled
'Treasurer at Wars.'   He married Elizabeth, daughter and heiress
of Sir Thomas Heneage, Chancellor of the Duchy of Lancaster,
Vice-Chamberlain of the Household, and one of the Lords of the
Council.

[1] Of Parma.

horsemen hither and footmen, if you hear not that the fleet [1] is scattered or beaten ; for surely if they come to the Narrow Seas, the Prince will play another manner of part than is looked for. I have written enough already. God send care with expedition with you there, and good success with us here ; specially with our sea forces. In all haste, 26th of July.

Yours assured,
R. Leycester.

There is no hope of a thousand men furnished, more than we have, out of Berkshire.

July 26.—SUSSEX [2] *TO WALSYNGHAM.*

[ccxiii. **40.**—Signed. Addressed.]

It may please your Honour :—I received a letter this day at two of the clock in the morning from Sir George Carey, the copy whereof I have sent unto your Honour herein enclosed, and also a letter from my Lord Admiral, which I received at six of the clock this morning, wherein he writeth for powder and shot, and saith he hath very great want thereof, by reason of three great fights which he hath had with the Spanish fleet. Whereupon I have sent him so much as that I have altogether unfurnished myself, as may appear by a note to your Honour herein sent ; which I shall desire your Honour to be a mean that it may be supplied, for that I shall have great want thereof if any attempt be offered. And

---

[1] The Spanish fleet.

[2] Henry Ratcliffe, Earl of Sussex, Constable of Porchester Castle, Warden and Captain of the town, castle, and isle of Portsmouth, joint Lord-Lieutenant of Hampshire. K.G. in 1589, and died in 1593. He was Howard's first-cousin.

so, hoping in my next letters to send your Honour some certain news of good success, I commit your Honour to God. From Portsmouth the 26th of July, 1588.

Your Honour's to his power,

Sussex.

Postscript.—I have considered of the proportion of powder and shot which is to come from the Tower, which is but five last of powder; and if I shall take out (as I must of force) so much as I have sent unto my Lord Admiral, there would none be left. Wherefore it were very requisite that there should be more sent hither, or into some place in Sussex where my Lord Admiral is like to come, or might have knowledge of it; for else it will be wanting.

July 25.—*SIR GEORGE CAREY TO SUSSEX.*

[**ccxiii. 43.**—Vera Copia. Endorsed.]

May it please your Lordship to understand that, finding by yours the copy and direction of the Lords' letters for supplying the Lord Admiral's wants, touching that, I have thus far proceeded. Two days since I sent his Lordship 4 ships and a pinnace sufficiently furnished with mariners and soldiers; from whom I have not yet heard any news; but sending yesterday another pinnace unto him with an hundred men, he returned them unto me this afternoon with great thanks, willing the captain to tell me that he had as many men as he desired or could well use. For your Lordship's news I humbly thank you.

This morning began a great fight betwixt both

fleets, south of this island 6 leagues,[1] which continued from five of the clock until ten, with so great expense of powder and bullet, that during the said time the shot continued so thick together that it might rather have been judged a skirmish with small shot on land than a fight with great shot on sea. In which conflict, thanks be to God, there hath not been two of our men hurt

The news in the fleet are my Lord Harry Seymour is hardly laid unto by the Dunkirkers, and that Scilla[2] is taken by the French or the Spanish.

The fleets keep the direct trade[3] and shot into the sea out of our sight by three of the clock this afternoon ; whereupon we have dissolved our camp wherein we have continued since Monday.   And so praying your Lordship to send this enclosed by the post, I humbly commit you to God.   From Carisbrooke Castle, this 25th of July, at 8 hours in the night.   Your Lordship's to command,

GEORGE CAREY.

July 26.—ROBERT SALMAN[4] TO BURGHLEY.

[ccxiii. 41.—Signed.   Addressed.]

Right Honourable, my duty considered :— Whereas I unworthy am chosen for this year to be Master of the Trinity House of Deptford Strond,

---

[1] As the fleets were well in sight at the time, the distance is enormously exaggerated ; but down to the beginning of this century there was no way in use to measure the distance of a ship, and the guesses were often extremely wild.

[2] Silly.

[3] The fairway of the Channel.

[4] Of Leigh, in Essex, where the family had been settled for upwards of two hundred years. A brass plate in Leigh Church records that 'he took to wife Agnes, with whom he lived thirty-

as I am a subject, my duty is to use all the means I
can for the preservation of her Majesty and our
country ; [and][1] my place doth require me, in my
opinion, to be more careful for my duty. If it may
please your Honour, as I do understand, my Lord
Admiral could be content to have some supply of
ships and men at this time. If it be so, your
Honour shall hear my poor opinion : that is, there
may be within this 4 days near 30 sail of serviceable
merchant ships ready to set sail, who are so furnished with ordnance and artillery of their own that
some small supply beside will suffice. As for their
men, they have 20 men a-piece, which they now
brought home with them; I mean those ships that
be come from Stade now. If they may have 5 or
6 mariners more a-piece, and 20 soldiers, every ship
to[2] those mariners, they may do very good services, as they are easily to be had now, and very
willing too in this needful service.

As for victuals,[3] if the victualler[3] can provide
for them in so small a time, he may be commanded
with all expedition to do it for some 14 days or
three weeks ; if they shall tarry longer, they may
have some more provided to send after them. If
he cannot provide for them in so short a time, if it
please your Honour to give me authority[4] and
provision,[5] and to command them that I will take
to me, your Honour shall see what haste there shall
be made. If there be not beef enough ready, then

two years, and had issue by her six sons and four daughters.'
He died September 6, 1591, in his 58th year. One of the sons,
Robert, was also Master of the Trinity House from 1617 till his
death, June 18, 1641, at which time he was Sheriff of London.
His monument is in Leigh Church. Barrett's *The Trinity
House of Deptford Strond*, pp. 135-8.

[1] MS. has *it*, apparently a slip of the pen.
[2] In addition to.   [3] MS. vetals, veteler.
[4] MS. atoryte.   [5] Sc. of money.

they shall have fish and peas, butter or cheese, and let them go. The brewer and baker will provide hastily for some 14 days or more; if it may be within this time done, it will be some good encouragement[1] to my Lord Admiral and those that be in service with him, and a discouragement to the enemy.

And thus I crave your Honour's pardon for my boldness, it wishing well to her Majesty and our country, if I could any ways do any services therein. And here I leave your Honour to the safekeeping of the Almighty. From Tower Hill, this 26th of July, 1588.

Your poor vassal to command,
ROBERT SALMAN, Master.

July 26.—SIR JOHN GILBERTE[2] AND GEORGE CARY, DEPUTY LIEUTENANTS OF DEVON, TO SIR FRANCIS WALSYNGHAM.

[ccxiii. 42.—Signed.   Addressed:—For her Majesty's affairs.]

Our humble duties to your Honour remembered:—Whereas the Roebuck hath brought into Torbay one of the Spanish fleet, Jacob Whiddon being captain of the said Roebuck, and these two gentlemen appointed by Sir Francis Drake for the conducting of the said Spanish ship into some safe harbour, but the present necessity of her Majesty's service so requiring for the speedy dispatch of the said Roebuck again to her Highness' navy, they have requested us to take the care for the safe harbouring of the said ship; which, by God's grace, we will take so good care of as possible we may.

[1] MS. incorydgment.
[2] Brother of Sir Humphrey Gylberte, and half-brother of Sir Walter Ralegh.

And for the better furnishing of her Majesty's navy with munition, we have taken out of the said ship all the shot and powder, and sent the same to her Highness' navy.   There is also taken out of the said ship one piece of ordnance for the better furnishing of a ship to join with the navy, wherewith we hope your Honour and the rest of my Lords will not dislike.   We have also sent to the seas all the shipping and mariners in all our county, to be employed as my Lord High Admiral shall appoint. And touching the ordnance and the residue of the goods that do remain in the said ship, there shall be a true and perfect inventory made, and the goods laid in safety as soon as the same shall be brought into Dartmouth, which we will forthwith do our best endeavours to perform ; and so acquaint your Honour and the rest of my Lords with the particularities thereof.   And so in haste we humbly [take] [1] our leave.   From Torbay this 26th of July, 1588.

Your Honour's to command,

JOHN GILBERTE.   GEORGE CARY.

July 26.—WALSYNGHAM TO BURGHLEY (?).

[Otho E. ix. f. 214 *b*.—Holograph.   A fragment, damaged by fire.]

I find by a letter written from my Lord Admiral unto her Majesty that, for lack of powder and shot, he shall be forced to forbear to assail and to stand upon his guard until he shall be furnished from hence.   There is 23 last of powder sent unto him with a proportion of bullet accordingly.

I hope there will be an 100 sail of Hollanders and Zealanders at the least to assist the Lord Admiral within these three days.

[1] Omitted in MS.

There are letters sent to the Lord Wyllughby, and in his absence to Sir William Russell, to send over 1000 of their best shot for the furnishment of the ships. [This,] in haste, I most humbly take my leave. The 26th of July, 1588.

Your Lordship's to command,

FRA. WALSYNGHAM.

July 27.—SIR JOHN GILBERTE AND GEORGE CARY TO THE COUNCIL.

[**ccxiii. 43.**—Signed. Addressed :—For her Majesty's affairs.]

Our humble duties to your good Lordships :— Whereas there is one of the Spanish fleet brought into Torbay (as your Honours have been heretofore advertised of), in which ship there is almost four hundred soldiers and mariners, all which for divers respects we have taken out of the ship and brought them under safe guard unto the shore, some 20 or 30 mariners only excepted, which we have left in the said ship to be the better help to bring the said ship into safe harbour,[1] being at this present, through the occasion of her Majesty's service, great want of mariners of our own country.

If it may so stand with your Lordships' pleasure, we desire to know your resolutions, what shall become of these people, our vowed enemies. The charge of keeping of them is great, the peril greater, and the discontentment [of][2] our country greatest of all, that a nation so much disliking unto them should remain amongst them. To her Majesty's commandment and your Honours' direction we refer this action, and likewise ourselves. Eftsoons praying your Lordships' resolved determinations, we are thus

---

[1] MS. harborowe.   [2] Omitted in MS.

bold, under your Lordships' correction, to give them their maintenance, touching [1] their sustenance of such provision as remaineth in the said ship.

There is one thing more that giveth us occasion to desire your Lordships' direction, for that the French King (as your Honours well know) being entered into the Holy League (as they term it) and vowed the extirpation of all others which are of the contrary, there are yet [2] divers French boats and vessels, that under pretence of transporting of passengers and other things, come into our ports and creeks. We greatly suspect and are much afraid lest their coming be rather to give intelligence, and understand her Majesty's proceedings in these perilous times ; and therefore do humbly pray your Lordships' directions herein, where [3] we shall stay them, or otherwise give them leave in peaceable manner to depart. And so very humbly take our leave from further troubling your Lordships. From Torbay this 27th of July, 1588.

Your Lordships' to be commanded,

JOHN GILBERTE.   GEORGE CARY.

Mr. Carew Ralegh [4] hath requested us to move your good Lordships that it would please you to give him warrant for some six pieces of ordnance which are in this Spanish ship to be placed in her Majesty's fort or castle of Portland, for the better strength thereof; for that your Honours (as he saith) hath been heretofore informed of the want of artillery which is to be required for the defence of the said castle.

---

[1] Taking. [2] MS. yeat.
[3] Whether. [4] Elder brother of Sir Walter Ralegh.

July 27.—SEYMOUR TO THE COUNCIL.

[**ccxiii. 50.**—Signed.   Addressed.]

May it please your Lordships :—I have received three letters in a packet of the 25th of this month, and with the same a single letter of the same date from Mr. Secretary, wherein is signified that by reason of advertisement that came after the making up of the packet from the Lord Admiral, her Majesty's pleasure was, notwithstanding all former directions from your Lordships, I should bend myself to stop the issuing of the forces of the Duke of Parma from Dunkirk. How easily [1] the lying of our ships against Gravelines, much more Dunkirk, I can say no more than I have many times written.   But seeing it is her Majesty's pleasure we will endeavour to perform it as near as wind and weather will give us leave.

Our victualling doth end the last of this month ; and for that your Lordships, by your writing, do reckon the galley to be in the Thames mouth for the guarding of the river, I have therefore taken order for Mr. Borough in the galley for the Thames, and [this] [2] was the only cause of the saving her and all the men's lives the last great storm.

I have besides to signify unto your Lordships that our fleet being from the first promised to be 78 sail, there was never yet, when the same was most, 36 ; and now we have not above 20 ; and of them, of her Majesty's shipping, as I have always written, but 8 sails besides pinnaces ; and for the

---

[1] So in MS., meaning, in fact, uneasily, or difficult. The following sentence shows this as well as the postscript, and Sir W. Wynter's letter of the same date.

[2] Omitted in MS.

coast men, I think[1] more than the hoys of Ipswich, the ships of Dover and Sandwich, the ships of Yarmouth and Lynn; few also of the coast that were set down for service,[2] little available. So giving your Lordships to understand that the Hollanders are not with us, and that I think they desire more to regard more their own coast than ours, do humbly take my leave. From aboard the Rainbow, the 27th of July, 1588, at anchor in the Downs.

I have also seen by experience, which I have likewise advertised, that our merchants' ships are not able to abide that stress upon these coasts which her Majesty's are able to endure, which is to be considered of.

Your Lordships' humble to command,
H. SEYMOUR.

So long as the wind holdeth West-South-West, your Lordships may not look to have us on the other coasts, neither can the enemy come out.

To make it more plain to your Lordships :—

Whensoever we ride upon the other coasts, if the wind come without the land our merchants' ships are enforced to forsake us, as not able to ride; so that our trust for this service is only upon her Majesty's ships, in number 8, besides pinnaces, which are not able to ride it out. I am driven to write this much, because, in my former letters,[3] your Lordships, having many matters, do forget them.

[1] There seems to be a 'no' omitted.
[2] 'And those' is perhaps omitted.
[3] Sc. though I have written it before, in my former letters.

Your Honour's letter of the 25th of this present I received this last night at 12 of the clock, being then within 4 miles of Calais, and according to your Honour's commandment I have dealt with Mr. Borough, who is most ready to obey your Honour's commandment, and will, I dare undertake, most faithfully perform it.   The long staying to the westwards of the King of Spain's army, which might have been here 4 days past if they had been disposed to have come so low, doth confirm the opinion which I have held that their intention is to surprise Portsmouth and to possess the Isle of Wight ; for if that were had, in my poor conceit [1] it were the only degree [2] to bring to pass their desires. And truly, I have ever loved and honoured my Lord Admiral ; but now, in respect of the wise and honourable carriage of himself in preventing of the army, that they gain not that place which, I do assure myself, is the only thing that they hunger for, doth double my service towards him ; and under your Honour's correction, speaking as to my honourable good friend, I do not think it wisdom nor discretion for my Lord with his army to put it to a journey, [3] for that were the hazarding of all.   Sir, these huge ships that are in the Spanish army shall have but a bad place to rest in, if they come so low as to the eastward of Portsmouth.

And now, Sir, you must look to the Thames mouth, which you may easily do by placing of shipping at the Nore-head ; which will serve two

[1] MS. concayht.   [2] Step.
[3] MS. jornaye : a day's fight, a pitched battle (*Fr. journée*).

turns, both touching Sheppey, and also the Thames. For those, how many so ever they be, you may victual and furnish them daily and hourly; and then if we, serving here, may be remembered in time with victuals and things needful (which hath been sent for), I doubt not but her Highness shall lie quietly at Greenwich in despite of any he whatsoever.

I humbly pray you that ye will so consider of your commandment there, as you do not danger us here. I mean, for riding afore Dunkirk. For if we should ride where you would have us, and as my Lord Admiral advises, I dare assure your Honour it is ten to one that we shall be put to Flushing or at the least to Yarmouth, as divers of us were of late; and of some of them no news is heard as yet. And if we should be so put from thence, then we shall leave the gap open to our enemy. What danger and hurts our fleet incurred and sustained in the last storm which did put us from the other coast, I do think is not made known to your Honour and the rest of my Lords. I know there hath been such as hath promised and took upon him to make warrants to your Honour and the rest of my Lords, that he would ride thwart of Dunkirk all weathers, to avoid, to impeach, and let [1] all passengers in and out; but I assure your Honours, his judgment and skill for that matter is neither grounded upon skill or reason, as I will be ready to prove it at all times.

I humbly beseech [2] your Honour to let me know whether your Honour did send away my letter to my Lord Admiral which I wrote of late to his Lordship, and sent the same open to your Honour to peruse by my servant Roger. Thus in haste I most humbly take my leave, praying God to preserve your Lordship. Written in the seas midway between Folke-

---

[1] Hinder.   [2] MS. beseek.

stone and Boulogne, the 27th of July at 6 of the clock in the [evening],[1] *anno* 1588.

Your Honour's most faithful to command,

W. WYNTER.

The best store of victuals that I and Sir Henry Palmer have at this time is your Honour's venison, for the which we humbly thank you.

July 27.—THE COUNCIL TO GEORGE TRENCHARD AND FRANCIS HAWLEY.

[ccxiii. 47.—Copy.   Endorsed.]

After our hearty commendations :—Whereas we are informed that the Spanish ship lately taken and brought into Portland hath good store of powder, bullets, and other munition and furniture, fit to be employed in her Majesty's service, we have thought good to require you, calling unto you for your assistance, Francis Hawley, esquire, Vice-Admiral of those parts, to take a diligent view and perfect inventory of all such powder, bullets, and other things of worth that shall be found in the said ship, and carefully to be kept until you receive our further direction ; but for the powder, you may not fail, with all the speed possible, to convey the same to Dover on some little bark fit for that purpose.   And touching the doubts delivered unto us by Captain Wye, we have sent our answer thereunto by way of apostilles [2] to your several demands.   And so we bid you heartily farewell.   From the Court at Richmond the 27th of July, 1588.   Your loving friends,

CHR. HATTON, Canc.   W. BURGHLEY.
FRA. WALSYNGHAM.   A. POULET.
                             J. WOLLEY.

[1] Torn off.   [2] Marginal notes.

July 28.—*THE COUNCIL TO SEYMOUR.*

[**ccxiii. 53.**—Rough draft.[1]   Endorsed.]

After our hearty commendations unto your Lordship :—Where[2] you were directed by letters written by me, the Secretary, in her Majesty's name upon an advice given unto her Majesty by the Lord Admiral that you should presently repair and lie before the town of Dunkirk :—Forasmuch as her Majesty seeth how greatly it importeth her service to have somewhat done to distress the Spanish navy before they shall join with the Duke of Parma's forces by sea, her pleasure is that you should join with the Lord Admiral to do your best endeavour, being joined together, to distress the said army, to be executed in such sort as upon conference between our very good Lord the Lord Admiral and you shall be agreed on. And further her Majesty's pleasure is that we should signify unto you that there is order given for the supply of your wants of powder, men, and munition, which shall be so sufficiently performed as you shall find no lack that way. And so we bid your Lordship heartily farewell. At the Court the 28th of July, 1588.

Your Lordship's loving friends.

And further her Majesty hath especially commanded us to signify unto your Lordship that she nothing doubteth, with the assistance of Almighty God, that when both your forces shall be joined together but that he will bless you with a most happy and glorious victoty, so as it be attempted before

---

[1] A difficult scrawl, full of erasures and corrections, (?) in Walsyngham's hand.
[2] Whereas.

the Spanish navy shall join with the Duke of Parma, and that upon conference between the Lord Admiral and you, you shall see no just cause to stay or delay the fight.

July 28.—*BOROUGH TO WALSYNGHAM.*

[ccxiii. 57.—Signed.   Addressed :—For her Majesty's service. Much stained and partially obliterated by damp.]

Right Honourable :—The Lord Henry [Seymour hath] appointed me [yesterday] in the forenoon to come with the galley to the mouth of Thames, for guarding the river ; and his Lordship told me it was meant that certain ships should come speedily from London furnished in warlike manner for like purpose, whereof I should have the charge.

That day in the afternoon, as I purposed to have come from the Downs hitherwards, news was brought that the two armies were between Folkestone and Boulogne near the other coast ; whereupon with the ebb, the wind South-West, the Lord Harry with all his fleet plied to windwards, and before night for as high up as Scales Cliffs,[1] where I suppose they had sight of the fleets.   I followed with the galley ; but ere I came half seas over, the wind forced me back into the Downs, where I remained all night ; and this morning, being little wind, I plied over towards Calais, in hope to have done some service if it had proved calm.   When I was three parts of the seas over, I perceived the English fleet at anchor against Scales Cliffs,[1] and the Spanish at anchor between them and Calais.   I could not fetch our [fleet] by [cause] of the leeward tide of flood, and therefore

[1] MS. Skaels Cleefes : so called from the village of Escalles. Now Calais Cliffs.

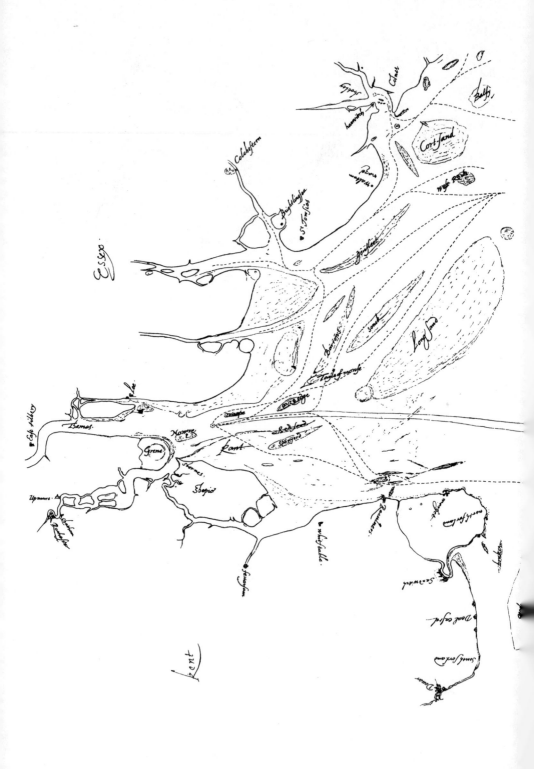

anchored; but the wind at South-South-West increased so as we could not ride; whereupon I weighed anchor, set sail and came room without the Goodwin Sand, to the North Foreland, and so longst up hither, where I anchored at 10 of the clock at night.

The pinnace that lately carried the Council's letters to Flushing returned back this day, and is gone to my Lord Harry with letters of answer to his. The master of her told me that the Lord Governor of Flushing willed him to tell my Lord Harry that there should be 30 or 40 sail of good ships sent to him from thence very shortly. The said master supposed they would be ready this day or to-morrow; but there was not one of their vessels abroad at sea. He told me further that he heard the mariners there use speeches that they would have their pay ere they went to the seas; but I hope they will not stick upon it now.

If it shall be thought good to appoint me to farther charge, to command any of the ships that shall guard the river, what shall be directed me therein [I will] observe and perform dutifully, with God's help, whilst life lasteth. I do send herewith a rough plot of this river's mouth, with the channels and shoals in it, to the end I may be appointed in the same plot where the ships should remain. The channels for shipping to come into this river, I have signified in the same with the red lines,[1] by which your Honour may perceive how they concur at the east end of the Nore. And therefore I think it were good they should be placed on each side of the ⊙ where I now ride with the galley. Bylanders[2] and small hoys and boats may come in at half flood, as I have drawn the double lines with black lead.[3]

---

[1] Here shown by dotted lines.
[2] MS. binlanders; cf. *ante*, p. 2 *n*.
[3] The double lines drawn east from the position at the Nore.

I send my servant of purpose herewith, to return me your Honour's pleasure where I shall attend, and in what order; and so with my duty to your Honour humbly acknowledged, commit you to the Almighty. From aboard the galley, in the Thames mouth, by east the Nore-head, this Sunday, the 28th of July, 1588, at 11 of the clock at night.

Your Honour's humbly at command
and most ready always,

W. Borough.

July 29.—GILBERTE TO THE COUNCIL.

[ccxiii. 59.—Signed. Addressed.]

My duty unto your Honour most humbly remembered :—I have received your Honour's letters of the 26th of July, for the sending away of 300 or 400 barrels of powder to the Earl[1] of Sussex out of the Spanish ship taken by her Majesty's fleet, all which powder and shot that could be found in her was sent away to my Lord Admiral, for that his Lordship sent to Weymouth this direction for powder and shot, and also sent a pinnace from the fleet of purpose for the powder and shot that was in the ship, which was but 88 barrels of powder and 1,600 shot that I could by any means learn of after I came to her ; and if I find any in unloading of the ship, I will with all speed send it to the Earl of Sussex, according to your Honour's directions, and will have special care for the putting in safety of the ordnance, and other munitions and goods in the ship whatsoever. Having no farther to trouble your Honour withal at this present, most humbly I take my leave. From Greenway, this 29th of July, 1588.

Your Honour's most humbly to command,

John Gilberte.

[1] MS. Earell.

July 29—*ARMAMENT OF THE LONDON SHIPS.*

[**ccxiii. 63.**—Endorsed :—29th of July, 1588. The number of men, ordnance and powder in the ten ships of the Merchants Adventurers. They are victualled for twenty days from the last of July.]

Ten ships, to be set out by the Adventurers for her Majesty's service, are to be furnished, as under followeth :—

Tons	Men	—	Demi-culverin	Sakers	Minions	Falcons	Fowlers	For every piece		Calivers	Muskets	Powder
								Round shot	Cross bar, langrell, and cloven			Barrels: every barrel containing 100 lbs.[1]
100	50	The Pansy of London. William Butler, Master		2	5	3	4	20	40	12	8	9
110	55	The Dolphin of Leigh William Hare,[2] Master		0	9	2	4	20	40	14	8	10
110	55	The Salamander of Leigh. William Goodlad,[2] Master		2	6	4	4	20	40	14	8	10
120	60	The George Noble of London Richard Harper, Master		2	8	4	4	20	50	14	10	11
120	60	The Antelope of London. Abraham Bonner,[2] Master		1	7	5	2	20	50	14	10	10
110	55	The Jewel of Leigh. Henry Rawlyn, Master		2	7	4	4	20	40	14	8	10
100	50	The Anthony of London. Richard Dove,[3] Master		1	7	4	2	20	40	12	8	9
120	60	The Toby of London. Robert Cuttle, Master	1[4]	1	9	2	3	20	50	14	10	11
100	50	The Rose Lion of Leigh. Robert Duke, Master		2	6	2	4	20	40	12	8	9
120	60	The Prudence of Leigh. Richard Chester,[2] Master		2	6	4	4	20	50	14	10	11
	555											100

[1] The MS. here has 100ᶜ, that is 100 cwt. or 5 tons : obviously a clerical error.

[2] All of Leigh. William Goodlad, presumably the son of the Master of the Salamander, was Master of the Trinity House in 1638, and died in 1639, aged 62. The family of Bonner was connected by marriage with that of Robert Salman, the Master of the Trinity House in 1588. Richard Chester's tombstone in the church of Leigh records that he was Master of the Trinity House in 1615 : that he lived in marriage with Elizabeth his wife about 49 years, by whom he had issue four sons and a daughter ; and that he died April 6, 1632 (Barrett, *The Trinity House of Deptford Strond*, pp. 135-37, 140-41).

[3] A shipowner of London in 1597 (*ib.* 140).

[4] The Toby's demi-culverin is written in later, by the same hand, but in different ink. Whether it had the same allowance of shot as the other guns does not appear.

Besides this furniture, these ships are to have
pikes, bills and swords sufficient, with convenient
fireworks. As part of the great ordnance is imprested by warrant, so doth there want to furnish
this proportion of small shot, 100 muskets, whereof
it is humbly prayed they may be furnished out of
her Majesty's store. It is purposed, if it may be,
that all the men for these ships shall be mariners.
But because thereof is no appearance, it is humbly
prayed that Mr. Captain Bellingham may have
warrant to furnish the want by press.

July 29.—HOWARD TO WALSYNGHAM.

[**ccxiii. 64.**—Signed ; first postscript, autograph ; the second postscript, on a separate scrap of paper, is in the same writing as
the letter. Addressed.]

Sir :—I have received your letter wherein you
desire a proportion of shot and powder to be set
down by me and sent unto you ; which, by reason
of the uncertainty of the service, no man can do ;
therefore I pray you to send with all speed as much
as you can. And because some of our ships are
victualled but for a very short time, and my Lord
Henry Seymour with his company not for one day,
in like[1] to pray you to dispatch away our victuals with
all possible speed, because we know not whether we
shall be driven to pursue the Spanish fleet.
    This morning we drove a galleass ashore before
Calais, whither I sent my long boat to board her,
where divers of my men were slain, and my lieutenant[2] sore hurt in the taking of her. Ever since
we have chased them in fight until this evening late,

[1] I have also, or in like manner, to pray you.
[2] Amyas Preston.

and distressed them much ; but their fleet consisteth
of mighty ships and great strength ; yet we doubt
not, by God's good assistance, to oppress them ;
and so I bid you heartily farewell.   From aboard
her Majesty's good ship the Ark, the 29th of July,
1588.

Your very loving friend,
C. Howard.

Sir :—I will not write unto her Majesty before
more be done.   Their force is wonderful great and
strong ; and yet we pluck their feathers by little and
little.   I pray to God that the forces on the land be
strong enough to answer so present a force.   There
is not one Flushinger nor Hollander at the seas.

Sir, I have taken the chief galleass this day before
Calais, with the loss of divers of my men ; but Monsieur Gourdan doth detain her, as I hear say.   I
could not send unto him, because I was in fight ;
therefore I pray you to write unto him, either to deliver her, or at leastwise to promise upon his honour
that he will not yield her up again unto the enemy.

July 29.—DRAKE TO WALSYNGHAM.

[ccxiii. 65.—Holograph.   Addressed.]

Right Honourable :—This bearer came aboard
the ship I was in in a wonderful good time, and
brought with him as good knowledge as we could
wish.   His carefulness therein is worthy recompense, for that God hath given us so good a day in
forcing the enemy so far to leeward as I hope in
God the Prince of Parma and the Duke of Sidonia
shall not shake hands this few days ; and whensoever they shall meet, I believe neither of them

will greatly rejoice of this day's service. The town
of Calais hath seen some part thereof, whose Mayor
her Majesty is beholden unto. Business commands
me to end. God bless her Majesty, our gracious
Sovereign, and give us all grace to live in his fear.
I assure your Honour this day's service hath much
appalled the enemy, and no doubt but [1] encouraged
our army. From aboard her Majesty's good ship
the Revenge, this 29th of July, 1588.

Your Honour's most ready to be commanded,

FRA. DRAKE.

There must be great care taken to send us
munition and victual whithersoever the enemy goeth.

Yours,

FRA. DRAKE.

July 30.—*ROBERT CECILL TO LORD BURGHLEY.*

[**ccxiii. 66.**—Holograph.   Addressed.]

My duty remembered to your Lordship :—
Although this bearer's letter to Mr. Secretary will
thoroughly advertise your Lordship, yet with remembrance of my duty, I thought good to acquaint
you with that which I have heard of a Spanish
gentleman taken yesterday in one of the galleasses,
which was run ashore at Calais, and there is seized
by Monsr. Gourdan. The captain of this ship,
named Moncada, one of the greatest personages in
the fleet, was killed with a small shot of a musket
that pierced both his eyes. The second of account
in that ship is taken and kept in one of the ships in
her Majesty's fleet. This man that is here is a
proper gentleman of Salamanca, who affirmeth that

---

[1] It hath.

there is great lack imputed to the Duke of Parma, in that he hath not joined with this fleet which hath lingered about Calais and Gravelines of purpose for him, and would not have stirred from those roads, if the device of the fireworks on Sunday had not forced them to slip their anchors and so make head away, in which instant my Lord Admiral gave them that fight which we saw upon the land yesterday; where, as terrible as it was in appearance, there was few men hurt with any shot, nor any one vessel sunk. For, as this man reporteth, they shoot very far off; and for boarding, our men have not any reason.

It is to be thought that Monsr. Gourdan will hardly part with this ship to her Majesty's use; and if he do not relieve her, and send them her again, yet it is the less harm. He sent, they say, a kind message to my Lord Admiral concerning it, which I am sure your Lordship is advertised of.

The opinion of this gentleman is that from Scotland they shall have aid; and for their own parts, he told me, they would think it sufficient if they could but draw away our fleet to the northward, thereby hoping *tenere il mare netto*, whereby, without impeachment, the Duke of Parma's men might land here; who, as he understandeth, is not in readiness; for his soldiers are yet unshipped, and as it is thought the Zealanders lie in the mouth of the haven to impeach their putting forth.

The powder your Lordship sent hither yesterday is gone now to our fleet in the Roebuck, which Sir W. Ralegh built, which is a fine ship and well furnished. Of my Lord of Derby I can hear nothing; wherefore I have determined to leave order here to be advertised immediately upon his arrival, that I may meet his Lordship from London upon the way, where I think to be to-morrow or next day, if the wind turn not to bring the ships upon this coast again. From Dover this 30th of July, 1588, at 12 of clock. I most humbly take my leave of your Lordship. In haste,

Your most obedient son,

Robt. Cecill.

July 30.—*RICHARD TOMSON*[1] *TO WAL-SYNGHAM.*

[ccxiii. 67.—Holograph.]

Since our first meeting of our enemies, which was on Sunday the 21st of this present, we have had four encounters such as, the Lord be praised, hath not a little daunted the minds of our enemies, but much impaired their great and unexpected forces, and to very little or no detriment of our English navy. At our first meeting of them, which was within two miles of Looe in Cornwall, they were 136 sail of ships and pinnaces, whereof 90 were very great ships, and the rest of smaller account; and at that time our English navy was not above 67 sail. By God's goodness and the good working of our commanders, we got the wind of

[1] Lieutenant of the Margaret and John of London; not improbably a brother of Lawrence Tomson, Walsyngham's servant or secretary. He had been for some years engaged in the Mediterranean trade, which, in 1582 and following years, had brought him into litigation with the Turkey Company. In 1583 he had made a voyage to Algiers to ransom captives. In September 1588 he was employed in arranging the ransom of the Spanish prisoners. At the end of the century he was living in London, writing occasional letters to Sir Robert Cecyll, then Secretary of State. He appears to have been a man of some education, conversant with French and Spanish, and may possibly have been a son of that Robert Tomson of Andover and Seville mentioned in the Introduction, though other indications seem to connect him with Norfolk.

them, which is a very great advantage and a special safety for the weaker part ; and ever since, God hath so blessed us that we have kept the same, to the great annoyance of our enemies ; and by that means, we have so daily pursued them at the heels, that they never had leisure to stop in any place alongst our English coast, until they came within two miles of Calais, where in the evening, very politicly, they came all upon a sudden to an anchor, being Saturday the 27th day, purposing that our ships with the flood should be driven to leeward of them ; but in happy time it was soon espied, and prevented by bringing our fleet to an anchor also in the wind of them.

The same night sent [1] ashore to Calais and forthwith to the Duke of Parma, advertising of their being there ; and one received answer that he with his forces would be in readiness upon Tuesday following, and come and join with them, with intent to come over and land their forces in England, about Margate [2] in Kent, as since I have thoroughly learned of the Spaniards that were taken in the chief galleass that the King had, hard under the jetty head at Calais. It hath appeared by many arguments that they Spaniards were not evil welcome to Monsieur Gourdan and the rest of his government, by permitting their messengers to go so speedily between the Duke and that place, as also by suffering the boats to go to and from the shore so usually, all Sunday the 28th of July, as they did ; and most of all, by sending his kinsman and lieutenant aboard the Duke of Medina with a great present ; whereof no semblance was made at all unto our Lord Admiral.

It pleased my Lord Admiral to appoint certain small ships to be fired on Sunday about 12 of the

[1] They sent.   [2] MS. Margarett.

clock at night, and let drive with the flood amongst the Spaniards; which practice, God be thanked, hath since turned to our great good; for it caused they Spaniards to let slip their anchors and cables, and confusedly to drive one upon another; whereby they were not only put from their roadstead and place where they meant to attend the coming of the Duke of Parma, but did much hurt one to another of themselves; and[1] now by the earnest pursuit of our Englishmen, very much weakened and dispersed, the Lord be praised; so that of the 124 sail that they were in Calais Road, we cannot now find by any account above 86 ships and pinnaces; so that I cannot conjecture but by the furious assault that my Lord and his associates gave them early on Monday morning, and did continue in vehement manner 8 hours, hath laid[2] many of them in the bottom of the sea, or else run with the coast of Flanders to save their lives, though unpossible to save their great ships, by reason of their evil harbours.

At the break of day upon Monday morning, my Lord and all the fleet setting sail after our enemies, we espied riding within shot of the town of Calais the greatest of the King's galleasses, the rest of the Spanish fleet being two leagues to leeward of her. My Lord Admiral began to go toward the galleass with his ship, the Ark, but finding the water to be shallow, other ships of less draught bare in with her and shot at her; whereupon she let slip and run the galleass aground hard before the town.

In our ship, which was the Margaret and John of London, we approached so near that we came on ground also; but afterwards came safely off again with the flood, being damaged by nothing but by the town of Calais, who, off the bulwarks, shot very

---

[1] Are.

[2] Sc. Many of them have been laid . . . or else forced to run.

much at us, and shot our ship twice through. And
the like powder and shot did Monsieur Gourdan
bestow upon sundry of our countrymen, and make
us relinquish the galleass, which otherwise we had
brought away, being masters of her above two hours,
and gotten by hard assault, to the great credit of
our country, if Monsieur Gourdan herein had not
showed his affection to the Spaniards to be greater
than our nation, or seemed by force to wrest from
us that which we had gotten with bloody heads.

My Lord Admiral, seeing he could not approach
the galleass with his ship, sent off his long boat unto
her with 50 or 60 men, amongst whom were many
gentlemen as valiant in courage as gentle in birth,
as they well showed. The like did our ship send
off her pinnace, with certain musketeers, amongst
whom myself went. These two boats came hard
under the galleass sides, being aground; where
we continued a pretty skirmish with our small shot
against theirs, they being ensconced within their ship
and very high over us, we in our open pinnaces and
far under them, having nothing to shroud and cover
us; they being 300 soldiers, besides 450 slaves, and
we not, at the instant, 100 persons. Within one half
hour it pleased God, by killing the captain with a
musket shot, to give us victory above all hope or
expectation; for the soldiers leaped overboard by
heaps on the other side, and fled with the shore,
swimming and wading. Some escaped with being
wet; some, and that very many, were drowned.
The captain of her was called Don Hugo de
Moncada,[1] son to the viceroy of Valencia. He
being slain, and the most part of their soldiers fled,
some few soldiers remaining in her, seeing our
English boats under her sides and more of ours
coming rowing towards her, some with 10 and some

[1] MS. Moncalla.

with 8 men in them, for all the smallest shipping were
the nearest the shore, put up two handkerchiefs [1]
upon two rapiers, signifying that they desired truce.
Hereupon we entered, with much difficulty, by
reason of her height over us, and possessed us of
her, by the space of an hour and half as I judge ;
each man seeking his benefit of pillage until the
flood came, that we might haul her off the ground
and bring her away.

It may please your Honour to understand that
during our fight to get her, the men of Calais stood
in multitudes upon the shore hard by us and
beholding all things, showing themselves at that
instant indifferent lookers-on ; but so soon as they
saw us possessed of so princely a vessel, the very
glory and stay of the Spanish army, a thing of very
great value and strength, as was well known to them
of Calais, for that they had been on board twice or
thrice the day before ; I say, Monsieur Gourdan,
seeing us thus [2] possessed, sent aboard to us that
were in her, in which boat came his kinsman and
another captain, desiring to parle [3] with us. None
being then in place that either understood or spake
French but myself, I asked them from whom they
came. They [4] answered, from Monsieur Gourdan,
the Governor of Calais. I demanded to know what
his pleasure was. They answered that he had stood
and beheld our fight and rejoiced of our victory,
saying that for our prowess and manhood showed
therein we had well deserved the spoil and pillage
of the galleass, as a thing due unto us by desert ;
and that he willingly consented that we should have
the pillage of her ; further requiring and commanding us not to offer to carry away either the ship or
ordnance, for that she was on ground under the

---

[1] MS. handkerchers.   [2] MS. this.
[3] Speak, confer.   [4] MS. the.

commandment of his castles and town, and therefore did of right appertain unto him. I answered
unto them that, for our parts, we thanked Monsieur
Gourdan for granting the pillage to the mariners
and soldiers that had fought for the same ; ac-
knowledging that without his leave and good will
we could not carry away anything of that we had
gotten, considering it lay on ground hard under his
bulwarks ; and that as concerning the ship and
ordnance, we prayed it would please him to send a
pinnace aboard my Lord Admiral, who was here in
person hard by, from whom he should have an honourable and friendly answer which we all are to obey
and give place unto. With this answer, to my
seeming they departed well satisfied ; but since I
have understood that some of our rude men, who
make no account of friend or foe, fell to spoiling the
Frenchmen, taking away their rings and jewels as
from enemies ; whereupon [1] going ashore and complaining, all the bulwarks and ports were bent
against us, and shot so vehemently that we received
sundry shot very dangerously through us. If this
have not incensed Monsieur Gourdan, I suppose that
he will easily, upon request made, either surrender
all or the better part of all things unto her Majesty ;
for the ship cannot be so little worth, with her
ordnance, as eighty thousand crowns ; having in her
four whole cannons, 8 demi-cannons, 12 culverins
and demi-culverins, 16 sakers and minions, all of
brass, 200 barrels of powder, and of all other things
great provision and plenty ; but very little or no
treasure that I can learn to be in her.

This is the substance and very truth of all that
passed in this action. Being thus departed from
the galleasses, my Lord with all the fleet pursued
the enemy, with all violent pursuit that our ordnance

[1] The Frenchmen.

and small shot could yield; little to our hurt, the Lord be praised, but greatly to the detriment of the enemy, as the bearer hereof, Mr. John Watts[1] of London, can amply inform your Honour; for he was present at the doing of most of these things happened within these two days, not without danger enough of his person both of cannon and musket shot, whereof his apparel beareth some tokens, although it pleased God to spare his life. At this instant we are as far to the eastward as the Isle of Walcheren, wherein Flushing doth stand, and about 12 leagues off the shore; and the wind hanging westerly, we drive our enemies apace to the eastward, much marvelling, if the wind continue, in what port they will direct themselves. Some imagine the river of Hamburg, which is a bad place for the receipt of ships of such charge; others suppose, because they have yet provision of victuals for three months, they will about Scotland, and so for Spain. I trust her Majesty may, by God's help, little fear any invasion by these ships; their power being, by battle, mortality, and other accidents, so decayed, and those that are left alive so weak and hurtless, that they could be well content to lose all charges to be at home, both rich and poor. There is want of powder, shot and victual, amongst us, which causeth that we cannot so daily assault them as we would. God grant the want may in time be supplied that so necessary a service be not neglected thereby. Thus I take my humble leave of your Honour, to whom Almighty God send all continuance of health and increase of happiness. Subscribed, RICHARD TOMSON.

[1] A merchant who, in connection with his partner, John Byrd, is repeatedly mentioned in the State Papers as exporting wheat, trading with Spain, sending intelligence, and, in 1590, capturing two Spanish ships. He seems (Lediard's *Naval History*, 277) to have been the owner of the Margaret and John.

July 31.—*KYLLYGREW TO WALSYNGHAM.*

[**Holland, lv.**—Signed, and autograph postscript. Addressed.]

It may please your Honour:—I could not let your Honour's own servant pass without some few lines, having at this present no great matter to write.

My Lord Governor of Flushing sent me of late a letter from my Lords of the Council unto him for the soliciting of the States of Holland to furnish out what shipping they could withal spare; wherein, as his Lordship hath moved them there, so here I have also done the like; and I understand the Admiral Justinus is gone out already with thirty sail from Flushing, besides some other which are presently to follow from those parts and North Holland, so as I doubt not her Majesty's fleet will be strong enough, especially the merchants being now returned from Stade and St. Nicholas,[1] as we understand. But, as I have signified unto your Honour heretofore, for any great assistance to be had from hence, it is not to be looked for at their hands. Their troubles and mutinies here have brought them so low, especially this last of Gertruidenberg, which hath cost them 215,000 fl., for the supplying whereof they have been fain to stretch their credits to the uttermost. So having moved them (according to your Honour's instructions sent unto me by Burnham) for the raising of some extraordinary contributions, I find no means to effectuate the same, considering as they say their extraordinary charges this year arise, through their preparations at sea, to a greater sum than many years heretofore, and that especially her Majesty's

---

[1] In the White Sea.

letter to them of Gertruidenberg was very acceptable to these men, as assuring them of her Highness'
honourable meaning towards them ; but coming now,
as it did, too late, they think it not convenient to
deliver it.

For your Honour's letter to my Lord General[1]
touching the articles[2] of peace, it was also very good
news unto them, and my Lord hath dealt for the
publishing thereof: but for the finding out of the
authors of such malicious slanders, they have no
other means than to learn of the Count William[3]
(who sent the same out of Friesland to the Count
Maurice) and of my Lord Governor of Flushing
(from whom also I received a like copy) from
whence they came into their hands.   To the Count
William, the Council of State will write to that
effect ; and to my Lord Governor of Flushing, I
have done the like.   They are in hand to dispatch
away Sir Martin Schenk[4] towards Bergen with
some horse and foot for the relief thereof, and to
furnish him with a bond of 30,000 fl. upon their
credit, to be paid after the enterprise is achieved.
Some of our horsemen lying thereabout in the
garrisons adjoining are to be drawn out to this
service.

The controversies of Utrecht are not yet ended,

[1] Lord Wyllughby.
[2] Certain articles, alleged to be the basis of the negotiations
for the treaty, had been published   They excited great indignation in Holland and Zealand, and were now vehemently denied
on the part of the Queen.
[3] Stadholder of Friesland, and brother-in-law of Maurice.
[4] A distinguished soldier of fortune, born in 1549, who after
serving with the Spaniards for several years, changed sides in
1585, in a pique with the Duke of Parma.   He was knighted by
Leicester in 1586, and after many valiant deeds was drowned by
the sinking of his boat in 1589.   A lively, but perhaps highly
coloured, picture of the man and his exploits is given by Motley
in the second volume of his *History of the United Netherlands.*

and rather grow worse and worse by reason of a request presented by the gentlemen of late, which hath made those of Utrecht more backward than before. In mine opinion it were not amiss if it might please her Majesty to address her letters unto them, requiring them in regard of the common cause to lay down their particularities.[1] For the 1,000 shot[2] to be sent over, my Lord General is very careful to dispatch them away presently, and to that end doth now repair into Zealand. Thus in haste, I most humbly recommend myself to your Honour's good remembrance, craving pardon for my rudeness. At the Hague, the 31st of July, 1588.

Your Honour's most assuredly

to be commanded,

H. KYLLYGREW.

I can but pray to God against the power and malice of Satan, for here there will be little more aid come than you have had. They make duty[3] to suffer any of her Majesty's people to return, because they stand in so great need themselves. Yet have they been dealt withal by all manner of persuasion. Their anchor hold is the treaty, and their towns in her Majesty's possession and the inability[4] they stand in to furnish Bergen and Ostend with any of theirs, who cashier[5] of their own daily, for want of means to keep them ; and sure if there come no money over to pay our companies their lendings, there will fall out great inconvenience, for here I see no relief to be had for them, unless some letters be written to our merchants at Middelburg to supply their needs at a pinch. My Lords may do well to advise upon this point, and under correction, the drawing of so

[1] Their personal interests or quarrels. [2] Musketeers.
[3] Sc. but not willingly. [4] MS. unhabillytye.
[5] MS. cassire : to break, disband.

many out of Flushing may prove more dangerous than by taking the whole number from Ostend.

I hear of great preparation in England to fight, but if London were trenched about as Paris was, it were a retreat in all events, and the only[1] way thought by good soldiers to break all the enemy's designs to his utter ruin. Many hands will make light work. The Lord of all power show us mercy.

These men are moved to set forth more ships, by name one that came from carrying[2] the Count Hohenlo to Hamburg [and][3] the wafters of the herring fleet newly come home. We have also moved the Count Maurice and the Council to go into Zealand, but yet the matter is in dispute, and will not be resolved this week by the States General who be here yet assembled.

I heard nothing out of England since the 11th of this present. Sir Thomas Morgan doth come over with the 2,000 shot, and hath been able to prevail in nothing here ; yet have I done for him what I could, though small thanks for my labour. I thank your Honour for remembering of Mr Gilpin ; I trust her Majesty shall receive good service by him. I write to no man at this time but to your Honour, and therefore it may please you to impart what your Honour shall think good.

July 31.—*MEMORIAL FOR RICHARD DRAKE.*

[ccxiii. 69.]

St. James, the last of July, 1588.

A memorial for Richard Drake, Esquire, being sent to the Lord Admiral, of such things as her Majesty doth desire to be informed of.

---

[1] We have heard something of this kind, even in our own time.
[2] MS. caring.   [3] Omitted in MS.

To be enquired :—

What number of ships are in service with my Lord Admiral, and of what burden?

How many are of the Queen's own ships? how many of them are ships of good bulk? how many are pinnaces, and how many of the country's charge?

What number of soldiers and of mariners serve in the Queen's ships?

How the Queen's ships are victualled?

How the other ships are victualled?

What powder and shot every ship hath?

How much powder and shot doth the navy use to spend in the fights with the enemies upon one day?

What quantity of powder and bullet hath been brought to the navy since the Lord Admiral met with the Spanish fleet near Plymouth? And from what places hath it been brought to the navy?

What losses of men and ships hath been on the Spanish side? and where were the losses? and where are the prisoners? And what powder, munition and any treasure hath been taken upon them? What losses hath happened to the Queen's army of ships and men?

What men hath been lost since the beginning of the services at Plymouth?

What causes are there why the Spanish navy hath not been boarded by the Queen's ships? And though some of the ships of Spain may be thought too huge to be boarded by the English, yet some of the Queen's ships are thought very able to have boarded divers of the meaner ships of the Spanish navy.[1]

And if his Lordship, upon good advice there

---

[1] This query is doubtless the explanation of Ralegh's celebrated defence of Howard's policy, quoted in the Introduction.

taken, shall find it more necessary to have those ten ships [1] to be used upon the coast of Flanders to imbarke [2] the Duke of Parma's shipping there, then, upon his commandment, the said ten ships shall repair to such place for that service as he shall appoint.

The Queen's Majesty would have Pedro de Valdes, that was the captain of the galleon distressed, to be sent safe into England; and such other Spaniards as have been taken and are now kept on seaboard; for that she thinketh very inconvenient to have any such kept upon any English ship, where either they may practise some mischief, or else come to understanding of the secrets of the services intended.

To inform the Lord Admiral that some Englishmen, and Spaniards also that are taken, do say that the intent of the Spanish navy is to draw along the English navy from the coast of Flanders; that the sea being clear, the Duke of Parma might come out with his forces to invade the realm, and namely to come to London. Some also do think that if this navy of Spain cannot prevail against the English, that they will sail to the river of Emden; whereof the Lord Admiral may see well to inform himself what may be probable to think thereof.

The Lord Steward,[3] who was at Dover the 29th of July, saith that a Hollander came to Dover declaring that he came in company with 30 or 40 sail of Hollanders, and came to the Spanish fleet in the night unawares, the night before when the fire was put by English boats, and that in the morning those Hollanders came to the Lord Admiral and joined with his navy. But by reason the Lord Admiral's

---

[1] The London ships under Bellingham. See *ante*, p. 339.
[2] So in MS. To embargo, embar, stay.
[3] The Earl of Leicester.

letters[1] written the 30th of this month reporteth that there was no Hollander nor Londoner upon the sea, it is to be enquired what may be thought thereof, and to enquire how the mouth of the Sluys is kept by any ships of Zealand, where it is said the Duke mindeth to set out a number of his by-landers.

You shall seek to learn the state of our commissioners at Bourbourg, whether they be come thence, and to what place, and with what surety they may come into England.

If any words can be sent to Sir Wm. Russell, to require him to send away 20 lasts of powder, and that if he may, some 8 or 10 lasts thereof may, in the way, be sent to the Lord Admiral.

Ex^m per W. WAAD.[2]

July 31.—GORGES TO WALSYNGHAM.

[ccxiii. 70.—Signed.   Addressed.]

Right Honourable :—According to your direction have done my endeavour, all that might be, for the coming to my Lord Henry Seymour with the eight ships of London ; and on the 30th of July, passing through the sands, we were becalmed and forced to anchor the same night in the New Channel.   The next morning, being the last of this month, we had the wind at South-East and blew very

[1] No letter of Howard's, of this date, is now known. It may be that it was read and re-read and handed about till it fell to pieces ; but the reference is, more probably, to the letter to Walsyngham of the 29th (*ante*, p. 341), which says no Hollander nor Flushinger. And in fact, there were, within Howard's knowledge, many London ships at sea—the Margaret and John among others—though Gorges was still in the river.

[2] William Waad, Clerk of the Council.

much, so that by no means we could recover the North Foreland. And thus riding in the New Channel we understood by a ketch that both the fleets weighed anchor on Sunday at night, and fell presently into fight, and so continued till they were out of sight of land plying to the North-East; but what course they have taken, as yet we cannot learn. But I mean with all diligence to ply into the Narrow Seas, to understand whether my Lord Henry hath left any order what I shall do ; and if there be order left for my service there, I mean to ply after the fleet with all possible means I can make. And thus, with my humble duty, I wish you increase of honour with all happiness. From aboard the Susan Parnell, at ten of the clock, this last of July.

Your Honour's most readiest to command,
NICHOLAS GORGES.

July 31.—*HAWKYNS TO WALSYNGHAM.*

[**ccxiii. 71.**—Signed and autograph postscript.   Addressed.]

My bounden duty humbly remembered unto your good Lordship:—I have not busied myself to write often to your Lordship in this great cause, for that my Lord Admiral doth continually advertise the manner of all things that doth pass. So do others that understand the state of all things as well as myself. We met with this fleet somewhat to the westward of Plymouth upon Sunday in the morning, being the 21st of July, where we had some small fight with them in the afternoon. By the coming aboard one of the other of the Spaniards, a great ship, a Biscayan, spent her foremast and bowsprit ; which was left by the fleet in the sea, and so taken up by Sir Francis Drake the next morning. The same Sunday there was, by a fire chancing by a barrel of powder, a great Biscayan spoiled and abandoned, which my Lord took up and sent away.

The Tuesday following, athwart of Portland, we had a sharp and long fight with them, wherein we spent a great part of our powder and shot, so as it was not thought good to deal with them any more till that was relieved.

The Thursday following, by the occasion of the scattering[1] of one of the great ships from the fleet, which we hoped to have cut off, there grew a hot fray, wherein some store of powder was spent; and after that, little done till we came near to Calais, where the fleet of Spain anchored, and our fleet by them; and because they should not be in peace there, to refresh their water or to have conference with those of the Duke of Parma's party, my Lord Admiral, with firing of ships, determined to remove them; as he did, and put them to the seas; in which broil the chief galleass spoiled her rudder, and so rode ashore near the town of Calais, where she was possessed of our men, but so aground as she could not be brought away.

That morning, being Monday, the 29th of July, we followed the Spaniards; and all that day had with them a long and great fight, wherein there was great valour showed generally of our company. In this battle there was spent very much of our powder and shot; and so the wind began to blow westerly, a fresh gale, and the Spaniards put themselves somewhat to the northward, where we follow and keep company with them. In this fight there was some hurt done among the Spaniards. A great ship of the galleons of Portugal, her rudder spoiled, and so the fleet left her in the sea. I doubt not but

[1] MS. schateringe : separation. Cf. *ante*, p. 13.

all these things are written more at large to your Lordship than I can do ; but this is the substance and material matter that hath passed.

Our ships, God be thanked, have received little hurt, and are of great force to accompany them, and of such advantage that with some continuance at the seas, and sufficiently provided of shot and powder, we shall be able, with God's favour, to weary them out of the sea and confound them. Yet, as I gather certainly, there are amongst them 50 forcible and invincible ships which consist of those that follow, viz. :—

Nine galleons of Portugal of 800 ton apiece, saving two of them are but 400 ton apiece.

Twenty great Venetians and argosies of the seas within the Strait, of 800 apiece.

One ship of the Duke of Florence of 800 ton.

Twenty great Biscayans of 500 or 600 ton.

Four galleasses, whereof one is in France.

There are 30 hulks, and 30 other small ships, whereof little account is to be made.

At their departing from Lisbon, being the 19th of May by our account, they were victualled for six months. They stayed in the Groyne twenty-eight days, and there refreshed their water. At their coming from Lisbon they were taken with a flaw, and four-teen hulks or thereabouts came near Ushant, and so returned with contrary winds to the Groyne, and there met ; and else there was none other company upon our coast before the whole fleet arrived. And in their coming now, a little flaw took them, fifty leagues from the coast of Spain ; where one great ship was severed from them, and four galleys, which hitherto have not recovered their company.

At their departing from Lisbon, the soldiers were twenty thousand, the mariners and others eight thousand ; so as, in all, they were twenty-eight

thousand men. Their commission was to confer
with the Prince of Parma, as I learn, and then to
proceed to the service that should be there concluded; and so the Duke to return into Spain with
these ships and mariners, the soldiers and their
furniture being left behind. Now this fleet is here,
and very forcible, and must be waited upon with all
our force, which is little enough. There would [1] be
an infinite quantity of powder and shot provided,
and continually sent abroad; without the which
great hazard may grow to our country; for this is
the greatest and strongest combination, to my understanding, that ever was gathered in Christendom;
therefore I wish it, of all hands, to be mightily and
diligently looked unto and cared for.

The men have been long unpaid and need relief.
I pray your Lordship that the money that should
have gone to Plymouth may now be sent to Dover.
August now cometh in, and this coast will spend
ground tackle, cordage, canvas and victuals; all which
would be sent to Dover in good plenty. With these
things, and God's blessing, our kingdom may be
preserved; which being neglected, great hazard may
come. I write to your Lordship briefly and plainly.
Your wisdom and experience is great; but this is a
matter far passing all that hath been seen in our time
or long before. And so praying to God for a happy
deliverance from the malicious and dangerous practice
of our enemies, I humbly take my leave. From the
sea, aboard the Victory, the last of July, 1588.

The Spaniards take their course for Scotland;
my Lord doth follow them. I doubt not, with God's
favour, but we shall impeach their landing. There
must be order for victual and money, powder and
shot, to be sent after us.

Your Lordship's humbly to command,

JOHN HAWKYNS.

This is the copy of the letter I send to my Lord
Treasurer, whereby I shall not need to write to your
Honour.   Help us with furniture, and, with God's
favour, we shall confound their devices.

Your Honour's ever bounden,

JOHN HAWKYNS.

I pray your Honour bear with this, for it is done
in haste and bad weather.

J. H.

July 31.—*BARREY TO WALSYNGHAM.*

[ccxiii. 72.—Signed.   Addressed.]

My most humble duty unto your Honour remembered :—Upon Sunday last Sir Henry Palmer
came unto Dover from the Lord Admiral for some
of the boats that were appointed to be laden with
bavens[1] and pitch, and had presently away with him
that night 19 boats of the ports laden with bavens;
and every boat one barrel of pitch of their own,
besides the 72 barrels sent down by your Honour,
the which were sent in one of those boats.   Sir
Henry Palmer embarked himself in one of those
boats, and departed from Dover on Sunday night
last, about 12 of the clock.   Before Sir Henry
Palmer's coming unto my Lord Admiral, there was
an attempt made by other vessels for the firing of
the Spanish fleet; by which means the fleet was
removed from the road before Calais, and so are
passed towards the North Seas, and all her Majesty's
navy in chase of them.   And I hope in the Almighty
God, he will give good success unto our navy.
Some of the boats that were sent out with the

---

[1] Faggots, bundles of brushwood.

bavens are returned from my Lord Admiral, who say that my Lord discharged them, But, for that it may be shift of wind may put back the fleet again, I make stay of all the boats that are here, as well of those that are returned as of the rest that were not yet sent forth.

Yesternight, about 6 of the clock, Jasper Swift[1] came unto me and showed me an order from your Honour for certain boats that should come unto Dover, which are not yet come, not above 3 of them; and if the Spanish fleet return not, here will be no use of them. The ports' men[2] deserve commendation for their willing readiness; for within one day after they received letters from me, with your Honour's letter, they sent 30 boats into this harbour. If there shall not be any further employment of them, may it please your Honour to signify your Honour's pleasure therein; for they are most of them fishermen of Rye and Hastings, and lie here at great charges, calling upon me every day to victual them. I gave my bills for victualling those that were sent with Sir Henry Palmer, as also for the bavens that were taken up, and the pitch that they brought in their own boats; and money also disbursed by me for sending to the ships and for labourers and boats in shipping of the bavens; most humbly beseeching your Honour that order may be taken by your good means for the satisfying thereof, the particulars whereof by my next I will send unto your Honour; and so I most humbly cease from troubling of your Honour. At Dover Castle, this last of July, 1588.

Your Honour's always most bounden
at commandment,
RYCHARD BARREY.

---

[1] Sergeant of the Admiralty.
[2] The men of the Five Ports.

July 31.—*DRAKE TO WALSYNGHAM.*

[ccxiii. 73.—Holograph. Addressed.]

Most Honourable :—I am commanded to send
these prisoners ashore by my Lord Admiral, which
had ere this been long done, but that I thought
their being here might have done something which
is not thought meet now.

Let me beseech your Honour that they may
be presented unto her Majesty, either by your
Honour, or by my honourable good Lord, my Lord
Chancellor, or both of ye.   The one Don Pedro is
a man of greatest estimation with the King of Spain,
and thought next in his army to the Duke of
Sidonia.   If they should be given from[1] me unto
any other, it would be some grief to my friends.   If
her Majesty will have them, God defend[2] but I
should think it happy.

We have the army of Spain before us and mind,
with the grace of God, to wrestle a pull[3] with him.
There was never anything pleased me better than
the seeing the enemy flying with a southerly wind
to the northwards.   God grant you have a good eye
to the Duke of Parma ; for with the grace of God, if
we live, I doubt it not but ere it be long so to
handle the matter with the Duke of Sidonia as he
shall wish himself at St. Mary Port among his
orange trees.[4]

[1] Sc. away from.   [2] Forbid.   [3] MS. wressell a poull.
[4] Cf. Nelson to Addington, 12th of August, 1801 : 'In my
command I find much zeal and good humour ; and should Mr.
Bonaparte put himself in our way, I believe he will wish himself
even in Corsica.'   The coincidence is only one of many which
occur in Nelson's letters, and raise the suspicion that he had read
much more than is commonly supposed.

God give us grace to depend upon him ; so shall we not doubt victory, for our cause is good. Humbly taking my leave, this last of July, 1588,
Your Honour's faithfully to be commanded ever,
FRA. DRAKE.

I crave pardon of your Honour for my haste, for that I had to watch this last night upon the enemy.
Yours ever,
FRA. DRAKE.

END OF THE FIRST VOLUME

STATE PAPERS

RELATING TO

THE DEFEAT OF

𝕮𝖍𝖊 𝕾𝖕𝖆𝖓𝖎𝖘𝖍 𝕬𝖗𝖒𝖆𝖉𝖆

ANNO 1588

EDITED BY

JOHN KNOX LAUGHTON, M.A., R.N.

Professor of Modern History in King's College, London

VOL. II.

SECOND EDITION

TEMPLE SMITH FOR THE NAVY RECORDS SOCIETY

1987

THE COUNCIL

OF THE

NAVY RECORDS SOCIETY

1893–4–5

———◆———

PATRONS

HIS ROYAL HIGHNESS THE DUKE OF SAXE-COBURG AND GOTHA, K.G., K.T., &c.

HIS ROYAL HIGHNESS THE DUKE OF YORK, K.G. &c.

PRESIDENT
EARL SPENCER, K.G.

VICE-PRESIDENTS

LORD GEORGE HAMILTON.
ADMIRAL SIR R. V. HAMILTON, K.C.B.

MARQUIS OF LOTHIAN, K.T.
PROFESSOR SIR J. R. SEELEY, K.C.M.G.

COUNCILLORS

H.S.H. PRINCE LOUIS OF BATTENBERG, G.C.B.
WALTER BESANT.
HON. T. A. BRASSEY.
REAR-ADMIRAL BRIDGE.
OSCAR BROWNING.
PROFESSOR MONTAGU BURROWS.
REV. H. MONTAGU BUTLER, D.D.
LIEUT.-GEN. SIR A. CLARKE, G.C.M.G.
VICE-ADMIRAL COLOMB.
ADMIRAL SIR EDWARD FANSHAWE, G.C.B.
C. H. FIRTH.

DR. RICHARD GARNETT.
MAJOR-GEN. GEARY, R.A., C.B.
LORD PROVOST OF GLASGOW.
DAVID HANNAY.
SIDNEY LEE.
REAR-ADMIRAL SIR LAMBTON LORAINE, BART.
SIR ALFRED C. LYALL, K.C.B.
CLEMENTS R. MARKHAM, C.B., F.R.S.
CAPT. S. P. OLIVER, late R.A.
COMM. C. N. ROBINSON, R.N.
J. R. THURSFIELD.
CAPT. WHARTON, R.N., F.R.S.
CAPT. S. EARDLEY WILMOT, R.N.

SECRETARY
PROFESSOR J. K. LAUGHTON, Catesby House, Manor Road, Barnet.

TREASURER
H. F. R. YORKE, Admiralty, S.W.

The COUNCIL of the NAVY RECORDS SOCIETY wish it to be distinctly understood that they are not answerable for any opinions or observations that may appear in the Society's publications. For these the responsibility rests entirely with the Editors of the several works.

DEFEAT

OF THE

SPANISH ARMADA

ANNO 1588.

Aug. 1.—*LORD H. SEYMOUR TO THE QUEEN.*

[**ccxiv. 2.**—Holograph.   Addressed :—To the Queen's most
excellent Majesty, my only Sovereign.]

MOST GRACIOUS LADY :—I received your most
favourable letters the 27th of July at the Downs, at
which very instant I had both message and letter
from my Lord Admiral to repair unto him with all
my forces, which I did incontinent, and met with his
Lordship off Scales Cliffs, about eight in the evening,
where both the armies anchored against the other,
and we somewhat to the westward.   The next day
in the morning, and in council with his Lordship, it
was resolved some exploit should be attempted the
night following by fire, which was performed ; and
what distress came thereof we certainly know not,
saving that the said put them from their anchoring,
by means whereof one of their galleasses came
athwart one of their own ships' hawses, whereby she

broke her rudder, and [was] constrained, for want of steerage,[1] to go into Calais Road, where certain of your hoys and pinnaces under my charge[2] followed, and after long fight was by some of them boarded, slaying sundry Spaniards; the rest of them saved themselves by boat and swam into Calais, where they were received; the governor whereof shot at our men, enforcing them to forsake her, leaving 30 pieces of ordnance in her, as was supposed.

The 29th of the said month, being resolved the day before my Lord Admiral should give the first charge, Sir Francis Drake the next, and myself the third, it fell out that the galleass distressed altered my Lord's former determination, as I suppose, by prosecuting the destruction of her, which was done within one hour[3] after. In the meantime Sir Francis Drake gave the first charge upon the Spanish Admiral, being accompanied with the Triumph, the Victory, and others. Myself, with the Vanguard, the Antelope, and others, charged upon the tail, being somewhat broken, and distressed 3 off of their great ships; among which, my ship shot one of them through six times, being within less than musket shot.

After this long fight, which continued almost six hours, and ended between 4 and 5 in the afternoon, until Tuesday at 7 in the evening, we continued by them, and your Majesty's fleet followed the Spaniards along the channel, until we came athwart the Brill, where I was commanded by my Lord Admiral, with your Majesty's fleet under my charge, to return back for the defence of your Majesty's coasts, if anything be attempted by the Duke of Parma; and therein have obeyed his Lordship much against my will, expecting your Majesty's further pleasure.

[1] MS. stirrege.   [2] Sc. of my squadron.   [3] MS. ower.

This, hoping God will confound all your enemies, and that shortly, do most humbly leave to trouble your most excellent Majesty. From aboard the Rainbow, this first of August, 1588.

Your Majesty's most bounden
and faithful fisherman,[1]

H. SEYMOUR.

Your Majesty's faithful servants, Sir William Wynter and Sir Henry Palmer, have faithfully performed their duties, and the more in respect of your Majesty's honourable remembering them.

August 1.—SEYMOUR TO WALSYNGHAM.

[ccxiv. 3.—Holograph. Addressed.]

Sir :—I have written to her Majesty at large of our proceedings upon my Lords' honourable letters directed unto me for the reinforcing my Lord Admiral's strength ; so was I likewise desired and written by my Lord Admiral himself to hasten my forces to join the same to his, which I did perform. And where his Lordship was altogether desirous at the first to have me strengthen him, so having done the uttermost of my good will (to the venture of my life) in prosecuting the distressing of the Spaniards, which was thoroughly followed the 29th of July, I find my Lord jealous and loth to have me take part of the honour of the rest that is to win, using his

---

[1] It is very doubtful what this ' fisherman' means. Possibly that, after taking his part in the glorious battle, he had been sent back to command coasting craft and fishermen (cf. *ante*, vol. i. p. 363), and was, in fact, being treated as if he was one. The next letter, to Walsyngham, shows that he was very much annoyed at having been ordered back.

authority to command me to look to our English
coasts, that have been long threatened by the Duke
of Parma.

So referring the rest unto her Majesty's letters
as[1] to these messengers, the one Mr. Brown[2] and
the other my lieutenant,[3] who both are witnesses of
our actions, do take my leave. From aboard the
Rainbow, this 1st of August, 1588, at anchor at
Harwich, at 3 in the afternoon.

Your assured friend to command,

H. SEYMOUR.

In the passage homewards from my Lord
Admiral, I received letters from Sir William Russell
that Justinus de Nassau cometh forth himself with
30 sail, and will be ready to perform anything what
her Majesty shall command, as you may perceive
by the effect of Sir William Russell's letters which
I send you.

I understand the French do arm to join with the
League, or at the least with Parma, and that all
passages are stopped for intelligence.

I pray God my Lord Admiral do not find the
lack of the Rainbow and that company; for I
protest before God, and have witness for the same,
I vowed I would be as near or nearer with my little
ship to encounter our enemies, as any of the greatest
ships in both armies; which I have performed to
the distress of one of their greatest ships sunk, if I
have my due.

We are in manner famished for lack of victuals,
although the same hath been drawn at length,[4] yet
by increase of soldiers the same is all wasted.

---

[1] As = as well as.
[2] Brute Brown, serving as a volunteer on board the Rainbow.
See *ante*, vol. i. p. 310.
[3] MS. lyftenant.   [4] Drawn out as long as possible.

I presume the Spaniards are much distressed for victuals, which I hope will be the cause to make them yield to her Majesty's mercy.

I do send my lieutenant the rather to give you perfect notice of our lacks, as also I pray you to use Mr. Brown with some favour, who of good will came to see the service two days before I joined with the Lord Admiral.

August 1.—*SHIPS WITH SEYMOUR.*

[ccxiv. 6.]

Ships on the seas with the Lord Henry Seymour the 1st of August :—

The Queen's Ships.

The Vanguard .	. 250	Sir Wm. Wynter.
Rainbow .	. 250	Lord H. Seymour.
Antelope .	. 250	Sir Henry Palmer.
Bull .	. 100	Turner.
Tiger .	. 100	
Tramontana .	70	Luke Ward.
Scout .	. 70	Cap. Ashley.
Achates .	. 60	Cap. Rigges.
Merlin .	. 35	Gower.
Sun .	. 30	White.
Cygnet .	. 20	a Mr. Ward.
George .	. 20	Hodges.
Galley .	. .	Mr. Borough.

13 ; whereof { Good ships, 5. Mean, 3. Pinnaces, 4.

1,255 men, besides the galley.

Coast Ships.

Ipswich and Harwich .	.	3 hoys.
Five Ports .	. . .	5 ships, 1 pinnace.
Colchester .	. . .	1
Aldborough	. . .	1
Yarmouth .	. . .	1 ship, 1 pinnace.
Lyme .	. . .	1 ship, 1 pinnace.
Hull .	. . .	2 ships, 1 pinnace.

Ships, 14.
Pinnaces, 4.

8 ships of London come with Nicholas Gorges to the Lord Henry Seymour the last of July.

In all, Ships . . . 30
Pinnaces . . 8

Aug. 1.—*RESOLUTION AT A COUNCIL OF WAR.*

[**B.M. Addl. MS. 33740, f. 6.**—Signed.]

1st of August, 1588.

We whose names are hereunder written have determined and agreed in council to follow and pursue the Spanish fleet until we have cleared our own coast and brought the Frith west of us ; and then to return back again, as well to revictual our ships, which stand in extreme scarcity, as also to guard and defend our own coast at home ; with further protestation that, if our wants of victuals and munition were supplied, we would pursue them to the furthest that they durst have gone.

C. HOWARD.   GEORGE COUMBRELAND.
T. HOWARD.   EDMONDE SHEFFEYLDE.
FRA. DRAKE.   EDW. HOBY.
JOHN HAWKYNS.
THOMAS FENNER.

2nd of August.

Determined by the council to return from thwart of the Frith.

August 1.—*WYNTER TO WALSYNGHAM.*

[**ccxiv. 7.**—Signed. Addressed.]

May it please your Honour :—Upon Saturday, the 27th of July, our Admiral, the Lord Henry Seymour, being with his fleet in the morning as high up as between Dungeness and Folkestone, attending the coming of the armies, we there spake with divers ships that came from the west, who said they saw none of the armies ; which put us in hope, our victualling being within three days of expiring, that we might bear into the Downs to see if the victuals were come, and to take in the same, and so to be in a readiness to do service. But we had not been scarcely there half an hour, the wind being SSW., but we received a letter from the Lord Admiral by a pinnace, declaring unto us what we should do ; and forthwith we made sail and gat out, not having any time to relieve ourselves with victual, and bare over with the French coast, whither we did see the fleet to draw ; and by that time we could recover over, which was about seven of the clock in the afternoon, the Spanish army was anchored to the eastward of Scales Cliffs, very round and near together, not far from the shore.

Our army not being past a mile and a half behind them, whom I had recovered with my ship, did also cast anchor thwart of Scales Cliffs ; and immediately, so soon as my Lord Admiral's ship was come to an anchor, his Lordship sent his pinnace aboard my ship for me, and a messenger in

the same commanding me to come aboard his Lordship, which I did ; and having viewed myself the
great and hugeness of the Spanish army, and did
consider that it was not possible to remove them
but by a device of firing of ships, which would
make them to leese[1] the only road which was apt
and meetest to serve their purpose, as also an
occasion to put many of them in danger of firing,
and at the least to make them to leese[2] their cables
and anchors, which could not be less than two for
every ship, I thought it meet to acquaint my
Lord withal at my coming to him at that time,
which was about 9 of the clock at night; and his
Lordship did like very well of it,[3] and said the next
day his Lordship would call a council and put the
same in practice ; and his Lordship and I were
reasoning of this matter in his Lordship's cabin,
there did drive with the tide aboard my Lord's ship
her Majesty's ship the Bear and three others, who
were all tangled together, so as there was some hurt
done by breaking of yards and spoil of tackle ; but
a great favour of God showed[4] that it had not made
a destruction of many [of] our ships.

Upon Sunday, being the 28th day, my Lord put
out his flag of council early in the morning, the
armies both riding still ; and after the assembly of
the council it was concluded that the practice for
the firing of ships should be put in execution the
night following, and Sir Henry Palmer was assigned to bear over presently in a pinnace for
Dover, to bring away such vessels as were fit to be
fired, and materials apt to take fire.   But because it

---

[1] Leese=lose.   [2] MS. lease.

[3] Wynter had only just joined the fleet, and it was his first
sight of the Spaniards. To the others his device would seem to
have occurred long before, and the combustibles had been sent
to Dover. See *ante*, vol. i. p. 362.

[4] Sc. showed itself in this, &c.

was seen, after his going, he could not return that
night, and occasion would not be over slipped, it
was thought meet that we should help ourselves
with such shipping as we had there to serve that
turn. So that about 12 of the clock that night six [1]
ships were brought and prepared [2] with a saker shot,
and going in a front, having the wind and tide with
them, and their ordnance being charged, were fired;
and the men that were the executers, so soon as the
fire was made they did abandon the ships, and
entered into five boats that were appointed for the
saving of them. This matter did put such terror
among the Spanish army that they were fain to let
slip their cables and anchors; and did work, as it
did appear, great mischief among them by reason of
the suddenness of it. We might perceive that
there were two great fires more than ours, and far
greater and huger than any of our vessels that we
fired could make. [3]

The 29th day, in the break of the day, my Lord
Admiral did bear with them with all his fleet; and
his Lordship perceived a galleass to go alongst the
French shore, as near as she might possibly,
striving to recover Calais, which could not use no
more but her foresail and oars. The which vessel
my Lord did cause to be followed with small vessels
and boats, which did force her to run aground upon
the bar of Calais haven, the tide being half spent.
Great fight was made there between our men and
them; and one William Coxe, master of a bark of
mine called the Delight, did first board her; who
sithen that time is slain. And so others, in boats
and small pinnaces, did very valiantly behave them-

---

[1] There were eight.

[2] Signalled; prepared to move when the gun was fired.

[3] None of the Spanish ships were burnt, and he wrote in the
belief that there were only six fire-ships.

selves ; which was better done by reason that my Lord Admiral did stay off and on, with some good ships with him, to give comfort and countenance to our men.

But after his Lordship perceived that our men had quietly possessed her, as we might judge of it, then his Lordship, with such as were with him, did bear room after the Spanish fleet, the wind being at the SSW., and the Spanish fleet bearing away NNE., making into the depth of the channel ; and about 9 of the clock in the morning we feat[1] near unto them, being then thwart of Gravelines. They went into a proportion of a half moon. Their admiral and vice-admiral, they went in the midst, and the greatest number of them ; and there went on each side, in the wings, their galleasses, armados of Portugal, and other good ships, in the whole to the number of sixteen in a wing, which did seem to be of their principal shipping. My fortune was to make choice to charge their starboard wing without shooting of any ordnance until we came within six score[2] of them, and some of our ships did follow me. The said wing found themselves, as it did appear, to be so charged, as by making of haste to run into the body of their fleet, four of them did entangle themselves one aboard the other. One of them recovered himself, and so shrouded[3] himself among the fleet ; the rest, how they were beaten, I will leave it to the report of some of the Spaniards that leapt into the seas and [were] taken up, and are now in the custody of some of our fleet.

The fight continued from 9 of the clock until six of the clock at night, in the which time the Spanish army bare away NNE. and N. by E., as much as

[1] Feat=fetched : the past tense of fett=fetch.
[2] Gunners seem to have counted then by paces. Cf. *post*, App. C.
[3] Concealed, sheltered.

they could keeping company one with another, I assure your Honour in very good order. Great was the spoil and harm that was done unto them, no doubt. I deliver it unto your Honour upon the credit of a poor gentleman, that out of my ship there was shot 500 shot of demi-cannon, culverin, and demi-culverin ; and when I was furthest off in discharging any of the pieces, I was not out of the shot of their harquebus, and most times within speech one of another. And surely every man did well ; and, as I have said, no doubt the slaughter and hurt they received was great, as time will discover it ; and when every man was weary with labour, and our cartridges spent, and munitions wasted [1]—I think in some altogether—we ceased and followed the enemy, he bearing hence still in the course as I have said before.

The 30th day the wind continued at WNW., very much wind ; and about three or four of the clock in the afternoon, my Lord Admiral shot off a warning piece, and put out a flag of council ; to the which myself, I was not able to go by reason of a hurt that I had received in my hip, by the reversing of one of our demi-cannons in the fight. But after the council was ended, my Lord Admiral sent aboard me a gentleman of his, both to see how I did, as also to tell me that my Lord Seymour had order to repair back again, to guard the Thames mouth from any attempt that might be made by the Duke of Parma ; and that I was to attend upon him, and [2] all the rest that were of his former charge ; and that we should bear away in the twilight, as [3] the enemy might not see our departing. And so, obeying the commandment which was brought unto me by Sir Henry Palmer, Sir John Hawkyns, Mr. Fenton,

---

[1] Expended.   [2] Sc. and so were all the rest.
[3] As = so that.

Mr. Beeston, and Mr. Baker, and likewise advertised to me from my Lord Henry Seymour, and by my nephew John Wynter, whom I did send aboard (being my lieutenant) to the council, to know what order should be taken, all agreeing with the message delivered unto me by my Lord Admiral's servant, I did about 8 of the clock in the night, a-being then little wind and veered to the N E., bear back again through our fleet ; and truly we had much ado with the staying of many ships that would have returned with us besides our own company.

The 31st day—we had the wind at SSW.—we recovered as high as Badsey Cliff; there we were forced to anchor in the sea (with very much wind), upon the ebb, about three of the clock in the afternoon, and so continued all that day, and the night following.

The 1st of August, as we were weighing of our anchors and to turn to windward in hope to win the North Foreland, the Lord Henry Seymour, our Admiral, sent the pinnace called the Delight, to show us that we should bear room for Harwich to take in our victuals ; and about one of the clock we came and anchored in Harwich. So that here I have declared unto you as much as I do know of that which hath happened from my coming lastly into my Lord Admiral's company, until this present time.

And now I will deliver unto you what I do think where the armies may be, and what my opinion is, and of the course that they, the Spaniards, mean to take.

First, when that I departed from my Lord Admiral as aforesaid, which was in the bottom of the channel, half way between the coast of Holland and the coast of England, I left them thwart of Lowestoft[1] ; and

---

[1] MS. Leistof.

for anything that I could perceive, and by the course that the Spanish army did hold, considering what a fresh wind it hath blown sithence that time, they cannot be less way now to the northward than at Flamborough Head upon our coast. If my Lord Admiral follow them, as he had in purpose, they dare not anchor, for fear of such a stratagem as lately hath been used ; to the which, if it should happen, it would put them by their ground tackle, and so should they be utterly undone. And to bear with Hamburg, I think it a very dangerous place for such huge ships and such a number ; and then, I do not know, except they go with the Naze of Norway or the Frith in Scotland, where they should take any succour, except it should be that they do bear about the north part of Scotland, and so go about to recover back into their own country again that way ; or else, they must be forced to abide their fortune, and to tarry [1] a wind to bring them back this way again ; which, by their flying, it seemeth they are not willing to do ; and in my conscience, I speak it to your Honour, I think the Duke would give his dukedom to be in Spain again. But the worst is to be reckoned of.

It were very necessary that victuals were provided ; [and that] munitions—powder, shot, match, lead, and canvas to make cartridges—which is greatly wasted, were likewise made ready to be sent to furnish the wants [of the ships], and especially of such as be good ; for I dare assure your Honour, if you had seen that which I have seen, of the simple service that hath been done by the merchant and coast ships, you would have said that we had been little holpen by them, otherwise than that they did make a show. May it please your Honour, in this

---

[1] Wait for. Cf. *Troilus and Cressida*, I. i. 15 : 'He that will have a cake out of the wheat must needs tarry the grinding.'

case there would[1] be no sticking for charge; for if they [be] well handled at this time, I trust your Honour and I shall never be troubled whilst we live with them; nor the Queen's Majesty during all the years of her life, which, I trust in God, shall be many and happy.

Thus most humbly taking my leave, I desire God long to preserve you with health and good life. Written aboard the Vanguard in Harwich Road, this 1st of August, 1588, at 7 of the clock at night.

Your Honour's most assured to his power,

W. WYNTER.

August 1.—SEYMOUR TO WALSYNGHAM.

[ccxiv. 4.—Holograph.   Addressed :—For her Majesty's affairs.]

Sir :—Upon our present arrival at Harwich, the first of August, and since the time I despatched my former letters, there came Mr. Nicholas Gorges with seven merchant ships of London, nothing well manned, but better appointed of munition and powder, and victualled for one month, whereof one week is past.

They would gladly be resolved at my hands what I shall direct them for service, either for my Lord Admiral or the Narrow Seas; which, when I shall know your further pleasures, they shall be thereafter directed.

So having nothing else to trouble you, do take my leave. From aboard the Rainbow, this first of August, 1588.

Your assured friend to command,

H. SEYMOUR.

[1] Should.

I met with Mr. Gorges upon the seas, unknow-ing[1] of his being there till I came to Harwich.   Sir, the gentleman is frequented with his old infirmity of bleeding, and therefore [I] could wish another in his place; albeit I hardly believe you can match him about London.

August 2.—THE MAYOR AND CORPORATION OF WEYMOUTH TO THE COUNCIL.

[ccxiv. 11.—Signed.   Addressed.   Endorsed.]

Right Honourable Lords, our duties premised :— Whereas long sithence we have made humble suit unto your Lordships that this town might be pro-vided of ordnance to remain here to her Majesty's use, for some defence of town and country ; and, for the better use thereof, [we] have with great charge builded a platform ; which places, notwithstanding this dangerous time, and peril of this coast, are hitherto unprovided.   And for that the 22nd of July last, upon the first sight of the enemy in these parts, [we] have sent forth four ships and pinnaces in war-like sort, to join with our very good Lord, the Lord Admiral, manned with 300 men at the least, leaving our town destitute :—May it please your Lordships to be advertised that a great ship or carrack, taken from that enemy, arrived the 23rd of the said July into the road of Portland ; in which was ordnance, powder, shot, and other commodities, in some part unladen, as in an inventory herein enclosed may certify your Lordships, and to what uses the same hath hitherto been employed : And, for that certain ordnance therein are now landed, yet remaining in this place, and in our understanding, some part

[1] MS. unknowen.

thereof fit to remain here for her Majesty's behoof[1] and safeguard of the coast :

Our most humble request unto your Lordships is that, in respect of the necessity of our former suit therefor, and the present want of ordnance, as well in this as in other times that may happen of danger, some part of the same ordnance may, by your Lordships' warrant, be continued in this place ; the choice whereof in number or otherwise we commit to your honourable consideration.

And forasmuch as divers commodities, as we suppose,[2] in that carrack may perish, without great care had, and some part vendible in this place, if it might further please your Lordships that we may buy any such, or refuse, before other, at reasonable prices, to be rated by such as shall be therefor authorised, we shall acknowledge all duty unto our good Lords, and beseech God to increase victory over her Majesty's enemies.   And do take our leave. Weymouth and Melcombe Regis, the second of August, 1588.

Your Lordships' ready at all commands,

RICHARD PITT, Mayor.

WM. DOTHERELL.[3]	HUGH RENDOLL.
JOHN BROOKE.	JOHN MOKET,[5] Bailiff.
JOHN BELLPYTT.	WILLIAM PIT.
BARTHOLOMEW ALLEN.[4]	JOHN WADE.

[1] MS. behofe.   [2] Suppose = are informed.
[3] In 1599 signed Dottrell.   [4] In 1599 signed Allein.
[5] Mayor in 1599 (*S.P. Dom. Eliz.* cclxxii. 19 and 33, I.)

ARTICLES FOR EXAMINATION OF PRISONERS.

[ccxiv. 16.—Endorsed :—Articles appointed by the Lords of the Council for the Spanish prisoners to be examined upon.]

1. When the fleet came from Lisbon ?

2. Whether, at their coming to the seas, there was any proclamation or denunciation publicly made of hostilities with England. What was the contents of the same ; and, if it were done by writing, where is the same ?

3. Whether the intention of the fleet was to invade and conquer England or no ; and who should have had the principal charge of that enterprise ?

4. Where they should have landed ; and whether their meaning were to take the City of London ; and what they meant to have done if they had taken it ?

5. What they meant to do with the noblemen, gentlemen, and other subjects of quality, as well of our religion as of the other ?

6. What the Englishmen should have done that came with them ; and whether they had not especial direction whom they should spare and whom they should kill ; or where were they to receive it ; and what it was ?

7. What they have heard or know of any help or succour that they should receive upon their landing in England ?

8. What forces did they look for out of France to join with them ?

9. Whether the King of Spain would have retained this realm for himself, or given it to any other ; and who that is ?

10. What principal noblemen of the Spanish or Italian nation be in this fleet?

11. What Englishmen they know to be in this fleet?

12. What treasure was taken in the ship wherein they were taken?

13. What ordnance, armour, munition, and other furniture; victuals, armour &c., was therein?

14. What was the number of the vessels; and where they missed any?

15. Whether there be any other preparation to come hereafter for the defence of this fleet; and what number of men, ships, and furniture there are?

August 2.—EXAMINATION OF SPANISH PRISONERS.

[ccxiv. 17.]

August 2nd, 1588.—The examination of the Spanish prisoners in Bridewell, which were taken in the ship called the Nuestra Señora del Rosario of Ribadeo, in the parts of Galicia, of the burden of 1,150 tons.

Vicente Alvarez, captain of the said ship.

To the 1st, he saith they departed from Lisbon the 29th of May, *stilo novo.*[1]

To the 2nd, that about four or six days before they departed from the port of Lisbon, proclamation was made with the sound of three drums in every ship, by special persons thereunto appointed,

---

[1] It will be seen that the date of leaving Lisbon varies between the 29th and 30th N.S.—that is, the 19th and 20th. Presumably they did not all go out in one tide.

who had the same delivered them in writing by the Duke of Medina Sidonia, at the commandment of the King, that all such ships as should be taken that did properly appertain to the Queen of England should be adjudged to the King, with their whole furniture and ordnance &c. ; and all ships appertaining to particular persons should be adjudged prize to the taker thereof ; and that there was no other proclamation of hostility, whether in the city of Lisbon nor elsewhere, that he heard.

To the 3rd, he saith that they were specially directed unto the Duke of Parma, who by the general report was the man that should take upon him the conquest of England ; and that the Duke of Medina Sidonia had order to deliver his forces over unto the Duke of Parma, and to follow his directions in all things.

To the 4th, he saith that it was openly spoken that the place of their landing should be within the river of London ; and it was resolved by the whole company, as well captains as soldiers, that in what place soever they should enter within the land, to sack the same, either city, town, village, or whatsoever.

To the 5th, he saith that they were determined to put all to the sword that should resist them, but they had no particular charge to use greater extremity to one than to another.

To the 6th, he saith he brought seven or eight Englishmen in his ship, but he never understood of any particular order that was given to them, either for the sparing or killing of one more than another.

To the 7th, he saith it was commonly bruited amongst them that a third part or one half of the realm of England would join to their aid so soon as they should enter on the land.

To the 8th, he saith that it was certainly understood there that the Duke of Guise would aid them with 30,000 men ; and that being offered to be crowned King of France, refused the same till the wars were ended with England.

To the 9th, he saith that he knoweth not any certainty thereof, but it was a question among them that if the Duke of Parma should conquer this land, who should then enjoy it, either the King or the Duke? and it was suspected that it would breed a new war between them. He also heard that the King of Spain would establish the Inquisition in this realm.

To the 10th, he saith that there are of men of great title and of the principal blood in this Armada, to the number of 52 persons ; whereof are these following : Duke of Medina Sidonia ; Príncipe de Ascoli[1] ; Conde de Xelves ; the son and heir of the Conde de Lemos[2] ; the cousin of the Duke of Medina ; the Marquis of Peñafiel ; the Earl of Parades ; the sons of Ruy Gomez de Silva ; the sons of Don Diego de Cordova ; the sons of the Earl of Barajas ; Don Alonso Martinez de Leyva, &c.

To the 11th, he saith that he knoweth not any of the English more than those seven which came in his ship, whereof two had come to the Court, one with Sir Francis Drake, and the rest, William Stucley, the pilot of the ship, Richard Brierley, and one more, passed forth of the ship before they were taken, promising to fetch them more aid.

To the 12th, he saith there was in the ship wherein he was taken, a chest of the King's, wherein there was 52,000 ducats, of which chest Don Pedro de Valdes had one key, and the King's Treasurer

[1] Antonio Luis de Leyva, Príncipe de Ascoli.
[2] D. Pedro de Castro.

or the Duke, another; besides 4,000 rials of this examinant's, and many other of the gentlemen had good store of money aboard the said ship. Also there was wrought plate of the Duke's and Don Pedro, but to what value he knoweth not ; and that there was great store of precious jewels and rich apparel ; and thinketh there was not four ships so rich in the whole armada.

To the 13th, he saith that there was in his ship 58 pieces of brass ordnance of the King's, great and small, of which the Duke commanded forth seven or eight of them into a pinnace; so as, he saith, there was 50 pieces, whereof some weighed 75 quintals,[1] 70, 65, 60, and the least 18 quintals, and to every piece, 200 pellets of iron at the least, and powder, 100 quintals. Corslets, 150; pikes, 250; calivers and muskets, 493, with swords and daggers. Wine of Xeres, Candy,[2] and Ribadavia, 130 or 140 pipes; vinegar, 10 pipes; oil, 2 pipes; rice, 16 pipes; beef, 10 pipes; fish, 3 pipes; biscuit, 700 quintals; neats' tongues and bacon, 3 pipes; calves, 3; sheep, 50. All which was left by them aboard when they were taken.

To the 14th, he saith that there were 152 sail of ships and galleys, great and small, which came out of the Groyne in Galicia; whereof there was but four galleys in all, and they were wanting, and two pinnaces, when they met with the English fleet.

To the 15th, he saith that there were, at their departure, 14 or 16 sail of great ships, from 800 to 1,000 ton, in preparation at Lisbon, to bring victual and furniture to the aid of this armada; and saith that there are with them, of all nations, English, Irish, Scottish, Flemish, French, and Italians; but what number he knoweth not.

[1] She had no guns of this weight. See *post*, August 29.
[2] Candia.

[The other examinants are Juan de Viana, master of the said ship; Gongoro, doctor of physic; Joseph Pelegrin, sergeant of the company to Don Alonzo de Gayas; Diego de Campos, a soldier; Marcos de Aybar, sergeant of a band; Don Sancho Pardo; Mateo de Fries, a soldier; Gregorio de Sotomayor, Portuguese; Alonzo de la Serna de Safra, entretenido; Luis de Ribera, del Puerto de Santa Maria; Alonzo Vazquez de Jaen; Pedro Martin Cabrito de Eijha. Their answers are not so full as those of Vicente Alvarez, but are in essential agreement. Another deposition of Gregorio de Sotomayor is given.

The examination of Giovanni Gaietano (ccxiv. 18), in Italian, sergeant of the company of Pedro de Leon, on board the Capitana of D. Pedro de Valdes, has no particular interest.]

CONFESSION OF GREGORIO DE SOTOMAYOR.

[**ccxiv. 19.**—Englished. The original Portuguese has not been preserved.]

The voluntary confession of Gregorio de Sotomayor, written under his own hand in the Portingal tongue, and translated verbatim.

To the 1st, that I am called Gregory de Sotomayor; and my brother's name, Stephen de Sotomayor, naturals of the town of Melgaço, in the kingdom of Portugal. My father's name was Gonçalo de Sotomayor, and my mother was called Lady Mary de Orasto. Trade or occupation, we have none; but do live by our goods and rents.

To the 2nd, where the soldiers were levied? I answer that at the time when they were prepared, I was at mine own house, which is 70 leagues from Lisbon, so that I knew not from whence nor where they were provided. In the kingdom of Portugal there was no preparation of men; but when they embarked themselves, they commanded 2,000 Portingals to go aboard upon pain of death.

To the 3rd, I answer that we set sail out of Lisbon the 28th of May, being in all 130 ships; and that there was in them 35,000 men in all, whereof 20,000 were fighting soldiers. We came to the Groyne, but what time I remember not. There we took in fresh victuals, as beef, water, fish, oils, and vinegar; from thence we set sail for this coast, to have joined with the Duke of Parma.

To the 4th, I say it was muttered among the soldiers that, joining with the Duke of Parma, they would divide their people into two parts; and that the one part should have come directly for London, and for the other, there was no speech whither they should go.

To the 5th, I say the common report was that in the realm there would rise great store of people in the favour of the King of Spain, but especially in this city of London; and the report was there should be in all 15,000 men.

To the 6th, concerning what treasure there was in the fleet, I say there was great stores of money and plate which came in the galleon wherein the Duke de Medina was, and in the ship of Don Pedro de Valdes which was taken, and in the admiral of the galleasses, and in the galley royal, and in the vice-admiral wherein was general John Martinez de Recalde, and in the vice-admiral whereof was general Diego Flores, and in the vice-admiral of the pinnaces, and in the vice-admiral of the hulks, and in a Venetian ship in whom came for general Don Alonso de Leyva. The report goeth that this ship brought great store, for that there came in her the Prince of Ascoli, and many other noblemen. This is all I know touching the treasure.

To the 7th, whether I know of any traitors? I say I do not know any, but would be glad to have known them, for to have given her Majesty understanding of them, as a good Portingal. And for the 30 ships which the report goeth are to come with succour for this fleet, it is said they bring great stores of treasure. This is all that I know as well of the interrogatories as otherwise, which I ratify with that which heretofore being examined I have said ; and would be glad that I knew more, both for the service of her Majesty and preservation of this kingdom.

I declare further that King Philip did command that the fleet should be victualled for 6 months, but Luis Hezar and Francisco Duarte of Cadiz did victual them but for 4 months, and with that which was nought and rotten. For which occasion the King commanded them to be apprehended ; and so they remained prisoners in Portugal at our coming away. And this is the very truth.

August 2.—*ARTICLES FOR THE EXAMINATION OF PRISONERS.*

[ccxiv. 20.—Autograph of Lord Burghley.]

In what place and time was the war published by the King against England ; and in what sort was the army limited to make advantage of their victories, of ships, of treasure ; and what part thereof should be to the King ; and what to the General, Admiral, and to the takers ?

How was it meant the spoils of London and other towns should be parted ; and what profit should be reserved for the King? Whether it was meant to have taken any to ransom or no ?

If they had possessed England, what was meant towards Scotland, and to the King, being of the religion?

In what sort was meant to have preceded with Ireland?

To inquire of him who were his first takers; what quantity of treasure he had on shipboard; to whom it was delivered?

What might be the value of the spoil of his ship?

ARTICLES FOR THE EXAMINATION OF PRISONERS.

[ccxiv. 21.]

Articles to be ministered to Don Pedro de Valdes and his associates.

1. What was the end and purpose of the King of Spain his sending so great an army by sea into these parts?

2. If his purpose were to invade the realm, with what honour and conscience the King could do the same, considering that her Majesty refused the sovereignty of the Low Countries, being offered sundry times unto her, as well by the general provinces[1] as the united provinces?

3. At what time the examinate was made privy that the investiture of this crown was conferred by the Pope upon the King of Spain, or upon that prince that should marry the King's daughter, and who that prince is?

[1] The 'general provinces' would seem to mean the provinces singly, as Holland, Zealand &c.; the 'united provinces' are the collective body.

4. Whether it were resolved that the said King should retain the crown, or the prince should have it that should marry his daughter?

5. How and in what sort they meant to have dealt with the King of Scots, who pretendeth to be a successor to this crown?

6. What princes Catholics were parties or contributories to this enterprise, and what each of them did contribute, upon what conditions, and what support they look for out of France, from whom, and from what place?

7. Whether they had any direction to harbour in France, in what place, and whether the same were with the French King's privity and assent?

8. Whether they had any direction to repair into Scotland, to what place, and what party they looked for to have had there?

9. Which were their two places where they should have made their descent here in this realm; how, by whom, and with what numbers the same should have been made, and what party they did look for here?

10. When the wars were proclaimed against England, and in what sort?

11. Whether, after their departure from Lisbon and their repair to the Groyne, they had any consultation whether it were fit to proceed in the enterprise or not; and whether they did impart unto their said King their resolution, and what direction they received thereupon from him?

12. Whether they had any intelligence that the Lord Admiral was in Plymouth before their departure from the Groyne; by whom they had the said intelligence; whether they had any meaning to attempt anything against him there?

13. What were the numbers of their ships at the time of their departure from Lisbon, and what were

the number of soldiers, mariners, and voluntaries in the same?

14. What money, jewels, and plate was in the ship wherein he was taken, and to whom the same was delivered at the time of his taking, and to whom he yielded prisoner?

15. What number of ships were prepared with men, munition, and victuals to be sent after them; and in what place they were prepared, and to what place they were directed to repair?

16. Which of the Englishmen in the army were privy to the secrets of the enterprise?

17. Whether there was any intent to attempt anything in Ireland; how, by whom, and with what forces?

August 4.—EXAMINATION OF DON PEDRO DE VALDES.

[ccxiv. 22.—Signed. Spanish.]

Examination of Don Pedro de Valdes, taken on the 4th of August, 1588.

1. He saith that the King sent this armada to the Prince of Parma for to clear the way, so as he might land in this kingdom and conquer it.

2. He saith that it lieth not with him to answer if the King did well or ill, being a subject, and unable to judge the actions of his prince.

3, 4, 5. He denieth any knowledge thereof; except that it was reported the Duke of Guise should have an understanding with the King of Spain in favour of the King of Scotland.

6. He answers that he hath no knowledge thereof.

7. He saith that they had no intention to touch at any port in France.

8. He saith that he knoweth not of any order to land in Scotland.

9. He saith that for the place where they were to land, it would be ordered by the Prince of Parma ; except that if they met with foul weather, they intended to anchor at the Isle of Wight for to repair their damage.

10. He saith that he knoweth not if war had been declared.

11. He saith that off of the Groyne they met with a tempest, by which the greater number of their ships were dispersed, whereof the most part put into havens on the coast of Biscay, others in Asturias, and others came on this coast ; after the which they took counsel whether they should proceed or no, and it was resolved to collect the whole army together and proceed ; which they notified the King of the same, who sent them order to do as they had resolved.

12. He saith that they received advertisement in Spain that the English fleet was at Plymouth, and should permit them to pass for to follow them. That on coming near this coast they took a fisher-man, which told them that the said fleet was at Plymouth ; whereupon the Duke called a council to consider of entering there and conquering the said fleet ; and this examinate was of opinion that it was not fitting to do so, because that the fleet was within the haven, whereof the mouth is so strait as not more than two or three ships could go in abreast, which was insufficient for that action.

13. The number of vessels, as well of great ships as of galleys and galleasses, should be about 100 ; of other vessels there might be 40. Of soldiers, sailors, gentlemen in the pay of the King, and volunteers, there were 29,000.

14. He saith there were near 20,000 ducats, as also vessels of silver worth another thousand.

15. He saith that ten ships were being made ready at Lisbon; he knoweth not how many were being armed in Andalusia; and they should receive order at the Groyne what they would do.

16. He saith that none of the English are privy to the design &c.

17. He saith there was not.

18. He saith that he knoweth not of any promise to take up arms in favour of the King.

19. He saith that the Duke of Parma hath 36,000 men, as well footmen as horsemen; and some vessels, but small and only meet for transport.

20. He saith that there was no order taken for the spoil on land.

21. He saith that the Duke of Parma sent a fly-boat to Lisbon to understand the state of the fleet, as also the cause of their so long stay; and that in company with the said flyboat, the Duke of Medina sent a pinnace[1] to the Duke of Parma, which did not return.

22. He saith that they have few pilots, whereof the most part are Spaniards and unexpert; and that there are few mariners.

23. He saith that when they parted from the Groyne they had victual for four to four and a half months, and water for three months.

August 3.—WM. BORLAS TO WALSYNGHAM.

[**Holland, lvi.**—Signed. Addressed.]

Right Honourable :—The last of July my Lord Governor was advertised by a small boat that came from the sea that there was one great ship of the

[1] MS. *zabra.*

Spaniards lying between Ostend and the Sluys. Whereupon my Lord sent out presently three men-of-war that lie here before the town, and I myself went out in them ; so that the same day about one of the clock we came where he was, having been beaten and dispersed from the fleet by her Majesty's ships ; yet he fought with us two hours, and hurt divers of our men ; but at the last yielded himself. The commander in her was Don Alonso[1] de Pimentel, the son and heir of the Marquis de Tavara. There was another marquis's son in her, and divers particular gentlemen of good account. I was the means that the best sort were saved ; and the rest were cast overboard and slain at the entry. There was slain in her two Englishmen ; the one was a brother of my Lord Mountagu's, as your Honour shall see by a letter that I found in the ship.

The same morning there was driven ashore between Nieuport and Ostend another great ship, where there was all the commanders that were in her fetched ashore by them of Nieuport. These are the names of them that were in her :—The Marquis de Peñafiel ; Don Francisco de Bobadilla, Master de Campo General ; a son[2] of Don Diego de Cordova, Master of the Horse to the King, and a great personage of their religion. The ships both are brought in here, with great store of ordnance and munition in them. This, with my most humble duty, I leave your Honour to the Almighty God. Flushing, the 3rd of August, 1588.

Your Honour's most dutiful to command,

WYLLIAM BORLAS.

[1] In error for Don Diego, camp-master of the Tercio de Sicilia, serving on board the San Mateo (Duro, ii. 77, 285).

[2] D. Felipe de Cordova ; according to Duro (ii. 66–7), both he and Peñafiel were in the San Marcos ; Bobadilla was with the Duke in the San Martin (ii. 246, 372).

August 3.—*WYLLUGHBY*[1] *TO WALSYNGHAM.*

[**Holland, lvi.**—Signed.   Addressed.]

Sir :—This morning I arrived here, having by a contrary wind staid on shipboard these two days and two nights.   I had well hoped that the men sent for hence had been despatched away before my coming, having been here three days at the least; but I find it far otherwise, neither any shipping provided for them.   I hope now there will be no great need to use them, seeing it hath pleased God so well to bless us and prevent the enemy's intention. Nevertheless, I will do my best to send them away presently, according to their Lordships' order.   But if there shall be no great need of employing them there, it were very needful they were returned hither again; for the enemy will not be idle, but, to repair their honour, will attempt something presently; and the want of them may greatly hazard some place of importance.

Upon my arrival here, I understand that the Duke of Parma, upon advertisement of the success of their fleet, hath earnestly protested to take revenge of these countries and islands.   In the meantime, he hath disarmed the burghers in the most towns they hold, by reason whereof great discontentment is fallen amongst them; and the mariners, which he had got together to be employed at sea, refuse the service, and are grown into a

---

[1] Peregrine Bertie, Lord Willoughby, or—as he chose to spell it—Wyllughby, of Eresby, the 'brave Lord Willoughby' of the ballad, was born in 1555.   At this time he was Lord General of the Queen's forces in the Low Countries.   He died in 1601, and was buried at Spilsby in Lincolnshire, where there is a monument to his memory.   His eldest son Robert, created Earl of Lindsay in 1626, was Admiral and Captain General at Sea in 1635.

mutiny.   The Duke himself hath thereupon ordered
to be slain ten or twelve of them ; but the rest, notwithstanding, are retired and dispersed, and refuse
to serve in that sort.

Those that are taken here cry out upon the
Duke of Parma, that they are betrayed by him,
because they were not seconded according to their
expectation.

And so leaving the success of all things to the
good pleasure of the Almighty, I commend you also
to his most holy protection.

From Middelburg, the 3rd of August, 1588.

Yours to be commanded,

P. WYLLUGHBY.

August 3.—*KYLLYGREW TO WALSYNGHAM.*

[**Holland, lvi.**—Signed.]

It may please your Honour :—In my last unto
your Honour, dated the last of July, I gave you to
understand of the President Vandermyle's motion
made in council, upon the report of a great battle
between her Majesty's navy and the Spanish.
Yesterday were assembled together about the same
matter all the colleges : the Council of Estate, the
States General, the States of Holland, the Council
of the High Court, and of the Provincial ; whom
the President Vandermyle, with a forcible and wise
oration, persuaded to this effect :—That, considering
the enemy hath stretched himself farther at this
time than heretofore, by raising of extraordinary
power both by sea and land for the invasion of
England, as it is thought, and consequently the
ruin and overthrow of these provinces, it might
please them to consider how necessary it were for

them, by some extraordinary means, to provide for
their own defence ; and if heretofore, at sundry
times, the private danger of some particular cities,
as of Haerlem, Leyden, Antwerp, and now lastly of
Gertruidenberg (which yet could not so nearly touch
the common cause), have moved them willingly to
bear a great charge, how much more now at this
time, when they see the enemy shoot directly at the
main mark, ought they to force themselves, and in
courage, forwardness, and liberality, to overcome
themselves in the defence of their lives, of their
wives and children, of their privileges and liberties,
of their religion and the cause of God, which, as
they have hitherto maintained so many years against
a prince so mighty, not by their own power, but
by the wonderful hand of God, so were all their
pains, all their charges utterly lost, if now at the
last gasp they should seem to relent.   And whereas
the enemy hath now advanced himself so far as to
come even before their doors, and, if he had not
found resistance of her Majesty's navy, might have
entered into their coast long ere this, if now in this
time of extremity they shall not yield some special
testimony of their forwardness to assist her Majesty
in the common defence, how just occasion shall be
given her more sparingly to afford them any aid
hereafter ; whereas no doubt, by their willingness
at this present, her Highness may be induced to
continue her favour towards them with increase.
The sum of all was this : that for the furnishing of
40 ships more it was necessary to levy some two
hundred thousand florins.   The motion was generally allowed, and the Council themselves, who
never heretofore have been taxed in such kind of
extraordinary contributions, have been contented at
this time to bear part of the charge for example to
the rest.

Now, what report cometh unto us here touching the Spanish fleet and her Majesty's, your Honour may perceive by the enclosed. I did also see a letter from the Admiral Justinus to Count Maurice, written the next day after the fight between Dover and Calais, wherein he signified 14 of her Majesty's navy were come to assist him[1] before Dunkirk, and protested he was resolved there to live and die.

The ships of North Holland, understanding the enemy was so near, made some stay to go to the fleet, but are now purposed, out of an hundred sail which lie in the Vlie, to send thirty choice ships thither, which they say shall be ready within 10 days. Her Majesty's letter unto them of Gertruidenberg was most acceptable to these men, and they would fain have had the original, as I suppose, to refute all such as might hereafter stand upon the like terms, under pretence of her Majesty's name ; but my Lord General excused himself, and gave them a copy. They do not find it convenient to deliver the letter, now that all matters at Gertruidenberg are appeased. For the effectuating of the President Vandermyle's motion, the Council are to take their journey some into one quarter, and some into another. The Chancellor of Gueldres[2] and myself are appointed to Utrecht, whither this day (3 *Augusti*) we are going.

Thus, with remembrance of my most humble duty to your Honour, I beseech the Almighty to preserve continually both you and yours. At the Hague, the 3rd of August.

Your Honour's most assuredly to be commanded,

H. KYLLYGREW.

---

[1] There is no mention of this in the letters from the fleet. They must have been some of the small craft, apt enough for such service, but useless in the clash of contending fleets.

[2] Or Gelderland.

It may please your Honour to impart the substance of these unto the rest of my Lords, with excuse that I cannot at this, being on my journey, write particularly to their Lordships.

August 4.—LEICESTER TO WALSYNGHAM.

[ccxiv. **23.**—Signed. Addressed.]

Mr. Secretary :—Your letters dated yesterday at the Court I received this morning at the camp. And albeit I do think that you have received such news as be brought me before this time, yet, notwithstanding, I will advertise [you] thereof likewise ; which is, besides the certainty of the Earl of Derby's arrival with [the] rest of the Commissioners at Dover yesterday, that upon Friday [1] last, two of the greatest carracks that the King of Spain had in his fleet, being scattered [2] from the rest, made the best sail they could to recover the Escluse [3] haven ; but being discovered by some Flushingers, they made out, with all the speed they could, certain men-of-war, which did encounter and fight with them ; but the carracks being great vessels, well manned and full of good artillery, defended themselves until certain other men-of-war, Zealanders that rid before Dunkirk and Flanders coast, hearing the fight, came to their aid ; and yet, nevertheless, these carracks fought it out until they saw no remedy ; but in the end they were taken and brought to Flushing, where they now be. This is written unto me for certain, and I do not doubt but that it is true. Thus

[1] By Borlas's letter (*ante*, p. 29) and Howard's Abstract (*post*, p. 58) it was on Wednesday.
[2] Separated. Cf. vol. i. p. 359.   [3] Sluys.

for the present I commit you to God.   In haste, at
Tilbury Camp, this 4th of August, 1588.

Your very loving friend,

R. LEYCESTER.

August 4.—SEYMOUR TO WALSYNGHAM.

[**ccxiv. 26.**—Holograph.   Addressed.]

Sir :—By the receipt of your two last letters
dated the 2nd of August, and sent by my servant
Floyd, it seemeth her Majesty is graciously pleased
with the service which happened the 29th of July
last past, which advantage God forbid our enemies
had had the like of us ; but I hope God alone doth
fight for us.

Concerning Mr. Nicholas Gorges' infirmity, his
good will and care is such to prefer her Majesty's
service, that I doubt both the gentleman and the
service ; and therefore would gladly favour him,
wishing he might be discharged by your honourable
direction.   Likewise, if you shall think it good, Mr.
Thomas Knyvet,[1] that hath accompanied him ever
since, may very well be admitted for sufficient among
a great many that have been allowed most serviceable.

As touching the Lords Commissioners, if you
had not forewarned me to have had care of them, I

---

[1] Probably Thomas Knyvet of Buckenham, knighted in 1603.
He was the grandson and representative of that Sir Thomas
Knyvet who perished in the burning of the Regent off Brest in
1512, and of Muriel, the sister of Sir William Howard, father of the
Lord Admiral and of the wife of Seymour's brother, the Earl of
Hertford.   It may, however, have been another Thomas Knyvet,
knighted in 1604, and raised to the peerage as Baron Knyvet of
Escrick in 1607.   He also was the grandson of the captain of the
Regent, and his relationship to Howard and Seymour was the
same as that of his cousin.

had not failed to have done my part therein, had I been a stranger unto them, in respect of the honour of her Majesty and my country.

I have likewise advertised Justinus de Nassau of our late conflicts, wishing[1] him to stand upon his guard, and that we will be ready to assist him with the next favourable winds.

I am likewise advertised that these Hollanders have lighted upon these argosies which we did distress, and that they have received great spoil thereof.

Thus, praying that God may continue these violent and strong winds to the further distressing of the Spaniards, do leave you to your infinite cares of this troublesome time. From aboard the Rainbow, this 4th of August, 1588, in Margate Road, at 11 of the clock in the night.

Your assured friend to command,

H. SEYMOUR.

If you think the [ships[2]] shall need any further supply of victuals, it would be considered in time; for, as I take it, Mr. Gorges' company do expire 3 weeks hence, and we have taken in our victuals at Harwich the 3rd of this month of August, which is almost 8 days difference.

I have not yet received my Lords' other letters, which you should[3] send me by my lieutenant.

August 4.—*FENNER TO WALSYNGHAM*

[ccxiv. 27.—Holograph. Addressed.]

Right Honourable :—I assure myself you are ascertained of our encounters with the enemy on

---

[1] Wishing=praying, desiring.　　[2] Word omitted in MS.
[3] I was told you would send.

Monday, the 29th of July, in long continuance and great force of shot on both sides ; many of their ships wonderfully spoiled and beaten, to the utter ruin of three of the greatest sort, beside the cutting off the galleass, the enemy thereby greatly weakened.

A thing greatly to be regarded, that the Almighty hath stricken them with a wonderful fear ; in that I hardly have seen any of their companies succoured of their extremities which befell them after their fights, but left at utter ruin, without regard,[1] bearing always as much sail as possible they might, holding the rest of their army together. The[2] want of powder, and shot, and victual hath hindered much service which otherwise might have been performed in continuance with them, to their utter subversion in keeping them from water. There were many ships in our fleet not possessed with three days' victuals.

The causes aforesaid considered in council, the second of this instant in the morning, pursuing the enemy until we came into 55 degrees and about two and thirty leagues from our coast in that height : it was thought meet for the safety of men's lives and shipping, the wind being southerly, to shape our course for the Frith in Scotland, to relieve our wants with water and such other things as the benefit of that place would yield, thereby to attain that place for the better regard both of England and Scotland.

It was intended, at our coming thither, that my Lord of Cumberland should have passed unto the King of Scots, to acquaint his Majesty of the accidents that had happened ; as also to stir his Majesty to provide some defensive power, if the enemy should draw unto his coasts ; wherein her Majesty's power should assist with all their force.

Two pinnaces were left to follow the fleet afar

[1] Notice taken of them.   [2] Our.

off, until they[1] were shot[2] beyond the Isles of Orkneys and Shetland, unto which place they continued their courses. And if, by any change of wind, they shaped their course otherwise, then, if wind would permit, the pinnaces [were] to advertise us at the Firth; and[3] not finding us there, to come alongst our own coast with the advertisement.

The 2nd of August, about 12 of the clock at noon, we hauled west, the better to recover our coast to attain the Frith, the enemy going away North-West and by North, as they did before.

Being hauled in fifteen leagues west, the 3rd of August in the morning, about ten of the clock, the wind came up at North-West. Counsel therefore taken—it was thought meet to take the benefit thereof for our reliefs of powder, shot, and victual, and so as to bear with all possible speed to the North Foreland; and as[4] if the enemy should return, we might be beforehand furnished of some of our wants, the readier thereby to offend[5] them.

I will deliver your Honour mine opinion, wherein I beseech your pardon if it fall out otherwise. I verily believe[6] great extremity shall force them if they behold England in sight again. By all that I can gather, they are weakened of eight of their best sorts of shipping, which contained many men; as also many wasted in sickness and slaughter. Their masts and sails much spoiled; their pinnaces and boats, many cast off and wasted; wherein they shall find great wants when they come to land and water,

[1] Sc. the Spaniards.
[2] Advanced, got. Cf. vol. i. p. 242, where the word is used in the same sense, also by Fenner.
[3] Or, if they did not find. [4] So that.
[5] Compare Milton, *Paradise Lost*, i. 187 : 'Consult how we may henceforth most offend our enemy.'
[6] That unless great extremity force them, they will not behold &c.

which they must do shortly or die; and where or
how, my knowledge cannot imagine. As the wind
serveth,[1] no place but between the Foreland and
Hull. Considering the shallows and sands[2] not
greatly to be doubted, the hugeness and great
draught of water in their ships considered, and
otherwise the wind as it is at North-West, they
have no place to go withal, but for the Scaw in
Denmark, which were an hard adventure as the
season[3] of the year approacheth. If the wind by
change suffer them, I verily believe they will pass
about Scotland and Ireland to draw themselves
home; wherein, the season of the year considered,
with the long course they have to run and their
sundry distresses, and—of necessity—the spending
of time by watering, winter will so come on as it
will be to their great ruin.

God hath mightily protected her Majesty's forces
with the least losses that ever hath been heard of,
being within the compass of so great volleys of shot,
both small and great. I verily believe there is not
three score men lost of her Majesty's forces. God
make us and all her Majesty's good subjects to
render hearty praise and thanks unto the Lord of
Lords therefor.

I will ever hold myself bound for your honourable and godly points in your letter of the 25th of
July, so as to depend upon the good providence of
God, unto whom I will, both in season and out of
season, call upon him, with a faithful assurance that
he will defend his from the raging enemy who
goeth about to beat down his word and devour
his people. My trust is their imaginations shall fall
upon themselves, as a just plague for their wicked-

---

[1] With the wind at N.W. by N., they can fetch no place but &c.
[2] The influence or effect of which is not greatly &c.
[3] Sc. the bad season.

ness and idolatry. God continue me such as your expectation in me and other of my name be not deceived ; and that we may continue as faithful servants and subjects to her Majesty ; not regarding the peril of life, to slack any one jot in that is meet for men to do in this her Majesty's needful service. God mightily defend my gracious mistress from the raging enemy ; not doubting but that all the world shall know and see that her Majesty's little army, guided by the finger of God, shall beat down the pride of his enemies and hers, to his great glory ; unto whom I betake your Honour. From aboard the good ship of her Majesty the Nonpareil, this 4th of August, 1588.

Your Honour's in all love and
duty for ever to command,
THOMAS FENNER.

Within two hours after the writing of this letter the wind came up at South-West, so as thereby the enemy was able neither to seize [1] England, Ireland, Scotland, Flanders, and hardly the out isles of Scotland. This 4th day and 5th, especially at night, continued very great storm at South-West, [we] being forced to ride out in the sea the extremity thereof. Which storm hath, in mine opinion, touched the enemy very near ; for divers considerations following viz. : the great sea-gate [2] about those isles ; the hugeness of their shipping, who were so light as in fair weather would hardly bear their topsails ; also the cold climate they are in toucheth them near, and will do daily more and more. Mine opinion is they are by this time so distressed, being

[1] 'Seize' appears to be used in the same sense as recover, or as the modern 'make' or 'fetch.'

[2] Swell ; cf. Manwayring, 85 : 'There can no great sea-gate come in.' 'Gate' means going, motion, and 'sea-gate' may be compared with the modern 'sea-way,' or 'run of the sea.'

so far thrust off, as many of them will never see Spain[1] again; which is the only work of God, to chastise their malicious practices, and to make them know that neither the strengths of men, nor their idolatrous gods can prevail, when the mighty God of Israel stretcheth out but his finger against them. God make all her Majesty's good subjects thankful.

THOMAS FENNER.

August 4.—BOROUGH TO WALSYNGHAM.

[**ccxiv. 24.**—Signed. Addressed :—For the affairs of her Majesty. Deliver this to the post at Rochester. Minuted :—Received at Rochester by a sailor which came afoot the 5th day of August at 8 in the forenoon.]

After my duty unto your Honour in most humble wise duly considered :—I have received from your Honour two letters; one, by my servant, bearing date the 30th of July; the other, of the first of this month, from the Court at St. James; which last came by way of post to Margate, and from Margate was sent me by water, which I received here yesterday in the forenoon; whereby I understand that Captain Bellingham hath the charge of ten merchant ships, with which he is appointed to go to the coast of Flanders, to join there with the Hollanders and Zealanders for keeping in the forces of the Duke of Parma at Dunkirk and Nieuport; and that my Lords of the Council have appointed me, with the galley, to continue at the Land's End,[2] to give warning to the army now lying at Tilbury, in case the Duke of Parma should, with the help of an easterly wind, slip upon this coast.

I suppose my Lords' and your Honour's meaning

[1] MS. Spayngne.
[2] The Land's End in Sheppey is Shell Ness.

is, that I should remain with the galley here, where I am ; which I mean to do. But because the last letter, sent by way of post, was directed to Margate, I may doubt that the Land's End [1] therein specified might be meant the point of Thanet by Margate, and if it be so, I will remove thither when I shall understand your further pleasure therein.

My purpose is, if I shall perceive the forces of the Duke of Parma to approach this place, to go up the river before the same ; and by the way to be shooting off great ordnance, to give warning, to the country and army at Tilbury, of the coming of the enemy, until I come as high as Gravesend, where I purpose to stay and stop a gap with the galley, at anchor or otherwise, between the two blockhouses there, with her prow towards the enemy, to join with those forts to impeach their landing and passage higher up the river. Where if I be not spoiled and overthrown by the enemy, and that they pass by that place up the river towards London, I will follow after them, by the permission of the Almighty, and will do them what spoil I can, so long as life shall last.

There are now riding against Leigh ten ships, which I suppose are those that Mr. Bellingham hath charge of. Captain Gorges, with seven ships, and certain hoys and barks laden with victuals for the Lord Henry Seymour and his fleet, put off from the North Foreland on Thursday last at night, to seek the Lord Admiral. The Lord Henry Seymour with his fleet (for want of victuals) put into Harwich upon Thursday last. I pray God bless her Majesty and all her forces, and send happy success and victory over our enemies.

Written aboard the galley, at anchor in the mouth of Thames, between the Land's End in

[1] Probably Fore Ness.

Sheppey and Little Wakering in Essex, the 4th of
August, 1588, at 8 of the clock in the forenoon.
                Your Honours' most humble and
                                ever ready at command,
                                        W. Borough.

Postscript, on the outside.—The ten ships set sail
at Leigh to come down the river, after this letter
was sealed.   W. B.

*August 6.—SEYMOUR, WYNTER, AND PALMER
                TO THE COUNCIL.*

[**ccxiv. 39.**—Signed.   Addressed.]

We have received your Lordships' letters, dated
at St. James the 4th of this present, delivered unto
us by John Wynter, riding between Margate and
the North Foreland, and troubled with a great
storm at the WSW., by the which it appeareth
that her Majesty would have us to consider upon a
fit strength to be left here in the Narrow Seas, for
the keeping in of the Prince of Parma, to be left
under the government of Sir Henry Palmer, knight ;
and that I, the Lord Henry Seymour, with Sir
William Wynter and the rest, should repair to the
North parts, for the better strengthening of the Lord
Admiral.   Whereupon conference hath been held
among us, to the which the wisest, skilfullest
masters and pilots of our companies hath been
called.
        First, it may please your Lordships to under-
stand that the last news we had of the Lord
Admiral being with our army was by a ship that
came to Harwich upon Friday last ; who declared
that the Wednesday before, about 3 of the clock

in the afternoon, he saw the Lord Admiral with his
army athwart of Yarmouth, more than half seas
over, bearing after the Spanish army, the wind
being then by the South-East, a indifferent wind to
have gone to the North or else to the South. But
he said the Spanish army bare away, with all the
sails they were able to make, North and by West ;
which doth argue a meaning in them not to return,
as we conjecture ; since which time the wind hath
been continually between the SSW. and WSW.,
blowing for the most part a storm, so that we do
reckon them to be very far to the northwards.
Emden or Hamburg we think they dare not bear
withal, with ships of such charge as they have ; and
then must they be forced to go with the Skaw, or
to bear, with some of the south winds, in Norway ;
for we think they can fett[1] no part of Scotland,
because that they are ships of no vantage in sailing. And if we should go the northwards to seek
the Lord Admiral, it would be a great chance
for us to meet his Lordship, the odds of ten to
one.

The weather hath been such as no man hath
been able to look upon the coast of Flanders this
seven or eight days past ; nor yet that any there
hath or can put forth. And if there were any
Flushingers or Hollanders attending about Dunkirk,
as it seemeth by your Lordships' letters that there
was, we do assure ourselves this weather, which of
late hath happened, hath put them all roome with[2]
Flushing. Herewithal your Lordships shall receive
a note of such ships of war as are now in our
company.

Your Lordships shall understand that, in plying
to get the North Foreland from Harwich, the

[1] Fetch.
[2] Hath forced them all to bear up for Flushing.

Vanguard hath spent her main topmast, the weather
was such ; which, by God's favour, shall be supplied
from Sandwich with a new one to-morrow ; and then,
although this wind be westerly, which doth keep in
the Dunkirkers and all those upon that coast, yet
we mean to show ourselves there, that they may
know we are ready to receive them, if their stomachs
will serve them to come forth when they have
opportunity of weather.

This long foul weather past may breed a later
summer ; wherefore we humbly pray your Lordship
that ye will send us victuals from time to time, as
we may make a reckoning never to have less in us
than three weeks' victuals at the least.   Also we
humbly pray your Lordships that there may be sent
us by the officers of the Tower, 500 ells of canvas ;
as also 200 quires of paper royal for to make
cartridges.

And lastly, for our opinions : If your Lordships
keep this force here in strength, with such help as
the Hollanders and Flushingers may join to ours,
we hope in God to put Parma and his consorts
besides all his Italian devices.   We know that the
Lord Admiral's purpose, at our departing, was not
to urge any further fighting with the Spanish army,
but to follow them, and to make head if need were ;
and for that purpose his Lordship's strength was
sufficient, as it was thought by my Lord and his
council.   And weighing the uncertainty of our
meeting with his Lordship, if we should seek after
him, and the certain service we shall be able to do
here, we conclude that it is better for us to keep our
strength here than otherwise to put it to hazard.
Nevertheless, we are to obey your Lordships'
pleasures.   So most humbly taking our leaves, do
beseech God long to preserve her Majesty and your
Lordships.   Written in the Downs, aboard the

Rainbow (with the wind West-South-West), the 6th of August, 1588.

Your Lordships' humbly to command,

H. SEYMOUR.

W. WYNTER.   HENRY PALMER.

August 6.—A LIST OF SHIPS WITH LORD HENRY SEYMOUR.

[**ccxiv. 39, I.**—Enclosed in the foregoing.]

The 6th of August, *anno* 1588.

A note of the names of all the ships that are now serving her Majesty under my charge, viz. :—

The Rainbow.

Vanguard.
Antelope.
Tiger.
Bull.
Scout.
Tramontana.
Achates.
Spy, absent by leave.
Merlin.

The Sun.

Fancy, absent by leave.
Cygnet.
George Hoy, absent at Flushing.
Bonavolia, absent at Nore-head.
Brigandine.

Coast Ships.

Hull . . .	The Griffin. Little Hare. Handmaid.
Ipswich and Harwich	William. Katharine. Primrose.
Hastings	Anne Bonaventure.
Rye	William.
Hythe	Grace of God.

Dover	The Elizabeth.[1]
Sandwich . . .	Reuben.
Feversham . . .	Hazard, absent at Harwich.
Yarmouth . . .	Grace.
Lynn . . .	Mayflower.
Colchester . . .	William.
Chichester and Romney .	John.

Ships which came from London under the charge of Mr. Nicholas Gorges, Esquire :—

The Susan Parnell.	The George Bonaventure.
Violet.	Jane Bonaventure.
Solomon.	Vineyard.
Anne Frances.	Samuel, absent.

Ships which came from London under the charge of Henry Bellingham :—

The George Noble.	The Antelope.
Anthony.	Jewel.
Toby.	Pansy.
Salamander.	Providence
Rose Lion.	Dolphin.

August 6.—THE STATES OF ZEALAND TO THE QUEEN.

[**Holland, lvi.**—Signed. Endorsed. French.]

Madam :—It greatly rejoiceth us to understand, by your Majesty's letters, your good contentment with our service, which, notwithstanding the exceeding charges arising out of the tumults in this country, we have willingly made for the common defence against the enemy before Dunkirk, whereby,

[1] MS. Elin Nathan.

besides the good effect of the same, we hope that
your Majesty, being truly instructed, will be the
more favourably disposed towards us ; for that our
fleet, under the charge of Count Justinus of Nassau,
being happily arrived and riding off of Dunkirk at
the very time of the discovery of the armada of
Spain, the forces of the Prince of Parma, then
ready to put to sea, were, by the same, closely
locked in and stayed within the said Dunkirk ;
whereby we have so seconded the victory of your
Majesty's ships of war, as not only have we thus
easily made ourselves masters[1] of these three
Spanish ships here, partly taken, partly wrecked,
but also that the battle[2] of the armada of Spain,
being pursued by the English ships, hath been constrained to bend its course northwards, seeing no
hope of succour from the Prince of Parma, whereon
they chiefly depended, as the prisoners report, who
say that the said armada was straitly commanded
by the King of Spain to bear at once with Calais
and Dover, where they should find or stay for the
forces of the Prince of Parma, having also no boats
fit[3] for landing withal, but should be furnished with
the same by the said prince. Which prince,
although he was ready and his soldiers embarked,
he has been and now is so closely locked in by our
ships in the havens of Nieuport and Dunkirk, that,
notwithstanding all his force, we hope by the grace
of God that he will be unable to come out, and that
your Majesty's ships shall have occasion to prevail
over the rest of the Spanish fleet, which we under-
derstand it to be altogether beaten and spoiled.

And whereby our said service, in keeping and
locking in the forces of the said prince, hath been

[1] MS. *impatronés.*
[2] MS. *le corps de l'armade,* the main body of the fleet.
[3] MS. *idoines.*

the chief cause of the overthrow[1] of the said
armada, we understand that in place of attributing
to us and to our fleet a part of the victory, that our
ill-wishers do unjustly blame us for that our ships
should have been withdrawn, as unwilling to assist
your Majesty's; although it is apparent that the
defeat of the said armada of Spain doth consist
chiefly and entirely in this, that the said prince, remaining where he still is, was unable to succour
and strengthen it with his forces; and especially do
we desire to assure your Majesty that we will not
cease to use all possible diligence, to the end he
may rest locked in where he is.

But to give your Majesty some intelligence of
that has passed here. It will please your Majesty
to understand that out of the Spanish ships which
were already utterly spoiled by the ordnance of your
Majesty's ships, there are 400 prisoners, whereof are
persons of quality as yet known, the following[2] :—
Don Diego de Pimentel, Don Juan de Velasco,
Don Juan de Toledo, Captain Martin de Avalos,
Captain [Francisco] Marques, Captain Alonso de Vargas. [Here enclosed is the confession of the camp-
master Pimentel,[3] and of others lately come to us
out of Holland, whereby your Majesty shall be fully
advertised of the truth, as also by the depositions of
two sailors[3] escaped from the Spanish fleet.[4]] The
prisoners do hold it for a miracle that amongst the
slain, as well the English ordnance as our own,
for the little it did, hath always struck down the
principal traitors, and amongst others hath slain the
banished English lords; the list whereof, according
to the confessions of the prisoners here—the chief

---

[1] MS. *désespoir*.
[2] MS. *lesquels pour encore avons sorti recognoistre*.
[3] See *post*, pp. 75, 77.
[4] This sentence is written as a note in the margin.

of them having been carried into Holland—is herein enclosed. Out of one ship, whereof D. Pedro de Toledo was captain, the said D. Pedro, with all the gentlemen of quality and their richest furniture, escaped in some boats sent out to them from Nieuport. The two ships brought here, the ordnance thereof hath been saved by us, but all else hath been pillaged with great disorder; and the said ships, as well as by cause of the damage they had received in fight, as by the bad conduct of the same, the one sank in the haven of Flushing, and the other athwart of Rammekens. The third sank between Ostend and Blankenberg, without anything being saved.

All the prisoners, as well the gentlemen of quality as those of the common sort, agree that their intent was, with the aid and forces of the Prince of Parma, to attack England straightway, there being embarked in Spain about 40,000 men, viz., 20,000 soldiers volunteers, 10,000 constrained to serve,[1] and 12,000 mariners. And to this end the said prince still holdeth his army in readiness, to the number of 25,000 men, with ships full of saddles, bridles, boots, spurs, and everything needful for such an enterprise. It is reported that the King of Spain should have sent him the crown and sceptre of England blessed by the Pope, and that he should have been made king if the enterprise had met with good success; and truly he hath much correspondence in the country, and receiveth certain advertisements therefrom.

[1] MS. *forçats*, pressed men, in opposition to the previous *soldats volontaires*. Cf. *ante*, page 23, 'they commanded 2,000 Portingals to go aboard, upon pain of death.' The word can here scarcely mean slaves, for, though these numbers are much exaggerated, the 2,000 galley slaves in the fleet could hardly be turned into 10,000. It must be remembered, too, that the French is that of a Dutchman.

As the prisoners do report—wherewith other things concur—the rest of the armada of Spain, pursued by your Majesty's fleet, will return hither with the first occasion, and that the Prince of Parma, to avoid further blame and to remove the stains of the past, wherewith he is much despited, will second it, whatever may be the cost of the same, so that it is necessary to be watchful on all sides. May God bless and prosper[1] the holy and virtuous plans and enterprises of your Majesty, and of your officers and servants ; hoping always that, by his grace, your Majesty shall gain renown and everlasting glory throughout the whole world in our just quarrel, seeking to cast down the heart of the hardened and *outrecuidé* Pharaoh by the hand of a lady who has never given him cause of offence, so as it is not to be doubted that, by the means and extra-ordinary succour of God, your Majesty's justice and innocence will prevail over his pride. This, humbly kissing your Majesty's valiant hands, we beseech your Majesty to hold us always in your protection and safeguard. From Middelburg, the 16th of August, 1588.

Your Majesty's most humble and
must obedient servants
The Council of the States of Zealand,
and by their order,

* * * *[2]

August 7.—SEYMOUR TO WALSYNGHAM.

[**ccxiv. 40.**—Holograph. Addressed.]

Sir :—We have omitted no time for taking in the Lords Commissioners, who are this day arrived at Dover. I perceive by my Lord of Derby that the

---

[1] MS *bienheurer*.   [2] The signature is undecipherable.

Duke of Parma hath withdrawn his sea forces to
Bruges and to Dixmude ; and that all the Spanish
commissioners, the Count Aremberg and the rest,
were met by the post of Antwerp at Bruges town's-
end ; also news came to Calais that Breda was
revolted ; and doubted at Calais, by common opinion,
that the withdrawing of the Duke's forces was either
for Ostend, Bergen-op-Zoom, or Breda, or some other
peece.[1] It seemeth the Duke is in a great chafe to
see his ships no readier at Dunkirk, also to find such
discomfiture of the Spanish fleet hard by his nose.
I can say no more, but God doth show his mighty
hand for protecting this little island, for his glory
and to the honour of our country. God in heaven
bless her Majesty and prosper all your honourable
proceedings. From aboard the Rainbow, the 7th
of August, 1588, at Dover, going to-morrow out
again with our navy.

Your assured friend to command,

H. SEYMOUR.

I am advertised that some supply of victuals
should come from Spain. I have again sent to the
Flushingers, to understand their minds, which as yet
I have no word [of]. Now her Majesty, if it please
her, may take upon her the absolute government of
Holland and Zealand. Also the India fleet could
be met withal.

August 7.—HOWARD TO WALSYNGHAM.

[ccxiv. 42.—Signed ; autograph postscript. Addressed.]

Sir :—In our last fight with the enemy before
Gravelines, the 29th of July, we sank three of their

---

[1] The writing is Seymour's, and is quite plain ; but surely he
meant to write 'place.' Cf. *post*, p. 121.

ships, and made four to go room with the shore so leak [1] as they were not able to live at sea. After that fight, notwithstanding that our powder and shot was well near all spent, we set on a brag countenance and gave them chase, as though we had wanted nothing, until we had cleared our own coast and some part of Scotland of them. And then, as well to refresh our ships with victuals, whereof most stood in wonderful need, as also in respect of our want of powder and shot, we made for the Frith, and sent certain pinnaces to dog the fleet until they should be past the Isles of Scotland, which I verily do believe they are left at their sterns ere this. We are persuaded that either they are past about Ireland, and so do what they can to recover their own coast, or else that they are gone for some part of Denmark. I have herewith sent unto you [2] a brief abstract of such accidents as have happened, which hereafter, at better leisure, I will explain by more particular relations. [3] In the meantime I bid you heartily farewell. From aboard the Ark, the 7th of August, 1588.

Your very loving friend,
C. HOWARD.

Good Mr. Secretary, let not her Majesty be too hasty in dissolving her forces by sea and land; and I pray you send me with speed what advertisements you have of Dunkirk, for I long to do some exploit [4]

[1] Leaky.

[2] Howard's secretary here wrote 'your Honour.' The 'r' and 'Honour' are erased, presumably by Howard's direction; but it is worth noting that the letter, with this significant erasure, was sent to Walsyngham.

[3] This is probably the Relation printed *ante*, vol. i. p. 1. In comparison with this Relation, and the Abstract of Accidents which here follows, see the Journal of Medina Sidonia, *post*, Appendix E.

[4] MS. dow some explyte.

on their shipping. If the Duke's forces be retired into the land, I doubt not but to do good. I must thank you for your favourable using [1] of my brother Hoby. He telleth me how forwards you were to further all things for our wants. I would some were of your mind. If we had had that which had been sent, England and her Majesty had had the most honour that ever any nation had. But God be thanked ; it is well.

A BRIEF ABSTRACT OF ACCIDENTS.

[**ccxiv. 42, I.**—Enclosure in the foregoing.]

A Declaration of the Proceeding of the two Fleets.

July 19*th, Friday.*] Upon Friday, being the 19th of this present month, part of the Spanish navy, to the number of 50 sail, was discovered about the Isles of Scilly, hovering in the wind as it seemed to attend the rest of the fleet ; and the next 20*th, Saturday.*] day, at three of the clock in the afternoon, the Lord Admiral got forth with our navy out of Plymouth, though with some difficulty, the wind being at South-West. Notwithstanding, through the great travail used by our men, they not only cleared the harbour, but also the next day, 21*st, Sunday.*] being Sunday, about 9 of the clock in the morning, recovered the wind of the whole fleet, which, being thoroughly descried, was found to consist of 120 sail, great and small.

At the same instant the Lord Admiral gave them fight within the view of Plymouth, from whence the Mayor,[2] with others, sent them continually supplies of men, till they were past their

---

[1] MS. yousyng. [2] William Hawkyns, brother of Sir John.

coast. This fight continued till one of the clock the same day, wherein the enemy was made to bear room with some of his ships to stop their leaks. The same day, by an accident of fire happening in one of their great ships of the burden of . . .[1] tons, there were blown up with powder about 120 men, the rest being compelled to leave her; and so she was by the Lord Admiral sent into the west parts[2] of England.

22nd, Monday.] Upon Monday the 22nd one of the chief galleons, wherein was Don Pedro de Valdes with 450 men, was taken, by reason of his mast that was spent with the breaking of his bow-sprit,[3] so as he presently yielded, with sundry gentlemen of good quality.

23rd, Tuesday.] On Tuesday the 23rd the Lord Admiral, chasing the enemy, who had then gotten some advantage of the wind, and thereupon seemed more desirous to abide our force than before, fell in fight with them over against St. Albans, about five of the clock in the morning, the wind being at North-East; and so continued with great force on both sides till late in the evening, when the wind coming again to be South-West, and somewhat large,[4] they began to go roomwards.[5]

24th, Wednesday.] The same night and all Wednesday the Lord Admiral kept very near unto *25th, Thursday.*] the Spanish fleet, and upon Thursday the 25th, over against Dunnose, part of the Isle of Wight, the Lord Admiral, espying Captain Frobiser with a few other ships to be in a sharp fight with the enemy, and fearing they should be distressed, did, with five of his best ships, bear up towards the admiral of the Spanish fleet; and

---

[1] Blank in MS.   The ship was the San Salvador, of 958 tons.
[2] Weymouth.   [3] MS. boare spitt.
[4] Strong, fresh.   [5] To leeward; they bore up.

so breaking into the heart of them, began a very
sharp fight, being within two or three score [1] one of
the other, until they had cleared Captain Frobiser
and made them give place.

26th, Friday.] The next day, being the 26th,
the Lord Admiral only continued his pursuit of the
enemy, having still increased his provisions, and
keeping the wind of them.

27th, Saturday.] Upon Saturday the 27th, about
8 of the clock at night, the Lord Henry Seymour,
Admiral in the Narrow Seas, joined with the Lord
Howard in Whitsand Bay, over against the cliffs of
Calais, and anchored together; and the Spanish
fleet rode also at anchor to leewards of the Lord
Admiral, and nearer to Calais road.

28th, Sunday.] The 28th, the Lord Admiral
prepared seven ships, fitted with pitch, tar, and
other necessaries, for the burning of some of the
enemy's fleet; and at 11 of the clock at night, the
wind and tide serving, put that stratagem in execution, the event whereof was this:—Upon Monday
29th, Monday.] the 29th, early in the morning, the
admiral [2] of the enemy's galleasses, riding next to
our fleet, let slip her anchor and cable to avoid the
fires; and driving thwart another galleass,[3] her cable
took hold of the other rudder,[4] and brake it clean
away, so that with her oars she was fain to get into
Calais road for relief. All the rest of the Spanish
fleet either cut or let slip their anchors and cables,
set sail and put to the sea, being chased from that
road.

After this the Lord Admiral sent the lieutenant [5]

[1] Sc. paces.
[2] The San Lorenzo.
[3] Really a galleon, the San Juan de Sicilia, of 800 tons.
[4] There is here a strange confusion of pronouns. It was the
San Juan's cable which took hold of the San Lorenzo's rudder.
[5] Amyas Preston.

of his own ship, with 100 of his principal men, in a
long boat to recover the galleass so distressed near
Calais ; who after some sharp fight, with the loss of
some men, was possessed of her, and having slain
a great number of the enemies, and namely their
captain-general of the four galleasses, called Don
Hugo de Moncada, son to the Viceroy of Valencia,
with divers gentlemen of good reckoning carried
prisoners to the English fleet. In this pursuit[1] of
the fireworks by our force, the Lord Howard in
fight[2] spoiled a great number of them, sank three,
and drove four or five on the shore ; so as at that
time it was assured that they had lost at the least 16
of their best ships.

The same day, after the fight, the Lord Admiral
followed the enemy in chase, the wind continuing
at West and South-West ; who, bearing room northwards, directly towards the Isles of Scotland, were
by his Lordship followed near hand, until they
brought themselves within the height of 55 degrees.

30*th, Tuesday*.] The 30th, one of the enemy's
great ships was espied to be in great distress by the
captain[3] of her Majesty's ship called the Hope ; ¨
who being in speech of yielding unto the said
captain, before they could agree on certain conditions, sank presently before their eyes.

31*st, Wednesday*.] It is also advertised that the
31st, two of their great ships, being in the like
distress, and grievously torn in the fight aforesaid,
are since taken by certain Hollanders and brought
into Flushing. The principal person of the greatest
of them is called Don Pimentel, being also one of
the Maestri del Campo.

---

[1] Sc. following up the effect of &c.
[2] The MS. has 'sight,' which appears to be a blunder of the
copying clerk.
[3] Captain Robert Crosse.

August 8.—HOWARD TO WALSYNGHAM.

[**ccxiv. 50.**—Holograph.   Addressed.]

Sir :—I did write yesterday by my Lord of
Cumberland, to her Majesty, to my Lord Treasurer,
and to you, being athwart of Harwich, a-seaboard
10 leagues.   My Lord bare with a pinnace into
Harwich ; I bare with some of the ships into Margate
road ; where the rest be gone I do not know, for
we had a most violent storm as ever was seen at this
time of the year, that put us asunder athwart of
Norfolk, amongst many ill-favoured sands ; but I
trust they do all well, and I hope I shall hear of
them this night or to-morrow.

I pray to God we may hear of victuals, for we
are generally in great want ; and also that I may
know how the coast ships of the west shall be
victualled ; and also that order be taken for the
victualling and for munition for the ships of London.
I know not what you think of it at the Court, but I
do think, and so doth all here, that there cannot be
too great forces maintained yet for five or six weeks,
on the seas ; for although we have put the Spanish
fleet past the Frith, and I think past the Isles, yet
God knoweth whether they go either to the Nase of
Norway or into Denmark or to the Isles of Orkney
to refresh themselves, and so to return ; for I think
they dare not return [1] with this dishonour and shame
to their King, and overthrow of their Pope's credit.
Sir, sure bind, sure find.   A kingdom is a great
wager.   Sir, you know security is dangerous ; and
God had not been our best friend, we should have
found it so.   Some made little account of the Spanish
force by sea ; but I do warrant you, all the world
never saw such a force as theirs was ; and some

---

[1] Sc. to Spain.

Spaniards that we have taken, that were in the fight at Lepanto, do say that the worst of our four fights that we have had with them did exceed far the fight they had there ; and they say that at some of our fights we had 20 times as much great shot there plied as they had there. Sir, I pray to God that we may be all thankful to God for it ; and that it may be done by some order, that the world may know we are thankful to him for it.

Sir, I pray you let me hear what the Duke of Parma doth, with some speed ; and where his forces by sea are.

Sir, in your next letters to my brother Stafford [1] I pray write to him that he will let Mendoza [2] know that her Majesty's rotten ships dare meet with his master's sound ships ; and in buffeting with them, though they were three great ships to one of us, yet we have shortened them 16 or 17 ; whereof there is three of them a-fishing in the bottom of the seas. God be thanked of all. Sir, I pray you let this gentleman receive thanks ; he hath well deserved it with great valour. Sir, Mr. Chidley [3] and Mr. Vavasour [4] are worthy of great commendation for

---

[1] Sir Edward Stafford, at this time ambassador at Paris.

[2] Don Bernardino de Mendoza, formerly ambassador of Spain in London, and at this time in Paris. He had received a letter from Calais announcing the utter defeat of the English fleet, and, eagerly accepting it as true, sent the news to Madrid and published it in Paris. The astounding falsehood to which he had thus carelessly given currency caused great indignation in this country, where it was translated and published with a commentary, under the title of *A Pack of Spanish Lies*. Mendoza's name naturally lent itself to many angry puns. See Duro, i. 175 and ii. 224.

[3] MS. Chydle. John Chidley, or Chudleigh, was lost the next year in the galleon Leicester, in command of an expedition to the Straits of Magellan.

[4] Probably Thomas Vavasour, who commanded the Antelope at the Islands in 1597, and was knighted by the Earl of Essex.

their valour.   Sir, being in haste and much occupied, I bid you most heartily farewell.   Margate
road, the 8th of August.

Your most assured loving friend,

C. HOWARD.

Sir, if I hear nothing of my victuals and munition
this night here, I will gallop to Dover to see what
may be [got] there, or else we shall starve.

August 8.—*DRAKE TO WALSYNGHAM.*

[ccxiv. 49.—Holograph.   Addressed.   In bad condition, and
very badly written.[1]]

Most Honourable.—The 8th of August I received your Honour's letter [of the] last of July, by
the which I understand [how hard] a thing it is upon
a sudden to procure [what] was and is most necessary for the defence [of such] an army as the King
of Spain had se[t forth].

To conclude, let us all with one accord [praise]
God the only [stock[2]] giver, who of his only [will]
hath sent this proud enemy of his truth where he
hath tasted of his power, as well by storm and
tempest, as he doth and did by putting away from
the coast of . . . . .[3]   Whether he mind to return
or not I [know] not, but my opinion to your Honour
is, that I [think] he neither mindeth nor is in case to
d[o so].   Certainly their people were many sick,
[and] without doubt many killed ; and that, [by
report] of such as are taken, their ships, [masts],
ropes, and sails much decayed by [shot], and more
it had been had we not [wan]ted powder and &c.

[1] Drake's writing, at its best, was very bad.   When he was
'half sleeping' it was not at its best.

[2] Perhaps in the sense of 'support.'   The MS. has 'steok'
plainly written, but the meaning of it is very doubtful.

[3] Torn away.   Probably Scotland.

For that I assure myself my Lord Admiral hath advertised at large both what hath past and also what is meet now to do, and his Lordship departed for Dover before my coming to an anchor, I leave to write farther, desiring of God [to] bless our gracious Sovereign, as he hath [done, and] give us all grace to live in his service. Aboard her Majesty's good ship the Revenge, this 8th of August, 1588.

Your Honour's most ready to be commanded,
but now half sleeping,

FRA. DRAKE.

August 8.—DRAKE TO WALSYNGHAM.

[ccxiv. 48.—Holograph. Addressed. Seal : the arms granted in 1581 (a fess wavy between two stars), with the old family crest, an eagle displayed.[1]]

Right Honourable :—This gentleman, Mr. Oseley,[2] hath carried himself most honestly ; and withal his advertisements of the King of Spain's army hath not done us little pleasure. His wants and some business hath procured him leave, but yet so as if there happen any service, he is presently to return.

I have not in my former letter touched whether it be meet or no for her Majesty to continue her forces, for that some haply will say winter cometh on apace. My poor opinion is, that I dare not advise her Majesty to hazard a kingdom with the saving a little charge. The Prince of Parma is very,[3] and will not let to send daily to the Duke of Sidonia, if he may find him. Thus in haste I humbly take my leave, this 8th of August, 1588.

Your Honour's faithfully,

FRA. DRAKE.

[1] It does not appear that Drake ever used the crest granted in 1581, which has been used by the later representatives of his family.
[2] See vol. i. p. 301.   [3] A word omitted.

August 8.—*HENRY WHYTE TO WALSYNGHAM.*

[**ccxiv. 43.**—Signed. Addressed.]

My duty most humbly remembered :—If it seem unto your Honour that I have been slack in this duty, impute it, I beseech you, to the long sickness and indisposition that haunted me.   When we heard of the arrival of the Spanish forces by sea upon the coast, weak as I was, I embarked[1] myself to wait upon my Lord Admiral, who with all diligence addressed himself to go meet them ; which the second day after he put from Plymouth he did.

The majesty of the enemy's fleet, the good order they held, and the private consideration of our own wants did cause, in mine opinion, our first onset to be more coldly done than became the value of our nation and the credit of the English navy ; yet we put them to leeward, kept the weather[2] of them, and distressed two of their best ships, whereof Don Pedro's was one.   After that, our fleet increased daily ; and as men and ammunition came, we plied them every day with more courage than other, until they came to an anchor before Calais, as your Honour may have heard.   There it was devised to put them from their anchor, and seven ships were allotted to the fire to perform the enterprise ; among the rest, the ship I had in charge, the Bark Talbot, was one ; so that now I rest like one that had his house burnt, and one of these days I must come to your Honour for a commission to go a-begging.

Sunday, the 28th of July, at night, about one of the clock,[3] the enterprise was undertaken, which took good effect, though not so good as was ex-

---

[1] MS. imbarked.   [2] The wind, the weather gage.
[3] More correctly, then, Monday morning, the 29th of July.

pected; for it drove[1] two of their galleasses to be
foul one of the other, so that the one plucked away
the other's rudder, which afterwards drove[1] into
Calais haven aground upon the sands.   The next
morning, by the dawning, we found all the fleet put
from their anchors, with the loss, by report of some
of them that were afterwards taken, of 100 or 120
anchors and cables.   Part of our fleet made haste
to overtake the enemy; my Lord Admiral, with
another part, lingered a space, to see what would
become of those he sent to attempt the galleon.   Of
their strength I say nothing, because I persuade
myself your Honour is already sufficiently informed
of it.   As soon as we that pursued the fleet were
come up within musket shot of them, the fight began
very hotly.   Myself was aboard the Mary Rose of
the Queen's, with Captain Fenton, whose value for
that day's service deserved praise.   We had not
fought above three hours but my Lord Admiral
with the rest of the fleet came up, and gave a very
fresh onset, which continued amongst us some six
hours more; and truly, sir, if we had shot and
powder sufficient to have given them two such heats
more, we had utterly distressed them.

The next day it was decreed the Narrow Seas'
fleet should go back; and my Lord Admiral with
the rest pursued the enemy, that fled before us
with all the sail they could make, until he had
brought them up well nigh as high as Berwick,
having weakened their fleet, first and last, to our
judgment of about twenty sail; so there rested of
them whole, when we parted, to the number of fourscore sail, and all at liberty, if wind and weather
hinder not, to practise in Scotland and attempt
Ireland, if so they resolve not to return again this
way, if weather serve as now it doth.

[1] MS. dryve.

By this my simple relation, your Honour may see how our parsimony at home hath bereaved us of the famousest victory that ever our navy might have had at sea. Our desire of victory is so great that we staid not to take the spoil of any of these ships we lamed ; but we understand some of them lighted to the lot of our friends in Flanders. I am now void of any charge in this service, and I would be loth to serve privately ; therefore I shall humbly beseech your Honour to have me in mind, according to your wonted goodness towards me ; for I assure your Honour, her Majesty's service hath utterly beggared me. But this comfort I have: her Highness, with your Honour's furtherance, may easily remedy my grief. This, craving pardon for my tedious troubling of your Honour, I shall humbly beseech Almighty God for your Honour's prosperity. From Margate, this 8th of August, 1588.
Your Honour's most bounden, ready to obey you,
H. WHYTE.

Aug. 8.—SIR T. MORGAN TO LEICESTER.

[**ccxiv. 44.**—Signed. Addressed.]

Right Honourable :—I am arrived here at Margate with 800 shot, musketeers, and small shot. And further I am to advertise your Honour that the Prince of Parma hath in readiness about thirty or forty thousand men, and intendeth, as we hear, this next spring tide to put out his forces for England, hoping to meet with the King's fleet ; for that he hath sent certain pilots with small pinnaces to conduct the navy.[1] Here is with me

---

[1] All this is mere hearsay. Parma had, in fact, but little over twenty thousand ; and, what with the Dutch fleet on the coast, and the English fleet in the North Sea, the sending out the small pinnaces seems very doubtful.

Captain Richard Wingfield and Captain Powell. Thus in great haste I take my leave of your Honour, humbly kissing your hands, and praying God to bless you in this honourable attempt. Margate, this 8th of August, 1588.

Your Honour's at commandment,

THO. MORGAN.

Aug. 8.—HAWKYNS TO THE LORD ADMIRAL.

[ccxiv. 46.—Holograph. Addressed:—For her Majesty's service. In the Downs, or elsewhere near Dover.]

The Queen's Ships:

The White Bear
Victory
Nonpareil
Hope

The Swiftsure
Foresight
Moon
White Lion
Disdain

The Ships of London:

The Minion
Golden Lion
Thomas Bonaven-
ture
Hercules
Red Lion
Royal Defence
Bark Burr
Galleon Leicester
Galleon Dudley
Tiger of Plymouth
Bark Bonner
Samaritan of Dart-
mouth
Delight

The Edward Bonaventure
Diamond of Dart-
mouth
Minion of Plymouth
Jacob of Lyme
Bark Hawkyns
Chance of Plymouth
John of Barnstaple
Acteon
Bark Flemyng
Solomon of Ald-
borough
William of Leigh
Katherine
Rat

My very good Lord:—This Thursday, being the 8th of August, we came into Harwich with these ships that are above noted. We are in hand to have out the ordnance and ballast of the Hope, and so to ground her. With the next fair wind we mind, with those ships that are here, to follow your Lordship into the Downs, or where we may hear of your Lordship, and to bring all the victuallers with us. There are three of the hoys[1] here already with beer and bread ; and the rest, being seven more, have order to come hither. We will relieve such as be in necessity, and bring away the rest with us.

The Bear hath a leak which is thought to be very low ; yet my Lord[2] will follow your Lordship.

The Elizabeth Jonas and the Triumph drave the last stormy night, being Monday ; since which time we have not heard of them. But, this fair weather, I hope your Lordship shall hear of them at the Foreland. As I write this letter more of the victuallers are come. There is 14 days' victual in them for the ships under your Lordship's charge, as I learn. And so, praying to God to send us shortly to meet with your Lordship, I humbly take my leave. From Harwich, the 8th of August, 1588.

Your honourable Lordship's most bounden,

JOHN HAWKYNS.

[**ccxiv. 45.**—A copy of the foregoing sent to Sir Francis Walsyngham, signed, with autograph postscript.]

This is the copy of the letter sent to my Lord Admiral, which I send to your Honour that ye may see in what state we are, and what we pretend. The wind is now bad for us to ply to my Lord, but we will lose no time.

Your Honour's most bounden,

JOHN HAWKYNS.

[1] MS. whoyes.   [2] Lord Sheffield.

August 8.—SIR F. DRAKE TO THE QUEEN

[ccxiv. 47.—Copy.]

The absence of my Lord Admiral, most gracious Sovereign, hath emboldened me to put my pen to the paper. On Friday last, upon good consideration, we left the army of Spain so far to the northwards as they could neither recover England nor Scotland. And within three days after, we were entertained with a great storm, considering the time of the year ; the which storm, in many of our judgments, hath not a little annoyed the enemy's army. If the wind hinder it not, I think they are forced to Denmark ; and that for divers causes. Certain it is that many of their people were sick, and not a few killed. Their ships, sails, ropes, and masts needeth great reparations, for that they had all felt of your Majesty's force. If your Majesty thought it meet, it [would not be] amiss you sent presently to Denmark to understand the truth, and to deal with their King according to your Majesty's great wisdom.

I have not written this whereby your Majesty should diminish any of your forces. Your Highness's enemies are many ; yet God hath and will hear your Majesty's prayers, putting your hand to the plough for the defence of his truth, as your Majesty hath begun. God, for his Christ's sake, bless your sacred Majesty, now and ever. Written aboard your Majesty's very good ship the Revenge, this 8th of August, 1588.

Your Majesty's faithful vassal,
FRA. DRAKE.

August 8.—WALSYNGHAM TO BURGHLEY.

[**B.M. Harl. MS. 6994, f. 136.**—Holograph. Addressed.]

My very good Lord :—Immediately upon my arrival at the camp I met with the Earl of Cumberland, sent hither unto her Majesty from the Lord Admiral. By his Lordship's letter, whereof I send your Lordship a copy, you may perceive where he left the Spanish fleet. It is hard now to resolve what advice to give her Majesty for disarming, either by sea or by land, until it shall be known what is become of the said fleet. The Earl of Cumberland telleth me that the Lord Admiral would be this night at the Downs. And so I most humbly take my leave. At the camp, in the Lord General's tent, the 8th of August, 1588.

Your Lordship's to command,
FRA. WALSYNGHAM.

The Commissioners landed this morning at Dover ; they write nothing touching the Duke of Parma's proceedings.

August 8.—WALSYNGHAM TO THE LORD CHANCELLOR.

[**Harl. MS. 6994, f. 138.**—Holograph. Addressed.]

By the copy of the Lord Admiral's letters brought this day to the camp by the Earl of Cumberland, your Lordship may perceive what is become of the Spanish fleet. I am sorry the Lord Admiral was forced to leave the prosecution of the enemy through the wants he sustained. Our half-doings doth breed dishonour and leaveth the disease uncured. The Earl of Derby and the rest of the Commissioners arrived this morning at Dover. The Lord Admiral cometh this night to the Downs. And so I most humbly take my leave. At the camp, the 8th of August, 1588.

Your Lordship's to command,
F<small>RA</small>. W<small>ALSYNGHAM</small>.

Aug. 8.—PRINCE MAURICE TO WALSYNGHAM.

[**Holland, lvi.**—Signed. Addressed. French.]

Sir :—For that I have caused the confession to be taken of Don Diego Pimentel, camp-master of the Sicilian regiment, a prisoner here, whereby you will be sufficiently informed as well of the designs of the King of Spain as of that hath passed betwixt the two fleets until the time of his imprisonment, it seemeth meet to refer the advertisement of these affairs to the said confession, as also to that the States-General and those of the provinces have written to her Majesty. Only this I will tell you : that, after the opinion of the said States, I have judged it fitting to put under sure guard all the prisoners brought hither from the two enemy's ships that were taken by our men, and that I have given commandment that the said Don Diego, belonging to one of the best families in Spain, and related to the greatest noblemen in the said kingdom, shall be treated according to his rank, as also all the other gentlemen and men of quality which hath been taken with them, to the number of about 25. The common soldiers have been divided in the prisons of the towns until it shall be seen what course their fleet taketh, and what may be the success of the *sortie* that the Duke of Parma seeketh to make from Dunkirk ; thereafter to be ordered concerning them as it shall be judged fitting.

Sir, I pray you to advertise me of her Majesty's pleasure therein, and of that you shall judge convenient, to the end I may pursue the same as far as we shall be able. This, I render you my most affectionate thanks for your good favour, and pray God to give you, with good health, a happy and long life. From the Hague, this 18th of August, 1588.

Your affectionate friend to be commanded,

MAURICE DE NASSAU.

August 8.—THE COUNCIL OF STATE OF THE UNITED PROVINCES TO THE QUEEN.

[**Holland, lvi.**—Signed. Endorsed. French.]

Madam :—For that God hath shown unto us his favour by inclining the heart of your Majesty to support the cause of these United Provinces, so many years assailed and troubled in this cruel war by the unhappy designs and violence of our enemies, which hath also for a long time practised by forcible and subtle means to offend your Majesty's royal person and kingdom, we do assuredly hope and believe that the same God hath, in his goodness, given your Majesty the victory over your enemies, and, before the whole world, everlasting glory, such as is fitting to your royal virtues ; whereof, after many and great difficulties, we now behold the happy effects in the pursuit that your Majesty's army hath made of the mighty and proud forces of the King of Spain and of his allies, shattering the powers of divers princes that have leagued together against your Majesty, the defender of God's church and of this country. We praise God for these great benefits, and pray him to bestow on your Majesty perfect victory over the said common enemy, which will be no less for the advantage of these provinces than for the honour of your Majesty.

We are sorely grieved that the rebellions and mutinies that have been in this State have taken away the most ready and apparent means that was prepared for the service of your Majesty, whereby your Majesty would have been further assured of the sincerity and good will there is here towards your Majesty's service, as is most meet, besides that the States do presently furnish, which hath showed themselves willing to pay another subsidy, to the end they may strengthen and increase their fleet, so as to be able as well for the service of your Majesty as for their own defence; which your Majesty will, without doubt, be more fully advertised of the same by his Lordship, the Lord Wyllughby, your Majesty's Lieutenant in these parts. Thus we cease to trouble your Majesty, most humbly beseeching you to continue your royal favour toward this country; and, humbly kissing your Majesty's hands, we pray Almighty God to preserve your Majesty, for the good of your subjects and servants, in a happy and long life. From the Hague, this 18th day of August, 1588.

Your Majesty's most humble and most affectionate servants, the Council of State of the United Provinces of the Low Countries.

CHR. HUYGENS.[1]

Aug. 8.— *THE COUNCIL OF STATE OF THE UNITED PROVINCES TO THE LORDS OF THE COUNCIL.*

[**Holland, lvi.**—Signed.   Addressed.   French.]

Sir :—We praise and glorify God exceedingly for that it hath pleased him at divers times to give

---

[1] Christian Huygens, secretary of the Council of State, born 1555, died 1624. He was father of Constantine Huygens the poet, and grandfather of Christian Huygens the mathematician and astronomer.

good success to her Majesty's navy against the
common enemy ; and we are glad that her Majesty
hath favourably considered of the service that hath
been done by us. It were greatly to be desired that
we could have seconded her with stronger forces
than we have here at this time, thereby to render
the victory more perfect. But the misfortunes which
have befallen this State, from the extraordinary and
unheard of mutinies excited amongst our soldiers,
have deprived us of the means whereby these
countries could have armed greater forces by sea,
so as better to have testified our zeal for the service
of her Majesty.

We cease not to travail with the States, moving
them to grant a new and extraordinary subsidy for
the strengthening and largely augmenting of our
said forces by sea, as that it may be prepared for
whatever may fall out, the resolution of our enemies
being apparent to persecute their pretences to the
uttermost ; as also, on the other part, we desire to do
our duty so far as lieth with us. Wherein we find
so much good will that, notwithstanding the manifold charges and contributions, we do already begin
to carry out our resolve, and arm for the sea about
40 more good ships of war. Nevertheless, for that
we are advertised that the Spanish army taketh a
course northward, we beseech your Honours to be a
mean that her Majesty may give commandment to
her army not to cease to pursue and follow up the
enemy, to the end they shall not be able to assure
themselves and renew their enterprise.

Certain of our captains have brought into these
parts some ships taken from the Spanish army, with
sundry persons, which we have examined the chief
of them, and have sent you, with these, copies of
their confessions, so as it may serve, with other
advertisements that your Lordships have, to make

known the pretences of the said King of Spain against her Majesty's kingdom. In like manner we do also send the confessions of certain mariners of this country, who have been stayed in Spain by the space of two years, and constrained to serve in the army of the King, but have now fled away from the army and yielded themselves here.

On the other hand, your Lordships will also see how sure and certain it is that the Duke of Parma, understanding of the ill success of his enterprise against England, will, in his fury, turn the great power that he has brought together in Flanders against this country, to revenge himself, if it may be, for the loss and shame his master and he have had at the sea. We beseech your Lordships to take order that the forces of her Majesty in these parts shall be sufficient in number and in quality, as well of footmen as of horsemen, whereof, at this present, there is great lack ; and, meantime, to continue your favours to this afflicted country in the great need that now is ; assuring your Lordships that, on our part, we shall not fail to do to the uttermost of our ability for the service of her Majesty and for our own safety.

The States-General do now consider of sending certain deputies to her Majesty, which will more fully inform your Honours of everything. This, commending ourselves to your good favour, we pray God to have your Lordships in his holy keeping. From the Hague, the 18th day of August, 1588.

> Your Lordships' very humble and very affectionate servants, the Council of State of the United Provinces of the Low Countries.
>   CHR. HUYGENS.

August 2.—DEPOSITIONS OF SPANISH PRISONERS.

[**Holland, lvi.**—Endorsed. Spanish, French, and English. The translations, the English especially, are very inaccurate ; the errors are noted by a reference to the Spanish.]

12 *Augusti, stilo novo,* 1588.

Don Diego Pimentel,[1] born at Valladolid, general of the forces of Sicily,[2] brother[3] to the Marquis of Tavara, of the age of 29 years, saith :—

He is of the order of St. Jacques ;[4] and saith, moreover, that the regiment of Sicily is of 32 companies, whereof the fifteen of foot old soldiers ;[5] that the said 32 companies were all in this army ; that they parted from the river of Lisbon the 30th of May with 145 sail, whereof 110 were men-of-war and 90 of them very great ; that the ship wherein he came is a galleass[6] of Portugal, of 700 tons.

He saith they came out with intention to join with the Duke[7] of Parma, and, with him, to cast themselves[8] upon England, and there to take some strong place, and afterwards to set all his forces on land. He saith that at the entry of the Channel one of their greatest ships lost itself and was taken, the captain whereof was Don Pedro de Valdes.

He saith in this army there were 20,000 Spaniards and 12,000 mariners and others, so as every day they received allowance for 32,000 men.[9]

[1] A sketch of Pimentel's earlier and later history is given by Duro, i. 171.

[2] *Maestro de campo del tercio de Sicilia* : commandant of the Sicilian regiment.

[3] He was the marquis's eldest son.   [4] *Santiago.*

[5] *Las quinze de infanteria vieja* : fifteen of which were veteran infantry.   [6] *Galeon.*

[7] *Principe.*   [8] *Se metter en.*   [9] *Davan 32 mil raciones.*

He saith the flower of the nobility of Spain was there, as of dukes, counts, marquises, barons, and gentlemen. Moreover, that the general, the Duke Medina, will not depart from hence till he have accomplished the charge which the King hath given him.

He saith the army was provided of all sorts for six months when they set forth out of Lisbon, and that his ship did carry 32 pieces of brass. He saith that when they counted the English fleet the last time, they found it of 130 sail.

He saith that, two months before they came from Lisbon the speech did run that the Queen of England was to make a peace with the Duke of Parma, and that they then had hope it would be made.

He saith that on Monday they strayed from the army, and that they left it complete and full, and that they had lost but three ships. He saith that the King spendeth in this army daily 12,000 pistolets, and that in the fleet there are 16 millions of ducats.[1]

Don Juan de Velasquez, of the age of 20 years, born at Valladolid, in a certain village called Primes. Roa, the father of the Count of Cerula, is lord of the said place; and he saith he is entertained of the King.[2]

Martin de Avalos, of the age of 50 years, captain of one company of the said regiment, saith he hath been heretofore at Maestricht.

---

[1] *Ducados.*

[2] *En un lugar que se llama Roa; hermano del Conde de Cerula, señor del mismo lugar, et que era entretenido del Rey:*—in a place called Roa; brother of the . . . , and that he was in the king's pay. The error is the more curious as the French has, correctly—un village qui s'appelle Roa; frère du . . . .

Francisco Marques, captain of one company, saith he hath also been at Maestricht twelve years ago.

Alonso de Vargas is come in the company of Don Diego.

Frantz Muelenpeert, of Herenthals, of 17 years old, saith he hath been nine years in Spain, and that almost he hath forgotten all his Flemish.

William Olyckers, of Luxemburg, of 20 years old, saith he hath also been there about nine years.

Don Diego saith that in his ship were three companies, to the number of 280 soldiers, and that in all there were 60 mariners. He saith they had been at Lisbon with the said army eleven months.

This ship was taken the 10th of August by Sir Peter Van der Does.[1]

Aug. 1.—DEPOSITION OF TWO DUTCH SAILORS WHO WERE IN THE ARMADA.

[Hist. MSS. Commission. Cecil Papers, iii. 343. Printed. French.]

[As this deposition has recently been printed in full, it is unnecessary to repeat here the statistics and details, which are, for the most part, wildly inaccurate. Their blunders, however, seem the natural exaggerations of ignorant men, rather than wilful lying, while some of their statements as to matters which came under their own observation appear to be true, and are in conformity with those of the Spanish State Papers edited by Captain Duro.

[2] *Par le Sieur Pierre.* This is an addition in the French and English copies ; it is not in the Spanish. Pieter van der Does, vice-admiral of the fleet of Holland, was born in 1562, at Leyden, to which town he now presented the flag of the San Mateo. He died at St. Thomas, in the West Indies, in 1599.

When they say that the greatest ships had 1,200 or 1,300 men on board, or that there were in the fleet 300 priests or monks, they are talking of things of which they had no knowledge; when they say that the Spanish ships sailed badly, that the English ships sailed better, easily took and kept the weather-gage, and fired three shot for one of the Spaniards, they are speaking of facts within the knowledge of every seaman in the fleet. So also when they say that :—

As they departed from Lisbon the fleet consisted of about 130 ships, great and small : about 40 of these were small ; about 70 were men-of-war, each of which might have, at a guess, 30 or 40 pieces of brass ordnance. Except the galleys, few of them had cannons.[1] Some of the ships had only 10, 12, 15, or 18 pieces of ordnance. There were about 10,000 old soldiers ; the rest were vine-growers, shepherds, and the like.]

August 3.—REPORT OF DESERTERS.

[Holland, lvi.—Endorsed.   Englished.]

The substance of certain mariners' report[2] touching the Spanish fleet, August 1588.

Certain mariners of this country,[3] to the number of 14, which have been in the Spanish fleet ever since they first put to sea, and are now fled away from them,[4] having made sails for their cockboat with their shirts, do report and say :—That all the fleet, being 150 sail, did set forth out of Lisbon the

[1] Sc. 40- to 60-pounders.
[2] This report seems of a totally different character from the foregoing. It is a mass of unblushing falsehood ; lies told apparently for the sake of lying. At the time, however, it presumably was accepted as true.
[3] Holland.
[4] The rascals took care not to fly till the fortune of war had declared against the Spaniards.

30th May, and, coming near England,[1] were driven
back again by contrary winds. That in all the
whole number of them was but 25 thousand men,
whereof 10,000 good soldiers, the rest common men.
That they were victualled for three months, and for
any great sickness, there was none as it was reported ; neither did they land any more sick persons
at the Groyne than 300, from whence they put to
sea the 22nd of July *stilo vetere*,[2] and came to the
Land's End by the 28th of the same ; and till they
came over against Plymouth they met with no man,
where 40 of her Majesty's ships did skirmish with
them, and one galleass was taken, another set on
fire by reason the captain falling into a rage with
the gunner and threatening to kill him if he shot no
righter. The gunner cast fire into the powder barrels
and threw himself overboard. In this ship, they
say, was the treasure and five ensigns of Spaniards.
After this again, at Portland and the Isle of Wight,
her Majesty's navy set upon them, but no great
hurt done ; but between Calais and the Blackness
most furiously,[3] where a great galleass was taken, and
three other great ships, with 1,000 men apiece, sunk
downright about the Goodwins,[3] besides another
Italian ship, which they take to be sunk also, because they made signs for help, but none made
towards them. That there about Calais they were
forced to cut their cables, by the ships of fire which
came upon them out of her Majesty's fleet, and so
from thence fled away with all speed. That they
were driven thus above Dunkirk, and there about
Blankenberg one of their great ships was grounded
on the Wielings, and taken by them of Flushing,
wherein were 800 Spaniards, of whom 180 are come

[1] A wilful lie ; they could not help knowing that the fleet did
nothing of the sort.

[2] So in MS. ; but, in fact, it was *stilo novo*.   [3] Quite false.

to Rotterdam, the rest cast overboard. That before their fight about Calais, which was on the Sunday,[1] the Duke of Parma sent them word he would assist them the next day;[2] but, for that he kept not promise, they generally cry out against him. That on the Saturday he did what he could to embark[3] his men, but it would not be, notwithstanding that with his own hands he did kill some soldiers and captains. That in all they had not above 300 horse and some mules for carriage of their field ordnance. That generally the Englishmen have greatly endamaged them with ordnance, and that in the fleet they did see, through the portholes, an Italian ship all full of blood, which yet maintained the fight in her rank three hours after. That one of her Majesty's ships valiantly passed through them to charge the Admiral, who fled away, and—as they say—doth seem to be wonderfully dismayed and discouraged. That when they left them and fled away, they were as high as Walcheren, yet about 100 sail, but uncertain what course to take, or where to turn in for relief. For into Spain they dare not return, because at their coming out they were all threatened hanging if they conquered not England;[4] and that they had brought great store of halters to hang up all Englishmen;[4] but they think they will round about Scotland. That her Majesty's navy followed them always hard, and drove them like a flock of sheep, but durst not aboard them, because they are so high built, so as 40 of ours were troubled to take one of their greatest armados[5] at the last

[1] The fight off Gravelines, which was the only one east of the Isle of Wight, was on the Monday.

[2] It might be so reported in the fleet, but could not possibly be known. In fact, no such message was sent.

[3] MS. imbarcque.   [4] More lies.

[5] They did not take one ; but of that these fellows might be ignorant.

fight on Monday. That—as they think—they should
have landed about the Isle of Wight. That three
days and three nights after they came upon the
coast of England they did hull without sails,[1]
minding to come to Dunkirk upon the spring tides.
That they have great need of mariners and especially of pilots, for that ship which came on ground
upon the Wielings had but one pilot, and he was of
Flushing. That when they set forth out of Lisbon
there were certain galleasses in their company, but
they came not with them from the Groyne.[2] That
a great Brittany ship was also taken or sunk by the
English.[2] In sum, they confess the Duke Medina
to be wonderfully amazed, and to stagger which way
he may turn himself. That there were a great
number of the hidalgos of Spain in their army, and
that now, their chief bulwarks and armados being
discomfited, they may easily be overthrown, if they
be followed as they should be.

The ship whose prisoners are brought to Rotterdam was taken between Dunkirk and Ostend, and
had been shot through 350 times. Being grounded,
five ships of this country took them to mercy.
Another was also taken by seven of this country's
fleet between Calais and Dunkirk. The names of
certain prisoners of account taken in the former ship
are these :—Don Diego de Pimentel, brother of
the Marquis de Tavara, camp-master of the tercio of
Sicily ; Don Juan de Velasco, brother of the Conde
de Siruela ; Captain Martin de Avalos ; Captain
Marquis Alonso de Vargas.

In the one ship were 34 pieces of brass, and in
the other 63.

---

[1] A very wilful lie.

[2] There were four galleasses, and they all came as far as
Calais. There were four galleys, and they all sailed from Corunna
with the fleet. There was no Brittany ship in the armada.

August 3.—This morning I understand, the Duke of Parma attempting to break out, two of his men-of-war are taken by the fleet lying before Dunkirk, and the rest driven in again. It is said, moreover, that 17 sail of the Spaniards are carried into England, and that still her Majesty's navy follow and pursue them.

August 9.—WALSYNGHAM TO BURGHLEY.

[**Harl. MS. 6994, f. 142.**—Holograph. Addressed.]

My very good Lord :—To the end that her Majesty might grow to some full resolution what forces were meet to be kept both by sea and by land, I moved her to send for my Lord Admiral, and to appoint both his Lordship and the Lord Steward to be at the court on Sunday next, at St. James's, there to confer with the rest of her Council what were fit to be done therein ; whereunto her Majesty assented. I wrote to my Lord Admiral yesternight, to advertise how many ships he thought meet to be entertained in pay, and that the lesser ships that were not thought serviceable might be discharged. At his repair to the court his Lordship may be dealt withal therein.

For the sending of some money to the fleet for the relief of the decayed men, I think the same may be deferred until her Majesty's return. Touching your Lordship's opinion for the sending of four ships well appointed to follow the Spanish fleet, I think, if it had been thought of in time, they might have been very well employed, but I fear it will be now too late.

This day, at noon, her Majesty, dining with the Lord Steward in his tent at the camp, had advertisement sent unto her from Sir Thomas Morgan, who

is arrived at Margate with the 1,000 shot, that the
Duke of Parma was determined this spring tide to
come out, and that he looked that by that time the
Spanish fleet would be returned, according to an
agreement between him and the Duke of Medina.
But this matter, though it were effectually apprehended at the first, yet her Majesty doth not so
much account of it as that it will work any stay
here, as was determined upon. A conceit her
Majesty had that in honour she could not return, in
case there were any likelihood that the enemy would
attempt anything. Thus your Lordship seeth that
this place breedeth courage. I fear now more the
hand of God, in respect of unseasonableness of the
weather, than the enemy ;[1] and so I most humbly
take my leave. At the court, in the camp, the 9th
of August, 1588.

Your Lordship's to command,
FRA. WALSYNGHAM.

August 9.—WALSYNGHAM TO BURGHLEY.

[Harl. MS. 6994, f. 140.—Holograph. Addressed. Another
letter of the same date, from Gravesend, enclosing letters from
Henry Kyllygrew, on the condition of the army and the Low
Countries, and the want of money, which may, perhaps, be
obtained from the Merchant Adventurers. The postscript is:—]

The Flushingers were forced to retire from
Dunkirk the last storm, and the gap left open being
not as yet retrieved. But I hope that through[2] the
Lord Admiral's care they will be stopped in their
passage. Sir W. Russell doth put me in hope that
there will be some powder sent hither from Amster-

---

[1] Of course he knew that Morgan's 'advertisement' was mere
garrison gossip, and that the Duke of Medina had left much too
hurriedly to have come to any agreement with Parma about his
return. [2] MS. thorrowghe.

dam, for in Zealand there is none to be had. The 1,000 shot under the conduct of Sir Thomas Morgan are arrived, which may be made part of the 6,000 footmen. It were not wisdom, until we see what will become of the Spanish fleet, to disarm too fast, seeing her Majesty is to fight for a kingdom. It were meet that the governor[1] of the merchant adventurers were sent to Stade, to take some money.

August 9.—BURGHLEY TO WALSYNGHAM.

[**ccxiv. 54.**—Holograph.   Addressed :—For her Majesty's affairs. At the camp at Tilbury.   At Tilbury or Gravesend, W. Burghley. Seal : the Burghley crest, a garb supported by two lions.]

Sir :—Both by the copy of the Lord Admiral's letter which you sent me, dated athwart Harwich, and by another to myself from my Lord Admiral, written yesterday at Sandwich, I perceive the cause of his Lordship's return with the navy, and the doubtful course of the Spaniards, whether about Scotland or to Denmark.   What shall now be determined by her Majesty I cannot judge, yet I mind to provide some money, in readiness to be carried down to the seaside, to relieve the decayed men for a time.   And I think Sir John Hawkyns will either come, or send to let us know what money were needful, though I will provide some 8,000*l.* or 9,000*l.* ; yet I will not send it from London before I shall hear from you what you or her Majesty shall think meet.   My Lord spake with Quarles at Sandwich, who telling him that the provision of victual was for 7 or 8,000 men, his Lordship saith they are near 10,000 ; but how that number is composed, I know not.   The 15 sail of victuallers are at Harwich, as my Lord of Cumberland saith.   More is making

---

[1] Richard Saltonstall.

ready in London. My Lord Admiral I think will discharge all sick men, and the refuse of the small vessels; but being absent here alone, I dare not direct anything to him; presuming that, with her Majesty's liking, you there will advise him how to keep his strength only of ships of value, considering there are in the Narrow Seas, with my Lord Henry, so many small vessels.

I am not of opinion that the Spanish fleet will suddenly return from the north or the east, being weakened as they are, and knowing that our navy is returned to our coast, where they may repair their lacks, and be as strong as they were afore. And without a north or east wind the Spanish fleet cannot come back to England. I wish if they pass about Ireland, that four good ships, well manned and conducted, might follow them to their ports, where they might distress a great number of them, being weather-beaten, and where the numbers of the gallants will not continue on shipboard.

As I perceive, the powder that was sent from Dover never came to my Lord Admiral. It is in vain to write any more for advice until, from my lord Cobham, we may learn something of the Duke of Parma, who now resteth the enemy to be withstood.   Yours assured,

W. BURGHLEY.

9th Aug. 1588.

August 9.—BURGHLEY TO TRENCHARD AND HAWLEY.[1]

[**ccxiv. 55**.—Copy. Endorsed.]

After my hearty commendations :—Whereas by letters of the second of this present to my Lords of

---

[1] George Trenchard and Francis Hawley, Justices of the Peace for Dorset.

her Majesty's Privy Council, from the mayor and
other of the town of Weymouth and Melcombe
Regis, earnest request is made that they may, for
the better defence of their town and country thereabouts, be provided of some great ordnance, to
remain with them to her Majesty's use ; wherein
opportunity being now offered to satisfy their desire
with the remain of such ordnance as [was] brought
to their town in the carrack lately taken from the
enemy : to wit, eight pieces of brass, four old iron
minions, and two old fowlers :

These are to require you to deliver all these
pieces of ordnance to the said mayor and town, by
inventory indented and subscribed between them and
you ; specifying in the indenture the property of the
same to be her Majesty's, and to what end the same
are delivered unto that town.   Which inventory, I
think good to be by you sent up to my Lords.

And moreover, whereas my Lords are let to
understand that in the said carrack were divers other
commodities, which for want of landing and looking
unto may perish or take much hurt, and also certain
Spaniards : for the same commodities, I pray [you],
taking unto you the said mayor, and one or two
other honest, skilful merchants of Weymouth and
Melcombe Regis, to see the same landed, and safely
preserved in some convenient storehouses there ;
sending up a perfect inventory to my Lords of the
same, and, as near as you and the said merchants
can estimate, the just value and prices of these commodities, according to their several kinds and goodness, that afterwards their Lordships may give
order for the sale of the same.

And touching the persons taken in the carrack,
you shall do well to commit them to safe custody
until further order be given you from here ; and in
the meantime, to examine whether there be any man

of quality or great account amongst them, and presently to certify hither the names of every of them.

Thus much, in the absence of her Majesty and the rest of the Lords from the city here, I have thought good to write unto you; and so commit you to God. From my house in the Strand, the 9th of August, 1588.

Your loving friend,
W. Burghley.

August 9.—MEMORANDA BY BURGHLEY.

[ccxiv. 56.—Autograph.]

9th of August, 1588.—The state of the victualling of the navy with the Lord Admiral and the Lord Henry. The like state for powder &c. :—

Lord Admiral.—24th of July, 1588.

Nota: the army under the Lord Admiral's charge, being 7,093, was victualled unto the 11th of August. Order and money delivered to victual them for 1 month of 28 days, to end the 7th of September, whereof was limited to be provided 14 days' victual at Portsmouth, and 14 days' at Dover.

Nota: he had for this victualling, to end the 1st of September, 6,000*l.*

Lord Henry Seymour.—27th of July.

There was order that the number 32 ships, 16 of her Majesty's ships, with 1,522 men, should be victualled from the 11th of August unto the 8th of September, for which 5,243*l.* with transport for 350*l.* was delivered to Mr. Quarles.

9th of August, 1588.

	£	s.	a.
Order to victual 7,664 men with the Lord Admiral, from the 9th of September unto the 15th there,[1] which is for 7 days	1,421	4	o[2]
Item, for 1,522 men with the Lord H. Seymour, for 14 days, which is from the 29th of August unto the 11th of September, being in 17 ships of her Majesty	612	14	o[2]
Item, for 784 men's victuals, being in 16 ships of the coast, for 23 days, from the 20th of August to the 11th of September	530	16	o[2]

Total from 9th of August .   . 2,564 14 0

Powder delivered out of the Office of the Ordnance for the seas since the 24th of July, 1588 :—

25th of July.

To Portsmouth, to the Earl of Sussex for to be sent to the Lord Admiral, 5 lasts, beside 2 lasts sent to Portsmouth.

Roebuck.—27th of July.

To Dover by sea by Nich. Gorges[3]   5 lasts ⎫
Eodem die, to Dover by land by   ⎬ 17 lasts
the Surveyor's clerk   .   . 12 lasts ⎭

---

[1] Thereof.

[2] These sums are calculated at 6*d.* per man per day, with 80 added to each for transport. (Shown in a formal account of these items, ccxiv. 57, 58.)

[3] MS. Gordy. It is impossible to say what the Roebuck had to do with it.

24th of July.

Sent to Dover to Sir Wm. Wynter,
  for the Lord Henry Seymour .   4 lasts

27th of July.

To Mr. Nich. Gorges, with the 8
  ships of the 8 merchants   .   4 lasts 4 cwt.
Total for the sea before the 28th
  of July, which was 1 day afore
  the fight [1]   .   .   .   .   .   32 lasts

25th of July.

Sent by water to the Lord Steward   5 lasts ⎱
Sent by land to the Lord Steward   5 lasts ⎰ 10 lasts

8th of August.

Sent to Harwich by Wm. Vaughan,
  for the Lord Admiral   .   .   .   5 lasts
                                        ⎯⎯⎯⎯⎯⎯
                                        47 lasts

Powder sent to the Lord Admiral from the Lord
  Buckhurst,[2] and 5,000 shot.

The Queen's navy holdeth under
  the Lord Admiral   5,775
The Londoners, 20 ships   1,240
The coast men   1,639
On the seas with the Lord Admiral . 10,000 ⎱
On the seas with the Lord Henry   ⎬ 12,000
  Seymour   .   .   .   .   .   2,300 ⎰

---

[1] Gorges, at any rate, did not join the fleet till after its return from the north.

[2] Thomas Sackville, created Lord Buckhurst in 1567, at this time Lord Lieutenant of Sussex. He was appointed Lord High Treasurer in 1598 ; was created Earl of Dorset in 1604, and died in 1608.

Besides 18 merchant ships having in them 8 ships 530 men.

In Essex with the Lord Steward {footmen {Northampton {Warwick {horsemen {Huntingdon {horse

In Kent {footmen {horsemen

About London under the Ld. Chamberlain {footmen {horsemen

The lords of the nobility and Councillors {footmen {horsemen

	Per diem		
	£	s.	d.
Footmen, 17,000 men	651	13	4
Horse, 1,200 men . . .	98	0	8
Principal officers of the field . .	28	0	0
500 pioneers	16	13	4
Total	783	14	8[1]

700 shot under Colonel Morgan.

August 9.—RETURN OF SHIPS, MEN &c.

[ccxiv. 60.]

My Lord Admiral hath under his charge at the seas 66 sail ; and the number of men that are in those ships and pinnaces are in all 7,644 men.

My Lord Harry Seymour hath under his charge, victualled by her Majesty, of her Majesty's ships (17) and the coast ships (16) the number of 33 ships and pinnaces ; and the number of men in those ships and pinnaces are in all, with the coast ships, their men are in all 1,306 men.

[1] So in MS.

More, there is lately sent out of the river of Thames by the merchant venturers the number of 18 sail of ships, and their numbers of men that were appointed for them were 1,150 men.

So my Lord Admiral hath in his charge of ships   .   .   .   . 66 sail
Also my Lord Harry Seymour hath under his charge the number of 33 sail with the coast ships   .   .   .   .   . 33 sail
The merchant venturers, their ships being at the seas are in number.   .   . 18 sail
So the number of all the ships with my Lord Admiral and with my Lord Henry Seymour that are under their charge are   . 99 sail
More, the merchant venturers, their 18 sail maketh in all, with my Lord Admiral's and my Lord Henry Seymour's, the ships, 119 sail in all

The numbers of men with my Lord Admiral and my Lord Henry Seymour are in all 9,970 men.

Adding the merchant venturers their men thereunto maketh 11,120.

August 9.—HOWARD TO WALSYNGHAM.

[**ccxiv. 61**.—Holograph.   Addressed.]

Sir :—After I had spoken with Mr. Quarles at Sandwich, I galloped hither to the Commissioners, to understand by them of the state of the Duke of Parma. I did understand by them that he was not in that readiness that I perceive since, by Welshe, that he is ; but I do assure myself he can do no great matter except the Spanish army return to them. I do understand, by a small bark of our company that lost us in the storm, [that she] met

with 20 great hulks going, as it seemed, after the
fleet. I doubt they be some victuallers that do
follow them. If they can water in any of the Isles
of Scotland, or in the north part of Scotland, it
is very likely that they will return; for, [in] my
thinking, they dare not go back with this dishonour
and shame; for we have marvellously plucked them.
I would think it were not amiss that her Majesty
did send one, in post, to the Scottish King, that he
would withstand their landing and watering; and
yet I fear more his [1] going into Denmark, and there
to be relieved, and to be helped with ships.

Sir, I hear that Colonel [2] Morgan is come to
Margate with 800 soldiers, and I do hear it should
be for our ships. If it should be so, we must have
victuals provided for them before we can receive
them; for the victuals that Mr. Quarles [3] hath provided will not serve our company above 3 weeks;
for the proportion is but for 7,600 men, and we
are near 10 thousand. There must be care taken
for it.

Sir, I do understand for certain [4] that there is
great preparation of shipping and men at Dieppe
and at Newhaven, and that they are ready to come
out. Sir, it were good that such ships as be of
service, either in the Thames or elsewhere in the
coast-towns, should be sent out with speed, for we
must divide ourselves into parts, to prevent all
danger. This is a thing cannot continue above 6
weeks, and for that time we must be strong. Some
of our company have spent their mast, and some
are grown with this last storm into leaks; and
therefore I do assure myself a good many will not
be able to sail.

There is a number of poor men of the coast

[1] Sc. their.   [2] MS. Courenell.
[3] MS. Quarelus.   [4] MS. carten.

towns—I mean the mariners—that cry out for
money, and they know not where to be paid. I
have given them my word and honour that either
the towns shall pay them, or I will see them paid.
If I had not done so, they had run[1] away from
Plymouth by thousands. I hope there will be care
had of it. Sir, money had need to come down for
our whole company. Sir, I am going to Margate.
In haste, fare ye well. From Canterbury, the 9th
of August. Your loving friend,
C. HOWARD.

Sir, I do not see but of necessity there must be a
magazine at Dover.

Aug. 9.—SIR THOMAS SCOTT TO LEICESTER.

[**ccxiv. 52.**—Signed. Addressed :—For her Majesty's affairs.]

My especial good Lord :—Being certified this
morning by Mr. Nevenson, our scoutmaster, who
was aboard this last night with Sir Francis Drake
at Margate, that Sir Francis did inform him that
the Spanish army did intend to land at Dungeness,[2]
near Lydd, and there to entrench themselves, and
to be supplied from time to time out of France with
victuals and all necessaries, I have thought it very
meet to certify your Lordship thereof, to the intent
that I, by your Lordship's directions, may draw
either the forces here, or some part thereof, towards
that place when your Lordship shall think it meet.

[1] MS. rone.
[2] It is difficult to believe that Drake said anything of the sort.
Probably he spoke of this as a place where they might possibly
have intended to land, had not the 29th of July come in the way;
but Drake knew perfectly well that they had no such intention on
August 8. Nevenson would seem to have misunderstood him.

The nature of the place is as followeth :—Lying between New Romney and Rye Camber ; [1] compassing about in manner of a half island ; good harbour for ships at all winds except one point, which I take to be some part of the north ; four miles in breadth ; very deep at the shore, whereby men may be landed without help of longboats ; this half island containeth by estimation six or seven thousand acres, all of loose beach.[2] The next ground adjoining to the same consisteth of 50 thousand acres of marsh, inhabited with few other than shepherds and herdsmen ; so as it is a place of all this shire farthest from aid of men, and the greatest desert.

Sir Francis Drake reporteth that the greater half of the Spanish navy is defeated, and that, so far as his judgment and skill doth serve, he left them so far beyond the farthest point of Scotland as they cannot return to do any hurt in England this summer. Nevertheless, he will not warrant it but that they may return.

Here are landed at Margate, as I am informed, six or seven hundred musketeers out of the Low Countries. We humbly pray your Lordship's direction for them, and that they may be joined to this camp here, except your Lordship have otherwise disposed them. And so, recommending your good Lordship to the protection of the Almighty, I most humbly take my leave. From the camp at Northbourne, this 9th of August, in haste, 1588.

Your Lordship's to command during life,

THOMAS SCOTT.

---

[1] 'Rye Camber' would seem here to mean, in an extended sense, the estuary of the Rother, then a considerable sheet of water. In the course of 300 years, the disposition of land and water near Rye has been very much altered.

[2] Shingle. The word is still in common use along the south coast.

August 9.—SIR THOMAS HENEAGE[1] *TO WALSYNGHAM.*

[**ccxiv. 53.**—Signed.   Addressed.]

Sir :—By the news my Lord of Cumberland brought yesterday, my Lord Admiral is like to be, with her Majesty's navy, near the North Foreland, having left the Spanish fleet for lack both of powder and meat, having not received a corn of all that was set down in paper by my Lord Treasurer, which I take to be above 30 last, and sent by us ; and they driven to such extremity for lack of meat, as it is reported (I wot not how truly) that my Lord Admiral was driven to eat beans, and some to drink their own water.[2]   Thus the Spaniards be gone whither it please them ; to Scotland or Ireland, they may ; or else home about both, they may, with this wind.   These things would[3] be timely considered on ; which I thought good to put you in remembrance of, because of Mr. Bodley's going.[4]   And concerning new provisions of victual and munition to her Majesty's navy, which need be more substantially done than it hath been, I hope anon to see you.   Till when and ever, the Lord Jesus bless and keep you as myself.   At Sawmunds,[5] near the Court, this 9th of August, 1588.

Yours all assured,

T. HENEAGE.

[1] Vice-Chamberlain of the Household.

[2] My Lord of Cumberland seems to have been 'greening' them.   There was no such absolute want.   [3] Would=should.

[4] Thomas Bodley, diplomatic agent, had just returned from a special mission to the King of France, and was now appointed Resident at the Hague, with a vote in the Council of State, an office which he held till 1596.   On the accession of James I. he was knighted, and died, without issue, in 1613.   He is now best known as the founder of the Bodleian Library.

[5] In Norden's map of Essex it is shown as 'Samons' a house

August 10.—*HOWARD TO BURGHLEY.*

[**ccxiv. 66.**—Signed.   Addressed.]

My good Lord :—Sickness and mortality begins
wonderfully to grow amongst us ; and it is a most
pitiful sight to see, here at Margate, how the men,
having no place to receive them into here, die in the
streets.   I am driven myself, of force, to come a-land,
to see them bestowed in some lodging; and the best
I can get is barns and such outhouses ; and the
relief is small that I can provide for them here.   It
would grieve any man's heart to see them that have
served so valiantly to die so miserably.

The Elizabeth Jonas, which hath done as well as
ever any ship did in any service, hath had a great
infection in her from the beginning, so as of the 500
men which she carried out, by the time we had been
in Plymouth three weeks or a month, there were
dead of them 200 and above ; so as I was driven to
set all the rest of her men ashore, to take out her
ballast, and to make fires in her of wet broom, three
or four days together; and so hoped thereby to have
cleansed her of her infection ; and thereupon got
new men, very tall and able as ever I saw, and put
them into her.   Now the infection is broken out in
greater extremity than ever it did before, and [the
men] die and sicken faster than ever they did ; so as
I am driven of force to send her to Chatham.   We
all think and judge that the infection remaineth in
the pitch.   Sir Roger Townshend,[1] of all the men
he brought out with him, hath but one left alive ;
and my son Southwell likewise hath many dead.

between Orsett and Horndon.   It must have been pulled down
soon after.

[1] It nowhere appears in what ship or in what capacity Townshend was serving.   It might seem from this that he commanded
the soldiers on board the Elizabeth Jonas.   Cf. vol. i. p. 25 *n.*

It is like enough that the like infection will grow throughout the most part of our fleet ; for they have been so long at sea and have so little shift of apparel, and so [few¹] places to provide them of such wants, and no money wherewith to buy it, for some have been—yea the most part—these eight months at sea. My Lord, I would think it a marvellous good way that there were a thousand pounds worth or two thousand marks worth of hose, doublets, shirts, shoes and such like, sent down ; and I think your Lordship might use therein the Controller of the Navy and Waker, Mr. Hawkyns his man, who would use all expedition for the providing and sending away of such things; for else, in very short time I look to see most of the mariners go naked. Good my Lord, let mariners be prest and sent down as soon as may be; and money to discharge those that be sick here ; and so, in haste, I bid your Lordship farewell.   From Margate, the 10th of August, 1588.

Your Lordship's most assured to command,

C. HOWARD.

August 10.—*DRAKE TO WALSYNGHAM.*

[ccxiv. 65.—Signed, and autograph postscript.]

Most Honourable:—The army of Spain I think certainly to be put either with Norway or Denmark. There are divers causes which moveth me so to think.   The first, we understand by divers prisoners which we have taken, that generally, through all their whole fleet, there was no one ship free of sick people.   Secondly, their ships, masts, sails and ropes were very much decayed and spoiled by our

¹ The clerk has here written ' shewe,' which is nonsense.   It seems a mere careless blunder.

great shot. Thirdly, at Calais, by fire, we forced them to cut many of their cables, whereby they lost many of their anchors, which of necessity they must seek to supply. Further, if they had had none of these former great causes of distress, yet the winds and storm, with the wind westerly, as it was, hath forced them thither. And I assure myself that whensoever her Majesty shall hear of their arrival in any of these coasts, that her Highness shall be advertised both of their great distress and of no small loss amongst them; for I assure your Honour, her Majesty's good ships felt much of that storm, and lost many of their boats and pinnaces, with some anchors and cables; yet were we fair by our own shore, and the wind right off the land.

Some amongst us will not let[1] to say that they are in Scotland. I cannot think so, for that we had no wind whereby they were able to recover any place of the mainland of Scotland; without it were some of the out isles, which are no meet places to relieve their so many great wants. Norway, or the out isles of Scotland, can relieve them but with water and a few cows, or bad beef, and some small quantity of goats and hens, which is to them as nothing. And yet these bad reliefs are to be had but in few places, and their roads[2] dangerous.

The only thing which is to be looked for is, that if they should go to the King of Denmark, and there have his friendship and help for all their reliefs, none can better help their wants in all these parts than he; for that he is a prince of great shipping, and can best supply his wants which now the Duke of Medina the[3] Sidonia standeth in need of, as great anchors, cables, masts, ropes and victuals; and what the King of Spain's hot crowns will do in

[1] Let = leave, cease.   [2] Roadsteads.
[3] So in MS.

cold countries for mariners and men, I leave to your good Lordship, which can best judge thereof.

We left a pinnace of her Majesty's, the Advice, and a fine caravel of my own to attend the fleet of Spain, when we left them; but what is become of them [in] that great storm, or whether they may be stayed in any other country, as they may, I know not. My poor opinion is, that it were most meet to send a good ship and some fine bark, with some very sufficient person, to deal effectually from her Majesty with the King of Denmark, as he shall find the cause to require; and to send the true report back with all speed possible, that they may be the better prevented[1]; for no doubt but that which they are able to do they will presently put it in execution. The winter will overtake them else in those parts. If they stay in the Sound this winter, I hope[2] many of the Spaniards will seek Spain by land.

The Prince of Parma, I take him to be as a bear robbed of her whelps; and no doubt but, being so great a soldier as he is, that he will presently, if he may, undertake some great matter; for his rest will stand now thereupon. It is for certain that the Duke of Sidonia standeth somewhat jealous of him, and the Spaniards begin to hate him, their honour being touched so near; many of their lives spent—I assure your Honour not so little as five thousand men less than when first we saw them near Plymouth—divers of their ships sunk and taken; and they have nothing to say for themselves in excuse, but that they came to the place appointed, which was at Calais, and there stayed the Duke of Parma's coming above 24 hours, yea, and until they were fired thence.

So this is my poor conclusion. If we may recover near Dunkirk this night or to-morrow morn-

---

[1] Forestalled.　　　[2] Hope=am confident.

ing, so as their power may see us returned from the chase, and ready to encounter them if they once sally, that the next news you shall hear will be the one to mutiny against the other; which when that shall come to pass, or whether they mutiny or no, let us all, with one consent, both high and low, magnify and praise our most gracious and merciful God for his infinite and unspeakable goodness towards us; which[1] I protest to your good Lordships that my belief is that our most gracious Sovereign, her poor subjects, and the Church of God hath opened the heavens in divers places, and pierced the ears of our most merciful Father, unto whom, in Christ Jesu, be all honour and glory. So be it; Amen, Amen.

Written with much haste, for that we are ready to set sail to prevent the Duke of Parma this southerly wind, if it please God; for truly my poor opinion is that we should have a great eye unto him. From her Majesty's very good ship the Revenge, this 10th of August, 1588.

Your Honour's faithfully to be
commanded always,
FRA. DRAKE.

For that we were very near to set sail, I most humbly beseech your Honour to pardon my pen, for that I am forced to write the very copy of that letter which I have sent to my Lord Chancellor. Since the writing hereof, I have spoken with an Englishman which came from Dunkirk yesterday, who saith upon his life there is no fear of the fleet. Yet would I willingly see it.   Your Honour's ever,
FRA. DRAKE.

[1] As to which.

August 11.—*DRAKE TO WALSYNGHAM.*

[ccxiv. 70.—Holograph. Addressed.]

Most Honourable :—The sudden sending for of my very good Lord, my Lord Admiral, hath caused me to scribble[1] these few lines. First most humbly beseeching your Honour to deliver this letter unto her Majesty as a testification of my Lord Admiral's most honourable using of me in this action, where it hath pleased his good Lordship to accept[2] of that which I have sometimes spoken, and commended that little service which I was able, much better than in either of them both I was able to deserve. Wherein, if I have not performed as much as was looked for, yet I persuade myself his good Lordship will confess I have been dutiful.

Touching any other causes that either hath been done or is to be done, let me pray pardon of your Honour, for I assure your Honour that my Lord Admiral hath so sufficiently instructed himself daily, as I faithfully believe his good Lordship will thoroughly satisfy her Majesty and your Honours what is now best to be done. Thus humbly taking my leave, I beseech God to bless the work of her Majesty's hands always. Written aboard her Majesty's good ship the Revenge, at midnight, this 11th of August, 1588.

Your Honour's faithfully to be commanded,

FRA. DRAKE.

Aug. 11.—*MATHEW STARKE'S DEPOSITION.*

[ccxiv. 63-4.—Copy, in duplicate.]

A note of certain speeches spoken by Sir Martin Frobiser at Harwich, in the presence of divers persons, as followeth :—

[1] MS. screbell.　　　　[2] MS. except.

The Lord Sheffield,
Sir John Hawkyns;
with others, whose names I cannot recite.

The 11th day of August, 1588, I arrived at Harwich, and delivered the letter sent by the Lord Admiral unto the Lord Sheffield, whom I found in his bed in the house of Mr. King.

First, after I had delivered my Lord's letter, the Lord Sheffield bade me depart, and so I did according to his commandment.

Then immediately he sent for me again; at which time of my return I found there Sir John Hawkyns, Sir Martin Frobiser, with divers others, who demanded of me in what surety the ships were in, and whether they were all at Margate or not.

Then Sir Martin Frobiser began some speeches as touching the service done in this action; who uttered these speeches following, saying :—Sir Fra. Drake reporteth that no man hath done any good service but he ; but he shall well understand that others hath done as good service as he, and better too. He came bragging up at the first, indeed, and gave them his prow and his broadside; and then kept his luff,[1] and was glad that he was gone again, like a cowardly knave or traitor—I rest doubtful, but the one I will swear. Further, saith he, he hath done good service indeed, for he took Don Pedro. For after he had seen her in the evening, that she had spent her masts, then, like a coward, he kept by her all night, because he would have the spoil. He thinketh to cozen us of our shares of fifteen thousand ducats ; but we will have our shares, or I will make him spend the best blood in his belly ; for he hath had enough of those cozening cheats already.

[1] MS. lowfe.

He hath, saith he, used certain speeches of me, which I will make him eat again, or I will make him spend the best blood in his belly. Furthermore he said, he reporteth that no man hath done so good service as he. But he lieth in his teeth; for there are others that hath done as good as he, and better too.

Then he demanded of me if we did not see Don Pedro over night or no. Unto the which I answered No. Then he told me that I lied; for she was seen to all the fleet. Unto the which I answered, I would lay my head that not any one man in the ship did see her until it was morning, that we were within two or three cables length of her. Whereunto he answered, Ay, marry,[1] saith he, you were within two or three cables length; for you were no further off all night, but lay a-hull by her. Whereunto I answered No, for we bare a good sail all night, off and on.

Then he asked me to what end we stood off from the fleet all night; whom I answered that we had scryed[2] three or four hulks, and to that end we wrought so, not knowing what they were. Then said he: Sir Francis was appointed to bear a light all that night; which light we looked for, but there was no light to be seen; and in the morning, when we should have dealt with them, there was not above five or six near unto the Admiral, by reason we saw not his light.

After this and many more speeches, which I am not able to remember, the Lord Sheffield demanded of me what I was; unto the which I answered, I had been in the action with Sir Francis in the Revenge, this seven or eight months. Then he demanded of me, What art thou? a soldier? No,

---

[1] MS. I marye.
[2] Scryed, or, in the duplicate, escryed = descried.

and like your Honour, answered I, I am a mariner. Then saith he, I have no more to say unto you ; you may depart.   By me, MATHEW STARKE.

All this written on the other side I do confess to be true, as it was spoken by Sir Martin Frobiser, and do acknowledge it in the presence of these parties whose names are hereunder written :—

> Captain Platt ;[1] Captain Vaughan ;[1]
> Mr. Gray, master of the Ark ;
> John Gray, master of the Revenge ;
> Captain Spindelow.

Moreover, he said that Sir Francis was the cause of all these troubles, and in this action he showed himself the most coward.

By me, MATHEW STARKE.

August 11 (?).[2]—*PETITION OF THE CAPTAIN, MASTER AND LIEUTENANT OF THE MARGARET AND JOHN OF LONDON.*

[ccxiii. 89.—Endorsed.   Addressed :—To my assured Friend.][3]

Whereas, Right Honourable, sundry reports have been spread concerning the taking of the ship wherein Don Pedro de Valdes was captain, and that

---

[1] Captain Platt is in Fenner's list (vol. i. p. 118), but neither he nor Vaughan had an independent command, they were probably masters of two of the great ships.   Spindelow, who is also in Fenner's list, had commanded the Thomas Drake till she was burnt on the morning of July 29.

[2] Not dated ; but it evidently refers to Frobiser's claim, and must belong to about this date.

[3] It would seem from this address that the petition was written by Tomson and privately sent by him to Walsyngham (cf. vol. i. 344 *n*.) to lay before the Council.

your Lordship's suppliants, John Fisher,[1] William Nash, and Richard Tomson, commanders of the Margaret and John of London, have been advertised that some others besides Sir Francis Drake (to whom the credit and honour of that prize doth most condignly appertain) have made challenge and enjoyed a good portion of the spoil thereof, we have thought good to set down unto your Honours, in a few articles, the service done by us and our said ship in that behalf ; humbly beseeching your Lordships, that if the said prize and prisoners are thought fit to be reparted[2] amongst such as were actors for her apprehension, or that, in your Honours' wisdoms, it be thought expedient that the forwardness of the willing be something considered, before such as never gave any attempt for the taking of her, that in such case, it may please your Lordships to vouchsafe to peruse our allegations, containing nothing but the truth of our own action, and do most dutifully submit ourselves to such consideration as to your Lordships' wisdoms shall seem expedient ; whom Almighty God long bless with health and increase of felicity.

1.—Your Lordships' suppliants, beholding upon Sunday, the 20th[3] of July, about 5 o'clock in the afternoon (upon which day we had our first encounter with

---

[1] Of Cley in Norfolk, a kinsman of the family which some years later gave birth to Christopher Myngs. In 1571 he commanded the Swift of Blakeney, trading to the Low Countries. Afterwards he commanded the Margaret and John of London, trading to the Mediterranean under charter to the Levant Company, or helping to burn the ships at Cadiz in 1587, and to fight the Spaniards in the Channel or off Gravelines in 1588. He brought away from the San Lorenzo a piece of plate, which is still in the possession of the family. He commanded the Centurion with Drake in 1589, was at Cadiz in 1596, and died at Salthouse in 1616.

[2] Divided.   [3] So in MS. It ought to be 21st.

the Spaniards), the opportunity that God had offered
into our hands by breaking the masts of Don Pedro
his ship, the which all the English navy beheld as
well as we, we only, with our ship, the Margaret and
John of London, as all the fleet can testify, bare
romer [1] with the ship, being accompanied neither
with ship, pinnace, or boat of all our fleet.

2.—At our approaching to the said ship, we
found left by her, for her safeguard, a great galleon,
a galleass and a pinnace, with order either to help her
repair her masts, and so follow the Spanish army,
gone before, or else to bring away the men, treasure
and munition thereof, and to fire or sink the ship;
all which three, upon the sudden approach of our
ship, only forsook Don Pedro, leaving him to the
mercy of the sea.

3.—If that present evening we had not followed
the opportunity, but delayed the same until the
morning following, as others did, then had the ship
been repaired and carried away; or else the men,
treasure and other things of value taken out by
such as were appointed to attend on her, and so all
of us frustrated of the prize. And this much hath
Don Pedro himself confessed, condemning and ex-
claiming much upon those that were left for his
comfort, in that they forsook him, upon the coming
of one small ship.

4.—About 9 of the clock the same evening we
came hard under the sides of the ship of Don Pedro,
which, by reason of her greatness and the sea being
very much grown, we could not lay aboard without
spoiling our own ship. And therefore, seeing not
one man shew himself, nor any light appearing in
her, we imagined that most of the people had been
taken out; and to try whether any were aboard or

---

[1] Romer : the more common form is room or roome ; bare
romer with=bore down to.

not, we discharged 25 or 30 muskets into her cage-work, at one volley, with arrows and bullet. And presently they gave us two great shot, whereupon we let fly our broadside through her, doing them some hurt, as themselves have and can testify.

5.—After this we cast about our ship, and kept ourselves close by the Spaniard until midnight, sometime hearing a voice in Spanish calling us ; but the wind being very great, and we in the weather,[1] the voice was carried away, that we could not well understand it, but were persuaded by our mariners, to be the voice of one swimming in the sea ; whereupon we put off our ship boat with 8 oars, to seek, call, and take them up ; but found nobody.

6.—About midnight, my Lord Admiral being about a league from us and lying a-hull, made sail after the whole fleet of the enemy's ; which when we perceived, fearing his Lordship's displeasure if we should stay behind the fleet, we made all the sail we could, and followed my Lord to overtake him. And the next morning betimes we went aboard the Ark, and certified his Lordship in what distressed state we had left the ship our enemy ; praying leave that we might be permitted to return to finish our attempt ; or that his Lordship would send a pinnace to Dartmouth or Plymouth, that some shipping might be set forth to fetch her in ; for that she could not possibly escape, if she were assaulted, and sought for.

7.—During this speech with my Lord Admiral, came up one Captain Cely in a pinnace, certifying his Lordship that Sir Francis Drake, staying behind the fleet all night, had taken the said ship of Don Pedro de Valdes, with 460 men in her, full of artillery, munition and some treasure. Therefore, if any do challenge or expect any recompense for

[1] In the weather=to windward.

service done against the said ship (except Sir Francis Drake, to whom she was wholly yielded), we hope that we cannot be in equity excluded, in that we drave away the three ships overnight, which otherwise, before the morning, might have carried all away; referring the examination of the truth unto your Honours, and the reward to your Lordships' ordering; whom the Lord long continue in health and felicity.

August 12.—*SEYMOUR TO WALSYNGHAM.*

[**ccxv. 1.**—Holograph.   Addressed.]

Sir :—I have received letters from Sir John Conway,[1] the which I send you to peruse, desiring you to return both it and Sir William Russell's letter. I sent Captain Musgrave [2] unto him, a very sufficient man, quick and careful. By the way he had two Dunkirkers in chase, who had the wind of him, otherwise he had had some hand of them.

This morning my Lord Admiral sent unto me, desiring very earnestly to speak with me and Sir William Wynter; and the message was no sooner delivered but there was descried almost 30 sails afar off. I sent him word I had her Majesty's pres[ent] service in hand, whereby I could not attend him; also I was directed by my Lords to have a vigilant eye to these coasts. But if my Lord himself should come into the Narrow Seas, and that Sir Francis Drake should attend as Vice-Admiral, I pray you let me be called home; for by that I find by experience, by good observation, some seers of antiquity are not the same persons they are deemed. And even so do commit you to God. In haste.

[1] Governor of Ostend.   [2] See vol. i. p. 233.

From aboard the Rainbow, this 12th of August, 1588, returned to the Downs.

Your assured friend to command,

H. SEYMOUR.

I am earnestly desired by Sir William Russell and Sir John Conway to visit them, which—if it were not in respect of her Majesty's services for Dunkirk, of the which truly, as I have always written in many my letters, the same was never to be feared by the Duke himself, except he were supported by the Spanish or French—I would gladly see them, so as I be warranted by my Lords' directions. But this withal, we must have our whole month's victuals; whereof we have received but one fortnight, and the same in manner expired.

August 12.—MEMORANDA BY BURGHLEY.

[**ccxv. 3**.—Autograph. Endorsed, in Burghley's hand :—12th of August, 1588. Charge of the navy with the Lord Admiral and Lord Henry Seymour. They are pleasing counsels in company.]

To spend in time convenient is wisdom.

To continue charges without needful cause bringeth repentance.

To hold on charges without knowledge of the certainty thereof, and of means how to support them, is lack of wisdom.

Sea.—Lord Admiral :

There is no knowledge given what are the monthly charges on the seas. By conjecture, there are 12,000 men in pay, and so many victualled; which is, by the month, in wages and victuals   .   .   . 16,800*l.*

Nota.—In the beginning of July, when the Lord Admiral went to the West Seas,[1] there was in wages with him . . . . . . 3,770 ⎫
And with Sir Francis Drake . 2,820 ⎬ 6,590

Afterward his Lordship and Sir Francis Drake took more ships into service, with the number of men . 399

Total in charge in the West Country, 4th of July . . . 6,989

In wages and victual per month, at 28s. a man . . . . . 9,784*l.* 16s.

Sea.—Lord H. Seymour :

In the charge of the Lord Henry Seymour with 16 ships were the number of men in charge . . 1,471 men.

Item. Afterwards were brought into her Majesty's charges ships of the coasts, in number of men . . 850 men.

Total in charge in the Narrow Seas with the Lord Harry . . 2,321

In wages and victuals . . 3,249*l.*

Total of all the numbers on the seas in the Queen's charge, per month 9,310 men.

Total in money . . . . 13,033*l.* 16s.

August 12.—*REPORT OF VICTUALS.*

[ccxv. 5.—Endorsed :—For my Lord Treasurer. And in Burghley's hand :—James Quarles' report of victuals, delivered to me 12th of August, 1588, at St. James.]

A declaration unto your Lordship what sums of money hath been received since the 14th of July, by order of your Lordship's warrant, out of the Ex-

---

[1] Actually, he went in the end of May. See vol. i. p. 179.

chequer, for the victualling of her Majesty's navy ; and how the same hath employed, viz. :—

Receipts.

	£	s.
First, Received the 14th day of July	6,000	0
Item, the 16th day of July	1,854	14
Item, the 29th of July	5,593	0
Sum	13,447	14

Of the which, Payments.

	£	s.
To Mr. Darell, the 15th of July, for the victualling 8,000 men for one month of 28 days, to begin the 8th of August, and to end the 5th of September, as appeareth by your warrant, at 6d. the man per diem	6,000	0
To Richard Peter, the 16th of July, for the victualling of 1,471 men, in 16 of her Majesty's own ships with my Lord Henry Seymour, for one month of 28 days, beginning the first of August, and ending the 28th of the same, at 6d. the man per diem	1,179	14
To him, more, for the victualling of 850 men, in ships out of divers ports, serving at the Narrow Seas, for one month of 28 days, beginning the 24th of July, and ending the 19th day of August, at 6d. the man per diem	675	0
To the said Richard Peter, more, the 29th of July, for the victualling of 7,664 men, serving under the charge of my Lord Admiral, for one month, by order of your Lordship's warrant ; to begin the 12th of August, and to end the 8th of September, at 6d. the man per diem, with transport	5,593	0
Sum	13,447	14

It will plainly appear unto your Lordship that
her Majesty's whole navy under the charge of my
Lord Admiral had been victualled for 6 weeks,
beginning from the first of August until the 30th of
September,[1] if by the sudden coming of the Spanish
fleet his Lordship was[2] enforced to take that victual
which was at that time on board, and to leave the
rest with Mr. Darell to be sent after; which, by
Mr. Darell's certificate unto your Lordship, will
appear; which victual is now at the seas with the
said Mr. Darell; which being delivered, my Lord
Admiral with the numbers of 7,671 men, with an
increase of 7 days' victual more, which lately your
Lordship hath given order for, shall be victualled
from the 12th of August unto the last of September.[3]

August 14.—*SEYMOUR TO WALSYNGHAM.*

[**ccxv. 8.**—Holograph.   Addressed.]

Sir :—There be five pinnaces that went unto my
Lord with provision of shot, powder and provision ;
and one at Yarmouth that went to seek my Lord
Admiral, and know not where to find him.   It were
very good they had intelligence of my Lord Admiral
here, to the end they may return, or otherwise abide
your pleasure.   So, having sent a perfect note of all
ships, their tonnages and number of men, according
to your last direction, do take my leave.   From
aboard the Rainbow, this 13th of August, 1588, in
the small Downs, where either for lack of wind, or
too much contrary winds, we abide ; and yet see all

---

[1] So in MS.

[2] 'Not' is surely omitted.   The sense clearly is, 'had not been
enforced.'

[3] The carelessness and inaccuracy of the wording and arithmetic in an important return of this nature is very noteworthy.

passengers, and do ne'er a whit fear the Duke of Parma's coming forth.

Your assured to command,
H. SEYMOUR.

A man of Rye, being a fisherman that came out of the North Seas, doth advertise this this morning, and that the Spaniards he judgeth to be about the Orkneys. Upon some occasions I have sent a pinnace to Ostend and Flushing.

August 14.—*SEYMOUR TO WALSYNGHAM.*

[**ccxv. 9.**—Holograph. Addressed.]

Sir :—Albeit I lie sometimes, and that very seldom, in the small Downs, yet do I take this order to send my spials abroad, as I think good, to discover news.

This day a skipper of Emden, being bound for Newhaven with pitch and tar, came aboard me, delivering me news, which himself saw, so far as he could descry, a great fleet off of Housdon[1] in Holland, and that great fleet did stand to the northward in his sight; and ever since the wind hath been for the most part southerly. Another, that is come from the Brill, did see no fleet at all.

For Dunkirk news, I send you Sir Thomas Scott's letter, and his advertisement from Doir, the same certified from Calais. Notwithstanding, I have sufficient forces this morning abroad along the coasts, besides a pinnace to bring me word if they should have any need of further help. It is advertised likewise that the Duke of Parma hath sent for the galleass, meaning to employ her, if she be of

---

[1] Huisduinen, near the newer and larger Helder. The church spire seems to have been a well-known landmark.

service; which if it should be so, then Monsieur
Gourdan playeth on both hands, and it had been a
good turn if she had been fired at the first.

Thus inferring[1] these and such like slight advertisements for matters rather of further charges to
her Majesty than otherwise, do take my leave.
From aboard the Rainbow, this 14th of August, in
the Downs, where with one tide, upon occasion of
their stirring, I can put over to them.

Your assured loving friend ever,

H. SEYMOUR.

I have taken order for Mr. Bodley, who came
unto me this morning, upon a postscript from you
revoking my Lords of the Council's letters, directed
to my Lord Admiral, and in his absence unto me.

I shall likewise know by to-morrow morning, by
these ships I sent this morning, more certain news
of the Duke of Parma, if any stirring be.   Besides
the spring of the tides is past, which is one of my
observations I had always observed.

I pray you procure us pay for our mariners, who
are more than four months behind.

August 14.—*SEYMOUR TO WALSYNGHAM.*

[ccxv. 10.—Signed.   Addressed.]

Sir :—I send you now more certain news of the
Duke of Parma his forces of Dunkirk, of the which
there is no likelihood or appearance of any issuing
forth, by reason the spring is past and altogether
declined.   And having had further conference with
one of the Flushingers sent unto me from his
admiral, doth assure me that there is not above 26
vessels great and small, wishing they were twice as

---

[1] Inferring=bringing in, reporting.

many more for them to deal withal, and to have the honour of the action ; who are of strength, of themselves, 40 good sails. And now, by reason the spring is past, they do mean likewise to attend the Duke of Parma's courses over again [1] Sluys, where some of his flat bottom boats be, meaning to return again towards Dunkirk the next spring, and as wind and weather shall give them leave.

I do send you likewise the admiral's letter itself, which I pray you to return, both that and others, after you have taken your pleasure. I perceive by him, likewise, they take a special care to send out 50 sails of North Hollanders in the pursuit of the Spaniards, for the better guarding of their coasts ; and have restrained their fishermen that go for herrings, so as yet they will not suffer them to go to sea in those affairs,[2] although the state of the country dependeth upon that fishing. And even so, do commit you to God. From aboard the Rainbow, the 14th of August, 1588.

Your assured friend to command,

H. Seymour.

Aug. 14.[3]—*SEYMOUR* (?) *TO PRINCE MAURICE.*

[**Holland, lvi.**—Copy. Endorsed. French.]

Sir :—To advertise you of our success since our meeting with the enemy and the great fight on Monday, being the 29th of July, you should understand that the Spaniards have lost about eight great ships, of which one is a galleass, and by my estimation, there are slain of their men from five to six thousand. My Lord the Admiral of England continueth to

---

[1] Against.   [2] Their business.
[3] The letter is dated on the 4th, but the postscript is ten days later.

follow them, keeping the advantage of the wind, and taking every occasion to fight with them. As for me, I have returned with our fleet, which will join you as soon as possible.[1] Meanwhile I do not doubt that you will have an assured watch, so as the enemy cannot undertake anything to your hurt, the more as you can keep them closely shut up in Dunkirk until the wind and other occasions permit us to join our forces with yours. In my opinion, this will be much better. Thus commending myself to your good favour, I pray God to help us with his pity, and to give you, Sir, a happy and long life. In haste, this 4th of August, 1588.

Postscript.—Sir, it is ten days past that I have written these letters, which the wind and other chances have delayed the passage of this captain. But for that I am since advertised that the Duke of Parma [2] is still unwilling to draw away his forces by sea, and hath manifested an intention to advance into the country, it seems to me very necessary to have a good eye to him. Therefore I pray you to send me word from time to time so as we shall be able to make our preparations for whatsoever occasions shall offer themselves. Likewise I pray you to advertise me of the forces which he has in Dunkirk, and if his ships are ready, with their number of mariners, and if there is any way of burning his ships in the haven; for now that he hath tasted of our strength in the encounter which we have had with the Spaniards, it is meet that we should pursue them to the uttermost, if you desire to live in better peace, as the Queen of England, my Sovereign Lady, desires it, as well for you as for herself. Meanwhile,

---

[1] This could scarcely be written by anyone but Seymour.

[2] MS. que le Duc de Parma ne veut point encore jetter arrière ses forces par mer comme il montre ses desseins pour aller plus avant au pays.

it is not possible that he should at this time undertake any enterprise by sea, because that the spring
is past ; nevertheless he may send some small
vessels northward, which you will easily be able to
overcome.

August 15.—*HOWARD TO WINCHESTER.*

[ccxv. 20.—Copy. Endorsed.]

To the Right Honorable my very good Lord
the Lord Marquis, and the rest of the Justices of
Peace in the county of Dorset.

After my hearty commendations :—Whereas the
Ryall of Weymouth hath served in her Majesty's
service of late against the Spaniards, in defence of
religion, our prince and country, for the space of
one month, wherein she and her company have
performed their duties very well, and that now, in
reward of their good service, they look for payment
and satisfaction :

These are therefore to pray your Lordship, and
the rest of the justices of your shire, to cause an
estimate to be first taken of the powder, shot,
victuals and other charges of pay, and such like ;
and afterwards to cause the sum to be levied by
equal contributions, as shall seem good to your
Lordship and the rest, out of your shire of Dorset ;
and therewith to reward and satisfy the good
service of the said ship and company.

And so, not doubting of your Lordship's favourable help herein, and the readiness of the rest, I bid
your Lordship and the rest heartily farewell.   From
aboard her Majesty's good ship the Ark, the 15th
of August, 1588.   Your loving friend,

C. HOWARD.

CHARGES OF THE RYALL OF WEYMOUTH.

[**ccxv. 20, I.**—Endorsed :—A note of the charge &c. Exhibited
by Thomas Middleton.]

A note of the charges expended by the Ryall of
Weymouth in her Majesty's service against the
Spanish fleet, under the Right Honourable the
Lord Admiral, set forth the 22nd of July, 1588, for
one month :—

	£	s.	d.
First, for 9 barrels of powder .	56	0	0
Item, 1 cwt. of match . . .	1	5	0
for cartridges in canvas. .	1	0	0
for one minion piece, broken in the fight . . .	6	0	0
for the hire of the ship, being of burden 160 tons, for one month	16	0	0
for the wages of 70 men for one month. . . .	50	0	0
for the victualling of the said 70 men, according to her Majesty's rate . . .	45	10	0
Sum total	175	15	0

Memorandum.—That there was one bowsprit
spent, and one anchor broken, with some other spoil
in the said ship, which is not charged in this account.

August 16.—*SEYMOUR TO WALSYNGHAM.*

[**ccxv. 21.**—Holograph. Addressed.]

Sir :—I have taken order for Monsieur de
Clermont [1] to pass him over safely to Flushing; also

[1] Clermont d'Amboise, one of the leaders of the French
Protestants, and at this time on an embassy from the King of

have directed another pinnace for Boulogne, being a matter of importance which requireth haste. And as for your news of the Spaniards for being at the Frith of Moray, and that the same should not be able to receive the whole fleet, I have inquired of the most sufficient pilots in our company, that do resolve me certainly that it is a great bay, able to contain two such fleets, being in distance 10 leagues over in the bay, within where they may ride along the shore, from[1] the North-North-West to SW. winds; but all easterly winds, it is open and a very ill place, such as if it blows any strength they are not able to ride. And as for my Lord Admiral coming hither, I am very glad, and could have wished his Lordship here all my time of abode, for the bettering of the service. But as touching my Lord's sending out to Dunkirk, I know well they have tasted of the same cup as Mr. Bellingham's company, which I sent this other day. So, having nothing else to write, do commit you to God. From aboard the Rainbow, this 16th of August, 1588.   Your assured friend to command,
                                   H. SEYMOUR.

The merchant ships lately set out from London, under the charge of Mr. Gorges and Mr. Bellingham,[2] their victuals do expire on Thursday next; which, if they be further to be employed, they must be supplied; as also ourselves, of her Majesty's old company, having but 12 days, at this present, of victuals.

Navarre to solicit Elizabeth's assistance. Cf. Wright's *Queen Elizabeth and her Times*, ii. 384.

[1] With the wind from &c.

[2] Henry Bellingham had commanded the Rainbow with Drake at Cadiz in the previous year. He was now the captain of the George Noble, and in command of the ten ships set forth by the city of London on July 29. See vol. i. p. 339.

August 16.—SEYMOUR TO THE COUNCIL.

[ccxv 22.—Holograph.   Addressed.   In bad condition.]

It may please your Lordships :—Whereas I
received a letter from Sir Thomas Scott, and other
advertisements besides, concurring with the said
letter, of the Duke of Parma's sudden reinforcing
his strength with present shipping to transport
40,000 men for England, albeit I could hardly be
persuaded in my own conceit, as well for not having
other aid than his own, as also being the last day of
the spring for any coming out of large ships from
Dunkirk, yet, nevertheless, I took order for Mr.
Bellingham, the 13th of this month, to go presently
thither with his charge of ships.   Withal I sent a
pinnace for advice, [and if] any service should
happen, to bring me word.   [Upon] which his being
there, the weather being most variable (by the
experience I have divers times bought dear), two of
his ships was aground and himself in great danger.
But, thanked be God, this morning they be come
over, all somewhat out of order by the distress of
weather.   So as I hope your Lordships will be
thoroughly resolved that those coasts are not to be
stayed upon.

I am further informed upon our seas, that the
Spanish fleet are in Scotland, in the Moray Frith,
and that the King of Scots should be enforced
to leave his country ; which if it be so, your Lordships do know it better than myself, and what is to
be done herein.

As for the Duke of Parma, what with the
Flushingers' good attendance on the one side and
our ships on the other, as I have always written, I
shall never be so happy to see him come out, but

rather fear him in other places, having [suspicion of mind] that it is not unlike he may attempt both Bergen-[op-Zoom] and Ostend at one time; so much the more because it is not unknown unto him how this country is weakened by sending over Sir Thomas Morgan [with] so many musketeers.

Lastly, I still perceive a continual recourse in transporting victuals to Calais, which is the only colour for the enemy now that the Lords[1] are absent from Bourbourg.

This, having overlong troubled your Lordships, I humbly take my leave. From aboard the Rainbow, this 16th of August, 1588, at anchor in Dover road.

Your Lordships' humble to command,

H. SEYMOUR.

August 16.—*THE COUNCIL TO BURGHLEY.*

[**B.M. Egerton MS. 1525, f. 14.**—Signed. Addressed.]

After our right hearty commendations to your good Lordship :—Whereas there was a Privy Seal directed to your Lordship, bearing date the 13th of July last past, for the defraying of the charges for the victualling of those ships which were at the seas, as well under our very good Lord the Lord Admiral of England as the Lord Henry Seymour, according to such certificates as[2] the numbers of men that shall from time to time serve in the said navy as your Lordship shall receive either from the said Lord Admiral, the Lord Henry Seymour, and Sir William Wynter, knight, or from six of us, from month to month, according as there shall be occasion for the continuance of the service :—Now, forasmuch

---

[1] The commissioners for the treaty.
[2] So in MS. As to, or of.

as it is thought most necessary that there should be a new supply of victuals to be made for the times ensuing ; viz., for 7,664 men's victuals to serve under the Lord Admiral for seven days, beginning the 9th of September next following, and ending the 15th day of the same month, the sum of one thousand three hundred forty-one pounds and four shillings, and for the transportation of the same proportion of victuals fourscore pounds ; likewise for the victuals of 1,522 men serving in her Majesty's ships under the said Lord Henry Seymour, for 14 days, beginning the 29th day of this present August, and to end the 11th of September following, the sum of five hundred thirty and two pounds 14s., and for transportation of the same fourscore pounds ; and also for 784 men's victuals serving under the said Lord Henry Seymour in sundry merchants' ships, for 23 days, to begin the 20th of this August, and to end the said 11th of September, 1588, the sum of four hundred fifty pounds 16s., and for transportation thereof fourscore pounds : These shall be to pray your Lordship, according to the said warrant, out of such her Majesty's treasure as remaineth in the receipt of the Exchequer, to pay or cause to be paid unto James Quarles, surveyor-general for the victualling of her Majesty's navy, the sums aforesaid, amounting together to the sum of 2,564*l.* 14s. : Wherein these shall be sufficient warrant and discharge to your Lordship in that behalf. So we bid your Lordship right heartily farewell. From the Court at St. James, the 16th of August, 1588.

Your Lordship's assured loving friends,

W. Burghley.   C. Howard.

H. Hunsdon.   W. Cobham.   F. Knollys.

T. Heneage.

Fra. Walsyngham.   Jamys Croft.   A. Poulet.

August 17.—*SEYMOUR TO WALSYNGHAM.*

[**ccxv. 24.**—Holograph. Addressed.]

Sir :—Monsieur de Nassau was driven over at the same time when Mr. Bellingham was with his company put to the same trump, and came yester-night to Dover, and this morning followed me to the Downs with 40 sails well appointed and furnished. When I anchored he came to dinner unto me, where he found Sir Henry Palmer, Edward Wynter and John Wynter, Sir William being ill at ease in his bed. Among many conferences which he ministered of our exploits, with the banquet which the Spaniards received of her Majesty's navy between Calais and Gravelines, he said that the enterprise was so proud and so *outrecuidé* of Parma to procure all the nobility of Spain to take upon them the conquest of England, that if there had been no blow given, but only the discovery of her Majesty's great forces both by land and sea,[1] had been enough to have mated[2] them, thinking that they will be better advised another time how to take in hand the like action. And as for the Duke of Parma his forces by Dunkirk, he thinketh them not to exceed 30 sails, altogether unfurnished of mariners, which he could never procure ; so in his opinion, his flat bottom boats should[3] never have enterprised anything upon England, but upon the present joining of both the navies, English and Spanish, where their last meeting was[4] ; wherein God hath mightily defended

[1] It.   [2] Confounded.   [3] Would.
[4] He appears to mean, upon the joining of the fleets and the defeat of the English ; but he does not say so.

us, considering the time of their anchoring nigh upon the spring tide.[1]

I find his service, with the Count de Nassau himself, much devoted to her Majesty; and so much the more, for that they find her Majesty hath always dealt most favourably with them when the peace was tendered. What is further to be advertised, I refer to his letters, which he desired me to see the same conveyed. I find the man very wise, subtle[2] and cunning, and thereafter do trust him.

This, having this morning set a-land Monsieur de Clermont returned to Boulogne, as otherwise despatched him to Flushing, do commit you to God. In some haste, from aboard the Rainbow, this 17th of August, in the Downs, 1588.

Your assured loving friend ever,

H. SEYMOUR.

Postscript.—I hope my Lord Admiral will be satisfied of our experience for riding on the other coasts; for had not Mr. Bellingham and two other ships have been aground, the Aid, and others which he sent at that time, had come to a worst reckoning, and were enforced to come away, for all they were commanded to ride there by his Lordship.

I shall be enforced to send Mr. Bellingham and his charge to-morrow hence, having not victuals for three days; and in like sort my cousin Knyvet[3] two or three days after, except the same be countermanded. Our own victuals expire ten days hence; and by that time another month be supplied, I hope her Majesty's cares and troubles will end for this year; but I do not believe so for the rest.

---

[1] Which would have allowed the larger vessels to get out of Dunkirk if the English had been defeated.

[2] MS. suttell.   [3] See *ante*, p. 36.

Aug. 17.—*COUNT JUSTIN TO WALSYNGHAM.*

[**ccxv. 25.**—Holograph. Addressed. French.]

Sir :—Being arrived yester evening, in the road
of Dover, with forty ships of war, I had the honour
to find my Lord Seymour in the same, where, when
I had particularly related to him that I had heard of
the designs of the Prince of Parma, he assured me
that it should be very agreeable to your Honour if
I were to inform you thereof by letter.   For this
cause, Sir, I think it my duty to make known to
you that, by the report of the espials which I sent
to Bruges, the Prince of Parma hath disembarked
his soldiers as well at Dunkirk as at Nieuport;
nevertheless, he still keepeth them together in the
western parts of Flanders, with the intention, as
many judge, of laying siege to Ostend, if he hath
not intelligence that the Spanish fleet is like shortly
to return hitherwards, which it is hard to be believed, as it was received so briskly the first time by
her Majesty's fleet.

There are now at Sluys 70 or 80 flat-bottomed
boats[1] of those that should be at Nieuport; wherefore I judge that the enemy may undertake something against the isles of Zealand; and though I left
before the said haven to the number of 25 crom-
sters,[2] to impeach their coming out, yet, as the tides
will not serve those of Dunkirk to come out, for
the more surety I will go thither myself with all

[1] MS. *pleytes.*
[2] MS. *crommestevens.*   The word, as the thing, was Dutch.   It
was a sort of hoy, and would seem to have been approved of, as
in December four were ordered for the English navy (*S.P. Dom.
Eliz.* ccxix. 6o), and after that they became common.   For small
craft, they carried a heavy armament : eight culverins, six demi-
culverins, and two sakers.

my ships, so as to fight them with more advantage, if perchance they should attempt anything against Holland or Zealand.   Nevertheless I will not fail to return before Dunkirk by the next full moon to impeach their coming forth, or to meet with them if they design to put to sea.   Thus I humbly kiss your Honour's hands, and beseech the Almighty to give you, Sir, good health and a long and happy life. From my ship, in the Downs, this 27th [1] of August, 1588.

Your very humble and affectionate servant,

JUSTINUS DE NASSAU.

August 18.—*SEYMOUR TO WALSYNGHAM.*

[ccxv. 27.—Holograph.   Addressed.]

Plain dealing is best among friends.   I will not flatter you, but you have fought more with your pen than many have in our English navy fought with their enemies;   and but that your place and most necessary attendance about her Majesty cannot be spared, your valour [2] and deserts in such places opposite to the enemy had showed itself.

For Mr. Henry Bellingham and his company, as I wrote yesterday by my servant, his victuals will scant carry him home to London ; which, if you find cause of further employment, you may use your authority.   Also Mr. Thomas Knyvet's company is in the like predicament, which is like to follow, except the same be countermanded.

But as touches our martial men, whom you have always respected, let a old servant of her Majesty's, Mr. Henry Bellingham, not be forgotten in that concerneth him, to make recompense of her Ma-

---

[1] New style.   [2] MS. valure.

jesty's favour towards him in his suit, for the which your favourable means will be a good help ; and for further experience of Dunkirk and Gravelines coasts, it seemeth he hath been heretofore acquainted with them.

For myself, as I have not spared my body, which I thank God is able to go through thick and thin, let not the same be spared to knit up all [harass] between her Majesty and her service, so far forth as God will give us leave ; I will not say as the Duke of Parma, by[1] Sir John Conway's letter which I sent you—I am bound to revenge, and I will do it, asking[2] God no leave. I will not trouble you any further; but if you have cause to employ me further, let all my wants be supplied, and refer the rest to God. From aboard the Rainbow, this 18th of August, 1588. Your assured friend ever,

H. SEYMOUR.

Sir, I should do the master of my ship wrong if I should not further his careful service, being a man of substance, most valiant, and most sufficient besides concerning his charge. I would desire you to prefer him to her Majesty coat[3] of ordinary, for I know ne'er a man in England that I would wish sooner to have care of the prince's person, if they were driven to the seas, than him.

Spare me not while I am abroad ; for when God shall return me, I will be kin to the bear, I will be haled to the stake, before I come abroad again.[4]

[1] Sc. as the Duke of Parma said, according to &c.

[2] MS. axing.

[3] To be one of the four masters attendant, who received annually, in addition to wages and victuals, a richly laced scarlet coat. Cf. *BM. Addl. MS.* 5752, f. 19 ; Monson's *Naval Tracts*, in Churchill's *Voyages*, iii. 284, 289.

[4] The extreme badness of the writing of this letter, and the inconsequence of the sentences, seem to suggest that it was written late in the evening.

August 19.—*SEYMOUR TO WALSYNGHAM.*

[**ccxv. 31.**—Signed, and autograph postscript.   Addressed.]

Sir :—I shall be glad to do her Majesty all the service I can which in duty I am bound, as otherwise for my country.   I find my Lord Admiral doth repair to these quarters, as I gather, to this end, to seek the Spaniards ; whom when he shall find, I wish him no better advantage than he had upon our last conflict with them.   But I hardly doubt the meeting of them this year, and for my own part desire to be spared at home for divers respects, which hereafter I may unfold.   I know I am envied, being a man not suitable with them, and therefore my actions and services shall be in vain.   Besides my summer ship, always ordained for the Narrow Seas, will never be able to go through with the Northern, Irish, or Spanish seas, without great harm and spoil of our own people by sickness.   I have hitherto (*invita Minerva*) maintained my honour and credit in all my services as best becometh me.   I would be loth now to stand *ad arbitrium Judicis*, and thereafter do pray you to respect your good devoted friend, who hath many weighty irons of his own to look unto ; and so do commit you to God.   From aboard the Rainbow, the 19th of August, 1588.

Your very loving assured friend,

H. SEYMOUR.

Postscript.—I shall be enforced to send away my cousin Knyvet and his company to-morrow to London, because of their short victuals and other lacks, which must be supplied, if the service be any more commanded.

August 19.—*SEYMOUR TO HOWARD.*

[ccxv. 33.—Signed, and autograph postscript. Addressed.]

My good Lord :—By the receipt of your Lordship's letter, and upon further consideration for my ship, I think it convenient to acquaint your Lordship beforehand in what sort she is, and how I was enforced, upon the discovery of our enemies, to alter her decks by cutting them and to make her fightable, so as now the time of the year is past, and the mariners of the ships do already complain of the great cold they find, and shall every day more and more sustain the like, except she be holpen and better repaired for their succour. Otherwise, in the summer time, the ship being repaired and mended as I say unto your Lordship, and those naked quarters which I find in her supplied with two pieces of ordnance more, I would not change her for many ships in the fleet.

And because your Lordship sets down the time of my Lady Sheffield's[1] repair to Dieppe not before the 26th of this month, and that our victualling doth expire within a day or two after, by the 28th of this month, I have made some stay of sending the Achates, to the end that Mr. Burnell, whom your Lordship appointed to come unto me, whom I do not yet see, may fulfil your pleasure therein. This, being glad to understand of your Lordship's repair to these coasts, do commit you to God. From aboard the Rainbow, the 19th of August, 1588.

Your Lordship's loving friend,

H. Seymour.

[1] Howard's sister Douglas, widow of the second Lord Sheffield, and wife of Sir Edward Stafford.

It would be known what shall become of Mr. Thomas Knyvet's company by to-morrow some time in the day, or otherwise I must send him away.

The men of my ship do begin to fall sick already, and did the last year die unreasonable, when Sir H. Palmer was in her, which is to be considered by your Lordship.

After I had sealed your Lordship's letter, being informed of some pilling[1] knaves between Beachy and the Ness,[2] I have despatched away the Achates, and the same to clear the coasts and to transport my Lady your sister, wishing them to prolong their victuals thereafter.

August 19.—SEYMOUR TO WALSYNGHAM.

[ccxv. 34.—Signed, and autograph postscript.   Addressed.]

Sir :—I have received letters from my Lord Admiral, by the which I perceive his Lordship is to repair to these coasts; whereof I am not a little glad, and hope I may now be discharged upon the time of his Lordship's coming.   For otherwise, if there be any reckoning for me to attend his Lordship northward or to the other seas, in seeking the Spaniards, whom I hardly believe we shall find, this ship is not for the purpose, except she be presently mended and repaired; for our men fall sick, by reason of the cold nights and cold mornings we find; and I fear me they will drop away far faster than they did the last year with Sir Henry Palmer, which was thick enough.   Otherwise, being repaired, and supplied with such necessaries as is

---

[1] To pill = to rob.   [2] Dungeness.

requisite for her, and which I find by experience most of her Majesty's ships have, I shall be glad to serve in her before many other ships. And even so do commit you to God. From aboard the Rainbow, the 19th of August, 1588.

> Your very loving assured friend,
> H. SEYMOUR.

I am taught to find the advantages and disadvantages of my ship, for that she is naked on both sides in one of her quarters, lacking two good brass pieces.

August 19.—*SIR JOHN PERROT*[1] *TO WALSYNGHAM.*

[ccxv. 30.—Signed. Addressed.]

Sir:—May it please you: as by chance two Irish merchants were put into this haven of Milford, that lately were at Bluet[2] in France, and yesterday came to my house; by whose reports it should seem certain galleys of the Spanish fleet were lost upon the coast of France, though not so many as I would there were. And inasmuch as I am glad to advertise the same, I have sent you herein the report of one of the merchants, signed with his hand; but how true I cannot warrant, but judge it to be so. I humbly take my leave. Carew,[3] the 19th of August, 1588.

> Yours whom you may command,
> J. PERROT.

---

[1] Formerly Lord Deputy of Ireland, but had been superseded in the preceding February, by Sir William Fytzwylliam.

[2] Blavet : on the south side of the river Blavet, where it falls into Port St. Louis.   [3] In Pembrokeshire.

August 18.—*NEWS OUT OF FRANCE.*

[ccxv. 30, I.—Copy.   Enclosure in Sir John Perrot's letter of
August 19.]

Written the 18th of August, 1588.

Nicholas Feld of Dublin, merchant, arrived at
Bluet in France the first of August, and there met
with a Spanish galley which was driven there by
foul weather.   By report of a ship that came from
Newfoundland, that there was a galley lost upon the
Sein, for proof, they found of the Spaniards upon
the water, and took them up, and took off their
clothes.   More, the admiral of the galleys commanded that they would bear up with him to
Bayonne de Buck[1]; and the pilot of one of the
galleys told the captain that if he had gone for
Bayonne that there was no way but death, and if
he had gone with him to France he would save
their lives with God's help, whereupon they did
agree to go with him, and did arrive at Bluet in
France, being so sore beaten with weather that they
had the carpenters 10 days repairing of the galleys.
Also the admiral with one galley in his company
went for Bayonne, and there was lost both.[2]   For
proof, the said Nicholas spake with one of their
galley slaves, which was a Frenchman of Bluet
that came away from thence, which told this news.

NICHOLAS FELD.

[1] Boucaut, the old mouth of the Adour.

[2] There were four galleys in the armada when it sailed from
Corunna.   They all parted company in crossing the Bay of
Biscay, and were driven by the fresh wind to the coast of France.
One was lost at Bayonne; the other three eventually returned to
Spain (Duro, i. 65 *n.*, 123; ii. 332).   Feld's story was therefore
false so far as he was repeating hearsay, but very possibly he did
see one of the galleys at Blavet.

August 21.—*DON PEDRO DE VALDES TO KING PHILIP*

[**ccxv. 36.**—Endorsed :—Copy of Don Pedro de Valdes' letter to the King his master. Englished.[1] August last, 1588, *stilo novo.*]

The 30th [*stilo novo*] of last month I acquainted your Majesty[2] with the proceedings of your fleet until that time ; now I will write what hath since happened unto me. The same day the Duke called to council ; and being within 10 or 12 leagues of Plymouth, where, by the report of a fisherman whom we took, he ,had understanding that the English fleet was at anchor,[3] it was resolved we should make to the mouth of the haven and set upon the enemy, if it might be done with any advantage ; or otherwise, keep our course directly to Dunkirk without losing of any time. Within two hours after, their fleet was discovered out of my ship four leagues off to leeward of ours, the haven of Plymouth remaining to windward[4] of us. I acquainted the Duke withal presently, desiring to know what he thought fit to be done ; wherein he neither took resolution nor made me answer, but, hoisting sail, spent all that day and night bearing but little sail, and by that means gave the enemy time to get the wind of us[5] by next morning, who presently set upon our rearward where Juan

[1] There is no copy of the original, which was most probably sent on to the King. See *post*, p. 149.

[2] Of this letter there is naturally no trace in this country. It is not mentioned by Duro.

[3] Cf. vol. i. p. xxxvii, and *post*, App. E.

[4] So in MS. In fact, it was to leeward, the wind being south-westerly.

[5] Though evidently, as they were running before the wind, the English would have got the wind of them still sooner if they had carried more sail.

Martinez de Recalde and I did sail with the shipping under our charge. Our ordnance played a
long while on both sides, without coming to hand
stroke. There was little harm done, because the
fight was far off.

When we had ended, I sent a pinnace unto Juan
Martinez de Recalde, to know whether he had
received any harm; his answer was that his galleon
had been sore beaten, and that his foremast was
hurt with a great shot; praying me that I would
come to relieve him, for that other-ways he should
not be able to abide any new fight if it were offered
the same day. Whereupon making towards him
with my ship, according to his desire, it happened
that another Biscayan ship of his company, lying so
in the way as I could neither pass by nor bear room,
on the sudden fell foul in such sort with the prow of
mine as she brake her spritsail and crossyard [1]; by
reason of which accident, and for want of sail, my
ship being not able to steer readily, it happened
again that, before I could repair that hurt, another
ship fell foul with her likewise in the self same
manner, and brake her bowsprit, halyards and forecourse. Whereupon, finding myself [2] in so ill case, I
presently sent word thereof to the Duke, to the end
he might stay for me until I had put on another
forecourse, which I carried spare, and put myself [2] in
order.

In the meanwhile I got to the fleet as well as I
could; and, being to leeward of them, struck the
crossyard of my foremast and the rest of my sail, to
repair my hurt the better, hoping that the Duke
would have done according to my request. While
I was in this case, the sea did rise in such sort that

---

[1] This seems to mean the spritsail yard, but lower down it is
clearly the fore yard.
[2] MS. meself.

my ship, having struck sail and wanting her halyard of the foremast, being withal but badly built, did work so extremely as shortly after, and before it could be remedied, her foremast brake close by the hatches,[1] and fell upon the mainmast, so as it was impossible to repair that hurt but in some good space of time. I did again send word thereof two several times to the Duke, and discharged three or four great pieces, to the end all the fleet might know what distress I was in, praying him either to appoint some ship or galleass to tow me ahead, or to direct me what other course I should take. Nevertheless, although he was near enough to me, and saw in what case I was, and might easily have relieved me, yet would he not do it; but even as if we had not been your Majesty's subjects nor employed in your service, discharged a piece to call the fleet together, and followed his course, leaving me comfortless in the sight of the whole fleet, the enemy being but a quarter of a league from me; who arrived upon the closing up of the day; and although some ships set upon me, I resisted them, and defended myself[2] all that night, till the next day, hoping still that the Duke would send me some relief, and not use so great inhumanity and unthankfulness towards me; for greater I think was never heard of among men.

The next day, finding myself in so bad case, void of all hope to be relieved, out of sight of our fleet, and beset with the enemies, and Sir Francis Drake, admiral of the enemy's fleet, bearing towards me with his ship, from whom there came a message that I should yield myself upon assurance of good usage, I went aboard him, upon his word, to treat of the conditions of our yielding, wherein the best conclusion that could be taken was the safety of our lives and courteous entertainment; for performance

---

[1] The deck.   [2] MS. meself.

whereof he gave us his hand and word of a gentleman, and promised he would use us better than any
others that were come to his hands, and would be a
mean that the Queen should also do the like; whereupon, finding that this was our last and best remedy,
I thought good to accept of his offer.   The next
day he brought me to see the general, by whom I
was courteously received, seeming to be sorry that
the Duke had used me so hardly, and confirming
the same promises that Sir Francis Drake had
made unto me.

   After ten days space that I had been in his
company, he sent me to London; and with me, the
captains of footmen, Don Alonso de Çayas[1] of
Laja, and Don Vasco de Mendoça y de Silva[1]
of Xerez de los Cavalleros, who had charge of the
companies that were levied in those places; and the
Queen at his request sent us four leagues off to a
gentleman's house, called Richard Drake,[2] that is
his kinsman, where we receive the best usage and
entertainment that may be.   About forty of the
better sort besides are bestowed in divers men's
houses in London; the rest, together with the ship,
were carried to Plymouth.[3]

   I have no other matter to impart unto your
Majesty until the return of Sir Francis Drake, who
is yet at sea, for then there will be some resolution
taken what shall become of us.   These captains do
humbly kiss your Majesty's feet, and we all beseech
your Majesty that it will please you to remember us,
and to comfort us with your princely letters in
answer hereof &c.   August last, 1588.

[1] Duro, ii. 80.   [2] Cf. vol. i. p. 356.
[3] She was sent to Torbay and Dartmouth.

Aug. 22.—SIR G. CAREY TO LORD HUNSDON.

[**ccxv. 37.**—Signed.   Addressed.]

My duty to your Lordship most humbly remembered :—It may please you to be advertised that this morning there arrived here divers mariners of this island, which came in a bark of Hampton, from Shetland [1]; who, upon oath, affirm that on this day fortnight, being the 8th of this present, they being come 12 leagues from Shetland, South-East, where they had been a-fishing, they descried a very great fleet of monstrous great ships, to their seeming being about 100 in number, lying just West, with both sheets aftward,[2] whereby their course was to run betwixt Orkneys and Fair Island ; Shetland lying North and by East of Orkneys 21 leagues, and Fair Island lying 10 leagues from Orkneys, about East-North-East.   Sithence which time, for 7 days together, they say they found at sea the wind most at South-East ; whereby they judge the Spanish fleet could fetch no part of Scotland except some of the out isles ; for themselves, lying by a wind, which a fleet will hardly do, it was 7 days before they could reach Moray Frith, which is far in the north of Scotland.

These good news of so peaceable a departure of our enemies, if before they have not been delivered, or not with so great certainty, I humbly beseech your Lordship to present them from me to her Majesty and the rest of the Lords ; to whom I spare to write, in respect I hope your Lordship will acquaint them with them.   Whereas also I sent a bark to see in what sort the Spanish ship that lay

---

[1] MS. Shotland, throughout.   [2] Aughtwarde.

at Hogge[1] Bay in France was to be set upon, having prepared men and shipping to have set forth to take her, what news I received from Alderney, both of that ship and otherwise, your Lordship shall also receive here enclosed.[2] And so, with the humble remembrance of my duty to my Lady, I humbly commit you to the tuition of the only Almighty. From the Park, this 22nd of August, 1588.

Your Lordship's most dutiful and obedient son,
GEORGE CAREY.

August 22.—HOWARD TO THE QUEEN.

[**ccxv. 40.**—Holograph.   Addressed :—To the Queen's most excellent Majesty.]

My most gracious Sovereign[3] :—The great goodness of your Majesty towards me that hath so little deserved, doth make me in case that I know not how to write to your Majesty how much I am bound to you for your infinite goodnesses, nor cannot be answered by any ways but with the spend of my blood and life in your Majesty's service, which I will be as ready and as willing to do as ever creature that lived was for their prince.

My most gracious Lady, with great grief I must write unto you in what state I find your fleet[4] in here. The infection is grown very great and in many ships, and now very dangerous ; and those that come in fresh are soonest infected ; they sicken the one day and die the next. It is a thing

---

[1] La Hogue. This was the Santa Ana, which had left the fleet after the fight on the 25th.
[2] Not now to be found.   [3] MS. Soferen.
[4] He had been summoned to the Court on the 9th, signed a Council letter at St. James's on the 16th, and arrived at Dover on the 21st.

that ever followeth such great services,[1] and I doubt
not but with good care and God's goodness, which
doth always bless your Majesty and yours, it will
quench again. The course that we here think meet
to be kept, both for the service as also for the safety
of your Majesty's people, we have written at large
unto my Lords of your Majesty's Privy Council, to
inform your Majesty, and have also sent this bearer,
Mr. Thomas Fenner, who is both wise and can
inform your Majesty how all things standeth here.
And because it requireth speed, the resolution of
your Majesty, I do leave to trouble your Majesty
any further, praying to the Almighty God to make
your Majesty to live more happier days than ever
creature that lived on the earth. From Dover, the
22nd of August.

Your Majesty's most bound, most
faithful and obedient servant,
C. HOWARD.

Even as I had written thus much, Mr. E.
Norreys [2] came, whose advertisement [3] doth alter the
case much.

August 22.—HOWARD TO THE COUNCIL.

[ccxv. 41.— Signed. Addressed.]

May it please your Lordships :— Upon my
coming back to Dover the 21st of August, about
three of the clock in the afternoon, I presently sent
for the Lord Henry Seymour, Sir William Wynter,
Sir Francis Drake, Sir John Hawkyns, Sir Henry
Palmer and Mr. Thomas Fenner, to come unto

---

[1] MS. sarvyses.
[2] Sir Edward Norreys, brother of Sir John. See vol. i. p. 306 *n.*
[3] See *post,* p. 142.

me, to confer with them for the present consideration of her Majesty's service ; who declared unto me the state of the fleet, which with sorrow and grief I must deliver unto your Lordships. As I left some of the ships infected at my coming up, so I do find, by their reports that have looked deeply into it, that the most part of the fleet is grievously infected, and [men] die daily, falling sick in the ships by numbers ; and that the ships of themselves be so infectious, and so corrupted, as it is thought to be a very plague ; and we find that the fresh men that we draw into our ships are infected one day and die the next,[1] so as many of the ships have hardly men enough to weigh their anchors ; for my Lord Thomas Howard, my Lord Sheffield, and some five or six other ships, being at Margate, and the wind ill for that road, are so weakly manned by the reason of this sickness and mortality, as they were not able to weigh their anchors to come whereas[2] we are.

Now, my Lords, sith the matter is of that moment for the service of her Majesty and this realm, we have entered into consideration what is fittest to be done, the extremity being so great ; the one touching the service of the realm, the other concerning the mortality and sickness ; and therefore thought this course which we here set down to be fittest to be done ; which is :—To divide our fleet into two parts ; the one to ride in the Downs, the other at Margate or Gorend[3] ; to bring our men, as many as conveniently we can, ashore, and there to relieve them with fresh victuals, and to supply such other their wants as we can ; and upon the hearing or discovery of the Spanish fleet, we shall be able,

[1] All this is quite incompatible with the sickness being dysentery, as has been very commonly alleged.
[2] Where.   [3] Gore-End.

with the help of soldiers[1] from the shore, for to be ready within a day for the service. And therefore, we are to pray your Lordships that Mr. Quarles may be sent down with all speed unto us, with that money that should have prepared the next victual-ling, therewith to provide fresh victuals upon the shore for the relieving of those men ; and so we will spare these victuals which we have aboard.

My Lords, we do not see, amongst us all, by what other means to continue this service ; for the loss of mariners will be so great as neither the realm shall be able to help it, and it will be greater offence[2] unto us than the enemy was able to lay upon us ; and will be in very short time answerable to their loss, besides the unfurnishing of the realm of such needful and most necessary men in a commonwealth. I know your Lordships will ac-quaint her Majesty with this great cause, which I leave unto your Lordships' honourable wisdoms to consider of.

My Lords, I must deliver unto your Lordships the great discontentments of men here, which I and the rest do perceive to be amongst them, who well hoped, after this so good service, to have received their whole pay, and finding it to come but this scantly unto them, it breeds a marvellous alteration amongst them ; and therefore I do not see but, of present necessity, there must be order sent down for the payment of them unto the 25th of August ; whereof I leave Sir John Hawkyns to certify the Lord Treasurer in more particular from himself.

The Roebuck is not yet come to the fleet, but, as I understand, she is employed by my Lord of Hun-tingdon[3] in the north service, whereby we are disappointed of the powder in her. And so I take

[1] MS. souldyoures.　　　　[2] Offence = injury.
[3] President of the Council of the North.

my leave of your Lordships. From Dover, the 22nd
of August, 1588.

    Your Lordships' most assured to command,

C. HOWARD.

August 22.—HOWARD TO WALSYNGHAM.

[ccxv. 42.—Signed.   Addressed.]

Sir :—Being about to write unto you of the
mortality and sickness in our fleet, and divers other
matters, I received intelligence by this gentleman,
Sir Edward Norreys, of the return of the Spanish
fleet. Wherefore, neglecting all things else, I bend
myself wholly unto such things as chiefly concern
the service, and refer the particular relation of the
same advertisements unto himself, praying you, with
all possible speed, to send down all the shipping and
mariners from London that you can, and that with
all speed. Besides, the Roebuck is not yet come,
whereby we miss that powder and shot in her.
Therefore I pray you that we may have supply of
all such things, in that greatest quantity you can.
And so, in greatest haste, I bid you heartily farewell.
From Dover, the 22nd of August, 1588.

Your very loving friend,
C. HOWARD.

Post.—Sir, there is here no provision of fireworks, nor boats, nor anything else ; for they rely so
upon my Lord Cobham, that without his warrant
they will do nothing ; for so Mr. Barrey sent me
word.

August 22.—HOWARD TO WALSYNGHAM.

[**ccxv. 43**.—Signed, and autograph postscript. Addressed.]

Sir :—The absence of the Roebuck doth hinder us wonderfully for lack of the powder in her. Mr. Barrey is sick, and there is neither fireworks nor boats ready here against any service, if the enemy should anchor anywhere. Therefore either my Lord Cobham must come down himself, or send such as hath authority, to provide us of such necessary things for service. We want pitch and tar here. It were good that some were sent to Sandwich. I pray you send me word the whether it was not appointed that a hundred sail of ships should be kept and retained in her Majesty's service by Sir Francis Drake and Mr. Hawkyns,[1] when they were sent down before me. And I bid you most heartily farewell. From Dover, the 22nd of August, 1588.

Your loving and assured friend,
C. HOWARD.

Sir, I do assure you I do not see that we are yet [arrived[2]] here, till they of London come again, above 60 sail great and small, and we are very ill manned. I pray let mariners be sent away with all expedition. I would my counsel had taken place, that the forces by land had been kept together till the full of the moon had been past.

[1] 'And Mr. Hawkyns' added in Howard's own hand.
[2] Conjecture.

August 23.—HOWARD TO WALSYNGHAM.

[**ccxv. 44.**—Holograph.   Addressed :—For her Majesty's affairs.]

Sir :—Mr. Barrey is dead, and we cannot learn where the pitch and tar is become ; nor no man now to deal for those things.   There must be some [1] sent down from my Lord Cobham,[2] to take order both for that and the boats that should be occupied [3] if Sir E. Norreys' advertisements be true, as it is very likely.   I am afraid it will be wished the forces had not been so soon dissolved.

I do assure you I doubt much that Hare's advertisement is not good ; for many hath met with them since that time that he speaketh of, that they should be passed betwixt Orkney and the Faroe Isles, 60 leagues a this side them.

Young North,[4] that served the Palatine, and hath been in the fleet all this time, came yesternight hither from Ipswich ; who declareth that there came one thither that came from the eastwards, and said to divers of the town that, as I take it, about the 16th of this present he saw them bear this ways, and that they were thwart of Berwick and kept the midst of the channel, and that they have but only their foresail to stem the tide, and sometime lay a-hull.   If it be true, then did they detract the time to come just with the spring.

[1] Some person.
[2] Barrey was Lieutenant-Governor of Dover ; Cobham, Lord Warden of the Cinque Ports.
[3] Occupied = employed, made use of.   So Luke xix. 13, 'Occupy till I come,' where the Revised Version has, 'Trade ye herewith till I come.'
[4] Sir Henry North, knighted by Leicester in 1586, younger son of Roger, second Lord North.   It does not appear what ship he had been in.

Sir, God knoweth what we shall do if we have no men. Many of our ships are so weakly manned that they have not mariners to weigh their anchors. The three ships that are gone to take the Spaniard at Newhaven, and the Elizabeth Jonas, that is at Chatham, hath weakened our fleet much. Well, we must do what we can. I hope in God that he will make us strong enough for them, for all men are of good courage here. That which will be done will be betwixt to-morrow and Wednesday. None of your lieutenants be in the ship; both needed not to have gone to London. My Lord Cobham's presence would do well here. That which must be done must be with speed. So fare you well. In haste, the 23rd of August.

Your assured loving friend,

C. HOWARD.

August 23.—SEYMOUR TO WALSYNGHAM.

[**ccxv. 45.**—Holograph. Addressed.]

Sir:—According to my leisure, I recommend these few lines, to the end you may think I am not altogether forgetful of that which may concern me and my services.

As I have written unto you lately, my Lord Admiral now returned, I am subject to his orders and directions so long as he is in place; and, as I perceive, his intention is to divide his company into two parts, whereof he wished me to take the road of Margate or Gorend, and himself the Downs or Dover; which, it it be so, I desire to be called home, for I never loved to be penned or moored in roads. But so long as there is an expectation of the Spaniards to return, I would not have the thought once to return before some better services be accomplished ; which I hardly doubt will fall out to such advantage as we had at our last bickerings.

I find my Lord and his company divided in manner to factions, which I would wish otherwise ; neither doth it appertain unto me to meddle much therein, or otherwise to advertise, so long as his Lordship is accountable for all.

I received direction from Sir Francis Drake and Sir John Hawkyns for the discharge of some of our navy, by order, as it should seem, of better authority ; which were discharged, to the number of some needless vessels, and yet had made stay of Mr. Thomas Knyvet's company, according to your last direction ; and withal, by good hap, upon these last intelligences of the Spaniards, have made stay of the rest. I am hastened by the Lord Admiral to repair with him to his lodging where he hath been these two days, whereby I find myself altered from my former courses by continuing a-seaboard. And even so do commit you to God. From Dover, this 23rd of August, 1588.

Your loving friend to command,

H. Seymour.

August 23.—DRAKE TO WALSYNGHAM.

[**ccxv. 46.**—Signed, and autograph postscript. Addressed. In very bad condition ; much torn, and almost illegible from damp.]

Right Honourable :—The uncertainty of the reports which daily come unto us out of Calais, Dunkirk, Ostend, Flushing, from my Lord of Huntingdon, Scotland, and such ships and pinnaces which have been sent out for discovery by my Lord Admiral, make me rather to rest upon mine own

conjecture than upon any of them, they disagreeing
so much as they do ; the one affirming that the
Duke of Sidonia, with his fleet, is coming back again,
that the Duke of Parma is marching presently to
embark to be conducted by him ; the other affirming that it is for certain that the fleet of Spain is
past without Scotland for their way homewards.
Which reports are quite contrary.

My poor opinion is, that if their fleet chance to
return, it is altogether for that the wind will not
permit them good passage to go about the other way
at this time of the year, because it is most subject tc
westerly winds. This wind that now bloweth, if it
be not more easterly there than it is here, could
hardly permit such a fleet, for that they shall feel a
great wind, for to set sail to pass on the back side [of]
Scotland and Ireland, which may be the cause that of
necessity they must be forced this way for Spain.

Farther, my judgment [is] that the Duke of
Sidonia, [with] his fleet, shall [needs] jump with fair
weather, the highest of a spring, [with] good wind,
and the Duke of Parma embarking all in one day.
This were very meet for them; for if any one of these
fail them, they shall never perform as much as they
have promised to the King, their master. My
reason is this. The most part of the ships of the
Duke of Parma are small, and, being pestered with
men of war,[1] must of necessity have fair weather ; and
—as I am credibly given to understand—they must
have a spring to bring their shipping both out of
Dunkirk, Nieuport, and Sluys.

Now, for the Duke of Medina his fleet, there is
[no] harbour for them upon that coast, so that to
stir it requireth fair weather ; which, when it happen
that we should find them there, he is like, God willing, to have unquiet rest. And yet, with my consent,

[1] Sc. soldiers.

we ought much more to have regard unto the Duke of Parma and his soldiers than to the Duke of Sidonia and his ships, for that our sands will take a strong party with us against his great ships, under water.   My poor opinion is that the Duke of Parma should be vigilantly looked upon for these 20 days, although the army of Spain return not this way ; for of them I have no great doubt, although there be great cause for us all to watch carefully and defend [1] mightily those many and proud enemies which seek to supplant the most honourable crown of England from our most gracious Sovereign, whom God defend, as he hath most graciously done for his great mercy's sake.

I would advertise your Honour of some defects in her Majesty's army, but that my very good Lord, the Lord Admiral, hath written unto your Honour thereof at large.

This is my poor opinion of her Majesty's [army], that the [threatening] of the enemy will put a great part of [their] weakness from her Majesty's good subjects, and no doubt but they will fight valiantly. Although I [find] my Lord Admiral well affected, when fair weather [is], to go for the coast of Flanders, yet I would your Honour should animate us forward ; for there are many causes that might move us to be there more than we are, and much better for us, and better service.   Thus humbly taking my leave of your Honour, I rest, desiring God to give us all grace to live in his fear, so shall we not need greatly to fear the enemy.   From aboard her Majesty's very good ship the Revenge, this 23rd of August, 1588.

Your Honour's most willing to be commanded,
FRA. DRAKE.

----

[1] Fend off, repel.

I have sent to your Honour a copy, Englished, out of a letter [1] sent from Don Pedro de Valdes to the [King his master], which doth deliver the time of their victualling, and of some discontentment which was between the Duke and him.

Let me humbly beseech your Honour that we may be put in mind here that it were good we saw the coast of Flanders as often as we might.[2] I think it one of the best services we can have in hand. It must be known I have written thus much to your Honour. God bless us all, and give us grace to fear his justice.

I crave pardon. I have no time to read that which I have caused to be written.

Your Honour's faithfully,
FRA. DRAKE.

August 24.—EDWARD WYNTER TO WALSYNGHAM.

[ccxv. 47.—Signed. Addressed.]

Sir :—Although I assure myself you are daily remembered by many others of the best sort amongst us, which write unto you of such things as happen worthy your notice, yet I thought it the least part of duty I can perform, honouring you unfeignedly, as you have ever given me cause, to acquaint you with such intelligences as this day hath for most certain been brought to my Lord Admiral ; and the rather, because, in his Lordship's cabin, myself had long discourse with the party that brought them, whom,

---

[1] This must be the letter *ante*, p. 133, but there is no word of their victualling in it.

[2] It will be noticed that Drake's opinion on this point is very different from that of Seymour and Wynter. Cf. vol. i. pp. 331, 333.

being a mariner, I found to be of good judgment and discretion.

This day, being the 24th of August, in the morning, he came from a village about a mile or two from Dunkirk, and came aboard my Lord Admiral about three or four in the afternoon, where this news he brings for certain.

First, that the Duke of Parma is retired in some haste with certain troops of horse from Bruges, up into Brabant, as high as Brussels, fearing, as it was thought, some sudden revolt. He hath commanded such victuals as were aboard his fleet in Dunkirk to be unshipped, which they are now performing; and already they have taken from many ships the sails from their yards. His mariners run away daily, many of whom he hath caught again and imprisoned sharply. They are all generally ill affected towards this service.

Great dissension of late grown between the Spaniards and Walloons, the Spaniards bitterly railing against the Duke of Parma, and that very publicly. Divers of them would have retired themselves into Gravelines, but none could be suffered to enter there. The Walloons, they demand for their pay very rudely. They are answered, it is brought them in the Spanish fleet, which they find now (although before they were persuaded otherwise) is retired and fearfully [1] fled. All such artillery as was left in the galleass driven ashore at Calais, by the consent of Mons. Gourdan, governor there, is taken out of her and sent to Dunkirk, where it now remains.

Young Norreys, that was sent after the enemy's fleet to discover which way they meant to take their course, brings certain news that he left them to the westwards of the Islands of Orkney, which is their course directly for Spain. God grant so happy and prosperous beginnings be in time so timely

---

[1] Full of fear.

prosecuted as may redound to his glory, and the honour and welfare of our country.

Now, Sir, for mine own particular, if it please you to know thus much. In hope that the Spanish fleet would ere this have returned, I have enforced myself to endure the seas, which (by reason of my late sickness) I find doth in no sort agree with me ; and therefore, because I am out of all hope now to see this year any service by sea, my humblest desire is, seeing I am resolved to follow the wars, that it would vouchsafe your Honour to be mindful of me if there happen any occasion that forces either of foot or horse should be employed. To be plain, Sir, I protest unto you my two journeys, the one to the Indies,[1] the other to the Low Countries, have already so dearly cost me as I would be loth, upon my own charge, absolutely to enter into the like ; and therefore do desire instantly to be advised by you what course to follow. I have nothing else to write but that I am ready to obey you with all duty and true inward affection in whatsoever service it shall best please you to employ me ; and do beseech God to make you ever happy, and yourself, Sir, to continue me in your honourable favour. Dover, the [2]4th[2] of August.

Your Honour's humbly at command,

EDW. WYNTER.

August 24.—*TRENCHARD AND HAWLEY TO THE COUNCIL.*

[ccxv. 49.—Signed. Addressed.]

Our duty most humbly done &c. :—Your Lordships' letters of the 27th of the last, touching the

---

[1] With Drake in 1585, when he was captain of the Aid.
[2] The ' 2 ' is omitted in the MS. ; but see *ante*, p. 150, line 2.

Spanish carrack, we received the 29th of the same,
and therein have performed your commandment in
as much as in us lay, having ever sithence attended
that service, as greatly delayed by reason of the far
distance of the ship in the bay from this town, and
by high winds. What therein we have found, and
what order have taken, by these enclosed shall
appear ; thinking it also some part of our duties not
to conceal from your Lordships the notable spoils
that were made upon the ship, which came to Portland road seven days before our dealing therein ;
and much more had been, if happily the Lord
Admiral had not sent Mr. Warner, a servant of his,
before our coming, to take some care thereof ; the
disorder growing so far, as we could very hardly
repress it ourselves, the great repair from all places
being such.

The bolting[1] out of particularities we do refer
to your Lordships' further order, for our commission
reacheth not thereunto ; except peradventure it may
appertain to the duty of mine[2] office, the deputy vice-
admiral.   Howbeit, if the fight had not been at that
instant upon the coast of Purbeck, that ship had
been better and sooner looked into.   We have also,
by virtue of the Lord Treasurer's letters of the
ninth of this present,[3] delivered to the mayor and
others of this port such ordnance as in these inden-
tures are specified ; so that now it resteth only in
your Lordships to set down your further pleasures
for the disposition of what remaineth.   Four other
iron pieces, as minion and falcon, are left out of this
indenture, as having no direction for the same.

The carrack is so great as that she cannot be
brought into this haven, and therefore we do attend
your Lordships' direction what shall be done with

[1] Bolting = sifting.   [2] Hawley.   See vol. i. p. 334.
[3] See *ante*, p. 86.

her. She is much [1] splitted, torn, and the charge
will be great in keeping her here, for we are forced
to keep therein ten persons continually to pump her
for fear of sinking. Surely, in the stealing of her
ropes and casks from her, and rotting and spoiling
of sails and cables &c., the disorder was very great.
It is credibly thought that there were in her 200
Venetian barrels of powder of some 120 [2] weight
apiece, and yet but 141 were sent to the Lord
Admiral. This very night some inkling came unto
us that a chest of great weight should be found in
the forepeak of the ship the Friday before our
dealing. Of what credit it may be, as yet we know
not; but do determine to examine the matter, and
to send for the party that hath reported it. All
search hath been made sithence our coming, but no
treasure can be found, and yet we have removed
some part of the ballast. We find here no Spaniards
of any account, but only one who calleth himself Don
Melchor de Pereda, [3] and nine others of the common
sort; two Frenchmen, four Almains, [4] and one Almain
woman; and since their landing here, twelve more
are dead. We humbly beseech your Lordships to
give some speedy direction what shall be done with
them, for that they are here diseased, naked, and
chargeable.

The charges necessarily disbursed for the performing and discharging of this ship, her ordnance
and loading, hath been so great, and so diversely
disbursed, and yet unlevied, as we cannot presently
particularise the same, but do think it will extend
well near to 200*l*., as by the accounts thereof, by the

---

[1] MS. mich. [2] Sc. pounds.
[3] No one of the name is mentioned by Duro. There are
several named Paredes, but with different Christian names. The
nearest to it is Melchor Perez, of the Sicilian regiment (ii. 84).
[4] Germans.

next messenger, shall to your Lordships particularly appear. And so we humbly take our leaves.
Weymouth, this 24th of August, 1588.

Your Lordships' humbly to command,

GEORGE TRENCHARD.
FRA. HAWLEY.

*August 24.—INVENTORY OF THE SAN
SALVADOR.*

[ccxv. 49, I.—Endorsed :—An indenture of the munitions in the
Spanish carrack brought to Weymouth.]

Goods unladen at the said port out of the great
carrack, viz. :—

Weymouth and Melcombe Regis.

Imprimis, of brass ordnance . . 14
Item, of iron pieces 4
  ,, of barrels of powder . 132
  ,, of shot : cannon, demi-cannon,
    and culverin . . . 2,246
  ,, of musket shot, firkins . . 6
  ,, of harquebus-a-crock [1] . . 6

Whereof sent to the Lord Admiral, by warrant
from his Lordship, viz. :—

Of brass ordnance . . . . 6 pieces
Item, of powder . . . . 132 barrels
  ,, of shot : cannon, demi-cannon,
    and culverin . . . 2,246
  ,, of musket shot . . . 6 firkins
  ,, of harquebus-a-crock . . 6

[1] Crock, akin to crutch, a stake, with a head like a boat's
crutch. It was driven into the ground and so formed a rest from
which the harquebus was fired. It could scarcely have been used
on shipboard, in that form, but may have been modified.

And so remainining in safe custody in this place, viz. :—

Brass ordnance 8
Iron pieces, minions, old pieces . . 4
Old fowlers. 2

[**ccxv. 49, II.**—Endorsed :—Inventory of the goods contained in the Spanish ship brought in at Portland.]

The inventory indented of the burnt Spanish ship called Le San Salvador, Almirante de Oquendo, together with her apparel, munition, and loading, which arrived in the road of Portland the 24th of July, 1588; priced and valued the 24th day of August, 1588, by Hugh Rendoll, Bernard Major, William Pit, John Pitt, Richard Belpytt, merchants, and Roger Guyer, mariner, by virtue of their corporal oaths in that behalf taken, as followeth, viz. :—

<table>
<tr><td></td><td>£</td><td>s.</td><td>d.</td></tr>
<tr><td>Imprimis, the hull, Biscayan built, by estimation of the burden of 600[1] tons, being by fire blown up and spoiled, riding in the road; having a mainmast, foremast, bowsprit, and mizen, with the foreyard, and shrouds for the two greater masts; two old junks, two other junks somewhat better; two anchors and cables which she rides by; four anchors more, whereof the one lies in the road of Portland; a maintopsail, a course, foretopsail, spritsail, and one other new main course; all worth by their estimation . .</td><td>200</td><td>o</td><td>o</td></tr>
<tr><td>Item, 6 pipes of wine valued at . .</td><td>30</td><td>o</td><td>o</td></tr>
<tr><td>„ 22 pipes of wine valued at . .</td><td>55</td><td>o</td><td>o</td></tr>
</table>

[1] She appears in the Spanish lists as of 958 (Duro, ii. 63).

	£	s.	d.
Item, 25 pipes of wine valued at . .	25	0	0
„ 67 empty casks at 3s. per piece .	10	0	0
„ 3 pipes beef, bad ; the cask [1] .	0	6	0
„ 1 pipe beans	0	10	0
„ 2 barrels vinegar . . .	0	13	4
„ 4 pieces lead, by estimation 4 cwt., [at] 6s. 8d. . . .	1	6	8

Brass ordnance.

	cwt.	lbs.
2 pieces, culverin and demi-culverin	28	66
1 cannon pedro [2]	20	19
1 other of the same	20	77
1 other of the same	23	18
1 other of the same	25	72
1 cannon	52	22
1 other cannon	53	29
	28 [3]	66

Sum, 8 pieces of brass, by the Spanish mark, 252 cwt. 2 qrs. 13 lbs. [4]

	£	s.	d.
The which, with their old carriages, do value at	505	0	0
Item, 3 old carriages like the other .	1	0	0
„ 1 old fowler and a bad sling .	2	0	0
„ 4 minions of iron, with their carriages	13	6	8
„ 108 cannon shot of iron, one with the other at 6s. 8d. the cwt. .	12	3	4
„ 14 cwt. match, at 9s. 4d. per cwt.	6	13	0
„ 4 gins, as we judge, to draw ordnance	1	6	8
Sum total	864	5	8

[1] Noted in margin :—'Mr Quarles.'   [2] MS. petrill.
[3] Apparently the demi-culverin in the first item.
[4] The addition should be 252 cwt. 2 qrs. 19 lbs., at 100 lbs. to the cwt.   Noted in the margin :—'To be brought up for the furnishing of her Majesty's ships.'

[**ccxv. 49, III.**—Endorsed :—The rest of the goods valued by the Commissioners.]

The note of the rest of the munition, goods and merchandise, belonging to the burnt ship aforesaid, not valued by the praisers aforesaid, by reason it never came to their view, but esteemed by us as followeth, viz. :—

	£	s.	d.
Imprimis, sent to the fleet the 26th of July, 1588, by a bark of Dartmouth appertaining to one Norris, at the appointment of Captain Flemyng, by direction from the Lord Admiral, before the date of your Lordships' letters dated the 27th of July, *anno predict.*, 100 Venetian barrels of powder, worth by our estimation	500	0	0
Item, sent to the fleet in the bark aforesaid, of cannon, demi-cannon and culverin shot, of iron, 2,000 shot, worth	200	0	0
Item, sent to the fleet at the same time, in Captain Flemyng his pinnace, 40 Venetian barrels powder, worth	200	0	0
Item, sent them one ton of match .	6	13	4

Delivered the last day of July, by our order, to John Somers of Lyme, by virtue of a warrant from my Lord Admiral, as followeth, viz. :—

	£	s.	d.
2 cannons, with their carriages [1] .	200	0	0
4 culverins, with their carriages [1] .	270	0	0
173 cannon pedro shot, worth . .	16	6	8

[1] Noted in margin :—' Letters to Sir W. Wynter to take charge.'

				£	s.	d.
99 culverin shot, worth	.	.	.	6	13	4
3 cross-bar shot, worth	.	.	.	1	0	0
8 barrels of musket shot	.	.	.			
6 harquebusses-a-crock, iron	.	.	.	3	0	0
1 barrel of powder	.	.	.	.	5	0	0
1 Milan corslet .	.	.	.	.	0	10	0
2 little pairs of iron-bound wheels	.	1	6	8

Summa totalis   1,411   0   0

GEORGE TRENCHARD.
FRA. HAWLEY.

August 25.—HOWARD TO WALSYNGHAM.

[**ccxv. 54.**—Signed, and autograph postscript.   Addressed.]

Sir :—Since I had made up my other letter, there came a Scottish gentleman in a passenger out of France unto me, and another Scottish man that hath served in the Duke of Parma his camp, which I send by this bearer, Mr. Cely, unto you, by whom you may find many things if he be well sifted. And so I bid you heartily farewell.   From aboard her Majesty's good ship the Ark, the 25th of August, 1588.   Your very loving friend,
C. HOWARD.

Sir, the gentleman, I think, came out of France. You shall hear much of the poor Scottish man, if you will examine him well.   I pray you let him be well used.   I have sent a good many of ancients [1]

---

[1] Ensigns.   These were probably the flags which were displayed at St. Paul's Cross on Sept. 8, at a sermon of thanksgiving, when 'there was openly showed eleven ensigns, being the banners taken in the Spanish navy, and particularly one streamer wherein was an image of our Lady with her Son in her arms, which was held in a man's hand over the pulpit.   The same banners the next day were

and banners by this bearer, Thomas Cely; but
Sir, they must be returned when they have been
used; they may be kept till I do come home.

August 26.—HOWARD TO WALSYNGHAM.

[**ccxv. 55.**—Signed, and autograph postscript. The second postscript is in the same writing as the body of the letter.
Addressed.]

Sir :—I have received your letter of the 24th of
August, touching the beer that was brewed at Sandwich. Mr. Darell hath been with me here, whom
I have dealt withal; and I perceive it hath been
refused, and upon that there were some appointed
to taste it, and so found it to be sour, and yet he
that hath the delivering of it[1]—and so saith Mr.
Darell too—that at the first it was good. But by
like there was some great fault in the brewer,
that within one month and less it would be sour;
and I perceive by Mr. Darell that the brewer
excuseth it by the want of hops. But, Sir, the
mariners who have a conceit (and I think it true,
and so do all the captains here) that sour drink hath
been a great cause of this infection amongst us;
and, Sir, for my own part I know not which way to
deal with the mariners to make them rest contented
with sour beer, for nothing doth displease them
more. There hath been heretofore brewed for the
navy, here at Dover, as good beer as was brewed
in London. This service being in the Narrow
Seas, and likely to continue, so long as we have to

hanged on London Bridge towards Southwark' (Nichols' *Pro-
gresses and Public Processions of Queen Elizabeth*, edit. 1823, ii. 537).
They were presumably given back to Howard, in accordance with
his request, but have long since disappeared.

[1] Sc. affirmeth.

do with the Low Countries, of necessity the victualling must be here at Dover, as it hath been in times
past; for being at London, it may fall out so as it
may be a great hindrance unto her Majesty's service
and the realm's.

Sir, I have caused Mr. Darell to make trial of
brewing here at Dover, in her Majesty's own offices
at the Messendewe,[1] and I doubt not but it will fall
out very well for the purpose. Mr. Darell makes
trial to brew the sour beer which came out of the
west country again, and so to mix it with other new
beer, which I hope will do well.

Sir, where you write that you would have the
hoys discharged of their victuals, I hope you do not
doubt but that if the weather had served to have
taken it in, or any hoy to come near us, but that we
would have taken in some part of it. And yet, Sir,
if this service should not continue, the overplus of
that which shall be taken in would be spoiled. The
weather hath been such here that all the victuallers
have been fain to go into the haven. The small
barks and pinnaces of our fleet, that likewise were
in the haven, have taken in their victuals; but else,
no great ship was able to take in any since I came
hither, the sea hath gone so high; but it shall be
done as conveniently as we may.

In the last part of your letter you do write that
I should consider what ships were meet to be
continued on the Narrow Seas. I do think your
meaning is only for defending of our seas and
keeping in of the Dunkirkers, in such sort as is to

[1] Maison Dieu. Originally a hospital for pilgrims, founded by
Hubert de Burgh in the reign of John. At the dissolution of the
monasteries and the wholesale plunder of Church property, it was
converted into Government storehouses, victualling offices and
brewery, and so continued till the present century, when—about
1834—it was bought by the Corporation and reconverted and restored into the Town Hall.

be continued all the winter. We have considered of it, and we think that until Michaelmas there would [1] some reasonable strength be continued; and after that time it may be lessened. And for that ships will grow foul and unsavoury, we have divided such ships as are most serviceable for the Narrow Seas into two parts, that the one company may be always ready when the other shall come in. I send you herein enclosed a breviate both of the ships that shall first serve, and also of the second. Sir, I pray you acquaint my Lord Treasurer herewith, and pray him to bear with me that I write not unto him; for I assure you I am so troubled with business that I have scarce leisure to write unto you at all. And so I bid you heartily farewell. From aboard her Majesty's good ship the Ark, the 26th of August, 1588.   Your very loving friend,

C. HOWARD.

Sir, It doth grieve me wonderfully to hear of my Lord Chamberlain's [2] sickness. I trust in the Almighty God that he shall recover. If he do, I pray let me have knowledge from you, or else I do not desire to hear anything. I know nothing, but my Lord Treasurer did write in a postscript this. I fear my Lord Chamberlain's sickness. God send him health, and that her Majesty and the realm do not lose in this time so good a servant.

Post.—Even as I had done this my letter, I had meant to have borne over to the other side; but it is grown so foggy upon the sudden that now I am determined to stay for fair weather.

[1] Sc. should.
[2] Lord Hunsdon, Howard's father-in-law.

[ccxv. 58.—In Howard's autograph. Much torn. Imperfect. Endorsed :—A note of the ships appointed to remain under the charge of Sir Henry Palmer and Sir Martin Frobiser for the guard of the Narrow Seas.]

Sir :—I do send you this, whereby you shall perceive what ships we do think meet to be continued in the Narrow Seas all this winter, and in what manner both for the ease of the ships, as also the captains and mariners, for this course must be kept, or else it would worry all men to continue still.

These to begin, and to continue two months under the charge of Sir Henry Palmer :—

	Men.
The Vanguard	[230]
Rainbow	230
Tiger	80
Bull	80
Tramontana	70
Achates	60
Sun	24
Moon	40
	814

These to [begin] when the [other] is ended, [and] be under [the] charge [of Sir] Ma. [Frobiser]:

	Men.
The Antelope	150

[*The rest is torn away.*]

August 26.—HAWKYNS TO BURGHLEY.

[ccxv. 56.—Signed, with an autograph postscript by Lord Howard. Addressed.]

Right Honourable mine especial good Lord :— This day my Lord Admiral called Sir William Wynter and me aboard his Lordship's ship, and

showed unto us your Lordship's letter of the 24th
of August, whereby your Lordship required to be
advertised what numbers of mariners and soldiers
there were in the ships that are here with my Lord.

Since I came down, the weather hath been such
as our fleet hath been divided, part in Dover road
and part at Margate and Gorend; and never could
come either of us to other, and those at the Margate
can hardly row ashore, or get aboard when they
were ashore.

Sir Francis Drake and I discharged and sent
away many of the western and coast ships, before
my Lord came down; which, upon some news that
Sir Edward Norreys brought, my Lord was somewhat displeased and misliked it.

I am not able to send your Lordship a better
particular of the numbers that are and were in her
Majesty's certain pay than that which I sent from
Plymouth, wherein was demanded about 19 thousand
pound to bring the pay to the 28th of July; wherein
there was no conducts demanded, for that no
discharge was then thought of; neither was there
any ships of the coast spoken of or voluntary ships
but those of Sir Richard Greynvile and those taken
into service by Sir Francis Drake then over and
above his warrant, yet by order from the Council,
as Sir Richard Greynvile and he hath to show.

Your Lordship may think that by death, by discharging of sick men, and such like, that there may
be spared something in the general pay. First,
those that die, their friends require their pay. In
place of those which are discharged sick and insufficient, which indeed are many, there are fresh
men taken, which breedeth a far greater charge, by
means of their conduct in discharge, which exceedeth
the wages of these which were lastly taken in, and
more lost by that than saved. We do pay by the

poll and by a check book, whereby if anything be spared, it is to her Majesty's benefit only. The ships I have paid, of those which were under Sir Francis Drake's charge, I find full furnished with men, and many above their numbers.

Those ships that are under my Lord Seymour, Sir William Wynter doth assure my Lord they have their full numbers. Beside there were sent aboard 500 soldiers, by Sir John Norreys and others; which stood them in little stead, for that they were imperfect men; but they kept them not above 8 days.

The weather continueth so extreme and the tides come so swift that we cannot get any victuals aboard but with trouble and difficulty, nor go from ship to ship. But as weather will serve, and time, to gather better notes,[1] your Lordship shall be more particularly informed of all things.

We think the conducts in discharge, with the double conducts, cannot grow to less than 2,500*l.*; and so I humbly take my leave   From the Ark Ralegh, in Dover road, the 26th of August, 1588.

Your good Lordship's humbly to command,

JOHN HAWKYNS.

There is a month's wages grown since the 28th of July, and ended the 25th of August, and so groweth daily till the discharge be concluded; therefore it were good your Lordship consider of it.[2]

My good Lord, this is as much as is possible for Mr. Hawkyns to do at this time. There is here in our fleet many lieutenants and corporals, which of necessity we were and are driven to have. Your Lordship knoweth well how services be far from that they were, and [I] assure your Lordship of necessity

[1] MS. nottes.
[2] This first postscript is in the same writing as the letter. The next is in Howard's autograph.

it must be so. God knoweth how they should be paid, except her Majesty have some consideration on them. The matter, it is not great in respect of the service. I think 500*l.*, with the help of my own purse,[1] will do it ; but howsoever it fall out I must see them paid, and will ; for I do not look to end with this service, and therefore I must be followed hereafter. My good Lord, look but what the officers had with Sir Francis Drake, having but 4 of her Majesty's ships. I do not desire half so much for all this great fleet.

My good Lord, it grieveth me much to hear of my Lord Chamberlain's sickness. The Almighty God help him. The Queen's Majesty and the realm should have as great a loss as of any one man that I do know. God send the next news to be of his amendment. God send you health, my good Lord.

Your Lordship's most assured to command,

C. HOWARD.

August 27.—BOROUGH TO WALSYNGHAM.

[**ccxv. 57.**—Signed. Addressed.]

After my duty unto your Honour always duly considered :—I have received your Honour's letter by this messenger, whereby I understand her Majesty's pleasure touching the discharge of most part of the navy, and that I should stay the sending of those ships &c., now at Chatham, which came in to be graved. May it please your Honour, I was yesterday at the Court, in the afternoon, at what time your Honour was with my Lord Treasurer at his Lordship's chamber, sitting, as it was told me, upon a commission. I was then in the outer chamber when your Honour came forth, and staid

----

[1] MS. pourse.

till my Lord came out. I showed my Lord that my coming was to know his Lordship's pleasure, whether I might not go down to Chatham, for the despatch of those ships to the seas that were there, and other business needful. His Lordship answered me that it was resolved that the most of the navy should be discharged and come in, saving a few that should remain at the seas under charge of Sir Henry Palmer, and therefore willed me to have care to husband things as well as I could. I could have no more words with his Lordship; he went straight to the Queen.

I then repaired to your Honour's chamber, to the end to have had some further speeches with your Honour therein. But then the show of horsemen began to appear, and your Honour was accompanied with divers of great honour, which were then in your chamber to see the sight. Being therefore out of hope to speak with your Honour in long time, I came thence, and straight sent order to Chatham to stay the Elizabeth Jonas and such other vessels as are there; and likewise to stay such other provisions as were, by order of my Lord Admiral, appointed in haste to be sent to the seas for the fleet.

Now that I have received your Honour's order, I purpose, in the morning, to go down to Chatham, but will return as speedily as I may, and will take order both here and there for saving such superfluous charges as her Majesty should sustain by sending provisions (now needless) that were appointed to be carried to the fleet, now at sea. And so I humbly take my leave, committing your Honour to the protection of the Almighty. From Deptford, the 27th of August, 1588.

Your Honour's at command most humbly,

W. BOROUGH.

August 27.—HOWARD TO WALSYNGHAM.

[**ccxv. 59.**—Holograph.   Addressed.   Endorsed, in Burghley's
hand :—Lord Admiral, by Sir Francis Drake.

Sir :—Upon [1] your letter, I sent presently for Sir
Francis Drake, and showed him the desire that her
Majesty had for the intercepting of the King's
treasure from the Indies.[2]   And so we considered of
it ; and neither of us finding any ships here in the
fleet any ways able to go such a voyage before they
have been aground, which cannot be done in any
place but at Chatham ; and now that this spring is
so far past, it will be 14 days before they can
be grounded.   And where you write that I should
make nobody acquainted with it but Sir Francis
Drake—it is very strange to me that anybody can
think that if it were that [some] of the smallest
barks were to be sent out, but that the officers must
know it ; for this is not as if a man would send but
over to the coast of France, I do assure you.

Sir Francis Drake, who is a man of judgment
and best acquainted with it, will tell you what must
be done for such a journey.   Belike it is thought
the islands be but hereby ; it is not thought how
the year is spent.   I thought it good, therefore, to
send with all speed Sir Francis, although he be not
very well, to inform you rightly of all, and look
what shall be there thought meet.   I will do. my
endeavour with all the power I may ; for I protest
before God, I would give all that I have that it [3]
were met withal ; for that blow, after this he hath,
would make him safe.

Sir, for Sir Thomas Morgan [4] and the discharging

[1] MS. Apone.   [2] MS. Indias.   [3] The King's treasure.
[4] Sending Morgan and his 800 shot back to Flushing.   See
ante, pp. 31, 65, 84.

of ships, I will deal withal when the spring is past; but before, I dare not venture. For them of London, I do not hear of them yet, but those that be with my cousin Knyvet.

Sir, I send you here enclosed a note of the money that Sir Francis Drake had aboard Don Pedro. I did take now, at my coming down, 3,000 pistolets, as I told you I would; for, by Jesus, I had not 3*l.* besides in the world, and had not anything could get money in London; and I do assure you my plate was gone before. But I will repay it within 10 days after my coming home. I pray you let her Majesty know so. And by the Lord God of Heaven, I had not one crown more; and had it not been mere necessity, I would not have touched one; but if I had not some to have bestowed upon some poor and miserable men, I should have wished myself out of the world. Sir, let me not live longer than I shall be most willing to all service, and to take any pains I can for her Majesty's service. I think Sir Francis Drake will say I have little rest day or night. The Ark, in Dover road, the 27th of August.   Your most assured,

C. HOWARD.

August 27.—TREASURE IN THE N. S. DEL ROSARIO.

[**ccxv. 59, I.**—Signed. The body of the document is in Drake's writing. Enclosure in Howard's letter of the same date.]

$$7,200$$
$$10,000$$
$$5,600$$
$$2,500$$
$$\overline{25,300}$$

This I confess to have.

Carried aboard to my Lord Admiral, by his Lordship's commandment, the 23rd of August 1588, three thousand pistolets. FRA. DRAKE.

C. HOWARD.

Taken out of the sum above written, by my Lord Admiral's knowledge, three thousand pistolets, the 27th of August, 1588. FRA. DRAKE.

August 27.—HOWARD TO BURGHLEY.

[ccxv. 61.—Holograph. Addressed.]

My honoured good Lord :—I received your letter, with the letter from the Earl of Sussex enclosed in it, about 5 of the clock in the morning ; and within an hour after I received your other letter. I have sent the Hope, with Captain Sampson, and 5 other ships ; four of them that are under my cousin Knyvet's charge. We do all think it very fit[1] to send strong ; for assuredly they of Newhaven will rescue them. It were a great shame that the matter should be taken in hand and not well gone through.

I do also hear that there are certain[2] ships riding under Beechy, that are laden with Spaniards' goods. I have sent one by land to discover them. If they be there, they shall be visited when the spring is past. They stay there but for a wind to bring them through. I must leave the report of all things to this bearer,[3] who is acquainted with all. And so my good Lord, Sir Francis Drake making great haste, I leave with my most hearty commendations to your

[1] MS. feet. [2] MS. sarten.
[3] Drake, as appears in the next line, who carried this with the preceding.

Lordship, whom God long continue with health. From aboard the Ark, the 27th of August.

Your Lordship's most assured to command,

C. HOWARD.

August 27.—ALDERMAN RADCLYFF[1] *TO WALSYNGHAM.*

[**ccxv. 60.**—Signed. Addressed. Endorsed.]

Right Honourable, my humble duty remembered &c. :—Upon the last moving of the matter unto your Honour by Sir George Barne[2] and myself, in the behalf of our poor house of Bridewell, it then pleased your Honour to show favourable liking thereunto. Since which time, according to your Honour's commandment, we have attended,[3] to understand your Honour's pleasure and the rest of my Lords, hoping to have obtained your Honour's warrant for the making choice of some 3 or 4 of the Spanish prisoners there, who might answer us for the charge of the rest. During which time of our attendance, the chiefest of the said prisoners have been taken away by others.

And forasmuch as the charge of keeping them is far more than the said house can bear, I thought it my duty once again to put your Honour in mind thereof, most humbly praying the continuance of your honourable favour herein ; assuring your Honour that, if some help be not obtained towards their maintenance by this means, we shall be compelled, in respect of the great poverty of the said house, to make a general collection through the city for the maintenance of those Spaniards ; which will

[1] Sheriff of London in 1585.
[2] Sheriff in 1576 ; Lord Mayor and knighted 1586–7.
[3] Waited.

be very unwillingly assented unto by the common sort, and we ourselves far more unwilling to do the same, if by any means it might be avoided ; which can be by no other way than by the obtaining your Honour's warrant as aforesaid. The which we do most humbly entreat.

Your Honour's most bounden
in all duty to command,
ANTHONY RADCLYFF.

August 28.—*HOWARD TO BURGHLEY.*

[**ccxv. 62.**—Holograph. No address nor endorsement. The letter fills the four pages of the sheet, and must have been sent in a cover, which is wanting.]

My good Lord :—I have received your letter concerning a French ship that should[1] be taken by a couple of pinnaces of her Majesty, and your Lordship hath written that the captain's name of the pinnace is Ware. My Lord, I protest I have inquired as much as possible I can. I can hear of no such thing, nor of any captain of that name. And where he saith that he[2] gave me notice of the Spanish fleet, I do assure you, on my honour, there was never any of any nation, English or other, that I knew anything of the discovery of the army,[3] but only Thomas Flemyng. Sir Francis Drake is now there. I pray let him be asked if he knew of any. The way for to know what pinnace and captain did it is for the party to come hither and see the pinnaces, for else I know not how to do it.

Newhaven men may do what they will. They have taken a hoy[4] of Thomas Gray's, my master,

[1] Is said to have been.
[2] Apparently the master of the French ship is meant—the party referred to eight lines lower down.
[3] Supply 'from.'   [4] MS. howy.

and stayed her, that went thither with coals [1]; and I
see nothing restored to our men, whatsoever they do.
But, my Lord, it is great dishonour to her Majesty
that such a town as Newhaven is, that is not at the
King's [2] commandment, but at the devotion of her
Majesty's great and villainous enemy, the Duke of
Guise, should have that favour they have, and our
men sustain the wrong they do by them. But, my
Lord, come of it what shall, I will lay rods in water
for them. I marvel the ambassador [3] is not ashamed
to speak for that town that the King his men cannot
command. I do assure your Lordship, I will not see
the seamen thus hardly dealt withal. There is now
here with me three or four complaints of Newhaven.
Good my Lord, as we shall and ought before God
and man to do justice, so for honour and justice to
our own people, let them have right. For, my Lord,
when I was in the west I took a pirate, and when I
charged him with his piracies, he cursed,[4] and said he
had dealt against none but Frenchmen; and he said
he was forced [5] to it, for he had complained two
years together of his losses by Frenchmen, and that
he was appointed at the last to go over into France
to follow it; so he and his partner went over. When
they had put up the complaint to the King, they
were threatened at the King's back, and the next
day his fellow, going from Paris to Rouen,[6] was
killed. This was complained on by the other party
at the council board at Greenwich,[7] and after at Oatlands. He followed the suit long, and saw no good
would come of it, and therefore sought other remedy.
The man I knew very well, and remembered his
suit, and so I am sure your Lordship and Mr.
Secretary doth, when you shall see him. My Lord,

[1] MS. colse.   [2] King of France.   [3] MS. imbasador.
[4] MS. corsed.   [5] MS. forsed.
[6] MS. Rone.   [7] MS. Grynwyge.

assure yourself if men have not justice they will be
pirates. My Lord, it is no answer to a man to say
the King's case is so that he can do no justice.
Thanks be to God, her Majesty's case is able to
make them to do justice.

My Lord, we have had here a wonderful storm
these two days, and it continueth still. No man was
able to come aboard of me for the discharging of
ships ; so we were fain, with the wind and tide, and
not without peril, to come to Dover town, to confer
about the discharge of the ships and the appointing
of those ships that shall remain in the Narrow Seas
under the charge of Sir Henry Palmer, which is fit[1]
to be something strong for a time. My Lord, it is
a wonderful trouble the discharging. Things in this
service hath grown so intricate with charging and
discharging ; as at Plymouth, we discharged many
ships because there was some opinion the Spaniards
would not come ;[2] within four days after, we heard
of their arrival on the coast ; then we were fain to
charge all again, and some others. Now here, Sir
Francis Drake and Sir John Hawkyns discharged
the day before my coming down hither many ships.
The next day, Sir E. Norreys brought those advertisements your Lordship do know. I sent presently
and stayed as many as I could. I think your Lordship doth[3] I had reason ; but upon advertisements

[1] MS. feet.

[2] This may be the origin of the story, which the Dutch
chroniclers got hold of, and Motley (*Hist. of United Netherlands*,
ii. 450) repeated, of the Queen sending Howard orders to pay off
the four great ships, and of Howard disobeying them at his own
risk. No such orders were given, or could have been given, for
the great ships could only be discharged at Chatham. The ships
to which Howard here refers were some of the smaller merchant
ships, such as Hawkyns had now also made haste to discharge.
Cf. *ante*, p. 163.

[3] MS. dowthe. There seems to be a word wanting, perhaps
'know.'

that I had from the other side, I did discharge, as the weather would give me leave to speak with them.

I have sent over to Calais crays of this town sundry times to bring me advertisements. Yesterday one returned from thence. The King's[1] bastard son, the Duke of Pascaredo,[2] came there yesterday. He sent to Monsieur Gourdan to desire that he might come thither with 150 horse ; but M. Gourdan desired him to pardon him, but he should come with 50 men, and so he did. He had 20 lackeys ran by him. There rode hard by his [side[3]] Don Juan Henriquez. They say his errand[4] is to see the galleass, that is utterly rewalted[5] and sunk in the sand, never to be recovered ; and also to speak with them at Calais that was within the galleass, and now to go into Spain. There came thither yesterday 4 small flyboats of Dunkirk to carry them away into Spain. The weather is so extreme as no man dare to venture[6] on that coast, the wind being at the North and North-East ; and with that wind may they go away. The ships that I had appointed and ready yesterday to go towards Newhaven, for the assisting of the Aid and the Charles, dare not yet put out of the road, the weather is so extreme ; but I hope to-morrow morning they will.

My Lord, we have rid here a bad road, and I am assured those ships at Margate worse. God send me to hear well of them. I have sent three posts to know. The ships that I have appointed to remain in the Narrow Seas with Sir Henry Palmer are these :—

---

[1] King of Spain.
[2] So in MS. Rodrigo de Silva, Duke of Pastrana, is meant.
[3] Word omitted.   [4] MS. arant.
[5] Laid, as corn ; tumbled down.
[6] MS. venter.

		Men
The Vanguard	. . . .	250
Rainbow .	. . .	230
Foresight	. . .	160
Aid .	. . . .	120
Tiger	. . . .	90
Tramontana	. . .	70
Achates .	. . .	60
Sun .	. . . .	25
Moon	. . . .	35
		1,040

My good Lord, it is good to be something strong for a while; it may be after lessened. Now your Lordship may perceive what victual is to be used. I have caused all the remain of victuals to be laid here and at Sandwich, for the maintaining them that shall remain in the Narrow Seas; but Mr. Quarles must help with better beer. This, my good Lord, I leave to trouble you for this time; though your Lordship and I must look ever to be greatly troubled as long as this world is. God send your Lordship your health. From Dover, the 28th of August.

Your Lordship's most ready to command,

C. HOWARD.

I thank God I perceive, by a letter of Mr. Secretary's, that my Lord Chamberlain hath missed a fever. God restore him to his health.

August 28.—HAWKYNS TO BURGHLEY.

[**ccxv. 63.**—Signed. Addressed. Endorsed, in Burghley's autograph :—Sir John Hawkyns, with answer to my letter for to know the state of the Queen's army.]

My honourable good Lord :—I am sorry I do live so long to receive so sharp a letter from your

Lordship, considering how carefully I take care to do all for the best and to ease charge. The ships that be in her Majesty's pay, such as I have to do for, your Lordship hath many particulars of them and their numbers; notwithstanding, I do send your Lordship all these again. I had but one day to travail in, and then I discharged many after the rate that I thought my money would reach; but after that day I could hardly row from ship to ship, the weather hath been continually so frightful.

I have six companies that do pay. Here are two clerks of Mr. Holstok's, two of Mr. Borough's, and Sir William Wynter in person, that helpeth what he can, and my brother [1]; and a clerk of the check, appointed by the officers to keep and order the books of those ships under Sir Francis Drake's charge, which I sent for post to Plymouth when I arrived at Harwich. I have six of mine own company that attend the pay, and so I furnish six companies; but now the ships go to Chatham, I do stay any payments saving sick men, such of the gentlemen that can be spared with their retinues, and soldiers; and discharge all the merchant ships that were in Sir Francis Drake's number, as near as I can.

Here is victual sufficient, and I know not why any should be provided after September, but for those which my Lord doth mean to leave in the Narrow Seas; which numbers will be about a thousand men, of which also I will send to your Lordship the names of the ships and their particular numbers, and never omit it more, though I may ill do it always. I do not meddle with any of the ships of London, for my Lord will discharge them all; neither do I write your Lordship anything of

[1] Edward Fenton, the husband of his wife's sister. He had only one brother in blood, William, the Mayor of Plymouth.

the coast ships ; but I am in gathering of a book [1] of all those that served, and the quality and time of their service, as I can overcome it. Your Lordship shall see it in the best order I can. Some are discharged with fair words ; some are so miserable and needy, that they are holpen with tickets to the victuallers for some victual to help them home ; and some with a portion of money, such as my Lord Admiral will appoint, to relieve their sick men and to relieve some of the needy sort, to avoid exclamation.[2] The sick men are paid and discharged, that are in her Majesty's pays ; the soldiers also, for the most part, we discharge here ; the retinues, some have leave to go to London, and are to be paid there ; and thus there is left but convenient companies of mariners and gunners to bring home the ships to Chatham. Your Lordship may consider by the numbers and the time they are to pay to the 25th of August, I required 19,000 pound, which I perceive your Lordship hath paid. At that time I knew of no thorough discharge, and till then I never demanded any conduct in discharge. The time will come over somewhat also for a good company before they come to Chatham ; but I will go with this as far as I can, and never demand more till extremity compel me.

There are some ships appointed to go to the coast of France for the great Spaniard. I will not forget to write your Lordship what they are, and their numbers, with those that stay in the Narrow Seas ; but my Lord will leave order they shall all so come to Chatham that are not of those companies in the Narrow Seas. Your Lordship doth know best what ships her Majesty will keep abroad, and can best give order to Mr. Quarles for the victual-

[1] This book does not seem to be in existence.
[2] Outcry.

ling of them.   My Lord hath now received order to
discharge the army, which [I] assure your Lordship
my Lord doth pass with all the speed possible ; and
Sir William Wynter and I am not behindhand to
further the easing of the charge.   This money,
which your Lordship hath delivered, is a prest
which is not sufficient to discharge that which is to
be paid ; howbeit her Majesty's charge shall cease [1]
with all the speed that may be ; and, as I wrote in
my last letters, the check book of every ship is kept
not by me, I assure your Lordship ; it is impossible
for me to spare time to peruse [2] them ; but when the
officers put their hands to confirm the pay books, I
give my men allowance of so much money as the
book maintaineth ; and with that her Majesty is
charged with, and no more ; and I never yet knew
any penny profit by sea books, nor know not what a
dead pay meaneth, as it hath been most injuriously
and falsely informed.   There are diets to the
captains, dead shares to the officers, and such like
accustomed pays to the officers, which are paid, and
no more.   It shall hereafter be none offence to your
Lordship that I do so much alone ; for with God's
favour I will and must leave all.   I pray God I may
end this account to her Majesty's and your Lordship's liking, and avoid my own undoing ; and I
trust God will so provide for me as I shall never
meddle with such intricate matters more ; for they
be importable [3] for any man to please and overcome it.   If I had any enemy, I would wish him
no more harm than the course of my troublesome
and painful life ; but hereunto, and to God's good
providence, we are born.

I have showed your Lordship's letter to my Lord
Admiral and Sir William Wynter, who can best

[1] MS seesse.   [2] Examine.
[3] MS. importyble = unbearable, intolerable, impossible.

judge of my care and painful travail, and the desire I have to ease the charge. Since we came to Harwich, the Margate, and Dover, our men have much fallen sick, whereby many are discharged; which we have not greatly desired to increase, because we always hoped of a general discharge; yet some mariners we have procured to divers of the ships, to refresh them. And so I leave, in great haste, to trouble your Lordship. From Dover, the 28th of August, 1588.

Your honourable Lordship's humbly to command,

JOHN HAWKYNS.

August 28.—*NOTE OF SHIPS IN THE QUEEN'S PAY.*

[**ccxv. 64.**—Endorsed by Burghley :—' 28th August, 1588 '; the rest partly in Hawkyns' hand, and initialled by him :—' A note of all the ships in her Majesty's pay. The ships that are to remain in the Narrow Seas, and the ships that seek the great Spaniard upon the coast of France.—J. H. This is badly written and in haste; I humbly pray your Lordship to bear with it. The hoys, with four ships of those under Mr. Thomas Knyvet, go also to seek the great Spaniard.' Added in Burghley's writing :—' 16th September, 1588.']

The ships that went to Plymouth with my Lord Admiral :—

	[Men]			[Men]
The Ark Ralegh .	425	The Swallow .		160
Bear . .	500	Foresight .		160
Triumph .	500	Charles .		40
Elizabeth Jonas	500	Moon . .		40
Victory . .	400	Disdain .		45
Mary Rose .	250	White Lion		50
Elizabeth Bona-		Hoy . .		30
venture .	250	Marigold .		20
Golden Lion .	250	Ketch . .		12
Dreadnought .	200	Lark . .		30
				3,862

Ships remaining with my Lord Seymour in the Narrow Seas :—

	[Men]			[Men]
The Rainbow .	250	The Spy . .		35
Vanguard .	250	Merlin .		35
Antelope .	160	Sun . .		30
Tiger . .	100	Cygnet .		20
Bull . .	100	George .		30
Tramontana .	70	Fancy . .		24
Scout . .	70	Ketch . .		12
Achates . .	60			
				1,246

				[Men]
The Galley				250
Brigandine				36
Victualler				14
				300

The ships under Sir Francis Drake's charge :—

	[Men]		[Men]
The Revenge .	250	The Swiftsure .	200
Nonpareil .	250	Aid . .	120
Hope . .	250	Advice .	35
			1,105

				[Tons]	
The Galleon Leicester . . .				400	160
Merchant Royal . . .				400	140
Roebuck				300	120
Edward Bonaventure . .				300	120
Gold Noble				250	110
Hopewell				200	100
Griffin . ' . . .				200	100
Minion				200	80
Thomas				200	80
Bark Talbot . . .				200	80
Spark				200	80

	[Tons]	[Men]
The Hope	180	70
Bark Bond	150	70
Bark Bonner	150	70
Bark Hawkyns	140	70
Eliz. Founes	100	60
Unity	80	40
Elizabeth Drake	50	30
Bear	140	70
Chance	60	40
Delight	50	30
Nightingale	40	24
Small Caravel	30	24
		2,993 [1]

The abstract of the whole charge in her Majesty's pay :—

	[Men]
My Lord Admiral . . .	3,862
Sir Francis	2,995
My Lord Seymour . . .	1,246
The Galley &c. . . .	300
	8,401
Ships taken by Sir Francis Drake .	614
	9,021

The ships of Sir Richard Greynvile's and others :—

	[Tons]	[Men]
The Galleon Dudley . .	250	100
God Save Her . .	200	80
Frigate	80	60
Bark St. Leger . .	160	80
Manington . . .	150	80

[1] Some ships seem to be omitted, and the total of men is in excess of the details ; but the arithmetic throughout is peculiar.

	[Tons]	[Men]
The Bark Buggins . . .	80	50
Bark Flemyng, Golden Hind	50	30
Bark Leman, Makeshift .	60	40
Diamond of Dartmouth .	60	40
Speedwell . . .	70	14
Bark Yonge . . .	70	40
		614

This is parcel of the abstract.

28th of August, 1588.

Ships appointed to stay in the Narrow Seas :—

		[Men]
The Hope . .	John Sampson [1] . .	250
Vanguard .	Sir Henry Palmer capt. .	250
Rainbow .	Thos. Gray [2] capt. . .	230
Aid . .	Willm. Fenner or Wm. Wynter . . .	120
Foresight .	Luke Ward capt. . .	160
Tiger . .	Mr. Bostocke capt. . .	90
Tramontana	Mr. Clifford capt. . .	70
Achates .	Mr. Riggs capt. . .	60
Sun . . }	Masters	25
Moon . . }		35
		1,290

This is no parcel of the abstract.

Ships abroad to seek the Spaniards :—

		[Men]
The Elizabeth Bonaventure	250
Foresight ; she is noted to remain.	
Aid ; she is also to remain . . .	120
The Charles	40

[1] This name is written in by Burghley. Sampson had probably been master of the Hope in the action ; but it does not appear what had now become of Crosse.
[2] Gray had been master of the Ark.

August 29.—HOWARD TO WALSYNGHAM.

[**ccxv. 66.**—Holograph. Addressed. In very bad condition.]

Sir:—This morning I have received a letter from Sir Thomas Morgan. The effect[1] is that he hath taken order for his men to [move] to Sandwich. I have taken order that the two hoys that served in the Narrow Seas with my Lord Ha. Seymour shall waft them, and also carry some of the soldiers in [them]. I doubt much the soldiers will not march before they have money. I am told they have no money come yet. I mean[2] to ride this afternoon to the soldiers to see what I can do with them, to embark them.

Sir, it is no small trouble that I have here in discharging of the ships of sundry places, both to the westwards as far as Bristol and Bridgwater. We are fain to help them with victuals to bring them [thither]. There is not any of them that hath one day's victuals, and many [of them] have sent many sick men ashore here, and not one penny to relieve them. I am driven to make Sir John Hawkyns to relieve them with money as he can [do]. It were too pitiful to have men starve after such a service. I know her Majesty would not, for any good. Therefore I had rather open the Queen's Majesty's purse something to relieve them, than they should be in that extremity ; for we are to look to have more of these services ; and if men should not be cared for better than to let them starve and die miserably, we should very hardly get men to serve. Sir, I desire [but] that there may be but double allowance of but as much as I [give] out of my own purse, and yet I am not the ablest man in [the realm] ; but,

¹ Effect = substance.   ² MS. min.

before God, I had rather have never penny in the world than they should lack.

It was this morning before those ships could go hence that should go to the helping of the Aid and the Charles, the storms have been so great these 3 days. I have sent over this morning the French gentleman of M. d'Éperon's[1] to Boulogne. I perceive by him he will [return] again to-morrow if he can.

There came into the road here yesternight against his will a very great hulk that came from Lisbon. I do understand by them that there were 12 ships laden with victuals to come to the [armada], thinking to find them here. They say certainly they will come this way.

I do hear there rideth divers ships under Beechy. Those ships that go with Captain Sampson and Mr. Knyvet shall speak with them, for it is in their [way. I have] gotten of the master of the hulk the names of the masters of [those] ships that bringeth the victuals out of Spain; so as I doubt not but if [they come] this ways but that they shall be met withal.

Even as I was writing [this present], George Morgan came to me, and told me that the soldiers were going to Sandwich. It shall be well done to hasten Sir Thomas Morgan from London, who is gone thither, as I learn, about earnest business; and also that the money for the soldiers be [sent] down with all speed to them. Sir, I thank God that my Lord Chamberlain hath [regained] his feet. God send him health. I do leave Sir William Wynter, Sir John Hawkyns and Sir Martin Frobiser, with the captains and one lieutenant, to [be] in the ships.

---

[1] The Duke d'Éperon, the celebrated 'mignon' of Henry III. At this period he was earning a nobler distinction as the leader of the King's army.

Sir, I think that myself, my Lord Ha. Seymour, my Lord Thomas Howard and [my Lord] Sheffield will be at the Court on Sunday ; for I trust by to-morrow [1] night to despatch all things here, and to leave order with Sir W. Wynter and Sir John Hawkyns for the rest ; as also with Sir Ha. Palmer, who remaineth with the charge of the ships in the Narrow Seas. I do leave these ships underwritten [with him], for it is good to have some good strength for a while.

Sir, God send you well to do, and so I bid you most heartily farewell. From Dover, the 29th of August.   Your assured loving friend,
                                        C. HOWARD.

Sir, Mr. Bodley is here, and [will] think he is forgotten. I think [there] is no cause of his farther [stay], but he will not depart till he knoweth her Majesty's pleasure.

The Vanguard	.	.	.	.	[250] [2]
Rainbow .	.	.	.	.	[230] [2]
Foresight	.	.	.	.	[160] [2]
Aid .	.	.	.	.	120
Tiger .	.	.	.	.	90
Tramontana	.	.	.	.	70
Moon	.	.	.	.	35
Sun	.	.	.	.	25
					1,040 [3]

[1] Friday.   [2] Torn away.
[3] This sum only amounts to 980. The Achates, 60 men, is omitted in error. See *ante*, p. 175.

August 29.—CARY TO WALSYNGHAM.

[**ccxv. 67.**—Holograph.   Addressed.]

Having now brought the Spanish ship[1] in safe harbour, bestowed the prisoners in sure keeping, and inventoried the ordnance and goods, we have sent unto your Honour the said inventory under our hands, with a note of the charges concerning the same, and with our humble request unto your Honours for some directions touching these Spanish prisoners, whom we would have been very glad they had been made water spaniels when they were first taken.   Their provision, which is left to sustain them, is very little and nought, their fish savours, so that it is not to be eaten, and their bread full of worms.   The people's charity unto them (coming with so wicked an intent) is very cold; so that if there be not order forthwith taken by your Lordships, they must starve.   They are many in number, and divers of them already very weak, and some dead. The pilot of the ship is as perfect in our coasts as if he had been a native born.   Divers of the rest are of the garrison[2] of Sicilia.

And touching the inventoring of the ordnance and goods, there are, I think, a 12 or 13 pieces of brass ordnance taken out of the ship, and so left out of our inventory, as your Honour may perceive by the empty carriages which are noted down on the inventory; of the which I take it Jacob Whiddon, captain of the Roebuck, had ten, and likewise divers muskets and calivers.   A pinnace of Plymouth, that came from my Lord Admiral for

[1] N. S. del Rosario.
[2] He uses 'garrison' as the English equivalent of *tercio*, which is rather the modern 'regiment.'

powder and shot, had other two pieces ; and the Samaritan of Dartmouth had the other, as also 10 muskets and 10 calivers. The Roebuck had also divers pipes of wine, and two of oil. None of these things could be allowed to be set down in the inventory, because my warrant from my Lords was for the inventoring of the goods whatsoever which were or are here remaining in the ship [sithence] their Lordships' first letters, and these things were taken out before. I was never much [1] experienced in these causes before this time ; but now I find that all these sea goods are mixed with bird-lime ; for no man can lay his hand of them, but is limed, and must bring away somewhat. Watch and look never so narrowly, they will steal and pilfer. There are four or five pipes of wine and vinegar privily hoisted over board, of which I have some under-standing of, and in my next letters your Honour shall have further knowledge what is become of them. And so they are not inventoried.

And now, having told you of others, I pray let me trouble your Honour and show a little of myself. It is reported unto us that there should a warrant come from my Lords for the receipt of the [ship] out of our hands ; and therefore Sir John [Gilberte] and I have left out of the inventory 4 pipes of wine, two for him and two for myself; but herewith I shall humbly beseech your Honour to acquaint my Lords ; for if it be not their pleasures to bestow the said two pipes on me, I will pay for them with all my heart as the rest are sold ; for in no case, nor under any colour, would I use any deceit, especially where trust is reposed in me ; neither will I touch the wines until I hear from your Honour what their Lordships' pleasures are. Thus, being sorry that I

---

[1] MS. mitch.

have troubled your Honour so long, I humbly take
my leave.   Cockington, this 29th of August, 1588.

Your Honour's most bounden,

GEORGE CARY.

*August 26.—GILBERTE AND CARY TO THE
COUNCIL.*

[ccxv. 68.—Signed.   Addressed.]

Our duties to your good Lordships most humbly
remembered :—Having received your Honours'
letters for the safe keeping and bestowing of the
Spanish prisoners, and likewise for the true and
perfect inventoring of the ordnance, munition, and
all other things whatsoever remaining in the ship
which was left in Torbay, and now in the haven of
Dartmouth:

And touching the said prisoners, being in
number 397, whereof we sent to my Lord Lieutenant[1] five of the chiefest of them, whom his Lordship hath committed to the town prison of Exon ;
and we have put 226 in our Bridewell, amongst
which all the mariners are placed, which are 61,
besides younkers and boys.   The rest, which are
166, for the ease of our country from the watching
and guarding of them, and conveying of their provision of their victuals unto them—which was very
burdensome unto our people in this time of harvest
—we have therefore placed them aboard the
Spanish ship, to live upon such victuals as do remain in the said ship ; which is very little and bad,
their fish unsavoury, and their bread full of worms,
and of so small quantity as will suffice them but a
very small time.

[1] The Earl of Bath.

And touching the ordnance and other things in the said ship, we have herewith, under our hands, sent your Lordships the true inventory, having left all the great ordnance aboard the ship ; but the small ordnance, lest that it should be embezzled[1] away, we have caused the same to be had on shore.

The wines, being 85 pipes, were so badly conditioned that they made but 67 full pipes, which are put in safe cellarage ; and the wines but indifferent, and many of them eager.[2] Thus much presuming of your Lordships' good allowance, we have bestowed four pipes of the said wines : the one on my Lord Edward Seymour,[3] for cumbering his house with these Spanish prisoners until the ship was cleared, not knowing otherwise where we should have bestowed them ; the other three pipes we gave to three gentlemen that this month have continually lain aboard and attended the said ship.   There are also sundry gentlemen and others which have demanded divers pipes of wine heretofore given unto them by the captains,[4] and some of them (as they say) have already paid their money for the same ;

---

[1] MS. imbeaselled.　　　　　[2] Sour. Fr. *aigre*.

[3] Second son of the Duke of Somerset, the Protector, by his first wife, whom he repudiated, disinheriting her children.   By the early death of his elder brother, he remained the eldest son ; but though this was acknowledged by Act of Parliament (7 Edw.VI.), it was a younger Edward, the eldest son of the Duke by his second marriage, that was created Earl of Hertford in 1559.   The older Edward lived retired at Bury Pomeroy, and died in 1593. His son was created a baronet in 1611.   It was his great-grandson, the third baronet, to whom, on his waiting on the Prince of Orange at Exeter in 1688, the Prince remarked :—'I think, Sir Edward, you are of the Duke of Somerset's family?'   'No, sir,' he replied, 'he is of mine.'   On the failure of the younger line, the title reverted to the elder in 1750.

[4] Possibly Flemyng, who brought her in, and Whiddon of the Roebuck, who had helped himself to 'divers pipes of wine' ; but the meaning is not clear.

but yet we have made stay thereof until your Lordships' pleasures be further known.

We have also sent your Honours a book of the charge which hath been defrayed about the said ship sithence she was left in Torbay, wind and weather not serving by the space of three weeks to bring her into safe harbour; wherein we humbly pray your Lordships' directions for the allowance of the said charges.

And so, resting to be commanded by your Lordships what your further pleasures are touching these Spanish prisoners and the rest of these causes, we cease from farther troubling your Honours, do most humbly take our leave. Greenwaye, 29th of August, 1588.

Your Lordships' most humbly to command,
JOHN GILBERTE. GEORGE CARY.

Aug. 28.—INVENTORY OF THE ROSARIO.

[ccxv. **67, I.**; **68, I.**—Signed. Duplicate. Enclosure in Mr. Cary's letter to Walsyngham of August 29, and the joint letter to the Council of August 29.]

The true inventory of all the ordnance, munition, wines, and all other things whatsoever aboard the Spanish ship in the haven of Dartmouth, taken the 28th day of August, 1588.

Ordnance of brass :

	lbs.	qrs.	lbs.
Imprimis, one fowler . . .	803	0	0
Item, more, one fowler . . .	186	0	0
„ a great base [1]	700	2	3

[1] According to Norton, an English base weighed 200 lbs., was 1¼ inch in the bore, and discharged an iron shot of 1 lb. Foreign patterns varied between 150 and 800 lbs., but the bore seems to have been the same.

				lbs.	qrs.	lbs.
Item, more, 1 great base	.	.	.	700	3	4
,, ,, 1 great base	.	.	.	600	3	0
,, ,, 1 great base	.	.	.	708	0	0
,, ,, a base	.	.	.	385	0	0
,, ,, 1 base	.	.	.	382	0	0
,, ,, 1 base	.	.	.	388	0	0
,, ,, 1 base	.	.	.	390	0	0
,, ,, 1 base	.	.	.	212	0	0
,, a falconet	.	.	.	700	3	0
,, 5 chambers of 23 case [1]	.	.	0	0	0
,, a cannon pedro	.	.	.	2,639	0	0
,, more, a cannon pedro	.	.	2,566	0	0
,, a demi-cannon, without number, of 6 inches height	.	.	0	0	0
,, more, 1 cannon pedro	.	.	3,032	0	0
,, 1 culverin	.	.	.	4,736	0	0
,, more, a culverin	.	.	3,200	1	9
,, ,, 1 culverin	.	.	4,728	0	0
,, 1 basilisco	.	.	.	4,840	0	0
,, more, 1 culverin	.	.	4,589	0	0
,, 1 cannon pedro	.	.	2,934	0	0
,, more, 1 cannon pedro	.	.	2,894	0	0
,, ,, 1 cannon pedro	.	.	3,021	0	0
,, ,, 1 demi-cannon	.	.	5,230	0	0
,, ,, 1 demi-cannon, without number, of 6 inches in height			0	0	0

Ordnance of iron :

Imprimis, 10 chambers	.	.	.	0	0	0
Item, 4 fore-locks	.	.	.	0	0	0
,, 1 minion	.	.	.	1,100	0	0
,, 1 demi-culverin	.	.	2,300	0	0

All which great pieces of brass and iron are mounted on their carriages a-shipboard.

[1] For case-shot. The case was a wooden cylinder. (Manwayring).

Item, 12 carriages without ordnance.
  ,,   2 field carriages without wheels.
  ,,   4 spare anchors within board.
  ,,   2 cables and anchors which the ship rides by.
  ,,   3 cables on shore, whereof 2 white and a tarred.
  ,,   2 kedging anchors.
  ,,   7 shear hooks[1] for yards.
  ,,   a graper[2] of iron with a chain.
  ,,   a main-course.
  ,,   1 mizen-sail.
  ,,   1 main-topsail wanting the wings, with sundry ropes, some whole, some broken, with divers sorts of pullies.[3]
  ,,   iron hoops 261
  ,,   empty casks 234
  ,,   sows of lead 5
  ,,   butts of wine taken overboard . . 85
  ,,   which filled 67
  ,,   a great lantern which was in the stern of the ship.

A brief of such charges as hath been bestowed about the Spanish ship during the time she remained in Torbay, till the time of her unlading :—

Imprimis, the wages for 50 men, after the rate of 10s. a month for a man . £ s. d. 25 0 0

[1] 'Shear hooks are great hooks of iron, about the bigness of a small sickle and more ; they are set into the yard arms of the main and fore yards ; the use whereof is that if a ship under sail come to board her that hath these hooks, she will cut her shrouds or tear her sails down with these hooks. Some use them, but they are most unuseful and unnecessary things, and dangerous for the breaking of a yard if the hook should catch in the other ship's mast.' (Manwayring.)
[2] Grapnel.
[3] MS. pullowes.

		£	s.	d.
Item, 1,700 of biscuit, at 7s. the hundred		5	19	0
,, 21 hogsheads of beer, at 8s. the hogshead		8	8	0
,, for beef, fish, and other necessaries		11	6	7
,, 8 boats to tow the ship about from Torbay into the haven of Dartmouth		1	6	0
,, carpenters to set up a jury mast in Torbay		0	13	4
,, to a boatman for carrying of ropes and other necessaries to set up the jury mast		0	16	0
,, for 20 pounds of iron spikes .		0	5	0
,, to 2 barks that landed the Spanish prisoners and brought certain ordnance from the ship into Dartmouth haven		8	0	0
,, for guarding and watching of the Spaniards 2 nights and a day at their landing		1	10	0
,, for 8 boats for carrying of victuals sundry times to the Spanish prisoners		2	0	0
,, for a boat of 12 tons to carry victuals to the Spanish prisoners to Bridewell		2	0	0
,, wood to dress the Spanish prisoners' meat ashore . . .		1	0	0
,, for lifters and labourers for the unlading of the ordnance, wine &c. .		4	17	0
,, for new hooping of the wines .		2	8	0
,, to Liddenton at his riding post to London to certify the arrival of the Spanish ship . . .		2	0	0
,, to a man of my Lord Admiral's that came for the powder out of				

		£	s.	d.
the Spaniard, and so came by post to Portsmouth . . .		2	o	o
„ for 500 of corr fish for the Spanish prisoners		5	o	o

Sum total 84 8 11

JOHN GILBERTE.   GEORGE CARY.

[Memorandum, in Burghley's hand.]

The charges laid out for the prisoners must be accounted for and repaid by the prisoners before they be delivered.

August 30.—SUSSEX TO THE COUNCIL.

[ccxv. 72.—Signed. Addressed. A singularly neat handwriting, though now somewhat faint, the ink having faded.]

It may please your Honours :—Upon Monday morning, being the 26th of this present, Captain Raymond in the Elizabeth Bonaventure, Captain Baker in the Foresight,[1] came from the coast of France, and found here at road Captain Fenner, captain of the Aid, and Captain Roberts, captain of the Charles, who were sent, being all of one concert, for the taking of the great Spanish ship that lay at the Bay of Hogges, and now in Newhaven road ; which captains, upon conference had amongst themselves for the execution of this exploit, found that there was among them lack of some victuals, powder and shot to perform the enterprise ; for that the Spanish ship was very well manned and appointed with ordnance and small shot, and meant to fight it out, besides the aid they might have of the French. Whereupon they came all unto me for supply of

---

[1] The words, ' and the pinnace called the Delight,' written in here, have been roughly scored out apparently by Sussex himself.

their wants, which I presently accomplished; as by the particulars thereof, herein sent to your Honours, may more plainly appear. So as upon Tuesday, about two of the clock after midnight, they set sail for the coast of France; so as I think they were yesternight, or this morning, at road by the Spanish ship, if she be not gone over the bar at Newhaven this spring tide; hoping[1] very shortly to hear some good news of their happy success in this their enterprise.

I have also received a letter from my Lord Admiral of the 23rd of this present, wherein he writeth that he hath received all the powder and shot that I sent unto his Lordship, and hath discharged all the ships[2] saving my Lord of Cumberland's. Having[3] requested me likewise, that forsomuch as he hath discharged them without their pay, that I would levy so much money hereabouts me, in this country, as will suffice to make pay and satisfaction unto them; the which, your Honours shall understand, I cannot by any means do, unless I will seek to be hardly thought of by the country— having been so greatly charged otherwise of late in these services—and thereby grow odious unto them; or else that the same may be levied by order and direction from your Honours of the Council, if you will so have it; for that of myself, I neither can nor will take it upon me.

I am sorry to write unto your Honours of the disorderly and dishonourable speeches uttered by Gray,[4] one of the masters of the Queen's Majesty's

---

[1] Sc. so that I hope.   [2] Cf. *post*, p. 211.
[3] Sc. But he has also requested.
[4] Probably Thomas Gray, the master of the Ark, and one of the 'masters of her Majesty's navy,' who had been appointed captain of the Rainbow, in the squadron with Sir H. Palmer (*ante*, p. 182). The only other Gray mentioned is John Gray, the master of the Revenge.

ships, of me ; and not contented therewith, but in offering to beat the captain of one of the barks sent by me, and strake [1] and beat divers of the company, and thrust the master overboard ; who then required that, if he would thrust them overboard, they might be considered for their wages.   Gray answered that if my Lord of Sussex did prest them, let him prest no more than he will pay ; and so turned them away, not suffering them to take either their apparel or furniture with them ; and took away from them two hogsheads of beer, which my Lord Admiral had assigned them to bring them home, and put it aboard his own hoy, as they said.   These dealings be very hard for a nobleman to receive at such a man's hands as he is ; for as Gray saith he knoweth me, I assure your Honours I know him, and some part of his doings ; but I make small account of his speeches, because I know the man's disposition ; but I fear his blows and beatings will not so easily be put up, if he come in place where they may be remembered ; for men and soldiers will hardly bear to be beaten.

Since the writing of my letters yesterday, and before the sealing up of the same this morning, the Queen's Majesty's ships which were sent for the coast of France—viz. the Elizabeth Bonaventure, the Foresight, the Aid, and the Charles—did come in sight.   The Charles having spent her mainmast, and finding the wind to blow very high at North-West, durst [2] not adventure the Queen's ships upon that coast ; and for that cause they returned, and do mean to pass over thither again with the next wind that will serve their turn.   And even so I commit your Honours to God.   From Portsmouth, the 30th of August, 1588.

Your Honours' most humbly at command,

SUSSEX.

---

[1] Struck.   [2] They durst not.

August 25.—NOTE OF SUPPLIES.

[**ccxv. 72, I.**—Enclosure in Lord Sussex's letter to the Council of
August 30, and is in the same writing.]

A note of such powder, shot, and victuals as
was delivered into the Queen's Majesty's ships, the
25th of August, 1588.

For the Aid, William Fenner :

Demi-culverin shot	20
Saker shot	50
Minion shot	50
Barrels of powder	5
Saker crossbar shot	12
Minion crossbar shot . . .	12

For the Charles, John Roberts :

Falcon shot	80
Demi-barrels of powder . . .	2
Falcon crossbar shot	12

For the Elizabeth Bonaventure, George Raymond :

Tons of beer	6
Bread	600
Demi-cannon shot	10
Culverin shot	10
[Saker shot][1]	20
Oars for the longboat . . .	6

For the Foresight, Christopher Baker :

Barrels of powder	4
Demi-culverin shot	30
Saker shot	30
Tons of beer	4
Biscuit	600
Oars for the longboat . . .	6

[1] The MS. has saylers, which has no meaning ; it is probably a
clerical error for saker shot.

[**ccxv. 73.**—Addressed.   Endorsed in Edmonds' writing.
Seal of the Seymour crest.]

Sir :—Since the time of my Lord Admiral's
repair hither, I have had some leisure to peruse all
your honourable letters, with them that come from
my Lords ; as [1] otherwise have examined all my own
copies ; wherein I find the sequel of this great cause
long prepared doth not much vary from my own
precedent private conjectured opinion ; chiefly in
respect of the Duke of Parma's exploits, the same
never to be enterprised by his own particular
strength, but always his attempts to proceed where
he doth assure himself of faction or civil discord, or
that he be otherwise supported of stronger forces
than his own.

Now finding the capital enemy, the Spaniard,
returned and brought even to his own home, with
greater shame and disgrace than before he set out
with pomp and glory, I imagine beforehand the
dispute that may arise between the King and the
Duke of Medina, [with] what controversies may
grow upon the authors of this mighty preparation,
what satisfaction the Duke of Parma can yield of
this course only directed by him ; for of these two
principal generals, the two foresaid Dukes, the
King must look to have a good account thereof,
and to whom he shall incline.   My opinion doth
give me the Duke of Parma is like to bear the
blame, who, I think, now may easily be entreated to
make a division of the Low Countries with her
Majesty. [2]   But, to proceed further herein I will

---

[1] As = and.

[2] This is very like a suggestion of the proposal actually made
in October by Palavicino to Parma.   Motley, in giving an account

omit, and leave the same to your graver conceits, meaning now to answer your last received letters, wherein I find myself ever remembered by your honourable good care.

And, to prevent her Majesty's good and gracious favourable remembrance of me, if so be that among you it shall be resolved to proceed with the charge of another month's victuals, which is already prepared, let not my service be spared. Albeit you may sit sure this year for the King of Spain ; yet, if you consider what I wrote in my last letters of the Duke of Parma, touching his desperate actions, finding himself foiled for not joining with the Duke of Medina, some unlooked-for enterprises to save his honour may be attempted for England, if we have a fair latter end of a summer ; and with my conceit, could never heretofore be so far forth carried, but now, upon the recovery of his honour at this time balanced. And even so, with my very loving commendations, and all manner of well-wishing unto yourself, do take my leave. From aboard the Rainbow, her Majesty's most honourable ship, the [1]

of its reception by Parma, adds : ' There is neither proof nor probability that the Queen's government was implicated in this intrigue of Palavicino's ' (*Hist. of United Netherlands*, ii. 512). There is certainly a probability that Walsyngham had spoken of the matter to Palavicino, with a hint that he might sound Parma respecting it.

[1] The letter ends thus abruptly, without date or signature. The writing is that of Seymour's clerk, as in the letters to Howard and Walsyngham of August 19 (*ante*, pp. 129, 130), and the mention of ' my Lord Admiral,' of ' the Rainbow,' as well as the seal and Edmonds' endorsement, leave no room for doubt as to its having been written and sent with Seymour's authority ; but a very casual perusal will show how different the wording of it is from letters of Seymour's own writing, or under his signature. It may perhaps be supposed that he told his clerk the substance of what he wanted to say, but did not dictate it, and was absent when it was written and sent off.

THE CHARGE OF CERTAIN SHIPS.

[**ccxv. 75.**—Signed. Endorsed :—The charge of certain ships sent to the seas by Sir John Gilberte to repair to the Admiral.]

A note of the charge of those ships sent unto the seas, for the supply of men to her Majesty's navy, the 22nd of July, 1588, and served one month.

The Roebuck victualled :—

	£	s.	d.
Imprimis, for 6 medernixes [1] for the Roe-buck	7	4	0
Item, 1 hogshead of beef . . .	3	11	3
,, 600 of Irish fish, at 50s. the hundred	15	0	0
Sum	25	15	3

To the Chance, my Lord Admiral's pinnace, which came for powder &c., and victualled :—

	£	s.	d.
Item, from the town of Dartmouth, 126 iron shot of all sorts, weighing 1 cwt.[2] 1 qr. 10 lbs., at 12s. the hundred	5	0	0
,, 2 hogsheads of beer . . .	1	0	0
,, 1 barrel of beef	1	10	7
Sum	7	10	7

The Phœnix of Dartmouth, Mr. Gawen Cham-

---

[1] A medernix, which appears in these papers under many different spellings—meddernix, or nex, methernix, and mederinax —and as mildernix in 'An Act against the deceitful and false making of mildernix . . . whereof sail-cloths for the navy and other shipping are made' (1 Jac. I. c. 24)—was a bolt of canvas.

[2] So in MS. Apparently in error for 8 cwt.

pernowne's[1] bark, burden 70 tons, with 50 men, and served one month :—

	£	s.	d.
Imprimis, 4 barrels of powder, weighing 493 lbs., at 12*d*. the pound . .	24	13	0
Item, 81 pieces of beef	2	0	0
„ 1 bushel of peas	0	2	8
„ 100 of fish	0	10	0
„ 1 cheese	0	0	8
„ for match and oakum . . .	0	8	6
„ for 9 lbs. of spikes[2] . . .	0	1	6
„ for 7 oars of 18 foot . . .	1	6	0
„ for cross-bars and round shot .	0	13	4
„ for 10 cwt. of biscuit . . .	3	10	0
„ 2 tons of beer	4	0	0
„ 7½ lbs. of plated lead . . .	0	1	3
„ for 24 lbs. of candles . . .	0	9	0
„ for all sorts of nails . . .	0	7	6
Sum[3]	38	3	5

Besides the ship and mariners.

JOHN GILBERTE.

The Command, Sir John Gilberte's ship, burden 120 tons, with 80 men, which served one month :—

	£	s.	d.
Item, 10 hogsheads of beer . . .	5	0	0
„ 1 hogshead of beef . . .	3	11	3
„ 100 of corr fish[3]	2	0	0
„ 11 cwt. of biscuit . . .	3	17	0
„ 6 cwt. of powder	30	0	0
„ 30 lbs of caliver powder . .	1	15	0
„ 750 lbs. of round shot, chain shot, and cross-bars, at 12*s*. the hundred	4	10	0

---

[1] First cousin of Sir Walter Ralegh : son of his mother's younger brother, Sir Arthur Champernowne of Dartington.

[2] MS. spukes.   [3] Salt cod.

	£	s.	d.
Item, 22 lbs of match, at 6*d.* the pound .	0	11	0
„ 6 yards of canvas for cartridges, at 10*d.* the yard	0	5	0
„ 20 lbs. of candles. . . .	0	6	8
„ for 500 of wood	0	13	4
„ for all sorts of nails . . .	0	10	6
„ 2 quarter cans	0	2	8
„ 54½ lbs. of plated lead . . .	0	9	2
„ 1 barrel of butter, 200 weight .	2	10	0
Sum	56	1	8

Besides the ship and mariners.

The Elizabeth, Mr. Adrian Gilberte's[1] ship, burden 70 tons, with 60 men, and served 1 month :—

	£	s.	d.
Imprimis, 20 cwt. of biscuit . . .	7	0	0
Item, 6 tons of beer	12	0	0
„ 2 hogsheads of beef and one barrel of pork	9	12	6
„ 1,000 of dry fish	5	0	0
„ 1 cwt. of butter	1	5	0
„ 1 cwt. of cheese	0	18	0
„ 3 bushels of peas	0	10	0
„ 700 of wood	0	18	0
„ 411 pounds of powder . . .	20	11	0
„ 30 pounds of candles . . .	0	10	0
„ 500[2] shot of all sorts . . .	3	0	0
„ waist cloths and cartridges, 40 yards	2	0	0
„ 20 lbs. of match	0	10	0
Sum	63	14	6

Besides the ship and mariners.

The head of the mainmast, with the topmast, sail and shrouds, spent.   JOHN GILBERTE.

[1] Brother of Sir John.
[2] So in MS. It would seem to mean 500 lbs. of shot at 12*s.* the 100.

The Samaritan of Dartmouth, burden 300 tons, with 150 men, which served one month :—

		£	s.	d.
Imprimis, 39½ cwt. of biscuit . .	.[1]3	16	6
Item, 30 hogsheads of beer . . .	14	0	0
„ 1,000 of dry fish	5	0	0
„ 1 hogshead of pork . . .	5	0	0
„ 60 lbs. of candles . . .	1	0	0
„ 800 of wood	.0	16	6
„ 12 bushels of peas . . .	2	0	0
„ 30 lbs. of match	0	15	0
„ of round shot and cross-bars, 700	4	0	0
„ 1 piece of lead, 110 lbs. . .	0	10	10
„ platters and dishes . . .	0	4	4
	Sum 47	3	2

Besides the ship and mariners.

JOHN GILBERTE.

SIR H. PALAVICINO'S RELATION.[1]

[**ccxv. 77.**—Italian. A peculiarly neat writing, the same as many of Palavicino's letters. Endorsed (in the writing of Edmonds):—Sir Horatio Palavicino : relation of the proceeding of our fleet with the Spanish navy. August 1588.]

Relation of the voyage of the Spanish armada, which departed from Lisbon to assail the kingdom of England :—

The Spanish fleet parted from Lisbon on the 29th of May, *stilo novo*, in number 130 sails great and small, with four galleasses of Naples and four galleys of Portugal, under the charge of the Duke

[1] As Palavicino went from Portsmouth on July 26, and presumably got on board the Ark in time for the battle of the 29th, it is curious to note the many inaccuracies in his relation, not only as to preceding events, which he heard of, but as to the later ones, which he witnessed.

of Medina Sidonia, general of the enterprise, with 25 or 30 thousand men, as well soldiers as mariners, and many noblemen.

They sailed for the port of the Groyne in Galicia, where they would receive some soldiers, munition and victuals; it being also the haven most near and convenient for passing into England. But in this voyage they had foul weather, which scattered them, so that when the Duke of Medina Sidonia arrived at the haven, he was not accompanied with more than 80 vessels, or thereabouts; which occasioned a longer stay, for that the rest came together only by little and little, and divers of them were wanting, amongst which were the four galleys of Portugal, whereof three suffered shipwreck on the coast of Bayonne in France, and the fourth with great difficulty recovered a certain haven.[1] And of the ships, there remained behind eight, which having spent their masts in the violence of the storm, they returned to Lisbon unable for the voyage. All the rest of the army, having refreshed and ordered themselves in the Groyne, and receiving continually commandment from the King to set out, they set sail on the 11th of July, according to our computation, and with a favourable wind arrived, on the 19th of the same, off of the Cape of Cornwall, in this kingdom, where it was first discovered by one of our pinnaces, and shortly afterward by the guard of the castle of Falmouth; intelligence whereof was carried to the Lord Admiral, who was in the haven of Plymouth with our fleet, having the conceit that the Spanish army would not come this year, because that the season was now almost past, and also of the

[1] It was so reported in England (*ante*, p. 132), but falsely (see App. E). The confusion between the first voyage, to Corunna, and the second, from Corunna, would seem to be Palavicino's own.

storm which should have spoiled them, and of the victual which was reported to be wasted ; so as he had great difficulty to bring some part of the ships out of the haven and to send the men aboard ; for that, the wind being fair for the Spanish army, he had sight of them the same evening, when as they were close to the port, with the intention of entering there and overcoming them, if they had not perceived our fleet.   Thus, their intention being prevented, they proceeded on their voyage alongst the Channel.   The whole of our fleet came out and followed them, often fighting with them and delaying their progress, because that they sailed in close order, without extending themselves.

The next day the fighting was hotter than on those which preceded it.[1]   One of our ships beat their galleasses, and was the cause that divers of their fleet were spoiled, so as, during the fight, a galleon of Seville, vice-admiral of the enemy's fleet, broke her mainmast[2] ; and a ship laden with munition of war[3] caught fire, so as her upper works were blown out, and she remained unable for the voyage, and a short time afterward was made a prize by our men. The aforesaid galleon likewise remained unable to follow their fleet, and was taken by our men.   There were in her 450 men ; the captain of her, which was Don Pedro de Valdes, accompanied with two gentlemen of quality, were all made prisoners ; also a great part of the King's treasure fell into the hands of our men.

When the fleets had come as far as the Isle of Wight, ours had grown daily because of the many ships and men which came to it from all sides ; where there was another fight, which continued

---

[1] Le precedenti.
[2] Il maggior albero.   Cf. *ante*, p 135.
[3] Una nave carrica di munitione di guerra.   Cf. *ante*, p. 56.

several hours, wherein our men more certainly perceived that the Spanish army wished not to fight,
and held themselves straitly to defence, with no
other intention than to arrive at the place appointed
for them.   During the whole voyage the wind was
favourable for them, so as, notwithstanding the stay
caused by the bickerings and by divers calms, they
arrived on the evening of the 27th of the aforesaid
month, by our account, off the port of the town of
Calais in France, where they anchored toward Dunkirk, from whence they expected the succour of the
Duke of Parma his forces.   Our fleet likewise anchored opposite to them, and the same evening were
joined by other ships, to the number of 20, which
had been guarding the mouth of Thames ; so as the
number of them amounted to near 140 sails.   On
the 28th of the said month, being Sunday, there was
held a consultation in what manner the enemy's fleet
might be moved from their place, and would be
fought withal.   It was resolved to prepare certain
ships with fireworks, and to endeavour to burn them
in the road, or to force them to put to the seas,
thereby to fight with them.   To this end six ships
were made ready, and two hours after midnight, the
tide and wind being favourable, they drew as near
the enemy as they could, where they were fired ;
which was no sooner seen by the enemy, than they
were seized with such great alarm as suddenly they
cut all their cables ; in which confusion, the chief of
the four galleasses became entangled among certain
other ships by her rudder, and was driven by the
current on to the shoals which are before the port of
Calais, where she was followed by our pinnaces and
barks, and was fought withal and overcome.   Many
Spaniards were there slain by the sword, and many
were thrown overboard and drowned, but some
were saved by swimming into the haven of Calais.

The captain-general, Don Hugo de Moncada, was likewise slain. Then was everything movable taken away, and such part of the King's treasure as was therein. The ship rested without value, which our men would have burnt it, if the governor of Calais had not prevented them, alleging the hurt it should cause to the town.[1]

Meanwhile, in the early morning our fleet assailed the enemy, which had put to sea, as aforesaid, in disorder, but had afterward arranged themselves in their usual[2] order of fight. There were made several very hot charges, and a great quantity of ordnance was fired on one side and on the other. Our fleet had the wind throughout, and gave always occasion to the enemy to open out and to fight; but they chose rather to be followed and to bear away, as well from Calais as from Dunkirk, than to open out and permit the fight to become general, so as it was not convenient to attack them thus together and in close order, for that our ships, being of smaller size, would have had much disadvantage; but in the continued assaults which they gave on them without entering, they made them to feel our ordnance; and if any ship was beaten out of their fleet, she was surrounded and suddenly separated from the rest. Amongst which, two galleons of Portugal, called the San Felipe and the San Mateo, were dispersed and so spoiled as, being unable to follow their fleet, and being almost full of water, they both fell the next day into the hands of our men, who conducted them to Flushing, having found [few] of their men living, who were all

[1] Allegando il preginditio del suo porto. This is repeated in almost the same words in Purchas *His Pilgrimes*, iv. 1908.

[2] Wynter says (*ante*, p. 10) in 'a half moon,' which, therefore, Palavicino understood to be their 'usual' order. This agrees with Pine's illustrations.

made prisoners, together with Don Diego de Pimentel, maestro de campo of the regiment of Sicilia, with divers gentlemen of quality. There was also therein a part of the King's treasure, which was sacked by the soldiers. In this same fight a great Biscayan ship was likewise dispersed from the fleet and sunk. There were also sunk two or three other ships of the enemy, so as they lost in that fight, besides the galleass, five or six great ships, and were pursued ten or twelve leagues beyond Dunkirk, being sorely beaten by our ordnance.

The next day they were driven farther, because, the same wind continuing to blow, they never endeavoured to force their way back, notwithstanding that they were not assailed.

On the next day, being the 31st, and also on the 1st of August, they had the same wind, but stronger. Then the enemy resolved to set all their sails, and by fleeing from the combat to secure their safety by flight. Nevertheless, for that it was doubted they might bear for Scotland, they were followed by our fleet not more than a cannon-shot off; which continued till the evening of Friday, the 2nd of August, when the fleets were thwart of Berwick,[1] where the enemy clearly showed their intention to hold another course, drawing northwards toward Norway, leaving Scotland on the left hand, and thus incurring the danger of a long navigation; wherein, because it would not have been prudent for our fleet to follow them in their peril, it returned home to the port of Harwich; which resolution was approved by the success, for that on the next Sunday, being the 4th of the month, there arose a great storm, which continued forty hours, the effects of which on the enemy's fleet as yet we know

[1] Essendo le armate pervenute sin nel mare fra l' Inghilterra e la Scotia. Cf. *ante*, p. 64.

not, but it is probable that they are dispersed and have suffered a great deal.

To conclude : the enemy, without having attempted anything, have lost 11 or 12 of their best ships, that we know of ; four to five thousand men ; three parts of the King's treasure, which was divided amongst five vessels ; are reduced to great extremity, not having a drop of water nor much victual, and very many sick, as all the prisoners report ; so as there is every appearance that very few of either ships or men will return into Spain.

NOTE OF CERTAIN PLUNDER.

[**ccxv. 78**.—Endorsed :—A note of the apparel taken by Captain Cely from the Spanish prisoners in Bridewell.]

Of Doctor Gongora : a girdle and a pair of hangers [1] embroidered with gold and silver.

Of the ancient bearer Luis de Ribera : a blue cloak of rash,[2] with a gold lace round about it ; a pair breeches of murrey tinsel of silk, with a gold lace ; and a buff jerkin, laid over likewise with gold lace.

Of the sergeant Pelegrin : a pair of blue velvet hose, with a gold and silver lace ; and a jerkin of wrought velvet, lined with taffety.

Of the sergeant Marcos de Biber : a jerkin of rash, lined with green taffety ; a pair of breeches of blue satin, laid with a gold lace ; with a cloak of rash, with a gold lace round about it.

[1] Sword slings.

[2] Rash is differently described as a smooth cloth, a coarse serge, and a glossy silk fabric. It would seem here to mean the cloth.

Of Don Sancho Pardo[1] : a pair of breeches of yellow satin, drawn out with cloth of silver.

Of the ancient bearer Cristobal de Leon : a leather jerkin, perfumed with amber, and laid over with a gold and silver lace.

Of Alonso de la Serna[2] : a coloured cloak, with a gold lace round about it ; a pair of breeches of cloth of gold ; a jerkin, embroidered with flowers, and laid over with a gold lace.

Of Diego de Carmona : a pair of breeches of cloth of gold, laid over with three gold laces.

Of Juan Becerill : a pair of black wrought velvet breeches.

Of the ancient bearer Bermudo : a cloak mandillion[3] ; and breeches of rash, laid over all with gold lace ; and a blue stitched taffety hat, with a silver band and a plume of feathers.

Of Santiago : a pair of black velvet breeches.

Of Mateo de Fries : a pair of black satin breeches

BOOK OF CHARGES.

[ccxv. 88.—Signed.]

Portsmouth.—A book mentioning such charges as were required to the setting forth of certain ships[4]

[1] This can scarcely be Sancho Pardo Osorio (Duro, ii. 189, 191), a man of too high rank to have been consigned to Bridewell. Possibly the Alferez Sancho de Paredes (*ib.* ii. 73).

[2] Duro, ii. 75.

[3] Mandillion = mantle ; 'a cloak mandillion' would seem to be a large cloak. So Chapman, *Iliads*, x. 120 :

'About him a mandillion . . .
Of purple, large and full of folds, curled with a warmful nap,
A garment that 'gainst cold in nights did soldiers use to wrap.'

[4] As these ships were still at Portsmouth on July 29 and later —the flyboat on August 11—they had no active part in the campaign. Except the Dragon, they were all discharged as soon

in her Majesty's service, when the Spanish fleet was upon our coast.

Abstract.

[The charges, certified by the Earl of Sussex, are for victuals and stores for the :

Dragon, of the Earl of Cumberland's, Mr. John Winckfield captain, William Maddocke master gunner, Morris Jones boatswain, 106*l*. 17*s*. 6*d*. ; and include beef at 13*s*. 4*d*. the hundred ; beer, 32*s*. the tun ; other beer at 28*s*. ; dry fish at 12*s*. the hundred ; large bank fish at 36*s*. the hundred ; biscuit at 6*s*. 8*d*. the hundred ; a quille of ropes weighing 25 lbs., at 23*s*. the hundred ; 'four hundred of bricks, to make up the Dragon's hearth and back, at 15*d*. the hundred.'

	£	*s.*	*d.*
Scout	5	9	11
Flyboat, Thomas Clyffe captain .	12	18	6
Blessing	9	3	11
Gift of God of Lowestoft . . .	10	5	8
Summa totalis of the charge of the whole book is	144	15	6]

These victuals were delivered by John Jennens of Portsmouth, for the victualling of 4 ships sent to the Lord Admiral by the Earl of Sussex.

SUSSEX.

September 4.—*HAWKYNS TO BURGHLEY.*

[**ccxvi. 3.**—Holograph.   Addressed :—For her Majesty's affairs.]

Right Honourable my very good Lord :—At this instant all her Majesty's ships arrived and met together in the Downs, Sir W. Wynter and I gave order to know what company of men were left in the ships ; and there was notice brought unto us from

as they joined the fleet (see *ante*, p. 195); and as the book is long, it seems unnecessary to print it in detail.

every ship of their companies they had at this present,[1] which I note to your Lordship herewith; and this is the first hour that there was any mean to do any thing in this matter.

At Chatham:

The Elizabeth Jonas		The Mary Rose	. 160
Triumph .	. 325	Bonaventure	. 200
Bear .	. 260	Lion .	. 180
Victory .	. 250	Revenge	. 176
Ark .	. 274	Nonpareil	. 180
		Hope .	. 250

Narrow Seas:

The Vanguard	. 250	The Tramontana .	70
Rainbow .	. 230	Moon .	. 40
Dreadnought	. 150	Charles .	. 35
Swiftsure	. 120	Spy .	. 35
Antelope .	. 160	Advice .	. 26
Swallow .	. 125	Merlin .	. 35
Foresight	. 110	Galley .	. 250
Aid .	. 120	Brigandine .	36
Bull .	. 96	White Lion .	50
Tiger .	. 90	Disdain .	30
Scout .	. 70	Fancy .	. 20
Achates .	. 60		
			4,453 [2]

These be the ships that remain in her Majesty's pay, and this is the company they have at this instant, which are in all 4,453. The companies do fall sick daily. It is not fit for me to persuade in so great a cause; but I see no reason to doubt the Spanish fleet, and our ships utterly unfitted and unmeet to

---

[1] A comparison of the numbers here shown with the complements of the several ships—*e.g.*, Triumph 500, Bear 500—would seem to give a measure of the fearful sickness and mortality.

[2] So in MS. The correct sum is 4,463.

follow any enterprise from hence without a thorough new trimming, refreshing and new furnishing with provisions, grounding and fresh men ; and so, with all duty, I humbly take my leave. From aboard the Ark, in the Downs, the 4th of September, 1588.

Your Honour's most bounden,
JOHN HAWKYNS.

I have no time to write to my Lord Admiral. Your Lordship may satisfy him at your pleasure.

September 6.—HAWKYNS TO WALSYNGHAM.

[**ccxvi. 4.**—Holograph. Addressed :—For her Majesty's service.]

I do send your Honour the book which I received from your Honour for the coast ships. There are many more besides these, whereof I think to be able to give a reason for at my coming to the Court, which are also to be considered with pay from the country or from her Majesty ; but that is a long matter, and will require mine own presence.

My Lord Treasurer, I understand, hath not been pleased for that I could not send his Lordship the certain number of such men as were in her Majesty's pay. The truth is the weather was such, and so cruel, as I could not ferry from ship to ship a long time ; and the fleet was dispersed, some at Dover, some at Margate, and some to seek out the great Spaniard upon the coast of France ; but now, the 4th of September, all the fleet met in the Downs, and presently, within two hours, I sent my Lord a perfect note, which was near about 4,300 men that remained in pay.

I would to God I were delivered of the dealing for money, and then I doubt not but I should as well deserve and continue my Lord's good liking as any man of my sort ; but now I know I shall never please his Lordship two months together, for which I am very sorry, for I am sure no man living hath taken more pain nor been more careful to obtain and continue his Lordship's good liking and favour towards him than I have been. My pain and misery in this service is infinite. Every man would have his turn served, though very unreasonable ; yet if it be refused, then, adieu friendship. I yield to many things more than there is whereof, and yet it will not satisfy many. God, I trust, will deliver me of it ere it be long, for there is no other hell. I devise to ease charge and shorten what I can, for which I am in a general misliking ; but my Lord Treasurer thinketh I do little, but I assure your Honour I am seldom idle.

I marvel we doubt the Spaniards. Surely there can be no cause ; and we put our ships in great peril, for they are unfitted of many things, and unmeet for service till they pass a new furnishing, both of men, grounding, and reforming of a world [1] of provisions, as it will be felt when we shall set forth again. The discourse which I wrote your Honour in December last [2] must take effect, and so her Majesty's charge shall cease, the coast of Spain and all his traffics impeached and afflicted, and our people set awork contented and satisfied in conscience ; and there is no other way to avoid the misery that daily groweth among our people. And so, being ever fatigated [3] with a number of troubles, I humbly take my leave. From the Downs, aboard the Victory, the 5th of September, 1588.

Your Honour's ever assured and bounden,

JOHN HAWKYNS.

[1] MS. worelld.
[2] *S.P. Dom. Eliz.* ccvi. 61. He repeated it on February 1 ; see vol. i. p. 58.
[3] MS. fattygatyd : fatigued, wearied.

September 8,—*TOMSON'S STATEMENT.*

[ccxvi. 9.—Holograph. Endorsed :—The speech that passed
between D. Pedro de Valdes and Ri. Tomson.]

I certified Don Pedro de Valdes that the Lords
of the Council were, of their honourable inclinations,
intended to take some favourable course for the
releasing of the soldiers and mariners taken in his
ship, by way of ransom, so far forth as he could
procure some means for the levying of such sum of
money as the same should arise unto, either by his
letter to the Prince of Parma or any other his friends
in the Low Countries, from whence the said ransom
might be the most soonest provided.

Don Pedro, with the rest of the prisoners,
seemed to be very glad that their Honours did
vouchsafe them that favour, adding that it was a
clemency sufficient to mollify the hardest heart of
any enemy ; that the news was as joyful unto them
as if it had been tidings of their own liberty, in
respect that the said poor people were raised by
them and were their neighbours, and came in this
employment for the love and zeal that they bare
unto them ; for that if they should perish by long
imprisonment or other want, it would be unto them
more grievous than all other accidents that might
happen to themselves. And said that they hoped,
as their Honours had been moved to show them
this courtesy, and the poor people this pity, so their
Honours would consider that they are very poor
men serving the King for four, six, and eight crowns
a month, and that according to the same their
Honours would appoint the ransom.

I answered that your Honours, as you were moved
in charity to release them, so you did not mind to

impose upon the poorer sort anything that should seem over burdenous. Notwithstanding as your pleasures was to let go the inferior sort for a month's pay or something more in respect of their charges, so likewise your Honours were determined to make a difference between the meaner sort and such as were officers that had a larger pension of the King, and they should be dealt withal according to their ways and calling. And further, that some such as were found to be of quality and well friended in Spain should be detained, and exchanged for others her Majesty's subjects in prison and in the galleys of Spain, or else released for sums answerable to their vocations.

They confessed that there were amongst them that had 15, 12, and 10 crowns a month, and that if such were limited according to their entertainment, it were but reason. And for any other that your Honours thought expedient to have detained in exchange of Englishmen in Spain, the cause is both reasonable and just.

They all desire your Honours to continue this favourable mind to their poor men, of whose misery they stand in great doubt if they should remain in prison until the cold of the winter approacheth; and say that in having answer from your Honours what number shall be released, and for what sum, that then, your Honours giving leave, they will write to the Prince of Parma or the Spanish ambassador in France for the provision of the money; and say that if it may stand with your Honours' pleasure to permit a prisoner to go with the said letters to solicit the matter, it should be a great furtherance for the speedy despatch thereof, as also to procure that shipping may be sent from thence to carry the said poor men into Spain. And this is the effect of so much as I have dealt with the said Don

Pedro and his company. At Esher, Sunday, the 8th of September, 1588.

Your Honours' according to duty,

RICHARD TOMSON.

September 8.—*DON PEDRO DE VALDES TO WALSYNGHAM.*

[ccxvi. 10.—Englished.]

There hath been with me, in the name of the Lords of her Majesty's Privy Council, Richard Tomson, to inform me of the favours which her Majesty is pleased to extend to the prisoners that came in the ship whereof I had charge ; that is, that they shall be delivered for one month's ransom apiece, according to the rate of their several pay. And for that I do perceive that this good work cometh chiefly by your Honour's procure, for the which I humbly thank you as for a singular favour ; and to the end that the matter may be brought to effect with such speed as is requisite, I think it would be necessary that there were some one sent to the Duke of Parma with my letters of credit, to deal for the said ransom and for shipping for transportation of the prisoners into Spain. And because your Honour hath been the worker of that which is begun, I beseech [you [1]] also to be a means to their Lordships to accept my word that the party to be sent shall return with safety, within the time to be limited, if God dispose not otherwise of him. And so, hoping that your Honour will in this continue your good favours towards us, I pray God &c. Esher, the 8th of September, 1588.

[1] Omitted in MS.

September 10.—*SIR J. POPHAM TO BURGHLEY.*

[Ireland, cxxxvi. 34.—Holograph.   Addressed.]

My duty unto your Lordship most humbly
remembered :—For that it is taken to be of importance here to certify unto your Lordship and the
rest of the Lords what hath happened here, by the
arrival of sundry of the ships of the Spanish fleet on
the north-west coast of this realm, with all expedition,
the Lord Chief Justice Anderson and others here
thought it best to despatch away a servant of mine,
this bearer, with the same in one of the barks stayed
here for the Chief Justice's return into England.
The advertisements are, that on Thursday last, and
sithence that time, there arrived first a bark, which
wrecked at the Bay of Tralee, another great ship
being also now near that place ; after that, two
great ships and one frigate at the Blaskets in the
Sound there ; seven other sail in the Shannon, by
Karryg-ni-Cowly,[1] whereof two are taken to be of a
thousand tons apiece, two more of 400 tons the piece,
and three small barks; at the Lupus Head [2] four great
ships, and toward the Bay of Galway four great ships
more.   It is thought that the rest of that fleet
wherein the Duke was, which were severed by a
late tempest, are also about some other part of this
land.   Before they were last severed, it seemeth, by
the Spaniards taken, there were not passing 70 sail
left.   The people in these parts are for the most
part dangerously affected towards the Spaniards, but
thanks be to God that their power, by her Majesty's
good means, is shorter than it hath been, and that
the Spaniards' forces are so much weakened as they
are, whereby there is no great doubt had here of

[1] Probably Carrigaholt.   [2] Loop Head.

any hurt that may grow thereby, although they use all the diligence and provision they may to provide for and prevent the worst of it.

[The rest of the letter refers to Irish business.]

September 12.—*EXAMINATIONS*[1] *OF SPANISH PRISONERS.*

[**ccxvi. 17.**—Englished. Endorsed :—The examinations of the Spaniards and Portingals sent from Dingle-i-couch. Other copies of these examinations are enclosures in **Ireland, cxxxvi. 41, 42,** and **43.**]

The examination of Emanuel Fremoso,[2] a Portingal.

He saith he was in the ship called St. John, of the Port[3] of Portugal, of one thousand one hundred tons, in which Don Martinez de Recalde is admiral of the whole fleet, and is next under the Duke, which is general ; in which ship, at her coming forth, there were 800 soldiers ; and for mariners, 60 Portugals and 40 Biscayans. This is the greatest ship of the whole navy. He saith they were in all, at their coming forth, 135 sail, whereof some were galleasses, some galleys, and 9 of them were

---

[1] Interesting as these examinations are, it is very easy to exaggerate their importance. In reading them, it should be remembered—first, that the men were common seamen, without any opportunity of knowing the things they deposed to ; second, that they were half dead with cold and hunger and half mad with terror, expecting that death which fell on most of them, and ready to say anything which they thought might be pleasant to their captors ; and third, that the interpreter, David Gwynn, was proved to be a liar and a scoundrel (see *post*, October 18, 19), and very probably did not know Spanish or Portuguese so well as he pretended.

[2] The name is differently written—Fernnoys, Fermoys, and Fremoso.   [3] Oporto.

victuallers. They came from the Groyne on the 15th day[1] next after midsummer last past, by their account. He saith they were directed to the Duke of Parma, and by him to be employed for England at such time as Parma should appoint.

He saith, after their departure from the Groyne about 8 days, the fleet came to the Lizard. He saith, about that place the general strake sail, whereupon they all strake sail all night, and the next morning they saw the English fleet, whereupon they hoisted their sails. He saith they were before informed that the English fleet was in Plymouth and Dartmouth. He saith, on the north-east of the Lizard the first fight began between the fleets, and in that fight their ship lost 15 men. He saith that there were other fights in a four or five days after, along the coasts, in which the ship this examinate was in lost 25 men. What were lost in those fights out of the other ships he cannot tell. And in those fights they lost two ships : the one in which Don Pedro was, and another, that was burned.

They anchored at Calais, expecting the Duke of Parma ; where, through the firing of the English ships, they were driven to leave their anchors, and to depart ; so as each of the ships lost two anchors at that place. The next morning the fight began about eight of the clock in the morning, and continued eight hours along the channel to the north ; all which time the English fleet pursued the Spanish fleet, in such sort as if they had offered to board the Spanish fleet, he saw their admiral so fearful, he thinketh they had all yielded.

He saith that in the same fight the Spanish fleet lost one galleass, which ran ashore about

---

[1] This absurd date, which appears in all the copies, is very likely a blunder of the interpreter's.

Calais ; two galleons of Lisbon, which were sunk, and one Biscay ship sunk, of between four and five hundred tons, and one other ship sunk also. After which fight the general took account of the whole navy, and found that there were left 120 sail of the whole fleet, as was delivered by those that came from the top ; but of his own sight he saw not passing four score and five sail, or thereabouts ; but what was become of the rest he cannot tell.

He saith that there were also in that fight three great Venetian ships which were in danger of sinking, being sore beaten and shot through in many places, but were for that time holpen by the carpenters ; and, as he hath heard, for that they were not able to keep the seas, took themselves towards the east [1] of Flanders, but what is become of them he cannot tell. He saith they were pursued by some of the English fleet about five days after this fight, northward, out of the sight of any land, and, as he thinketh, off the north part of Scotland.

He saith that about four days next after the English fleet left them, the whole fleet remaining being towards 120 sail, as it was said, came to an island, as he thinketh, off the north part of Scotland, where they staid not nor had any relief ; but at this place the general called all the ships together, giving them in charge that they should with the best they could haste themselves to the first place they could get to of the coast of Spain or Portugal ; for that they were in such great distress through the great want of victuals. And otherwise he saith they came forth the worst furnished thereof, for that they expected to be relieved of those things more amply by the Duke of Parma.

He saith that out of this ship there died four or five every day of hunger and thirst, and yet this

[1] So in MSS. It would seem to be in error for 'coast.'

ship was one that was best furnished for victuals;
which he knoweth, for out of four of the other ships,
some people were sent to be relieved in this ship.

After this, for a ten days, the whole fleet remaining held together, holding their course the best
they could towards Spain. He saith that at the same
time, which is now about 20 days or more past, they
were severed by a great storm, which held from four
of the clock in the afternoon of one day to ten of
the clock in the morning of the next day, in which
storm the admiral came away with 27 sail, and that
one of them was a galleass of 28 oars a-side. What
is become of the rest of the navy, he cannot tell.
He saith, also, that about ten days past they had
another great storm with a mist, by which storm
they were again severed, so as of these 27 sail there
came into the coast of Dingle-i-couch but the admiral,[1]
another ship of 400 ton, and a bark about 40 ton;
and what is become of the rest of those 27 sail he
knows not, but of one great hulk of 400 ton, which
was so spoiled as she cast towards the shore about
20 leagues from Dingle-i-couch. He knoweth not
who was captain of this hulk.

He saith that, of all sorts, there be now remaining
in the admiral[1] near about 500 men, of which there
be 25 Basques[2] and 40 Portingals which are mariners;
the master being very sick, and one of the pilots.
He saith there be 800 soldiers and 20 of the mariners
in the admiral very sick, and do lie down and die
daily, and the rest, he saith, be all very weak, and
the captain very sick and weak.

He saith this admiral[1] hath in her 54 brass pieces
and about 800 quintals of powder.

He saith they were so near the coast before they

---

[1] It will be remembered that the word 'admiral' means either
the man or his ship: here it is the ship.
[2] MS. Biskes, Biskerns.

found it, that by means of the strong westerly wind
they were not able to double out from it. There is
in this admiral left but 25 pipes of wine, and very
little bread; and no water, but what they brought
out of Spain, which stinketh marvellously; and their
flesh meat they cannot eat, their drouth [1] is so great.
He saith no part of the navy, to his knowledge, ever
touched upon any land, until such time as they came
to this coast at Dingle-i-couch [2]; nor hath had any
water, victual, or other relief, from any coast or place
sithence the English fleet left them.

He saith that when they lay before Calais there
came a pinnace to their fleet from the Duke of
Parma, who told them the Duke could not be ready
for them until the Friday following; but by reason of
this fight of the English fleet with them they were
not able to tarry there so long.

He saith that the admiral's purpose is, upon the
first wind that serveth, to pass away for Spain.
He saith also that it is a common bruit among
the soldiers, if they may once get home again, they
will not meddle again with the English. He saith
there be of principal men in the admiral, Don John
de Luna,[3] a Spaniard, which is chief captain of the
soldiers of that ship; Don Gomes, a Spaniard,
another captain; Don Sebastian, a Portingal gentleman, an adventurer, and a marquis, an Italian,
who is also an adventurer; and another Portingal,
whom he knoweth not; but that they are principal
men, that had crosses on their garments. Other
mean gentlemen there be also in the said ship. He
saith all the soldiers in this ship were Spaniards.

[1] MS. druth : thirst.
[2] The old Irish name is given as Dangean-ni-Cushey, which is
frequently transformed in these papers into Dengenechoush, in
various spellings. The modern name is commonly shortened to
Dingle.   [3] Duro, ii. 39.

He saith there are in the small bark that is with them about 25 persons. How many are in the hulk that is there, he knoweth not.

He saith he thinketh that the Duke is passed towards Spain, for that he was seen 12 leagues more westerly than the admiral was in the last storm. He saith that the great galleon, which came from the Duke of Florence, was never seen sithence they were in the fight at Calais. He saith the people of the galleass were most spoiled by the English fleet.

Emanuel Francisco examined, saith in all things as the former examinate till the fight at Calais ; in which fight he saith he knoweth there was left a galleass, that ran ashore at Calais ; two galleons of the King's, the one called St. Philip of the Brando, the other called St. Matthew, of 800, a Biscay ship of about 500, and a Castile ship of about 400, all sunk.

This he knoweth for that some of the men of those ships were divided into the admiral's ship, in which this examinate was.

He saith after this fight ended, it was delivered by him at the top that there was 120 sail left of the Spanish fleet, and saith that those were very sore beaten, and the admiral was many times shot through ; and are shot in their mast, and their deck at the prow spoiled ; and doth confess that they were in great fear of the English fleet, and doubted much of boarding. He saith the admiral's mast is so weak, by reason of the shot in it, as they dare not abide any storm, nor to bear such sail as otherwise he might do ; and for the rest, he agreeth in everything with the former examinate, saving he saw not, nor understood not, of any pinnace that came from the Parma, nor remember that he saw above 20 sail with the admiral after the first storm ; and saith that those in the

ship that he is in do say that they will go into the
ground sooner than they will come such a journey
again for England; and saith the best that be in the
admiral's ship are scarce able to stand; and that if
they tarry where they are any time they will all
perish, as he thinketh. And for himself, he would
not pass into Portugal again if he might choose, for
that he would not be constrained to such another
journey.

John de Licornio, of Lekyte[1] in Biscay, mariner,
saith he was in the ship that the admiral is in; and
that he told[2] the navy after the fight ended at Calais,
and that there were then remaining not passing 110
or 112 of the whole Spanish fleet left; and saith that
a leak[3] fell upon one of the galleasses about 15 days
past, which he taketh to be fallen upon the north
coast of this land.

He saith he doth not remember that there [were]
above 20 sail left in the company of the admiral
after the first great storm which fell on them, about
30 days sithence. He saith the Duke did give
them express commandment that they should not go
in any place on land without his order.

He confesseth the navy that remained after the
last fight were marvellously beaten and shot through,
and the tackle much cut and spoiled with the shot;
and for the rest of the matters, he agreeth with the
former examinate in every point in effect, and saith
there was an English pilot with the Duke.

He saith that the Scot that is taken was taken
in the north part, after the English fleet parted from
them, in a ship of 500 ton (in which was about 12[4]
men), which the fleet hath carried with them, both
the ship and people. Six of the Scots were aboard

---

[1] Lequeitio.   [2] Counted.
[3] MS. leck.   [4] So in MSS.

the admiral, whereof one is he that is taken.   He
saith, after the English fleet parted from them, the
Spanish fleet cast out all their horses and mules into
the sea, to save their water ;[1] which were carried in
certain hulks provided for that purpose.

Pier o Carr,[2] a Fleming, examined the 10th of
September, 1588.   Examined from what port in Spain
he came, he saith from Lisbon, and that there came at
the same time therehence 133 ships, wherein he saith
there were two and twenty thousand soldiers, besides
mariners, whose certain number he knoweth not.
The general of the army, he saith, is the Duke of
Medina Sidonia, and that they were all bound towards the Prince of Parma ; and after his forces
taken in, they meant to come for England.   In their
way they met with the Queen's fleet and navy near
Plymouth, who pursued them to the coast of Scotland, where the English fleet returned from them ;
and they being then about one hundred and eighteen
ships, and not knowing at that time in what part
they were.   Of the ships then left, there were two
Venetians of 11 or 12 hundred tons apiece ; and 9
other ships about 900 or 1,000 tons apiece ; 16 ships
out of Sicily, of 600 or 700 tons apiece ; the rest, in
particular, he cannot recite.   Of the ship that he
was in, called St. John, a galleon, 900 tons, whereof
is captain John Martinez de Recalde, vice-admiral
of 20 ships, next in government unto the Duke,
in which ship was 500 soldiers.   There are two
hundred dead : twenty slain in the fight with
the Queen's ships, the rest dead of the sickness.
What is lost by the rest of the ships he knoweth
not.
Twenty days since he departed with 12 ships
more from the Duke, he having with him about

---

[1] So also Duro, ii. 286.   [2] So in MSS.

46 ships, from the which they were severed by tempest.

They lost the Duke upon the coast of Norway, and they were wind driven upon this coast, their ships being much spoiled with the English fleet. The Duke, he saith, by this time is in Spain, unless he be taken on the seas ; and ever after his departure from the English fleet intended to go back to Spain, being frighted and dismayed.

How many ships are lost he do not certainly know, but he verily thinketh that half the number of people do not return that came out in this army.

One galleass was lost at Calais, wherein was fifty [1] rowers and a great number of soldiers. There was slain Don Francisco Pacheco, master of the camp. Don Pedro de Valdes, a man of great account with the King, was taken with the ship, being of very great burden. Who else are taken or lost, he knoweth not. His coming this way was to seek Cape Clear, therehence to make into Spain.

They never heard from the Prince of Parma, nor ever had any favour or intelligence from any since their coming from Spain, to his knowledge.

In the ship that he came in thither, besides the vice-admiral before named, there are five captains, Don John Luna, Don Gomes de Galanayar,[2] Don Pedro de Manrique, the Count of Paredes, Don Felice. There is also there an Italian marquis of Piedmont, called the Marquis of Farnara.[3]

---

[1] Gwynn ought to have known better than this. What was said was, no doubt, fifty oars.

[2] Carvajal (Duro, ii. 333) : r and l are frequently interchanged ; and the confusion between u and n is still common.

[3] Garres (*ib*. ii. 66), where he is styled *cuñado*—brother-in-law of the Duke of Savoy ; but the Duke had no legitimate sister, and was married to the daughter. of the King of Spain.

In the other ship at the Dengen,[1] being 600 or 700 tons, who are in her he knoweth not.

The third hath but 40 men in her, and is about 40 tons.

They have bread sufficient ; their beef is corrupt ; water they want ; many of them are sick.

Re-examined the 12th of September, 1588, he saith the navy of the Spaniards were so far north as unto sixty-two degrees. He saith, also, that the admiral, after such time as the fight was at Calais, came not out of his bed till this day sennight, in the morning that they came upon this shore.

He saith this admiral is of Biscay, either of Bilbao or Laredo, and of 62 years of age, and a man of service. He saith that there were in this navy, of old soldiers of Naples, under the conduction of Don Alonso de Sono,[2] and of the old soldiers of Sicilia, under the conduction of Don Diego de Pimentel,[3] whose ship was lost at Calais. There was also Don Alonso de Leyva, master of the camp, of the chivalry of Milan. He saith there is a bastard son of King Philip, called the Prince of Ascoli in Italy, in ship with the Duke. This Prince passed from them in a pinnace about Calais.

[1] Dingle.   [2] Luzon.   [3] MS. Peamentela.

September 12.—*HAWKYNS TO BURGHLEY.*

[**ccxvi. 18.**—Signed. Addressed.]

My bounden duty humbly remembered unto your good Lordship :—I do send unto my Lord Admiral an estimate of such money as is now to be had for a full discharge of her Majesty's army. And because your Lordship may be the better satisfied of every demand, I do set down particulars to maintain them in the same book following.

1. The first demand, and the speciallest, is for a month's wages, from the 28th of July to the 25th of August, which was not demanded in the estimate sent from Plymouth of the 19,000 pounds which your Lordship hath paid.

2. The second is for the wages of 2,951 men that have now served in her Majesty's ships from the 25th of August to the 15th of September ; besides the Hope, which was appointed to serve in the Narrow Seas, and is now returned to Queenborough.

3. The third is for conduct in discharge, which hitherto hath not been demanded ; whereof there can be set down no certainty before it be set out upon the sea-books. But I am sure the demand is far under that which it will grow into, but with time your Lordship shall know it more certainly.

4. The fourth is for the tonnage of the ships that served westward, under the charge of Sir Francis Drake, knight, the particulars whereof appeareth in the estimate No. 4.

5. The fifth is for an increase of pay to be made to preachers, lieutenants, and corporals, whereof the estimate doth show to what ships they are allowed particularly, in the No of 5

6. The sixth, and last, is for money appointed to be paid by my Lord Admiral to certain ships of the coast for the continuance of them in service, and to relieve their companies at their departing, which appeareth by particular in the estimate in No. 6.

I have sent this estimate to my Lord Admiral, for his Lordship to confirm it under his hand, that it may be a warrant to your Lordship for the payment of the money ; and have sent this bearer of purpose to attend upon your Lordship for order for payment of the same, humbly praying your good Lordship to help him to his despatch as soon as it may be ; and I will not fail in the meantime to ease her Majesty of the charge of the multitude, and put over the greater sums, that may abide sometime without loss to her Majesty. There were 7 or 8 ships fired by my Lord Admiral's appointment, for the removing of the Spanish fleet out of the Calais road, for which the owners demand 5,000*l.*, which may be considered of by some commissioners from your Lordship and my Lord Admiral, what their value might be. And so praying to God for your Lordship's health and prosperity, I leave to trouble your Lordship. From Queenborough, aboard her Majesty's good ship the Victory, the 12th of September, 1588.

Your honoured Lordship's humbly to command,
JOHN HAWKYNS.

Since I wrote this letter, I understood by my servant Walter that your Lordship had paid 1,600 pound, which your Lordship may abate in this demand.   J. HAWKYNS.

[**ccxvi. 18, I.**—Estimate No. 5, referred to in the foregoing. The other estimates only repeat the names of ships, number of men and tonnage.]

An increase of wages to preachers, lieutenants, corporals, and secretaries:—

—	Preachers	Lieutenants	Corporals
	per mensem	*per mensem*	*per mensem*
The Ark . .	1 at 3*l.*	1 at 50*s.*	4 at 17*s.* 6*d.*
Eliz. Jonas .	1 at 40*s.*	1 „	4 „
Bear . .	1 at 40*s.*	1 „	4 „
Triumph .	—	1 „	4 „
Victory . .	—	1 „	4 „
Rainbow .	1 at 40*s.*	1 „	4 „
Vanguard .	—	1 „	4 „
Lion . .	1 at 40*s.*	1 „	4 „
Mary Rose .	—	1 „	4 „
Bonaventure .	—	1 „	4 „
Nonpareil .	—	1 „	4 „
Hope . .	—	1 „	4 „
Revenge .	1 at 40*s.*	1 „	4 „
Dreadnought .	—	1 „	2 „
Swiftsure .	—	1 „	2 „
Swallow .	—	1 „	2 „
Foresight .	—	1 „	2 „
Antelope .	—	1 „	2 „
Aid . .	—	—	2 „
Galleon Leicester .	—	1 „	2 „
	6	19	66

An abstract.

  1 preacher at 3*l. per mensem.*
  5 preachers at 40*s.*   ,,
19 lieutenants at 50*s.*   ,,
66 corporals at 17*s.* 6*d.*   ,,
  2 secretaries at 30*s.*   ,,

All which, for the time of their service, may amount unto, by estimation, over and above 10*s. per mensem* allowed unto them by the ordinary medium, 800*l.*

Sept. 15.—*THE CHARGES OF THE LYME SHIPS.*

[**ccxvi. 27.**—Endorsed :—An abstract touching the charges of the ships set forth out of sundry ports, taken out of sundry letters written concerning the same.]

Dorset—Lyme. Somerset—Chard. Devon—Axminster.

Sir Robert Denys, for Devon.

Being charged with a collection of 700*l.* for the setting forth of two ships, Axminster is taxed at a third part ; offer 140*l.*, and desire the residue may be borne by the other two towns, for the reasons following :—

That all the confining [1] hundreds to them within his division have contributed towards the charge of 1,300*l.* with Exon, the town and hundred of Axminster only being left untaxed, to contribute with Lyme.

That the same are to bear a new charge of 240*l.* for 3 other barks set forth.

That the county of Somerset hath been only charged with a small bark for this service, in which county Chard is.

That the county of Dorset (wherein Lyme is) hath borne but little charge.

Justices of Somerset.

According to your Lordships' letters, they have yielded to contribute one third part of the said sum

[1] Adjoining, neighbouring.

of 700*l.*, and desire they may not be further charged, in respect they have been burdened with the charge of 6,000*l.* or 7,000*l.* for the late setting forth of the 4,000 trained footmen and 300 horse ; and that they are to contribute, with other port towns in the said county, and namely to Bridgwater, for 447*l.* 15*s.* 6*d.*

Sir George Sydenham and George Trenchard, Esq., together, for Somerset and Dorset.

They have yielded to contribute two third parts of the said charge, according to the direction of your Lordships' letters.

In the behalf of the Mayor of Lyme, by petition.

That if Axminster be exempted from contributing a third part, he having already disbursed the whole charge, seeth not how he shall be satisfied. These are his reasons why the same should not be exempted :—

That it hath not been charged with any former contributions.

That according to this assessment they are rated but at 2*s.* in the pound, and the said town of Lyme at 5*s.* 6*d.*

George Trenchard, Esq., for Dorsetshire.

That he hath yielded to contribute a third part, though hardly the same can be levied.

That in respect that they hath been burdened with other charges, the same may be eased in that contribution of a third part rather than Axminster ; the chief merchants inhabiting in Somersetshire and Axminster, Lyme being only the port town.

That if Axminster be by their Lordships eased, the same may be supplied by the towns and county of Somerset.

In the behalf of the town of Bridgwater, by petition.

That they have been at the charge of 447*l*. 15*s*. 6*d*. in setting forth a ship of 60 tons, which they are not able to sustain, being impoverished through want of trade ; whereupon they obtained your Lordships' letters for the levying thereof by contribution from the inhabitants of the county of Somerset, which is not performed by reason the certain sum, till now, was not known. They desire your Lordships' letters to the justices again to collect the said sum.

By letters from the citizens of Bristol.

They have sustained the charge of 1,000*l*. in setting forth 3 ships and a pinnace, which is not yet levied, nor hardly can be, though the wealthier sort are taxed at 13*s*. 4*d*. in the pound, by reason there are many merchants decayed there through want of trade.

The owners and mariners have due to them for tonnage and wages 11,000*l*. more, whereof, in consideration of the premises, they desire to be discharged, and that order may be given for the payment thereof by such other means as your Lordships think meet.

The late Lord Steward,[1] by his letter sent by Floyd, his secretary, desired they may be favoured, supposing their disability such as they allege.

[1] The Earl of Leicester : he died on September 4.

By letters from your Lordships, Mr. Darell hath made provision of the victual of the said ships, since the first two months' victual provided by them of the city. They desire to be discharged from the answering thereof; also, by direction to the said Darell, to release their security given in that behalf.

Minute.—Sir Fras. Drake is to examine what the wages of the said mariners amounteth unto from the end of two months until the day of the discharge.

Captain Nicholas Webb, by petition.

The city of Gloucester, with the county of the city, and the town of Tewkesbury, were charged with the setting forth of a ship of 80 tons, to join and continue in service with her Majesty's navy; at which time, in respect of occasion for the present employment of such ship, they were advertised by your Lordships' letters, and particularly from my Lord Admiral, that his Lordship would appoint a ship, being ready furnished, to serve in lieu of that to have been set forth by them, and therefore might forbear to provide any, and that hereafter, upon due account, they should answer the charge which the said ship should be signified by his Lordship to amount unto.

The said towns, notwithstanding—his Lordship then being at sea—suggesting to your Lordships that there was not any ship in service for them, obtained order to set forth a ship of their own appointment. Nevertheless, there hath not any such ship served in the navy since the beginning of the service hitherto. This the Lord Admiral will approve. The suppliant hath served with a ship, appointed by his Lordship, from the beginning to the end of the service, and borne all the charge of her setting

forth and victualling for all that time, being five
months and ten days, which amounteth to
643*l.* 0*s.* 4*d.* This [his] Lordship will also certify.
Desireth, he having performed the service and defrayed all the charge aforesaid, their Lordships
would be pleased to take order for his satisfaction
thereof.

September 20.—*DECLARATION OF ACCOUNTS.*

[ccxvi. 34.]

Charge of victualling her Majesty's ships and
others in the West Country :—

A brief declaration of the account of James
Quarles, Esquire, general surveyor of the victuals
for the marine affairs, for victualling sundry the
Queen's Majesty's ships and others, at Plymouth in
the West Country, for 300 days, begun the first day
of December, and ending the 20th day of September, Anno regni dominæ Elizabethæ nunc
Reginæ, 30°.

Charge and receipts, viz. :—

	£	s.	d.
Ready money by him received and had	22,428	4	10

Whereof

Allowance and payments, viz. for :—

	£	s.	d.	£	s.	d.
Rigging and other extraordinary victualling and harbour	1,118	8	8	1,125	8	8
Transportation of victuals, with lighterage and other charges	7	0	0			

Sea-victualling :—

7*d.* the man per diem, 7,546*l.* 11*s.* 8*d.* 6*d.* the man per diem, 9,081*l.* 5*s.* 0*d.*	16,627	16	8					
Transportation of victuals, with lighterage and other charges . .	1,071	16	8		20,030	8	4	
Leakage, ullage, and filling beer . .	108	9	0					
Victualling on shore at Plymouth, at 6*d.* per diem . .	2,222	6	0					

Sum total of the allowance and payments aforesaid 21,155 17 0

And so he remaineth in debt the sum of 1,272*l.* 7*s.* 10*d.*

17th day of January, 1588.

Exd. by Jo. CONYERS, Auditor.

Sept. 21.—*SIR R. BINGHAM*[1] *TO FYTZWYLLIAM.*[2]

[Ireland, cxxxvii. 1, I.—Copy. Endorsed.]

It may please your Honour, what I write unto your Lordship now is no more in effect, but a con-

[1] Sir Richard Bingham, born in 1528, had served with the Spaniards at St. Quentin in 1557 and at Lepanto in 1572, and against them in the Low Countries as a volunteer with the Dutch. In 1579 he was serving in Ireland against Desmond, and in 1580 was captain of the Swiftsure under Wynter at Smerwick. In 1584 he was knighted by Sir John Perrot, the Lord Deputy, and was appointed Governor of Connaught, which office he held, with little interruption, till his death in 1599. He is said to have exercised extreme severity towards the Irish. His conduct towards the Spaniards did certainly not err on the side of mercy.

[2] Sir William Fytzwylliam, a lawyer, born in 1526, after being Treasurer and Lord Justice of Ireland, was Lord Deputy from 1572

firmation of my last letters, which I sent by Cotgrave the messenger. For sithence that time here hath not happened any great alteration of news. And yet it is delivered unto me by some of the prisoners of certain, that the Duke of Medina himself was in the great ship, which received the 600 from land at Ballycroy, and then by all likelihood he is cast away, for the wind fell contrary immediately after they put to sea, and became very stormy and foul weather, as not possible he could escape, except his ship were most strong and good, for he was marvellously pestered with such numbers of men. And in the seven ships which lay at Raviskeith[1] on Thomond side, whereof two were lost and one burned, was the galleon St. John, wherein went[2] John Martinez de Recalde, admiral of the whole fleet, who put to sea the same day the Duke did. And sithence I have learned by a Breton, which came to Galway loaded with salt, that these four ships rode[3] at anchor against the Blaskets[4] in Munster, which may haply get home if any do. But by this may appear the great handiwork of Almighty God, who hath drowned the remain of that mighty army, for the most part, on the coasts of this province, which was the very place they themselves most doubted, as may appear by the instructions the Duke gave them after the Queen's ships had left them, the copy whereof your Lordship shall here inclosed receive.

This morning I am going to Galway to take order for some things there, and to despatch a man

to 1575, and again from February 1587–8 to 1594. He died in 1599.

[1] Possibly Labasheeda in the Shannon. Thomond was, roughly, County Clare. The seven ships would seem to be those spoken of by Popham, *ante*, p. 218.

[2] Bingham's Spanish service will account for his use of this peculiarly Spanish idiom, *en que iba*.

[3] Rydd.   [4] Blaskeyes.

unto your Lordship with Don Luis de Cordoba, the prisoner, which we have yet gotten ; and till now I could not satisfy your Lordship's desire therein, for the great floods, and other urgent occasions I had in hand, unless I should have sent some of the basest sort. And by him I shall be better able to advertise your Lordship the full particularities of all things which have happened in this action.

I had intelligence sent me from my brother that the 700 Spaniards in Ulster were despatched, which I know your Lordship heareth before this time. And this I dare assure your Lordship now, that in a 15 or 16 ships cast away on the coast of this province, which I can in my own knowledge say to be so many, there hath perished at least a 6,000 or 7,000 men, of which there hath been put to the sword, first and last, by my brother George, and in Mayo, Thomond, and Galway, and executed one way and another, about 7 or 800, or upwards, besides those that be yet alive, of which Don Luis de Cordoba is supposed to be the best, for Pedro Mendoza was slain in Clare[1] Island by Dowdaraugh O'Mayle before he would yield in time of the execution. So as now —God be thanked—this province stands clear and rid of all these foreign enemies, save a silly poor prisoners, except O'Rourke[2] do keep any contrary to our general order and proclamation, sithence the publication whereof I have not heard from my brother how he hath answered him in that point.

And touching the ordnance and other munitions lost here, all diligence shall be used to save as much as may for her Majesty's use ; but the great ship at Ballicro, and the rest cast away about those islands, are now all broken in pieces, and the ordnance and everything else utterly lost, I fear me. Treasure and great wealth hath been taken, no doubt, but that by

¹ Cleare   ² Orwoorke.

such unworthy persons as it will hardly be ever any thereof come by at all, they be such as hath it as before now have always been upon their keepings; albeit it is possible in time some of it may be had. This is all worthy your Lordship's advertising for this time. And so I humbly take my leave. At Shrowle,[1] the 21st of September, 1588.

Your Lordship's most humbly at commandment,
RICHARD BINGHAM.

[**Ireland, cxxxvii. 1, II.**—Copy.   Endorsed :—Direction given by the Duke of Medina for the course which the Spanish navy should hold on their return to Spain.]

The course that shall be held in the return of this army into Spain.

The course that is first to be held is to the North-North-East, until you be found under 61 degrees and a half; and then to take great heed lest you fall upon the island of Ireland, for fear of the harm that may happen unto you upon that coast. Then parting from those islands, and doubling the Cape in 61 degrees and a half, you shall run West-South-West until you be found under 58 degrees; and from thence to the South-West to the height of 53 degrees; and then to the South-South-West, making to the Cape Finisterre, and so to procure your entrance into the Groyne or to Ferrol, or to any other port of [the[2]] coast of Galicia.

[1] Shrule, County Mayo.   [2] Omitted in MS.

September.—*REPORTS OF SURVEY.*

[ccxx.]

25th of September, 1588.—A survey of the
tackle and apparel, cables, cablets, anchors and other
provisions remaining in her Majesty's ships, taken
at their coming from the seas as well by the view
of John Austyne and Richard Poulter, two of the
masters of her Highness's said ships ; as also by
Roger Monnox, clerk of the survey of the same.

[The survey of each ship is signed by Austyne and
Poulter, and in most cases by the boatswain, generally
with a mark. The ships included, with the names of the
signing boatswains, are :—
Triumph, Simon Fernandez ; Elizabeth Jonas, John ×
Woodroffe[1] ; Bear, Robert × Baxter ; Ark, John × Wright ;
Victory, John × Edmonds ; Hope, John × Vayle ; Golden
Lion (not signed) ; Mary Rose, John × Heath, for Law-
rence Cleer ; Elizabeth Bonaventure, Tristram Searche ;
Revenge, Richard × Derrick ; Nonpareil, I.C. ; Rainbow,
Richard Laine ; Dreadnought, × Harvye ; Swiftsure,
Willm. Mychell ; Antelope (not signed) ; Foresight,
James Andrews ; Swallow, John × Bourman ; Aid, John
× Russell ; Bull, Myhyll Pyrkyne ; Tiger (not signed) ;
Scout (not signed) ; Tramontana, John Pratte ; Achates
(not signed) ; Charles (not signed) ; Disdain ; Advice,
Tristram × George ; Cygnet, George Wilkynson ; Spy ;
Merlin ; Moon.
It seems unnecessary to print the whole ; the survey of
the Ark will probably be thought the most interesting, and
may be taken as a fair specimen. Not one speaks of any
great damage or serious defect. The survey of the Ark is
given in the original spelling, which is singularly good and
consistent.]

[1] × These signed with a mark.

September 23.—THE ARK ROYAL

The Rigginge of the Bolsprite :—

The bolsprite—good ; the spritesale yarde—good ; the clulyns—decayed—xl fadoms—ii inche ½ ; the braces—decayed—l fadoms—i inche ½ ; the spritesale shuts[1]—half-worne ; the spritesale hallyards —half-worne ; the false tye—decayed—xvi fadoms —vi inches.

The Rigginge of the Formaste :—

The formaste—good ; the foreyarde—good ; the forestaye—half-worne ; the forepennants—good ; the ronners—good ; the falls of the tackells—half worne ; the falls of the swifters—half-worne ; the pennants of the swifters—half-worne ; the backe-stayes—decayed—xvii fa : apece—vii inches ; the foretyes—decayed—xxxvi fa :—vii inches ½ ; the forehallyards — half-worne ; the backestayes — de-cayed—xvii fa : ; the foretacks—half-worne ; the foreshuts—half-worne ; the foreshrouds—half-worne ; the forebolings — half-worne ; the clewgarnetts—de-cayed—lx fa :—ii inches ; the martnetts[2]—decayed— lx fa :—ii inches ; the trusses—good ; the pennants of the forebraces—half-worne ; the falls of the fore-braces—decayed—l fa :—ii inches ; the parrell—good ; the forelifts—half-worne ; the jeer—decayed xl fa :—vi inches ½.

The Rigginge of the Foretopmaste :—

The foreputtocks[3]—decayed —xxx fa :—iii inches ; the foretopmaste—good ; the foretopmaste yarde—

---

[1] Sheets.   [2] Leech-lines.
[3] Futtock-shrouds.

good ; the foretopsale—half-worne ; the foretopmaste
shrowds—good ; the foretopmast staye—good ; the
pennants and falls of the tackles of the foretopmast
—good ; the lifts—half-worne ; the braces—decayed
—lx fa :—i inch ½ ; the clulyns—decayed—iiii[xx] [1] fa :
—ii inches ; the foretopsale shuts—decayed—iii[xx]
fa :—v inches ; the wyndrope [2] for the topmaste—
decayed—xlviii fa :—vii inches ; the hallyards—decayed—xlii fa :—viii inches ½ ; the parrell—good ;
the foretopsale bolings—decayed—lxiiii fa :—i inch
rope ; the backestaye of the foretopmaste—good ;
the martnetts and their falls [3]—half-worne.

The Rigginge of the Mayne-maste.

The mayne-maste—good ; the mayne yarde—
good ; the mayne shrowds—half-worne ; the mayne
staye—good ; the pennants of the garnetts [4]—good ;
the falls thereof : vi good, the other decayed—xl
fad :—iiii inche ; the pennants of the tackles—half-
worne ; the ronners of the tackles—half-worne ;
the mayne tacks—good ; the mayne shuts—half-
worne ; the mayne bolings—half-worne ; the clew
garnetts—decayed—lx fa :—i inche ½ ; the mayne
parrell and trusses—good ; the mayne tyes—decayed—xl fa :—viii inches ½ ; the mayne hallyards—half-worne ; the mayne lifts—half-worne ; the
mayne braces with pennants and falls—decayed—
iii[xx]x [5] fa :—iii inche ; the jeer—decayed—xxxviii fa :
—vii inches ½ ; the mayne martnetts and falls—decayed—lx fa :—i inche.

---

[1] Four-score.   [2] Probably the mast-rope.
[3] 'The fall of the martnets of the top-sails comes no farther
than the top, where it is hauled. When they are to haul these
martnets, the term is " top the martnets "' (Manwayring).
[4] Gurnet-pendants.
[5] Three score and ten.

The Rigginge of the Mayne topmast.

The mayne topmaste—good ; the mayne topmaste yarde—good ; the mayne topmaste staye—good ; the puttocks—decayed—lxiiii fad :—iiii inche ; the mayne topmaste shrowds—good ; the tackells—good ; the parrell and trusses—good ; the lifts—half-worne ; the martnetts—decayed—ii coyle of small lyne ; the braces—decayed—l fad :—i inche ½ ; the clulyns—decayed—xlv fad :—ii inche ½ ; the mayne topsale bolings—decayed—xliiii fad : — ii inche ½ ; the backestayes—good ; the mayne topsale shuts—decayed—c fa :—vi inche ½ ; the wyndrope —decayed—xlviii fad :—vii inches ; the topsale tye —decayed—viii fa :—v inches ; the topsale hallyards—half-worne ; the lanyards and brest ropes for the mayne parrell and fore parrell—decayed—iii^{xx} fa :—iiii inche ½.

The Rigginge of the Mayne mysson maste.

The maste — good ; the yarde — good ; the shrowds—good ; the lifts—decayed—iiii^{xx}—ii small lynes ; the staye—good ; the parrell and trusse—good ; the tye—decayed—xii fad :—vi inches ; the hallyards—decayed—xl fa :— iii inches.

The Rigginge of the Bonaventur mast.

The maste—good ; the yarde—good ; the shrowds —good ; the tye—decayed—x fads :—vi inches ; the hallyards—decayed—xxxvi fads :—iiii inches ; the swifters parrell and trusse—good ; the staye—half-worne ; the shuts—decayed—xxx fads :—iii inches.

JHON AUSTYNE.
RYCHARD POULTER.

Great anckers for bowers. . . iii

Great anckers cracked in the crosse
and caried to Harwich out of the
Downes i

Sheate anckers i

Boate anckers i

Grapnells loste with the boate and a
hawser of iiii inches . . . i

Cables of xvii inches, whereby the
ship is mored to the eastwarde . i half-worne

Cables of xvi inches in a shot, whereby the ship is mored to the west-
warde . . . . .
{ ii whereof one is to be cut of, being more then qr. worne

Cables of xvi inches in a shot . { ii more then qr. worne

Cables of xv inches . . . { ii worne and noughte

Fathoms of a cable of xv inches . l fath : worne

Cables of xv inches, whereof one
broken at Flushinge . . . ii worne

Cables of xi inches for a kedger . { ii more then qr. worne

Cables of x inches for a bote rope,
beinge a great parte cut of at the
losinge of the boate . . . i half-worne

Gest rope of viii inches . . . i worne

Cabletts of viii inches cut out in iii
booye ropes of xxv fath : a pece . i newe

Cabletts of viii inches . . . i newe

Cabletts of vii inches . . . i newe

Cabletts of vii inches . . . i qr. worne

Cabletts of vi inches . . . i half-worne

Hawsers of viii inches . . . i newe

Hawsers of vii inches . . . i qr. worne

Hawsers of vi inches . . . i qr. worne

Hawsers of iiii inches . . .	iiii newe
Coyles of v inches	iiii newe
Of ii inches, do. . . .	xvi newe
Coyles of ii inches and inche ½	v
Tarde lynes	iii
Ratlyne	iiii bolts
Marlyne	iiii bundells
Twyne, white and blacke .	x skeynes
Sale nedells	ii dozen
Bolts of medernex . .	lviii
Streamers	xiiii
Pendants	xvi
Shovells and spades . .	x
Bowles	iii
Bucketts	{x of lether & iii other
Scowpes	iiii
Ballost basketts . . .	vi
Compasses	iii
Roninge glasses . . .	iiii
Flaggs of St. George . . .	{iii & ii of the Q. armes, rotten
Ensignes of silke	{i taken awey either by Mr. Gray or my Lord's man
Soundinge lynes	{iiii new & ii oulde
Soundinge leads . . .	iiii
Fidds of yron . . .	viii
Catte hooks	iiii
Can hooks	i pair
Loof hooks	ii
Leech hooks	i
Boate hooks	ii

Fishe hooks	ii
Bilbowes with x shackells . .	i pair
Spare shevers of brasse . . .	xx
Crowes of iron	ii
Pitche potts of iron . . .	i ⎱ consumed at
Pitche potts of copper . . .	i ⎰ the firing of the shipps
Baricos	xxxii
Bote oars	xviii
Nettings for the forecastle, for the waste, & for the half-decke . .	viii
Waste clothes	ii rotten
Kettles for the cooke rome . .	ii
Toppe armors for the myzon toppe	ii
Trevetts	i
Spitts	i
Cobyrons [1]	i pair
Furnesses of copper . . .	i
Cratchetts for lights . . .	i

The Sailes of the saide Ship, viz. :—

The spritesale with a bonnet [2]—half-worne ; the forecourse & bonnet doble, with a single drabler —half-worne ; the fore topsaile—half-worne ; the mayne corse & bonnet doble, with a single drabler

[1] Irons hung on the bars of the range to support the spit.

[2] The bonnet was a strip of canvas which laced on to the foot of the sail. 'Lacing on the bonnet' or 'bringing to the bonnet' was equivalent to shaking out a reef. The drabler, in the same way, laced on to the foot of the bonnet. 'The bonnet is commonly used with none but the mizen, main and fore-sails, and the sprit-sails. I have seen—but it is very rare—a top sail bonnet. . . . When we do speak of the sail in any correspondence to the bonnet, we call it the course, and not the sail ; as we say, when a ship hath those sails out—course and bonnet of each, not mainsail and bonnet and foresail and bonnet. Shake off the bonnet : that is, take it off' (Manwayring).

—qr. worne ; the mayne topsale—half-worne ; the mayne myzon saile—qr. worne ; & the bonaventure myzon saile—half-worne ; the ii bonnetts belonginge to the myzon sailes, lost in the bote. Item, one topgallant saile, newe. Item, the botes saile & ii pinnesse sailes were also lost in the boate.

The long boate with a shyver of brasse in the hedd, with the oares and dyvers other things lost at sea, the boat being splitte. Item, the pynnesse being also lost, & a cocke. Item, one oulde pynnesse used for a shifte.

Note, that there was lent, by my Lord Admeralls comaundment, unto one Nicholas Wrighte, captaine of a ship called the Bartholomew of Apsam, one cable of x inches, being a qr. worne, for the which he delyvered his bill to be restored agayne.

Moie, lent to one Rafe Hawse of Dartmouth, cne cablet of vii inches, by my Lord's comaundment. More, lent to a ship of Lyme, by my Lord's comaundment, iii parts of a hawser of vii inches.

JHON AUSTYNE.
RYCHARD POULTER.

John Lights marke.

[But the ‘ declaration of the wants ’ of the Ark is signed, with the same mark, ‘ Signum Joh^is Wright, boteswayne.’]

[At the end of the volume is :—
‘ A declaration of all the several wants of anchors, cables, cablets, hawsers &c., as is to be provided as well for the perfect rigging of all her Majesty’s ships and pinnaces hereafter particularly set down, as also for ground tackle and sea store fit for the said ships for one setting forth to the seas, as followeth.’

The wants are entirely cables, hawsers, rope &c., anchors, and grapnels. The chief points of interest about them are that the Ark demanded a sheet anchor of 22 cwt.

and a bower anchor of 20 cwt. ; and that the Spy demanded six bolts of ' mederinax ' for binding of sails and for store.

The following from the different surveys may also be noted :—

Triumph.—The long boat lost at sea. 'Item, one newe longe botte, with a shyver of bras in the hedd and one in the davith.' Flags of St. George, one new, and one carried away by Mr. Eliot. Ensigns of silk, carried away by Sir Martin Frobiser, one. ' Ronynge glasses, viii ; compasses, v.'

Elizabeth Jonas.—' The grete botte lost at sea.' Flags of St. George, three, whereof one delivered to the dock ; ensigns of silk in John Austyne's chest, one. ' Compasses, v ; ronynge glasses, xii.'

Bear.—' The great boate with all her furniture lost, with the saile.' Flags of St. George, two, and one of the Queen's arms. Ensigns of silk, taken away by my Lord's lieutenant or his man. 'Compasses, vi ; ronninge glasses, viii.'

Victory.—' Item, the longe boate, with a shever of iron in the hedd & one other in the daffid.' Flags of St. George, two ; ensigns of silk, one. ' Bolts of medernex, xxiiii.'

Golden Lion.—' The longe boate not serviceable, with a shyver of iron in the hedd & one in the davith.' Flags of St. George, two, old.

Elizabeth Bonaventure.—Flags of St. George, two, and ' a bluddey flagge.' Ensigns of silk, one, spoiled with shot and given to the captain.

Revenge.—' Medernex, lix ; streamers, small & great, xi ; waste clothes, iiii^{xx} yards ; flagges of Sainte George, ii, worne ; ensignes, i.'

Rainbow.—Flags of St. George, two, old ; ensigns of silk, one ; streamers, ten, old and nought.

Dreadnought.—' Flagges of St. George, i ; ensignes of bewpers, i. Item, a longe boate, with ii shyvers of yron, the one in the hedd, & the other in the davitte.'

Similarly for the rest. All the long boats were fitted with a davit. All the ships had one ensign, one or more flags of St. George, and—some of them, but not all— streamers and pendants.]

September 28.—*A SURVEY OF THE NAVY.*

[ccxvi. 40.—Signed.   Endorsed.]

All such ships as were at Chatham, at this instant 28th of September, 1588.

The state of her Majesty's ships, ship-boats, and pinnaces examined and surveyed by the master ship-wrights and other the masters attendant at Chatham, according to the directions and order given unto them from her Majesty's officers of the navy, the 28th of September, 1588.

The Elizabeth Jonas.—The same ship being so pestered in the hold, which most special places could not be examined; and so generally throughout the fleet.   And being exactly examined and surveyed by the master shipwrights the 12th of October, 1587, and the same exhibited to the Lord Admiral, unto the which we thought good to have a relation only such other imperfections as is since made known, we are to set down the same; as in this ship, the decayed fashion-pieces; the weakness of the forecastle; the altering of the form thereof, whereby more shot may be used forward.   Also divers knees are to be placed for her more strength, and accordingly caulked and ransacked for her better preservation.

The Triumph.—In the same ship appeareth divers imperfections about the loof[1] and forepart, growing of decayed timber, which is to be strengthened; as also the forecastle is to be reformed, as in the Elizabeth; certain parts in the ship is to be strengthened with knees; and two beams that are cracked or given way are to be amended; the stem before and the fashion-pieces abaft are to be examined; sundry places in

---

[1] The after part of the bow, before the chess-tree.

the cage-work are to be renewed, and the outward and inward places to be ransacked and caulked. Also she is to have a new bonaventure-mizzen and a new boat.

The White Bear.—In the same ship appeareth divers imperfections : growing of decayed timber, which procureth the leakiness at the seas ; besides, the stem and sternpost is imperfect ; all which as they are to be reformed, so can it not be done to any perfection without a dry dock. Also she is to have a new mainmast, a foremast, a bowsprit, a main-yard, a foreyard, a spritsail yard and a bonaventure-mast. Also she wanteth a new boat and a new pinnace.

The Victory.—The same ship, as the timber and fashion-pieces be in great decay, yet there is hope and no less show of her service than of the rest, so that a small charge for the present is to be bestowed, besides ransacking and caulking ; only she wanteth a new bowsprit and a new boat ; also a main-mizzen mast.

The Ark.—The same ship, her upper overlop in the waist is to be taken up and brought to a less cambering,[1] for the better use of the ordnance. There is a beam cracked, which is to be amended ; and the ship ransacked and caulked. Also she wanteth a new boat and a pinnace.

The Hope.—In the same ship appeareth great imperfections and weakness, which procureth leaki-ness at the sea ; and by the disorderly graving which hath been used upon her, hath hastened her decay ; for reforming whereof no help can well be had without dry docking. The mainmast is decayed, and she wanteth a new boat and a pinnace.

The Bonaventure.—In this ship there is a show of imperfection growing from under the sheathing,

[1] Curve ; made more level.

which is to be removed ; as also the sternpost, fashion-piece and rudder are much decayed ; all which are not to be remedied without dry docking. Besides, she wanteth a new bowsprit and a new pinnace.

The Mary Rose.—This ship at this instant is very leaky, which may not only proceed of the imperfections of her timbers, but much more of her decayed stem and sternpost, which appeareth to be a cause thereof, as well at the sea as otherwise ; the remedy whereof cannot well be done but in a dry dock. Besides, her mainmast is decayed, and her boat and pinnace is to be repaired.

The Lion.—The same ship is at this instant in order for the seas, both graved and caulked within board and without ; the cook room is removed and made upon the lower overlop in the midships ; the mainmast and foremast are fished, and such other needful works done.

The Revenge.—The same ship is to have a new mainmast, being decayed and perished with shot as otherwise ; more, she is to have a new jeer capstan, and certain other places to be amended. Also the boat is to be new, and the pinnace to be repaired.

The Nonpareil.—The same ship's mainmast is to be taken out, and the same to be fished, or else to make a new ; also the foremast, bowsprit, with the main-mizzen-mast, are all to be made new, and likewise the bonaventure-mast. More, she is to have a new boat, and all new tops, as also the pinnace repaired ; besides ransacking and caulking.

The Dreadnought.—The same ship hath been lately reformed of some imperfections. Notwithstanding, her many decayed timbers remaineth, and for her leak at the sea is to be amended at the next graving, with other needful ransacking and caulking. Her bow is to be repaired, and to have a new pinnace.

The Swiftsure.—In this ship her imperfect timber remaining, divers other imperfections to be reformed, as the beak-head and the stem under the same; also the step of the foremast is decayed; also she is to be graved and new caulked under water, for doing whereof it is determined to have her into the wet dock at Chatham. Also she is to have a new foremast, a foreyard, and a new boat.

The Antelope.—The same ship, being an old bottom, at her next graving is to be dubbed and well ransacked and caulked. Also she is to have a new rudder, a new capstan, a broken knee renewed, her boat repaired, a new foretop, and a new pinnace.

The Swallow.—In which ship some weakness appeareth; for strengthening whereof, divers standing knees are to be placed, a new fore-knight is to be made, the main capstans new whelped, her bow to be amended, and a new pinnace to be made, and a new maintop.

The Tiger.—In this ship appeareth some leakiness under the beak-head, which is to be amended; divers ports are to be reformed; a new maintop is to be made, a new boat and a pinnace.

The Bull.—The same ship being often in hand, and sundry times repaired, and now in that decay as will be a charge of such a new one to bring in good order, and being without hope of her service or continuance, we leave her to a further consideration of such as may deal further in her by authority and their better discretions.

The Merlin.—The same pinnace, her mainmast is to be new headed and her footwaling something raised for the ballast in the midships. She is to have a new bilge pump and a new maintop, besides ransacking and caulking.

The Charles.—The same pinnace hath had a new mainmast, mizzenmast, certain knees and other needful things done ; and is ransacked, caulked, and graved, and in readiness for any sudden service, only she wanteth a boat.

The Spy.—This pinnace hath had a new head and certain bindings within board ; as also all her masts new, and is now in readiness for the service.

The Scout.—This bark hath had divers things reformed in her, specially about the bows ; her cook room removed up upon the overlop; a new bowsprit ; ransacked, graved, and caulked, and in readiness to service.

The Achates.—The same bark being often repaired, and so much done for her strength as may be, nevertheless it is reported by the captain, master, and boatswain that her leakiness is such in foul weather, and complaineth so sore, as they think her state dangerous to be continued at the sea.   To remedy the same, cannot well without bringing her upon a dry shore, to do it to any perfection.

The Galley Eleanor.—The same galley is so near worn as her service is of small continuance.

Per PETER PETT.   MATHEW BAKER.
JHON AUSTYNE.[1]

PETITION OF ANTHONY POTTS.

[ccxvi. 66.—Endorsed :—The humble petition of Anthony Potts of Bridgwater, mariner.]

To the right honourable the Lords and others her Majesty's most honourable Privy Council.

In most humble wise complaining, showeth unto your Honours your continual suppliant and daily orator, Anthony Potts :—That whereas your said

[1] This man could scarcely write even his name, and here signed it 'Astyne.'

suppliant was lately employed in her Majesty's service in a certain ship of his own, called the Charity of Newcastle, of the burden of 180 tons, with victuals and the wages of 80 men belonging thereunto; and also of one other bark of 30 tons, with victuals and wages also of 20 men the space of two months, over and above the charges allowed him by the town of Plymouth; and for that, Right Honourable, your said suppliant hath been a continual suitor unto your Honours the space of six weeks past for such money as is due unto him, as well to his great cost and intolerable expenses, as also to the utter undoing of him and his for ever, by reason of his great charge and absence : May it therefore please your Honours, of your accustomed goodness, with pity to regard your suppliant's estate, and of your honourable clemency to grant that he may have present payment of his said money due unto him. And he, with his, as most bounden, shall daily pray unto God for your Honours, in all prosperity, long ife, with all increase of honour, long to continue.

Autograph minute, signed.—Sir Francis Drake is to certify how long his ship hath served, and with what numbers, and what is due unto him for the time of his service.   FRA. WALSYNGHAM.

THE PETITION OF THE CAPTAINS &c., OF SANDWICH AND DOVER.

[**ccxvi. 67.**—Endorsed :—Not mentioned in Mr. Hawkyns' book.]

To the Right Honourable Sir William Cecill, Knight, Baron of Burghley, Lord High Treasurer of England, and one of her Majesty's most honourable Privy Council.

Most humbly beseecheth your Honour, the captains, masters, mariners, and soldiers, with others of the two ships lately set forth by the towns of Sandwich and Dover :—That whereas, upon letters of demand sent by your Honours to the said townships, they have dutifully and faithfully (as they trust) served her Majesty by the space of two months now passed, at their own great and excessive cost and charges, and did for the great and weighty considerations remembered in your Honour's letters double the charge requested ; and those two months being expired, were commanded by the Honourable the Lord Henry Seymour, then admiral in the Narrow Seas, to take in victuals of her Majesty's and to serve other two months, which we have accordingly very sufficiently performed, as by his Lordship's and Sir William Wynter's their discharge under their hands may and doth appear : It may therefore please your Honour to grant speedy order for pay to be made of the said two last months behind unpaid, the rather for that the great outcries and pitiful complaints of the poor needy mariners and soldiers, daily made for want thereof, cannot otherwise be relieved and appeased. And we the said humble suppliants shall, as we are most bounden, continually pray unto the Almighty for the long and happy estate of your Honour, to his glory.

MEMORIAL OF THE TOWN OF HASTINGS.

[ccxvi. 68.—Engrossed.]

Remembrance for the Right Honourable the Lord Burghley, Lord High Treasurer of England.

The Anne Bonaventure, of the burden of 70 tons, manned with 49 men.

The said ship served in the Narrow
Seas with her Majesty's navy five
months, of which time they were victualled by the inhabitants of Hastings
for three months, and by her Majesty's
officers for two months.   They have,
according to the Right Honourable Sir
Francis Walsyngham's direction, repaired unto Mr. Holstok and Mr. Borough
for the rating of their allowances, who have
not all only abated unto them their tonnage, for which they pay 13*l.* 6*s.* 8*d.* per
month, the sum of 26 13   4
but also of their men's wages as they
have paid them, the sum of .   .   . 17   3   6
the which amounteth unto 43*l.* 16*s.* 10*d.*
over and above the sum of 403*l.* 7*s.* 9*d.*,
the charge the poor township hath been
at for the three months they themselves
victualled.

    Their humble petition is beseeching
your Honours of your warrants for
their payment to be despatched, for
avoiding of charges by long suit ; the
sum being rated at 69 10 10

    They beseech also your honourable
regards to be carried towards their allowance of their victualling and manning of
11 crayers, furnished with 80 men, who,
upon the sight of the Right Honourable Sir Francis Walsyngham's letters,
were set forth to attend upon the Lord
Admiral in the Narrow Seas, where
they continued 15 days, the sum of   . 36   0   0

    They pray also your honourable
warrants to be granted unto them that,
where they have no allowance of ton-

£   s.   d.

nage, the said warrants may be directed   £ *s.*   *d.*
unto the owner of their said ship, to
enjoin him to take her Majesty's allowance, and to repay back again what he
hath received for the later two months
above her Majesty's said allowance ; as
also to be directed unto those which
refuse to pay their contribution, as they
are assessed unto the said charge.

The like, they of the town of Hythe
most humbly desire to be allowed, as by
their bill rated appeareth ; as also allowance for five crayers, manned with 40 men
and 4 boys, for the like time, the sum of   18   o   o

September 30.—*WM. THOMAS TO BURGHLEY.*

[Holland, lvii.—Signed. Addressed.]

The God of all wisdom and power govern. and
direct you ever in all your counsels as may be most
to his glory, the honour of her Majesty's people and
country, and to the utter overthrow of all her
enemies.

Whereas, Right Honourable, at this time, as also
at other times,[1] I have been bold to write to your
Honour, the rather presuming of your Honour's
favour, in that my desire or request tendeth for the
honour of her Majesty and your Honours all, and
for the better service to be done against the enemy ;
for the which, Right Honourable, a petition was

---

[1] *S.P. Dom. Eliz.* clvii. 42 : the petition is not dated, but
would seem from this to have been written in 1585. In it Thomas
proposes that the ships should have 5 gunners to every 100 tons ;
which, notwithstanding his present complaint, is about what the
ships had.

made to your Honour and to the rest of her
Majesty's honourable Privy Council of long time,
but more plainly made known three years past. The
suit was to have the corporation for the gunners
which was given by that famous prince of memory,
Henry the Eighth, that the said charter, with other
articles needful, then made known, to be annexed for
the better service of her Highness, might be renewed
and confirmed; the cause of so great a benefit
requested only for the better strengthening and
defending of her country, and being to be proved no
charges more to her Highness, neither to her people,
but from the same would have proceeded great
profit, not only to her country, but also even to her
Majesty's coffers, as, if it had pleased God I might
have been permitted to have answered, should have
been more plainly showed.

But our sins and our unworthiness caused that
suit so little to be regarded, as it may plainly appear
at this day; for if it had pleased God that her
Majesty's ships had been manned with a full supply
of good gunners, according to the forces they carry,
when the Spanish fleet came through the Narrow
Seas and her Highness's navy so long in fight, it
could not otherwise have come to pass, the Lord
being not against them, but that it would have been
the woefullest time or enterprise that ever the
Spaniard took in hand; and no otherwise to be
thought or doubted of, but that the most noblest
victory by the sea that ever was heard of would
have fallen to her Majesty. What can be said
but our sins was the cause that so much powder
and shot spent, and so long time in fight, and, in
comparison thereof, so little harm?

And although, Right Honourable, our gracious
God hath dealt mercifully with us, in that our enemies hath had no success at this time against us, yet

it were greatly to be wished that the same suit with
the articles were stirred up again, and that it might
come before your Honours all, to be more deeply
considered of ; and also it were greatly to be wished
that your Honours were more truly certified of that
blind exercise and unskilful teaching by the name of
scholars in the artillery, whereby her Highness may
no longer be deceived, neither your Honours therein
any further abused.[1]   And as we are bound, Right
Honourable, to give God most hearty thanks for
that her Highness and your Honours hath so great
care for the keeping and the maintaining of so royal
a navy, and also sparing of no charges for the
furnishing of them plentifully with great and forcible
ordnance, every one of them according to their
burden, so it were greatly to be desired of the Lord
that he would also work with her Majesty and your
Honours that there might be such good policies
and means by her established and confirmed, as
thereby in our science knowledge may be more
and more known and increased ; whereby her
Majesty, in all her affairs, may be the better
served, and her enemies thereby the more terrified.
Thus, Right Honourable, I cease, craving your
Honour's favour in this my boldness ; and so for
this time I humbly take my leave, praying continually to the Almighty for your Honour's happy
health, with long increase of the same.   Flushing,
the last of September.

   Your Honour's to use
         at your commandment till death,
      Wm. Thomas, master gunner in Flushing.

[1] The spelling of this letter is rather a curiosity. Here is a
sample :—yt were grettly to bey wesshed that yowr onors were more
truly sartyfyed of that blynde exsarsyes and own skelfell techen
by the name of skolors. In the artelayry. Where by her heyght-
nes may no leyngar be dessavyd. nayther yowr onors. thare In.
any forthar a beusyd.

Oct. 1.—*SIR R. BINGHAM TO WALSYNGHAM.*

[**Ireland, cxxxvii. 3.**—Signed.   Addressed.]

It may please your Honour :—Although the
Lord Deputy (I know) hath from time to time
acquainted your Honour with the particular occur-
rences of this province, as well as the general state
of things else in this action of the Spanish shipping, yet consideration of duty bindeth me to
deliver unto your Honour somewhat briefly the
accidents that have happened within my charge,
with such honour and praise unto Almighty God
as so glorious a victory, first at sea and since by
their confusion of shipwreck, is worthy of, beseeching the same God that for these his infinite blessings we may ever rest much more thankful.

After the Spanish fleet had doubled Scotland
and were in their course homewards, they were by
contrary weather driven upon the several parts of
this province and wrecked, as it were by even
portions, 3 ships in every of the 4 several counties
bordering upon the sea coasts, viz., in Sligo, Mayo,
Galway, and Thomond.   So that 12 ships perished
that all we know of on the rocks and sands by the
shore side, and some 3 or 4 besides to seaboard
of the out isles, which presently sunk, both men
and ships, in the night time.   And so can I say,
by good estimation, that 6 or 7,000 men have
been cast away on these coasts, save some 1,000
of them which escaped to land in several places
where their ships fell, which sithence were all put
to the sword.

Amongst these were many gentlemen of the
middle sort, and some reserved alive, but none of
their greatest commanders have happened into our

hands.　The Duke himself was upon the coast of Erris in Mayo, and there received into his ship Don Alonso de Leyva, with a 600 men that had been cast ashore out of the Rata, Sir Horatio Palavi-cino[1] his ship, which ship lies there all to split in pieces.　And John Martinez de Recalde, their admiral, with some 6 or 7 ships more in his company, fell into the mouth of the Shannon, and is since departed for Spain; but I am persuaded that neither of them both will ever recover home, and especially the Duke, for they wanted both victuals and fresh water, and have since been hindered with continual contrary winds.　The like opinion I hold of as many more of their ships as touched upon these coasts, and have from hence taken their course for Spain.

Other great wrecks they had both in Munster and in Ulster, which being out of my charge I have not so good notice of, but the same (I doubt not) is fully made known unto your Honour.

For saving of the artillery and other munitions for her Majesty's store, there shall not anything be omitted here that may possibly be done to the furtherance thereof.

And thus craving pardon for my boldness, with my humble duty remembered unto your Honour, to my Lady, and to my good lady and mistress, with the like from my wife, I humbly take leave for this time.　At Athlone, the first of October, 1588.

Your Honour's most humble at command,

RY. BINGHAM.

---

[1] In confusion for Horatio Donago (*post*, p. 276).　Palavicino had, of course, nothing to do with it; but the Christian name suggested the surname.

October 6.—*CARY TO THE COUNCIL.*

[ccxvii. 10.—Holograph.   Addressed.]

My duty to your good Lordships most humbly
remembered :—I have received your Honours' letters
of the last of September, touching the continuance of
my service concerning the safe keeping of the goods
which were in the Spanish ship.   Though none of
them do remain in my custody, yet will I in all duty
have care of your Lordships' commandment as ap
pertaineth, trusting that hereafter others in like case
will use better husbandry than heretofore hath been.
And in discharge of my duty and conscience, I
think it meet to acquaint your Lordships with some
things left out of our last inventory, namely, two
pieces of brass delivered out of this ship into a pinnace of Plymouth ; another piece of brass delivered
into the Samaritan, a ship of Dartmouth ; as also in
the same ship 12 muskets and 12 calivers.   The ship
and bark are returned from her Majesty's service,
yet these things remain unanswered to her Majesty.
Your Honours' directions I humbly pray.   Jacob
Whiddon had also 10 or 12 pieces of brass into the
Roebuck.   For the liberal disposing of the wines
and other things, it will be over long to trouble your
Honours therewith.   To be plain, it goeth against
my conscience that we cannot yield so just an account
of our doings as in duty it appertaineth.

It pleased your Honours to direct your letters
of the 6th of this last month unto Sir John Gilberte
and myself, signifying thereby her Majesty's pleasure that the Spanish prisoners for their relief should
be allowed to everych [1] of them 4*d.* per diem.   In
this service Sir John Gilberte and I do not agree :

---

[1] Every each, every one.

for he, being unwilling to take any pains where no
profit ariseth, would fain thrust the 226 prisoners
which remain at Bridewell, 16 miles from my house,
to my charge. And he would take upon him the
charge of 160 of the said Spanish prisoners remaining a-shipboard hard by his house, and every day
hardly labouring in his garden in the levelling of
his grounds, so that he is too wise for me (as he
thinketh), to have their daily labour and yet allowance
from her Majesty of 4*d*. per diem to each of them.
I have no grounds to level nor work to set them
unto, so far from my house ; and therefore, under
your Lordships' favours, the match he offereth me is
not equal.   The service by your Lordships commanded was jointly sent us both.   By this means
your Honours' directions are neglected.

These persons, under your Lordships' correction,
would, with good discreet order, be sufficiently relieved for 2*d*. per diem, and so a moiety of the charge
saved, if your Honours would but direct a course
from whence the money should be disbursed, either
from the Sheriff or from the Receiver, and so to be
allowed upon their accounts.   And in this I humbly
beseech the assistance of some others that may always
be an eye [1] witnesses of my just proceedings herein.
It is requisite (if it so stand with your Honours'
pleasures) to direct some good course herein, for there
is no order taken as yet ; and if they had not been
relieved by Mr. Justice Peryam's and others' good
means, they had starved ere now.   And so, with
my humble duty, I rest from further troubling your
Honours.   Cockington, this 6th of October, 1588.

Your Lordships' to be commanded,

GEORGE CARY.

[1] Yee.

October 6.—ORDER TO QUARLES FOR
PAYMENT.

[**B.M. Egerton MS. 1525, f. 16.**—Signed. Addressed. Endorsed.]

The charge of victualling 258 men serving her Majesty in these ships of Bristol following, for two months :—

The Minion	. . . 110	
Unicorn	. . . 66	258 men
Handmaid	. . . 56	
Aid	. . . 26	

	£	s.	d.
Victualled for 5 days, begun the 19th of June, ended the 23rd of the same, at 7*d.* a man per diem . . .	37	12	6
And for 51 days, begun the 24th of June, and ended the 14th of August, at 6*d.* a man per diem	328	19	0

Sum, 366*l.* 11*s.* 6*d.*

Ex^d per DARELL.

We do acknowledge that these ships have served her Majesty all this time, and were victualled by Mr. Darell for the said time.

C. HOWARD.   JOHN HAWKYNS.
W. WYNTER.   WILLM. HOLSTOK.

Make an order for payment hereof.
W. BURGHLEY.

October 8.—COMPARISON OF CHARGES.

[**ccxvii. 12.**—Wynter's autograph, but not signed.[1] Endorsed, in
   Burghley's hand :—A comparison betwixt the expenses for
   five years afore Mr. Hawkyns' bargain and of the five years
   since the bargain of Mr. Hawkyns.   Sir Wm. Wynter's declaration.]

It may please your Lordship to call to mind that
in February,[2] 1584, there was an account delivered to
your Lordship by me and other of my fellows,
wherein is showed what the charge was of ordinary
and extraordinary for her Majesty's navy, in harbour,
for 5 years last before the first undertaking of the
bargain for the ordinary ; the which, besides the
new building and repairing of ships in dry docks, did
amount to the sum of 29,413*l.* 16*s.* 9*d.*,[3] which being
divided into 5 parts, maketh the charge of each year
to be 5,882*l.* 15*s.* 5*d.*

By the same account was also showed that the
like charge for ordinary and extraordinary, besides
new buildings and repairing of ships in dry docks, for
five years next ensuing the first undertaking of the
said bargain, did stand her Majesty in the sum of
25,377*l.* 14*s.* 8*d.*, which being divided into 5 equal
parts, showeth the charge of each year to be
5,075*l.* 10*s.* 11*d.* So as, by comparing the said
accounts together, it may seem her Highness hath
saved in the latter 5 years 4,036*l.* 2*s.* 6*d.*, which falleth
out for each of the 5 years 807*l.* 4*s.* 6*d.*

But it is to be considered that, in the five years

---

[1] Though not signed, there is no pretence at anonymity. The
paper is a serious charge against Hawkyns ; but between Wynter
and Hawkyns there was not much love.

[2] MS. Phebr.   The account referred to does not seem to be
extant.

[3] All these sums are interpreted in the margin, in Burghley's
hand, thus :—xxix^m iiii^c xiii^{li} xvi^s ix^d.

before the bargain, there was bestowed upon the ordinary, for ransacking,[1] repairing and trimming of the said ships in harbour, in wages and victuals of carpenters, caulkers and labourers, and provisions for the same works, the sum of 2,200*l.* yearly, which in my conscience was no more than needed ; and if there were any evil dealing in the expending thereof (as I know none), the same was in the master shipwrights whom we trusted.

Likewise it is to be considered that the latter 5 years of the bargain there was assigned out of the 4,000*l. os. od.* which was appointed for the ordinary but 1,000*l. os. od.* for the doing of the like works and charges before declared, viz., wages and victuals of carpenters, caulkers and labourers, and provision for the same works ; and so it appeareth that there was laid out in the former 5 years 6,000*l. os. od.* more than in the latter 5 years for the like works in repairing and trimming of the ships, which was yearly a charge of 1,200*l. os. od.* more than in the latter 5 years. And if the office had forborne the expending of the said 1,200*l. os. od.* yearly for the former 5 years (as in duty it was not thought convenient), then the charge of the ordinary and extraordinary in harbour, besides the new building and repairing of ships in dry docks, would have been for the said 5 years 1,963*l.* 17*s.* 6*d.* less than was spent in the latter 5 years, which is yearly 392*l.* 15*s.* 4*d.*

It may be alleged that her Majesty's ships, with the 1,000*l. os. od.* yearly since the bargain, hath been as well and sufficiently ransacked, trimmed, repaired and done as they were in the former 5 years with the charge of 2,200*l.* yearly ; the which in my conscience is most untrue. And for better trial, if her Majesty be pleased to call the master shipwrights,

[1] Ransacking appears to mean thoroughly overhauling and examining.

workmen of all sorts, clerks, and any other that had dealings in the works in the former or latter times, to declare their knowledge and conscience, upon their oaths, then I doubt not but the truth will be manifested.

And if these reasons before set down may not satisfy, then let the whole charge for ordinary and extraordinary, since the first taking of the bargain to this day, be collected and truly set down. In the doing thereof there must be good regard had to the new titles used in the account of this latter time, viz., charges for provisions of double furniture, charges of new buildings of wharves and houses, transportations, and such like, which in the former time, before the bargain, were comprised under the titles of ordinary and extraordinary in harbour ; and thereby shall manifestly appear that the said sparing of the ordinary in repairing, trimming and ransacking of her Majesty's ships in this latter time, hath bred a far greater charge to her Highness than was in the like time before the bargain ; besides the clouterly [1] patching and doing of the same, very discommodious in the use of the ships.

Oct. 9.—THE CHARGE OF THE LONDON SHIPS.

[**ccxvii. 13.**—Signed. Endorsed, with a minute by Burghley :—To be considered by the officers of the Admiralty of the reasonableness of the demand and time of the service.—W. Burghley.]

A note of the 8 ships appointed to be sent to the Lord Harry Seymour, into the Narrow Seas, the 25th of July, 1588, under the conduct of Mr. Nicholas Gorges, Esquire.

---

[1] Clumsy.

The names of the ships and their numbers of men :—

	Men
The Susan Parnell of London . .	80
Solomon	80
George Bonaventure. . .	80
Anne Frances	70
Vineyard	60
Violet	60
Samuel	50
Jane Bonaventure	50

Sum of the men 530

The 26th of July the ships and men entered into pay, and, from that day, was victualled for one whole month.

	£	s.	d.
The victualling of 530 men for one month, after 14s. per man—sum .	371	0	0
For press of 530 men, at 12d. per man .	26	10	0
For the pressors due, after 4d. per man	8	16	8
Sum	406	6	8

October 12.—*INSTRUCTIONS FOR THE LORD PRIMATE AND OTHERS.*

[S P. Ireland, cxxxvii. 14.]

W. Fytzwylliam.—Instructions for the Lord Primate, Sir Henry Wallop, knight, and David Gwynn, gent., or any two of them, to be dealt in with the Spanish prisoners at Drogheda.

1. Imprimis :—You shall inquire from whence they came, by whom they were entertained ; in what ship they came forth, for what cause, and how many of them came on land here ?

2. Item.—You shall inquire what quality the persons were that came forth in their said ship, and how many of them are dead, or drowned, or killed since their coming forth?

3. Item.—You shall inquire how they came into the north, either by shipwreck or otherwise; how they were entertained and relieved upon their landing, and by whom; how many of them were killed before they were taken, how many after, and how many escaped with their lives that be now in the country, and in what manner and order they themselves were taken and used?

4. Item.—To know what money, jewels, plate, apparel, or furniture for the war the captains took from them, or from any of their company, and what any of the soldiers or Irishry likewise had of them?

5. Item.—To inquire what he is that is with O'Donnell's wife, and what those were that remained with the Earl of Tyrone, and how many in number?

6. Item.—What they were that were killed between their coming out of O'Donnell's country and the Newry, being such as were not able to travel?

7. Who brought them any chains, jewels, or money since they came to Drogheda, and who sent the same unto them?

8. Item.—Whether any of Drogheda have any chains, jewels, or money of theirs in custody, and who they be?

9. To know of them who of this country's birth were with them in Spain, and what their names be that were shipped either with them or in any other of their ships?

10. Item.—To know whether James Fitz-morris's son came out of Spain; if he did, in what ship, and what became of him?

11. Item.—To know whether they left any plate, money, jewels, or other things with the Earl of Tyrone, or with O'Donnell, or his wife, and what the same were?

12. Item.—To know what friendship they have received since they came to Drogheda, and what their names be that showed the same?

13. Item.—To know how many ships fell upon this north coast where they landed, and how many were in every ship?

14. Item.—To know if the captains upon their first landing did make any promise unto them, and if they did, what the same?

October 13.—*EXAMINATION OF PRISONERS.*

[Ireland, cxxxvii. 15.]

13th of October, 1588. *Apud* Drogheda.

Examination taken of the Spanish prisoners remaining at Drogheda, by virtue of a commission from the Lord Deputy and Council, dated the 12th of October, 1588, and certain interrogatories to the same annexed, directed to the Lord of Ardmaugh, Sir Henry Wallop, knight &c., and David Gwynn, gent., or any two of them.

1. Imprimis:—Don Alonso de Luzon, master of the camp of the tercio of Naples, being 10 ensigns containing 1,800 men, examined upon the first interrogatory saith, upon his oath, they came from Naples aforesaid, and were entertained by King Philip, being of his old garrison of Naples, and sent on this journey to go into Flanders to the Duke of Parma. But what they should do further than ot be at the same duke's direction was known

to the Privy Council, and not to him.   He saith
they landed in O'Doherty's country, out of the ship
called Valencera de Venecia,[1] being a very great
ship, but of what certain burden he knoweth not,
about 400 and 50 men, whereof many sick and
weak, besides which, 100 and upwards were
drowned in coming to the shore, being common
soldiers and mariners.   In this ship, when she came
from Lisbon, there were, as he saith, 400 soldiers
and 4 score and odd mariners and gunners, of which
men that were drowned and did land here, 4 days
before their coming to shore they took out of the
hulk called the Bark of Hamburg[2] 100 men, and
the captain of them, called Don Beltran del Salto,
and the master of the said hulk, called Jaques
Flamenco.

2. To the 2nd interrogatory he saith that he and
other of his company have set down under their
hands the names of all the men of quality that was
in the same ship.   He saith that they did lack,
besides the 3 gentlemen that died in Drogheda, 8 or
9 of those men of quality who landed with the rest ;
but what is become of them, whether they be dead
or alive, he knoweth not.

3. To the 3rd interrogatory he saith they landed
by shipwreck as many of them as they could in a
broken boat of their own, some swam to shore,
and the rest were landed in a boat of O'Doherty's
country, for the use of which they gave in money
and apparel 200 ducats.   Touching their entertainment when they came on land, he saith that he
and 5 more of the best of his company landed first,
only with their rapiers in their hands, where they

[1] La Trinidad Valencera, of 1,100 tons, 42 guns ; 281 soldiers,
79 mariners (Duro, ii. 63).
[2] Barca de Amburg, of 600 tons ; 239 soldiers, 25 mariners
(*ib.*, ii. 64).   Except these 100, they seem to have been all lost
(see *post*, p. 275).

found 4 or 5 savage people—as he termeth them—
who bade them welcome and well used them, until
some twenty more wild men came unto them, after
which time they took away a bag of money containing 1000 reals of plate and a cloak of blue rash,
richly laid with gold lace.   They were about two
days in landing all their men, and being landed, had
very ill entertainment, finding no other relief of victual in the country than of certain garrans,[1] which they
bought of poor men for their money, which garrans
they killed and did eat, and some small quantity of
butter that the common people brought also to sell.
Who they were that brought those things unto them
he knoweth not, only it was in O'Doherty's country ;
and saith that before he and the rest of the gentlemen
of the company yielded themselves, none were slain
by the savage people.   Item, he saith that the
killing by the soldiers and the savage people was
the same night that he and the rest of the gentlemen had yielded, at which he was not, and therefore
knoweth not how many were slain, nor how many
remain alive.

He saith he and the whole company yielded
themselves, within 6 or 7 days after their landing,
to the captains that carried the Queen's ensigns,
O'Donnell and his wife being present, upon condition
that their lives should be saved till they came to the
Viceroy, and that they should be suffered to repair
unto him, every private soldier with one suit of
apparel, and every gentleman with two ; incontinent
whereupon they laid down 350 muskets and calivers
and some few pikes to her Majesty's use, because
they yielded in her name, all which were seized on
by John Kelly, whom they term sergeant-major, and
Captain Richard Hovenden's lieutenant ; after which

---

[1] Horses : Irish, *gearran.*

their promise was not kept with them, but the soldiers and savage people spoiled them of all they had.

4. To the 4th he saith he knoweth not what money, jewels, plate and apparel was taken from the whole company, but for his own part he lost in plate, jewels, money and apparel, that was taken from his servants, above the value of 3,000 ducats; but who took the same he knoweth not, only one of his men told him that he who termed himself sergeant-major to the two captains took his plate, which he esteemeth worth 1,000 ducats and more; and further than he hath said in the 3rd interrogatory touching the artillery he cannot say.

5. To the 5th he saith he certainly knoweth not who it is that is remaining with O'Donnell's wife, but thinketh it is Captain Miranda, who was captain of a ship and a company also, but being discharged of his company at Lisbon, he left his ship also and came unto this as a private man, who was very sick when this examinate saw him last. He also saith that there staid with the Earl of Tyrone, that were sick, Don Alvaro de Mendoza, Don Antonio Manrique, Rodrigo Ponce de Leon, auditor of the tercio of Naples, and one soldier whose name he knoweth not; and these are as many in number as he knoweth that did stay with the Earl of Tyrone.

6. To the 6th he saith there were none killed in the coming between O'Donnell's country and the Newry, but certain gentlemen of account died on the way, whose names ensue:—Don Garcia de Avila, Don Gaspar de Avila, his brother, Don Christobal Maidonado. Hernando Cañaveral dead, and Don Diego de Guzman he thinketh is also dead.

7. To the 7th he saith that since their coming to Drogheda there was neither chains, jewels, nor money sent to him, or any of the rest, to his knowledge.

8. To the 8th he saith that none of Drogheda have any money, chains, or jewels in custody of his or any of the rest, that he knoweth of.

9. To the 9th he saith he knoweth not the names of those of this country's birth that were in Spain when he came from thence, but did see a tall young gentleman, with a red beard and of sanguine complexion, of whose name he knoweth not. He heard of three others; but the said young gentleman came forth with the navy, but in what ship he knoweth not.

10. To the 10th he saith he knoweth not James Fitzmorris' son, nor any that doth call himself by the name of Earl of Desmond.

11. To the 11th he saith that neither he nor any of his company, to his knowledge, did leave any plate, jewels, or money with the Earl of Tyrone or O'Donnell's wife, or any other, more than what was taken by force, as aforesaid.

12. To the 12th he saith that since his coming to Drogheda he hath received no friendship, neither hath any of his company to his knowledge.

13. To the 13th he saith he knoweth not that any other ship fell upon the north coast, saving the same that he was in.

14. To the 14th, more then he hath said in his answer to the 3rd interrogatory he cannot say.

Being asked what became of the admiral of the hulks and the hulk called the Black Castle,[1] who were in company when the Bark of Hamburg sank, he saith they lost the sight of them at the same time, and never heard of them since.

Being further examined what store of ordnance came in his ship, he saith 32 pieces of brass and iron, whereof 4 were cannons of brass; but of what kinds

[1] Castillo Negro, of 750 tons, 279 soldiers, 34 mariners (Duro, ii. 64).

the rest were, how many of brass, or how many of iron, he knoweth not, neither whether the same will be saved or not.

Being asked what treasure of the King's there was in this ship, he saith none. Being demanded whether any were in the ship of greater degree than himself or those here, he saith none were.

Being asked of his knowledge what treasure the King sent in the whole navy, he saith of himself he knoweth not, but hath heard some say 600,000 ducats and some 700,000, part whereof was shipped in the vice-admiral to Admiral Oquendo, and the rest in other ships, whose names he knoweth not.

Being asked in what sort Horatio Donago entered into this voyage, he saith he was taken and pressed by the King's officers at Sicilia to bring part of the 2,000 men of the tercio of Sicilia to Lisbon, where he laboured to procure his discharge, but could not, as the camp-master of the tercio of Sicilia told this examinate; and of himself he knoweth that the Marquis of Santa Cruz did command the said Horatio to grave his ship, who refused so to do because he would have been discharged of the voyage.

October 14.—*CARY TO THE COUNCIL.*

[ccxvii. 21.—Holograph.   Addressed.]

My humble duty to your good Lordships :— Sithence the writing of my last letters unto your Honours, I have been advertised that the Spanish prisoners remaining in our house of correction near the city of Exeter, and which are in number 211, are in some distress for want of relief to sustain them ; and therefore inasmuch as my associate

refuseth to follow those directions it pleased your
Honours jointly to command us both in this service, the necessity of the case so requiring, I have,
with the advice of Sir Thomas Denys and of the
Mayor of Exeter and his brethren, taken order, for
these 14 days, to relieve their misery, in allowing to
each of them $1\frac{1}{2}d$. per diem, and to some of them $2d$.
per diem; and have disbursed the money out of my
purse, to make provision for victuals at the best and
cheapest hand; for otherwise they must needs have
perished through hunger, and possibly thereby have
bred some infection, which might be dangerous to
our country.

And therefore, presuming of your Lordships'
good allowance of my doing herein, do humbly
desire your Honours' directions to have some others
to be joined unto me; for that I am loth to
meddle in such a charge without the assistance of
some others, that may always be an eye-witness of
my just dealings; and that it would please your
Lordships to appoint from whence there might
be some money had beforehand, to provide their
victuals in good order, wherein a third part of the
charge would be saved; for I dare assure your
Lordships that $2d$. per diem, with some other allowances for fire and other necessaries, will suffice for
their maintenance. There hath also heretofore
been defrayed for their relief the sum of fifteen
pounds, for the which I have also given my word
to see it repaid; and therefore shall humbly desire
your Honours' allowance of the same. And touching your Lordships' letters of the last of September
concerning the Spanish goods, I see there is such
havoc made thereof that I am ashamed to write
what spoils I see. And though I have spoken and
written to Sir John Gilberte to understand of his
proceedings, and what is become of all the wines

I left in his custody, yet I can receive no direct answer from him ; but this I know by others, that all the best wines are gone. It were well, if it so stood with your Lordships' pleasures, that we both might answer our doings before your Honours. And so, humbly beseeching your Lordships to receive your directions in these causes, as also concerning the Spanish prisoners, I cease from further troubling your Honours. Cockington, this 14th of October, 1588.

Your Lordships' to be commanded,

GEORGE CARY.

October 14.—*CARY TO WALSYNGHAM.*

[**ccxvii. 22.**—Holograph. Addressed.]

Sir :—I think I shall never rest troubling your Honour ; for sithence my last letters unto you, I am so exclaimed on to give some relief to these Spanish prisoners to keep them from famine, that I am eftsoons enforced to be an humble suitor to your Honour and the rest of my Lords for some other directions for their maintenance ; for Sir John Gilberte is not disposed to take pain where no gain cometh, and the authority that their Lordships gave was jointly unto us both, and so I can do little by myself. Notwithstanding, with the advice of some others, I have presumed, under the favourable allowance of my Lords, to disburse some money out of my own purse, to make some provision to buy victuals to sustain their present miserable estate, allowing unto some of them $1\frac{1}{2}d$. per diem and to others $2d$. per diem. And whereas their Lordships, by their former letter to Sir John Gilberte and myself, did allow $4d$. per diem to each of them, I will assure your Honour that they may be very well maintained for 2*d.* per diem, so[1] that their Lordships will appoint some money to be received beforehand, to buy in their provision. In this I humbly beseech your Honour's and their Lordships' speedy directions. And touching the Spanish goods, notwithstanding their Lordships' letters, and though I have spoke and written to Sir John Gilberte to be acquainted with his proceedings, and how he hath disposed of the wines and some other of the goods, I can yet receive no direct answer. The best wines are all gone ; the tackle of the ship so spoiled by his negligent looking unto, that 200*l.* in ropes and other necessaries will not suffice to set her to the seas again. My Lords should do well to examine these spoils, either by themselves or by some others they shall appoint. Thus, with my humble duty to your Honour, I most humbly take my leave. Cockington, this 14th of October, 1588.

Your Honour's most bounden,

GEORGE CARY.

October 18.—*LORD DEPUTY AND COUNCIL TO THE PRIVY COUNCIL.*

[**Ireland, cxxxvii. 25.**—Signed.]

It may please your Lordships :—There hath been lately delivered unto us an information of the lewd and undutiful behaviour of David Gwynn, sent hither by your Lordships to view the Spanish prisoners in Tredagh[2] and other places, by a gentleman named Eustace Harte, who met him at Rochelle soon after his escape out of the galley. The report,

---

[1] Provided that.   [2] MS. Tredath : Drogheda.

as we have learned, hath been since here spread at
some tables abroad, and being lately in secrecy
delivered by the gentleman himself to the Master of
the Rolls at length, it was by him revealed to me,
the Deputy, and six others of this Council, con-
ferring together for a preparation against the
Spaniards in Tyrconnel.[1]   Whereupon we caused
the gentleman to set down his information under his
hand ; which the next day he did before us whose
names are hereunto subscribed, who likewise have
in duty thought good not only to send the same
enclosed verbatim unto your Lordships, but also
therewith both the accuser and the accused, to receive
their due deserts.   We would with all willingness
have here proceeded to the correction and punishment of the offender, had not your Lordships signified
your pleasure for the speedy return of Gwynn, whom,
as in other things—as, namely, in the embezzling,
impairing and concealing of such chains, gold and
money as he took from the Spanish prisoners at
Tredagh, to the value of 160*l.*—we have found a
most lewd man, so in this information we are most
assuredly persuaded in our consciences that he hath
most injuriously abused that honourable gentleman ;
and herein hath committed so great a villainy as
justly deserveth most severe punishment.   And
therefore we earnestly wish that, in regard of this
new and rare precedent of most extreme villainy,
the offender may be made a public example, to terrify
others from the like offence, the rather because the
honour, credit, innocency and loyalty of the best and
greatest personages in the world is interested in this
cause, which we humbly refer to your grave considerations.   And so, with the remembrance of our

[1] Nearly identical with the modern Donegal.

humble duties, take leave. From her Majesty's castle of Dublin, the 18th of October, 1588.

Your Lordships' ever most humble to command,

W. FYTZWYLLIAM.

AD. DUBLIN, Canc. THOS. MIDENSIS.
ROBT. DILLON. VALENTINE BROWNE.
H. WALLOP. LUCAS DILLON.
RO. GARDENER. GEFF. FENTON.[1]
G. BOWRCHIER.

Oct. 16.—DECLARATION OF EUSTACE HARTE.

[Ireland, cxxxvii. 25, I.—Signed. Endorsed.]

A declaration of me, Eustace Harte, gentleman, before Sir William Fytzwylliam, Knight, Lord Deputy of Ireland, and others of her Majesty's Council, the 16th day of October, 1588, concerning David Gwynn.

I, the said Harte, had been some eight or nine months in a town of garrison of the King of Navarre, under the government of Monsieur de Plasack, called Pons,[2] and did take my leave of the governor the 30th of July last, with letters to his Majesty, then lying at Rochelle. But having some occasion of business with one Monsieur de Treilleboys, dwelling in the Isle of Allvart,[3] did stay some 5 or 6 days, and from thence did take

[1] The Members of the Council here signing are: Adam Loftus, Archbishop of Dublin and Lord Chancellor of Ireland; Sir Robert Dillon, Chief Justice of the Common Pleas; Sir Henry Wallop, Vice Treasurer and Treasurer at Wars; Sir Robert Gardener, Chief Justice of the King's Bench; Sir George Bowrchier; Thomas Jones, Bishop of Meath, afterwards Archbishop of Dublin; Sir Valentine Browne; Sir Lucas Dillon, Chief Baron of the Exchequer; and Sir Geoffrey Fenton, Secretary of the Council.
[2] In Charente Inférieure; then a place of some strength.
[3] The Peninsula of Arvert.

boat towards Rochelle, thinking to find his Majesty there, and to have passage for England. In which boat were 3 galley slaves that came lately from the galley cast on shore near to Bayonne in France; which galley slaves reported unto me, and the rest that were in the boat, that the galley, being sore broken with the weather at sea, were driven to take shore to save themselves, and that the governor of the galley and the rest of the Spaniards did remain with the governor of the town of Bayonne until the King of France's pleasure were further known. And asking them what Englishmen were in their galley with them, answered but some two or three. Then at my arrival at Rochelle, which was upon Thursday, the 13th of August,[1] or thereabouts, which very day the King went from Rochelle and took his voyage to meet with Duke Mercœur,[2] Governor of Brittany. And on the Friday following, an English galley slave, whose name was David Gwynn, came to Rochelle with divers others which saved themselves as the rest. And this Gwynn, being in necessity and want, sought for some relief of the English merchants; and telling them much news of the Spanish fleet—as they affirmed to me —and of divers intelligences that the Spaniards should have out of England, did make report that, amongst others, a Spanish secretary had showed him a letter which should come from Mr. Secretary Walsyngham, whose name he did see in writing —Francisco Walsyngham (not permitted to see any more than his name); but that the said Spanish secretary said he was wholly for them, and he would deliver her Majesty's person into their hands. Which merchants, hearing him to report thus lewdly, one amongst the rest, named Thomas Hayward, a

---

[1] August 13 was a Tuesday ; or by New Style, a Saturday.
[2] MS. Marcurye.

merchant of Chester, lodging with me at one Patrick Hughes, an Irishman, told unto me the report of this galley slave ; and for the better confirmation of the tale was desirous to bring this Gwynn to my chamber, that I might hear the speeches which he had uttered to the merchants. The said David Gwynn, being asked by the said Thomas Hayward in the presence of me, did there confirm that which he had before spoken ; saying, further, that he had divers and sundry times wrote unto her Majesty, and that he had yet to disclose many things at his coming over into England unto her Majesty of her enemies in England, and that of the best sort ; and, moreover, did take forth a paper out of his pocket, wherein were written certain verses by him of her Majesty, concerning the estate of England, and did name her Majesty by the name of Bess.

Mr. Hayward, being offended in his mind, desired me that if it were possible to get that lewd prating fellow punished ; but I wished this merchant to bestow somewhat of him, and to let him alone in that place, whereby there might more be gathered of him, saying that the Council of England would soon find him. EUSTACE HARTE.

Signed by the said Eustace Harte in the presence of us. , W. FYTZWYLLIAM.

AD. DUBLIN, Canc. THOS. MIDENSIS.
H. WALLOP. ROBERT DILLON.
RO. GARDENER. G. BOWRCHIER.
LUCAS DILLON. N. WHITE.
GEFF. FENTON.

Oct. 18.—*FYTZWYLLIAM TO WALSYNGHAM.*

[Ireland, cxxxvii. 26.—Signed. Addressed.]

Sir :—What event hath here fallen out upon Gwynn's employment albeit by letters sent by this bearer from me and this Council to their Lordships and your Honour doth appear, yet could I not be satisfied without writing these few lines unto you, to manifest how far it is from me to think that you— whose long approved zeal and loyalty to God's church and her Majesty hath the attestations of all men in general, and of myself, with my life and all I possess, in particular, to clear you—should be guilty of the least minute wherewith this caitiff—un- worthy of life—hath so villainously charged you; and therefore do most earnestly beseech you so to construe of this our proceeding as of that which, I protest, we have specially done in the love and honour we bear you, and the desire we have had that so detestable a fact might be severely punished; and withal for myself, to assure you that to the utter- most of my power I will stand for and defend your loyalty and innocency—even with the loss of my blood—as I will mine own, which God and my conscience know to be unspotted. All which refer- ring to your honourable consideration, and myself to all the honour and service I may do you, I humbly take leave. From her Majesty's castle of Dublin, the 18th of October, 1588.

> Your Honour's ever assured to command,
> W. FYTZWYLLIAM.

October 18.—*N. WHITE*[1] *TO WALSYNGHAM.*

[Ireland, cxxxvii. 28.—Signed. Addressed.]

My humble duty remembered to your Honour :— It may please the same to understand it hath been my hope of late to be made acquainted with a cause that toucheth you, wherein I did seek to use all the

---

[1] Sir Nicholas White, Master of the Rolls.

good means that might express my dutiful affection towards you, as Sir Harry Wallop and Sir Lucas Dillon can witness, and do hope that your Honour will even so accept of it. The matter is this. A young gentleman, Eustace Harte, nephew to Mr. Auditor Peyton, who professeth greatly to love and honour you, did of himself, upon like opinion conceived of me and through my acquaintance with his uncle, reveal unto me certain false and slanderous speeches given out in his hearing, of you, by one Gwynn, lately come hither, requesting me to impart the same to the Lord Deputy, to the end the party might not escape unpunished, which I did, of a reverend regard and faithful meaning towards your Honour. And upon Harte his avouching of the speeches under his handwriting, delivered to the Lord Deputy, the said Gwynn was committed, and is now sent over to receive his well deserved punishment, having been also condemned afore us here of manifest falsehood and perjury touching the embezzling of certain chains of gold and coin received by him of the Spaniards to her Majesty's use. After some muttering abroad of this fellow's speeches, and afore I had heard anything hereof, it was thought that through the guiltiness of his own conscience he meant to have stolen away, if he had not been apprehended. And for that I was not at the signing of the letters written by the Lord Deputy and Council to your Honour touching this matter, I thought it my part to signify unto you how far and upon what occasion I dealt therein, humbly craving your favourable construction of my good meaning in the same ; and so humbly take my leave. From Dublin, this 19th of October, 1588.

Your Honour's humbly and heartily to command,
N. WHITE.

October 28.—FYTZWYLLIAM TO WALSYNGHAM.

[Ireland, cxxxvii. 48.—Signed.   Addressed.]

Sir :—Having for the more expedition sent afore by my man Morris, as well such letters as advertise the state of our occurrents here, as also those which particularly concern Harte and Gwynn, committed to the charge of this bearer my servant, likewise sent for the safe bringing of them unto their Lordships, I thought it meet, to the end both he and they might have the better and more convenient access unto you, to accompany him with these few lines only to signify the same.   And so, with remembrance of my duty, I humbly take leave, and commit your Honour to the Almighty's protection.   From the castle of Dublin, 28th of October, 1588.

Your Honour's ever assured to command,

W. FYTZWYLLIAM.

I send you enclosed the copy of a letter, which I received from Captain Merriman while this was in writing, which confirmeth that there cannot be gone above 300 of all the men which landed, neither have they now any one vessel left to carry the rest away ; and since it hath pleased God, by his hand, upon the rocks to drown the greater and better sort of them, I will, with his favour, be his soldier for the despatching of those rags which yet remain.

[Ireland, cxxxvii. 48, I.—Enclosure in preceding.   Endorsed :— A copy of a letter of Captain Merriman.]

Right Honourable :—With regard of my most humble duty, I thought good to acquaint your Honour with the occurrents here, that the Spanish ship which arrived in Tyrconnel with the McSweeny was on Friday the 18th of this present descried over against Dunluce, and by rough weather was perished, so that there was driven to the land, being drowned, the number of 260 persons, with certain butts of wine, which Sorley Boy hath taken up for his use. All these his messengers told me, whom I met passing hitherwards with the same news. Thus most humbly &c. &c.

October.—*ALLOWANCE FOR SHIPS BURNED.*

[**ccxvii. 71.**—Endorsed.]

Rate for allowances for the ships burned for the firing of the Spanish navy :—

	£	s.	d.
Captain Yonge's[1] flyboat, of the burden of 140 tons, or thereabouts, valued at	550	0	0
Cure's ship,[2] of the burden of 150 tons, valued at	600	0	0
The Angel of Hampton, of the burden of 120 tons, valued at	450	0	0
The Thomas[3] of Plymouth, of the burden of 200 tons, valued at	1,000	0	0
The Bark Talbot,[4] of the burden of 200 tons	900	0	0
The Bark Bond,[5] of the burden of 150 tons	600	0	0
The Hope,[6] of the burden of 180 tons	600	0	0
The Elizabeth of Lowestoft, of the burden of 90 tons	411	10	0
Sum	5,111	10	0

[1] The Bear Yonge (ccxxii. 74); Captain Yonge owner (ccxvi. 18, I.).

[2] It nowhere appears who or what Cure was. It may be an eccentric way of spelling Cary, but neither this ship, nor the Angel, is in any other list.

[3] Belonged to Sir Francis Drake (*ib.*).

[4] A west country ship (*ib.*).

[5] Seems to have belonged to Sir J. Hawkyns (*ib.*).

[6] Of Plymouth, William Hart owner (*ib.*).

[ccxvi. 74.]

The particulars of such goods and provision as Thomas Meldrum, merchant, had burnt at Calais road :—

	£	s.	d.
Imprimis, the ship called the Elizabeth of Lowestoft, of the burden of 90 tons, with all anchors, cables, ropes, masts, sails, tackle and furniture thereto belonging	300	0	0
Item, for four fowlers containing 24 cwt., at 24s. per cwt.[1]	28	16	0
Item, over and above the foresaid tackle, 1 cable of 10 cwt., one cable of 6 cwt., and a warp of 390, at 20s. per cwt.	19	10	0
Item, 8 double bases	16	0	0
,, 12 calivers	6	0	0
,, in shot, 1 cwt.	1	0	0
,, in powder, 150 lbs. . . .	7	10	0
,, 12 pikes	1	4	0
,, 6 tons of beer, at 42s. per ton .	12	12	0
,, in biscuit,[2] 15 cwt. . . .	5	0	0
,, 3 barrels of beef	6	0	0
,, 4 firkins of butter . . .	2	13	4
,, in fish, 1 cwt. and a half of North Sea cod	7	10	0
,, one wey of cheese . . .	2	0	0
,, 4 doz. of candles	0	14	8
Sum	416	10	0

[1] The cwt., or rather the c., was at this time 100 lbs., and the qr. was 25 lbs.

[2] It seems improbable that in the threatening scarcity of victuals this biscuit, beef, &c., was burnt. Meldrum was very likely trying to get as much as he could, and if the Treasury would pay for the victuals twice over, so much the better for him ; but it nowhere appears that he got it.

Item, he asketh allowance for the ship's service, and for bringing of 30 men from Dartmouth to my Lord Admiral's and other her Majesty's ships, and for his wages.

November 5.—*CARY TO THE COUNCIL.*

[**ccxviii. 4.**—Holograph. Addressed.]

My humble duty unto your good Lordships :— Forthwith upon the receipt of your Honours' letters of the 21st of the last month, I rode presently to Plymouth, where, understanding that the Roebuck being there then in harbour, and ready, as they said, with the next good wind to depart, I signified unto the mayor of the town of Plymouth and the officers there, and likewise to Jacob Whiddon, captain of the said Roebuck, what your Lordships' pleasure was—that such brass pieces that were taken out of the Spanish carrack whereof Don Pedro had charge should be laid on shore and put in safe keeping to her Majesty's use. And for the better satisfying of them for that point, did show unto them your Honours' warrant, which they promised to obey and perform. The said Jacob Whiddon confesseth the having but of 10 brass pieces, whereof he saith he laid one on shore at Portland. I did appoint Mr. William Hawkyns to receive those other 9 brass pieces, and likewise the 2 brass pieces in Founes' pinnace, and keep them to her Highness's use until your Lordships' pleasure were further known.

And during my abode there, having understanding that one of the Spanish fleet was cast on shore (at a place called Hope near Salcombe), and the great pilfering and spoils that the country people made, I rode thither and took order for the restoring and rehaving again of all such things as either by search or inquiry I could find out, and have put the same in inventory. And took order, for the orderly saving of the rest, as weather would give leave, to have the same on land, appointing two head constables to attend that service, and they and others to keep several inventories. The ship is a hulk, and called St. Peter the Great,[1] one of those two ships which were appointed for the hospital to the whole navy. She is in burden, as they say, 550 tons, but I think not so much. The ship is not to be recovered ; she lieth on a rock, and full of water to her upper decks. They confess that there were put into her, at her coming out of Spain, 30 mariners, 100 soldiers, 50 appertaining to the hospital. There are now remaining about a hundred forty, or thereabouts. There was put into her as much drugs and pothecary stuff as came to 6,000 ducats, of which I think there will come little good of the same, being in the water almost this sennight, the weather such as none could get aboard. There hath been some plate and certain ducats rifled and spoiled at their first landing, both from their persons and out of their chests. The ship, I think, will prove of no great value ; the ordnance is all iron, and no brass ; their ground tackle all spent, save only one new cable. There are no men of account in the ship—soldiers and such as have risen by service, and bestowed all their wealth in this action. I have severed the captains and chiefest of them, to the number of 10 persons, from the rest ; eight of them I left to the charge of Sir William Courteney, and two of them, the one being the pothecary, the other the sergeant, I took to myself ; the others are put in safe keeping, and guarded both day and night ; and

[1] See Appendix F.

have appointed 1½*d.* a day to every of them, to
make provision for their sustenance, until your
Lordships' pleasures were further known ; which I
humbly desire may be with some speed, for that the
charge of these, and those of Bridewell, grow somewhat heavy unto me. I disburse the money myself,
for money is not to be received for the wines, Sir
John Gilberte having disposed already of all the
best ; the rest, through ill usage in this country, will
yield but little, nor good for anything, as I think,
save only to make aquavitæ of, or such like. I
would humbly desire the gift of those two Spaniards
which I have, not for any profit, but I make trial
what skill is in them. I am given to understand
that there is remaining 14 barrels of powder in the
Samaritan, of such as I caused to be taken out of
the Spanish carrack and appointed to have been
sent and delivered unto my Lord Admiral in the
late service, according to my Lord's direction ; but
the same was never delivered, and doth yet remain
in the Samaritan, as I am informed. And so I
humbly take my leave. Cockington, this 5th of
November, 1588.

Upon the finishing of my letter I received a
letter from the Mayor of Plymouth and other the
officers there, which I send herein enclosed unto
your Honours.

Your Honours' always to be commanded,
GEORGE CARY.

November 7.—GILBERTE TO THE COUNCIL.

[**ccxviii. 6.**—Signed. Addressed.]

My duty unto your Honours most humbly remembered :—I have this day received advertisements
by one Richard Blackater of Totness, merchant, that

came presently from St. Malo ; and the report there is, by a ship that came lately out of Spain, that the Duke of Medina was arrived, and hurt in one of his legs.   Being at the Court, the King would not see him, but commanded him to his house.   And there are 50 of the fleet arrived on the coast of Spain. The King prepared for another fleet, to be of 150 sail of ships and 50 galleys ; he says French ships and all others of 80 tons and upwards.   The King is coming in person to see the performance of this fleet into Biscay, and hath executed sundry of his officers that had the charge of the victualling of this last navy, for that the victual was bad, and not the quantity that they ought to have provided.

He further says that there is 1,000 tons of the best and serviceablest ships of St. Malo's freighted for Spain, and they determine to carry victual, and expect plenty of Newfoundland fish, and pilchards to come to them out of these west parts.   And hereupon, I have sent to the justices of Cornwall to make stay of the pilchards there, and to Plymouth and Dartmouth, that no victuals be transported till your Honours' pleasure be herein known.   In Dartmouth there are some ready to depart with fish to St. Malo, which I have sent to the mayor to stay.   Hoping of your Honours' good acceptance of this my duty, till further direction from your Honours, most humbly I take my leave.   Greenway, this 7th of November, 1588.   Your Honours' most humbly to command,

JOHN GILBERTE.

November 12.—*ANTHONY ASHLEY TO THE COUNCIL.*

[ccxviii. **14**.—Signed.   Addressed.]

May it please your Lordships :—Having received letters of the fifth of this present, I have accordingly

acquainted the gentlemen with your Lordships' pleasure for the deferring of the execution of the Spaniards, and do herein enclose a schedule of the names
of those of the best sort, with their offices, quality,
and their offers for ransom, as also of all the rest of
the meanest sort, and likewise such of other nations
as came in the ship; with such other particularities
touching the said persons as I thought necessary.
But concerning the drugs, we have not found any of
value, though by confession of the apothecary of the
Spaniards, there were to the value of 6,000 ducats
at the time of their arrival here; but the simples
which are of value cannot yet be found out; those
drugs which are saved are compounds, and therefore
esteemed nothing worth. We have used what means
we thought meetest, by examination and otherwise,
to cause such money, ordnance and other goods as
have been embezzled to be restored, the particularities whereof as of all other things committed to my
charge as soon as may be shall be advertised to
your Lordships.[1]

By late examinations taken of the Spaniards, I
find that certain bezoar[2] stones and other simples, to
the value abovesaid, were purloined out of the ship,
of which bezoar stones I hope to recover the most of
them. I have been bold to stay this messenger
hitherto, thinking I should have been able to have
advertised some certainty of them, but must now
leave the same to my return, which shall be as speedily as I may. The ship being run upon rocks by
the Spaniards, is now through the tempestuous weather broken in pieces and scattered on the seashore,
and order is taken for the saving of such things of
the same as are anything worth.

It may please your Lordships to signify your

[1] Note in the margin : The inventory not perfected.
[2] MS. besar.

pleasure touching such of the company that are not Spaniards, as of the rest, as soon as your Lordships shall think convenient, for avoiding of the charge of their diet. Those Spaniards that offer ransom will also pay for the charge of their diet until their departure, if so your Lordships be pleased to order; and for the loan of the money for their liberty and growing charges, they would send some one or two to collect and bring over the same. 10 or 12 of the best sort are placed in a town called Kingsbridge, where order is taken for the provision of their wants and account kept of their expenses; the rest, until your Lordships' further pleasure known, are remaining together in one house, whither they were first committed, where they are safe kept and provided of necessary food.

I am put in great hope to discover things of great value which belonged to the ship wherein Don Pedro was, that are embezzled, where,[1] as soon as this business is ended, I will do her Majesty the best service I can.

I have found Mr. Cary very carefully to travail in this service, to the great furtherance thereof. So I humbly take my leave. From Ilton, Sir Wm. Courteney's house, the 12th of November, 1588.

Your Lordships' most humble,
A. ASHLEY.

[ccxviii. 14, I.—Signed. Endorsed.]

The names, offices and quality or place of all those persons that came in the hulk called St. Peter the Great, which was driven into a bay called Hope, adjoining unto the grounds of Sir William Courteney, and within two miles of Salcombe:—

[1] Wherein.

The monthly pay of officers and of private soldiers	—	Offers for ransom
Ducats.[1]		Ducats
40	Diego de Aler, captain of 100 soldiers embarked in the hulk, hath served in the Low Countries in the time of Don Juan, as ancient in the tercio of Don Fernando de Toledo.	—
15	Diego de Salvateria, ensign to the said captain.	20
12	Francisco de Silva, captain of the ship.	—
25	Rodrigo de Calderon, comptroller of the hospital, brother to Coque Calderon, Auditor-General of the army.[2]	80
8	Alonso de Muñoz, gentleman, sergeant of the company.	20
18	Pedro de Samillon, overseer of the hospital.	60
—	Gonzalo and Luis de Castillo, brothers, gentlemen adventurers, of Granada.	150
30	Lopes Ruiz, of Aledida in Estremadura, the chief pothecary of the army.	—
—	Gregorio de Taguada, had the chief charge of the sick.	30
10	Francisco de Medina, the wardrobe keeper.	30
6	Diego Martinez, keeper of the victual and diet of the sick ; is brother to the physician of Juan Martinez de Recalde's.	30
10	Juan Martinez, of Melgar, clerk of the hospital.	20
—	Diego Soliez, gentleman, page to Don Alonso de Leyva ; thinks his master will redeem him.	—
—	Francisco de la Dezima, distributor of the victual and diet of the sick.	--
6	Pedro de las Gueuas, steward of the hospital.	20
7	Pedro Hernandez, corporal of the company.	15
6	Martin Ximenes, assistant to the pothecary.	15

[1] Silver ducats, worth about 3s.
[2] The Auditor-General was Martin de Aranda. Pedro Coco Calderon was a *contador*, an accountant (Duro, ii. 84)

These following, being ordinary private soldiers, their pay 4 ducats the month. [28 of them, offer ransom of 12, 15, 20, two of 30 ducats; three out of the burnt ship.]

Spaniards that can give no ransom, being soldiers [67 in number], and mariners [11].

Portugal soldiers [13].
French mariners [10].
Italian mariners [2].
Dutch mariners [10].

JOHN GILBERTE.   A. ASHLEY.
GEORGE CARY.   CHR. HARRIS.

November 15.—*JOHN THOMS*[1] *TO HOWARD.*

[ccxviii. 24.—Signed.]

Right Honourable, my humble duty remembered:—And may it please your Lordship to be advertised of the great Spaniard[2]; she was lost at Studland, but, God be praised, there is saved 34 of our best men; and there was lost 23 men, whereof 6 of them was Flemings and Frenchmen that came in the same ship out of Spain; and by good hap there came out of Studland a small man-of-war and saved these men. It may please your Honour, the ship had a new foresail, which was in Nicholas Jones' hands, of Portland Castle, well approved by Mr. George Trenchard. So said Mr. Jones: ' I pray send for it; you shall have it, and a dozen of oars.' But it was least part of his meaning, for the next day the

---

[1] Clerk of the prick and check at Portsmouth. In the accounts of the yard, the name appears as Thomas.

[2] The San Salvador, on her way from Weymouth to Portsmouth.

said Jones rode away to London, and left no order
to deliver the same sail, neither none could be
had. And please your Lordship, I charge him
before Mr. Trenchard, that the ship or men should
miscarry, that he should answer it ; for truly, if
Mr. Jones had not a promised me the sail, I would
not a defrayed any moneys upon her, but should a
lien still. There be of his neighbours that are saved,
and others of the company, that will venture their
lives whenever they meet with him ; for all those
that are saved will depose that he was the casting
away the ship and the death of the men. Sithence,
and please your Honour, I have been westward, to
belay[1] all such masts, yards, shrouds and small ropes
or sails that should come ashore, to be kept for the
Queen's use or any of her 2 pinnaces. Their
anchors,[2] and please your Honour, there are marks
taken where they lie, and I have given order that if
they may have any fair weather they will sweep for
them. There are 4 which weighs 30 hundred a
piece, which I hope will help to quite[3] this charge.
The Lion, and please your Honour, is come into Portsmouth, and have spent her mainmast, yard, topmast
and yard, and topsail; wherein I have taken order to
have it brought into the dock, and I have promised
to pay the charges ; but I know not, and please your
Honour, whether it be the Queen's charge or my
Lord of Cumberland's. Here is no provision in my
custody to help any of the Queen's ships if they
should need ; not a cable, neither ropes, masts,
anchors, spikes, nails ; but 7 bolts medernexes,
which is most of them cut afore I came. I humbly
rest, praying for your Lordship's health with much

[1] To secure, take possession of. The *N. E. D.* has no instance
exactly corresponding to this.
[2] As regards their anchors.
[3] Requite.

increase of honour.   From Portsmouth, the 15th of November, 1588.

    At your Honour's commandment
          to my poor service,
              JOHN THOMS.

    The ship's masts were oak and clampered[1] together, nothing worth.

November 26.—*CHARGE OF VICTUALLING.*
[ccxviii. 43.]

    xxvi[to] die Novembris, 1588.—An estimate of the charge of the victualling, as well her Majesty's own ships, as also all other ships taken to serve with them in warlike manner, from the first of July, 1587, unto the last of December, 1588, being one whole year and half :—

	£
First, the charge of the victualling of her Highness' own ships, by estimation, for one year and a half, beginning and ending as aforesaid	42,161
Item, for the victualling of her Majesty's ships in harbour, within the said time, by like estimation.	3,730
Item, for the victualling of sundry ships, as well on the Narrow Seas as also in the west country and coast of Spain, being taken from sundry parts to join with her Majesty's navy for their better strength, within the said time, by like estimation	20,440
Summa totalis	66,331

[1] Patched up, built.

Dec. 3.—SIR R. BINGHAM TO THE QUEEN.

[Ireland, cxxxix. 2.—Signed. Addressed :—To the Queen's most
excellent Majesty.]

Most gracious and dread Sovereign :—My long
silence in not acquainting your Majesty with the
occurrents of this your Highness's province hath
proceeded rather through fear to offend your Majesty
by pressing too far into your Highness's presence
with my rude and uncomely letters, than any way
for want of a serviceable care to answer the trust
and charge it hath pleased your Highness to lay
upon me. Albeit, finding the manifold benefits and
blessings of Almighty God poured upon us, your
Highness's subjects, under the excellency of your
sovereignty, daily to exceed all others your Majesty's
neighbours, I have adventured, in the consideration
of my duty and bounty of your Highness's favour
towards me, your poor and faithful soldier, to present
your Highness now with these humble and few lines,
as a thanksgiving to Almighty God for these his
daily preservations of your sacred person, and the
continual deliverance of us, your Majesty's subjects,
from the cruel and bloody hands of your Highness's
enemies, and that lastly from the danger of the
Spanish forces, defeated first by your Majesty's
navy in the Narrow Seas, and sithence overthrown
through the wonderful handiwork of Almighty God,
by great and horrible shipwrecks upon the coasts of
this realm, and most upon the parts and creeks of
this province of Connaught, where it hath pleased
your Majesty to appoint my service under your
Highness's Lord Deputy. Their loss upon this
province, first and last, and in several places, was
twelve ships, which all we know of, and some two or

three more supposed to be sunk to seaboard of the
out isles; the men of which ships did all perish in
the sea, save the number of 1,100 or upward, which
we put to the sword; amongst whom there was
divers gentlemen of quality and service, as captains,
masters of ships, lieutenants, ensign-bearers, other
inferior officers and young gentlemen, to the number
of some fifty, whose names I have for the most part
set down in a list, and have sent the same unto your
Majesty; which being spared from the sword till
order might be had from the Lord Deputy how to
proceed against them, I had special direction sent
me to see them executed, as the rest were, only
reserving alive one, Don Luis de Cordova,[1] and a
young gentleman, his nephew, till your Highness's
pleasure be known. Other gentlemen of special
reckoning we had none, for the Count Paredes and
Don Alonso de Leyva, with other gentlemen, being
thrown ashore in Erris, the remotest place in all this
province, and their ship all to broken, did afterwards
by chance embark themselves in another of their
ships and departed to sea; but being again driven
back upon the northern coast in Ulster, and from
thence putting to sea again, are sithence, as I hear
say, cast away about the isles going for Scotland.
My brother George had one Don Graveillo de
Swasso[2] and another gentleman, by licence, and
some five or six Dutch boys and young men, who
coming after the fury and heat of justice was past,
by entreaty I spared them, in respect they were
pressed into the fleet against their wills, and did
dispose them into several Englishmen's hands, upon
good assurance that they should be forthcoming at
all times. And this,[3] God be praised, was all the
province quickly rid of those distressed enemies, and

[1] Brother of the Marquis of Ayamonte (Duro, ii. 364).
[2] So in MS.   [3] In this way, thus.

the service done and ended without any other forces
than the garrison bands, or yet any extraordinary
charge to your Majesty.   But the Lord Deputy,
having further advertisements from the north of the
state of things in those parts, took occasion to make
a journey thither, and made his way through this
province, and in his passing along caused both these
two Spaniards, which my brother had, to be executed,
and the Dutchmen and boys which were spared
before, reserving none but Don Luis and his nephew,
whom I have here.   I was glad in one respect that
his Lordship should take his way through Connaught, for that thereby he might the better satisfy
himself of what we had before performed here,
and accordingly had written of.   Other wrecks
they had both in Munster and Ulster, which being
out of my charge I have not so good notice of.
And this much I have boldly presumed to deliver
unto your Majesty, though somewhat late, for which
I most humbly crave your Highness's pardon,
beseeching the Almighty God for your long and
prosperous reign over us, and withal that we, your
Highness's people, may daily grow in more thankful-
ness towards our mighty God and Protector, who
ever preserve your Majesty to our continual com-
forts.   From your Majesty's castle of Athlone, the
third day of December, 1588.

> Your Highness's most loyal
> and humble soldier,
> Ry. Bingham.

[Ireland, cxxxix. 2, I.]

Don John de Quintanilla.[1]
Don Pedro Girosque.[2]
Don Alonso de Argotta.

[1] The surname, with different Christian name, appears in Duro.
[2] Mentioned by Duro.

Don Antonio de Ulloa.[1]
Don Diego de Cordova.[1]
Don Diego Sarmiento.[2]
Don Fernando la Serna.[1]
Michell Dicas, ancient bearer.
Pedro de Arechaga, captain of the ship.[3]
Bartolomé Bravo, captain.[2]
Serjeant Calderon.[2]
Francisco Maria Centeno.[2]
Don Diego Martell.
Don Alonso Ladron de Guevara.[4]
Don Jaques de Mires.
Giovanni Avauncye, master of the Rata.
Gaspar de los Reyes, master.[5]
Bartolomé de Arboleda.
Antonio Moreno.[2]
Felipe Cornetes.
Francesco Cortes, ancient bearer.[2]
Diego de Allyon.[2]
Francisco de Espinosa, ancient bearer.[2]
Juan Medrano.[1]
Pedro de Acuña.[2]
Diego del Roncon.
Francisco de Leon.[2]
Don Diego de Santillana.[1]
Antonio Bazan, ancient bearer.[1]
Juan Gil.[6]
Alonso de la Serna.[2]
Bernardo Pineto.
Sebastian de Carvajal, ancient bearer.[2]

[1] The surname, with different Christian name, appears in Duro.
[2] Mentioned by Duro.
[3] Captain of the Falcon Blanco Mediano (*ib.* ii. 140).
[4] A captain of soldiers. He is differently mentioned as in the Gran Grin (*ib.* ii. 37) and in the Rata (*ib.* ii. 67).
[5] Master of the Gran Grin (*ib.* i. 391).
[6] Alferez, or ensign bearer, at first serving on board the San Martin, on the staff of the Duke. As he could speak English,

December.—*HOWARD TO BURGHLEY.*

[**ccxix. 23.** —Signed.   Addressed.]

My very good Lord :—Whereas I do perceive, by a note subscribed by the auditor, which I do here-withal send your Lordship, that there hath grown a surcharge unto her Majesty of 623*l.* 10*s.* 11*d.* in this late service, by reason of certain extraordinary kinds of victuals, as wine, cider, sugar, oil, and certain fish, provided and distributed amongst the ships at Plymouth by my order, and Sir Francis Drake's, which was done as well to relieve such men withal as by reason of sickness or being hurt in fight, should not be able to digest the salt meats at sea, as also for the better lengthening of our ordinary victual when we should have gone for the coast of Spain, and which afterwards did stand us in great stead, both when we came to spend of that biscuit and beer which was sent us from London, whereof a great part was much wasted and spoiled in the carriage, and besides in making us able to help many of the coast ships with victual, which we did oftentimes when they were in want, but espe-cially at our being northwards in the pursuit of our enemies : I am therefore to pray your Lord-ship (albeit I must acknowledge this charge to be such as the like, I think, in former times hath not been), yet in regard of the greatness of this service above others, and that these provisions were used for the relief and encouragement of such upon whose forwardness and valours the good success of

he was sent away in a pinnace (*zabra*), and picked up the Fal-mouth boatmen on the night of July 20 (see vol. i. p. xxxvii) ; afterwards he was sent on to the Duke of Parma (Duro, ii. 229, 233, 273, 275), and presumably rejoined the fleet at Calais.

the service did much rest, that your Lordship will use all the favourable consideration you may in the allowance of them, which I hope her Majesty will not mislike of. There was also a further supply of beer and wine distributed amongst the fleet by my order, which I have now caused to be stricken out of the book, and for which I will myself make satisfaction as well as I may, so that her Majesty shall not be charged withal. And so, leaving all to your Lordship's good consideration, I take my leave for this time. From Deptford, this . . .[1] of December, 1588. Your Lordship's very loving friend,

C. HOWARD.

[ccxix. 23, I.—Enclosure in the foregoing.]

A conference[2] between the charge of the extraordinary victuals delivered in gross by order and warrant, and her Majesty's ordinary allowance due by the day, as hereafter followeth :—

The ships serving under the Lord Admiral :

	£	s.	d.
There was due for the victualling of 3,770 men serving in the Triumph and 15 other her Majesty's ships, under the charge of the Lord Admiral, by the space of 14 days, begun the 14th of July and ended the 27th of the same, after the foresaid rate of 6d. to each man by the day	319	10	0

Against the which :—There was sent from London by Mr. Quarles and distributed amongst those ships, biscuit at 7s. the cwt., 52,304 lbs.,

---

[1] Blank in MS. [2] Comparison

£   s.   d.

183*l*. 1*s*. 3*d*., and beer at 33*s*. 4*d*.
per ton, 217 t. 2 puncheons 1 hhd.,
364*l*. 3*s*. 10*d*. In all, as by certificate under the hand of Richard
Peter may appear . . .   547   5   1

Not allowed in Mr. Darell's account, but
only set down here to prove the loss.

And also there hath been distributed
amongst them at Plymouth, by Mr.
Darell, certain extraordinary victuals in gross, by order and warrant, viz., at one time 243*l*. 6*s*. 8*d*.,
and at another time 942*l*. 12*s*. 2*d*.
In all, as by the particulars thereof
may appear   1,185   18   10
And for their ordinary allowance of
necessaries and lading charges
during that time, by reason of the
victualling in gross and not by the
day   31   18   8

Sum   1,765   2   7

And so there hath grown a loss unto
her Majesty within the said time
of 14 days, by these extraordinary
victuals, to the sum of . . .   445   12   7

The ships serving under Sir Francis Drake:

There was due, according to her
Majesty's allowance, for the victualling of 2,820 men serving in the
Revenge and 30 other ships, under
the charge of Sir Francis Drake,
by the space of 7 days, begun the
4th of August, 1588, and ended

	£	s.	d.
the 10th of the same, after 6d. to a man by the day	493	10	0
Against the which :—There hath been delivered to those ships certain extraordinary victuals in gross, by order and warrant, amounting unto, as by the particulars thereof may appear	671	8	4
And so there hath grown a loss unto her Majesty within the said time of 7 days, by these extraordinary victuals, to the sum of . . .	177	18	4
Sum total of the losses aforesaid	623	10	11

I have examined the premises by the particular book subscribed by the officers of the Admiralty.

8th of December, 1588.

Exd. per JOHN CONYERS, Auditor.

December 14.—*PETITION OF SIR J. HAWKYNS.*

[ccxix. 28.—Engrossed. Endorsed.]

Your humble suppliant, as well by reason of sundry great payments growing by his office of treasurership of her Majesty's marine causes, and by the bargain made with her Highness for the defraying of the ordinary charges of the same, as through the last extraordinary accidents and charges about the late sea services, is thereby as well greatly indebted to divers her Majesty's subjects, as by reason of his late service against the Spaniards many great and unlooked for charges is thereby grown, and his accounts great and far out of order, and not speedily to be reduced and brought into form and perfection without great travail, pains and time to be spent in performing and finishing of the same; besides the private estate of your suppliant by these great payments both dangerous and much encumbered, and his accounts, which he is, both in conscience and duty, to yield unto her Majesty, is thereby grown so great and intricate as, unless your Honours will be pleased to be a mean to her Majesty to spare him some convenient time for the better perfecting and reducing of the same to some good form and order, he shall neither be able to do her Majesty that service which in duty and fidelity he is bound and most desirous to perform, nor answer your Lordships' expectations for matters pertaining to his place. In tender consideration whereof it may the rather please your Honours to deal with her Majesty that Mr. Edward Fenton, one of her Majesty's servants, both honest and of great fidelity, and for whom your said orator and his sureties already given into the Exchequer will undertake and still stand bound for, as also myself enter into any further bond your Honours shall reasonably devise for the better surety of her Majesty therein, may receive and disburse, from the first of January next until the last of December, 1589, in his own name and by his own acquittance, all such sums of money as is to be disbursed and laid out for and during that time in and about the ordinary and extraordinary charges of her Majesty's marine causes; which to that effect (standing with your Honours' good likings and favours, and not prejudicial or anyways hurtful to her Majesty) her gracious letters patents of the said office, granted to your said orator as treasurer of her Highness's marine causes, doth permit, suffer and allow. And yet, nevertheless, your said orator, to the uttermost of his power, and according to the duty and fidelity he oweth to her Majesty (reserving fit and convenient time for the reducing of his said account into good form and order, whereby her Majesty may be justly answered all such sums of money as may happen to grow thereby due to her or any of her subjects), will also endeavour himself to do all those good offices which may best maintain and be most profitable for the good continuance, well ordering and preservation of her Majesty's most royal navy, or anything concerning or belonging to the same. And your said orator shall be bound daily to pray for your Honours' long and good estates.

December [14].—*WARRANT OF THE QUEEN.*

[ccxix. 29.]

Right trusty and well beloved, we greet you well. Whereas we are made to understand, by a petition exhibited unto you (our Treasurer and Admiral), that our servant Sir John Hawkyns, knight, is desirous for one whole year, to begin the first of January next and to end the last of December, 1589, to substitute and appoint in his place, as his lawful deputy, our servant Edward Fenton, for the receiving of all such sum and sums of money as shall be anyways allotted during that year for the payment as well of our ordinary as extraordinary charges which shall happen to grow in and about our marine causes during that time, to the end that the said Sir John Hawkyns may thereby have better liberty to reduce and put in order such his accounts, as he is to be accountable and answerable to us for such sums of money as he hath formerly received, by virtue of his office of treasurership for our marine causes sithence his entry into the same, whereby it may the rather appear in what manner of estate and condition he standeth, as well with us for those accounts, as what may further grow due thereby to any of our subjects by that occasion: We have thought good, for the reasons specified in his petition, as well to grant him liberty for the time he requireth to compound and finish those his accounts, as also, at his humble and earnest suit, to admit and allow of our servant Edward Fenton to execute his place for that time, so as (in all sorts) his self and former surety and bonds may be answerable to us for such sum and sums of money as the said Edward Fenton shall, during that year, receive of our treasure for any our marine causes whatsoever. Commanding, nevertheless, that our said servant Sir John Hawkyns shall, from time to time, be aiding and assisting with his travail and counsel to further such our services as shall happily grow fit and necessary to be managed and handled in that time. Given &c.

December 20.—*WYNTER TO WALSYNGHAM.*

[ccxix. 36.—Signed. Addressed.]

The service and duty I owe to her Majesty and love to my country forceth me to make choice of your Honour, by reason of some weakness in me that I cannot attend upon her Majesty as otherwise I would, to utter and discover a cause that, in my poor opinion, is to be regarded, which is a danger that this her Majesty's realm may be in by the malice of God's enemies and her Highness's, and what the means were, with God's grace, to prevent it. And albeit I presume to deal in a matter of so great weight, yet I hope, if I commit any fault herein, your Honour will shadow the same with your cloak,

the rather because I was encouraged to it by your
Honour, and for the secret choice I have made in the
uttering of it ; most humbly beseeching your Honour
when you have read this, and that you do not like of
it, that then you will be so much my honourable
friend as to suppress it.   Your Honour is the only
person that ever I uttered this cause unto in particular.

Of what importance London is to the crown of
England your Honour doth know ; and how much
the same in all likelihood was desired by the enemies
before declared, besides others that lay hidden, the
coming and adventuring of the King of Spain's army
into the Narrow Seas, and the preparations of the
Prince of Parma made in the Low Countries, doth
bewray it ; for before the armies coming as far forwards as the Narrow Seas, I wrote a letter by your
Honour's commandment, for answer to one of yours
which it pleased your Honour to vouchsafe to write
me, touching what I thought the Prince of Parma's
meaning was for the employing of his flat-bottomed
boats &c., that among other my answers, I doubted
the Isle of Sheppey and the river of London.[1]   But
had I seen and known that which since I have done,
I would have said flatly that their meaning was for
the river of Thames and London ; which plot being
then in their heads, no doubt but that it remaineth
there still, and will hardly be removed until they see
their hope made void, which is not likely without the
providence of God, except that London be fortified
as it may be able to make resistance for a time against
an army, and that also certain points of the shore
lying in the river of Thames may have sconces made
on them, for both must go together.   Which being
done, I do verily think that neither the King of Spain,
yea, although Holland and Zealand should revolt to

[1] Cf. vol. i. p. 213.

him, which I hope in God never to see, and that also the French king would join with them, but that our gracious Lady and mistress shall preserve herself and her kingdom in despite of them.

The working and doing of it being carefully looked unto at the beginning, will amount to little in respect of the wonderful benefit that will grow by it, and the works brought to an end in short time. It may be thought that her Majesty's navy had, and hath had, through the favour of God, so victorious a hand over the enemy that in likelihood it will be so hereafter, if any such attempt be made. I would I might not live to advise her Majesty to diminish the strength of her Highness's navy, for what a jewel the same hath been to the kings and queens of England in my lifetime, my eyes are witnesses thereof; as in the most noble King Henry the 8th time, both at Wight against the French king, and also in Scotland, as well in the east as in the west side of the same realm; also in his son's time, King Edward, the army into Scotland, and the journeys to the islands of Guernsey and Jersey; likewise in his daughter Queen Mary's time, the army to Conquet, and the recovering again of Alderney; and now, lastly, in the Queen's Majesty's our most gracious mistress's time, her army to Leith in Scotland, the like to Newhaven, the several journeys into Ireland, the journeys into Spain and the Indies, and lastly this last God's gift against the Spaniards, besides a number that I leave unrehearsed. So that, weighing these triumphant things, the world might condemn me for a rash and careless person if I did not that which lay in me to advance the maintenance of them. But when I consider that ships are subject to wind, weather, and other haps, it were not good, as I think, for[1] to build our defence only upon them; for I speak of

---

[1] MS. or.

knowledge, as no person shall be able to prove against it, if the King of Spain had men sufficient at Sluys, Nieuport, and Dunkirk, with reasonable shipping to transport them and their provision, the wind being at the North-East, and so to the eastward, and the Queen's Majesty having an army as great as that which her Majesty had any time this year, riding, as commonly they do with the like winds, between Blackness and Boulogne, the King of Spain's army might be in the Thames and danger [1] the principal matter, before knowledge could be given to our ships lying so upon the coast of France as aforesaid. I leave to speak of any army that might come out of Spain to annoy us, and to be thought of by such as are wise, what in probability so mighty a king as the King of Spain may do with his wealth, and what the puissance and force of a gross army of trained soldiers can do against a number of raw men, unexperienced, after they had once settled themselves in places of strength in the Thames (as by God's grace I shall never see it), your Honour can judge as a person of experience.

It would greatly help that Sandwich might be fortified, being apt for that purpose ; also Harwich in Essex, and likewise Yarmouth in Suffolk ; [2] and how the same may be best compassed your wisdom, with others of honour, can best consider ; and thus you should put a defence to the face of your enemies, to the comfort greatly of her Majesty's good subjects everywhere.

It may be alleged that if London be fortified, danger might grow by stubbornness of the citizens or practice of some great personages that might oppose themselves against their prince. Surely if any such should be intended, in my simple opinion the same might easily be prevented.

[1] Endanger.   [2] So in MS.

Thus I thought meet to speak of as one that is desirous the work might proceed without gainsaying. And fearing I have been too tedious, for the which I crave your honourable pardon, I rest, beseeching God to increase you with honour and health. Written the 20th of December, 1588.

If I might know that her Highness and your Honour do favour or like of this, I will draw a plate of the river of Thames, and set down upon [it [1]] the places needful where I imagine the sconces might be best placed (such one I left with my Lord Treasurer at my going lastly to the seas), for your Honour.

Your Honour's in all dutifulness to command,

W. WYNTER.

Dec. 27.—THOMAS FLEMYNG TO BURGHLEY.

[**ccxix. 40.**—Neither written nor signed by Flemyng. Addressed.]

Right Honourable :—Whereas, by warrant and commandment from the Lord High Admiral of England, I was charged to serve her Majesty at the seas for the space of five months against the Spaniard, in part [2] whereof I received by the appointment of the Lord Admiral only for three months and half; and for the other six weeks, having charge of 36 men in a small bark of mine own, to be furnished with all necessaries, as of victuals as wages, I have hitherunto received no allowance, the which, with his loss of cables, anchors, and masts, amounteth to the sum of 70*l.* at the least. My very good Lord, forasmuch as my charge in the said service hath been very great and chargeable unto me, and my attendance since my return from the seas, by these 15 weeks past, very

---

[1] Omitted in MS.   [2] Sc. part payment.

tedious, I beseech your Honour therefore to have regard to my present state, and to take some good order for my present satisfaction in respect of this said charge, to my further encouragement in service, and daily prayer for the continuance of your Honour in all happy state. And so I most humbly take my leave, this 27th of December, 1588.

Your Honour's most bounden,
THOMAS FLEMYNG.

SCALE OF PAY.

[**ccxxxvii. 62.**—A late report or copy, *circ.* 1628.]

Expeditions at Sea. *Anno* 1588.

A brief report made of the charge of the wages, diets, and entertainments of the Lord High Admiral of England; 7 other admirals upon special occasion of service at sundry times; 3 vice-admirals; one rear-admiral; and divers captains, masters, mariners, gunners, and soldiers, appointed to serve her Majesty in the seas against the Spanish forces for one whole year, ended at Christmas, *Anno* 1588, according to the several differences of numbers of men, continuance of time, and rates of allowances and other charges, as hereafter followeth :—

The regiment under the charge and conduct of the Lord High Admiral of England.—Men 3,868.

To himself, per diem, 3*l.* 6*s.* 8*d.* ; the Lord Henry, Lord Seymour, vice-admiral, 2*l.* per diem ; Sir John Hawkyns, rear-admiral, 15*s.* per diem; and for the wages of 19 captains at 2*s.* 6*d.* per diem apiece, with 22 masters and 3,824 mariners, gunners, and soldiers, and sometimes fewer, serving under them, as the exigent of time and need of service required, viz. :—Wages of mariners, gunners, and soldiers, at their accustomed wages, at several times as aforesaid, between the 22nd of December, 1587, and the 15th of September following, 1588 ; with 1,431*l.* 19*s.* 6*d.* for conduct in discharge of the said companies, the sum of . . 22,597*l.* 18*s.* 6*d.*

Regiment of the Lord Henry Seymour, admiral, viz.—Men 1,658.

For himself, being captain and admiral, per diem 40*s.*, from the 14th of May until the 15th of August ; Sir Hen. Palmer, at 20*s.* per diem, from the first of January to the 13th of May ; Sir Willm. Wynter and Sir Martin Frobiser, at 20*s.* apiece per diem ; Thos. Gray, vice-admiral, at 6*s.* 8*d.* per diem ; for the wages of 12 captains, at 2*s.* 6*d.* per diem, and 16 masters, and 1,625 other officers, mariners, gunners and soldiers, and sometimes a less number, as the services required, serving under the aforesaid Sir Hen. Palmer and the rest, at several times, from the first of January to the last of December following, 1588 ; with 222*l.* 10*s.* 10*d.* for conduct in discharge of the said men . . 11,031*l.* 13*s.* 8*d.*

Regiment of Sir Fra. Drake, Knt. Men 2,737.

For himself, being captain and admiral, at 30*s.* per diem ; Tho. Fenner, vice-admiral, at 15*s.* per diem ; 28 captains, at 2*s.* 6*d.* per diem ; 30 masters, and 2,677 other mariners, gunners and soldiers, and sometimes fewer, as services required, serving under them at several times, between the first of January, 1587, unto the 10th of September, 1588 ; in all, with 552*l.* 9*s.* 9*d.* for conduct in discharge ; 3,758*l.* 13*s.* 8*d.* for tonnage, and 343*l.* for sea store of sundry merchants of London . . . 19,228*l.* 12*s.* 5*d.*

Sea wages of merchant coasters serving her
Majesty.—Men 2,789.

Nicholas Gorges, Esq., admiral, for him and his
lieutenant, at 13*s.* 8*d.* per diem ; 50 captains, 51
masters, and 2,686 mariners, gunners and soldiers,
serving under him, after the rate of 14*s.* every man
per mensem, shares and rewards in the same accounted; in all, with 2,264*l.* 6*s.* 8*d.* for tonnage, 65*l.*
14*s.* 2*d.* for prest and conduct, and 39*s.* for rewards;
serving by the space of seven weeks, from the 25th
of July to the 11th of September following, 1588,
and 853*l.* 11*s.* 4*d.* for the sea victuals, sum of
7,330*l.* 10*s.* 9*d.*

Wages of voluntary ships.—Men 840.

Captains, 17 ; masters, 17 ; and 806 other mariners, gunners and soldiers serving under them,
between the 17th of July, 1588, and the 9th of
September following, after the rate of 14*s.* every
man, diets, shares and rewards in the same accounted, with 563*l.* 10*s.* for sea victuals, 202*l.* for
tonnage, and 40*l.* for a reward, sum is 1,622*l.* 17*s.* 6*d.*

Other sea wages and victuals, viz. :

Francis Burnell, captain and admiral of the **Mary
Rose** of London, for her wages and tonnage, and
of 24 other ships appointed to transport victuals to
the navy southwards   .   .   .   1,006*l.* 4*s.* 5*d.*
Thomas Cordell of London, for victual delivered
for 530 men serving under the charge of the Lord
H. Seymour, for one month, begun the 26th of July,
and end the 22nd of August following, 1588, 400*l.*
16*s.* 8*d.*

Sea wages of 13 preachers, 26 lieutenants, 24 corporals, 2 secretaries, and two ensign bearers, men 62, 852*l*. 6*s*. 1*d*.

Provisions, emptions and extraordinary disbursements for the same service, within the time aforesaid.

Regiment under the charge and conduct of the Lord High Admiral of England.

Emptions and provisions, viz., boats, oars, masts, anchors, iron and ironwork, timber, boards, lead, rosin, flags, ensigns, streamers, and such like, 5,388*l*. 0*s*. 9½*d*. ; water carriage, 920*l*. 13*s*. 7*d*. ; wages and entertainments, 48*l*. 4*s*. 6*d*. ; task work, 269*l*. 10*s*. 11*d*. ; rewards,[1] 220*l*. 10*s*. 8*d*.; travelling charges, 440*l*. 14*s*. 2*d*.; allowance for a diet for the Lord Thomas Howard and Lord Sheffield, 433*l*. ; in all, as by the particulars appear .   . 8,742*l*. 1*s*. 2*d*.

Regiment of Sir Fra. Drake, Knt.

Emptions and provisions, viz., of canvas, masts, timber, boards, planks, and such like, 1,322*l*. 5*s*. 4*d*. ; water carriage, 83*l*. 3*s*. ; wages and entertainments, 201*l*. 6*s*. 8*d*.; task works, 330*l*. 4*s*. 9*d*., and rewards, 160*l*. 4*s*. 6*d*. ; in all, as by the particulars appear, 2,445*l*. 17*s*. 5*d*.

Regiment under Sir Martin Frobiser.

Emptions and provisions, viz., of anchors, iron works, flags, ensigns, leadline &c., and such like, 223*l*. 6*s*. 11*d*. ; carriage, 8*l*. 10*s*. 6*d*. ; task works, 72*l*. 6*s*. 8*d*. ; travelling charges, 54*l*. 1*s*. 7*d*. ; in all, as by the particulars   .   .   . 436*l*. 10*s*. 8*d*.

---

[1] MS. has 'record,' which is nonsense ; a blunder of the copying clerk.

A new supply.

Emptions and provisions, viz., of pinnaces, boats, masts, oars, sails, canvas, anchors, cordage, iron work &c., and such like, 3,108*l.* 0*s.* 8½*d.* ; carriages, 16*l.* 14*s.* 10*d.* ; wages and entertainments, 26*l.* 9*s.* 4*d.* ; task works, 176*l.* 10*s.* 10*d.* ; travelling charges, 15*l.* 14*s.* 4*d.* ; in all, as by the particulars thereof appear . . . . 3,379*l.* 8*s.* 0½*d.*

MISCELLANEOUS ACCOUNTS.

[Pipe Office Declared Accounts,[1] 2224.]

Prest, conduct, and coat money of mariners, gunners, and soldiers from divers places prested to serve in the aforesaid ships, viz. in calling to service after the rate of 1*d.* the man for every mile, according to the distance of the places from whence they were prested, 2,295*l.* 13*s.* 1*d.* ; together with the prest, conduct, and coat money of the several retinues, viz. of the Right Honourable the Lord Charles Howard, Lord Admiral 120*l.* ; the Lord Henry Seymour, 60*l.* ; the Lord Thomas Howard, 30*l.* ; the Lord Edmund Sheffield, 30*l.* ; Edward Fenton, Esq., 20*l.* ; George Beeston, Esq., 15*l.* ; Benjamin Gonson, Esq., 15*l.* ; and Sir Robert Southwell, Sir William Wynter, knight, and William Borough, Esq., 90*l.*

In all . . 2,275*l.* 13*s.* 1*d.*

Conduct homewards being discharged from service at ½*d.* the mile to every man 123*l.* 9*s.* ; and for

---

[1] For 1587. These volumes contain the naval accounts for each year in full detail. A few only of the entries are here given, those being selected which have some interest besides the market price of stores.

the charge of the presters for presting of the said mariners, gunners, and soldiers, 151*l.* 4*s.* 2*d.*

In all the sum of 2,950*l.* 6*s.* 3*d.*

Anthony Jenkinson[1] Esq., for his pains and charges sustained in attending the Council's pleasure by the space of 6 weeks for her Majesty's service intended on the Narrow Seas, with sundry her Highness' ships under his charge, the sum of 20*l.*

Diets to Thomas Lane and 135 other mariners by the space of one day, being the 12th of June, 1587, attending at Deptford Strand for the launching of the Ark Ralegh, by agreement of the said officers of her Highness' ships, the sum of 71*s.* 2*d.*

William Byford, upholster, for the trimming of the captain's cabin and others for gentlemen in her Highness' ship the Vanguard, being garnished with green cotton,[2] finding at his own charges all manner of stuff and workmanship .   .   . 15*l.* 8*s.* 8*d.*

William Byford upholster, for the trimming of the captain's cabin in the Ark Ralegh, finding at his own charges all manner of green cotton,[2] darnix,[3] lace, copper nails, tacks, curtain rings, green and yellow fringe, mockado[4] and other necessaries, with the workmanship thereto belonging . . 39*l.* 6*s.* 8*d.*

---

[1] The celebrated Russian traveller and merchant. He did not actually have any naval employment at this time, though his name occurs in lists drawn up in 1587, of sea-captains available for the Queen's service.

[2] This early use of 'cotton,' probably some sort of chintz, is noticeable. Whether the colour green was a reference to the Tudor liveries, green and white, or mere fancy must be uncertain.

[3] A coarse sort of damask used for curtains &c. : made of different materials—silk, wool, or thread. Originally manufactured at Tournay ; Flemish, *Doornik.*

[4] Mock velvet, made of wool ; similar to what is now known as Utrecht velvet.

[Pipe Office Declared Accounts,[1] 2225.]

Provisions for sea causes extraordinary, for the furniture of divers ships appointed against the Spanish forces, under the charge of the Lord High Admiral of England.

Flags, ensigns, streamers, and pennants &c. bought for the use of her Highness' ships in the foresaid service against the Spanish forces, viz.—

Flags of St. George of divers prices, 32 ; whereof one flag at 4*l.* ; one other at 3*l.* 10*s.* ; 20 flags at 3*l.* the flag, 60*l.* ; one flag at 2*l.* 10*s.* ; 5 flags at 2*l.* the flag, 10*l.* ; and 4 flags at 20*s.* the flag, 4*l.*

	£	s.	d.
All for the flags aforesaid	84	0	0

Ensigns of divers prices, 15 ; whereof one of silk for the Bonavolia, at 8*l.* 6*s.* 8*d.* ; one other of silk for the Rainbow, 5*l.* 6*s.* 8*d.* ; 3 ensigns of fine bewper[2] at 4*l.* every such ensign, 12*l.* ; 2 other ensigns of fine bewper at 3*l.* 10*s.* the ensign, 7*l.* ; 4 other ensigns of fine bewper at 3*l.* 6*s.* 8*d.* the ensign, 13*l.* 6*s.* 8*d.* ; two other of fine bewper at 3*l.* the ensign, 6*l.* ; one other of bewper at 2*l.* 12*s.*, and other of bewper at 2*l.* 10*s.*

	£	s.	d.
In all for the ensigns aforesaid	57	2	0

Streamers in all, 70 ; whereof 24 streamers at 22*s.* every streamer,

---

[1] For 1588.

[2] A woollen fabric, similar to, if not quite the same as, the modern bunting.

	£	s.	d.

26*l.* 8*s.* ; and 46 streamers for the Ark,[1] the Victory, the Mary Rose, and the Swallow at 20*s.* the streamer, 46*l.*

In all for the said streamers . . . 72 8 0

Pennants of sundry prices, to discern their company from the enemy, 110; whereof 10 pennants at 20*s.* the pennant, 10*l.*, and 100 other pennants at 25*s.* the piece, 25*l.*

In all for the foresaid pennants . . 35 0 0

More, for 102 yards of calico for flags at 9*d.* the yard. 3 16 6

In all amounteth to the sum of . . 252 6 6

Glass and glazing employed in and about her Majesty's ships, viz. new, 236½ foot, whereof 216½ foot at 6*d.* the foot, 108*s.* 3*d.* ; and 20 foot at 7*d.* the foot, 11*s.* 8*d.*

In all, for new glass 5 19 11

Leading of 127½ foot of old glass, viz. 95½ foot at 3*d.* the foot, 28*s.* 10½*d.*, and 32 foot at 4*d.* the foot, 10*s.* 8*d.*

In all, for new leading . . . 1 19 6½

Mending of 8 casements . . . 2 8

New quarrells[2] set in 485½ quarrells[2] at 1*d.* the piece 2 0 5½

And making and mending of glass and lanterns by agreement, viz. new making of two lanterns, 39*s.* Mending of a lantern, 8*s.*, and for glazing of 10 new casements in the Van-

[1] The Ark, as the ship of the Lord Admiral : the other three, as representing the Hawkyns family.

[2] A quarrell was a pane of glass (Low Lat. *quarellus* ; Norm. Fr. *quarel* ; Fr. *carreau*). It appears here to mean also the frame in which the glass was set.

	£	s.	d.
guard, 18s. 2d., and for mending the glass windows in the Lion, 4s. 10d. | | | |
For mending of glass by agreement . | 3 | 10 | 0 |
In all, for glass and glazing . . | 13 | 12 | 7 |

Overplus of diet,[1] viz. To the Lord Thomas Howard for his diets serving her Majesty as captain in the Ark Ralegh and the Golden Lion against the Spanish forces from the 22nd of December 1587 unto the 25th of August next, being 248 days, after the rate of 20s. per diem, as by a warrant from the Lord Admiral to the treasurer of the ships for payment thereof did appear, amounting to the sum of 248*l.*, whereof 2s. 6d. per diem is borne upon the sea books for the foresaid ships, and the residue, being 17s. 6d. per diem, is by the said warrant here to be allowed, amounting to the sum of 217*l.*

And to the Lord Edmund Sheffield for his like diets, serving her Majesty as captain in the Victory, the Dreadnought, and the White Bear during the whole time aforesaid and after the same rates, and allowed by virtue of the aforesaid warrants, the sum of 217*l.*

Amounting in all to the sum of 434*l.*

[Pipe Office Declared Accounts,[2] 2226.]

William Byford for new laying, repairing, and trimming the captain's cabin in the Ark Ralegh, finding at his own charges all manner of baize, cotton, lace, tacks, thread, &c. . . 6*l.* 18s. 4d.

---

[1] The accounts of the ships for pay are all given. In all, the captain's diet is given at 2s. 6d. per diem. It is not to be supposed that the captain of the Charles, the Moon, or the Golden Hind got the same emoluments as the captain of the Mary Rose or the Hope ; but the difference does not appear in these accounts. No 'overplus of diet' is shown for any but these two.

[2] For 1589.

The said William for the garnishing and lining of the captains' cabins in the Vanguard and the Elizabeth Bonaventure, finding at his own charges all manner of stuff and workmanship . 5*l.* 10*s.* 9*d.*

Lewis Lyzarde and Richard Jackson, painters, for the painting of the Mary Rose, dry-docked at Deptford Strand, the colours being laid with oil and her Majesty's arms, gilded and laid with fine gold, they finding all manner of charges and workmanship . . . . . 65*l.* 0*s.* 0*d.*

LIST OF THE FLEET.

[ccxv. **76.**—Signed. Compared with **ccvi. 59, ccix. 46, ccxiii. 2 II., ccxv. 82, ccxxxvii. 15** (a later copy), **B.M. Harl. MS. 168, f. 176,** and very many other documents.]

[No dependence can be placed on the tonnage of even the Queen's ships; it is given differently in almost every different list, and the differences are sometimes very great. The Triumph, for instance, varies between 900 and 1,100 ; the Victory between 600 and 800 ; the Tiger between 160 and 200 tons. As for the merchant ships, the tonnage, with a few exceptions, is not given in the State Papers, and is here taken from the Harleian MS. referred to, and is probably not more incorrect than that officially given for the Queen's ships. The number of men is official, and, as it was checked by the pay lists and victualling accounts, cannot be very far wrong, though the frequent errors in the arithmetic do not give a favourable impression of the accuracy of the clerk who wrote the list, or of Langford, who attested it. In the partial lists the arithmetic is here corrected, but the abstract at the end is printed as it stands in the MS. The names of the ships are given in modern spelling. Wherever possible, the names of men (here distinguished by a *) are from their signatures ; failing which, from the signatures of known relations—by no means a certain comparison (see vol. i. p. lxxxii)—from the form now in use, or after a careful collation of the different MSS.]

Her Majesty's whole army at the seas against the Spanish forces, in *Anno* 1588 :—

No	Ships' Names	Tons	Men			Total	Captains and Officers
			Mari-ners	Gun-ners	Sol-diers		
1	Ark . .	800	270	34	126	425	The Lord Admiral *Sec.* Sir *Ed. Hoby *Mr.* Thomas Gray *Lt.* Amyas Preston *Capt. of Soldrs.* Morgan *Mr. Gunr.* Saml. Clerke *Btsn.* John Wright *Volrs.* Ri. Leveson Thos. Gerard [Willm.] Harvey [John] Chidley [Thos.] Vavasour *Adml's. men* : Fra. Burnell Newton
2	Elizabeth Bonaventure	600	150	24	76	250	Earl of Cumberland George Raymond *Mr.* James Sewell *Btsn.* *Tristram Searche *Vol.* [Robert Carey]
3	Rainbow .	500	150	24	76	250	Lord *Henry Seymour *Btsn.* *Ri. Laine *Volrs.* Sir Chas. Blount Fra. Carey Brute Brown
4	Golden Lion .	500	150	24	76	250	Lord *Thos. Howard
5	White Bear .	1000	300	40	150	500	Lord Sheffield *Mr.* *Richard Poulter (?) *Lt.* H. Sheffield *Btsn.* Robt. Baxter
6	Vanguard .	500	150	24	76	250	Sir *Willm. Wynter *Lt.* John Wynter
7	Revenge .	500	150	24	76	250	Sir *Fra. Drake *Mr.* John Gray *Lt.* Jonas Bodenham *Prsr.* Martin Jeffrey (?) *Btsn.* Ri. Derrick *Volr.* *Nich. Oseley
8	Elizabeth Jonas	900	300	40	150	500	Sir Robt. Southwell *Mr.** John Austyne (?) *Btsn.* John Woodroffe
9	Victory . .	800	270	34	126	400	Sir John Hawkyns *Mr.* [Barker] (?) *Btsn.* John Edmonds
10	Antelope .	400	120	20	30	160	Sir *Henry Palmer

No.	Ships' Names	Tons	Men			Total	Captains and Officers
			Mari-ners	Gun-ners	Sol-diers		
11	Triumph .	1100	300	40	160	500	Sir *Martin Frobiser *Lt.* Eliot (?) *Btsn.* *Simon Fernandez
12	Dreadnought .	400	130	20	40	200	Sir George Beeston *Btsn.* Harvey
13	Mary Rose .	600	150	24	76	250	Edward Fenton *Btsn.* Lawrence Cleer *Volr.* *Henry Whyte
14	Nonpareil .	500	150	24	76	250	*Thomas Fenner *Btsn.* I. C.
15	Hope . .	600	160	25	85	250	*Robert Crosse *Mr.* John Sampson (?) *Btsn.* *John Vayle
16	Galley Bona-volia	—	—	—	—	250	*William Borough
17	Swiftsure .	400	120	20	40	180	Edward Fenner *Btsn.* Willm. Mychell
18	Swallow .	360	110	20	30	160	*Richard Hawkyns *Btsn.* John Borman
19	Foresight .	300	110	20	20	160	Chr. Baker *Btsn.* *James Andrews
20	Aid . .	250	90	16	14	120	W. Fenner *Prsr.* Richard Blucke (?) *Btsn.* John Russell
21	Bull . .	200	80	12	8	100	Jeremy Turner *Btsn.* *Myhyll Pyrkyne
22	Tiger . .	200	80	12	8	100	John Bostocke
23	Tramontana .	150	55	8	7	70	Luke Ward *Btsn.* *John Pratte
24	Scout . .	120	55	8	7	70	Henry Ashley
25	Achates .	100	45	8	7	60	Gregory Riggs
26	Charles .	70	36	4	—	45	John Roberts *Volr.* [Willm. Monson]
27	Moon . .	60	34	4	—	40	Alexr. Clifford
28	Advice . .	50	31	4	—	40	John Harris *Btsn.* Tristram George
29	Merlin . .	50	20	4	—	35	Walter Gower
30	Spy . .	50	31	4	—	40	Ambrose Ward
31	Sun . .	40	26	4	—	30	*Mr.* Richard Buckley
32	Cygnet . .	30	—	—	—	20	*Mr.* John Sheriff *Btsn.* *Geo. Wilkynson
33	Brigandine .	90	—	—	—	35	Thomas Scott
34	George hoy .	100	16	4	—	24	*Mr.* Ri. Hodges

Merchant ships appointed to serve westwards under
the charge of Sir Francis Drake :—

No.	Ships' Names	Tons	Men	Captains and Officers
35	Galleon Leicester .	400	160	George Fenner
36	Merchant Royal .	400	160	Robert Flicke
37	Edward Bonaventure	300	120	James Lancaster
38	Roebuck. . .	300	120	Jacob Whiddon
39	Golden Noble . .	250	110	Adam Seager
40	Griffin . . .	200	100	William Hawkyns
				Mr. Samuel Norfolk
41	Minion . . .	200	80	William Wynter
				Mr. Nicholas Maunder
42	Bark Talbot . .	200	90	*Henry Whyte
				Mr. John Hampton
43	Thomas Drake .	200	80	Henry Spindelow
				Mr. John Tranton
44	Spark . . .	200	90	William Spark
				Mr. Richard Loarie
45	Hopewell . .	200	100	John Marchant
46	Galleon Dudley .	250	96	James Erisey
47	Virgin God save her	200	70	John Greynvile
48	Hope Hawkyns .	200	80	John Rivers
				Mr. Roger Haley
49	Bark Bond . .	150	70	William Poole
				Mr. John Rock
50	Bark Bonner . .	150	70	Charles Cæsar
				Mr. William Loggin
51	Bark Hawkyns .	150	70	Prideaux
				Mr. William Snell
52	Unity . . .	80	40	Humphrey Sydenham
				Mr. William Cornish
53	Elizabeth Drake .	60	30	*Thomas Cely
				Mr. Thomas Clerke
54	Bark Buggins . .	80	50	John Langford
55	Elizabeth Founes .	80	50	Roger Grant
56	Bark St. Leger .	160	80	John St. Leger
57	Bark Manington .	160	80	Ambrose Manington
58	Hearts-ease . .	—	24	Hannibal Sharpham
59	Golden Hind . .	50	30	*Thomas Flemyng
60	Makeshift . .	60	40	Piers Lemon
61	Diamond of Dart-mouth	60	40	Robert Holland
62	Speedwell . .	60	14	*Mr.* Hugh Hardinge
63	Bear Yonge . .	140	70	John Yonge
64	Chance . . .	60	40	James Founes
				Mr. Hugh Cornish
65	Delight . . .	50	40	William Coxe
66	Nightingale . .	40	30	John Grisling
				Mr. Habakkuk Percy
67	Small caravel . .	30	20	—
68	Flyboat Yonge .	50	50	Nicholas Webb

34 ships ; 2,294 men.

Ships set forth and paid upon the charge of the City of London.

No.	Ships' Names	Tons	Men	Captains and Officers
69	Hercules .	300	120	George Barne
70	Toby	250	100	Robert Barrett
71	Mayflower	200	90	Edward Bancks
72	Minion .	200	90	John Dale
73	Royal Defence	160	80	John Chester
74	Ascension	200	100	John Bacon
75	Gift of God	180	80	Thomas Luntlowe
76	Primrose	200	90	Robert Bringborne
77	Margaret and John .	200	90	John Fisher
				Mr. John Nash
				Lt. *Ri. Tomson
				Volr. John Watts
78	Golden Lion .	140	70	Robert Wilcox
79	Diana .	80	40	Edward Cock
80	Bark Burr	160	70	John Serocold
81	Tiger	200	90	William Cæsar
82	Brave	160	70	William Furthow
83	Red Lion	200	90	Jervis Wilde
84	Centurion	250	100	Samuel Foxcraft
85	Passport .	80	40	Chr. Colthurst
86	Moonshine	60	30	John Brough
87	Thomas Bonaventure	140	70	William Aldridge
88	Release .	60	30	John King
89	George Noble .	120	80	*Henry Bellingham
				Mr. Richard Harper
90	Anthony .	100	60	George Harper
				Mr. Richard Dove
91	Toby	120	70	Christ. Pigot
				Mr. Robert Cuttle
92	Salamander	110	60	Damford
				Mr. William Goodlad
93	Rose Lion	100	50	Bar. Acton
				Mr. Robert Duke
94	Antelope .	120	60	Denison
				Mr. Abraham Bonner
95	Jewel	110	60	Rowell
				Mr. Henry Rawlyn
96	Pansy	100	70	*Mr.* William Butler
97	Prudence	120	60	*Mr.* Richard Chester
98	Dolphin .	110	70	*Mr.* William Hare

30 ships and barks ; 2,180 men.

Merchant ships serving under the charge of the
Lord Admiral, and paid by her Majesty :—

These 8 served about 7 weeks in her Majesty's pay :

No.	Ship's Names	Tons	Men	Captains and Officers
99	Susan Parnell . .	220	80	Nicholas Gorges
100	Violet . . .	220	60	Martin Hawkes
101	Solomon . . .	170	80	Edmund Musgrave
102	Anne Frances . .	180	70	Charles Lister
103	George Bonaventure	200	80	Eleazar Hickman
104	Jane Bonaventure .	100	50	Thos. Hallwood
105	Vineyard . . .	160	60	Benj. Cooke
106	Samuel . . .	140	50	John Vassall

These ships and barks following served the whole
time only for her Majesty's pay :

No.	Ships' Names	Tons	Men	Captains and Officers
107	White Lion . .	140	50	Charles Howard
108	Disdain . . .	80	45	Jonas Bradbury
109	Lark . . .	50	20	[Thos.] Chichester
110	Edward of Maldon .	186	30	Willm. Pierce
111	Marigold . .	30	12	*Mr*. Willm. Newton
112	Black Dog . .	20	10	*Mr*. John Davis
113	Katharine . .	20	10	—
114	Fancy . . .	50	20	*Mr*. John Paul
115	Pippin . . .	20	8	—
116	Nightingale . .	160	16	*Mr*. John Doate

The 15 ships that transported victuals westward:

No.	Ships' Names	Men	Captains and Officers
117	Mary Rose . . .	70	Francis Burnell *Mr.* William Parker
118	Elizabeth Bonaventure .	60	Richard Start
119	Pelican	50	John Clarke
120	Hope	40	John Skinner
121	Unity	40	John Moore
122	Pearl	50	Lawrence Moore
123	Elizabeth of Leigh . .	60	William Bower
124	John of London . .	70	Richard Rose
125	Bearsabe . . .	60	Edward Bryan
126	Marigold . . .	50	Robert Bowers
127	White Hind . . .	40	Richard Browne
128	Gift of God . . .	40	Robert Harrison
129	Jonas	50	Edward Bell
130	Solomon . . .	60	George Street
131	Richard Duffield . .	70	William Adams

33 ships and barks ; 1,561 men.

Coasters under the charge of the Lord Admiral, and paid by her Majesty :—

No.	Ships Names	Tons	Men	Captains and Officers
132	Bark Webb . .	80	50	—
133	John Trelawney .	150	30	Thomas Meek
134	Hart of Dartmouth .	60	70	James Houghton
135	Bark Potts . .	180	80	Anthony Potts
136	Little John . .	40	20	Lawrence Clayton
137	Bartholomew of Apsam	130	70	Nicholas Wright
138	Rose of Apsam .	110	50	Thomas Sandye
139	Gift of Apsam . .	25	20	—
140	Jacob of Lyme .	90	50	—
141	Revenge of Lyme .	60	30	Richard Bedford
142	Bark of Bridgwater .	70	30	John Smyth
143	Crescent of Dartmouth	140	75	
144	Galleon of Weymouth	100	50	Richard Miller
145	John of Chichester .	70	50	John Young
146	Katharine of Weymouth	66	30	
147	Hearty Anne . .	60	30	John Wynnall
148	Minion of Bristol .	230	110	John Sachfield
149	Unicorn of Bristol .	130	66	James Langton
150	Handmaid of Bristol	80	56	Christ. Pitt
151	Aid of Bristol . .	60	26	William Megar

20 ships and barks ; 993 men.

Coasters appointed under the Lord Henry Seymour, whereof some were paid by her Majesty, but the greatest part by the port towns, according as order was taken :—

No.	Ships' Names	Tons	Men	Captains and Officers
152	Daniel　.　.　.	160	70	Robert Johnson
153	Galleon Hutchins　.	150	60	Thomas Tucker
154	Bark Lamb　.　.	150	60	Leonard Harbell
155	Fancy　.　.　.	60	30	Richard Fearne
156	Griffin　.　.　.	70	35	John Dobson
157	Little Hare　.　.	50	25	Matthew Railstone
158	Handmaid　.　.	75	35	John Gattenbury
159	Marigold　.　.	150	70	Francis Johnson
160	Matthew　.　.	35	16	Richard Mitchell
161	Susan　.　.　.	40	20	John Musgrave
162	William of Ipswich .	140	50	Barnaby Lowe
163	Katharine of Ipswich	125	50	Thomas Grymble
164	Primrose of Harwich	120	40	John Cardinal
165	Anne Bonaventure　.	60	50	John Conny
166	William of Rye　.	80	60	William Coxon
167	Grace of God　.　.	50	30	William Fordred
168	Elizabeth of Dover .	120	70	John Lidgen
169	Robin of Sandwich .	110	65	William Cripps
170	Hazard of Feversham	38	34	Nicholas Turner
171	Grace of Yarmouth .	150	70	William Musgrave
172	Mayflower　.　.	150	70	Alexander Musgrave
173	William of Colchester	100	50	Thomas Lambert
174	John Young　.　.	60	30	Reynold Veysey

23 ships and barks ; 1,090 men.

Voluntary ships that came into the fleet after the coming of the Spanish forces upon our coast, and were paid by her Majesty for the time they served :—

No.	Ships' Names	Tons	Men	Captains and Officers
175	Sampson.　.　.	300	108	John Wingfield
176	Frances of Fowey　.	140	60	John Rashley
177	Heathen of Weymouth	60	[30]	—
178	Golden Ryall of Weymouth	120	[50]	—
179	Bark Sutton of Weymouth	70	40	Hugh Pearson
180	Carouse　.　.　.	50	25	—

No.	Ships' Names	Tons	Men	Captains and Officers
181	Samaritan of Dartmouth	250	100	—
182	William of Plymouth	120	60	—
183	Gallego of Plymouth	30	20	—
184	Bark Halse .	60	40	Grinfild Halse
185	Unicorn of Dartmouth	76	30	Ralph Hawes
186	Grace of Apsham .	100	50	Walter Edney
187	Thomas Bonaventure	60	30	John Pentire
188	Rat of Wight . .	80	60	Gilbert Lee
189	Margaret. . .	60	46	William Hubbard
190	Elizabeth . .	40	30	—
191	Raphael . . .	40	40	—
192	Flyboat . . .	60	40	—
193	John of Barnstable .	—	65	—
194	Greyhound of Aldborough	—	40	—
195	Elizabeth of Lowestoft	90	30	—
196	Jonas of Aldborough	—	25	—
197	Fortune of Aldborough	—	25	—

23 ships and barks ; 1,044 men.

An Abstract :

		Men
34 of her Majesty's ships, great and small .		6,705
34 merchants' ships with Sir Francis Drake, westward		2,294
30 ships and barks paid by the city of London		2,130
33 ships and barks with 15 victuallers, under the Lord Admiral		1,651
20 coasters, great and small, under the Lord Admiral, paid by the Queen . .		993
23 coasters under the Lord Henry Seymour, paid by the Queen		1,093
23 voluntary ships, great and small . .		1,059
		15,925

Totalis : 197 ships, 15,925 men.

ROG. LANGFORD.

NOTES ON THE LIST OF THE FLEET.

Ships.

The following details have been gathered from many different documents in the Public Record Office and the British Museum. But the mass of these is so great that, notwithstanding the assistance which the Editor has received from Mr. Oppenheim, the examination of them has been far from exhaustive, and further research may very possibly modify some of the statements. It may be well to explain at the outset that the term rebuilding, which continued in use till the middle of the eighteenth century, had a very wide and varied signification, and meant almost any thing the authorities chose, from a slight repair to absolute breaking up and working such of the timber as was found serviceable into a new ship, of totally different lines and tonnage.

1. Built by Richard Chapman for Sir Walter Ralegh. Launched June 12, 1587 (*ante*, p. 319). Before she was launched, she was sold to the Queen for 5,000*l.*, which amount was, in 1592, struck off Ralegh's debt to the crown (*S.P. Dom. Eliz.* ccxlii. 21). It will be noticed that in the letters here printed Howard always calls her simply the Ark. Hawkyns frequently calls her the Ark Ralegh, i.e. Ralegh's Ark, in the same way that the Thomas (No. 43) is, in the list, called the Thomas Drake, or the Hope (No. 48) is called the Hope Hawkyns. She was sometimes, but as yet very rarely, spoken of as the Ark Royal ; later on, this name became more common. In 1596 she again carried the flag of the Lord Admiral in the expedition to Cadiz. In 1608 she was rebuilt, and renamed the Anne Royal. She carried the flag of Lord Wimbledon in the expedition to Cadiz in 1625, and got home with great difficulty, leaking like a sieve. It does not appear that she was ever at sea afterwards, and in April 1636, while lying in the Thames, she bilged on her own anchor and sank. She was raised, but on examination was found so much damaged and so decayed that she was judged not worth repairing, and was broken up.

2. Built in 1561 and named the Elizabeth Bonaventure, expressing a confidence in the future, as the Elizabeth Jonas (see *post*, No. 8) had been named in prayerful gratitude for the past. She was more commonly called simply the Bonaventure. Rebuilt in 1581. No ship of the time had such continuous and distinguished service. She was Drake's flagship in the West Indies in 1585–6, and at Cadiz in 1587. In 1590 she was commanded by Thomas Fenner in the expedition to the coast of Portugal under Hawkyns, and by Crosse in 1591 in the voyage to the Azores under Lord Thomas Howard. In 1595–6 she was with Drake and Hawkyns in the West Indies. In 1597 she was with Essex in the Islands voyage, her captain being Sir William Harvey. Broken up about 1610.

3. Built by Peter Pett, at Deptford, in 1586 (cf. vol. i. p. xlvi). She, as well as the Vanguard (No. 6), is described by Monson (p. 321) as 'low and snug in the water,' 'like a galleass,' though the San Lorenzo is spoken of (vol. i. p. 348) as high out of the water. Henry Bellingham was her captain in Drake's expedition to Cadiz in 1587 ; Sir George Beeston commanded her in 1590, in the expedition to the coast of Portugal. In 1594 she was at Brest, with Frobiser, under the command of Thomas Fenner ; in 1596 was at Cadiz, commanded by Sir Francis Vere ; and in 1597 was in the Islands voyage, commanded by Sir William Monson. Was partly rebuilt in 1602 ; and rebuilt as a larger ship in 1618.

4. More commonly called the Lion. Built in 1557 ; rebuilt in 1582. Portugal, 1590 ; Azores, 1591 ; with the Earl of Cumberland, 1593 ; Cadiz, 1596 ; Islands voyage, 1597. Broken up in 1609.

5. More commonly called the Bear. Built in 1563. Like the others of the four great ships, she was thought too big for foreign service, and was not again employed during the war. She was rebuilt in 1600.

6. Built by Matthew Baker, at Woolwich, in 1586 (cf. vol. i. p. xlvi). Was commanded by Frobiser in 1594 in the attack on Crozon, when he received his mortal wound. Cadiz, 1596. Rebuilt in 1615. Was vice-admiral, commanded by Sir Richard Hawkyns, in Mansell's expedition to Algiers in 1620. Rebuilt as a larger ship in 1630.

7. Launched at Deptford in 1577. Carried Drake's

flag in 1589, and Frobiser's in 1590. Was captured at the
Azores by the Spaniards on September 1, 1591, after a
stubborn fight, which has been celebrated in immortal prose
and glowing verse ; and sank five days afterwards. According to Monson (Churchill's *Voyages*, iii. 194), judging by
'the Revenge's precedent misfortunes, she was designed,
from the hour she was built, to receive some fatal blow ;
for to her, above all other her Majesty's ships, there
happened these unfortunate accidents : In 1582, in her
return out of Ireland, where she was admiral, she struck
upon a sand, and escaped by miracle. Anno 1586, at Portsmouth, being bound upon a southern expedition, coming
out of the harbour she ran aground, and against the
expectation of all men was saved, but was not able to
proceed upon her voyage. The third disaster was in 1589,
as she was safely moored in Chatham, where all the
Queen's ship's lay, and as safe, one would think, as the
Queen's chamber ; and yet by the extremity of a storm,
she was unluckily put ashore and there over-set, a danger
never thought on before, or much less happened.'

8. 'The 3 day of July, 1559, the Queen's Grace took
her barge at Greenwich unto Woolwich to her new ship,
and there it was named Elizabeth Jonas, and after her
Grace had a goodly banquet, and there was great shooting
of guns, and casting of fire about made for pleasure' (*Diary
of Henry Machin*, Camden Society, p. 203). The ship
'was so named by her Grace in remembrance of her own
deliverance from the fury of her enemies, from which in
one respect she was no less miraculously preserved than
was the prophet Jonas from the belly of the whale' (*Egerton
MS.* 2642, f. 150). This refers, of course, to the Jonas.
It had been the custom for nearly two hundred years,
and has been so ever since, to name one of the largest
ships in the navy after the reigning sovereign ; so that this
great ship was called the Elizabeth very much as a matter
of course. She was rebuilt in 1598, and carried Lord
Thomas Howard's flag in the Downs in 1599 ; but had no
other service against the enemy, and was sold in 1618.

9. Launched in 1561. In 1586 she was 'altered into
the form of a galleon,' at a cost of 500*l*. Except a voyage
under the command of the Earl of Cumberland in 1589
she had no other service during the war. In 1610 she was

rebuilt as a ship of 1,200 tons and renamed the Prince Royal (*P.O.D.A.*, 2248). After the death of Charles I. the ship's name was again changed to Resolution, as which she bore Blake's flag in the battle of the Kentish Knock, and Monck's in the battles of June 2–3 and July 31, 1653. After the Restoration her name was changed back to Royal Prince; she carried Sir George Ayscue's flag in the Four Days' fight, in the course of which, June 3, 1666, she grounded on the Galloper shoal, and was burnt by the Dutch.

10. Built in 1558. Rebuilt in 1581. She does not seem to have served in any of the principal expeditions during the war. Rebuilt as a larger ship in 1618.

11. Built in 1561. Rebuilt in 1595. Sold out of the service in 1618.

12. Built at Deptford in 1573. Constantly employed through the war. Cadiz in 1587, Thomas Fenner; Portugal, 1589, Thomas Fenner; Brest, 1594, and Cadiz, 1596, Alexander Clifford; Islands, 1597, Sir William Brooke; on the coast of Portugal with Leveson and Monson, 1602, Captain Manwayring (Sir Henry Manwayring, author of the *Seaman's Dictionary*). Rebuilt in 1613. Sold about 1644.

13. Built by Edward Bright in 1556 (*Cott. MS., Julius,* F. iii., f. 105). Rebuilt 1589. Portugal, 1590, Sir John Hawkyns; Cadiz, 1596; Islands, 1597; Portugal, 1602, Captain Slingsby. In 1618 she was made into a wharf at Chatham.

14. Built in 1556 as the Philip and Mary. Rebuilt in 1584, and renamed the Nonpareil. Portugal, 1589, Captain Sackvile; Azores, 1591, Sir Edward Denny; Cadiz, 1596, Sir Robert Dudley; Islands, 1597, Sir Thomas Vavasour; in the Downs, 1599, Sir Robert Crosse; Portugal, 1602, Captain Reynolds. She was again rebuilt in 1603, and her name changed to Nonsuch (*P.O.D.A.*, 2220; 2243).

15. Built in 1558. In 1584 she was 'brought into the form of a galleass' (cf. No. 3). Portugal, 1590, Bostocke; West Indies, 1595–6, Gilbert Yorke; Islands, 1597, Sir Richard Leveson. Rebuilt in 1603, and name changed to Assurance.

16. Built about 1585. Proved quite useless as a ship of war.

17. Built at Deptford in 1573. Portugal, 1589 and 1590 ; Cadiz, 1596, Sir Robert Crosse ; Islands, 1597, Sir Gilly Merrick. Rebuilt in 1607, and name changed to Speedwell (*P.O.D.A.*, 2246). Wrecked in 1624.

18. Built in 1558. Rebuilt in 1580. Condemned in 1603.

19. Built in 1570. Portugal, 1587, William Wynter, jun. ; Azores, 1591, Captain Thomas Vavasour ; at the capture of the great carrack in 1592, Robert Crosse ; West Indies, 1595-6, Wynter. Condemned in 1604.

20. Built in 1561. Appears to have been rebuilt about 1580. West Indies, 1585-6, Frobiser ; Portugal, 1589, William Fenner, who was mortally wounded in the attempt on Lisbon. Condemned in 1603.

21. Built 1570. Condemned 1593.

22. 'So called of her exceeding nimbleness in sailing and swiftness of course'—that is, in anticipation (*Egerton MS.* 2642, f. 150). Built 1570. Condemned 1605.

23. Built by Chapman, at Deptford, in 1586. Cadiz in 1596. Broken up in 1618.

24. Built 1577. Condemned in 1604.

25. Built at Deptford in 1573. Condemned in 1604.

26. Built by Baker, at Woolwich, in 1586. Sold in 1616.

Of the merchant ships there is but little recorded, and that rather by accident than design. The names, too, of many of them can scarcely be considered distinguishing marks.

35. Was built apparently about 1580 as the Galleon Ughtred, the property of Henry Ughtred. In 1582 the Earl of Leicester, in conjunction with Ughtred, Drake, and others, fitted out an expedition designed for the South Seas, in which this ship was the admiral, commanded by Edward Fenton. Her name was then changed, out of compliment to Leicester, who was by far the largest sub-scriber and not improbably became her owner. She was afterwards the rear-admiral with Drake in the West Indies in 1585-6, and was the ship in which Cavendish made his last voyage in 1591.

36, 37. Both of these belonged to the Levant Company, represented by Thomas Cordell, merchant. No. 37 was with Fenton in 1582, commanded by Luke Ward. Both of them sailed in 1591 for India round the Cape of Good Hope,

Lancaster being captain of the Edward Bonaventure. The Merchant Royal came home from the Cape with invalids ; and the Penelope, the admiral of the voyage, went down in a storm off Cape Corrientes. The Edward Bonaventure pursued the voyage alone, and returned safe in 1593 with a very valuable cargo. This was the first voyage to India made by an English ship, and led directly to the foundation of the East India Company.

38. Belonged to Sir Walter Ralegh.

41. In the West Indies in the expedition of 1585–6. She was then commanded by Thomas Cely, presumably the same who, after being in prison for many years at St. Mary Port, commanded the Elizabeth Drake (No. 53) against the Armada.

42. In the West Indies, 1585-6. She was burnt at Calais on the night of July 28–29, 1588.

43. The Thomas belonged to Sir Francis Drake, and was with him in the West Indies, 1585–6, commanded by his brother Thomas. She was burnt at Calais.

47. Belonged to Sir Richard Greynvile.

48. Belonged to William Hart ; was burnt at Calais.

49. In the expedition of 1585–6, commanded by Robert Crosse. Belonged to Sir John Hawkyns. Was burnt at Calais.

50. In the expedition of 1585–6.

59. The pinnace that brought in the news of the Armada being off the Lizard. She must not be confused with the Golden Hind in which Francis Drake went round the world, which was more than twice her size.

63. The Bear, belonged to John Yonge ; was burnt at Calais.

65. Belonged to Sir William Wynter.

77. Belonged to John Watts (*B.M. Lansd. MS.* cxliii. 39). For her size, she took a prominent part in the fighting of the year (see vol. i. p. 346 ; *ante*, pp. 104-8). In 1590 she was one of a squadron of merchantmen coming home from the Mediterranean, and fought a severe action with the Spanish galleys off Cadiz, which they succeeded in beating off. With her, in this action, were ships of the same name as Nos. 74, 84, 100, 101, 106, 131 ; but it cannot be certainly said that all of these were the same ships, though it is probable that they were.

87. 99. 103. Belonged to the Levant Company, represented by Thomas Cordell (*S.P. Dom. Eliz.* ccxix. 86 ; *B.M. Lansd. MS.* cxliii. 33).

107. Appears to have been a Queen's ship.

108. Though spoken of as the Lord Admiral's pinnace, she was really a Queen's ship (see *ante*, p. 241), built by Chapman in 1585. She was the ship that opened the engagement on July 21.

110. Belonged to Edward Pycke—probably Peek.

114. Appears to have been a Queen's ship.

125. The name, sometimes written Bearsabee, has no apparent meaning. Bathsheba is one of many suggestions. Very possibly it was originally a compound, similar to Bear Yonge (No. 63), the last half of which is hopelessly corrupt.

131. Mr. Duffield's ship Richard, one of those with No. 77 in 1590.

137. Apsam, now Topsham.

148-151. Belonged to John Sachfield.

168. In many lists is called Elinathan ; probably a clerical blunder, which has been repeated.

175. Belonged to the Earl of Cumberland.

178. Belonged to Thomas Middleton (see *ante*, p. 118).

193. Belonged to Sir Richard Greynvile.

195. Belonged to Thomas Meldrum. Was burnt at Calais (see *ante*, p. 288).

Men.

Most of the men named in the list, of whom anything is known, have been already noticed and can be referred to in the index. A few notes are here added. The names in brackets are supplied from other sources : they are probably correct, but are not absolutely certain.

2. The Earl of Cumberland held an anomalous position. He is returned in the official list as captain of the E. Bonaventure, but appears to have been, in reality, only a volunteer. There is no mention of his having any pay ; and on the other hand, in the accounts of the ship (*Pipe Office Declared Accounts*, 2225), Raymond is recognised as sole captain and receives the captain's diet. James Sewell (*S.P. Dom. Eliz. Addenda*, xxx. 12) may perhaps be the same as the Captain Sewell spoken of by Monson (p. 175)

as having escaped from the Spanish galleys, in which he had been prisoner for four years, and swum off to the English prior to the attack at Cezimbra on June 3, 1602. The identification is, however, quite uncertain.

5. Richard Poulter was one of the Principal Masters. He is named (*P.O.D.A.* 2226) as master of the White Bear in 1589. That he was so in 1588, with Howard's nephew, is very probable, but doubtful.

7. Martin Jeffrey, purser of the Revenge in 1589 (*P.O.D.A.* 2226); most probably also in 1588.

8. John Austyne, one of the Principal Masters of the Navy (see *ante*, p. 249). It seems natural that Howard, who had one of the Principal Masters in his own ship, should have another with his son-in-law.

9. Captain Barker is said by Hakluyt to have been in command of the Victory. This he certainly was not, but may have been her master.

11. Eliot (see *ante*, p. 249). He may have been the master, or only a volunteer. A Lawrence Eliot was with Drake in the Golden Hind, not improbably the master (*S.P. Dom. Eliz.* cliii. 49). Simon Fernandez was with Amadas in the Virginian voyage of 1584, and in 1585 was master of the Tiger, with Sir Richard Greynvile, the admiral of the expedition. Hakluyt (iii. 253) says that, going into the harbour of Wocokon, 'through the unskilfulness of the master the admiral struck on ground and sunk.' That was on June 29; but as the Tiger sailed for England on August 25 and arrived at Falmouth on October 6, her sinking did not do her much harm.

15. John Sampson (see *ante*, p. 182).

18. Richard Hawkyns, son of Sir John, was captain of the Duck, with Drake in the West Indies, in 1585–6; and in 1590, of the Crane, with his father on the coast of Portugal. In 1593 he sailed in command of the Dainty on a voyage to the South Seas; and in June 1594 was captured in the bay of San Mateo. He was sent a prisoner to Spain, and did not return to England till 1602. In 1620 he was vice-admiral of the expedition against Algiers, under Sir Robert Mansell; and died suddenly in 1622. He was the author of 'Observations in his Voiage into the South Sea,' first published in 1622, and twice reprinted by the Hakluyt Society.

20. Richard Blucke was purser of the Aid in 1589.

26. William Monson, knighted at Cadiz in 1596; after-wards admiral of the Narrow Seas and vice-admiral of England. Author of the *Naval Tracts*. He himself says he was the lieutenant of the Charles; but the Charles was not allowed a lieutenant.

27. Alexander Clifford commanded the Dreadnought at Brest in 1594, and again in the expedition to Cadiz in 1596, when he was knighted.

40. William Hawkyns was probably the son of the Mayor of Plymouth; but the name was not uncommon, and the identification is doubtful.

45. Marchant is spoken of as 'brother,' that is, brother-in-law, of Robert Crosse (Wright's *Queen Elizabeth*, ii. 421).

46. James Erisey, captain of the White Lion in the West Indies in 1585-6. His grandfather, James Erisey, married Christiana, youngest daughter of Roger Greynvile of Stow. This would seem to be an older Roger than Sir Richard Greynvile's father; but the name was common in the family. Erisey himself married Elizabeth, daughter of Thomas Carew of Anthony (*Visitation of Cornwall*, 1620, Harl. Soc. pp. 160-4).

51, 82, 93. Prideaux, Furthow, Acton, may probably be identified with the men of these names who were with Lane in Virginia in 1585-6 (Hakluyt, iii. 254).

77. John Watts (see vol. i. p. 350), a wealthy merchant and ship-owner; knighted in 1603, Lord Mayor in 1606. He married a daughter of Sir James Hawes, Lord Mayor in 1574; and, dying about 1616, left large estates in Norfolk and Herts to his sons.

107. This may have been the Lord Admiral's son; but probably a more distant relation. His name does not appear elsewhere in these papers.

131. In 1598 William Adams sailed as pilot-major of a fleet of merchant ships fitted out from Rotterdam, and after many adventures and hardships arrived in Japan, where he entered the service of the Shogun and was mainly instrumental in the first opening of the country to European trade. He died in Japan in 1620, and three years later the English factory was broken up.

133. A Thomas Meek was in the Golden Hind with Drake in his voyage round the world (*S.P. Dom. Eliz.* cliii. 49).

148. There can be little doubt that this name is a corruption of Sackvile. Probably the Captain Sackvile who commanded the Nonpareil in 1589.

188. The following Report (*B.M. Lansd. MS.* lvii. 25) was not found in time to insert it in its place in the body of the work ; it is of no great importance, and its facts are grossly inaccurate ; but as embodying the current rumours picked up by an intelligent man, is not without interest. The examination was presumably made by the Earl of Sussex, but it is not so stated.

The Report of Mr. Gilbert Lee, lately come from the coast of Spain and arrived here at Portsmouth the 5th of July, 1588.

He saith that upon the 25th of May after their computation, there departed out of Lisbon for England one hundred and threescore sail of small and great ships, viz. four galleys, four galleasses, thirty hulks, thirty small ships, the rest armados and galleons. In the same fleet there is 30,000 footmen beside mariners, which fleet arrived in the Groyne, all saving the thirty hulks, which hulks are yet missing. The vice-admiral of the whole fleet is dead, and the sickness increaseth in the fleet. The general, being the Duke of Medina, hath written to the King to know his pleasure for the proceeding in his voyage. The fleet lieth within the Groyne, in three several roads, three leagues one from another ; and he saith that if there had come but 50 sail of ships, by reason of the sickness and being so dispersed, they might have burned them all. There is a preparation for a second fleet in Lisbon, which shall likewise come for England. The King of Spain and the Turk hath concluded league for a certain time. This news he learned by three several ships, which he stayed and took upon the coast of Biscay ; in one of them this news was confirmed by several Spanish letters directed for Antwerp.

One that is part merchant and a passenger, being in a ship that is here now, saith that he will affirm upon the loss of his life that all this is true. This ship came from Bayona about 20 days past, and saith he left all this whole fleet in the Groyne, saving the 30 hulks that be missing, wherein all the horses be ; since which time he saith they have had no southerly wind whereby the fleet could well come out of the Groyne, until this three or four days ; and upon receipt of the King's answer, they were presently determined to come for England. He saith also that the soldiers and gentlemen that come on this voyage are very richly appointed, assuring themselves of good success ; in so much as they might take up any wares there to repay it upon the booty they should take in England. The Duke of Parma did send a ship from Dunkirk to Lisbon, wherein there was an ambassador and four score pilots, upon whose arrival the fleet departed presently.   There was a report there that the Duke of Parma had come with his force out of Flanders and entered the Thames and taken London without resistance, whereupon they were about to make bonfires.

The Englishmen that be in Spain do report very foul speeches of the Queen's Majesty ; and they and the Spaniards desire but to set foot on land and all shall be theirs. He saith they made a just account to be received in Scotland.   He saith also that he met with 25 sail of Frenchmen upon the coast of Biscay, which came from Lisbon, and after some conflict between them and hurt done on both parts, they departed, and whither they went he knoweth not.

I asked Captain Lee whether he saw my Lord Admiral at sea or not, and he saith he saw none of the fleet.

It is not impossible that, whilst staying these merchant vessels and gathering these rumours, Lee did not neglect his own interests.   A series of depositions from Rouen and Dieppe dated in June (*B.M. Lansd. MS.* cxlviii. 148–153) accuse him of plundering a harmless French trader of Rouen ; and a letter from Prince Maurice to the Council (*S.P. Holland,* lvi. August 20) charges him with having seized certain Dutch ships trading to Bayona, brought them to the Isle of Wight, and there sold their goods without any legal process.   On the other hand, it is quite possible that the ships and goods were, under the circumstances, lawful prize.   The evidence in support of Lee's claim, or the decision of the Admiralty Court, has not been found ; but the French depositions distinctly name the Rat, and there is no doubt that the Rat was, at the time, in the Queen's service.

APPENDIX A.

CAPTAIN CELY'S LETTERS FROM PRISON IN ST. MARY PORT.

December 12, 1579.—*TO THE QUEEN.*

[**S.P. Spain, xvi.**—Holograph.]

In Andalusia, the 12th of December, in Puerto Santa Maria, 1579.

My duty remembered, your poor obedient servant, Thomas Cely of Bristol, wisheth your Majesty health and prosperity to God's good will and pleasure, Amen. For that my bringing up hath not been such to write dutily unto your Majesty, I crave pardon if my pen run astray, for that I am where I cannot attain to counsel, neither will I that any man shall understand that I write, for that I am sworn by the Inquisition of Spain neither to speak, neither yet to write nothing touching the secrets of the Inquisition or their house, where I was three years in close prison, for God's cause and yours, and all my goods taken from me most unjustly ; for God I take to witness, I never did anything contrary to Spain in all the days of my life.

Notwithstanding these great injuries, they have condemned me to the galleys for four years. Three of them within 2 months be past. My friends hath procured your Majesty's favourable letters for me, but they do not avail, but I pray God I may be thankful for your Highness's good will towards me. There is in the galley where I am a woman, which woman is a courtesan, and is daily in the company with the captains where she doth hear much.

She is of Alexandria and is *amiga* to one of the captains of the infantry. This woman doth talk with me very often, and I make fair weather with her, and for such talk as passeth with the captains I am sure to understand. I am in one of the chambers in the galley where I do her pleasure to suffer her friends to talk with her, so she doth what she can for me. I thought it good to move your Majesty, for that their communications hath been such that a-force I must needs venture my life to write, for that they touch your Majesty and your country very much.

I do think it good to trouble my Lord Treasurer with these affairs, for that I will not trouble your head with a long letter. My Lord Treasurer's wise and politic head will, with forty words, put into your head more in a quarter of an hour than I shall with writing of 10 sheets of paper. I have written unto your Majesty 2 letters touching other affairs; but I wrote in the last letter, which I sent by one Pease of Weymouth, that I would be worth a hundred thousand pounds a year to your subjects and forty thousand pounds a year to your coffers. I hear nothing from you. I fear you doubt I work for my liberty. Truly liberty I desire, and one year I have to accomplish and 2 months, and have nothing but ill biscuit and water: but my trust is in God, to attain to my country; and if I may be heard, I trust God will give me the grace to accomplish my word, if not, strike off my head as a traitor.

I am in a galley called the Estrella, otherwise called the Espera, in misery. I thank God I am whole of my rackings. All my study in close prison hath been for your common wealths. Send me, for God's love, to pass this year to come, and bear with my rude and bold manners. I marvel you have not the fruitfullest [1] island in the world. You may if you will put to your hands.

I would fain copy out this letter for that I doubt your Majesty will be troubled with reading of it. Have patience [2] with you, and take some pains with reading of it, for that I dare not write any longer. This I omit, committing your Majesty to God's good will and pleasure, Amen, and all his elect wheresoever. My prayer daily you have and shall have, as my bounden duty. Peruse my Lord Trea-

---

[1] MS. frutefools.   [2] MS. pasie.

surer's letter, and keep well the Queen of Scots, and sure. This counsel I need not give, but my pen will not otherwise do. I beseech God give me the grace to see the court of England ere I die.

Your poor obedient servant,
THOMAS CELY of Bristol,
Of your guard extraordinary.

December 12, 1579.—*TO LORD BURGHLEY.*

[**S.P. Dom. Eliz. Add. xxvi. 35.**—Holograph.]

Laus Deo.

In Andalusia in Puerto Santa Maria, the 12th of December, 1579.

Right Honourable my duty remembered.—For that I am where I cannot have time to write dutily,[1] for God's love bear with my hasty inditing if my pen run astray. Read the Queen's letter first, so shall your Honour pick out some matter and the meaning of my good will towards my Sovereign Lady and Mistress, and towards her honourable Council and her whole dominions. First to touch the great preparation for war with us now making ready in Spain, but whither, or for what place, God knows. Some says it is to conquer Portugal[2] by sword; some says it is for Algiers in Barbary; others says it is for El Arish[3] and Tetuan[4] in Barbary, two ports where the galliots do harbour. This woman hath told[5] me that she hath heard the captains say it is only[6] for Ireland[7] or for Flanders; farther they say that they shall have great aid out of Scotland and Ireland, and that there be some more of their friends in the north part of England; and a worse matter than all this she hath heard them say, that there will be means made to set the navy on fire. God forfend!

[1] MS. dewtely.
[2] MS. Portyngegaell. Portugal was actually conquered and annexed in 1580.
[3] MS. Alarache.   [4] MS. Twetwan.
[5] MS. toweld.   [6] MS. wonly.   [7] MS. Erland.

Disperse them, for God's love, in time, some in one place,[1] and some in another.   I need not to counsel your Honours.

They be not ashamed to say that there be daily of the Council, waiting upon the Queen, that will be ready to help them.   I pray God give them better grace.[2]   I trust the Queen will be careful of herself, and her honourable Council will, I doubt not, have great care of these affairs. If the Queen's Majesty will do in England as they do now in Spain, I think she should do very well.   All the Moriscoes that they do mistrust in Spain, they do remove them a hundred leagues from their country,[3] some to one place and some to another.   So may the Queen enquire of suspected persons, and remove them, and put others[4] in their room ; I say in the north part of England and Wales and Ireland and elsewhere.   Good my Lord, bear with me.   The very zeal I bear unto my mistress and unto my country moveth me to write.   I well know there is careful heads of her Council[5] ; and I am sure there is a great grudge borne[6] unto England, for Englishmen did the Spaniards great injury in Flanders, as they say.[7]

There is great store of fireworks made, great store of scaling ladders, great provision of yokes to draw ordnance by mules and horses, and terrible[8] cannons and many, with all other provision for wars.   One thing there is provided which makes me to muse : four thousand ploughs for tillage, which is made ready in Cartagena : all other provision I have seen ; but those I have not seen, but I have heard 20 soldiers talk of them, which be accounted of credit.   They embarge in Italy all the great shipping and in Mallorca and in other parts of the Straits[9] ; and in Cadiz[10] they have embarged[11] 16 great ships of Genoa[12] and of other parts.   Notwithstanding all this, there is no money for soldiers, and great scarcity of victual.   A soldier is allowed 24 ounces of ill biscuit, which is sufficient[13] if it were good ; but for meat, they have but 2 ounces of peas and 6 ounces of newland[14] fish, or 6 ounces of salt tunny[15]

---

[1] MS. plaes.   [2] MS. graes.   [3] MS. contre.
[4] MS. pot wothers.   [5] MS. Cowencell.
[6] MS. ys a gret gruege boren.
[7] Rymenam was fought on August 1, 1578.   [8] MS. tyreble.
[9] The Mediterranean.   [10] MS. Caels.   [11] MS. ynbargyd.
[12] MS. Jenaweys.   [13] MS. sofysien.
[14] Newfoundland.   [15] MS. sawelte toney.

or 6 ounces of bacon, which comes once in a month; and they should have 10[1] ounces of fresh flesh every Sunday, but it is [seldom][2] that it comes. Wheat is here worth 23 ry[als] a hanik. There comes hither much English wheat. [I][2] do believe your Honour do not know of it. It we[re well][2] done to give order to your officers and let[3] them forci[bly]. If I had liberty I would do you to understand [great][2] things. I lack some trifle present to give my [guard].[2] If I had it, I should go ashore when I list, as [others][2] do of my countrymen. Great pity it is that a tr[ue] subject, doing his prince's commandment, should lose all his goods and to be tormented and made a galley slave for 7 years, three in close prison and four in the galleys. I have lost little less than [two][2] thousand ducats, besides my cruel torments, and [wife][2] and children undone for ever. God mend it when His [good][2] will and pleasure is.

My Lord, there is here great talk how that the King of France's brother is a suitor unto the Queen's Majesty. They doubt the making away of the King of France[4] and then, say they, if [France] and England join together it will grow to a foul piece of work. The common people be afeared of their own shadow.

I beseech your Honour bear with my rude and bold manners, and desire the Queen's Majesty to be good unto me. My duty and conscience hath moved me to write these few lines, for that I am her servant and beareth good will to my country. This I omit, committing your Honour to God and to His Holy Word. Your Honour may always hear of me in this port, at the house of one Thomas Butlers, an Englishman and here a dweller.

Your poor orator,

THOMAS CELY of Bristol.

Written in haste.

Good my Lord, have patience with you in reading, for that it is ill written. Consider where I am, in a miserable prison.

---

[1] Doubtful. The x is clear, but as the edge of the paper is torn, it is uncertain whether it was not followed by ii.

[2] Conjecture. The edge of the MS. torn away.

[3] Hinder.   [4] MS. Frawens.

APPENDIX B.

THE TRADE.

Down to the beginning of the seventeenth century, the Trade was the recognised name of the sea immediately outside Brest, the inshore part of the Broad Sound, now known as the Passage de l'Iroise. It is so marked in the Mercator's Atlas of 1616. The earliest mention of it, as yet noted, is in 1338 (Rymer's *Fœdera*, orig. edit., iv. 836), when complaint was made on behalf of the King of Spain, that certain English mariners of the ship Margaret of Southampton meeting a Spaniard named Juan Gomes 'in loco vocato la Trade Sancti Mathæi,' had plundered him of merchandise and goods to the value of 40*l*. sterling. Many instances of the name occur in the State Papers of Henry VIII., showing it in common use in English ; but as the previous one, so also the following shows that it was at least accepted by foreigners ; though the word *ultra* seems to point out the English origin of these sentences. . In the treaty concluded in 1511 between Henry VIII. and Ferdinand of Aragon, it is agreed that, for the guard of the sea, a sufficient number of men and ships of war shall be provided by each of the two kings ; viz.:—the King of England shall furnish 3000 men and ships properly equipped, 'qui mare inter le Trade et ostium Thamisiæ ab incursu inimicorum et hostium pro viribus tuebuntur, custodient et defendent ' ; and similarly the King of Aragon shall furnish 3000 men, 'qui mare ultra le Trade ab incursu inimicorum &c.' (*ib*. xiii. 315).

The history of the name has not been traced with sufficient exactness to render the meaning of it quite certain. It has been suggested that it is a corruption of 'le rade' ; but the Trade could never be a roadstead, nor is it easy to see how 'le rade' could turn into 'le Traad,' so as to be used in formal State Papers. Again 'le raz' is suggested as the origin, with special reference to Saint Mathieu, to which, according to Littré, the name 'raz' distinctively belongs; but to this there is the same difficulty about the change into 'le Traad.' It may, perhaps, seem more probable that the name was English and denoted the route of the trade from England, Flanders and Normandy to Bordeaux and the South of France, which, even before the time of Henry II., was relatively very great, and would certainly keep as close inshore as possible. It will be seen that wherever the trade came from, or wherever it was going to, outward or homeward, it must have passed through the Trade, just as now every ship not bound directly across the Atlantic must pass by Ushant.

By the time of Queen Elizabeth, when the name had dropped out of common use, it seems to have been occasionally extended to the 'fairway' off Ushant. The flyboats that went through the Trade on their way from Rochelle to Holland (vol. i. p. 215) may have been keeping close inshore, but more likely passed outside Ushant; nor does it seem probable that Drake went, with half a score ships, to look for the expected armada (vol. i. p. 246) in the Goulet or the bay of Douarnenez. On the other hand, complaint was made in July 1576 that the admiral of the Queen's ships in the Narrow Seas lay in the Downs, 'and keepeth not the trade where the ships are used to pass to and fro' (Acts of the Privy Council, ix. 170), and Sir George Carey clearly applies the name to the fairway of the Channel (vol. i. p. 324), from which it would seem that the use of the word as denoting the trade route was already becoming general. Its application, in the modern sense, to the Trade winds, is comparatively recent; its limitation to them, still more so. Dampier used the word as meaning a persistent wind, whether permanent or not, and applied it to the African or Indian Monsoons, as well as to the Trade Winds proper. Cook used it only with its modern limitations.

APPENDIX C.

THE SECRETS OF THE [USE] OF GREAT ORDNANCE.

[**Dom. Eliz. ccxlii. 64.**—Signed.]

—	Height of the piece	Weight of the piece	Weight of the shot	Weight of the powder	Breadth of the ladle	Length of the ladle	Number of shot in a last of powder	Point blank by the Quadrant	Random
	inch	lbs.	lbs.	lbs.	inch	inch		paces score	paces
Cannon Royal . . .	8½	7,000	66	30	13¼	24½	80	—	1,930
Cannon	8	6,000	60	27	12	24	85	17	2,000
Cannon Serpentine . .	7½	5,500	53⅓	25	10½	23⅓	96	20	2,000
Bastard Cannon . .	7	4,500	41¼	20	10	23½	120	18	1,800
Demi-Cannon . . .	6½	4,000	30¼	18	9⅓	23¼	133	17	1,700
Cannon Pedro . .	6	3,000	24¼	14	9	23	171	16	1,600
Culverin	5½	4,500	17⅓	12	8½	22⅓	200	20	2,500
Basilisco	5	4,000	15¼	10	7½	22	240	—	—
Demi-Culverin . .	4½	3,400	9⅓	8	6⅓	21	300	20	2,500
Bastard Culverin . .	4	3,000	7	6¼	6	20	388	18	1,800
Saker	3½	1,400	5⅓	5⅓	5½	18	490	17	1,700
Minion	3¼	1,000	4	4	4½	17	600	16	1,600
Falcon of 2⅓″ . . .	2⅓	800	3	3	4¼	15	800	15	1,500
Falconet	2	500	1¼	1¼	3¼	11¼	1,950	14	1,400
Serpentine . . .	1½	400	⅓	⅓	2½	10	7,200	13	1,300
Robinet	1	300	½	½	1½	6	4,800	12	1,000
Falcon	2½	660	2¼	2¼	4¼	15	1,087	15	1,500

The last of powder containeth in weight 2,400 lbs. after five score to the hundred at 16 oz. to the pound.

Forasmuch as there is difference of strength between sundry sorts of powder, that is to say powder usual heretofore for great artillery, and powder in use for small ordnance, as for muskets, calivers, petronels, dags and pistols, the one bearing the name of serpentine powder being in meal only, and in these days corned with some more strength allowed to the same, and is now called cannon corn powder, and the powder usual for small ordnance aforesaid is commonly called by the usual name of fine corn powder, the which is or ought to be in strength and force a quarter more than the powder for great artillery, and if so it happen that you have no more sorts of powder but one for all as is aforesaid, being fine corn powder, to serve the great ordnance, then abate one-fourth part of the allowance of powder as is set down in the rules above specified ; and in like sort, with your rule, compass-callipers and shears, cut off one-fourth part of the length and breadth of your ladle and so charge your ordnance ; for this was often done and tried by John Sheriffe with cannon and culverin at battery, being in her Majesty's service, and found by him by good experience to be just, good, serviceable and without danger.

Per JO. SHERIFFE.

To this account of sixteenth-century ordnance the following titles of books on the subject may be added. They are all in the British Museum.

'Three Books of Colloquies concerning the Art of shooting in great and small pieces of Artillery ; written in Italian by Nicholas Tartaglia, and now translated into English by Cyprian Lucar. Whereunto is annexed a Treatise named Lucar Appendix.' London, 1588, fol.

'The Gunner, showing the whole Practice of Artillery, with all the appurtenances thereunto belonging. By Robert Norton, one of his Majesty's gunners.' London, 1628, fol.

'The Complete Cannonier, or the Gunner's Guide. By John Roberts.' London, 1639, 4°.

APPENDIX D.

Dec. 28, 1585.—*PROPOSED INCREASE OF WAGES.*

[**Dom. Eliz. clxxxv. 33 II.**   Enclosure in a letter from Hawkyns to Lord Burghley.]

The 28th of December 1585.

A note to show the commodity that would grow to her Majesty and country by increasing the wages of the servitors by sea in her Highness' ships.

First.   If it might please her Majesty to allow for the medium of all servitors an increase of 4*s.* 8*d.* the man by the month, it would fall out to be to every man, one with the other, 6*d.* by the day, so as the common man, that had but 6*s.* 8*d.* by the month, shall have 10*s.*, and so every officer will be increased after that rate, a third part more in his wages.

By this mean her Majesty's ships will be furnished with able men, such as can make shift for themselves, keep themselves clear without vermin and noisomeness which breedeth sickness and mortality, all which would be avoided.

The ships would be able to continue longer in the service that they should be appointed unto, and would be able to carry victuals for a longer time.

There is no captain or master exercised in service, but would undertake with more courage any enterprise with 250 able men than with 300 of tag and rag, and assure himself of better success.

The wages being so small causeth the best men to run away, to bribe and make mean to be cleared from the service, and insufficient, unable and unskilful persons supply the place, which discourageth the captains, masters and men, that know what service requireth.

If it shall please her Majesty to yield unto this increase, her Highness' service would be far safer and much bettered, and yet the charge nothing increased.   As for example :—

The charge of the Lion for one month's wages and victuals of 300 men, after the old rate of 23*s*. 4*d*. per man, doth amount unto 350*l*.

The same ship being now furnished with 250 able men, after the new rate of 28*s*. wages and victuals, for every man per mensem, will amount unto (even as before) monthly, 350*l*.

So as all the commodities are obtained without any increase of charge to her Majesty.

The sailors also (in consideration of her Majesty's gracious liberality) shall be bound for to bring into the said service, every man his sword and dagger.

APPENDIX E.

RELATION OF MEDINA-SIDONIA.

[This relation, enclosed in a letter to the king, dated August 11–21, was sent by the hands of Don Baltasar de Zuñiga, who had served on the Duke's personal staff on board the San Martin, and was now described as one who could give full information on all details. Mr. Barrow had access to a copy of the MS., and refers to it as 'Spanish Narrative' (*Life of Drake*, 287), but without knowledge of its author. The original is printed in *La Armada Invencible*, tom. ii. p. 228, from which it is here translated.]

Journal of the armada in the English expedition under the charge of the Duke of Medina-Sidonia, from the time of their sailing from the Groyne.

July[1] 12.]   On the 22nd of July, 1588, the Duke and all the armada departed from the Groyne with a south-west wind, which they held for some days and thereby made good progress.

July 15.]   On the 25th the Duke sent the captain Don Rodrigo Tello to Dunkirk, to advertise the Duke of Parma of his coming, and to bring back word of what state Parma should be in, and where it seemed to him best for them to join their forces.

July 16.]   The 26th at dawn, the weather was calm and cloudy, and so continued until noon, when the wind came from the north, and the armada stood eastwards until midnight, when the wind shifted to WNW. with much rain.   This day the vice-admiral of the galleys, named the

---

[1] Old style, according to the English Calendar.   The dates in the text of the Relation are New Style, according to the Spanish Calendar.

Diana, making much water, separated from the armada and returned to port.[1]

July 17.] The 27th, the same wind but stronger, with a heavy sea, which continued until midnight, whereby many ships were dispersed from the armada, as well as the three other galleys.

July 18.] Thursday, the 28th, the day dawned clear and bright, the wind and sea more quiet than the day before. Forty ships were counted to be missing, and the three galleys. The Duke gave order to sound, which was done in 75 fathoms, 75 leagues from the Scilly Islands; after which he sent away three pinnaces, whereof one should go to the Lizard to see if the missing ships were there, with order for them to stay his coming; another should discover land and examine the same; and the third was to turn back and order all the ships to make more sail, and especially the missing ships if they were found lagging behind.

July 19.] Friday, the 29th, the wind was West. The pinnace which had been to the Lizard returned with news that the missing ships were in front, under the charge of Don Pedro de Valdes, who had collected them and was staying for the armada. At evening all the ships of the armada were joined, except the *capitana*[2] of Juan Martinez, in which was the camp-master Nicolas de Isla, and the three galleys, which it was not known what course they had taken. This same day the coast of England was seen, and was said to be the Lizard.

July 20.] The 30th at dawn, the armada was near with the land, so as we were seen therefrom, whereupon they made fires and smokes. And in the evening the Duke sent the ensign-bearer Juan Gil, in a boat to gain intelligence. In the evening many ships were seen, but by cause of mist and rain, we were unable to count them This night the ensign-bearer Juan Gil, returned with four Englishmen in a boat. The same said they were of Falmouth, and had that evening seen the English fleet go out of Plymouth under the charge of the Admiral of England and of Drake.

July 21.] Sunday, the 31st, at dawn, the wind had

---

[1] She was wrecked near Bayonne.

[2] The Santa Ana, No. 13 in the list, Appendix G.

shifted to the WNW.; 80 ships were discovered in the
weather, and to leeward, near the land, there were 11
others, amongst which were three great galleons, that
fought with some of our ships, and continued turning to
windward until they joined their fleet. Our armada placed
itself in order of battle, and the *capitana* put abroad the
royal standard at the foremast. The enemy's fleet passed,
firing on our van under the charge of Don Alonso de
Leyva, which drove into the rear [1] under the charge of the
Admiral Juan Martinez de Recalde, who stood fast and
abode the assault of the enemy, although he saw that he
was being left unsupported, for that the ships of the rear-
guard were shrouding themselves in the main body of the
armada. The enemy assailed him with great discharging of
ordnance, without closing, whereby his ship suffered much
in her rigging, her forestay was cut, and her foremast had
two great shot therein. In the rear, supporting Juan
Martinez de Recalde, were the Grangil,[2] with D. Diego
Pimentel and D. Diego Enriquez, the Peruvian.[3] The
capitana real struck her fore-topsail and let fly the sheets,
and coming to the wind, awaited the rear to gather it into
the main body of the fleet. Whereupon the enemy drew
off and the Duke collected his fleet, being unable to do
anything more, because the enemy having recovered the

[1] According to Adams' charts, reproduced in Pine's Illustrations, the formation of the Spaniards was a deep crescent, with the
convexity in front, the concavity towards the English. No vanguard or rear-guard is shown; and it is difficult to understand
how a van-guard proper could be driven into the rear-guard, the
main body of the fleet being between them. It seems probable
that, in connection with this formation, the terms were used as
denoting the right and left wings or horns; and so Captain Duro
(i. 78-9) has understood them.

[2] There is no ship of this name in the list. No doubt it means
the Gran-Grin, the *almiranta* of the Biscay squadron (Appendix
G, No. 14).

[3] The Sp. has *el del Peral*, which seems to have no meaning, and is probably a misprint for *del Peru*. He is spoken of afterwards as the 'son of the Viceroy of Peru,' to distinguish him from
another Diego Enriquez, son of the late *commendador* of Alcantara,
who was at first in the *capitana*, and afterwards in the San Juan
de Sicilia. This one, the son of the Viceroy, was in the San Juan
of Diego Flores.

wind, and their ships being very nimble and of such good steerage, as they did with them whatsoever they desired.

This day in the evening, Don Pedro de Valdes ran foul of the ship Catalina of his squadron, so that he spent his bowsprit and his foresail, and withdrew into the main body of the armada to repair the damage. Our fleet continued until 4 in the afternoon endeavouring to recover the wind of the enemy. At this hour, on board the vice-admiral of Oquendo, some of the powder barrels caught fire, and her two decks and her poop were blown up ; in which was the Paymaster General of this armada with part of the King's treasure ; and the Duke seeing this ship remaining behind, turned the *capitana* towards her, and discharged a piece of ordnance, to the end the fleet should do the same, and gave order to send boats to her assistance. The fire was extinguished, and the enemy's fleet, which was standing towards that ship, desisted when they saw our *capitana* bear with her, so as the ship was shrouded and brought into the main body of the armada.

In this casting about, the foremast of Don Pedro's ship was broken off by the hatches, and fell on the main yard. The Duke turned to succour him, by giving him a hawser ; but though great diligence was used, neither weather nor sea permitted of it, and so she was left without sails, because it was now night, and Diego Flores told the Duke that if he shortened sail to stay for her it was not possible for our fleet to see him, because they were much in advance ; and that without doubt, by the morning more than half the fleet would be missing ; and that the enemy's fleet being so near, all the armada should not be imperilled ; esteeming it certain that by shortening sail the expedition would be ruined.[1] Upon hearing this opinion, the Duke ordered Captain Ojeda with four pinnaces to remain by the *capitana*,[2] as also the *almiranta*[3] of Don Pedro, the *capitana*[4] of Diego Flores, and a galleass, so as to take her in tow and remove her people ; but neither the one nor the other was found possible, owing to the heavy sea, the darkness and the weather ; and the Duke proceeded on

[1] For this especially, and his counsel generally Diego Flores, on his return to Spain, was thrown into prison.

[2] Sc. of Don Pedro.   [3] San Francisco.

[4] San Cristóbal.

his course, rejoining the fleet and taking care to keep it united for whatever might happen the following day. This night they removed the wounded and burnt men from the vice-admiral of Oquendo. The sea and wind increased greatly this night.

July 22.] Monday, the 1st of August, the Duke ordered Don Alonso de Leyva to pass with the van and join himself to the rear, thereby making one squadron of the van and the rear, with the three galleasses and the galleons San Mateo, San Luis, Florencia, and Santiago, numbering in all 43 of the best ships of the armada, to confront the enemy, so as there should be no hindrance to our joining with the Duke of Parma ; and the Duke with the rest of the armada should go in the van, so as the whole fleet was divided but into two squadrons, Don Alonso de Leyva taking the rear under his charge, while Juan Martinez refitted his ship, and the Duke having charge of the van.   He called to him all the sergeant majors and commanded them to go in a pinnace, and range the fleet according to the prescribed order, giving it to each of them in writing that they should put every ship in her appointed place, and also that any ship, which did not keep that order, or left her appointed place, that without further stay they should hang the captain of the said ship ; and that for this purpose they should take with them the provost-marshals of the *tercios*[1] and their men ; and that three sergeant majors were to attend to the rear, and the other three to the van, so as the better to carry out this order.

At eleven this same day the captain of the *almiranta* of Oquendo advertised the Duke that the ship was sinking, whereupon the Duke ordered the King's money and the people to be taken out of her and the ship to be sunk.

---

[1] Sp. *los capitanes de campaña.*   In each *tercio*, consisting nominally of 30 companies of 100 men each, one company was told off for police duty, the captain of which had an office roughly equivalent to that of provost marshal.   The order which they were here appointed to carry out marks the extreme subordination of the captains of the ships.   It will be noticed in the course of the Relation that the credit of each ship's action is always given to the officer in command of the soldiers, and that the captain of the ship is never named or referred to, in connection with the fighting.

This day in the evening the Duke despatched the ensign-bearer Juan Gil in a pinnace to the Duke of Parma, to give him advertisement as to where the fleet was.

July 23.] Tuesday, 2nd of August, the day dawned fine, and the enemy's fleet, being to leeward, was standing towards the land, endeavouring as much as they could to recover the wind. The Duke also made a board towards the land in order to keep the weather. The galleasses went with him in the van, and the rest of the fleet followed. The enemy seeing our admiral standing towards the land, and that they could not in this way recover the wind, cast about to seaward ; whereon those of our ships that had the weather of the enemy, bare room with them and assailed them. Captain Bertendona[1] very gallantly as-saulted their admiral, offering to board her ; but as he came near her, she bare room and stood out to sea. In this fight there were also the San Marcos, San Luis, San Mateo, the Rata, Oquendo,[2] San Felipe, San Juan de Sicilia, in which was Don Diego Tellez Enriquez, who had been in fight with the enemy from the morning, the galleons Florencia, Santiago, San Juan of Diego Flores, in which was Don Diego Enriquez, son of the viceroy of Peru, and the Valencera of the Levant squadron, in which was the camp-master Don Alonso de Luzon. The galleasses of the vanguard being carried by the current almost within culverin-shot, the Duke sent them order that by oar and sail they should endeavour to close with the enemy, to which end also he turned the *capitana* towards them. The galleasses bore with the ships of their rear which were in conflict with some of ours that had closed with them and were endeavouring to board them. These were the galleons Florencia, in which was Gaspar de Sosa[3] and the *capitana* of Ojeda,[4] and the Begoña,[5] in which was

[1] In the Regazona, of the Levant squadron.

[2] In the Sp. this is erroneously printed in italics, as a ship's name : presumably the *capitana* of Oquendo is meant.

[3] The commandant of a body of 2,000 Portuguese soldiers, not embodied in a *tercio*, as were the Spaniards (Duro, ii. 81).

[4] Ojeda must be an error of transcription or print for Oquendo. There were two Ojedas in the fleet, but not men of the first importance.

[5] Of Diego Flores : No. 37 in the list. The other vessel of the same name, No. 105, was only a pinnace.

Garibay, and the Valencer, in which was D. Alonso de
Luzon, and the galleon Juan Bautista, in which was
D. Juan Maldonado and D. Luis de Maeda; but all to
little effect, because the enemy, seeing that we endeavoured
to come to hand-stroke with them, bare room, avoiding our
attack by reason of the lightness of their vessels; and afterwards they returned with tide and wind in their favour,
and assailed Juan Martinez de Recalde, who was in the
rear. D. Alonso de Leyva went to his assistance, during
which time our *capitana* was in the hottest of the fight,
supporting those ships which were closely engaged with
the enemy's rear at a distance from both fleets; and
Captain Marolin[1] was ordered to go in a boat and command those ships which were near at hand to succour Juan
Martinez de Recalde; which they did; whereupon the
enemies left Juan Martinez, and turned against the *capitana*
which was going alone to the assistance of the ships named;
and our *capitana* seeing the enemy's admiral in the van,
turned towards her, and lowered her topsails; and the
enemy's admiral and all the fleet passed her, shot at her,
ship by ship, whilst she, on her part, fired her ordnance
very well and fast, so as half the enemy's fleet did not
approach, but shot at her from afar. When the fury of
the assault had spent itself, there arrived to her support
Juan Martinez de Recalde, D. Alonso de Leyva, the
Marquis of Peñafiel, who was in the San Marcos, and
Oquendo; whereupon the enemy bare room and stood out
to sea; their admiral shortening sail, having, as it seemed
to us, sustained some damage, and collecting those of his
ships which had been in fight with our van. In this conflict, which lasted more than 3 hours, the galleon Florencia
was one of the foremost ships, and was in close fight with
the enemy.

July 24.] Wednesday the 3rd, Juan Martinez de
Recalde again took the rear under his charge,[2] Don Alonso

[1] Marolin de Juan, on the Duke's staff on board the San
Martin (Duro, ii. 48).
[2] It would seem probable that at this time he moved from the
Santa Ana to the San Juan. If after the 21st he was obliged to
give up the charge of the rear on account of the damage his ship
had sustained, he could scarcely resume the command in the same
ship after the further pounding she got on the 23rd.

de Leyva remaining with him, reparting between them the 40 or more ships that were therein. The enemy bore with our rear, and assaulted the Admiral ; the galleasses discharged their stern pieces, as also did Juan Martinez and D. Alonso de Leyva, and the other ships of the squadron, without quitting their station. And so the enemy retired without any other success, the galleasses having spoiled their admiral's rigging and shot away his mainyard.

July 25.] Thursday the 4th, Feast of St. Dominic, the Santa Ana and a Portuguese galleon were somewhat astern, which the enemy assaulted with great fury. The galleasses, Don Alonso de Leyva [1] and other ships went to their assistance ; and the galleasses did so well, that they rescued them although they were surrounded by many of the enemy. At the same time that this conflict was in the rear, the enemy's admiral and other great ships assailed our *capitana* ; they came nearer than the first day, discharging their large pieces from the lower deck, and cut the *capitana's* mainstay, slaying also some soldiers ; there came to his succour the San Luis, in which was the maestro de campo Don Augustin, [Mexía], who confronted the enemy, Juan Martinez de Recalde, and the San Juan of the squadron of Diego Flores, in which was D. Diego Enriquez, and Oquendo, which placed themselves in front of our *capitana*, being by the currents prevented from keeping together, and the other ships did the same. Thereupon the enemies retired, but their admiral being much damaged, rested somewhat to leeward of our fleet. Our *capitana* cast about towards her, and Juan Martinez de Recalde, and the San Juan de Sicilia, and the *capitana* of the galleons of Castile, and the Grangin,[2] and all the other ships of our armada, the enemy's fleet recovering the wind, and guarding their admiral which was so spoiled in the fight, that she struck the standard and discharged pieces to show her need of succour, and was now towed by eleven of the enemy's long boats. Our *capitana*, and the *almiranta*, and the rest of the ships were gaining on her so much, that the enemy stood towards her, to support her, so as it appeared certain that we would that day succeed in boarding them, wherein was the only way to victory. But at this moment

---

[1] In the Rata.   [2] Another misnomer for the Gran-Grin.

the wind freshened in favour of the enemy's admiral, whereby she began to slip away from us, and to leave the boats which were towing her; whereupon the enemy's fleet recovered the wind, which meantime had fallen somewhat to leeward. The Duke seeing that in the proposed assault the advantage was no longer with us, and that we were now near the Isle of Wight, discharged a piece and proceeded on his course, the rest of the armada following in very good order, the enemy remaining a long way astern. The same day the Duke despatched Captain Pedro de Leon [1] to Dunkirk, to the Duke of Parma, to advertise him as well of the place wherein he was, and of his success, as also that it was fitting he should come out with as little delay as possible to join with this fleet. He gave the squadron of D. Pedro de Valdes in charge to D. Diego Enriquez, son of the viceroy, having seen him to be careful and able in matters belonging to the sea.

July 26.] Friday the 5th dawned calm, the fleets being in sight of each other; and the Duke despatched a pinnace to the Duke of Parma with the pilot Domingo Ochoa, to obtain from him shot of four, six and ten lbs., because much of his munition had been wasted in the several fights; praying him also eftsoons to send 40 flyboats to join with this armada, to the end he might be able with them to close with the enemy, because our ships being very heavy in comparison with the lightness of those of the enemy it was impossible to come to hand-stroke with them. He was also to notify the Duke that it should be well that he would be ready to come out and join with this armada the day that we should arrive in sight of Dunkirk, whither the Duke proceeded cautiously, suspecting that Parma was not there, seeing that D. Rodrigo Tello had not returned, nor had any other messenger come from him. At sunset the wind rose, whereupon our armada pursued its course towards Calais.

July 27.] Saturday the 6th at daybreak, the two fleets were very near to each other, though without firing; our armada sailing with a fair wind, and the rear close up and in very good order. At ten a clock, we discovered the

---

[1] Of the *tercio* de Sicilia, serving on board the N. S. del Rosario (see *ante*, p. 22 ; Duro, ii. 35), but had, apparently, been sent to the San Martin before the Rosario was captured.

coast of France, being that near to Boulogne. We proceeded towards Calais, where we arrived at four in the
afternoon. There were divers opinions as to whether we
would anchor there or go on further ; but the Duke, understanding from the pilots who were with him that, if he
went on further, the currents would carry him out of the
English Channel and into the North Sea, he resolved to
anchor off of Calais, seven leagues from Dunkirk, from
whence the Duke of Parma could join with him ; so as at
five a clock in the afternoon, order was given for the whole
fleet to anchor ; and the Duke sent Captain Heredia[1] to
visit the Governor of Calais, Monsieur de Gourdan, as well
to advertise him of the cause of our presence there, as to
offer him our friendship and good offices. This evening
36 ships joined the enemy, whereof five were large
galleons, which were understood to be the squadron that
Juan Acles[2] had under his charge before Dunkirk, and
they all anchored about a league from our armada. This
night Captain Heredia returned from Calais, and said that
the governor made great offers of service on the part of
his Majesty, and showed his goodwill by offering the same
on his own part. This night also the Duke sent the
Secretary Arceo to the Duke of Parma, to advertise him
of the place where he now was, and that he could not
tarry there without endangering the whole fleet.

July 28.] Sunday the 7th, at dawn Captain D. Rodrigo
Tello arrived, which came from Dunkirk ; the Duke [of
Medina-Sidonia] had sent him away on the 29th of the
past month ; who said that the Duke [of Parma] was at
Bruges, whither he had repaired to him, and that although
he had shown great satisfaction at the news of the armada
being arrived, that on the evening of Saturday, the 6th, of
this present, when he departed from Dunkirk, the Duke
had not yet come thither, and that they were not embarking either the men or the munition. This day in the

---

[1] Pedro de Heredia, serving in the San Martin. Writing on
May 28 at Lisbon, the Duke described him as 'a soldier of great
experience' (Duro, ii. 46).

[2] Acles was Hawkyns, who, as we know, had not had charge
of the squadron before Dunkirk ; but to Medina-Sidonia Acles
was a familiar name, and he had probably never heard of Lord
Henry Seymour.

morning, the governor of Calais sent his nephew to visit
the Duke and with him a present of refreshments, and to
acquaint him that the place wherein he had anchored was
very dangerous to remain in, because the currents and
counter-currents of that channel were very strong. The
Duke seeing the goodwill of the governor of Calais, sent
the purveyor general, Bernabé de Pedroso, to buy victuals,
and with him went the comptroller. That night likewise
the Duke sent D. Jorge Manrique to the Duke of Parma
to urge him to come out suddenly. On Sunday night the
Secretary Arceo sent one from Dunkirk to advertise the
Duke that Parma had not arrived there, and that the
munitions were not embarked, and that it seemed to him
unpossible that all things could be prepared within a fortnight. On Sunday at sunset, nine ships joined the enemy,[1]
and with them a squadron of 26 ships moved nearer to the
land, which the same made us suspect that they had come
with some design of fire ; whereupon the Duke ordered
Captain Serrano [2] to go in a pinnace, taking with him an
anchor and cable, so as if any fire-ship should be set forth
he might tow it to land. Also he sent to warn all the
ships to be on their guard, and to that end to have ready
as well boats as soldiers. At midnight two fires were seen
kindled [3] in the English fleet, which increased to eight; and
suddenly eight ships with sail set, and fair wind and tide,
came straight towards our *capitana* and the rest of the
fleet, all burning fiercely. The Duke seeing them
approach and that our men did not hinder them, fearing

[1] This is not mentioned in any of the English papers. Most
probably it was some ships shifting berth ; but neither have we
any mention of the movement of the 26 ships. Certainly Howard
and all the English believed that the fire-ships took the Spaniards
altogether by surprise ; and it is possible that Medina-Sidonia,
wishing to put his conduct in the best light, confused the time at
which he first suspected the designs of the enemy.

[2] Antonio Serrano, in command of the fore-castle of the San
Martin ; a man of distinguished valour, in whom the Duke placed
great confidence.

[3] This does not seem to be quite accurate. The English
accounts, which agree with common sense, are that the fires
were first lighted when the barks were approaching the Spanish
fleet.

that they should be explosion-machines,[1] gave order to weigh, and also for the rest of the armada to do the same, intending when the fires had passed to return and recover the same position. The admiral galleass, in keeping clear of one ship, came entangled with the San Juan de Sicilia, and so damaged herself that she had to remain near the shore. The current was so strong that it drove our armada in such manner as, although our *capitana* and divers of the ships that were near her anchored again, firing a piece of ordnance, the rest did not see her, and were so driven as far as off of Dunkirk.

July 29.] Monday the 8th, at daybreak, the Duke seeing that his armada was very far off and that the enemy was coming under a press of sail, weighed anchor to collect his fleet and therewith endeavour to recover the place they had been in. The wind was blowing strong from the NW.,[2] nearly straight on to the coast, and the enemy's fleet, wherein were 136 ships, came on suddenly with wind and tide in their favour, so as the Duke, who was in the rear, seeing that if he bare room with his fleet, it would be to their destruction, for that it was already very near the banks of Dunkirk, as he was assured by his Flemish pilots, chose rather to save it by abiding the enemy's fleet ; and so cast about to meet them, discharging his ordnance, and sending off pinnaces to order all the ships to keep a close luff, as otherwise they should drive on to the banks of Dunkirk. The enemy's admiral, with the greater part of their fleet, assaulted our *capitana*, with great shooting of ordnance, approaching within musket-shot, or even harquebus-shot. This continued without ceasing from daybreak ; nor did the *capitana* bear room until the fleet was clear of the shoals. And during all this time, the galleon San Marcos, in which was the Marquis of Peñafiel, continued hard by the *capitana*.

The admiral galleass, not being able to follow our armada, turned towards Calais, and ran on ground at the entrance of the haven, whither divers of the enemy followed her. It is reported that the French in the castle of Calais

---

[1] Sp. *maquinas de minas*. In Benbow's time such ships were called 'machines' or 'machine-ships' ; in Lord Cochrane's, they were distinguished as 'explosion-vessels.' These, of course, were simple fire-ships. [2] Cf. *ante*, p. 10.

supported her with their ordnance, and that her people reached the land.

Don Alonso de Leyva and Juan Martinez de Recalde, and the *capitana* of Oquendo, and all the ships of the camp-masters, as well Castillians as Portuguese, and the *capitana* of Diego Flores, and that of Bertendona, and the galleon San Juan of Diego Flores, in which was D. Diego Enriquez,[1] and the San Juan de Sicilia, in which was D. Diego Tellez Enriquez,[2] sustained the assault of the enemy as stoutly as was possible, so as all these ships were very much spoiled, and almost unable to make further resistance, and the greater part of them without shot for their ordnance. In the rear D. Francisco de Toledo abode the coming of the enemy, and endeavoured to grapple with them ; whereupon they assailed him, and by shooting of ordnance brought him to great extremity. D. Diego Pimentel came to relieve him, and both were hardly pressed ; seeing which, Juan Martinez de Recalde came to their assistance, with D. Agustin Mexía, and rescued them from this strait. Notwithstanding which, these ships returned and again assaulted the enemy ; as likewise did D. Alonso de Luzon, and the Santa Maria de Begoña, in which went Garibay, and the San Juan de Sicilia, in which went D. Diego Tellez Enriquez. These came near to boarding the enemy, yet could they not grapple with them ; they fighting with their great ordnance, and our men defending themselves with harquebus-fire and musketry, the distance being very small.

Whenas the Duke heard the harquebus-fire and the musketry in the rear, but by reason of the smoke was unable to see from the top what it was, except that two of our ships were surrounded by the enemy, and that their whole fleet, having quitted our *capitana*, were assailing them, he gave order to cast about to succour them, although the *capitana* was sorely distressed by great shot between wind and water, so as by no means could the leak be stopped, and her rigging was much spoiled. Nevertheless, when the enemy perceived our *capitana* approach, they left the ships they were assailing, which were the ships of D. Alonso de Luzon[3] and of Garibay, of D. Francisco de

---

[1] The son of the Viceroy.   [2] The son of the Commendador.

[3] Namely, the Valencera, Begoña, San Felipe, San Mateo, and San Juan de Sicilia.

Toledo, of D. Diego Pimentel, and of D. Diego Tellez Enriquez. These three last had been most closely and hotly engaged with the enemy, and had all suffered much damage and were unable for the service, all their people being slain or wounded, only the ship of D. Diego Tellez Enriquez was able to follow us, though much spoiled. The Duke collected his armada and the enemy did the same.

The Duke ordered boats to go to bring away the people from the San Felipe and San Mateo; whereby all the people were taken out of the San Mateo,[1] but D. Diego Pimentel would not leave the ship, and sent D. Rodrigo de Vivero and D. Luis Vanegas to the Duke, to ask him to send some to see if it were not possible to save her ; whereon the Duke sent a pilot and a diver from this galleon, though there was much peril in remaining without him ; but because it was now late, and the sea very heavy, they could not reach the San Mateo, beyond seeing her afar off, going towards Zealand. The galleon San Felipe came alongside of the hulk Doncella, which all the people got into her ; and D. Francisco being in her, heard a cry that the hulk was sinking ; whereupon the captain Juan Poza de Santiso sprang back into the San Felipe, and so also did D. Francisco de Toledo,[2] which was a great misfortune ; for it was not true that the hulk was sinking, and D. Francisco was carried in the San Felipe towards Zealand, the Duke having been told that he and all his people were in safety on board the hulk Doncella. The sea was so high that nothing more could be done, nor could the damage be repaired which the *capitana* had suffered from great shot whereby she was in danger of being lost.

This day the Duke wished to turn on the enemy with the whole armada, so as he would not leave the Channel ; but the pilots told him that it was unpossible, because with the sea and wind from the North-West, setting straight on

[1] Apparently the Duke did not know how many were brought away. It can only have been a few (cf. *ante*, pp. 30, 70, 77).

[2] 'Don Francisco said that if he was to be lost, he would be lost in his own ship, and therewith he returned to her and went towards Zealand' (Duro, ii. 263). He, however, made good his escape to Nieuport (*ante*, p. 30, where he is confused by Borlas with Don Francisco de Bobadilla).

to the coast, they must by force go into the North Sea, or else that the whole armada would drive on to the banks. Thus in no way could they avoid leaving the Channel ; nearly all the best ships being spoiled and unable to resist longer, as well from the damage they had received as from not having shot for their ordnance.

July 30.] Tuesday the 9th, eve of San Lorenzo, at 2 o'clock in the morning, the wind increased, so as our *capitana*, which had stayed in the hope of returning to the Channel, was driven towards the coast of Zealand, although keeping as close a luff as possible. At daybreak the NW. wind was not so strong, and the enemy's fleet with 109 vessels was discovered astern little more than half a league off. Our *capitana* remained in the rear with Juan Martinez de Recalde and D. Alonso de Leyva, and the galleasses, and the galleons San Marcos and San Juan of Diego Flores, the rest of our fleet being far to leeward. The enemy's ships stood towards our *capitana*, which lay to ; the galleasses also abode their coming, as also did the other ships which were in the rear ; whereupon the enemy brought to. The Duke shot off two pieces to collect his armada, and sent a pinnace with a pilot to order them to keep a close luff, because they were very near to the banks of Zealand ; for which cause the enemy remained aloof, seeing that our armada must be lost ; for the pilots on board the *capitana*—men of experience of that coast—told the Duke at this time that it was not possible to save a single ship of the armada ; for that with the wind as it was, in the NW., they must all needs go on the banks of Zealand ; that God alone could prevent it. Being in this peril, without any sort of remedy, and in six and a half fathoms of water, God was pleased to change the wind to WSW., whereby the fleet stood towards the North without hurt to any ship, the Duke sending order to every ship to follow the *capitana*, for that otherwise they would go on the banks of Zealand.

This evening the Duke summoned the generals and D. Alonso de Leyva, to consider what was best to be done ; and when the Duke had explained the state of the armada and the lack of shot—for that all the greatest ships sent to ask for them—he wished them to say whether it were best to turn back to the English Channel or to return to Spain by the North Sea; seeing that the Duke of Parma had not sent word that he would be presently able to come out. The Council was wholly of opinion that they should go back to the Channel if the weather would permit it; but if not, that then, constrained by the weather, they should return by the North Sea to Spain, seeing there was such great lack of provisions in the fleet, and that the ships were spoiled and unable, that hitherto had resisted the enemy. The wind continued to increase in the SSW., and the Duke stood to seaward, the enemy's fleet following him.

In regard to the fighting, and the turning to relieve and assist his ships, and the abiding the coming of the enemy, the Duke took counsel with the camp-master D. Francisco de Bobadilla, whom, on account of his many years' experience of war by land and sea, he had ordered at the Groyne to come on board the *capitana*, quitting the S. Marcos, which belonged to the same squadron. The Marquis de Peñafiel who also was in the S. Marcos, remained there, for that he did not wish to remove to the *capitana*, quitting the gentlemen that were with him. But in regard to the conduct of the fleet, and such matters as related to the sea, the Duke had the council of the general Diego Flores, whom he also ordered to move into the *capitana*, because he was one of the oldest and most experienced in sea affairs.

July 31.] Wednesday the 10th, our armada pursuing their course with a strong wind from the SW. and a high sea, the enemy's fleet continued to follow us, and in the evening the force of the wind becoming less, they came on under all sail towards our rear; whereupon the Duke, for that in the rear there were but few ships with Juan Martinez de Recalde, struck his topsails and lay to, waiting for the rear, and shot off three pieces so as our fleet should also lie to, and wait for the rearguard and the *capitana*. What our armada did thereupon, D. Baltasar de Zuñiga will say. But when the enemy saw that our *capitana* had brought to, and that the galleasses of the rearguard and as many as 12 of our best ships had done the same, they also brought to and shortened sail, without shooting of ordnance against us. This night Juan Acles[1] turned back with his squadron.

---

[1] He continues in the same mistake; it was, of course, Seymour who parted company.

August 1.] Thursday the 11th, we continued our voyage with the same strong wind, the enemy's fleet keeping a long way off; at evening they came under all sail towards our armada, and we counted the ships of Juan Acles to be missing, and again the galleasses and our *capitana* brought to and abode their coming; whereupon they also brought to, not coming within cannon shot.

August 2.] Friday the 12th, at daybreak, the enemy's fleet was close up with ours, and seeing that we were in good order and our rearguard strengthened, they rested and turned back towards England, until we lost sight of them. Sithen that time we had always the same wind, until we went out of the channel of the Sea of Norway without it being possible to return to the English Channel [*August* 10] though we desired it, until to-day, the 20th of August, when having passed the isles at the north of Scotland we are now sailing towards Spain with the wind at North-East.

APPENDIX F.

RELATION OF GONZALO GONZALEZ, A PRISONER IN ENGLAND.

[Paris, Archives Nationales. K. 1592. (Dossier B. 81.)—Spanish.]¹

Memorial that I, Gonzalo Gonzalez del Castillo, natural of Granada, made for his Majesty, of divers things which I saw and heard in England whilst I was a prisoner there.

The 7th day² of the month of November, 1588, the hulk San Pedro el Mayor, of the squadron of Juan Gomes de Medina, was cast ashore in England, on the land of Sir William Courteney, where she was pillaged and her people imprisoned.

The 11th day of the said month, there arrived a commissioner from the Queen, with order to separate twelve from the rest of the prisoners and to put them in prison, apart by themselves,³ which was done; and to each of these they gave 4d. for his daily sustenance, and to each of the rest they gave 1d.⁴

The 24th of November of the year 1589, the Spanish prisoners there were released by the Queen's order, excepting twelve which the Queen gave to Sir William Courteney, who eftsoons straitly imprisoned us, requiring from us 5,000 ducats for our ransom; which sum was not paid, for that there were none save only poor men.

¹ For the transcript of this Relation the Editor is indebted to the good offices of M. Alfred Spont.
² October 28, Old Style. Cf. *ante*, p. 289.
³ This agrees with Ashley's report (see *ante*, p. 294), which says they were imprisoned at Kingsbridge.
⁴ Cary says he allowed them 1½d. (*ante*, p. 291).

The 11th of August, 1590, being told by the said Sir William Courteney that he required of us 12,000 ducats for our liberty, and seeing that we had little remedy, we wrote a letter to the Queen, beseeching her that as she had given liberty to all the Spaniards which had been in her kingdom, she would give us our liberty for the like sum as had been judged sufficient for the others. This letter falling into the hands of the said Courteney, he thrust us into a strong prison, giving us for our diet but bread, broth, and water. We were in such straits that, seeing ourselves dying, we resolved to break out of prison and appeal to the justices for a remedy; but they answered that they were unable to relieve us, because he was a powerful man, with whom they could not meddle. So that we were sent back to our prison and remained therein seven months, suffering great hardship.

The 7th of February, 1591, the said Sir William Courteney sent one William Blake, an Englishman, to this province of Brittany to treat with the Duke of Mercœur for our ransom, as well for our liberty as for our better treatment; who came to no agreement about the same, because they required 25,000 ducats, so that the prisoners remain there to this day.

The 24th of December, 1591, I departed from Exeter for Brittany; but having put out to sea, the wind changed and drove us into the haven of Artamu,[1] where we stayed for a wind seven weeks.

On the 8th of February of this present year,[2] Francis Drake passed through the town by the post, having been summoned by the Queen.

On the 23rd of the said month, order came to this port to prepare the five ships[3] of her Majesty's which were there, and likewise six that were in the port of Plymouth, which was done, for to go to the Seine mouth,[4] to prevent the King our master from relieving Rouen. Whenas the ships were prepared, they desired to embark the infantry, but it was found unpossible to do so, for that a great many of those who were on the muster-roll were absent. Whereof

---

[1] Probably Dartmouth.　　　　[2] 1592.

[3] There were certainly not five of the Queen's ships at Dartmouth.

[4] Sp. *á la costa de rruan.*

word was sent to the Court so as provision should be made ; whereupon there came order to imprest peasants— men whom arms do not arm—and embark the same.[1]

I have ofttimes spoken with divers persons of all conditions, as well men as women, which have told me the good wishes they had for our victory in that land, as also the zeal they had and have for the Catholic religion ; and that if they have not declared themselves, it is that they may not lose house and property. There are others who avow themselves Catholics ; for the which they have suffered divers punishments, and yet openly say that they must needs be Catholics and will die in that religion. Many complaints were made about the number of declared Catholics, and they had prayed the Queen to have them punished ; who had given order that such complaints should not be preferred against the Catholics, and that each one live freely as he wished.[2]

They stand in great fear of the galleys and of the general thereof, which they well know his name, and that he is a good knight and an able mariner. They hold it for certain that the galleys will some day offend them, for they say that as they go on the coast of Brittany, they will likewise come on their coast, because it is much better for them than that of Brittany, the passing over to it being the only difficulty. They say the galleys will be their utter ruin, and therefore there is nothing that they fear so much.[3]

They have great lack of soldiers because of the losses they have had of the same. I am a witness that from the journey of Portugal, of more than 15,000[4] men which embarked, not 4,000 disembarked, because of the pestilence there had been in the ships, and of the mortality and of the Spanish prisons. Likewise of the 4,000 men set forth

[1] There is not a word of all this in the State Papers.

[2] We may suppose that he was told this, but most certainly it was not true.

[3] Compare Fenner's 'Twelve of her Majesty's ships were a match for all the galleys in the King of Spain's dominions' (vol. i. p. xxxii) ; but Gonzalo was not a seaman.

[4] This refers to the expedition of 1589. The loss is scarcely exaggerated ; but as the writer has already said that he was a close prisoner at the time, he cannot have been a witness.

from Plymouth to the support of the prince, there are not 500 remaining; and of five ships which were sent to the succour of Rouen, all perished in a storm, wherefrom not one man escaped.[1] Thus they are forced to levy men from the isles of Holland and Zealand.

Whilst in this port there arrived a flyboat from the isles with about 80 men therefrom, who, going in company with other 20 towards the Seine mouth, were all lost in a storm, within a week.

They have been much pained by the loss of one of the Queen's galleons at Terceira, called the [Revenge]; they say that she was the best ship that the Queen had, and which they had the most confidence in for her defence.[2]

They are not such as speak against the King our master; they say nothing more but that if it were not for the pope he would be the best prince ever born; and thus in all honesty they pray for peace, for they say that if they have not peace within two years they will be all irremediably ruined.

They are fearful that his Majesty may take a port in Brittany, for they say that when he is stablished there his fleet shall be in England, and that there are so many of his party in this kingdom that there will be no let to his winning it.

There is no one who is well affected to Francis Drake; for the people of quality say that he is but of a mean family to have risen so high; and the rest say that he is the cause of the wars. He is well looked on by the Queen, who showeth him much favour.

They cannot away with the name of Dom Antonio whom they call King of Portugal, for they say that he was the cause of the loss of the people which died in Portugal. They seek to stone him, and they say that the Queen keepeth him in a stronghold from whence he never goeth out. He is so poor, lacking money and servants, as it is not to be believed.

Don Pedro de Valdes abideth five miles from London as hitherto; for although they imputed to him a desire to escape and imprisoned him for the same, Francis Drake, to whom always he hath recourse, hath arranged every-

[1] The State Papers know nothing of this.
[2] Compare note No. 7, *ante*, p. 334.

thing, so as he goeth a-hunting and to other pleasure parties as in the time when he was not in prison. The chief persons of the island do not regard him with favour, for they say that he was the cause that certain gentlemen (a general of the Queen's and others of her council) were executed, which they were all of the party of the king ; but this is not credible, for Don Pedro would have lost his life ere he would have spoken of it.

They hourly attend the armada of the king our master, and they plainly say that they know that England must be his Majesty's, and that the cause of her ruin will be the galleys.

I left Artamu, a port of England, and was at Plymouth on the 5th of February of this year, 1592. These are the best havens which the Queen hath, wherein her armadas are gathered ; and in none of them is any other sort of armada to be seen, neither machine of war, than what I have said.

That I have here written is the truth of such things as I saw and heard whilst I have been in that kingdom ; and I sign it with my name in the town of Blavet, on the 9th day of March 1592.

GONZALEZ DEL CASTILLO

APPENDIX G.

LIST OF THE SPANISH ARMADA.

[From *La Armada Invencible* of Captain C. Fernandez Duro, tom. ii. p. 60 ; copied from the original sent to the king by the Duke of Medina-Sidonia. Compared with *La Felicissima Armada,* printed at Lisbon in 1588 : a copy of which, with autograph notes by Burghley, is in the British Museum. No attempt has been made to rectify the arithmetic, which is in a hopeless muddle.

Relation of the galleons, ships, patasses and zabras, galleasses, galleys, and other ships that go in the most Happy Armada which his Majesty has ordered to assemble in the river of this city of Lisbon, whereof the Duke of Medina-Sidonia is Captain-general ; with the tonnage of the ships and the number of soldiers, mariners, etc.

[Armada of Portugal, under the charge of the Duke of Medina-Sidonia.]

No.	Ships' Names	Tons	Guns	Soldiers	Mariners	Total
1	San Martin, capitana general .	1,000	48	300	177	477
2	San Juan, almiranta general .	1,050	50	321	179	500
3	San Marcos	790	33	292	117	409
4	San Felipe	800	40	415	117	532
5	San Luis	830	38	376	116	492
6	San Mateo	750	34	277	120	397
7	Santiago	520	24	300	93	393
8	Florencia	961	52	400	86	486
9	San Cristobal	352	20	300	78	378
10	San Bernardo	352	21	250	81	331
11	Zabra Augusta . . .	166	13	55	57	112
12	Zabra Julia	166	14	44	72	116
	12	7,737	347	3,330	1,290	4,623

Armada of Biscay, whereof Juan Martinez de Recalde
is Captain-general.

No.	Ships Names	Tons	Guns	Soldiers	Mariners	Total
13	Santa Ana, capitana . .	768	30	256	73	329
14	El Gran Grin, almiranta . .	1,160	28	256	73	329
15	Santiago	666	25	214	102	316
16	La Concepcion de Zubelzu .	486	16	90	70	160
17	La Concepcion de Juanes del Cano	418	18	164	61	225
18	La Magdalena . . .	530	18	193	67	260
19	San Juan	350	21	114	80	194
20	La Maria Juan . . .	665	24	172	100	272
21	La Manuela	520	12	125	54	179
22	Santa Maria de Monte-Mayor .	707	18	206	45	251
23	Patax la Maria de Aguirre .	70	6	20	23	43
24	,, la Isabela . . .	71	10	20	22	42
25	,, de Miguel Suso . .	36	6	20	26	46
26	,, San Estéban . . .	96	6	20	26	46
	14	6,567	238	1,937	863	2,800

Armada of the galleons of Castille, whereof Diego
Flores de Valdes is General.

No.	Ships' Names	Tons	Guns	Soldiers	Mariners	Total
27	San Cristóbal, capitana . .	700	36	205	120	225
28	San Juan Bautista . . .	750	24	207	136	243
29	San Pedro	530	24	141	131	272
30	San Juan	530	24	163	113	276
31	Santiago el Mayor . . .	530	24	210	132	343
32	San Felipe y Santiago . .	530	24	151	116	267
33	La Asuncion	530	24	199	114	313
34	Nuestra Señora del Barrio .	530	24	155	108	263
35	San Medel y Celedon . .	530	24	160	101	261
36	Santa Ana	250	24	91	80	171
37	N. S. de Begoña . . .	750	24	174	123	297
38	La Trinidad	872	24	180	122	302
39	Santa Catalina . . .	882	24	190	159	349
40	San Juan Bautista . . .	650	24	192	93	285
41	Patax N. S. del Socorro . .	75	24	20	25	45
/42	Patax San Antonio de Padua .	75	12	20	46	66
	16	8,714	384	2,458	1,719	4,177

Armada of the ships of Andalusia, whereof D. Pedro de Valdes is Captain-general.

No.	Ships' Names	Tons	Guns	Soldiers	Mariners	Total
43	N. S. del Rosario, capitana .	1,150	46	304	118	422
44	San Francisco, almiranta. .	915	21	222	56	278
45	San Juan . . .	810	31	245	89	334
46	San Juan de Gargarin . .	569	16	165	56	221
47	La Concepcion . . .	862	20	185	71	256
48	Duquesa Santa Ana . .	900	23	280	77	357
49	Santa Catalina . . .	730	23	231	77	308
50	La Trinidad	650	13	192	74	266
51	Santa Maria del Juncal . .	730	20	228	80	308
52	San Bartolomé . . .	976	27	240	72	312
53	Patax el Espiritu Santo . .	—		33	10	43
	11	8,762	240	2,325	780	3,105

Armada of the Province of Guipúzcoa, whereof Miguel de Oquendo is General.

No.	Ships' Names	Tons	Guns	Soldiers	Mariners	Total
54	Santa Ana, capitana . .	1,200	47	303	82	385
55	N. S. de la Rosa, almiranta .	945	26	233	64	297
56	San Salvador . . .	958	25	321	75	396
57	San Estéban . . .	736	26	196	68	264
58	Santa Marta . . .	548	20	173	63	236
59	Santa Bárbara. . .	525	12	154	45	199
60	San Buenaventura . .	379	21	168	53	221
61	La Maria San Juan . .	291	12	110	30	140
62	Santa Cruz . . .	680	16	156	32	188
63	La urca Doncella . .	500	16	156	32	188
64	Patax la Asuncion . .	60	9	20	23	43
65	,, San Bernabe . .	69	9	20	23	43
	12	6,991	247	1,992	616	2,608

Armada of Levant ships, whereof Martin de Bertendona has charge.

No.	Ships' Names	Tons	Guns	Soldiers	Mariners	Total
66	La Regazona, capitana . .	1,249	30	344	80	424
67	La Lavia, almiranta . .	728	25	203	71	274
68	La Rata Coronada . . .	820	35	335	84	419
69	San Juan de Sicilia . . .	800	26	279	63	342
70	La Trinidad Valencera . .	1,100	42	281	79	360
71	La Anunciada . . .	703	24	196	79	275
72	San Nicolas Prodaneli . .	834	26	374	81	355
73	La Juliana	860	32	325	70	395
74	Santa Maria de Vison . .	666	18	236	71	307
75	La Trinidad de Scala . .	900	22	307	79	386
	10	7,705	280	2,780	767	3,527

Armada of hulks, whereof Juan Gomes de Medina hath charge.

No.	Ships' Names	Tons	Guns	Soldiers	Mariners	Total
76	El Gran Grifon, capitana .	650	38	243	43	286
77	San Salvador, almiranta .	650	24	218	43	261
78	Perro Marina . . .	200	7	70	24	94
79	Falcon Blanco Mayor . .	500	16	161	36	197
80	Castillo Negro . . .	750	27	239	34	273
81	Barca de Amburg . .	600	23	239	25	264
82	Casa de Paz Grande . .	650	26	198	27	225
83	San Pedro Mayor . . .	581	29	213	28	241
84	El Sanson . . .	500	18	200	31	231
85	San Pedro Menor . . .	500	18	157	23	180
86	Barca de Anzique . . .	450	26	200	25	225
87	Falcon Blanco Mediano . .	300	16	76	27	103
88	Santo Andres . . .	400	14	150	28	178
89	Casa de Paz Chica . .	350	15	162	24	186
90	Ciervo Volante . .	400	18	200	22	222
91	Paloma Blanca . . .	250	12	56	20	76
92	La Ventura	160	4	58	14	72
93	Santa Bárbara . . .	370	10	70	22	92
94	Santiago	600	19	56	30	86
95	David	450	7	50	24	74
96	El Gato	400	9	40	22	62
97	Esayas	260	4	30	16	46
98	San Gabriel	280	4	35	20	55
	23	10,271	384	3,121	608	3,729

Patasses and zabras, whereof Don Antonio Hurtado de Mendoza hath charge.

No.	Ships' Names	Tons	Guns	Soldiers	Mariners	Total
99	N. S. del Pilar de Zaragoza capitana	300	11	109	51	160
100	La Caridad, inglesa . .	180	12	70	36	106
101	San Andres, escoces . .	150	12	40	29	69
102	El Crucifijo	150	8	40	29	96
103	N. S. del Puerto . . .	55	8	30	33	63
104	La Concepcion de Carasa .	70	5	30	42	72
105	N. S. de Begoña . . .	64	—	20	26	46
106	La Concepcion de Capetillo .	60	10	20	26	46
107	San Jeronimo . . .	50	4	20	37	57
108	N. S. de Gracia . . .	57	5	20	34	54
109	La Concepcion de Francisco de Latero	75	6	20	29	49
110	N. S. de Guadalupe . .	70	—	20	42	62
111	San Francisco . . .	70	—	20	37	57
112	Espíritu Santo . . .	75	—	20	47	67
113	Trinidad	—	2	—	23	23
114	N. S. de Castro . . .	—	2	—	26	26
115	Santo Andres . . .	—	2	—	15	15
116	La Concepcion de Valmaseda	—	2	—	27	27
117	La Concepcion de Somanila .	—	—	—	31	31
118	Santa Catalina . . .	—	—	—	23	23
119	San Juan de Carasa . .	—	—	—	23	23
120	Asuncion	—	—	—	23	23
	22	1,131	91	479	574	1,093

Galleasses of Naples, under the charge of D. Hugo de Moncada.

No.	Ships' Names	Tons	Guns	Soldiers	Mariners	Total
121	Capitana San Lorenzo . .	—	50	262	124	386
122	Patrona Zuñiga . . .	—	50	178	112	290
123	Girona	—	50	169	120	289
124	Napolitana	—	50	264	112	376
	4 with 1,200 rowers . .	—	200	873	468	1,341

Galleys of Portugal, under the charge of D. Diego Medrano.

No.	Ships' Names	Tons	Guns	Soldiers	Mariners	Total
125	Capitana	—	5	—	106	106
126	Princesa	—	5	—	90	90
127	Diana	—	5	—	94	94
128	Bazana	—	5	—	72	72
	4 with 888 rowers . .	—	20	—	362	362

General Summary.

	Ships	Tons	Guns	Soldiers	Mariners	Total
Armada of Portugal . .	12	7,737	347	3,330	1,293	4,623
,, Biscay .	14	6,567	238	1,937	863	2,800
,, Castille . .	16	8,714	384	2,458	1,719	4,171
,, Andaluzia .	11	8,762	240	2,327	780	3,105
,, Guipuscoa .	14	6,991	247	1,992	616	2,608
,, Levant Ships .	10	7,705	280	2,780	767	3,523
,, Hulks .	23	10,271	384	3,121	608	3,729
Patasses and Zabras . .	22	1,121	91	479	574	1,093
Galleasses of Naples . .	4	—	200	773	468	1,341
Galleys	4	—	20	—	362	362
	130	57,868	2,431	19,295	8,050	27,365
Rowers . . .						2,088
Summa Totalis .						29,453

NOTES ON THE LIST OF THE ARMADA.

Of the age or previous history of the Spanish ships, nothing is known in this country. Of the fate of a great many of them even the Spaniards are ignorant. In the majority of cases, so total was the destruction, that all they could say of any particular ship was that she did not come home. Nor were the English always better informed. If a ship went down in the open seá, nothing was heard of her ; if she was cast ashore, it often happened that there

were no survivors, and the English officials could only
report that a great ship had been split to pieces, and that
the shore was strewn with dead bodies, or that the Irish had
brained all that came to land, or that a miserable remnant
had been despatched by order of their own officers.
Captain Duro supposes (i. 201) that English writers have
been studiously silent on the subject in order to conceal
'the foul stain on the character of a people who pride
themselves on their humanity.' In this he is mistaken.
English writers have never concealed the broad facts as far
as they were known ; but it is only within the last few
years that Mr. Froude's History and, more fully, the
Calendar of the Irish State Papers have made the details
public. This Calendar was not yet issued when *La
Armada Invencible* was published ; still, with Mr. Froude's
last volume before him (i. 204–5), Captain Duro's suggestion is more than a little curious. Nothing, indeed, can
be clearer than that the actors in the terrible tragedy felt
neither shame nor sentiment in the part they were called
on to play ; and if they had thought excuses necessary,
would doubtless have found them in the conduct of the
Spaniards on several occasions, notably in that of Alva in
the Low Countries, and of Santa Cruz after his victory at
Terceira.

Captain Duro's researches permit him to give the
following tabular statement of losses; it is probably as
fair an approximation as can be arrived at.

Abandoned to the enemy	2 [1]
Lost in France (stores saved) . . .	3 [2]
Lost in Holland	2 [3]
Sunk in the battle	2 [4]
Wrecked in Scotland and Ireland . .	19 [5]
Fate unknown	35
	63

[1] Nos. 43, 56.   [2] Nos. 13, 121, 127.   [3] Nos. 4, 6.
[4] Not specified ; possibly Nos. 14, 69.
[5] He has not given their names ; one, No. 83, was lost on the
coast of Devonshire. The Irish accounts speak of 17 as known to
have been lost in Ireland alone.

which he classes thus :—

Galleons and ships	.	.	.	.	.	26
Hulks	.	.	.	.	.	13
Patasses	.	.	.	.	.	20
Galleasses	.	.	.	.	.	3
Galleys	.	.	.	.	.	1

63

It is of very few that any particulars can be given.

1. Notwithstanding the battering to which she had been subjected, by dint of having a capable pilot, she returned safely to Santander, having lost 180 men dead and almost all the rest sick. The Duke of Medina-Sidonia is described as having lost all heart and making no attempt to keep the fleet together, or to exert himself for the common safety. His one anxiety was to reach Spain ; and when, off Santander, the wind came foul, he hurried to shore in the pilot-boat, leaving the ship to the care of Diego Flores de Valdes. His court favour preserved him from punishment or rebuke, and the guilt of having deserted the disabled Rosario was attributed to Diego Flores, who had indeed counselled the measure which Medina-Sidonia adopted. Captain Duro accepts the opinion, current at the time, that Diego Flores was actuated by personal enmity to his cousin, a crime surely deserving a severer punishment than the 15 months' imprisonment which it received.

2. From being designated the *almiranta* before the fleet left Lisbon, it would seem that Juan Martinez de Recalde was then on board her. He probably continued so till the night of July 21, when he took command of the rear in the Santa Ana (No. 13), from which he returned to the San Juan on the 24th. Captain Duro (i. 210) describes him as putting into a strange port in Ireland, landing his men, and by force of arms obtaining the water of which his ships were much in need. The unknown port would seem to have been Dingle ; and in this skirmish, the men, whose examinations are given *ante* p. 219, were presumably made prisoners. The S. Juan arrived at Corunna, and there Recalde—worn out with vexation and hardships—died in the middle of October.

He was a man of long experience in maritime affairs, and is spoken of as 'one of the greatest seamen of the age.' The ship was burnt by Drake at Corunna in 1589 (*S. P. Dom. Eliz.* ccxxiv. 24).

3. 4. 5. 6. 8. These were all reckoned as amongst the most powerful ships in the armada, and with 1 and 2, bore a great part of the brunt of the fighting. The S. Felipe and S. Mateo, after being captured by the Zealanders, sank in the mouth of the Scheldt. The S. Marcos was lost on the coast of Ireland (Duro, i. 125).

13. Is said to have been missing on July 20 (*ante*, p. 355). She must have rejoined the fleet during the night, though Medina-Sidonia has not mentioned it ; for there seems no doubt that she was the ship which, with Juan Martinez de Recalde on board, was so sorely beaten on July 21 and again on the 23rd (*ante*, pp. 134, 356, 360). Juan Martinez probably left her on the 24th, when he resumed the command of the rear-guard (p. 360 ; cf. Duro, i. 61) ; and on the 25th, being ' scattered' from the fleet (vol. i. p. 359 ; *ante*, p. 361) she was very roughly handled by the Victory and others of the ships with Hawkyns ; so that, being unable to keep the sea, she parted company during the night, and drifted across into the Bay of La Hogue, whence she went to Havre. There were sundry proposals to attack her there (*ante*, pp. 179, 195–6), but they came to nothing ; and the Santa Ana, trying to go into the river for her better security, struck on the bar and became a complete wreck (Duro, i. 171).

30, *en que iba* Diego Enriquez. Of the ship herself there is no direct account ; but the ship in which Diego Enriquez was at the time, was lost on the coast of Ireland. A detailed account of the miserable death of this brave man is given in *La Armada Invencible*, ii. 342.

43. After being pretty well cleared out at Dartmouth, she was patched up and taken round to Chatham (*P. O. D. A.* 2226). She was probably found not worth repairing, and was broken up. D. Pedro de Valdes remained a prisoner more or less at large (*ante*, p. 374) for about 3 years, when he paid a ransom of 3,000*l.* and returned to Spain. In 1602 he was appointed Governor of Cuba. He held the office till 1608, during which time he built the Castilla del Morro to defend the Havana. On his return,

he retired to Gijon, his native place, and died there in 1614.

48. With D. Alonso de Leyva and the survivors from the Rata on board, was lost in Glennagiveny Bay, a few miles to the west of Inishowen Head (*S. P. Ireland, Eliz.*, cxxxvi. 36, III.) Many were drowned ; some were killed or taken prisoners ; D. Alonso and the rest were taken off by the Girona, No. 123.

54. Got back to the Passages, where she accidentally caught fire and blew up. Oquendo, who had been in all the expeditions of his time, a man of fiery courage and vehement temper, did not live to witness this last blow, dying of vexation on the 22nd of September.

55. 56. The Almirante of the Guipuzcoan squadron would seem to have left the Nuestra Señora de la Rosa and gone on board the San Salvador, probably at the Groyne. Both Spanish and English accounts speak of the ship that was partially blown up on the evening of July 21 as the *almiranta* or vice-admiral of Oquendo, and it is perfectly certain that this ship was the San Salvador (*ante*, p. 155). But misled by his list, Captain Duro has insisted (*La Armada Invencible*, i. 197) that 'the burnt ship' was the N. S. de la Rosa, which was actually lost among the Blaskets (*S. P. Ireland, Eliz.*, cxxxvi. 41, V.).

66. According to the list, the largest ship in the armada, though apparently not the most heavily armed. Her commander, Bertendona, having distinguished himself in the fighting (*ante*, pp. 359, 366), more fortunate than many of his companions in arms, succeeded in reaching Spain. In the next year, he took part in the defence of Corunna against Drake, and burnt his ship to prevent her falling into the hands of the enemy. In 1591 he commanded a ship in the armada at the Azores under D. Alonso de Bazan, and is said by Captain Duro (i. 212) to have been the actual captor of the Revenge.

68. In *La Felicissima Armada* the name is given as La Rata Santa Maria Encoronada. She was cast ashore on the coast of Erris, and split in pieces (*ante*, p. 262), when Alonso de Leyva with most of his men were said to have got on board the San Martin. Afterwards he removed to the Duquesa Santa Ana.

69, *en que iba* Diego Tellez Enriquez. From the

terrible battering which she got on July 29, and from the
fate of the San Mateo and San Felipe her companions in
the fight, it seems extremely probable that she foundered
during the night or was the ship that went down whilst in
treaty with Captain Crosse. Her name does not appear
afterwards.

70. Lost on the coast of Ireland. The examination of
D. Alonso de Luzon is given *ante*, p. 271.

71. 74. Their armament is given vol. i. p. xlv. It does
not appear from the list that they ought to be regarded as
exceptional.

76. A ship of Rostock ; was lost on Fair Island, where
Juan Gomes de Medina and his men remained through the
winter. In the following year they crossed to Scotland
and reached Edinburgh, whence they obtained a passage to
Spain. The coincidence of the name gave rise to a rumour
long prevalent that it was the general of the expedition,
the Duke of Medina-Sidonia, who was wrecked on Fair
Island.

79. A Hamburg ship. On January 22, 1588–9, as she
was returning to Hamburg from Lisbon, she was captured
and taken into Plymouth (*B.M. Lansd. MS.* cxliv. 282).

83. Wrecked in Bigbury Bay (*ante*, pp. 289–90), though
how she got there is a puzzle, to which Gonzalez' Relation
(*ante*, p. 371) does not offer any solution. It would seem
that after passing round Ireland she ran into the Channel,
under the impression that she was on her way to Spain,
till she was rudely brought up by the Devonshire coast. It
was on the Bolt Tail, the southern headland of Bigbury
Bay, that the 90-gun ship Ramillies was lost in 1760.

87. Lost on the coast of Ireland (*ante*, p. 302 ; Duro,
ii. 332).

121. Driven ashore and captured at Calais. She was
left aground and became a complete wreck.

122. Is said to have arrived on the coast of Ireland
about September 4, with 80 men dead of hunger and thirst
and the rest dying. From the Irish they could get no
relief, but obtained it from a French ship which they met,
and so succeeded in reaching Havre, where they were hos-
pitably received (Forneron, *Hist. de Philippe II.*, iii. 347).
The story seems doubtful in its details, for it is difficult to
imagine what a French ship could be doing on the west

coast of Ireland at that time, and the Spanish records return her as missing (Duro, ii. 332). Her purser fell into the hands of the English, possibly when he had come on shore in hopes of obtaining victuals and water. From his examination on September 9 it does not appear that the ship had been then lost.

123. After narrowly escaping the fate of the Duquesa Santa Ana (No. 48), she received the survivors on board, including D. Alonso de Leyva, the Count of Paredes, and other men of distinction, and putting to sea, was dashed to pieces near the Giant's Causeway. It was believed that every soul on board perished. The place of the wreck, pointed out by tradition, still bears the name of Spaniard Rock, the western head of Port-na-Spagniagh. Don Alonso, knight of Santiago, Commendador of Alcuesca, having served with honour in the Low Countries and as captain-general of the Sicilian galleys, had been appointed captain-general of the horsemen of Milan, but had resigned the office to take part in the English expedition, with a secret commission as commander-in-chief in case of the death of Medina-Sidonia. It is said that the king felt more grief for his death than for the loss of the fleet.

124. Returned to Spain.

125. 126. 128. Returned to Spain. Burghley noted on his copy of *La Felicissima Armada* that 126 was 'driven into Blavet.'

127. Wrecked at Bayonne.

APPENDIX H.

BIBLIOGRAPHICAL NOTES.

When the first volume of this work was issued, the
Editor was unable to speak with certainty as to the origin
of the Relation of Proceedings printed at pp. 1–18, although he felt little doubt that it was drawn up under
Howard's direction.   The correspondence between it and
the account printed by Ryther in 1590, under the title of
A Discourse concerning the Spanish Fleet, was at once
pointed out, and it was suggested that this Relation, as well
as Ryther's Discourse, was a translation from the Italian of
Petruccio Ubaldino.   The suggestion was probably made
without a close comparison of the two, for Ryther's Discourse
contains many details which are foreign to the other, and is
evidently of a later date.   The question, however, is definitely set at rest by the discovery in the British Museum
of Ubaldino's MS. (*O.R.,* 14. A. x), with a dedication to
Lord Howard of sufficient bibliographical interest to warrant its reproduction here.   It is to this effect :—

Most excellent and noble Lord :—
Your Lordship's own relation of what happened against
the enemy's fleet in these seas, first written in English, now
returneth to you in Italian, to the end that the abundant
content won for the English nation by the happy success of
those days, may also bear witness to other nations, in a
language which they understand, of the valour and conduct
of your Lordship, by the favour, wisdom and good fortune
of her Majesty the Queen, High Admiral of this kingdom,
supreme commander and chief of all that was therein
achieved, as also of the honour that was gained, and of the
security to the public quiet.   And in truth, as appertaining
to my office, I have sought to adorn the relation and the

subject thereof, written plainly in your own tongue, with
words which seem more suitable in Italian, and are requisite
as well for the clear understanding of the matter, as for in-
struction in every sort of history, but none the less free from
all adulation and partiality, so as the simple verity, looked
for by those who read, may be found therein, which otherwise I know that your Lordship would not receive it.

It remains now that I should thank your Lordship for
your favour in vouchsafing to entrust me with this charge,
and for that I being an Italian, your Lordship should have
wished the relation of your achievements to be translated
into the Italian tongue sooner than into any other, to the
end the same should be known by other nations and people.
And two things there are which, without doubt, will prosper
the same, inasmuch also as the Queen's Majesty's pleasure
appears therein.   For first, the opinion is confirmed which
hath long been held, that her Majesty hath ever been and
still is affectioned with royal constancy unto this tongue
and this nation ; and if I am not deceived, her Majesty
doth also desire and procure that the same should appear.
And for the other, the achievements of your Lordship shall
be openly showed to these distant nations and these noble
princes, like as the clear and honoured prowess of many of
your name, which are set forth in history to the honour and
great glory of the English crown ; an aim, in truth, praise-
worthy and desirable, the special mark of noble minds.

I have also added to the tenor and course of the story
some notes by way of apostilles, which seemed to me the
more necessary to the end they that read may not lack the
means whereby to attain a better understanding thereof
than they would procure by their own travail ; knowing
that there is nothing which tendeth more surely to the
perfect teaching of men to win praise for their own actions,
than the imitation of the deeds of others well and clearly set
forth in order.

I therefore humbly beseech your Lordship to receive
this my travail with that favour which those of your name
have ever used towards their humble friends ; and that you
will vouchsafe to be a mean that the Queen, your sovereign
Lady, and mine—foreigner though I be—may believe my
zeal and fidelity, for that in long service with the pen, I
have never wearied in setting forth the virtues of her

Majesty, and that in this matter, for her particular glory and for that of the crown, I have sought not to fail of my duty in any place.

Meanwhile may the good God grant to your Lordship prosperous success to your honourable thoughts, for the honour of her Majesty and the advantage of this realm. From London, the 15th of April 1589.

Your most illustrious Lordship's
affectionate and humble servant,
Petruccio Ubaldino
the Florentine.

It follows then that the very interesting document printed in vol. i. pp. 1–18, is the original of which Ubaldino's narrative is an avowedly ornate translation, and that it was drawn up, as already conjectured, under Howard's direction. The identity of the author it is impossible to guess. It is more literary in style than any of the letters written by Howard, or his secretary or his secretary's clerk. But as far as the present work is concerned, it is sufficient to know that it emanated directly and immediately from Howard ; and that, after being translated into Italian, and translated back into English, it formed the basis of the accounts given by Camden and Stow, who reared thereon a weighty superstructure of very questionable matter, and was largely reproduced by Entick in his *Naval History*. Lediard and Morant alone have referred to the original MS., but without any knowledge of its absolute value.

The celebrated Tapestry hangings of the old House of Lords, which were burnt with it in 1834, had an historical value which ought not to be overlooked. Within a very few years of the events portrayed they were designed and woven for Howard, and were already decorating the walls of Arundel House in 1602 (Chamberlain's *Letters*, 169). They were afterwards sold to King James and by him presented to the House of Lords. They were thus accepted by Howard and such friends as we may suppose he consulted —Leveson, Hoby, Preston, Seymour, 'old' Gray and others— as fair representations of the battles and the formation of the fleets. It is not of course to be supposed that they were rigidly accurate ; we know by our own experience of later pictures—such as Loutherbourg's ' First of June '—how impossible it is to arrive at accuracy of detail ; but these pictures by Cornelis de Vroom were accepted by competent judges as not outrageously unlike, which is, perhaps, the most that can be said of any battle picture. They were destroyed by the fire sixty years ago; but fortunately had been engraved, nearly 100 years before, by John Pine (fol. 1739), whose work has thus something of the value of an original record. The engravings are accompanied by a careful narrative drawn up by the Rev. P. Morant, which is sufficient for the purpose intended, but has no original authority. The maps and plans, on the other hand, are taken from the plates drawn by Robert Adams and engraved by Ryther in 1590 as illustrations to the *Discourse* already mentioned. They are thus strictly contemporary and have a real value.

A short narrative, void of all detail, was published in 1588, under the title of *The copie of a Letter sent out of England to Don Bernardin Mendoza, Ambassador in France for the King of Spain.* It is little more than a pamphlet, and has no special authority, though its age gives it a kind of respectability. Another pamphlet of the same date (1588), entitled *Certain advertisements out of Ireland concerning the Losses and Distresses happened to the Spanish Navie,* contains some of the depositions of prisoners and a general summary of the losses. All other early accounts are directly or indirectly based on the *Discourse* published by Ryther, with a larger or smaller intermixture of current gossip or Dutch imaginings, and have little or no value.

Towards the end of last century Bruce's *Report* (see vol. i. p. lxxxi) was printed for the Government, but was not then offered for sale and is now rare. Whether in accordance with his instructions or from his own judgment, Bruce dealt most fully with the defensive preparations on shore, and such naval papers as the book contains were printed from very inaccurate transcripts. Barrow, in his *Life of Drake,* has since then printed some few others ; and Mr. Motley and Mr. Froude have embodied in their Histories the substance of many extracts. But extracts, or selections, may and often do leave a very false impression on the mind of the reader ; and the full story of the campaign, from the English point of view, is—to the best of the Editor's knowledge—now printed for the first time.

INDEX

* prefixed to a man's name indicates that the spelling is taken from his signature

Achates, the, survey of, ii. 254 ; note on, 336

Acles = Hawkyns, i. 73 *n.* ; ii. 363, 369

Acton, Bar., ii. 340

Adams, William, ii. 340

Advertisements ; from Nantes, i. 90 ; by Capt. Story, 120 ; by Robert Keble, 121 : from New-haven, 122 ; from Rouen, 169 ; from Lisbon, 175, 281 ; by Rochelle ships, 215 ; from Con-quet, 240 ; from Rochelle, 230, 281 ; from Bayona, 272 ; from St. Sebastian, 292 ; from the Lord Admiral, ii. 69 ; from Blavet, 131–2 ; from the Shetland Isles, 137 ; contradictory, 146 ; by Gilbert Lee, 341

Advice, the, ii. 39

Against = again, i. 241 *n.*

Aid, the, i. 35, 126 ; ii. 124 ; to take the Santa Ana, 184, 194, 196–7 ; note on, 336

Aid of Bristol, the, ii. 338

Albert, the Cardinal Archduke, i. 93 *n.*

Alderney, recovering of, ii. 311

Allen, Cardinal, his book, i. 209 *n.*

Allin, Thomas, i. 95 *n.*

Alvarez, Vicente de, Captain of the Rosario, his examination, ii. 18

Anderson, Sir Edmond, Lord Chief Justice, i. 291 ; ii. 218

Angel of Hampton, the, burnt at Calais, ii. 287

*Anson, Commodore, his opinion on scurvy, i. p. lxiii ; adminis-ters a quack medicine to cure it, *ib.*

Antelope, the, i. 29, 66 ; with Sey-mour at Gravelines, ii. 2 ; survey of, 253 ; note on, 335

Antonio, Dom, i. 201 *n.*

Anunciada, the, i. p. xlv ; ii. 386

Aquavitæ, made out of poor wine, ii. 291

Arceo, Jeronimo de, Secretary of the Duke of Medina-Sidonia, ii. 363–4

Arderne, Robert, i. 318 *n.*

Aremberg, Count, the chief of the Spanish Commissioners for the treaty, ii. 53

Ark, the ; mentioned, *passim* ; bought for 5,000*l.*, i. 85 *n.* ; the odd ship in the world, 85 ; sails well, 86 ; the best ordered for all conditions, 96 ; a leak stopped, 138 ; waits with the stranded galleass, 346 ; survey of, ii. 242–8, 251 ; launch of, 319 ; up-holstering of her cabin, *ib.*, 322 ; streamers for, 321 ; note on, 332

Arm = to equip, i. 213

Armada, la felicísima ; not officially known as the Invincible, i. p. xxix ; popular exaggerations, pp.

xxxii, xxxiii ; ii. 51 ; faulty equipment of, i. p. xxxiii ; puts into Corunna, *ib.* ; numerical strength of, pp. xl, xli ; tactical cause of its defeat, p. li ; great preparations for, i. 2 ; equipment of, 176, 360 ; sailed from Lisbon, 194 ; reported as being at Ushant, 206, 214, 219 ; crews of many nationalities, 242 ; ii. 21 ; sighted off the Lizard, 6 288 ; is fought with off Plymouth, i. 7, 288–90, 358 ; ii. 55–6, 356–7 ; off St. Albans, i. 10–12 ; ii. 56, 359–60 ; off the Isle of Wight, i. 13–14, 359 ; ii. 56, 361–2 ; anchors before Calais, i. 15, 345, 359 ; ii. 7–9, 57, 363 ; driven from its anchors by fireships, i. 15, 346, 359 ; ii. 9, 57, 364–5 ; completely defeated off Gravelines, i. 15–17 ; ii. 10–11, 58, 207, 365–8 ; flies to the north, i. 17–18 ; ii. 39, 59, 208, 369–70 ; principal persons in, ii. 20 ; victuallers to follow, 21 ; knew that the English fleet was at Plymouth, 28 ; in want of pilots, 29 ; men wasted with sickness and slaughter, 39, 61 ; will probably pass about Scotland and Ireland, 40 ; may possibly return, 52 ; the world never saw such a force, 59 ; weakened of about 20 sail, 64 ; list of, 376–81 ; summary of losses, 382–3

Armado = great ship, i. 13 *n.*

Armament, comparison of English and Spanish, i. pp. xliv–xlviii ; of the London ships, i. 339

Arme = Herm, i. 121

Armour, price of, in Middelburg, i. 312

Arnemuiden, well affected to the Queen, i. 71, 100–1, 104 ; entertains Howard at supper, 99 ; has disbanded its company, 233

Ascoli, Prince of, i. 177 *n.* ; ii. 23

Ascott, i. 25

*Ashley, Sir Anthony, i. 25 *n.* ; his report to the Council about the San Pedro, ii. 292–6

Ashley, Henry, i. 25 *n.*

Assurance, the, ii. 335

Aumale, Duke of, his civility to Seymour, i. 177 *n.* ; besieges Boulogne, 178–9

*Austyne, John, ii. 241, 248–9, 254, 339

Axminster refuses to pay, i. 259 ; ii. 232

*Ayscue, Sir George, ii. 335

Bacon, Sir Francis, i. 98 *n.*

*Baeshe, Edward, i. 52 *n.*

Baker, Christopher, ii. 12, 194, 197

*Baker, Mathew, reports on Hawkyns' bargain, i. 38–44 ; mentioned, ii. 254, 336

Baker, Thomas, i. 86–7

Barca de Amburg, ii. 272, 275

Barfetnes = Barfleur, i. 120

Barne, Sir George, ii. 170

Barnevelt, i. 114

Barrett's *Trinity House of Deptford Strond*, referred to, i. 325 *n.*, 339 *n.*

*Barrey, Richard ; letter to Burghley, i. 86 ; to Walsyngham, 362 ; is sick, ii. 143 ; dead, 144

Barron, Sir John, Mayor of Bristol, i. 259

Barrow's *Life of Drake*, referred to i. pp. xlii, xlviii ; ii. 354, 391

Bartholomew, the, ii. 248

Bavens = faggots, i. 363

Bayona, no Spanish ships at, i. 273 ; some are there, 281 ; advertisement from, ii. 341

Bayonne de Buck, ii. 132

Beach = shingle, ii. 94

Bear, the White, i. 8, 14, 23, 26, 58, 76, 97 ; ii. 322, 339 ; hath a leak, ii. 67 ; is very sickly, 96 ; defects, 249 ; survey of, 251 ; note on, 333

Bear Yonge, the, burnt at Calais, ii. 287 *n.*, 337

Beard, a long grey, i. 49

Bearsabe, the, ii. 338

Bedford, Richard, i. 139

Beer, Howard complains of the, i. p. lxii ; ii. 159 ; had gone sour within a month, *ib., ib.* ; similar complaints by Hawke, i. p. lxii ; Darell trying to brew it again, i. p. lxiii ; ii. 160 ; better beer wanted, ii. 175

Beeston, Sir George, knighted, i. 14 *n.* ; conduct for retinue, ii. 318 ; mentioned, i. 16, 76 ; ii. 12

Begoña, the Santa Maria de, ii. 359, 366

*Bellingham, Henry, i. p. xli, 311 ; ii. 42–43, 48, 119 *n.*, 120, 123–4

Bergholt, East ; the Justices of, to the Council, i. 163–5 ; the place is poor and decayed, 164

Betake = commit, i. 208, 281

Bezoar stones, ii. 293

Bibliographical note, ii. 388

Billingsgate oyster-boat, i. 256

Bingham, George, ii. 300

*Bingham, Sir Richard, ii. 237 *n.* Letter to Fytzwylliam, 237 ; to Walsyngham, 261 ; to the Queen, 299

Blackater, Richard, ii. 291

Black-ness = Gris-nez, i. 280 and *freq.*

*Blake, General Robert, referred to, ii. 335

Blakeney, belongs to the port of King's Lynn, i. 144

Blessing, the, ii. 211

Blount, Sir Charles, i. pp. lxxvi, lxxvii, 310 *n.*

Blucke, Richard, ii. 340

Bluet = Blavet, ii. 131

Boatswains of the Queen's ships, names of the, ii. 241

Bobadilla, Francisco de, ii. 30, 367, 369

Bodenham, John, i. 229 *n.*

Bodenham, Jonas, i. 229 *n.*

Bodenham, Roger, i. 229 *n.*

*Bodley, Sir Thomas, ii. 95 *n.*, 114, 185

Bonaventure, Elizabeth, the, i. 15 *n.*, 16 ; fire on board, 26 ; runs ashore, 96 ; gets off without damage, 97 ; is 27 years old, *ib.* ; never was a stronger ship, *ib.*, 111 ; goes to Plymouth with Howard, 179 ; had been in the

Trade, 215 ; had been to take the Santa Ana, but returned, ii. 194, 196–7 ; wants of, 249 ; survey, 251 ; upholstering of cabin, 323 ; note on, 333

Bonavolia, the, ought to be abroad, i. 133 ; if not fit to sail, is fit for the fire, *ib. n.* ; not able to keep the sea, 287, 336–7 ; note on, ii. 335

Bond, Sir George, letter to, i. 193

Bond, Thomas, i. 193

Bond, the Bark, burnt at Calais, ii. 287, 337

Bonner, Abraham, i. 339

Bonner, the Bark, ii. 337

Bor, unduly credulous, i. p. lxxix

*Borlas, William, letter to Walsyngham, ii. 29

*Borough, William, his quarrel with Drake, i. p. lxxv ; abused by Drake, 74–5 ; his flight, 148 ; his chart of the Thames, 337 ; conduct for retinue, ii. 318 ; mentioned, i. 51, 80, 332 ; ii. 176, 257. Letter to Burghley, i. 74 ; to Howard, i. 76 ; to Walsyngham, i. 336 ; ii. 42, 165

Bostocke, John, i. 28 *n.* ; ii. 182, 335

Bostocke, Thomas, letter to Sir G. Bond, i. 193

Boulogne, siege of, i. 177–8

*Bowrchier, Sir George, ii. 281 283

*Braye, William, i. 136, 163

Brierley, William, ii. 20

Bright, Edward, built the Mary Rose, ii. 335

Bristol, Darell to victual the ships of, i. 253

Brockinge, Robert, i. 259

Brook, H., i. p. lxxvi

Brooke, Sir William, ii. 335

Brouage, trade to, i. 120–1

Brown, Brute, i. 310 *n.* ; ii. 4–5

Browne, Mr., i. 101

*Browne, Sir Valentine, ii. 281

Bruce, John, his *Report*, i. p. lxxxi ; ii. 391

Buckhurst, Lord, ii. 89 *n.*

*Burghley, Lord, Lord High Treasurer, *passim* ; advocated the use of the rack, i. p. xix; his arithmetic, p. lviii *n.*; memoranda by, i. 127; ii. 87, 109; is in great pain, i. 142; his daughter dead, 198; signs an order for money, 261; ii. 265; much troubled, i. 284; want of money, *ib.*; has conferred with Palavicino and Saltonstall, 285; is providing money, ii. 84. Letters to Walsyngham, i. 141, 268, 284; ii. 84; to Darell, i. 268; to Trenchard and Hawley, ii. 85

Burgundian flag, i. 236 *n.*

Burnell, Francis, i. 186; ii. 129, 316; family of, i. 186 *n.*

*Burnham, Edward, i. 351; letter to Walsyngham, i. 312

Bull, the, survey of, ii. 253; note on, 336

Butler, William, i. 339

Byford, William, ii. 319, 322–3

Bylander, i. 2, 337

Bytack = binnacle, i. 87 *n.* (Smith's *Seaman's Grammar* has bittack)

Cables, to be made in Muscovy, i. 95

*Cæsar, Sir Julius, i. 25 *n.*

Calais Cliffs, i. 282

Calico, for flags, ii. 321

Camden, his list of volunteers, i. p. lxxvi

Campvere, well affected to the Queen, i. 71, 100-1, 104; entertains Howard at dinner, 99; has dismissed its soldiers, 233

Carey, Francis, i. 310 *n.*

*Carey, Sir George, i. 14, 188 *n.*; has not authority to levy money, 132. Letter to Walsyngham, 131; to Sussex, 323; to Lord Hunsdon, ii. 137

Carey, Robert, i. pp. lxxvi, lxvii; ii. 195 *n.*

Carr, Pier o, deposition of a prisoner so called, ii. 226

*Cary, George, i. 187, 188 *n.*, 304; ii. 294, 296. Letters to: Walsyngham, i. 326; ii. 186, 278; the Council, i. 328; ii. 188, 263, 276, 289

Castillo Negro, the, ii. 275

Catalina, the, ii. 357

*Cecill, Robert, i. pp. lxxvi, lxxvii, 98 *n.*, 151. Letter to his father, 342

*Cecill, Thomas, i. pp. lxxvi, lxxvii

Cely, Dorothy, her petition, i. p. xxi

*Cely, Thomas, the case of, i. p. xxi, xxii; brought intelligence to the Admiral, 262; advocates a sharp war and short, 264; was accused of meddling with councillors' matters, *ib.*; went away with a flea in his ear, 265; in the Inquisition, 265; ii. 343-7; has lost 2,000*l.* in serving the Queen, i. 265; strikes the Inquisitors' Secretary, 266; his son's vessel taken by the French, 267; asks for leave to take a Frenchman, *ib.*; brings the Admiral word of the capture of the Rosario, ii. 107; takes two Scots to London, 158; and a good many flags, 158-9; plunders the Spanish prisoners, 209; commanded the Minion in 1585, and the Elizabeth Drake in 1588, 337. Letters to Burghley, i. 261; ii. 345; to the Queen, ii. 343

Centurion, the, i. 10

Champernowne, Sir Arthur, ii. 201 *n.*

*Champernowne, Gawen, ii. 200-1, *n.*

Chance, the, charges for, ii. 200

Chapman, Christopher, i. 135-6, 162

Chapman, Richard, ii. 332, 336

Chard, refuses to pay, i. 259; question of its share, ii. 232-3

Charges, ii. 232, 236, 268. See Estimates

Charles, the, i. 99; rescues two English barks, 100-1; to take the Santa Ana, ii. 184, 194, 196-7; survey of, 253; note on, 336

Chatham Church, i. 107

Check with = fight with, i. 280

Chester, Richard, i. 339

Chidley (? Chudleigh), John, i. 173 *n.*; commended, ii. 60 *n.*

Chopping up = clapping in prison, i. 47
Cinque Ports, men of the, commended, i. 363
Clayton, a messenger, i. 73
Clermont d'Amboise, M., i. 118 *n.*, 124
Cley, belongs to the port of King's Lynn, i. 144
Clifford, Sir Alexander, ii. 335, 340
Clothing should be sent to the fleet, ii. 97
Clyffe, Thomas, ii. 211
Cobham, Lord, i. 66, 142 ; ii. 85, 142-5
Collye, Reuben, i. 153
Command, the, ii. 201
Commissioners for the treaty, the, i. 3 ; go to the Low Countries, i. 81, 200 ; should be called home, 207 ; dishonourable if they do not come safe, 219; hard for them to be informed, 268 ; enquiry as to their state, 357; arrived at Dover, ii. 35-6, 52, 69
Concur = converge, i. 337
Condé, the Prince of, his death, i. 106 *n.*, 120
Conway, Sir John, ii. 108-9, 127
Conyers, John, ii. 237, 306
Cooke, Sir Anthony, i. 98 *n.*
Cordell, Thomas, ii. 316, 336, 338
Cordova, D. Luis de, ii. 300-1
Corporals, their pay, ii. 231
Cotton, for upholstering cabins, ii. 319, 322
Cotton, Richard, i. 119
Council, the Privy, resolutions of, i. 170. Letters of : to Darell, i. 248 ; to the Deputy-Lieutenants, 250; to Howard, 317; to Trenchard and Hawley, 334 ; to Seymour, 335 ; to Burghley, ii. 121
Council of State of the United Provinces, letter of, to the Queen, ii. 71 ; beg for a continuance of the Queen's support, *ib.* ; letter to the Queen's Council, 72 ; are endeavouring to strengthen their fleet, 73 ; hope her Majesty's fleet will follow up the Spanish, *ib.* ; send the examination of prisoners, *ib.* ; and of deserters, 74 ; fear that Parma will turn his great power against their country, *ib.*
Council of War, i. 6, 8, 210 ; ii. 1, 6, 8
Council of War, Spanish, i. p. xxxviii ; ii. 28, 133, 368
Courteney, William ; letter to Walsyngham, i. 127 *n.*
*Courteney, Sir William, ii. 294, 371-2
Covenanters, persecution of the, i. p. xix
Coxe, William, i. 11 *n.* ; brings intelligence, 92-4 ; note on, 92 ; boards the San Lorenzo, ii. 9 ; is slain, *ib.*
Crane, the, ii. 339
*Croft, Sir James, i. 49 *n.*, 219
Cromster, ii. 125 *n.*
*Crosse, Sir Robert, i. 17 *n.*, 25, 263 ; ii. 58, 335-7, 340. Letter to Drake, i. 171
Cumberland, Earl of, i. 16 ; ii. 6, 59, 69, 84, 95, 195, 211, 297, 338
Cure's ship, burnt at Calais, ii. 287 *n.*
Cut sail = set sail, i. 82 *n.*, 84, 179
Cuttle, Robert, i. 339

Dainty, the, ii. 339
Dancers, the, gallantest, i. 201
*Darell, Marmaduke, i. 137 *n.*, 197 *n.*, 234-6, 268, 296 ; ii. 111-2, 235, 265, 305. His wise and well doings, i. 197, 199; his care, 218 ; money should be sent to, 228 ; time of victualling, 243 ; to send word when the victuals will be ready, 248-9 ; to victual the Bristol and Lyme ships, 253 ; reprimanded by Burghley, 270 ; will prepare victuals for the London ships, 293 ; money to be sent by a draft on some merchant in Exeter, *ib.* ; the statements in his former reports are true ; begs he may not be condemned until the contrary is proved, 294 ; begs for payment, 295 ; declares

the sour beer was good at first, ii. 159 ; is to brew it over again, 160. Letters : to the Council, i. 243, 252, 289 ; to Walsyngham, i. 244 ; to Burghley, 293. Letter to, from Burghley, 268

Darnix, ii. 319 *n.*

*Darrell, William, i. 197 *n.*

Davey, John, i. 126

Deadmen, the pay of, i. 284

Dead-shares, i. p. lxix, 32 *n.* ; ii. 178

Defend = repel, i. 264 ; ii. 148

Defiance, the, i. 229 *n.*

Delight, the, i. 11 ; ii. 12, 337

Denmark, the King of, may relieve the Spanish ships, ii. 98-9

Denny, Sir Edward, ii. 335

Denys, Sir Robert, i. 304 ; ii. 232

*Denys, Sir Thomas, ii. 277

Derby, Earl of, i. 343

Derrick's *Memoirs of the Royal Navy*, referred to, i. p. xlv

Desmond, Earl of, ii. 275

Determination = ending, i. 243

Detract time, i. 200, 203

Diet, i. p. lxix, 32 *n.* ; ii. 178, 322

Digges, Thomas, 55 *n.*

*Dillon, Sir Lucas, ii. 281, 283, 285

*Dillon, Sir Robert, ii. 281, 283

Disdain, the, i. 7 ; ii. 338

Donago, Horatio, ii. 262 *n.*, 276

Doncella, the, receives some of the men of the San Felipe, ii. 367

Doria, Andrew, i. 123 *n.*

Douglas, Archibald, i. 233

Dove, Richard, i. 339

Dover, inspected by the Lord Admiral, i. 82 ; by Wynter, *ib.*, 180 ; beer to be brewed at, ii. 159-60

Downs, the small, i. 254

Dragon, the, ii. 211

*Drake, Sir Francis ; his career, i. pp. xiii, xiv, lxxiii–lxxvi ; Admiral in the west, 4 ; Vice-Admiral of the fleet, 5 ; pursues some merchant ships, 8 ; ii. 103 ; captures the Rosario, i. 9 ; ii. 108, 135-6 ; commands the second squadron, i. 12 ; attacks the Spanish fleet, 16 ; a man

killed by bursting of a gun, 48 ; his quarrel with Borough, 74-5 ; urges the advantage of going on the coast of Spain, 124, 200, 203, 237 ; want of powder, 125 ; demands muskets and arrows, 126 ; meets the Lord Admiral at Plymouth, 179 ; fear of, at Cadiz, 182 ; commended by the King of Spain, 183 ; bears himself lovingly and kindly, 202 ; one of the Admiral's council, 210 ; advanced money for victuals, 218 ; sent into the Trade, 246 ; lying towards Ushant, 247 ; places the men at six upon four, 252 ; takes measures to procure intelligence, 256 ; is ready for sea, 273 ; Parma and Medina-Sidonia shall not shake hands, 341 ; victuals should be sent, 342 ; takes possession of the Rosario, 358 ; the prisoners of the Rosario are his, 364 ; Medina-Sidonia shall wish himself among his orange trees, *ib.* ; his seal and crest, ii. 62 *n.* ; his friendly relations with Howard, 101 ; is railed at by Frobiser, 102-3 ; in council about the infection, 139 ; Medina-Sidonia is like to have unquiet rest, 147 ; carries a letter to the Court, 167 ; his note of the Rosario's treasure, 168-9 ; to report what is due to Potts, 255 ; his rate of pay, 315. Mentioned, i. 7, 73, 103, 107-8, 113, 115, 126, 139, 143, 150-1, 170, 173, 201, 235, 249, 257-8, 270-1, 276-81, 296-7, 300-1, 326 ; ii. 6, 93-4, 110, 143, 163, 165, 173, 176, 229, 287, 303, 305, 317, 336-7, 339. Letters : to the Council i. 123 ; to the Queen, i. 147, 165 ; ii. 68 ; to Seymour or Wynter, i. 289 ; to Walsyngham, i. 228, 341, 364 ; ii. 61, 62, 97, 101, 146

Drake, Richard, sent to the Admiral, i. 354 ; his instructions, 355 ; had charge of D. Pedro de Valdes, ii. 136

Dreadnought, the, i. 11, 16; ii. 322; wants of, ii. 249; survey of, 252; note on, 335

Dublin, Archbishop of, ii. 281, 283

Duck, the, ii. 339

Dudley, Sir Robert, 335

Duke, Robert, i. 339

Dunkirk, two ships of, stayed, i. 222; pilots from, 236; not a place for ships to lie off, 331, 333; ships ought to be there more than they are, ii. 148–9

Dunwich, petition of, i. 154

Duro, Captain C. Fernandez de, his *La Armada Invencible*, i. p. xxiv *n.*; referred to, *passim*; on the proceedings of the Armada off Plymouth, i. pp. xxxviii, xxxix

Dutch chroniclers had no special opportunities, i. p. lxxix

Dutch fleet off Dunkirk, ii. 49; the chief cause of the overthrow of the Armada, 50

Dutch seamen will not go to sea till they are paid, i. 337; deposition of two, ii. 77; of fourteen, 78; lies told by, 78–81

Dutch ships to join Seymour, list of, i. 230; thirty or forty coming over, 337

Eager = sour, ii. 189

Eddystone, the, i. 7

Edward III., gold noble of, i. p. ix

Edward VI., expedition to Scotland in reign of, ii. 311

Edward Bonaventure, the, note on, ii. 336–7

Edward of Malden, the, ii. 338

Eleanor, the, ii. 254

Elephant, the, i. 130

Elinathan = the Elizabeth of Dover, i. 186 *n.*; ii. 338

Eliot, Mr. (? Lawrence), ii. 249, 339

Elizabeth, Queen of England, approves of Drake's conduct and knights him, i. p. xiv; her grievances against Spain, xv; not hoodwinked by Parma, xxxv;

her object in the negotiations, *ib.*; alleged parsimony as to the men's victuals, lvii; a groundless charge, *ib.*; so also as to the lack of powder, lxiv; careless for her surety, 133, 320; relieth on a hope that will deceive her, 133; if time is lost, money or jewels will not help, *ib.*; reads a letter from Robert Cecill several times, 151; may have a good peace, 209; should have a care for her person, 217, 220; commends Howard's care, 217; is implored to awake, 225; might take on herself the absolute government of Holland and Zealand, ii. 53; dined with Leicester at the camp, 82; could not in honour leave the camp, 83; wishes to intercept the Spanish treasure ships, 167; warrant to Fenton, 308

Elizabeth of Lowestoft, the, burnt at Calais, ii. 287, 338; estimate for, 288

Elizabeth Bonaventure, the. See Bonaventure

Elizabeth Jonas, the, i. 10, 11, 14, 97; drove, ii. 67; very sickly, 96; measures to cleanse her of the infection, *ib.*; unavailing, *ib.*; at Chatham, 145, 166; wants of, 249; survey of, 250; note on, 334

Elizabeth, the, ii. 202

Embargo, on English shipping in Spain, i. p. xxiii; a general, ordered, i. 127; of Scottish ships, 134; of French, *ib.*; of the great Swede, *ib.*

Emptions, ii. 317–8

English fleet, numerical strength of, i. pp. xli, xlii; beats out of the Sound, 288; ii. 55; has not lost threescore men, ii. 40; very great sickness in, 96, 138; list of, 323–42

Englishmen, feigning to be Scots, i. 134; in the Armada, ii. 19–20; expected to favour the King of Spain, 23

Enriquez, Diego, son of the Viceroy of Peru, his gallantry, ii. 356, 359, 361, 366 ; put in command of the Andalusian squadron, 362 ; his death, 384

Enriquez, Diego Tellez, son of the Commendador of Alcantara, his bravery, ii. 356 *n.*, 359, 366–7. See San Juan de Sicilia

Eperon, Duke d', ii. 184 *n.*

Erisey, James, ii. 340

Estimates and charges, i. 27, 29, 30, 64, 114–5, 140–1, 275 ; ii. 298 ; the London ships, i. 251 ; for the boom at Tilbury, 287 ; for wages and provisions, 296 ; for payment in discharge, ii. 229 ; rewards to certain officers, 231 ; extraordinary victual, 304 ; miscellaneous accounts, 318

Exeter, the Mayor and Citizens of, pray that the several places belonging to the port may be ordered to assist in preparing the ships, i. 143

Falcon Blanco Mayor, the, note on, ii. 386

Famars, M. de, i. 83, 313

Fancy, the, 338

Feat = fetched, ii. 10

Feld, Nicholas, his intelligence, ii. 132

Fenner, George, i. p. xlviii

*Fenner, Thomas, i. 16, 263, 286 ; ii. 6, 335 ; his estimate of the Spanish galleys, i. p. xxxii ; points out the danger of being caught without victuals, i. 92 ; sends list of available officers, 118 ; in favour of going on the coast of Spain, 203, 238 ; one of the Admiral's council, 210 ; considerations by, 238 ; his armorial bearings, 279 *n.* ; a faithful servant of the Queen, ii. 41 ; sent to the Queen to explain about the infection, 139. Letters to Walsyngham, i. 90, 117, 279 ; ii. 37 ; to Drake, 171

Fenner, William, i. 172 ; ii. 194, 197 ; mortally wounded, ii. 336

Fenton, Edward, i. 16, 17 ; ii. 11, 64, 176, 336 ; to assist Hawkyns in making up the accounts, ii. 307–9 ; conduct for retinue, 318

*Fenton, Sir Geoffrey, ii. 281, 283

*Fernandez, Simon, ii. 339

Fett = fetch, ii. 45

Fighting, new method of, i. p. lxv

Finch, i. 312

Finch, Sir Moyle, i. 312 *n.*, 320 *n.*

Fire on board the Bonaventure, i. 26

Fireships, i. 345 ; fitted out at Dover, 364 ; sent back, 365 ; resolved on in a council of war, ii. 1, 8 ; fitted out, 9, 57 ; their success, *ib.*, 364–5

Fisher, John, memorial of, ii. 105 *n.*

Fishing, good, i. 198

Fitzmorris, James, ii. 270, 275

Flag ; Spanish ships fly the English, i. 125, 236 ; the French, 236 ; the Burgundian, 236 *n.* ; of St. George, ii. 246, 249, 320 ; of the Queen's arms, 246 ; ensigns, streamers and pennants, 246, 249, 320–1

Flamenco, Jaques, ii. 272

Fleet, list of the English, ii. 323–24 ; of the Spanish, 376–87 ; comparative strength of the two, i. pp. xl-lii

*Flemyng, Thomas, brings the news of the Armada off the Lizard, i. 6 *n.* ; ii. 171 ; takes the San Salvador to Weymouth, i. 9 ; carried her powder to the fleet, ii. 157, 189 *n.* ; letter to Burghley asking for pay, 313

Fletcher, Mr., resident at Cadiz, i. 182

Flores de Valdes, Diego, ii. 23, 357 *n.*, 369 ; imprisoned, 383

Floyd, Seymour's servant, i. 234 ; ii. 36

Floyd, Leicester's secretary, ii. 234

Flushing, the squadron before, i. 28–9 ; visit of the fleet to, 96–106 ; Bonaventure on shore at, 96–7, 104 ; three men-of-war from, capture the San Mateo, ii. 30

Foresight, the, ii. 194, 196–7 ; note on, 336

France, the victim of Spanish intrigue, i. p. xxxi ; the King of, one of Howard's Trinity, 48 ; will not assist the Spanish, 245 ; has joined the League, 329

Francisco, Emanuel, deposition of, ii. 224

Fraser, Sir William, his *Book of Carlaverock* referred to, i. 232 *n.*

Fremoso, Emanuel, deposition of, ii. 218

French, the, expected to join with Parma, ii. 4 ; boats spying at Torbay, i. 329 ; ship, said to be on the west of Ireland, ii. 386 ; ships, expected to join the Spanish, i. 237, 245 ; great preparation of, ii. 92

Fridays, only one meal on, i. 109

*Frobiser, Sir Martin, his family and early career, i. p. lxxvi ; his good service and death, *ib.* ; had no book learning, lxxvii ; commands the fourth squadron, i. 12 ; is knighted, 14 ; returned from a cruise, 106, 150 ; in favour of going on the coast of Spain, 200, 203 ; one of the Admiral's council, 210 ; in sharp fight, ii. 56–7 ; rails against Drake, 101–3 ; to command a squadron in the Narrow Sea, 162 ; rate of pay, 315. Mentioned, i. 25, 103, 150 ; ii. 184, 317, 336

Froude, Professor, on Dorothy Cely's petition, i. pp. xxi, xxii ; on the sour beer, lxiii ; his *History of England* referred to, 48 *n.*, 213 *n.* ; ii. 391

Fuentes, Count of, i. 177 *n.*

Furthow, William, ii. 340

*Fytzwylliam, Sir William, ii. 237 *n.*, 273, 281, 283, 301 ; memoranda for the examination of prisoners, 269 ; joint letter to the Council, 279. Letters to Walsyngham, 283, 286

Galleass, the great. See San Lorenzo

Galley slaves, Englishmen as, i. p. xviii, 181 ; ii. 282, 343–7

Galleys, reported to be lost, ii. 132 ; note on, 387

*Gardener, Sir Robert, ii. 281, 283

Garibay, Juan de, ii. 360, 366

Garrans = nags, ii. 273

George, the, an old hoy, i. 286

George Bonaventure, the, ii. 338

Gerard, Thomas, a volunteer, i. 15

Gertruidenberg, mutiny at, i. 314 *n.* ; 351–2 ; ii. 34

Gift of God of Lowestoft, the, ii. 211

Gil, Juan, put to death, ii. 302 *n.* ; captures a fishing-boat, 303 *n.*, 355 ; sent to Parma, 359

Gilbert, is oppressively charged at Orford, i. 155

Gilberte, Adrian, ii. 202

*Gilberte, Sir John, i. 304 ; ii. 296 ; has set apart two pipes of wine for himself, ii. 187 ; ships sent out by, 200–3 ; his sharp practice, 263–4, 277–9, 291. Letter to Walsyngham, i. 326 ; to the Council, i. 328, 338 ; ii. 188, 291

Girona, the, note on, ii. 387

Glass and glazing, charge of, ii. 321

Goddard, Anthony, i. 73

Godolphin, Sir Francis, advertisement from, i. 211 *n.*

Golden Hind, the, i. 6, 9 *n.* ; ii. 337

Golden Hind, Drake's, ii. 337, 339–40

Golden Lion, the. See Lion

Golden Rose of Enkhuysen, the, i. 280

Gomes de Medina, Juan, ii. 386

Gonson, Benjamin, Sir John Hawkyns' father-in-law, i. p. lxxiii

Gonson, Benjamin, Sir John Hawkyns' brother-in-law, conduct for retinue, ii. 318

Gonzalez del Castillo, Gonzalo, his Relation, ii. 371–5

Goodlad, William, i. 339

Gorges, Arthur, i. p. lxxvii

Gorges, Sir Edmund, i. 55 *n.*

Gorges, Sir Edward, i. 55 *n.*

*Gorges, Sir Ferdinando, i. 55 *n.*

*Gorges, Nicholas, i. 55 *n.*, 311,

315 ; ii. 48, 88–9, 119 ; in command of eight London ships, i. 357 ; becalmed in the river, *ib.* ; joins Seymour, ii. 6, 14, 43 ; is in bad health, 15, 36 ; his victuals will run out, 37 ; his rate of pay, 316. Letter to Walsyngham, i. 357

Gourdan, M. de, i. 16, 222, 282–3, 311 ; ii. 174 ; detains the San Lorenzo, i. 341–3, 348–9 ; ii. 2, 114, 150 ; welcomed the Armada, i. 345, 347, 363

Gran-Grifon, the, note on, ii. 386

Gran-Grin, the, ii. 356, 361

Gravelines, the battle of, i. pp. lii, liv, lv, 16–7, 359 ; ii. 2, 7–11, 58, 365–8 ; contradictory statements as to the wind, ii. 58, 365, 367

Gray, John, ii. 104, 195 *n.*

Gray, Thomas, i. 70 *n.* ; ii. 104, 171, 182, 195 *n.* ; pay as vice-admiral, 315

Green cotton for upholstering cabins, ii. 319

*Greynvile, Sir Richard, i. 172, 187, 277, 297 ; ii. 163, 181, 337–40

Greynvile, Roger, ii. 340

Guise, the Duke of, places a force at St. Omer, i. 66 ; accepted by the Parisians, 184 ; his demands of the King, 195 ; in league with the King of Spain, 203 ; ii. 27 ; and with Parma, i. 207 ; to support the armada with 30,000 men, ii. 20 ; is the Queen's enemy, 172. Mentioned, i. 223

Gunners, need of, on board the ships, ii. 259–60 ; corporation of, 259

Guns, description of, i. p. xliv ; ii. 350–1 ; considered ignoble by the Spaniards, i. xlix ; great windage allowed, *ib.*

Gwynn, David, the fictitious story of, i. pp. lxxvii, lxxviii ; the true story of, lxxviii, lxxix ; to conduct the examinations of prisoners, ii. 219 *n.*, 269, 271 ; charges against him, 279–85 ; a most lewd man, 280 ; a caitiff unworthy of life, 284 ; con-

demned of manifest falsehood and perjury, 285 ; sent to England, 286

Gwysans, partisans of the Duke of Guise, i. 67

*Gylberte, Sir Humphrey, i. 326 *n.*

Handmaid of Bristol, the, ii. 338

Hare, William, i. 339

Harper, Richard, i. 339

Harquebus-a-crock, i. 12 *n.* ; ii. 154 *n.*

Harvey (? William), i. 15

Harwich, inspected by Howard, i. 33, 45 ; fleet arrived at, ii. 67 fifteen victuallers at, 84

Hart, William, ii. 287, 337

*Harte, Eustace, his charge against Gwynn, ii. 279–85 ; his declaration, 281–3 ; nephew of Mr. Auditor Peyton, 285 ; is sent to England, 286

Hastings, petition from, ii. 256

Hatches = deck, ii. 135

*Hatton, Sir Christopher, i. 317, 334

Hatton, William, a volunteer, i. p. lxxvi

Haul the coast, i. 239

Hawes, Mr., of London, 239

Hawes, Sir James, ii. 340

Hawes, Ralph, i. 257 ; ii. 248

*Hawkyns, Sir John, overwhelmed at San Juan de Lua, i. p. xiii ; intrigues with the King of Spain, *ib.* ; marries Gonson's daughter, lxxiii ; becomes Treasurer of the Navy, *ib.* ; is accused of peculation, lxxiv ; commands an expedition to the coast of Portugal, *ib.* ; dies in the West Indies, *ib.* ; boards the San Salvador, i. 9 ; commands the third squadron, 12 ; attacks the Santa Ana, 13 ; is knighted, 14 ; his bargain for the navy, 34–7 ; his conduct criticised, 38–44 ; ii. 266–8 ; proposes resolute war, i. 60 ; has left his bargain without warrant, 77 ; commended by Howard,

79 ; the shipwrights are hostile to him, 87 ; advises a squadron on the coast of Spain, 200, 203 ; of the Admiral's Council, 210 ; advanced money to Darell, 218 ; lying towards Scilly, 247 ; hard speeches against, 273 ; his account of the fighting, 358–61 ; arrived at Harwich, ii. 67 ; in council about the infection, 139 ; to pay money to relieve the men, 183 ; his pains to win Burghley's favour, 214 ; is seldom idle, *ib.* ; thinks nothing more is to be feared from the Spaniards this season 214 ; begs that Fenton may be appointed to assist him with the accounts, 307 ; which is done, 309 ; his pay as rear-admiral, 314. Letters to Burghley, i. 33, 87, 95, 111, 274 ; ii. 162, 175, 211, 229, 352 ; to Walsyngham, i. 58, 358 ; ii. 67, 213 ; to Howard, ii. 66 ; petition to the Queen, ii. 306. Mentioned, i. 24, 51, 73, 80, 112–13, 115, 117, 135–6, 141, 159, 271, 296, 311 ; ii. 6, 141, 143, 173, 184–5, 265, 287, 335, 337

*Hawkyns, Richard, i. 16 ; ii. 339

*Hawkyns, William, Mayor of Plymouth, i. 73 *n.* ; is graving the ships, 73 ; draws a bill on his brother, *ib.* ; the Plymouth ships will be revictualled, 260 ; letter to the Council, the Spanish fleet is in view, 289 ; to receive the brass guns from the Roebuck, ii. 289

Hawkyns, William, ii. 340

*Hawley, Francis, letter to, from the Council, i. 334 ; letter to, from Burghley, ii. 85 ; he is to take charge of the ordnance and stores of the San Salvador, and send up an inventory, 86 ; joint letter to the Council, 151. See Trenchard

*Heneage, Sir Thomas, i. 312, 317, 321. Letter to Walsyngham, ii. 95

Henriquez, D. Juan, ii. 174

Henry V., his killing the prisoners, i. p. xvii

Henry VII., his right to the throne, i. p. xxvii

Henry VIII., supplies of victuals under, i. lix, 137 *n.* ; the Mary Rose and Swallow were ships in his time, 79 *n.* ; expedition to Leith under, 213 ; granted a corporation for the gunners, ii. 259 ; the engagement with the French in 1545, 311

Heredia, Pedro de, sent to Gourdan, ii. 363

*Hoby, Sir Edward, i. 98 *n.*, 105, 279 ; ii. 6, 55. Memorandum by, i. 262

Hoby, Sir Thomas, i. 98 *n.*

Hogge Bay, Bay of Hogges = La Hogue, i. 120 ; ii. 138 ; a Spanish ship there, *ib.*

Hohenlo, Count, gone to Hamburg, i. 354

Holland, to arm forth shipping, i. 213

*Holstok, William, i. 68, 80, 311 ; ii. 176, 257, 265

Holy Office, the. See Inquisition

Hope = feel confident, ii. 99

Hope, near Salcombe, Spanish ship wrecked at, ii. 289–91, 294

Hope, the, i. 126 ; ii. 58 ; graved and tallowed, i. 73 ; came in with a leak, 273 ; to be cleared and out and grounded, ii. 67 ; sent to Newhaven, 169 ; survey of, 251 ; note on, 335

Hope Hawkyns, the, burnt at Calais, ii. 287, 337

Horsemen, show of, ii. 166

Hortop, Job, doubtful credibility of, i. pp. xix, xx

Hovenden, Richard, ii. 273

*Howard, Charles, Lord, his family, i. pp. lxx–lxxiii ; nearly related to the Queen, lxxi, lxxii ; his nepotism, lxxiii ; his writing, lxxx ; his spelling, lxxxi ; takes command of the fleet, i. 4 ; his commission as Lord Admiral, 19 ; inspects Dover and Harwich,

33; his report on Harwich, 45; goes at his own expense, 47–8; his Trinity, 49; his visit to Flushing, 96; dines with Sir W. Russell, 98; with the citizens of Campvere, 99; sups with those of Arnemuiden, *ib.*; detains a flyboat of Calais, 102; joins Drake at Plymouth, 179; is ordered not to go on the coast of Spain, 192; complains of want of victuals, 198; will catch fish, *ib.*; thinks it would have been better to go on the coast of Spain, 200, 203–4; danger of lying off and on, 204; hopes his wife may have his boy, 212; and the keeping of Hampton Court or Oatlands, *ib.*; the Queen should have care for her person, 217; the negotiations cannot have a good end, 219; urges the necessity of sending victuals, 220; implores the Queen to awake, and see the villainous treasons round about her, 225; to trust no more to Judas kisses, 227; lies in mid channel, 247; sent to the Groyne for intelligence, 247; has placed the men at six upon four, 252; takes measures to procure intelligence, 256; durst have gone to Venice in the Hope, 274; doth not ground with his ship, 275; otherwise occupied than with writing, 288; in fight with the enemy, 289; put to sea in haste, so that some of the ships did not complete their victual, 294; all available reinforcements to be sent out, 299; two of the enemy's ships taken, *ib.*; his wise and honourable carriage, 332; 'we pluck their feathers by little and little,' 341; stayed to capture the galleass, ii. 2, 10; 'set on a brag countenance,' 54; his 'Abstract of Accidents,' 55; a strong force ought to be maintained, 59; 'sure bind, sure find; a kingdom is a great

wager,' *ib.*; forced to leave the pursuit, 69; is sent for to Court, 82; said to have been driven to eat beans, 95; returns from the Court, 139; finds a grievous infection in the ships, 138, 140; consults as to the measures to stop it, 139–41; sends many flags to London, 158 *n.*; officers and men must be paid, 165, 183; will open the Queen's purse, 183; will contribute himself, *ib.*; is not the ablest man in the kingdom, *ib.*; will be at the Court, 185; ordered extraordinary victual to be issued, 303; the charge ought to be allowed, *ib.*; will pay for the extra beer and wine, 304; his pay, 314; conduct for retinue, 318; his 'Relation of Proceedings' (i. 1–18) translated into Italian by Ubaldino and dedicated to him, 388. Letters to Burghley, i. 23, 25, 45, 71, 78, 79, 83, 87, 96, 102, 137, 150, 159, 179, 186, 189; ii. 96, 169, 171, 303; to Walsyngham, i. 46, 48, 50, 56, 65, 69, 103, 106, 133, 195, 199, 202, 208, 219, 226, 245, 256, 271–2, 288, 340; ii. 53, 59, 142–4, 158–9, 167, 183; to the Queen, i. 224; ii. 138; to the Council, i. 217, 228; ii. 139; to Sussex (?), i. 299; to Winchester, ii. 117. Mentioned, *passim*
Howard, Charles, ii. 340
Howard, Sir Edward, his complaint about the victualling, i. p. lix
Howard, John, the philanthropist, i. p. xvii
*Howard, Lord Thomas, boards the San Salvador, i. 9; is knighted, 14; a most gallant gentleman, 210 *n.*; great sickness on board his ship, ii. 140; going to the Court, 185; his diet, 317, 322; conduct for retinue, 318. Mentioned, i. pp. xxxiv, lxxii, 16, 24; ii. 6, 11, 84
Howe, Mr., i. 193

Hoys, proposal to substitute them for ships, i. 127-9 ; suitable for the defence of the river, 207, 286

Hunsdon, Lord, i. pp. lxxii, lxxiii, 69 *n.*; his sickness, ii. 161, 165, 175 ; hath regained his feet, 184. Letter to, from his son, ii. 137

Hunter, a Scottish gentleman, i. 107

Huntingdon, Earl of, ii. 141, 146

Hurleston, Thomas, i. 86

Hussey, Dr., i. 272

*Huygens, Christian, ii. 72 *n.*, 74

Importable = unbearable, ii. 178

Incommend = recommend, i. 175

Infection, on board the Elizabeth Jonas from the beginning, ii. 96 ; measures to cleanse her of it, *ib.*; unavailing, *ib.* ; in many ships, and very dangerous, 138, 140

Inferring = reporting, ii. 114

Inquisition, the ; charges against, i. p. xvi ; exaggerations of, *ib.* ; strong feeling aroused by, xxiii ; Cely's sufferings in, i. 265-6 ; ii. 343 ; rumour that the King of Spain would establish it in England, ii. 20

Invasion, how it might be done, ii. 312

Ipswich, the bailiffs of, letters to Walsyngham, i. 145, 160

Ireland, Spanish ships on the coast of, ii. 218, 238-40, 286, 299

Jacks, to be upon their, i. 196

Jackson, Richard, ii. 323

James VI., King of Scotland, his claim to the throne of England, i. p. xxvii ; one of Howard's Trinity, i. 49 ; the Spaniards will force him to leave his country, ii. 120

Jeffrey, Martin, ii. 339

Jenkins, David, i. 135

Jenkinson, Anthony, ii. 319

Jennens, John, ii. 211

John of Barnstaple, the, ii. 338

John of Gaunt, the ancestor of the King of Spain, i. p. xxvii

Jones, John, Mayor of Lyme, i. 259, 304

Jones, Morris, ii. 211

Jones, Nicholas, ii. 296-7

Juan Bautista, the galleon San, ii. 360

Justinus of Nassau, Count, i. 255 *n.*; coming out with thirty ships, ii. 4 ; his letter to Prince Maurice, 34 ; joined off Dunkirk by fourteen of the Queen's ships, *ib.*; warned by Seymour, 37 ; off Dunkirk, 49 ; dines with Seymour, 123 ; very wise, subtle and cunning, 124. Letter to Walsyngham, ii. 125

Keble, Robert, i. 121

King's Lynn, memorial from the Mayor and Aldermen of, i. 144 ; they ask that the towns which belong to the port may bear part of the charge, *ib.*

Kingston-upon-Hull, letters from the Mayor and Aldermen of, i. 135, 161 ; all the mariners have been pressed, 135 ; all the best ships are abroad, 136 ; the Privy Council is displeased by their letter, 161 ; their ships have returned and will be fitted out at once, 162

*Knollys, Sir Francis, i. 317

Knyvet, Thomas (according to Monson, 327, this was the future Lord Knyvet of Escrick. It is not improbable ; but Monson's testimony on such a point is by no means conclusive), ii. 36 *n.*, 124, 126, 128, 130, 146, 168, 179, 184

*Kyllygrew, Henry, i. 98, 313 ; advertisements from, ii. 83. Letters to Walsyngham, i. 351 ; ii. 32

Lancaster, James, i. pp. xxxiv, xlviii

Land's End, the, i. 33 *n.*; ii. 42-3 *n.*

Lane, Thomas, ii. 319

Lanterns, cost of, ii. 321

Lee, Gilbert, his intelligence, ii. 341-2

Lee, Richard, a volunteer with Seymour, i. 310

Leese = lose, ii. 8

Leicester, Earl of, i. 56, 151, 280, 304 ; ii. 234 ; is cook, cater and hunt, i. 305 ; commends the spirit of the soldiers, 305, 318 ; complains of Norreys and Williams, 306–9 ; insists on the respect due to his place, 307 ; was at Dover on July 29, 356 ; sends advertisements, ii. 35 ; the Queen dining with, 82 ; powder sent to, 89 ; his death, 234 *n.*; an adventurer in Fenton's voyage, 336. Letters to Walsyngham, i. 298, 305, 318, 321 ; ii. 35

Leicester, the galleon, i. 11, 280 ; note on, ii. 336

Leighton, Sir Thomas, i. 181

Lepanto, the battle of, i. p. lxv ; ii. 60

Leveson, Sir Richard, i. 78 *n.*, 99 ; ii. 335

Leveson, Sir Walter, ordered to make compensation to a Dane, i. 78

Leyva, D. Alonso de, i. 177 ; ii. 23, 300, 358, 360, 366, 368, 387

Licornio, John de, deposition of, ii. 225

Lieutenants, a necessity of the service, ii. 164 ; pay of, 231

Lion, the Golden, i. 10, 11, 13 ; ii. 322 ; is very sickly, ii. 140 ; wants of, 249 ; survey of, 252 ; defects of, 297 ; note on, 333

Lonck van Roozendaal, Cornelis, i. 230 *n.*

Low Countries, the English dread of a hostile occupation of, i. p. xxiii.

Lucar, Cyprian, *The Art of Shooting*, ii. 351

Luzon, D. Alonso de, ii. 359–60, 366 ; his examination, ii. 271

Lyme Regis, letters from the Mayor of, i. 138, 259 ; their larger ships are absent, i. 139 ; their merchants have suffered great losses, 140 ; Darell to victual their ships, 253 ; Axminster and Chard ought to assist, 259 ; as to the payment of the levy, ii. 232

Lyon Quay, i. 57

Lyzarde, Lewis, ii. 323

Machine-ships, ii. 365

Maddocke, William, ii. 211

Maeda, Luis de, ii. 360

Maldonado, D. Juan, ii. 360

Malines, Gerald, i. 174

Mammer = hesitate, shilly-shally (Cf. *Othello*, III. iii. 71), i. 59

Mandillion = a mantle, ii. 210

Manrique, Jorge, ii. 364

*Mansell, Sir Robert, ii. 339

Manwayring, Sir Henry, ii. 335

Marchant, John, ii. 340

Margaret and John, the, warmly engaged on July 23, i. 10 ; at the capture of the San Lorenzo, 346 ; her share in the capture of the Rosario, ii. 104–8 ; note on, 337

Marques, Francisco, ii. 77

Mary, Queen of England, ii. 311

Mary, Queen of Scots, effect of her death on Spanish policy, i. p. xxvi ; referred to, i. 197 *n.*

Mary of Hamburg, the, stayed at Plymouth, i. 189

Mary Rose, the, i. 10, 11, 14, 16–7, 79 *n.*; ii. 64 ; survey of, ii. 252 ; streamers for, 321 ; painting, 323 ; note on, 335

Master, the, an officer of high standing, i. p. lxx ; his pay, *ib.*

Masters attendant, principal masters of the Queen's ships, ii. 127 *n.*, 195, 241, 339

Masts, a cargo of, i. 134 ; of 'oak and clampered together,' ii. 298

Mated = confounded, ii. 123

Maurice, Prince, at Middelburg, i. 83 ; his ill-feeling towards the English, 84 *n.*; Howard writes to him, 98 ; he goes to Lillo, *ib.* ; and thence to Holland, 99 ; his departure from Middelburg, 101, 105 ; writes to Howard, 99, 105 ; is led by Villiers and Famars, 313. Letter to Walsyngham, ii. 70. Mentioned, 1. 352, 354

Maxwell, Lord, imprisoned, i. 232 *n.*

Mayflower of London, the, i. 11
Mayflower of Lynn, the, i. 145
Meath, Bishop of, ii. 281, 283
Medernix, a sort of canvas, ii. 200 *n.*, 249, 297
Medina-Sidonia, Duke of, takes command of the armada, i. p. xxix ; his character, *ib.*, xxxviii ; his instructions, xxxv ; his movements off Plymouth, xxxvii, xxxviii ; was warned against the English artillery, l ; sent a message to Parma, 345 ; shall wish himself at St. Mary Port among his orange trees, 364 ; his proclamation, ii. 19 ; to be under Parma, *ib.* ; sends a message to Parma, 29 ; has agreed with Parma to return, 83 ; jealous of Parma, 99 ; said to be returning, 147 ; 'like to have unquiet rest,' *ib.* ; his directions for the armada's return to Spain, 240 ; his Relation, 354–70 ; his return to Spain, 383. Mentioned, i. 7, 11, 109, 177, 301, 341, 345 ; ii. 148, 198–9, 292, 341
Meek, Thomas, ii. 340
Meldrum, Thomas, ii. 288, 338
Men, the reduced numbers, i. 27–33; the full numbers to be raised, 62–3 ; should be paid six weeks wages, 71 ; the gallantest company of, 190 ; at six upon four, 252 ; never nobler minds, 273 ; demand their pay, 283 ; as many as could be used, 323 ; sick, to be discharged, ii. 85 ; said to have drunk their own water, 95 ; great sickness among, 96 ; die in the streets, *ib.* ; in want of clothes, 97 ; and money, *ib.* ; full numbers, 164 ; imperfect men, *ib.* ; being paid off, 177 ; sick, are discharged, 179 ; better men are to be got by higher wages, 352
Mendoza, D. Bernardino de, his false advertisement, ii. 60 *n.* ; *Copie of a Letter to*, 391
Merchant Royal, the, i. 10 ; note on, ii. 336–7

Merlin, the, survey of, ii. 253
Merrick, Sir Gilly, ii. 336
Merriman, Captain, letter to Fytzwylliam, ii. 286
Messendewe = Maison Dieu at Dover, ii. 160. Cf. Jameson's *Scottish Dictionary*
Mexía, D. Augustin, ii. 361
*Michell, Captain Mathew, his opinion of scurvy, i. p. lxiii
Middelburg, i. 71, 83, 84, 312 ; the burgomaster invites Howard to dinner, 99
Middleton, Thomas, ii. 118, 338
Minion, the, note on, 337
Minion of Bristol, the, 338
Mockado = woollen velvet, ii. 319
Moncada, D. Hugo de, slain i. 342, 347 ; ii. 58
*Monck, George, referred to, ii. 335
Monson, Sir William, ii. 335 ; his *Naval Tracts* referred to, *freq.*
Morant, Rev. P., his narrative mentioned, ii. 391
Morgan, Captain, Howard's man, i. 50 ; a tall gentleman, *ib.* ; is extreme sick, *ib.* ; commands the soldiers in the Bear, *ib.*
Morgan, Sir Thomas, to bring over the thousand shot, i. 354 ; brings over 800 shot, ii. 65, 82, 90, 92, 121 ; his letter to Leicester ; his advertisements mere gossip, 83 *n.* ; to be sent back, 167, 183
Morris, Fytzwylliam's man, ii. 286
Morrys, Ralph, of Ipswich, refuses to pay the rate, i. 161
Mortality in the fleet, i. 258, 269 ; ii. 212 ; in the Elizabeth Jonas, ii. 96
Motley, his *History of the United Netherlands* referred to, i. p. lxxviii, 11, 49 ; ii. 173, 199
Mountagu, Lord ; his brother slain, ii. 30
Mousehole, a small cove on the west side of Mount's Bay, a few miles to the south of Newlyn, i. 221
Muelenpeert, Frantz, a prisoner, ii. 77
Musgrave, Captain, a very suffi-

cient man, ii. 108 ; the brothers, deserve thanks, i. 233

Musketeers. See Shot

Mutinies of Dutch towns, ii. 33, 72. See Gertruidenberg

Names, the spelling of, i. p. lxxxii

Napper, Giles, his declaration, i. 181 ; rows in the Spanish galleys, *ib.*

Narrow Seas, the, to be well guarded, i. 211, 219. See Frobiser, Sir Martin ; Palmer, Sir Henry ; Seymour, Lord Henry

Nash, William, joint memorial of, ii. 105

Navarre, the King of, i. 95 ; ii. 281 ; reported poisoning of, 106 ; good success of, 282 ; hath small means, 313

Navy, the survey of, ii. 250–4

Navy Board, the, abolished, i. 80 *n.*

Nelson, referred to, i. 148 *n.*, 364 *n.*

Nevenson, Mr., ii. 93

Newhaven men will defend the Santa Ana, ii. 169 ; have taken a hoy of Gray's, 171 ; are at the devotion of the Queen's enemy, 172. See Santa Ana

Newport, Isle of Wight, a poor market, i. 132

Newton, Margaret, wife of John Bodenham, i. 229 *n.*

Newton, Mary, wife of Sir Francis Drake, i. 229 *n.*

Newton, William, Howard's man, i. 66 *n.*

Nile, the battle of the, referred to, i. p. lii

Nonpareil, the, i. 10, 14, 16, 126 ; graved and tallowed, 73 ; on the coast of Brittany, 279–81 ; survey of, ii. 252 ; note on, 335

Nonsuch, the, ii. 335

Norreys, Sir Edward, brings news of the return of the armada, ii. 139, 142, 144, 163, 173 ; a different version of his news, 150

*Norreys, Sir John, i. 306 *n.*, 321 ; ii. 164 ; his expedition to Lisbon, i. p. lxxvi ; marshal of the foot-

men at Tilbury, 306 ; Leicester's complaint against, 306–9 ; at Dover, 310

North, Sir Henry, ii. 144

Northumberland, Earl of, said to have served as a volunteer, i. pp. lxxvi, lxxvii

Norton, Robert, his *Practice of Artillery*, ii. 351

Occupied = made use of, ii. 144 *n.*

O'Doherty, ii. 272–3

O'Donnell, ii. 270, 273–5

Officers, Burghley's list of, i. 27–8 ; Fenner's list of, 118–9 ; list of, with Seymour, ii. 5 ; list of, in fleet, 324–31 ; notes on, 338–42

Ojeda, Captain, ii. 357, 359

Olderne, a money of account (?), i. 183 *n.*

Olyckers, William, a prisoner, ii. 77

Oquendo, Miguel de, General of the squadron of Guipuzcoa, ii. 276, 357–9 ; his death, 385

Orange, the Princess of, i. 100 *n.*, 313 *n.*

Ordnance, Books relating to, ii. 351. See Guns

Orford, to furnish a ship, i. 153 ; petition from, 154

*Oseley, Nicholas, a spy for the Government, i. 301 *n.* ; his letter to Walsyngham, 301 ; a volunteer on board the Revenge, *ib.* ; ii. 62

Oxenham, John, his death, i. p. xvi

Oxford, Countess of, her death, i. 198 *n.*

Oxford, Earl of, said to be a volunteer in the fleet, i. pp. lxxvi, lxxvii

*Palavicino, Sir Horatio, Burghley confers with, i. 285 ; letter to Walsyngham, 304 *n.* ; is going to join the Admiral, *ib.* ; his proposal to Parma, ii. 198–9 *n.* ; his Relation, 203–9 ; confused with Donago, 262

Palmer, Sir Henry, i. 25 *n.*, 84, 85, 101, 216, 334; ii. 11, 130, 185; commands a squadron off Flushing, i. 28-9, 49; convoys the commissioners for the treaty, 81, 83; goes to Dover for the fireships, 364-5; ii. 8; joint letter to the Council, ii. 44; in council with Howard, 139; to command a squadron in the Narrow Seas, ii. 162, 166, 173-4; rate of pay, 315

Paredes, Count of, i. 177 *n.*; ii. 387

Parma, the Duke of, nephew of the King of Spain, Governor-General in the Low Countries, is to form an army of invasion, i. p. xxvi; will seek to land at Sheppey, Harwich or Yarmouth, i. 213; cannot put to sea, 214; has not sufficient shipping, 231; his pride abated, 241; is watched by Seymour, 246; proposal to send a messenger to, from the Queen, 268; may show his courage, 309; expected to come out, 321-2; shall not shake hands with Medina-Sidonia, 341; great lack imputed to him, 343; sends message to the armada, 345; ii. 29; to be watched, i. 364; was to command the expedition, ii. 19, 27; to be King of England, 20; will have revenge on the Dutch, 31; accused of having betrayed the cause, 32; blocked in by Justinus, 49; is in a great chafe, 53; will turn his power against Holland, 74; is determined to come out, 83; can do nothing unless the armada return, 91; is as a bear robbed of her whelps, 99; hated by the Spaniards, *ib.*, 150; has disembarked his soldiers, 125; has seventy or eighty flat-bottomed boats at Sluys, *ib.*; is expected to lay siege to Ostend, *ib.*; his speech, 127; said to be preparing to embark, 147; his ships are small, *ib.*; ought to be regarded, 148; said to have retired into Brabant, 150; may be entreated to make a division of the Low Countries with the Queen, 198; may attempt some unlooked-for enterprise, 199; his further preparations, 310. Mentioned, i. 2, 3, 15, 47, 57, 82, 103, 107, 124, 178, 206-7, 223, 335, 343, 356, 359, 361; ii. 4, 40, 60, 100, 114-6, 120, 123, 217, 221, 354, 358-9, 362-4, 369

Pastrana, the Duke of, ii. 174

Pay, irregularity of, i. p. lxvii; not exceptional, *ib.*; prompt payment, a modern thing, *ib.*; the men demand their, lxviii; ii. 141, 163; system of, in the sixteenth century, i. lxviii; rates of, ii. 314-7; proposed increase of, 352

Penelope, the, lost off Cape Corrientes, i. 17 *n.*, ii. 337

Pent, the, i. 82 *n.*

Peñafiel, Marquis of, ii. 30, 360, 365

Pereda, Melchor de, a prisoner, ii. 153

*Perrot, Sir John, sends intelligence, ii. 131

Peruse = examine, i. 305

*Peryam, John, Mayor of Exeter, i. 260; ii. 277

*Peter, Richard, i. 261; ii. 111, 305

*Pett, Peter, notice of, i. 38 *n.*; his report on Hawkyns, 38-44; plans a boom at Tilbury, 298-9, 321; signs report of survey, ii. 254

Peyton, Mr. Auditor, ii. 285

Philip II., King of Spain, his grievances against England, i. p. xv; foments rebellion in Ireland, *ib.*; determines to invade England, xxv; disapproves of Santa Cruz' plan, xxvi; his descent from John of Gaunt, xxvii; different estimates of, xxix; sensible of the difficulty of the task, xxxi; one of Howard's Trinity, 48; will have all things perfect, 203; hath engaged his honour, 209; effect of his hot crowns in cold countries, ii. 98;

will not attempt more this year,
199 ; will have no success against
England, 310 ; possible danger
from, 312 ; alluded to, *freq.*
Philips, Miles, his story, i. pp. xix,
xx ; needs confirmation, *ib.*
Phœnix of Dartmouth, the, ii. 200
Pilchards for Spain, stayed, ii. 292
Pilling knaves, ii. 130
Pimentel, D. Diego de, captured
in the San Mateo, ii. 30, 50, 58,
70 ; his examination, 75 ; is in
the thickest of the fight, 356,
366–7 ; refuses to leave his
ship, *ib.*
Pine, John, his engravings of the
tapestry hangings of the House
of Lords, ii. 391 ; referred to,
i. p. liv ; ii. 207, 356
Pirates, might be summarily slain,
i. p. xvii ; losses by, 130 ; if
men have not justice, they will
be, ii. 172–3
*Pitt, Richard, Mayor of Wey-
mouth, i. 153, 303 ; ii. 16
Platt, Captain, ii. 104
Polwhele, Captain, i. 171–3
Poole, petition of Mayor and
Alderman of, i. 129 ; decayed
state of the town, 130
*Popham, Sir John ; letter to Wal-
syngham, i. 191 *n.* ; to Burghley,
ii. 218
Porter, John, Mayor of Saltash,
i. 260
Posa de Santiso, Juan, Captain of
the San Felipe, ii. 367
Potts, Anthony, petition of, ii. 254
*Poulet, Sir Amyas, i. 49 *n.*, 317,
334
Poulter, Richard, ii. 241, 248, 339
Powder, alleged short supply of,
i. lxiv ; no available reserve, *ib.* ;
unprecedented expenditure of,
lxv ; insufficient supply of, 125–6 ;
more wanted, 289 ; requisition
for, 303 ; from the Spanish prize,
338 ; want of, ii. 11, 13 ; that
sent from Dover did not reach
the Admiral, 85
Powell, Captain of soldiers, ii. 66
Preachers, wages of, ii. 231, 317

Prest, imprest, money paid on
account or as an earnest, 89 *n.*,
and *freq.*
Preston, Amyas, i. 15 *n.* ; ii. 57–8
Pretended = intended, i. 229 *n.*
Prideaux, Captain, ii. 340
Primrose of Poole, the, i. 129
Prince Royal, the, ii. 335
Prisoners, articles for examination
of, ii. 17, 24–5, 269–71 ; examinations of, ii. 18, 22, 27, 50, 75,
215-28, 271 ; under sure guard,
70 ; maintenance of, 170–86, 188,
264, 276–7 ; should have been
made water spaniels, 186 ; plundered by Cely, 209 ; ransom of,
215–7 ; many of them poor men,
ib. ; put to the sword, 259 ; made
to work in Gilberte's garden,
264 ; names of, from the San
Pedro, 295–6 ; names of, killed
in Ireland, 301–2
Proclamation, for the maintenance
of discipline, issued by Howard,
i. 36 ; no proclamation of war by
Spain, ii. 17, 19
Puntales, the Castle of, i. 182
Pycke, Edward, ii. 338

Quarles, James, his conditions, i.
52–4 ; his book, 234 ; instructs
Darell, 243 ; report by, ii. 110 ;
to be sent to the fleet, 141 ; victualling accounts, 236 ; order to
265. Mentioned, i. 112–3, 117
141, 187, 244, 261, 284, 298 ; ii.
87, 91–2, 122, 175, 177
Quarrells = panes of glass ; also
the frames for the panes, ii. 321

Radclyff, Anthony ; letter to Walsyngham, ii. 170
Rainbow, the, her armament, i. pp.
xlv, xlvi ; gone to Dover with
the Lord Admiral, 33 ; new sails
for, 111 ; Seymour moves into,
179 ; the Admiral may find the
lack of, ii. 4 ; her part at Gravelines, *ib.* ; her lieutenant, 4-5 ;
her master, a most valiant and
sufficient man, 127 ; is a summer

ship, 128; not fit for winter service, *ib.* ; wants of, 249 ; note on, 333

Ralegh, Carew, wants guns for Portland, i. 329

*Ralegh, Sir Walter, his defence of Howard's tactics, i. p. lxvi, 355 *n.* ; said to have served in the fleet, lxxvi ; which seems improbable, lxxvii. Mentioned, i. 85, 257, 326 *n.*, 343 ; ii. 201 *n.*, 332, 337

Rammekens, the, design to burn the squadron before, i. 45

Ransom, question of, ii. 215-7, 371-2 ; of D. Pedro de Valdes, 384

Rat, the, ii. 342

Rata, la = the French *la Forte* ; note on, ii. 385

Rawlyn, Henry, i. 339

Raymond, George, i. 16 *n.* ; ii. 194, 197, 338

Recalde, Juan Martinez de, Admiral of the fleet, commander of the Biscay Squadron, i. 7, 15 *n.*, 301 ; ii. 23, 219, 361, 366, 368 ; his ship beaten and spoiled, ii. 134, 356, 358, 360 ; his death, 383

Redbird, sends intelligence from St. Sebastian, i. 292

Regazona, the, note on, ii. 385

Reparted = divided, ii. 105

Reprisals, cause loss, i. 94 ; Sir George Carey has not gained by, 182 ; Lyme has received no benefit from, 140 ; nor Ipswich, 147 ; nor Weymouth, 152 ; Southampton much impoverished by, 157

Resolution, the, ii. 335

Revenge, the, i. 9, 16, 33, 126, 301 ; ii. 339, 374 ; wants of, 249 ; survey of, 252 ; note on, 333-4

Revenge of Lyme, the, i. 139

Rewalted = fallen over, ii. 174

Rewards, system of, i. pp. lxix, lxx, 32 *n.*

Reynolds, Captain, ii. 335

Rich, Penelope, Lady, i. 308 *n.*, 310 *n.*

Rich, Robert, Lord, afterwards Earl of Warwick ; a man much respected and loved, i. 308 ; except by his wife, *ib. n.*

Richard, the, ii. 338

Roberts, John, ii. 194, 197

Roberts, John, his *Complete Cannonier*, ii. 351

Roebuck, the, helped to capture the Rosario, i. 9 ; took the Rosario to Torbay, 326 ; a fine ship, 343 ; powder sent by, ii. 88 ; has not come to the fleet, 141-3, 186-7 ; charges for, 200 ; had guns from the Rosario, 263, 289 ; note on, 337

Roger, Wynter's man, i. 333

Room, romer = to leeward, 7 *n.* and *passim*

Rosa, the N. S. de la, note on ii. 365

Rosario, the N. S. del, brought into Torbay, i. 326 ; an inventory is to be made, 327 ; the men sent on shore, 328 ; the powder to be sent to the Admiral, 338 ; taken by Drake, 358 ; dismasted and captured, ii. 56, 134-6 ; prisoners from, 18, 22 ; dispute as to the capture of, 101-8 ; treasure on board of, 168 ; inventory of guns and stores, 190-2 ; charges for, 192-4 ; has been shamefully plundered, 278-9 ; some of her guns in the Roebuck, 289 ; note on, 384

Roscoff, ships of, i. 165, 282-3, 287

Rose of Exeter, the, i. 143

Russell, Sir William, i. 45 *n.*, 104, 254-5, 337, 351-2 ; ii. 4, 29, 108-9 ; entertains Howard and his officers, i. 97 ; to send over powder, i. 357 ; ii. 83

Russia, trade with, i. 188

Ryall of Weymouth, the, has rendered good service, ii. 117 ; order for her payment, *ib.* ; her charges, 118

Rye Camber, ii. 94

Rymenam, battle of, i. p. xxx; ii. 346 *n.*

Sachfield, John, ii. 338, 341
Sackvile, Captain, ii. 335
St. Aldegonde, M. de, i. 313
St. Leger, Mrs., i. 172
*Salman, Robert, Master of the Trinity House, i. 324 *n.* ; letter to Burghley, *ib.* ; proposes to fit out thirty sail, 325
Salto, D. Betran del, ii. 272, 291
Saltonstall, Richard, i. 285; ii. 84
Samaritan, the, ii. 187, 203, 263
Sampson, John, ii. 169, 182, 184, 339
Sampson, the, ii. 338
San Felipe, loss of, ii. 30, 384 ; beaten and disabled, 367
San Juan, the, ii. 383–4
San Juan of Diego Flores, the, ii. 356 *n.*, 359, 361, 366, 368
San Juan de Sicilia, fouls the San Lorenzo and breaks her rudder, ii. 57 ; in the thickest of the fight, 359, 361, 365–6 ; note on, 385
San Lorenzo, the, driven on shore at Calais and captured, i. 15, 340–3, 346–9 ; ii. 2, 9 ; breaks her rudder, ii. 57, 64 ; is ' utterly rewalted and sunk in the sand,' 174
San Marcos, the, ii. 30 *n.*, 359–60, 368, 384
San Mateo, the, capture of, ii. 30, 384 ; in the thickest of the fight, 358–9, 366–7 ; disabled and sinking, 367
San Pedro Mayor, wrecked near Salcombe, ii. 290, 371, 386 ; the hospital ship, 290 ; names of the prisoners, 295 ; their treatment, 371–5
San Salvador, the, damaged by an explosion, i. 8, 301, 359 ; ii. 56, 357–8 ; horrible state of when taken, i. 9 ; brought to Weymouth, i. 9, 334 ; an inventory to be taken, 334 ; ii. 86; great stealing on board, 153 ; the inventory, 154–8 ; lost at Studland, 296 ; note on, 385
Sandwich, battle of, i. p. lii ; beer of, is sour, ii. 159 ; store of victuals at, 175 ; petition from, 255

Santa Ana, the, beaten out of the fleet and wrecked at Havre, ii. 360–1, 384 ; ships to go to her, 170, 177, 179, 182, 195–6
Santa Ana of Oquendo, note on the, ii. 385
Santa Ana, the Duquesa, note on, ii. 385
Santa Cruz, Marquis of, defeats Strozzi at Terceira, i. p. xxiv ; gives in his plan for the invasion of England, xxv ; which is not approved, xxvi ; his death, xxviii, 101 ; referred to, ii. 276, 382
Save = to shake casks, i. 241 *n.*
Scales Cliffs, the fleets anchored near, i. 336 *n.* ; ii. 1, 7
Scantyings, i. 219
Scattered = separated, i. 359 ; ii. 35
Schenk, Sir Martin, i. 352 *n.*
Sconces, suggested for the defence of the river, i. 207 ; ii. 310
Scotland, King of. See James VI.
*Scott, Sir Thomas, ii. 113, 120. Letter to Leicester, ii. 93
Scout, the, ii. 211 ; survey of, 254 ; note on, 336
Sea-gate = swell, ii. 41 *n.*
Secretaries, pay of, ii. 231, 317
Seize = recover, ii. 41 *n.*
Serrano, Antonio, ii. 364
Sewed = dried, i. 16 *n.*
Sewell, James, ii. 338
Seymour, Sir Edward, ii. 189 *n.*
Seymour, Edward, Earl of Hertford, eldest son of the Duke of Somerset by his second marriage, i. p. lxxii. *Cf.* ii. 189 *n.*
*Seymour, Lord Henry, a near connexion of Howard's, i. p. lxxii ; Admiral in the Narrow Seas, i. 4, 14, 16, 17, 24, 211, 261, 296–8, 337 ; ii. 12, 87–91, 110–1, 121–2, 160, 256 ; has a bad cold, i. 70 ; in command of the E. Bonaventure, 96, 104 ; his honourable mind, 95 ; moves into the Rainbow, 179 *n.* ; advises hoys for the defence of the river, 207 ; his force should be strengthened,

211 ; stays two Dunkirk ships, 222 ; descried thirty sail, 223 ; victuals sent to, 235 ; watches Parma, 246 ; stays two Roscoff ships, 282 ; munition, men, and powder not come, 310 ; choicest 'shot' to be sent to, 317 ; goes to join the Admiral, 321 ; lying off Dunkirk is dangerous, 330-1 ; goes off Scales Cliffs, 336 ; is short of victuals, 340 ; his charge at Gravelines, ii. 2 ; has returned to the Narrow Seas, 2, 4, 43 ; the Queen's 'fisherman,' 3 ; thinks Howard is jealous of him, 3 ; sends intelligence, 113 ; entertains Count Justin, 123 ; commends Walsyngham's zeal and ability, 126 ; will be 'kin to the bear' before he comes abroad again, 127 ; wishes to go home, 128 ; is a man not 'suitable' with his colleagues, *ib.* ; in council with Howard, 139 ; never loved to be penned in roads, 145 ; regrets that there are factions in the fleet, 146 ; questions the authority of Drake and Hawkyns, *ib.* ; to be at the Court, 185 ; suggests that the Queen and Parma might divide the Low Countries between them, 198 ; his pay, 314-5 ; conduct money for retinue, 318. Letters to Walsyngham, i. 104, 173, 184, 206, 222, 231, 233, 253, 285, 309 ; ii. 14, 36, 52, 108, 112-3, 114, 118, 123, 126, 128, 145, 198 ; to the Council, i. 300, 330 ; ii. 44, 120 ; to Burghley, i. 177 ; to the Queen, ii. 1 ; to Howard, ii. 129 ; (?) to Prince Maurice, ii. 115

Sheffield, Lady, i. 46 *n.*, 211 *n.* ; ii. 129-30

Sheffield, Edmund, Lord, knighted, i. 14 ; his valour, 16 ; commands a Queen's ship, 24 ; enquires into the religion of his barber, 65 ; is a zealous protestant, 66 ; one of the Admiral's council, 210 ; a most gallant gentleman, *ib.* ; note on, 211 *n.* ; at the council of war, ii. 6 ; hears Frobiser's complaint, 102-3 ; his ship very sickly, 140 ; to be at the Court, 185 ; his diet, 317, 322 ; conduct for retinue, 318

Sheffield, Mr. Henry, examines the barber, i. 65-6

Sherbrooke = Cherbourg, i. 120

*Sheriffe, John, his note on ordnance, ii. 350-1

Ships, the Queen's, commended, i. 79, 81, 201, 274 ; great number needed to transport an army, 213 ; French, will join the Spanish fleet, 237 ; the, have been supplied with fresh victuals in harbour, 244 ; charges of the London, 251 ; those to come in first that are most in need of victuals, 253 ; were victualling when the Admiral put to sea, 294 ; by sparing and mortality, they have a store of extra victuals, 295 ; the Queen's ships better sea-boats than the merchantmen, 331 ; thirty or forty Dutch to be expected, 337 ; the smaller, will be discharged, ii. 85 ; four good, might follow the Spanish fleet, *ib.* ; return of, 90-1 ; are infectious and corrupted, 140 ; three gone to take the Spaniard at Newhaven, 145 ; survey on the Queen's ships, 241, 250 ; burnt off Calais, 287 ; notes on, 332-8

Ships, the four great, ought to be abroad, i. 107 ; estimate for fitting out, 114 ; charges for, 140-1 ; the reports against, are false and villainous, 201 ; are in most royal and perfect state, 274 ; their pay, 276 ; alleged order to pay them off, ii. 173 *n.*

Ships, list of, i. 27, 30, 62-4, 68-9, 72 ; repaired by Hawkyns, 44 ; of eight which left Queenborough with the Lord Admiral, 75 ; that went west with the Admiral, 167 ; ii. 179 ; that remained in the Narrow Seas, i. 168 ; ii. 180 ; coast ships with Seymour, i. 185, 255 ; Dutch ships, 230 ; of the

West country, 260 ; ii. 181 ; with Gorges, i. 311, 315 ; ii. 269 ; of ten, with Bellingham, i. 339 ; with Seymour on August 1, ii. 5 ; with Seymour on August 6, 47 ; at Harwich with Hawkyns on August 8, 66 ; in the Narrow Seas with Palmer and Frobiser, 162, 175, 182, 185, 212 ; with Drake in the West, 180–1 ; at Chatham, 212 ; of the Queen's whole army at the seas, 323–31

Ships, the Spanish, were undermanned, i. p. xliii ; not lost by storm, lvi ; but by reason of the damage they had received, *ib.* ; seen near Scilly, xxxiii, 5, 206, 221, 225, 246, 257, 360 ; memorandum of, 56 ; wearing English flags, 125 ; their sails crossed with a red cross, 221–2 ; have returned to Spain, 237 ; 'not half of them men-of-war,' 290 ; 'wonderfully spoiled and beaten,' ii. 38, 68 ; three sunk, 53 ; one sunk, 58 ; two taken to Flushing, *ib.* ; 'ships, masts, ropes, and sails much decayed by shot,' 61, 97 ; without anchors, 98 ; riding under Beechy, 169 ; one at Havre, *ib.* ; wrecked on the coast of Ireland, 261–2, 299 ; list of the armada, 376 ; notes on, 382

Shore, Commander, his *Smuggling Days* referred to, i. 165 *n.*

Shot = advanced, i. 242 *n.* ; ii. 39

Shot = musketeers or harquebusiers, a good number of the best, to be sent to the fleet, i. 317 ; a thousand to be sent from the Low Countries, 353–4 ; ii. 31. See Morgan, Sir Thomas

Shrouded = sheltered, ii. 10

Sickness, very prevalent in the fleet, i. p. lxiv, 258 ; grows wonderfully, ii. 96 ; very great, 138 ; numerical estimate of, 212 *n.*

Sidney, Sir Philip, his death, i. 101 *n.*

Sike = so as, i. 211

Simons of Exeter, advertisement by, i. 212, 225

Sleeve, the, i. 5 *n.*, 205, 224, 245–6 ; a large room for men to look unto, 247

Slingsby, Captain, ii. 335

Sluys, importance of the battle of, i. p. ix ; flat-bottomed boats collected at, ii. 125

Smerwick, the butchery at, i. p. xvi ; ii. 237 *n.*

Sonoy, Colonel, i. 83 *n.* ; 99, 101, 105, 314

Sotomayor, Gregorio de, his deposition, ii. 22

Sound, the, insecure anchorage, i. 195

South Cape = Cape St. Vincent, i. 187

Southampton, petition of the Mayor and Aldermen of, i. 155 ; the town is much decayed, 156 ; unable to pay the charge, 157 ; not one gentleman remaining in the town, *ib.* ; all the seamen have been pressed, 158

Southwell, Sir Robert, Howard's son-in-law, i. pp. xxxiv, lxxii ; commended, 17 ; captain of a Queen's ship, 24 ; his ship sickly, ii. 96 ; conduct money for retinue, 318

Spain, the great power of, i. pp. xxx, xxxii

Spain, King of. See Philip II.

Spale = Seville, i. 240

Spaniards, drowned, ii. 261 ; put to the sword, *ib.* ; names of several, 274

Spanish forces, the, were to land in the Thames, ii. 19 ; were to put all that resisted to the sword, *ib.* ; have lost many sick and slain, 68 ; marvellously plucked, 92 ; very sickly, 97 ; can get no sufficient relief in Norway or the isles of Scotland, 98 ; on the coast of Ireland, 218 ; their men dying of hunger and thirst, 221

Speedwell, the, ii. 336

Spindelow, Henry, ii. 104 *n.*

Spy, the, survey of, ii. 254 ; note on, 336

Stade, trade with, i. 188, and *freq.*

Stafford, Sir Edward, i. 46 *n.*, 142, 245 ; ii. 60

Stanley, Sir William, i. 85 *n.*

Starke, Mathew, his deposition, 101

States General of the United Provinces, the, vote extraordinary contributions, ii. 33

Storm, a great, 'considering the time of year,' ii. 68. See Weather

Story, Captain, his advertisement, i. 120

Stucley, William, a traitor, ii. 20

*Studley, Andrew, Mayor of Southampton, i. 159

Sun, the, i. 286

Surgeons, prest by the company of, i. 66 ; the barber-surgeon of the Bear accused of papistry, 65 ; is a zealous, honest man, 66

Susan Parnell, the, ii. 338

Sussex, Earl of, i. 14, 322 *n.* ; ii. 169, 341 ; sends intelligence, i. 119 ; letter to Walsyngham, i. 322 ; has sent powder to the Admiral, *ib.* ; desires that powder may be sent to Portsmouth, 323 ; powder to be sent to, 338, ii. 88 ; letter to the Council, ii. 194 ; complains of Gray's insolence, 195 ; has sent powder and stores to certain ships, 197 ; victualling account of, 211

Swallow, the, i. 11, 16, 55, 66, 79 *n.* ; survey of, ii. 253 ; streamers for, 321 ; note on, 336

Swansey, Richard, a messenger, i. 228

Swanson, Richard, a messenger, i. 243, 259. Probably the same as the preceding

Swift, Jasper, i. 363

Swiftsure, the, i. 32, 126 ; survey of, ii. 253 ; notes on, 336

Sydenham, Sir George, ii. 233

Talbot, the Bark, burnt at Calais, ii. 287, 337

Tare up = disparaged, i. 88. Cf. *Faery Queen*, III. vii. 39

Tarry = wait for, ii. 13

*Teddeman, Sir Thomas, i. 86 *n.*

Tello, D. Rodrigo, sent to Parma, ii. 354 ; detained, 362 ; returned, 363

Terceira, Spanish victory at, i. pp. xxiv, lxv, lxvi ; ii. 382

Thomas, John, i. 158

Thomas, Pascoe, his *Voyage to the South Seas* referred to, i. p. lxi

*Thomas, William, on the necessity of a full supply of gunners, ii. 258–60

Thomas of Plymouth, the, burnt at Calais, ii. 287, 337

Thomas Bonaventure, the, ii. 338

*Thoms, John, his letter to Howard, ii. 296

Tiger, the, survey of, ii. 253 ; note on, 336

Tiger, the, another ship, ii. 339

Tilbury, boom at, i. 287 *n.*, 298–9

Toledo, Francisco de, escaped to Nieuport, ii. 30 (where he is erroneously called Bobadilla), 51 (where he is, by another error, called Pedro) ; resolves to stick to his ship, 367

Tomson, agent for Archibald Douglas, i. 233

*Tomson, Richard, i. 233 *n.*, 344 *n.* ; ii. 104–5 ; letter to Walsyngham, i. 344 ; boards the San Lorenzo, 347 ; treats with D. Pedro de Valdes for the ransom of the prisoners, ii. 215–7

Tomson, Robert, his story, i. p. xx ; needs corroboration, *ib.*

Tonnage, very differently estimated, ii. 323

Townshend, Sir Roger, is knighted, i. 14 ; has a command in the fleet, 25 *n.* ; ii. 96 *n.*

Trade, the, a geographical term, i. 196, 215, 246, 324 ; ii. 348–9

Tramontana, the, i. 99 ; note on, ii. 336

Treasure, in the armada, ii. 23 ; in the Rosario, ii. 20, 29, 168 ; Spanish, to be intercepted, ii. 167

Treaty, the, a fraud, i. 200, 203. See Commissioners

*Trenchard, George, letter to, from the Council, i. 334 ; letter to, from Burghley, ii. 85 ; to send an inventory of stores on board the San Salvador, ii. 86 ; letter to the Council, 151 ; enclosing the inventory, 152 ; there have been great charges, 153. Mentioned, ii. 233, 297

Triumph, the, i. 10, 11, 97 ; with Drake at Gravelines, ii. 2 ; drove, ii. 67 ; wants of, 249 ; survey of, 250 ; note on, 335

Tydyeman, Henry, i. 86

Tydyeman, William, i. 86

Tyrone, Earl of, ii. 274

*Ubaldino, Petruccio, relates the story of the campaign, ii. 388 ; dedicates it to Lord Howard, *ib.*; it is translated for Ryther, 390

Ughtred, Henry, a ship owner, ii. 336

Unicorn of Bristol, the, ii. 338

*Valdes, D. Pedro de, General of the squadron of Andalusia ; his account of the proceedings off Plymouth, i. xxxviii ; his ship dismasted, i. 7-8, ii. 134-5, 357 ; and captured, i. 9, 301, ii. 56, 135-6 ; ordered to be sent on shore, i. 356, 364 ; articles for his examination, ii. 25 ; his examination, ii. 27 ; his account of the proceedings until his capture, ii. 133-6 ; is treated with touching ransom, ii. 215-7 ; was deserted, ii. 357-8 ; his residence in England, ii. 374-5 ; ransomed, ii. 384 ; memoir of, ii. 384-5. Letter to the King of Spain, ii. 133 ; a copy of it sent to Walsyngham, ii. 149. Letter to Walsyngham, ii. 217. Mentioned 22-3, 355

Valencera, La Trinidad, of Venice, ii. 272, 362, 366, 386

Valke, M. de, Councillor of Zealand, dines with Sir W. Russell, i. 98

Van der Myle, president of the Dutch Council of State, his forcible and wise oration, ii. 32-3

Vanegas, Luis, ii. 367

Vanguard, the, at Gravelines, ii. 2, 10-11 ; spent her main-top mast, 46 ; fitting of her cabin, 319, 321, 323 ; note on, 333. Mentioned, i. 16, 33

Vargas, Alonso de, his examination, ii. 77

Vaughan, Captain, ii. 104

Vaughan, William, a messenger, ii. 89

Vavasour, Thomas, ii. 60 *n.*, 335-6

Velasquez, Juan de, his examination, ii. 76

Venetian ships, sore beaten and in danger of sinking, ii. 221

Victory, the, defects, ii. 249 ; survey, 251 ; streamers for, 321 ; note on, 334-5. Mentioned, i. 9-11, 16, 97 ; ii. 2, 322, 339

Victuallers, for the armada, i. 194 ; ii. 21, 53

Victuals : cost of, i. 53-4 ; order for, 68-9 ; scale of, 109, proposal for saving, 110 ; estimate for, 113 ; Henry VIII.'s practice, p. lviii, 137 *n.*; two months insufficient, 149 ; might be provided at Dover, 181 ; should be supplied for six weeks, 184 ; rice purchased for, 189 ; danger of their not being ready, 92 ; danger of being without at the enemy's coming, p. lix, 137 ; short supply of, 198 ; danger of short supply, 203 ; delayed, 218 ; getting in, 225 ; fresh, in harbour, 244 ; men at six upon four, 252, 269 ; misconception regarding this, p. lxi ; common practice in the navy, *ib.* (Cf. Tucker's *Memoirs of the Earl of St. Vincent*, i. 230, 241) ; many of the ships incomplete, p. lx, 294 ; victualling of London ships, 325 ; want of, 430; ii. 4, 6, 13, 59 ; allegations concerning this, i. p. lviii-lx ; no provision of, i. p. lviii ; fresh to be provided, ii. 141 ; extraordinary, issued, ii. 303

Villiers Marshal, besieges Medem-
blick, i. 83. Mentioned, i. 313
Villiers, the preacher, i. 313
Virgin, God save her, the, ii. 337
Vison, the Santa Maria de, i. p.
xlv ; ii. 386
Vivero Rodrigo de, ii. 367

*Waad, William, i. 357
Waker, Hawkyns' man, ii. 97
Wakerland = Walcheren, i. 286
Walcheren, probable attack on, i.
67 ; well affected to the Queen,
100
*Wallop, Sir Henry, ii. 269, 271,
281, 283, 285
*Walsyngham, Sir Francis, Prin-
cipal Secretary of State. Letters
to Howard, i. 192 ; to Burghley, i. 327 ; ii. 69, 82-3 ; to the
Lord Chancellor, ii. 69
Walter's *Voyage round the World*
referred to, i. p. lxiii
Walton, Roger, i. 102 n.
War ; causes of the, with Spain, i.
pp. xiii, xxiii ; comparison of, with
that of the French Revolution,
i. p. xxiii ; Hawkyns proposes
resolute, i. 60 ; open, would ease
her Majesty's purse, 207 ; Cely
advocates 'a sharp war and a
short,' 264
Ward, his 'pill and drop,' i. p. lxiii
Ward, Luke, i. p. xxxiv ; ii. 183,
336
Ware, accused of piracy, ii. 171
Warwick, Earl of, i. 308 n.
Water-works, hard, i. 282
Watts, Sir John, i. 350 n.; ii. 337,
340
Weather ; winter's, i. 81, 86 ;
stormy, i. 199, 253-4, 282-3, 331 ;
ii. 2, 3, 45, 163-4 ; will greatly
endanger the Spaniards, i. 254 ;
foggy, ii. 161
Weather = to windward, i. 195
Webb, Nicholas, ii. 235
Wells, belongs to the port of King's
Lynn, i. 144
Wentworth, Thomas, Lord, i. 308 n.
Weschester = Chester, i. 26

Weymouth, memorials of the Mayor
and Corporation of, i. 151 ; ii.
15 ; a town in part decayed, i.
152 ; ask for some guns, ii. 15 ;
they are given guns from the San
Salvador, ii. 86
Whiddon, Jacob, i. 326 ; ii. 186,
189 n., 263, 289
*White, Sir Nicholas, ii. 283. Letter
to Walsyngham, 284
White Bear, the. See Bear
White Lion, the, ii. 338, 340
*Whyte, Henry ; letter to Wal-
syngham, ii. 63 ; his ship burnt,
ib. ; his story of the fight, ib. ;
on board the Mary Rose, 64
Wight, Isle of, has no ships fit for
warlike service, i. 131 ; levy of
money illegal, 132 ; probable
place for the Spaniards landing,
190 ; prize said to be illegally
sold in, ii. 342
William of Nassau, Count, i. 352
Williams, Sir Roger, of the Ad-
miral's Council, i. 210 n. ; with
Leicester at the camp, 306 ; ab-
sents himself, 307 ; returns, 321
Willoughby, Ambrose, i. p. lxxvi
Winchester, Marquis of, Lord-
Lieut. of Dorset, letter to the
Council, deprecating men being
sent out of the county, i. 316
Winckfield, John, ii. 211
Wind ; on July 20, i. p. xxxix ; on
July 21, ii. 355-6 ; on July 29, ii.
10, 365 ; on July 30, ii. 11, 368
*Windebank, Sir Francis, i. 142 n.
*Windebank, Sir Thomas, i. 142 n.
Wingfeild, Sir John, i. 314 n.
Wingfield, Richard, ii. 66
Wishing = requesting, ii. 37
*Wolley, J., i. 317, 334
Woodbridge, should belong to the
port of Orford, i. 155
Wright's *Queen Elizabeth and her
Times* referred to, ii. 119
Wright, John, ii. 248
Wright, Nicholas, ii. 248
Wye, Captain, 334
*Wyllughby, Lord, i. 314 n., 352-3 ;
ii. 31 n., 72. Letter of, to Wal-
syngham, ii. 31

*Wyngfeld, Sir Robert, i. 153 *n.*
*Wynter, Edward, ii. 123 ; letter to Walsyngham, ii. 149 ; wishes to serve on shore, ii. 151
Wynter, George, commands on coast of Ireland, i. 188 *n.*
Wynter, John, Burghley's man, i. 45
Wynter, John, lieutenant of the Vanguard, ii. 12, 44, 123
*Wynter, Sir William ; his long experience, i. p. x ; his insight into the conditions of naval war, *ib.* ; his account of the battle of Gravelines, p. lv ; ii. 7 ; inspects the works at Dover, i. 82, 180 ; suggests sconces for the defence of the Thames, i. 207, 286 ; ii. 310 ; was at Leith in 1544, i. 213 ; asks Walsyngham to send him a buck, i. 216 ; thanks him for the same, 334 ; proposes ships to lie at the Nore, 332 ; charges the starboard wing at Gravelines, ii. 10 ; is wounded, 11 ; ordered back, *ib.* ; speculates as to the course the Spaniards may take, 13 ; ill at ease in bed, 123 ; in Council with Howard, 139 ; prefers charges against Hawkyns, 266–8 ; his rate of pay, 315 ; conduct for retinue, 318. Mentioned, i. 11, 14, 16–17, 24 *n.*, 86, 159, 188, 206, 272, 290 ; ii. 89, 108, 121, 157, 162, 164, 176, 178, 184–5, 211, 256, 265, 336–7. Letters to Howard, i. 77 ; the Principal Officers, i. 80 ; Burghley, i. 180 ; Walsyngham, i. 212, 332 ; ii. 7, 309 ; the Council, ii. 44
Wynter, William, junr., ii. 336

Yonge, John, ii. 287, 337
Yorke, Edmund, with Leicester at the camp, i. 307 *n.*
Yorke, Gilbert, ii. 335
Yorke, Rowland, i. 85 *n.*, 307 *n.*
Younge, John, i. 158

Zealand, to arm forth shipping, i. 213 ; should be looked to, i. 233 ; letter from the States of, to the Queen, ii. 48
Zuñiga, D. Baltasar de sent with a letter to the King of Spain, ii. 354 ; and to give a verbal account, 369
Zutphen, battle of, i. p. xxxi, 101 *n.*

THE END

PRINTED BY
SPOTTISWOODE AND CO., NEW-STREET SQUARE
LONDON